Arguments & Arguing

FOURTH EDITION

Arguments & Arguing

The Products and Process of Human Decision Making

FOURTH EDITION

Thomas A. Hollihan
University of Southern California

Kevin T. Baaske
California State University, Los Angeles

WAVELAND PRESS, INC.

Long Grove, Illinois

For information about this book, contact:
Waveland Press, Inc.
4180 IL Route 83, Suite 101
Long Grove, IL 60047-9580
(847) 634-0081
info@waveland.com
www.waveland.com

Photo Credits
p. 195, Thomas Koch / Shutterstock.com; p. 196, Malcolm P Chapman / Shutterstock.com; p. 196, Thomas Koch / Shutterstock.com; p. 198, Julia Le Duc / AP Images; p. 201, Pence Nicholas Pfosi / Reuters / Alamy Stock Photo; p. 202, Jonathan Ernest / Reuters / Alamy Stock Photo; p. 204, refrina / Shutterstock.com; p. 205, DCStockPhotography / Shutterstock.com; p. 205, Gale S. Hanratty / Alamy Stock Photo; p. 206, Richard Ellis / Alamy Stock Photo; p. 207, UMA Press, Inc. / Alamy Stock Photo; p. 208, João Paulo Tinoco / Alamy Stock Photo; p. 210, Hayk_Shalunts / Shutterstock.com; p. 210, Hayk_Shalunts / Shutterstock.com; p. 210, Tom Brenner / Reuters / Alamy Stock Photo; p. 211, Milica Lamb / PA Images / Alamy Stock Photo

Copyright © 2022, 2016, 2005, 1994 by Thomas A. Hollihan and Kevin T. Baaske

10-digit ISBN 1-4786-4769-8
13-digit ISBN 978-1-4786-4769-0

All rights reserved. No part of this book may be reproduced, stored in a retrieval system, or transmitted in any form or by any means without permission in writing from the publisher.

Printed in the United States of America

7 6 5 4 3 2 1

*We dedicate this fourth edition to
Riley Anita Crawford,
a small but mighty spirit who has already
demonstrated that she can express herself vocally.*

Contents

Preface xi
Acknowledgments xiii

PART I
Principles of Argumentation 1

1 Argumentation as Human Symbolic Activity 3
Shared Symbol System 3
Senses of the Term *Argument* 6
Argumentation and Individual Decision Making 9
Argumentation and Democratic Deliberation 10
Argumentation and Values 12
Ethics and Argumentation 15
SUMMARY 17 / KEY TERMS 18 / ACTIVITIES 18
RECOMMENDED READINGS 18 / ENDNOTES 19

2 The Foundations of Argument 21
Value Implications of Arguments 21
The Narrative Paradigm 29
The Limits of Argument 35
The Study of Argumentation 37
SUMMARY 37 / KEY TERMS 38 / ACTIVITIES 38
RECOMMENDED READINGS 39 / ENDNOTES 39

3 Audiences and Fields of Argument 43
Knowing Your Audience 43
People Evaluate Arguments Differently 52
The Principle of Presence 53
Argument Fields 55
SUMMARY 58 / KEY TERMS 58 / ACTIVITIES 59
RECOMMENDED READINGS 59 / ENDNOTES 60

4 The Language of Argument   63
Understanding Language 63
Language and Good Stories 66
Metaphor 79
SUMMARY 82 / KEY TERMS 82 / ACTIVITIES 82
RECOMMENDED READINGS 83 / ENDNOTES 83

5 Argumentation and Critical Thinking   87
Propositions 87
Types of Propositions 89
The Techniques for Analyzing Propositions 92
SUMMARY 104 / KEY TERMS 105 / ACTIVITIES 105
RECOMMENDED READINGS 106 / ENDNOTES 106

6 Types of Arguments   107
Inductive Arguments 107
Deductive Arguments 113
The Deductive Syllogism 115
The Toulmin Model 118
SUMMARY 122 / KEY TERMS 122 / ACTIVITIES 123
RECOMMENDED READINGS 123 / ENDNOTES 124

7 The Grounds for Argument   125
Premises 126
Examples 133
Statistics 134
Testimony 140
SUMMARY 145 / KEY TERMS 146 / ACTIVITIES 146
RECOMMENDED READINGS 146 / ENDNOTES 147

8 Building Arguments   151
Defining Research 151
Planning the Research Process 152
Sources of Information 153
How to Record the Evidence 163
What to Look for When Researching 165
Organizing Your Advocacy 168
SUMMARY 170 / KEY TERMS 171 / ACTIVITIES 171
RECOMMENDED READINGS 171 / ENDNOTES 172

9 Refuting Arguments — 173

The Refutation Process Defined 173
Focused Listening (Step One) 174
Critically Evaluating Arguments (Step Two) 175
Formulating a Response (Step Three) 183
Presenting Your Response (Step Four) 188
SUMMARY 190 / KEY TERMS 191 / ACTIVITIES 191
RECOMMENDED READINGS 191 / ENDNOTES 192

10 Visual Argument — 195

Physical Images 199
The Power of Images 212
Tests of Visual Arguments 214
SUMMARY 217 / KEY TERMS 217 / ACTIVITIES 218
RECOMMENDED READINGS 218 / ENDNOTES 219

PART II
Argumentation in Specialized Fields 221

11 Academic Debate Overview — 223

The Debate Orientation 223
The Resolution 224
Three Types of Academic Debating 225
Format 226
The Nature of Debate Arguments 229
Flow Sheeting as Systematic Note Taking 237
SUMMARY 241 / KEY TERMS 241
ACTIVITIES 241 / RECOMMENDED READINGS 242

12 Advanced Academic Debate — 243

The Resolution 243
Hasty Generalizations 246
Plans and Counterplans 248
Thinking Strategically 251
Specialized Debate Formats 253
SUMMARY 257 / KEY TERMS 257 / ACTIVITIES 258
RECOMMENDED READING 258 / ENDNOTES 258

13 Argumentation in Politics: Campaigns and Debates   261
Issues and Voters   263
Voter Attitudes   266
Campaigns as Stories   268
The Structure and Form of Campaign Arguments   274
Political Debates   275
SUMMARY 278   /   KEY TERMS 278   /   ACTIVITIES 278
RECOMMENDED READING 279   /   ENDNOTES 279

14 Argumentation and the Law   283
The U.S. Judicial System   284
The Assumptions of the System   285
The Role of Attorneys in Pretrial Phases   288
The Role of Attorneys in the Trial   293
SUMMARY 299   /   KEY TERMS 299   /   ACTIVITIES 299
RECOMMENDED READINGS 300   /   ENDNOTES 300

15 Argumentation in Business and Organizations   303
Competing Interests in Organizations   303
Preparing Arguments to Meet Objectives   308
Shaping the Message: Devising Strategies   310
The Oral Presentation   314
Encountering Resistance   315
Follow-Up Activities   317
The Challenge of Working at a Distance   317
SUMMARY 318   /   KEY TERMS 318   /   ACTIVITIES 318
RECOMMENDED READINGS 319   /   ENDNOTES 319

16 Argumentation in Interpersonal Relationships   321
Arguing and Conflict Mediation Strategies   322
A Conversational Theory of Argument   325
Strategic Dimensions of Conversational Argument   328
Argumentation and Self-Esteem   330
The Importance of Empathic Listening   331
SUMMARY 331   /   KEY TERMS 332   /   ACTIVITIES 333
RECOMMENDED READINGS 333   /   ENDNOTES 334

Appendix A: Transcripts of Two Convention
  Acceptance Speeches, 2020   337
Appendix B: Eulogy Speech   351
Appendix C: Case Study for Analysis   357

Index   377

Preface

Arguments and Arguing: The Products and Process of Human Decision Making, Fourth Edition, is intended to meet the needs of students enrolled in courses in argumentation, critical thinking, and media literacy. Because the text also introduces students to rhetorical theory, and to many of the most important theorists, the book may also be suitable for courses in rhetoric. The book offers chapters on arguing in specialized fields and contexts including academic debate, law, politics, business and organizations, and interpersonal communication. Thus, it may also be of interest for courses in those areas.

WHY THIS BOOK AT THIS TIME?

This is the fourth edition of this book. The first edition appeared in 1994, the second in 2005, and the third in 2016. Revisiting this manuscript every few years has been an interesting experience. We have discovered much that has remained the same even as we experience a world that seems markedly different than it was before. With each new edition we have tried to keep up and write about new events, new challenges, new technologies, and new anxieties and risks. Although there have been many advances in argumentation theory and research over the life of this book, we have discovered that the fundamental principles of argumentation, critical thinking, and public deliberation that we wrote about in earlier editions are still relevant today.

Instructors who are familiar with the book will find that this new edition attempts to remain faithful to the general outline and structure of earlier editions. Our task in this new edition is to include fresh, new, and recent examples so that today's generation of readers recognize the application of concepts and theories to controversies and topics that shape their daily lives. Some topics reappear here because they revolve around issues that have proven resistant to meaningful solutions. Wars in the Middle East, arguments about income inequality or inadequate access to health care, racial injustice and police violence, to name just a few, are topics that continue to challenge us. Although we have updated most of the discussions to include more recent examples, the issues are familiar. We have also introduced new topics, including a deeper conversation about fake news and misinformation campaigns, incivility and its consequences, and arguments about individual rights and communal responsibilities, especially those shaped by the COVID-19 global pandemic. This edition continues to highlight the complexities of an ever-evolving networked social media environment.

Our interest in an argumentation book developed because we both taught courses in argumentation at the undergraduate and graduate level and because we both are former high school and college debaters and college debate coaches. Although neither of us has coached debate for decades, our love for the activity persists, and we both continue to participate in a community of scholars devoted to the study of argumentation. We are delighted that the study of argumentation is now a global phenomenon and that argumentation conferences and argumentation research are conducted around the world. We were especially pleased when our friend and colleague Deng Xinxin translated the third edition of this book into Chinese so that it was more widely accessible to students and teachers in the Middle Kingdom.

We hope that we have produced a new edition that manages to preserve the most useful elements of the earlier editions and that also engages today's students who were likely born well after the first edition was published.

Acknowledgments

In this edition, as in earlier editions, our ideas were formed and deepened by interactions with our students and our colleagues. We also want to thank our families for engaging us and, for the most part, patiently tolerating our exchange of views in so many productive (and a few less productive) arguments. Patti Riley, Alexandra Riley Hollihan Crawford, Justin Crawford, Sean Hollihan, Nancy Baaske, Megan Baaske VandenBoss, and Brett VandenBoss have all demonstrated their ability to develop and defend their positions, and they have earned our love and respect.

We also want to thank Neil and Carol Rowe and Waveland Press for their support for this fourth edition and for their help in producing this volume. We especially want to express our appreciation for Carol, who is a thorough and insightful editor.

TAH
KTB
Los Angeles, California
2021

PART I

PRINCIPLES OF ARGUMENTATION

Our goal in this book is to demonstrate the important role that arguments play in helping you understand complex issues, form opinions, and resolve disagreements. We therefore present argumentation as an essential dimension of the human communication process. Part I of the book introduces you to argumentation theory and principles, and part II considers the unique characteristics of argumentation in specialized fields and contexts.

In chapter 1 we discuss human reliance on symbols to create and share meaning. Because humans create different meanings and hold different opinions, the urge to argue is natural. We focus on the different meanings of the term *argument*, the importance of argumentation in decision making, and the role that our values play in the arguments we develop. Finally, chapter 1 discusses the importance of ethics in argumentation.

Chapter 2 examines the stories people use to structure and create their arguments. These stories help people understand and evaluate arguments, and they provide an important means for using arguments to explore complex issues.

Chapter 3 makes the case that because arguments are typically generated to influence someone's opinions or actions and are shaped by human values, arguers should consider the beliefs and values likely held by their audience when creating their claims.

In chapter 4 we focus on the language that gives life to arguments. Specifically, this chapter looks at the use of linguistic devices in the creation and evaluation of stories.

In chapter 5 we consider the role that argumentation plays in the development of critical thinking skills. The chapter discusses different strategies used in argumentation analysis and offers specific recommendations that will sharpen your analytical skills.

Chapter 6 discusses different types of arguments and focuses on the differences between inductive and deductive reasoning. This chapter also introduces the syllogism and offers insights into how arguments can be diagrammed.

In chapter 7 we turn our attention to the grounds for argument. We include a discussion of how arguments are discovered and evaluated. This chapter considers the different types of grounds available to arguers and also contains a brief discussion of the unique challenge that the use of statistical support poses for advocates.

Chapters 8 and 9 are companion chapters. In chapter 8 we focus on the process of building arguments. The chapter discusses the importance of research, offers suggestions regarding how best to conduct your research, suggests strategies for note taking, and gives advice on how to organize your findings into arguments. Chapter 9 then focuses on how to refute arguments—the process of undermining the argument claims that have been advanced by others. This chapter also discusses how to avoid using and how to refute misinformation and disinformation, sometimes referred to as "fake news." The chapter discusses some common fallacies (arguments that are logically flawed) and provides advice on how to detect fallacies.

Chapter 10 examines nondiscursive arguments, specifically how visual images (photographs, illustrations, paintings, sculptures, films, television programs, video games, and even themed architectural environments) function as arguments and, as a result, have profound impact upon human opinions and decision-making.

By the time you have finished part I of *Arguments and Arguing,* you should have a well-formed understanding of the component parts and principles of argumentation. This groundwork should prepare you for the discussion of the unique traits of argumentation in specialized settings offered in part II.

Argumentation as Human Symbolic Activity

The feature that most distinguishes humans from other creatures is the capacity for using **symbols**. Through symbols humans are able to name objects, give meaning to experiences and events, and accumulate and share knowledge with peers and later generations. The ability to acquire and share knowledge enables humans to collaborate to develop useful technologies. As Andrew Buskell argued, "While it is true that some animals build structures (think, for instance, of beaver dams) and that some use tools (with the New Caledonian crow being an exceptional instance), humans not only have a large and varied tool-kit, but also use this tool-kit to survive in almost all the terrestrial territories of the globe."[1]

This symbolizing permits the creation of a "cumulative culture," and it involves all of the elements of human creativity. As Christine H. Legare noted:

> Technological complexity is the outcome of our species' remarkable capacity for cumulative culture; innovations build on each other and are progressively incorporated into a population's stock of skills and knowledge, generating ever more sophisticated repertoires. Innovation is necessary to ensure cultural and individual adaptation to novel and changing challenges, as humans spread to every corner of the planet. Cultural evolution makes individuals more innovative by allowing for the accumulation of prefabricated solutions to problems that can be recombined to create new technologies. The subcomponents of technology are typically too complex for individuals to develop from scratch. The cultural inheritance of the technologies of previous generations allows for the explosive growth of cultural complexity.[2]

SHARED SYMBOL SYSTEM

Symbols can be defined as special types of signs. As the definition of sign implies, "signs call attention to significances: they relate to what has been perceived; they point to, indicate, or denote something other than themselves."[3] The ability to share in a symbol system permits humans to build social communities and to discover, assess, and evaluate situations to address problems jointly to improve the quality of our daily lives. Symbols are circulated in stories, fables, biographical narratives, books, journals, manuscripts, films, and even ballads. Symbols teach us about the values and experiences of those who lived before us and permit us to create aspirational notions of the possibilities to be discovered in our imagined futures. Symbols transmit our anxieties, hopes, and desires. They express our regrets, and they celebrate our achievements. Through our symbols we express our tribal, national, cultural, and political identities. In short, to paraphrase the enlightenment philosopher Rene Descartes, "because we symbolize we are."[4]

Kenneth Burke, a noted rhetorical theorist and literary critic, declared that this symbolic capability created humans as "political animals."[5] As symbol users and political animals, we are constantly seeking ways to better our lives. No matter how satisfying our current situation, we are apt to imagine ways in which our lives, our society, and our world can be improved. Burke wrote that this makes us "rotten with perfection."[6] Much of our symbolic "tinkering" is designed to achieve such improvements. Because we experience the world somewhat differently—and encounter different circumstances, problems, and experiences—this symbolic tinkering naturally leads us to arguing with our family, friends, teachers, coworkers, media sources, and public and political figures. As was on full display in the public conversations and protests regarding police violence and the Black Lives Matter movement, the arguments that were most likely to resonate with people were often shaped by their racial identity and their personal experiences, or the experiences of their family members or friends with police officers.

Through our use of symbols, we create and negotiate a complex web of interpersonal, public, and professional relationships that manage our sometimes-competitive interactions as we seek to resolve our problems and create harmonious and productive lives. Some of the problems that we encounter seem to be ours alone; others are shared broadly. The years 2020 and 2021 will forever be remembered as the time of the COVID-19 pandemic that struck nations around the world, rich and poor, and killed millions of people. Yet, even as we all experienced the same storm, we really did not share the same boat. People who were more affluent and highly educated could often work from home via digital technology. Their incomes did not suffer, and they were largely able to seclude themselves from the virus—often in comfortable single-family homes, where they binged on Netflix videos and experimented with home-baked sourdough bread. Others, however, lost their jobs when businesses were forced to close. Without work they found themselves unable to pay their rent or even buy groceries. Still others were deemed "essential workers," and they were compelled to go to work as doctors, nurses, first-responders, grocery store clerks, delivery drivers, etc. They may have been fortunate to continue to earn their salaries, but they were also unable to hide from the virus. They, and those who lived with them, were thus far more likely to become sick and possibly to die from the virus. There were stark differences, too, in the experiences of those who became ill. Some, especially younger people, experienced few if any debilitating symptoms. Others, especially older people and those with comorbidities (such as diabetes, obesity, or heart disease) were far more likely to need hospitalization, supplemental oxygen, and possibly admission to an intensive care ward. Even among those who became very ill there remained important differences. Those who had access to health insurance and sophisticated health care systems achieved much better outcomes than did those living in developing countries with chronically underfunded medical care systems. Horror stories emerged from nations such as India where the medical caregivers often ran out of oxygen, and people were reported to be dying outside of the hospital because there were no more open beds inside. Given these significant differences in situations and circumstances, should it be surprising that the health crisis created many opportunities for arguments about the need to shut down businesses, parks, beaches, churches, or schools? In the United States we also argued about whether or not people should have been legally obligated to wear masks or to take the vaccines once they were approved—if not to protect themselves, to protect their grandparents or others?

Because humans are fundamentally social beings, we derive satisfaction from our interactions with others. The pandemic represented the greatest challenge to the fundamental character of how these interactions were permitted to occur. We substituted virtual "Zoom" classrooms for face-to-face interactions. We did drive-through graduations and socially distanced wedding ceremonies. We cancelled or modified basketball, baseball, and football seasons. We did without state fairs, Pride parades, and even the venerable Rose Parade in Pasadena, our annual event to celebrate the start of a New Year. We also argued about each of these sacrifices. Were they really necessary to protect our health? Was it right to ask business owners to surrender their enterprises and years of hard work to stop the spread of the virus? Was it fair and necessary to ask high school and college students to forgo proms and graduation ceremonies? Was it legitimate to classify those underpaid, often immigrant workers in meat processing plants as "essential workers," even though doing so put them at far greater risk to catching and even dying from the disease?

Arguments that engaged us helped us understand the threat that we faced and inspired us to search for appropriate actions in response. Scientists and health care providers argued about possible treatments and immunization strategies. Others among us argued about our social and political responsibilities to protect ourselves and others from exposure to the virus. Political leaders and engaged citizens argued about the consequences of incurring unprecedented levels of public debt to provide financial support to individuals and to companies devastated by the sudden decision to close down the economy. We argued about the sufficiency of the actions our governments and institutions took to prevent or halt the virus, and we argued about the origins of the virus and whether or not it should be blamed on China. Many of these arguments will never really be finished. They are ongoing today, and they will be revisited for a hundred years or longer by historians seeking to make sense of this calamitous pandemic. It is through arguments that we make sense of experiences, identify solutions, and prevent future occurrences.

In our personal and our public lives—in relationships between friends and lovers, colleagues and coworkers, nations and cultures—we use arguments to negotiate, resolve conflicts, and find ways to live together in situations where our interests sometimes align and sometimes differ. Sometimes we find amicable solutions through such arguments, and sometimes we discover problems that seem to be intractable and beyond solution. Argumentation and deliberation are typically the best way forward to find places to collaborate, to discover grounds for compromise, or to develop strategies for amicable accommodation.

From personal experience as well as from the accumulated understanding of history, we have learned that when communication fails and people cannot reach agreement, the potential for conflict and even war increases dramatically. We have also learned, however, that the situations that spark conflict will never disappear. Learning how to identify, analyze, name, reach understanding about, and then solve the problems that we individually and collectively face is essential if we are to live in harmony.

This book seeks to teach the communication skills required for human problem solving and decision making and for the maintenance of effective and harmonious social relations. This book is about ***arguments***—the claims that people make when they are asserting their opinions and supporting their beliefs—and ***arguing***—the process of resolving differences of opinion through communication.

SENSES OF THE TERM ARGUMENT

Two different, but equally important, senses of the term *argument*[7] correspond to two of the most important objectives for the use of arguments: effective decision making and the desire to achieve social harmony. The first, which can be called *argument1*, refers to the claims that people make. As we have mentioned, when people encounter problems they seek solutions. To find the solutions they must consider the causes of the problems, and they must weigh the costs and benefits of different solutions. Advances in all aspects of human intellectual life are testimony to the creativity and the reasoning capacity of humans as they reach decisions. Our intense desire to understand our world and to improve our condition in it combined with our ability to reason and to evaluate opinions through arguments prompt us to assert our knowledge claims about the world that we inhabit. We continually find ourselves testing and challenging these knowledge claims as they are subjected to new events, new information, new problems, and new interactions with others who may see the world and experience these new conditions differently than we do.

We know that people respond to problems in a variety of ways. As a result of differences in experience, culture, education, values, interests, objectives, economic circumstances, and so forth, people will choose to focus on and assign priority to different problems—and they will propose or reject different solutions. The problems that are of the greatest concern to well-clothed, well-fed, and well-housed people might seem trivial to those who are impoverished. Thus, even within the same nation, culture, and/or political community, profound differences can be found.

Political liberals and conservatives have deep differences of opinion both about the problems they believe are most important in society and about the possible solutions to those problems. Likewise, those who adhere to fundamentalist Christian doctrine often hold markedly different theological beliefs than do those who follow more liberal or reformed religious doctrines. Sometimes these differences of opinion may be highly technical in nature. For example, scientists may argue about alternative approaches to conducting research or critics may comment on the value and/or meaning of a particular artistic creation. The more knowledge or expertise someone possesses about a subject, the more nuanced and specific may be the quality of the arguments that they advance. We are thus exposed to myriad alternative arguments and symbolically expressed claims each day of our lives. Some of those claims may interest and matter to us a great deal. Other claims involve issues in which we have little interest or exceed our capability to comprehend.

In a robust, pluralistic, and democratic society these different claims and opinions compete for our attention and acceptance. We grant some opinions and some arguments more credibility than we do others. Our differences cause us to identify and form opinions in unique ways, and those differences also cause us to evaluate arguments differently.

"The marketplace of ideas" is a common expression that could be interpreted as a marketplace for competing arguments. "Sellers"—arguers hawking their worldviews—seek to find "buyers" who might be convinced to accept their claims. The best test of the truth of an idea is the ability of an idea to gain adherents in competition with other ideas.[8] However, the argumentative marketplace, much like the economic marketplace of modern capitalism, is not always a place of free and fair competition. Not all arguments are given an equal opportunity to be aired or considered, and some arguments are much more likely to receive a favorable hearing than others. Particular argumentative positions may be more likely to be presumed as true because, for example, they are advocated by persons perceived to have greater competence or credibility, because many people already believe them, or because they have been accepted as probably true for a long period of time. Some arguments are not given a "fair" hearing, perhaps because they represent distinctly minority viewpoints, because those who are perceived to be experts in the relevant fields do not accept them, or because they counter accepted historical understandings. Even though the argumentative marketplace may be less than perfect, arguments do compete against each other. Some arguments will win support and perhaps even gain wide public agreement, while other arguments will fall by the wayside and eventually be forgotten. Why some arguments win support while others fail is among the primary issues discussed in this book.

The second sense of the term *argument*, which can be called *argument2*, refers to the types of interactions in which claims are developed—interactions characterized by disagreement. To argue is to have a dispute with someone. From this perspective, an argument does not exist until some person in the exchange perceives what is happening as an argument.[9] Many textbooks in argumentation emphasize the first sense and not the second sense. These books primarily want to help people learn how to become better arguers—meaning more insightful, skilled, and analytical arguers. Although we share these objectives, we believe the second sense of the term argument is also important. The ability to conduct a civilized and polite argument with someone—the ability to argue and disagree with others while also managing to protect your relationship with them—is one of the most important things people must learn. It is an important measure of what Daniel Goleman described as emotional intelligence, which he argued is perhaps the most important predictor of career and personal success in life.[10]

The two senses of the term argument are:

Argument1: Claims offered by arguers (in a later chapter we will distinguish between arguments and assertions).
Example: Access to comprehensive health care is a right that should be enjoyed by all people regardless of their income or ability to pay for the services they need. Advocates might support this claim by making moral and value claims about not turning people away from needed care and by discussing those who lose their health insurance when they lose their jobs and cannot find new insurance that will cover their preexisting medical conditions.

Argument2: Types of interactions in which people engage.
Example: People with different opinions about access to comprehensive health care could dispute one another's claims. For instance, someone could respond to the claim offered above by arguing that access to health care is a privilege and not a right; it is the responsibility of all people to provide for their own health care needs and the needs of their family. They might support that argument by claim-

ing that if people were able to access the health care system without needing to pay, they could overuse doctors, hospitals, and prescription drugs to treat very minor ailments thus consuming valuable resources that should be devoted to sicker patients. Or they might argue that providing access to health care for all people might encourage those without legal residency to enter the country seeking the free care. Finally, they might argue that providing free access to health care for everyone would be so expensive that it would require a very steep tax increase that could damage the growth of the economy, lead to a loss of investment by businesses, and increased unemployment. It might be better, such advocates could argue, to lower taxes to stimulate the growth of the economy to create access to health care for all citizens and legal residents.

It is possible to make arguments (argument1) without engaging in disputes or disagreements (argument2). If everyone agreed that it would be a wise policy to assure access to health care for all people regardless of their ability to pay, for example, there would be no argument2 in the above example. However, it is not possible to have disputes (argument2) without having people making claims (argument1). Disagreements are a potential consequence of argument1.

The distinction offered here between argument1 and argument2 is important because it illustrates that argumentation is not merely a problem-solving capability. Argumentation is a very basic social and communication skill, and it has profound importance for the quality and character of our interactions with others in personal, family, workplace, and public social settings.

Many people have been taught and have come to believe that arguments are unhealthy and thus they should be avoided if possible. Women may especially be discouraged to display argumentative assertiveness in many cultures around the world because to do so is to signal traits or behaviors that have been deemed nonfeminine.[11] Regardless of gender, to describe someone as **"argumentative"** is generally not considered flattering. Those who are too quick to argue, too intense or passionate in their arguments, or too unwilling to surrender their positions when confronted by superior arguments are often viewed as disagreeable or even unpleasant people.[12] Although the U.S. culture is certainly more argumentative and more confrontational than some other cultures (e.g., most Asian cultures), even among people living in the United States there seems to be a strong presumption that arguments are not good for human relationships. A simple Google search can link you to hundreds of websites that inform you about how to avoid unhealthy arguments, arguments about disputed facts, repetitive or circular arguments, or divisive or hostile arguments.[13] The linguist and popular author, Deborah Tannen, laments that an "argument culture" causes people to "approach the world—and the people in it—in an adversarial frame of mind."[14] Tannen protests that this human tendency toward argument accentuates differences, discourages compromise, falsely polarizes opinions, and encourages aggressive behavior. Although Tannen does not mention it, we cannot help but note the irony that exists when she offers such forceful arguments to support her case about the dangers and negative consequences of this argument culture. Given the nature of our book, readers will not be surprised to learn that we disagree with most of the arguments that Tannen advances.

While Tannen worries that humans are too quick to argue, we believe our language system actually conditions us for critical analysis and gives us the tools to reach agreement. We believe arguing can be—and often is—healthy both for relationships and for societies. People argue to negotiate their social perspectives with others and to enhance their understanding of complex problems. They argue to resolve their disagreements and problems and to make tough decisions about how to move forward. The problem, as we see it, is not that arguments per se are unhealthy; rather, too many people have never learned how to argue in a constructive and socially beneficial fashion. Our goal for this book is thus to help students learn some strategies and techniques that will enable them to improve their argumentation skills and to argue constructively. Constructive arguments permit disagreements to surface so people can examine alternative ways to view and understand problems, identify different solutions, and select the most compelling position.

We believe relationships and communities are created through communication and, yes, through argument. The values of the community are shaped through people coming together to share their opinions, offering reasons in support of their beliefs, and deliberating. There is some danger that demands for civility can privilege the voices of those who already have platforms and silence those who do not have significant power but who may have legitimate reasons to protest the injustices found in society. However, we believe that civil discourse and respectful disagreement is also foundational to the creation of an ethical society. We believe that civility is more than interacting with others with good manners or politeness, it means acting toward others with restraint and respect that honors the humanity even of those with whom we may strongly disagree.

ARGUMENTATION AND INDIVIDUAL DECISION MAKING

We are challenged every day to make decisions in our personal lives. Some of the differences are small and relatively insignificant; others are major and will end up shaping our lives. Certainly, even the accumulated consequences of small decisions can have very significant long-term impacts on us. Should I go out and socialize with my friends, or should I stay home and study? What college should I attend? What should be my major? Should I take on the debt to buy a new car? Do I have the money to take the spring break vacation that I have planned? Should I accept the job offer that would require me to move across the country and away from my friends and family? Which candidate should I vote for in the next election? All of these decisions, and thousands of others like them, that we are called upon to make every day, test our analytical and argumentative abilities. Whenever we are compelled to consider alternative choices, we make use of arguments. Thus, as a problem-solving activity, argumentation may involve decisions and choices that are distinctly personal in nature, many of which we might not even bother to disclose to our friends or families.

Often, however, we are called upon to discuss or even to account for our decisions. In such discussions we explain our actions to those people whose opinions matter to us. We want them to understand why we made the choices we made, and often we seek their approval and respect for our decisions and our reasoning processes. We make our choices based on our understanding of the unique problems we face, our knowledge and view of the world, and our goals and values. We strive to be rational, and we want others to validate our rationality and to confirm that our choices were, in fact, the right ones. Depending on the nature of the decision, we may be accountable to a wide range of different people. For example, most of us are accountable to our parents because even after we are adults, we are driven by the desire to please them and to make them proud of us. We are also accountable to our lovers and partners, to other family members, to friends, teachers, coworkers, and to employers. Thus, even intensely personal decisions may be argued or reasoned out with an assumed audience in mind.

ARGUMENTATION AND DEMOCRATIC DELIBERATION

The ability to make and evaluate arguments is a fundamental survival skill for life in a democracy. Democratic political systems assume that citizens have the knowledge and the ability to decide complex issues and to evaluate competing arguments involving both values and public policy. The continued health and vitality of any democratic government depend on the respect that citizens have for each other and for a democratic process that permits people to express their opinions, register their agreements and/or disagreements, evaluate the alternatives available to them, and then select a policy or strategy to move forward. A democratic political system requires an informed, capable, and interested citizenry that will deliberate about their political choices.

The preservation of democracy also demands that people meet certain standards of civility and decorum in their public lives. We suggest that arguing advocates should focus on the ideas of others—not on the person or persons advancing the ideas. Separating the idea from the advocate enables us to test the wisdom of the idea itself. Wise and unwise people can make good and bad arguments. We can reject an idea without rejecting the person who advocated the idea. Focusing on the idea increases the likelihood of civility and decorum because it reduces the role of the advocate unless the advocate's trustworthiness and competence are also a focus.

Positive models of deliberative discourse are needed to help citizens make well-reasoned and respectful arguments. As Mary Stuckey and Sean Patrick O'Rourke argue, "Rhetoric, community, and civility are united in the idea that good rhetoric requires good faith, and that such rhetoric somehow involves the avoidance of willful deception and the readiness to speak and listen with respect."[15] One of the most troublesome characteristics of our contemporary politics in the United States is the decline in the quality of our civil discourse. Political leaders who repeatedly lie or misrepresent the truth, engage in name-calling and personal attacks, and who use arguably racist or divisive discourse are terrible role models for how we should conduct our public democratic discourse.

It is unfortunate that the quality of our political arguments has deteriorated so markedly and is now characterized by negative attacks, scurrilous charges, and demeaning and divisive discourse. While it may be funny to watch a manager in a baseball game kick sand onto the umpire's pants and gesture wildly while protesting a call on the baseball diamond, these same tactics should alarm us when they occur in the halls of Congress, on the campaign trail, on a presidential debate stage, or in a White House press conference. In the news today, as this section is being written, is a story reporting that Representative Ted Yoho (R-FL) accosted Representative Alexandria Ocasio-Cortez (D-NY) on the steps of the capitol.

> In a brief but heated exchange, which was overheard by a reporter, Yoho told Ocasio-Cortez she was "disgusting" for recently suggesting that poverty and unemployment are driving a spike in crime in New York City during the coronavirus pandemic.

> "You are out of your freaking mind," Yoho told her.
>
> Ocasio-Cortez shot back, telling Yoho he was being "rude."
>
> The two then parted ways. Ocasio-Cortez headed into the building, while Yoho, joined by Rep. Roger Williams (R-Texas), began descending toward the House office buildings. A few steps down, Yoho offered a parting thought to no one in particular.
>
> "F . . . g b . . . ch," he said.[16]

The example illustrates a negative, demeaning personal attack disparaging a person rather than a disagreement over a claim.

A 2019 poll discovered that "the vast majority of Americans—93%—identify incivility [in our daily lives and in our politics] as a problem, with most classifying it as a 'major' problem (68%)."[17] The results are extraordinary, because it is almost impossible to imagine any other issue or social problem that would result in polling data illustrating such a high level of agreement. The poll also reported that,

> Eight in 10 or more point to risks to society as dangerously high; almost nine in 10 respondents identify serious ramifications from incivility, including cyberbullying (89%), harassment, violence and hate crimes (88%, equally), intimidation and threats, intolerance, and people feeling less safe in public places (87%, equally).[18]

Fully 50 percent of the respondents in this poll blamed the White House [this poll was taken during the Trump administration] for sparking this incivility, and 47 percent blamed politicians in general.[19] While contemporary politicians may indeed too often model very negative behavior, this study suggested that fully 89 percent of respondents reported that they personally encountered incivility most frequently in their interactions online.[20] In online communications, it is easy to "flame" or insult someone with whom you disagree. The restraints of politeness are greatly diminished because the social ties seem more loosely defined.

As we briefly mentioned above, we also want to emphasize that calls for civility and decorum can be used to silence those who hold minority opinions. Participating in protests and offering dissenting views are legitimate ways to participate in democratic decision making. Certainly, attempting to silence such expression by saying it lacks civility or decorum is also contrary to the goals of democracy.[21] The notion of civility that we embrace therefore demands that all persons be encouraged to exercise their right to speak, offer their opinions, and be heard and welcomed into civic dialogue. This kind of civility is frequently challenged in many public presentations, and these situations may themselves inspire interesting topics for debate and discussion about free speech and democratic deliberation. Should, for example, speakers be permitted to speak on your college campus without interruption if they use racist or homophobic provocations? Is it an appropriate response for the assembled audience to shout the speaker down so that their message cannot be heard?

The relationship between citizens and their elected officials is one that depends upon well-nourished forms of communication and public deliberation. As citizens of a democratic nation we surrender certain powers to our elected officials. We acknowledge the right of these officials to set limits on how fast we may drive, to require that we wear seat belts, to assess taxes, to determine what chemicals we can legally ingest, and so forth. Nonetheless, when encountering new restrictions created in response to new problems or situations, we may respond by offering arguments signaling our resistance. Think, for example, about the intense public debate that arose when some states, localities, schools, or businesses imposed the requirement that people should wear face masks to prevent the spread of the COVID-19 virus. In order to overcome such resistance, those who would impose this new requirement must convince us that they are acting in our best interests either in protecting our own health or in preventing us from infecting others. If a majority of our citizenry (or even a substantial, well-organized, vocal minority) decide not to accept the legitimacy of the established political order—or the correctness, fairness, and justice of the laws—our society could quickly disintegrate.

Given that people do not always agree and that there are always differences of opinion about what the government should do, argumentation is the primary means for shaping the course of public policy. As citizens, we participate in public debates, express our opinions, and listen to and evaluate the arguments made by competing politicians. Ultimately, we pledge our support to one candidate or another and to one political position or another by the way that we cast our vote. Lively public arguments occur around almost all of the complex policy issues that shape our daily lives. Issues such as abortion, gun control, immigration rights, or capital punishment, for example, are sure to spark heated debates. Political candidates seek to create arguments that will attract public support and win elections. They must listen to public arguments in order to understand and to best carry out the will of their constituents. Public policies are formed, deliberated upon, and ultimately passed or rejected by decision makers engaged in the creation and evaluation of arguments in legislative hearings and in debates on the floor of Congress, in state legislatures, or in city council chambers.

Argumentation skills are important for our political life because they enable us to express our opinions in a coherent manner, to make ourselves understood, and to convince others that they should share our beliefs. These same skills also help us as consumers and critics of public arguments. People who understand argumentation principles are more careful and critical audiences for arguments. We are exposed to myriad different arguments on a daily basis. Advertisers, political figures, reporters, and sales personnel all attempt to influence our opinions. Knowledge of argumentation theory should make you a more skeptical listener who is better able to analyze the merits of the arguments you hear. Such knowledge will also help create an informed electorate—one that is less susceptible to the deceptive or exaggerated claims made by political demagogues.

ARGUMENTATION AND VALUES

As we have mentioned, people are continually trying to make sense of their worlds by naming and structuring their experiences. Burke observed:

> Our philosophers, poets, and scientists act in the code of names by which they simplify or interpret reality. These names shape our relations with our fellows. They prepare us for some functions and against others, for or against the persons representing these functions. The names go further: they suggest how you shall be for or against. Call a man a villain, and you have the choice of either attacking or cringing. Call him mistaken, and you invite yourself to attempt to setting him right.[22]

The very act of naming—the choice of one symbolic referent over another—helps to form our attitudes and *values*. It thus should come as no surprise that all arguments, to some extent, concern human values. Certainly, some arguments concern more important or substantive values than do others. For example, an argument about who makes the best pizza in town may center on the value of thin versus thick crust. Perhaps to a true pizza aficionado this is a value of great significance, but most of us can enjoy both thick- and thin-crusted pizzas. On the other hand, an argument about abortion will involve assessments of such competing values as a woman's right to control her own body and her right to privacy versus the need to protect the life of the unborn. These are certainly more significant and complex value questions.

Arguments can become even more "sticky" and difficult to resolve when the symbols themselves provoke intense feelings or emotions. An example would be the public debate over "late term" abortions. Such abortions have for many years been allowed by law when they were deemed medically necessary, either due to the discovery of a severe fetal abnormality or to protect the health of the mother. When opponents of abortion chose to label these procedures "partial-birth" abortions, however, they sparked an even more intense public debate. The debate over this procedure, and whether it should be permitted by law, further polarized public deliberations about the legality and morality of all abortions. What was perhaps obfuscated by the intensity of the disagreement, however, was that these "late term abortions, though long accepted as an appropriate or medically necessary treatment in some cases, were rarely undertaken. The Centers for Disease Control (CDC) tracks the number of abortions in the United States. In 2018, 38.6% of abortions were nonsurgical interventions at or before the 9th week of gestation, 92.2% of abortions were performed at or before 13 weeks, 6.9% at 14–20 weeks, and 1% at or after 21 weeks.[23]

The declaration that all arguments concern human values does not suggest that all values are equally significant. Still, issues of value underlie virtually all concerns about which people are inspired to argue. This also means that some issues will prove especially difficult to resolve because they reveal fundamental differences in the ways in which people conceive of themselves. Milton Rokeach, probably the best-known social scientist contributing to scholarship about how people are shaped by their values, defined the term as "abstract ideals, positive or negative, not tied to any specific attitude, object, or situation, representing a person's beliefs about ideal modes of conduct and ideal terminal goals."[24]

Although persons hold many different attitudes and beliefs, Rokeach argued that they include only a few, perhaps a dozen, core values.[25] Our values are formed early in our lives. While they may be changed by our education and experience, they are for the most part stable touchstones from which we can draw lessons and create meaning for our experiences.[26] We learn values from our parents, our schools (teachers and coaches), religious instruction, our peers, and the media. We also learn them by experiencing day-to-day life in our culture. Thus, to grow up in the United States is to be influenced by the U.S. value system.

However, there is not just one U.S. value system; rather, there are many different and often competing conceptions of values that exist and even thrive in different communities.[27] For example, the values that guide daily life in the rural Midwest may be quite unlike those operating in a city on the East Coast or in a suburb on the West Coast. The values that shape the social and political culture in the South are markedly different than those in the North. We see some of these differences in the voting patterns in rural versus urban America; they are revealed in the public debates over hotly contested issues regarding such topics as whether citizens should be required to wear face masks to prevent the spread of the COVID-19 virus. The fault line is a dispute over which should be valued more—individual liberty or community responsibility.[28] There also may be important differences in values that are reflected in particular socioeconomic experiences, ethnic communities, subgroups, or families. Furthermore, people acquire their political beliefs and values as they acquire a vocabulary of symbols that carry ideological meaning. Citizens who have acquired the values that are deemed appropriate to their culture have also learned how to function as effective, although not necessarily compliant, members of that society.[29]

Values dramatically shape the arguments people make and the arguments they find convincing. We argue in accordance with the truths that we accept.[30] The values to which people cling are also influenced by how people conceive of their self-interests. Because our values are shaped by the situations in which we find ourselves, our objective both in making and evaluating arguments will be to improve our place in the world and to reinforce our conceptions of ourselves. It makes intuitive sense, therefore, that young single women may be more inclined to favor a pro-choice position on abortion and that middle-aged and older men may be more inclined to oppose the right of women to terminate an unwanted pregnancy. It is reasonable to assume that poor people may be inclined to support increased government spending on social programs to help provide for human needs, while more affluent citizens might be more likely to argue that people need to be self-sufficient, that such programs lead to a culture of dependency, and that government spending should be reduced so that taxes are lower. People are influenced by values, and their values are shaped in part by the particular problems and needs that they face as they attempt to create a more perfect and satisfying life for themselves and their loved ones.

Acknowledging the role of human values in argumentation makes us aware that while arguments may be designed to reach the truth, there may be more than one "truth." People's opinions regarding what is true are shaped by their values and experiences. Thus, complex value questions are often complex precisely because there is no single answer that will be accepted as true by all people. Reasonable people can and do differ on issues such as abortion, euthanasia, capital punishment, and access to pornography. Arguers who choose to participate in the public dialogue on these issues should recognize the role of their values in shaping their arguments. Arguers debating such controversies should also be aware that the persons with whom they are arguing might see the world through the lens of a different set of values and value hierarchies.

The values that people hold shape what claims they see as worthy of argument. The claim that the government should not concern itself with regulating the safety of food or prescription drugs might not spark much controversy at a convention of the Libertarian Party, but it would probably seem preposterous to most of the delegates at a Democratic Party convention. Democrats would probably not take this argument seriously, and thus might not even deem it worth arguing. As another example, Democrats would likely enthusiastically support setting aside more wilderness areas in the West to protect them from future development, while Republicans might support privatizing or selling land that the government already holds so that it can be mined, used for agricultural production, or developed. Indeed, Democratic President Barack Obama in 2016 issued a proclamation creating the Bears Ears National Monument in Utah to preserve two spectacular buttes. In 2017, President Trump greatly reduced the size of the land set aside by 85%, opening it up for private use.[31]

The values that people hold function as the lens through which they see the world. The way in which one views the world largely determines what one accepts as true and what one believes must be contested. We may evaluate and change our values when we encounter new information, live new experiences, confront new realities, or acquire new perspectives. Think for example, about the evolution of public values and attitudes regarding acceptance of gays in the United States. When President Clinton was in office, the best that he could achieve was a policy of "don't ask don't tell" where gays could serve in the military only if they kept their sexual preferences a secret. Only a few years later, however, values in the society had changed to the point where President Obama could create a policy where gays could openly serve, and the courts ruled in favor of same-sex marriage. This is not to say that all resistance was eliminated or that gays do not continue to face homophobia, discrimination, persecution, and even violence today. Nonetheless, it is clear that significant value changes did occur and that people can change their minds.

Values play a dramatic role in determining argument sufficiency. It should be easier to convince a farmer that the government should set minimum price supports for agricultural products than to convince an urban consumer. The farmer presumably would value the stability of markets and the preservation of small family farms and rural communities that agricultural price supports might provide. The urban consumer presumably would value a competitive free market that kept grocery prices lower; the growth of large agribusiness factory farms and the accelerated decline of rural communities would have less value than reasonable pricing. When people have fundamentally different values there will likely be more conflict, and it will be far more difficult to reach agreement. Likewise, arguers facing audiences that hold fundamentally different values from their own will find it especially challenging to persuade those audiences to support the positions they are defending.

We often hear it claimed that when values come into conflict we might as well forget about arguments—that people cannot, or will not, reason about issues of value. Although arguing about fundamental differences in values is not easy, there is no satisfactory alternative.[32] History teaches us that value disagreements cannot be ignored. If the underlying differences in values are substantial, they may eventually lead to armed conflict. The situation in the Middle East provides an example. The Israelis and their Arab neighbors have been in or near a state of war for more than 70 years as a result of unresolved conflicts rooted in religious beliefs, cultural traditions, political autonomy, national and cultural identity, economic inequality, and history. Young Arabs and Israelis have been raised in a climate of fear and distrust. The creation and maintenance of an effective argumentative dialogue given the magnitude of such long-standing problems, although enormously difficult, is clearly better than the alternative—the building of high walls, terrorist assaults, the bulldozing of homes, and other violent acts that could easily escalate to a full-scale war that might kill thousands of people.

The fact that all arguments are to some extent shaped by human values suggests that people must learn how to reason about issues, even when those issues are characterized by profound differences in values. We will discuss arguing about propositions of value in greater detail in chapter 5. When we use reason, we attempt to discover and account for value differences, to accommodate people who hold values different from our own, and to preserve a sense of civility and respect—acts that make for a far more hospitable and safer world.

ETHICS AND ARGUMENTATION

We have already made several references to the importance of maintaining a climate of civility and decorum when engaging in argument. Decorum and civility are foundations for the conduct of ethical argumentation. We believe the issue of ***ethics*** is of vital concern for any student of argumentation theory and practice. Ethics can be understood as a philosophy of human action, as a set of rules for appropriate conduct, and as a way of being and relating to others.[33] Examining ethics in argumentation generally means considering the motives and means used by an arguer. We believe that arguers should seek to be honest, kind, empathetic, patient, and sensitive to the needs and interests of others.

As we have already argued, the values people hold dear are a product of their upbringing, culture, religious training, and even their ideology. We would submit, however, that most of the values such as those identified above transcend the particularities of culture, faith, and ideology. Truthfulness, justice, kindness, respect, and so forth are—or certainly should be—esteemed by all arguers, and thus these values should guide our argument choices.

Wayne Brockriede, a distinguished argumentation theorist, suggested that the images that arguers have of each other are particularly important in shaping the nature of argumentative exchanges. Brockriede argued that it is important that arguers not see those with whom they are arguing as objects or as inferior human beings that they can coerce or manipulate. Such arguers, Brockriede claimed, focus so much on prevailing in the argument and on achieving their desired outcome that they may humiliate their opponents, damage the possibilities for future interactions, create a climate of conflict, and undermine the possibility for trust in the relationship.[34] Brockriede also warned that some arguers seek to take advantage of others through charm or deceit. Such arguers may attempt to beguile others by misrepresenting themselves or their positions so that they can pursue their own objectives without regard for the desires, feelings, wishes, needs, or emotional consequences that those deceptive strategies might have for other people.[35]

What the two types of arguers identified by Brockriede have in common is a belief that they know what is true and correct. Someone who disagrees with them is, by definition, wrong. If individuals are certain they alone know the truth, then they do not have to listen to others. The individual can interrupt, bully, and silence the other. The second type of arguer can pretend to care about the other person and pretend to listen to what the other person is saying, in order to deceive and manipulate the other person. To refuse to even consider the perspectives of others is to deny their humanity.

Brockriede emphasized that arguers should attempt to see others as humans and not as objects and that people should seek power parity rather than a power advantage. The goal for arguers should thus be to develop argument strategies, techniques, and goals that enable people to discover mutually beneficial outcomes that will help establish positive, ongoing, and mutually reinforcing relationships.[36] This form of argumentation is intrinsically dialogic. It requires that arguers speak and listen to others and reflect carefully on what they hear in an effort to understand.[37] Ethical arguers have to enter the interaction with the recognition that the other may have a better conception of truth, that truth might lie somewhere between the two perspectives, or that neither has truth. Arguers who have respect for those with whom they argue acknowledge the intellect, ability, and wisdom of others to decide themselves what they wish to believe after being exposed to competing arguments. Those who argue from this perspective are willing to put themselves on the line for the positions they believe in, and they argue with a sense of genuineness and conviction that demonstrates argumentative integrity. The arguers recognize that they could lose the argument and thus have to confront the fact that their beliefs and/or long-standing opinions could be unwarranted. Arguments thus entail an element of risk and require a capacity for self-reflection.

We find this view of argument compelling. All of us would prefer to engage in arguments with people who value and respect us rather than see us as objects to be used. How can you create such a climate for argumentative encounters? We suggest a principle much akin to the "golden rule" that you were taught as a child: "Do unto others as you would have them do unto you," or its corollary, "if you want a friend, be one." Some manipulative and unethical arguers will always exist; indeed, some continually benefit from their bullying, aggressive, and deceitful behaviors. However, we think the best way to counteract them is to be certain that you do not resort to the same tactics. Always model desirable elements of integrity and empathy for others in your behavior. By living up to high ethical standards yourself, you will encourage others to do the same. If enough people embrace this philosophy there will be fewer unethical, deceptive, and coercive arguers in our society. The contrast between those who conduct themselves in an ethical fashion and those who do not will create strong social pressure to interact honorably.

Ethical arguers are honest and truthful arguers. They discover and investigate the relevant facts carefully. They do not misrepresent those facts; they do not conceal information that would cause people to interpret their arguments differently; and they do not attempt to persuade others to embrace positions or viewpoints they themselves know are not true. Ethical arguers do not try to get people to do things that work against their best interests. At a minimum, they freely acknowledge the possibility that their claims and the resulting actions could be incompatible with the interests of others. Walter Fisher argued that our ethical standards are "intersubjectively created and maintained through symbolic transactions over time. They are neither irrational nor rational; they are historically, and culturally created 'goods' we acquire through socialization, the stuff of the stories we tell, hear, read and enact every day."[38]

Ethical arguers respect the views of others. They enter the argumentative marketplace with the assumption that all parties are persons of integrity and good will—persons who will be open to other ideas. They acknowledge that force and coercion do not lead to effective decision making. People will make better choices if given the opportunity to consider the issues on both sides of a question carefully and systematically.

Learning how to argue effectively means learning how to argue in an ethical and positive manner. We believe if you set high standards for yourself as an arguer and treat others with respect and dignity, they will be more likely to treat you in the same way. In the process, the argumentative marketplace will become a more civilized and valuable place for the free exchange of ideas and for the pursuit of policies and programs that will improve all our lives.

Summary

The ability to argue is necessary if people are to solve problems, resolve conflicts, and evaluate alternative courses of action. While many people are taught that arguing is a counterproductive activity and that arguments should be avoided, we believe arguing is an essential and fundamental human activity. Learning how to argue effectively entails learning not just the strategies and principles of analysis and logical reasoning but also the importance of arguing in an ethical, positive, and socially constructive fashion.

KEY TERMS

arguing
argumentative
arguments
ethics
symbols
values

ACTIVITIES

1. Keep a log for a day. Note the occasions when you were exposed to advocacy.
   a. How many times were you exposed to advocacy?
   b. What was the form of the advocacy? Was it written? Oral? Nonverbal?
   c. What individual decisions were you called upon to make?
   d. What shared or communal decisions were you called upon to make?
2. Recall a recent situation in which you engaged in argumentation2 (an interaction characterized by disagreement).
   a. What was the point of the disagreement?
   b. What values informed your standpoint? What values were reflected in the views of the other person in the interaction?
   c. How was the disagreement resolved?
   d. Were you satisfied with the outcome of the interaction?
3. Consult the opinion section of a daily newspaper or news website. Analyze the arguments that are offered in one of the editorials or op-eds. What value assumptions did the author make? What values would inform someone taking the opposite viewpoint?
4. Make a list of the five values you hold most dear in order of importance. Ask a friend, classmate, sibling, parent, or significant other to do the same. Compare the lists.
   a. How many values appear on both lists?
   b. How similar were your rankings?
   c. What accounts for the similarities?
   d. What accounts for the dissimilarities?

RECOMMENDED READINGS

Aristotle, *The Nichomachean Ethics,* translated by W. David Ross (London: Oxford University Press, 1998).
Bowell, Tracy, Robert Cowan, and Gary Kemp, *Critical Thinking: A Concise Guide*, 5th ed. (New York: Routledge, 2020).
Brodie, Sarah, *Ethics with Aristotle* (Oxford: Oxford University Press, 1991).
Dawes, Mark, Ruth Matthews, Andrew Roberts, and Geoff Thwaites, *Cambridge International AS & A Thinking Skills: Coursebook,* 3rd ed. (New York: Cambridge University Press, 2018).
Fisher, Alec, *Critical Thinking an Introduction,* 2nd ed. (Cambridge: Cambridge University Press, 2011).
Gass, Robert H. and John H. Seiter, *Arguing, Reasoning and Thinking Well* (New York: Routledge, 2019).
Walton, Douglas, *Fundamentals of Critical Argumentation* (New York: Cambridge University Press, 2006).
Zarefsky, David, *The Practice of Argumentation: Effective Reasoning in Communication* (New York: Cambridge University Press, 2019).

ENDNOTES

[1] Andrew Buskell, "What Makes Humans Special?" *London School of Economics*. March 3, 2016. http://www.lse.ac.uk/philosophy/blog/2016/03/03/what-makes-humans-special/

[2] Christine H. Legare, "What Scientific Concept or Theory Ought to be More Widely Known," *Edge*. 2017. https://www.edge.org/response-detail/27143

[3] Joyce O. Hertzler, *A Sociology of Language* (New York: Random House, 1965), 21. See also: Kenneth Burke, *Language as Symbolic Action* (Berkeley: University of California Press, 1966), 3.

[4] Descartes's original declaration was translated as "I think, therefore I am." In Latin the phrase was "Cogito ergo sum," and it was originally pronounced in his text *Discourse on Method*. See: Burns, William E. (2001). *The Scientific Revolution: An Encyclopedia* (Santa Barbara, California: ABC-CLIO) 84. ISBN 978-0-87436-875-8.

[5] Kenneth Burke, "Definition of Man," in *Language as Symbolic Action* (Berkeley: University of California Press, 1966): 16.

[6] Ibid.

[7] For a more complete discussion of this concept, see Daniel J. O'Keefe, "Two Concepts of Argument," *Journal of the American Forensic Association* 13 (1976): 121–128.

[8] "The origins of translating market competition into a theory of free speech was John Stuart Mill's 1859 publication *On Liberty*. In Chapter 2, Mill argues against censorship and in favor of the free flow of ideas." . . . "The first reference to the marketplace of ideas was by Justice Oliver Wendell Holmes Jr. in *Abrams v. United States* (1919). Dissenting from a majority ruling that upheld the prosecution of an anarchist for his anti-war views under the Espionage Act of 1917, Holmes stated: "But when men have realized that time has upset many fighting faiths, they may come to believe even more than they believe the very foundations of their own conduct that the ultimate good desired is better reached by free trade in ideas—that the best test of truth is the power of the thought to get itself accepted in the competition of the market, and that truth is the only ground upon which their wishes safely can be carried out." See: David Schultz (updated by David L. Hudson in June 2017), "Marketplace of Ideas," *The First Amendment Encyclopedia*. https://www.mtsu.edu/first-amendment/article/999/marketplace-of-ideas

[9] Wayne Brockriede, "Where Is Argument?" *Journal of the American Forensic Association* 11 (1975): 179.

[10] Daniel Goleman, *Emotional Intelligence: Why it Can Matter More than IQ* (New York: Bantam Books, 1995).

[11] Emily T. Amanatullah and Michael W. Morris, "Negotiating Gender Roles: Gender Differences in Assertive Negotiating Are Mediated by Women's Fear of Backlash and Attenuated When Negotiating on Behalf of Others," *Journal of Personality and Social Psychology* (2010), 98, 2: 256–267.

[12] Sally Jackson and Scott Jacobs, "Structure of Conversational Argument: Pragmatic Bases for the Enthymeme," *Quarterly Journal of Speech* 66 (1980): 251–265. See also: Susan Heathfield, "Dealing with Difficult People," July 13, 2020. https://dealingwithdifficultpeople.org/category/confrontation-skills/

[13] For example, see: Elizabeth Earnshaw, "How Lack of Communication Can Ruin Relationships and How to Fix It," *MindBodyGreen*, February 22, 2020. https://www.mindbodygreen.com/0-14106/5-communication-mistakes-that-kill-relationships.html

[14] Deborah Tannen, *The Argument Culture: Stopping America's War of Words* (New York: Ballantine Books, 1998), 3.

[15] Mary E. Stuckey and Sean Patrick O'Rourke, "Civility, Democracy and National Politics," *Rhetoric and Public Affairs* 17 (4): 711–736, 712.

[16] Mike Lillis, "Ocasio-Cortez Accosted by GOP Lawmaker Over Remarks: 'That Kind of Thing Hasn't Ever Happened to Me,'" *The Hill*. July 21, 2020. https://thehill.com/homenews/house/508259-ocasio-cortez-accosted-by-gop-lawmaker-over-remarks-that-kind-of

[17] Civility in America 2019: Solutions for Tomorrow, *Weber Shandwick*. https://www.webershandwick.com/wp-content/uploads/2019/06/CivilityInAmerica2019SolutionsforTomorrow.pdf

[18] Ibid., p. 3.

[19] Ibid.

[20] Ibid.

[21] This argument is developed in greater detail by Stuckey and O'Rourke.

[22] Kenneth Burke, *Attitudes Toward History* (Boston: Beacon Press, 1937; rpt. 1961), 3–4.

[23] CDC's Abortion Surveillance System FAQs, Centers for Disease Control, November 2020. https://www.cdc.gov/reproductivehealth/data_stats/abortion.htm

[24] Milton Rokeach, *Beliefs, Attitudes and Values* (San Francisco: Jossey-Bass, 1968), 124.

[25] Ibid., p. 124.

[26] Michelle Fyfe, "What Are Your Personal Core Values?" *Medium,* April 23, 2019. https://medium.com/real-life-resilience/what-are-your-personal-core-values-622a04e1127b

[27] Joseph W. Wenzel, "Toward a Rationale for Value-Centered Argument," *Journal of the American Forensic Association* 13 (1977): 150–158.

[28] Josh Katz, Margot Sanger-Katz, and Kevin Quealy, "How Many People Report Wearing Masks? It All Depends Where You Live," *The New York Times*, July 18, 2020, p. A8.

[29] Thomas A. Hollihan, *Uncivil Wars: Political Campaigns in a Media Age,* 2nd ed. (New York: Bedford St. Martin's, 2009), see especially chapter 3.

[30] Malcolm O. Sillars and Patricia Ganer, "Values and Beliefs: A Systematic Basis for Argumentation," in J. Robert Cox and Charles Arthur Willard, Eds., *Advances in Argumentation Theory and Research* (Carbondale: Southern Illinois University Press, 1982), 184–201.

[31] Julie Turkewitz, "Trump Slashes Size of Bears Ears and Grand Staircase Monuments," *The New York Times,* December 4, 2017. https://www.nytimes.com/2017/12/04/us/trump-bears-ears.html

[32] One of the classic texts in philosophy, law, and rhetoric, focusing on the role of values in human argumentation was authored by a Belgian philosopher who was active during WWII in the anti-fascist resistance movement and who was prompted to think deeply about the challenge of making difficult choices about who might live and who might die when there was no clear legal or moral framework to guide the decisions. See: Chaim Perelman and L. Olbrechts-Tyteca, *The New Rhetoric: A Treatise on Argument* (Notre Dame, IN: The Notre Dame University Press, 1969). The book explains how arguers can learn to develop their argument skills so they can improve the quality and criticism of arguments in value disputes. See especially pp. 54–114.

[33] Walter R. Fisher, "The Ethics of Argumentation and Practical Wisdom," in Thomas A. Hollihan, Ed., *Argument at Century's End: Reflecting on the Past and Envisioning the Future* (Annandale, VA: National Communication Association, 2000), 1–15.

[34] Wayne Brockriede, "Arguers as Lovers," *Philosophy and Rhetoric* 5 (1972): 1–11.

[35] Ibid.

[36] Ibid.

[37] Christopher W. Tindale, *The Philosophy of Argument and Audience Reception* (Cambridge: Cambridge University Press, 2015).

[38] Fisher, p. 4.

The Foundations of Argument

People make arguments when they express, justify, or explain their opinions. These arguments both reflect and have implications for the values that people hold. Arguments have value implications because they reveal how people have constructed their views of the world and how they have interpreted and assigned meaning to their experiences. Consequently, an examination and analysis of arguments tells us a great deal about the people who created them, those who accept them as convincing, and the societies and/or cultures in which those people live.

People are continually challenged by new experiences and situations that they must interpret and make sense of in order to make their way in the world. Events acquire meaning as we think about them, interpret them—and most importantly, as we talk about them with others. It is through discussing our experiences that human culture is created, shared, and re-created. Human values develop largely because those who came before us learned the utility of living their lives according to certain principles. Some of these principles are revealed through the teachings of religious prophets, priests, and other clergy. We learn other values from the proverbs, fables, and historical lessons we are taught. Still other values are taught by our parents, teachers, and civic leaders. Finally, our values are shaped and influenced by our experiences and our interactions with friends, classmates, or fellow team members. That people's values differ reflects how their experiences and cultures differ.

This chapter considers how values influence how people select and evaluate arguments and the formation of the argumentative marketplace. Throughout our lives we both hear and tell stories, *narrative* forms that help us make sense of the world. We enjoy, find useful, and believe some *stories*; because we find them appealing, we repeat them. Other stories we find unbelievable; we discredit and discard those stories. Through storytelling, we give form to the world around us. The stories we tell do more than merely reflect our views of the issues we regard as significant—they become our reality.

VALUE IMPLICATIONS OF ARGUMENTS

Some stories are simple and straightforward, such as those learned in childhood. They often contain moral lessons that are intended to guide us in our life decisions. For example, all of us can probably recall the simple moral lesson in the story of the three little pigs. The first pig built a house of straw, a second pig built a house of sticks, and the third pig labored long and hard to build a sturdy structure of bricks and mortar. Only the pig that took the time and effort to build the secure brick home had shelter when the wolf appeared and blew the houses of straw and sticks away. Obviously, the point of the story goes far beyond the relative merits of alternative porcine dwellings. The intended moral is that hard work will be rewarded; one should anticipate the possibility of adverse conditions and circumstances (perhaps not just nasty and aggressive wolves but also high winds and raging fires). People, like pigs, need to exert the energy to prepare for the future. From such stories, children learn important lessons that should help them later in life. These narratives are easily comprehended, remembered, and eventually passed on to their own children.

Narrative forms communicate core values to guide our lives. Childhood fables taught most of us the importance of doing good deeds for others (e.g., the child who removes the thorn from the paw of the angry and wounded lion is not only spared injury but also makes a friend). We learned what happens to those who raise false alarms (e.g., the boy who always cries wolf discovers that no one takes him seriously when he really needs assistance). Another narrative communicated the importance of always telling the truth (e.g., George Washington admitted to his father that he used his new hatchet to chop down the cherry tree; as a result of his honesty, he was not punished). The exposure to so many different fables teaches us how to craft and tell our own stories as well as how to reason in narrative form. As our intellects develop and become capable of more complex processing, our stories require a greater degree of nuance to account for situations that are morally ambiguous. They also begin to make use of more sophisticated language, storytelling techniques, and plot devices. Despite these developments, however, the nature of the narrative reasoning remains fundamentally the same.

Complexity of Storytelling

Details about the Crimean Peninsula provide an example of the complexity of storytelling. The narrative reveals how stories will be seen and judged differently based upon one's perspectives, interests, and objectives—and the demands of the current moment. Nikita Khrushchev, as leader of the Soviet Union, ceded Crimea from Russia to the neighboring Ukraine in 1954. At that time, Russia and the Ukraine were yoked together under the ruling Communist Party in the Union of Soviet Socialist Republics. The peninsula was transferred from the Russian Republic to the Ukraine Republic with little fanfare via a simple official declaration:

> Decree of the Presidium of the USSR Supreme Soviet transferring Crimea Province from the Russian Republic to the Ukraine Republic, taking into account the integral character of the economy, the territorial proximity and the close economic ties between Crimea Province and the Ukraine Republic, and approving the joint presentation of the Presidium of the Russian Republic Supreme Soviet and the Presidium of the Ukraine Republic Supreme Soviet on the transfer of Crimea Province from the Russian Republic to the Ukraine Republic.[1]

Sixty years later the situation had changed dramatically. When the Soviet Union collapsed, Ukraine and several other republics broke away and became independent nations. Despite Khrushchev's transfer, the Crimean Peninsula had long been considered part of the Russian homeland. In 1954, there were three ethnic Russians living in

Crimea for every Ukrainian, as there were in 2014. Although there was no land connecting Crimea to Russia, several large Russian military installations on the peninsula served as the home base for Russia's strategically important Black Sea fleet. In 2014, Russian leader Vladimir Putin took advantage of political disruptions in Ukraine to encircle Ukrainian armed forces inside their own Crimean bases. He then demanded a public election to poll Crimean residents on whether they would prefer to remain in Ukraine or become part of Russia. The election went Russia's way, and Putin welcomed Crimea into the Russian Federation. He also promised to begin construction on a bridge to connect the peninsula to the Russian mainland. The 12-mile long bridge was completed in 2018, tightening the Kremlin's grip on the Crimean Peninsula.[2] Recognizing that their own forces were no match for the military power of the Russians, the Ukrainians eventually evacuated their forces from Crimea.[3]

The United States and most European governments loudly protested Russia's tactics in seizing the territory of a weaker neighbor, but Putin's popularity at home soared. "Recovering the region that was part of Russia for centuries has boosted Putin's standing among countrymen nostalgic for Moscow's lost superpower status."[4] Former Secretary of State and the Democratic presidential candidate in 2016, Hillary Clinton used strong political language and a historical narrative to protest Putin's aggressive strategy.

> Now if this sounds familiar, it's what Hitler did back in the '30s. . . . The ethnic Germans, the Germans by ancestry who were in places like Czechoslovakia and Romania and other places, Hitler kept saying they're not being treated right. I must go and protect my people, and that's what's gotten everybody so nervous.[5]

In February 2022, Putin claimed Ukraine was a Nazi regime committing genocide against ethnic Russians. He invaded Ukraine in the largest ground war since World War II.

The Hitler Narrative

Clinton's 2014 comparison of Putin's actions to those of Hitler stirred international and diplomatic tensions about Russia's strategy, and her comments received significant attention in the global media. Some media accounts have speculated that Hillary Clinton's Hitler comparison and her speculation that Putin "may not have a soul," deeply offended the Russian leader, "who is considered as vain as he is ruthless," and that her criticism "crossed over from the political into the personal."[6] There is further speculation that this deep hatred may have led to his decision to hack into the Democratic National Committee's email servers to steal emails that were damaging to her campaign in order to help defeat her in the 2016 presidential election.[7]

Perhaps Putin would have been less upset or surprised at the comparison if he understood that the invocation of Hitler in a foreign policy argument was not all that unusual for a U.S. politician. President George H. W. Bush invoked the Hitler analogy to justify his decision to send U.S. troops to the Middle East in the "Desert Storm" war against Iraq in 1991. Bush argued that the troops were necessary because the United States had an obligation to counter the Iraqi aggression against Kuwait. If we did not intervene, he argued, Iraqi leader Saddam Hussein would eventually try to capture Saudi Arabia and the other nations of the region. Hussein's goal, according to this story, was to capture all of the oil reserves in the region so he could hold the United States and other oil-dependent countries hostage. Furthermore, he sought to oppress the people in the region. President Bush claimed that Hussein was utterly ruthless and had no respect for the sanctity of human life. Hussein was said to have seized power by force, to have silenced his critics, and to have used chemical weapons against the Kurdish residents of his own nation.

U.S. military forces, and those of other nations who joined the war effort, quickly ejected the Iraqi invaders from Kuwait and inflicted severe damage on the retreating armies. President Bush chose to end the conflict without capturing the Iraqi capital of Bagdad, however, and without toppling Saddam Hussein's regime. The reasoning offered at the time was that capturing the city would result in a terrible loss of life, and it was believed that Hussein's grip on power would be so weakened by the battlefield losses that he would likely be toppled by his own citizens. President Bush also believed that overthrowing Saddam Hussein was beyond the scope of the mission agreed to by our allied partners and might have ended up splitting the coalition and thus causing political tensions to worsen in the region.[8]

A dozen years later in 2003, President George W. Bush, the son of President George H. W. Bush, invaded Iraq to finish the work his father had begun. Saddam Hussein had not only managed to hang on to power in Iraq but also continued to stir up trouble in the region. He was believed to have plotted an unsuccessful attempt to assassinate the first President Bush.[9] President George W. Bush, the devoted son, again developed his argument for war in a narrative that emphasized Saddam Hussein as an evil actor, a dictator who oppressed and murdered his own citizens—and someone who, because he possessed weapons of mass destruction, also represented an existential threat to the United States and to our allies in the region. Although the claim regarding the weapons of mass destruction was never substantiated, the narrative of Saddam Hussein as a villain rang true for many Americans. Bush won significant public support for his decision to invade Iraq and overthrow the regime.[10] The war in Iraq ultimately lead to the collapse of Saddam Hussein's regime and his eventual arrest and execution, but the nation—and indeed the region—has not realized peace in the years since. Even today, political candidates in the United States are called to account for how they voted on the resolution to support the invasion of Iraq in 2003.

Although there was some disagreement as to whether Saddam Hussein was a Hitler-clone who urgently needed to be defeated, it is important to note that there have been countless other brutal dictators in the world that the U.S. government not only tolerated but also befriended and claimed as allies. For example, August Pinochet of Chile, Ferdinand Marcos of the Philippines, and Chiang Kai-shek of China (after the communists defeated his regime in 1949, he fled to Taiwan) were capable of great cruelty and corruption, but all received aid and military assistance from the United States. Indeed, in previous years Saddam Hussein had been depicted as a U.S. ally because his opposition to Iran was seen as furthering U.S. strategic interests—later he was depicted as a cruel villain. How were these inconsistencies reconciled? Why did the United States intervene to overthrow the brutal dictator Muammar Gaddafi of Libya in 2011 but allow the equally brutal dictator Bashar al-Assad of Syria to remain in power even after he crossed the "red line" warning laid down by President Obama in August 2012 and in 2013 used sarin nerve gas against his own citizens?[11]

The decision to invade or not to invade is made following a pragmatic analysis of how important a particular nation is to the interests of the United States and how likely it is that an intervention will produce the desired outcome. We would argue, however, that public support for military action would almost certainly be stronger if the public becomes convinced that the enemy leader is an immoral actor who poses a threat to the peace and security of the United States. The American people, or at least a significant percentage of them, were convinced that Saddam Hussein and Muammar Gaddafi constituted such a threat. They were not convinced that Bashar al-Assad did because there were not stories circulating that linked his behavior to direct risk to U.S. interests or people.

To return to our earlier discussion of Adolf Hitler, we would argue that Hitler is arguably the most notorious figure in history. He embodied deliberate evil in its most horrific form. The claim that any other foreign leader, whether it is Hussein or Putin, is another Hitler gains its power by reminding people to recall the lessons of World War II—lessons relived in the stories of the great conflict and the Holocaust. World War II narratives often begin with accounts of how British Prime Minister Neville Chamberlain sought to appease Hitler and negotiate with him in an attempt to prevent a broader conflict. Ultimately, of course, Hitler could not be appeased, and a total and complete state of war was necessary to unseat the German dictator and to thwart his murderous territorial ambitions. The lessons of history tell us it would have been better had Great Britain, France, and the United States responded more aggressively to Hitler much earlier, before he had acquired so much power. A columnist in the *London Daily Telegraph* drew the following conclusion: "A pre-emptive strike against Hitler at the time of Munich would have meant an immediate war, as opposed to the one that came later. Later was much worse."[12] If one is to extend the narrative logic, for example, between Hitler and Hussein, it is more desirable to act immediately to topple his regime before he is able to consolidate power or develop more powerful weapons.

The power of invoking the Hitler narrative is obvious. Hitler, the most heinous of modern villains, was capable of unthinkable brutality and industrialized genocide. He, and his Nazi followers, were so morally bankrupt and damaged that they were beyond the reach of rational argument or a sense of shame. Hitler was willing to destroy his people and his nation in the pursuit of his delusional, grandiose plans. Hitler was stopped only by extreme force. If Saddam Hussein is akin to Hitler, then he is also an evil force who must be dealt with quickly and definitively. As James Fallows argued, "Nazi and Holocaust analogies have a trumping power in many arguments, and their effect in Washington was to make doubters seem weak—[the] Neville Chamberlains versus the Winston Churchills who were ready to face the truth."[13] Fallows further argued, however, that the Nazi analogy paralyzed the debate about Iraq rather than clarifying it. Like any other episode in history, the Iraqi situation was both familiar and new. The ruthlessness of Hitler and Hussein was similar, but their countries differed. Unlike Germany, Iraq had no industrial base and no military allies nearby. Both countries had large armies, but Iraq did not have the military experience, training, discipline, or advanced weapons enjoyed by Germany. Iraq also was, and still is, split by regional, religious, and ethnic differences that complicated mobilization compared to Nazi Germany's mobilization of "Aryans" against Jews.[14] As the crisis unfolded, arguments that asserted that Hussein was not a mad Hitler clone or that Iraq was not Nazi Germany were less convincing to most Americans because they lacked the narrative power of the Hussein as Hitler analogy.

Applying Historical Lens to Current Events

As these examples demonstrate, people naturally seek to understand current world events by comparing them to historical events. As we apply the lessons of history, the stories that we share become the lens through which we view our current situation. Historical narratives that have acquired meaning in our lives provide the patterns for our reasoning and problem-solving deliberations. It is in this sense that people can be said to reason through narrative structures.

Another example of an attempt to explain a new event by searching for a historical narrative was provided by the terrorist attacks on the World Trade Center in New York and on the Pentagon in Washington, D.C., on September 11, 2001. The events of that day, now widely known in the public lexicon as 9/11, were so dramatic, tragic, and terrifying that ordinary citizens, media spokespersons, and elected officials alike searched for the appropriate stories to explain them. Many storytellers, including President George W. Bush, likened these terrorist attacks to the Japanese attacks on the U.S. Navy base at Pearl Harbor on December 7, 1941. As a result, many of these storytellers declared that the United States should respond to the 9/11 attacks with a declaration of war and a strategy of military conflict. Those who told such stories noted that the events were similar because both represented an attack on U.S. soil, similar numbers of lives were lost, both attacks came without warning, and the United States had done nothing to provoke them.

What these storytellers seemed to miss in offering the analogies between the two events, however, was that the 9/11 attacks were not made by a nation or by the military forces of a standing army. Instead, they were the work of a loosely structured terrorist network. Consequently, a declaration and pursuit of war might not be as appropriate or as effective as it had been in World War II.

The terrorist network that planned and perpetrated the attacks operated in and attracted members from a variety of locations around the world, including the Middle East, Asia, Africa, and even Europe. Was the United States prepared to engage the terrorists in a declared war in all of these locations? There was convincing evidence of collusion between the terrorists and the ruling Taliban government in Afghanistan that made that nation a logical primary target for a military response, but what about those nations where the evidence of cooperation with the terrorists was present but less overwhelming? What should be the U.S. response in those cases? Indeed, it was soon proven that many of the terrorists who hijacked the planes that were used to crash into the World Trade Center and the Pentagon were citizens of Saudi Arabia, a nation that the United States had long considered an ally, the supplier of much of the foreign oil we were importing, and a client-state that purchased a vast quantity of U.S.-manufactured weapons. What was the appropriate response given these findings? Furthermore, President Bush declared that the United States was engaged in a war against terror. But terror is an emotion. The strategic device used by terrorists is the provocation of fear. So, just how does a nation use military force to win a war against fear? And, how does one prove that such a war has been successfully concluded?—when we are no longer afraid? We would submit that day will never come. As a result of how the narrative case for the war was made, we believe that the United States in 2001 committed its forces to a war in which clear resolution was unlikely. The conflict in Afghanistan raged on for twenty years and became the longest war in U.S. history. President Biden withdrew U.S. military forces in August 2021 and the Taliban regained power in Afghanistan. The Taliban now is locked into a conflict with warriors from the Islamic State, and terrorists continue to strike fear into people around the globe.[15]

Our point is that stories can serve as powerful resources in the construction of narratives to understand events—but storytellers need to recognize that the choice of a particular narrative may lock people into worldviews and resulting policy actions that do not address a perceived threat as well as an alternative narrative might. Did President Bush have a better narrative frame available to him in 2001? Perhaps, but perhaps not. He might, for example, have argued that the terrorists who struck our country were criminals participating in a conspiracy to harm us—and that all who directly or indirectly participated in this criminal enterprise should be subject to arrest and prosecution. This response would not have locked us into a military conflict; in that sense, it might have been a superior response. We have serious doubts, however, that the American people would have accepted such a response as sufficient given the scope of the loss (approximately 3,000 killed and another 6,000 injured), the extent of the public grief and rage, and the conviction that if we did not respond we would appear weak and vulnerable to another similar attack. In short, although there were negative consequences to the story that Bush selected when he spoke of the tragedy, there were likely negative consequences—and substantive risks—to any alternative narrative.

Narratives and Identity

Stories serve an important formative purpose for the people who choose to tell and believe them and ultimately for the cultures that come to accept them. As U.S. citizens, many of us have developed an understanding of our identity as a nation on the basis of stories about our founding fathers and—far too infrequently—stories about our founding mothers. In elementary school we are taught to respect George Washington's honesty, Benjamin Franklin's inventiveness and ingenuity, Thomas Jefferson's concern for equality, and Abraham Lincoln's humility. Our teachers, at least not in the primary grades, did not dwell on the facts that George Washington was accused of padding his expense accounts, that Benjamin Franklin and Thomas Jefferson were philanderers, or that Abraham Lincoln was a successful corporate attorney (representing railroads, the most powerful corporations of the day). These aspects of our founding fathers' life stories are not recounted as frequently because they serve our contemporary needs less well. In short, the stories that are retold time and again are those that fulfill contemporary needs.

This explains why our society, shocked at video footage of the murder of George Floyd when he was detained by the Minneapolis Police in May 2020 and prompted by the Black Lives Matter Movement, has undertaken a more robust conversation about the history of racial oppression in the United States. As part of that conversation, there are increasing calls to tear down statues and to revisit our praise for many of our founding fathers, particularly George Washington and Thomas Jefferson who owned slaves. Many conservatives have attempted to prohibit the teaching of what is known as "critical race theory" in elementary schools, high schools, and public universities because they do not want students to question the history that ignores the oppression of black bodies.[16] Judging historical figures by the standards of today is a common occurrence. Even Abraham Lincoln, long hailed as "the Great Emancipator" because his actions led to the end of slavery, has come under attack for statements that he made that supported segregation. In an 1858 debate with Senator Stephen A. Douglas, Lincoln said: "I'll have no purpose to introduce political and social equality between the white and black races. There is physical difference between the two, which in my judgment will probably forever forbid their living together upon the footing of perfect equality."[17]

When most U.S. citizens are asked to recount the story of the first settlers of their nation, they mention the Pilgrims who landed at Plymouth Rock in Massachusetts in 1620. The story details a landscape bare of people—yet indigenous peoples already inhabited North America. These populations are largely written out of history. In addition, it is worth noting that these stories also ignore other European settlers. The first European settlement on the East Coast of North America was in 1607 at the colony in Jamestown, Virginia. Why does this colony not come to mind when people are asked about our origin story? We suggest there are likely several reasons. First, the Pilgrims came for religious freedom while the Jamestown colony was intended to be a profit-driven enterprise. It is far more compelling to anchor your national origin story in a morally compelling religious narrative. Second, the Jamestown colony failed, and the settlement was briefly abandoned in 1610. How glorious can it be to tell your origin story in a narrative of failure?

There are consequences to sharing stories about the Pilgrims' search for religious liberty and stories emphasizing the achievements of our founding fathers. These narratives establish a collective national identity and invite citizens to follow a particular course of action. Our self-image includes the moral purpose inherited from the Pilgrim settlers and the love of freedom-by descendants of patriots such as Washington, Franklin, Jefferson, and Lincoln. Is it not our moral duty to live up to this heritage by eliminating evil actors such as Hitler, Saddam Hussein, Muammar Gaddafi, or Osama bin Laden? As long as there are terrorists or dictators trying to kill innocent people or thwart the free will of their citizens, the United States is prepared to assert the moral authority to end the oppression.

Creating Stories to Fit our World and Creating a World to Fit Our Stories

The confidence that we, as U.S. citizens, have in the moral certainty of our actions, is thus a result of our narrative experience—we have created a world to fit our stories, as much as we have created stories to fit our world. The purpose of this discussion is not to discredit the stories that make up U.S. history, nor do we mean to suggest that this process is a negative one. All humans reason through narratives, which helps to explain why the citizens of Iraq believed in the legitimacy of Iraq's invasion of Kuwait and admired the courage of Saddam Hussein. For most U.S. citizens Osama bin Laden was a terrorist and a murderer, but for many in the Middle East and beyond he was a hero because he was willing to strike at the very heart of U.S. power.[18] How can international diplomacy be conducted and reasoned arguments occur when people tell such completely different stories—and, as a result, construct their reality in such incompatible ways?

One lesson that quickly becomes apparent from this discussion is that patriotic stories that on the surface seem so positive to the formation of values of a political culture may have negative consequences. For example, the patriotic stories about Washington, Franklin, Jefferson, and Lincoln previously discussed may have led many U.S. citizens to have an unquestioning faith in the legitimacy of their nation, making them unwilling or unable to see any faults. This, in turn, leads to believing that what is good for the U.S. interests is also good for everyone else's interests. We may be too inclined to believe that our way is the best way, if not the only way, to solve problems. This view is sometimes referred to as "American exceptionalism."[19] Can those of us who live in relative prosperity and privilege in a nation that cherishes pluralism and democratic values really believe that we tell the same stories, live the same experiences, and share the same worldviews as those who live in repressive, undemocratic, tribal, or impoverished nations? We also want to be clear that other nations similarly tell their origin stories in ways that serve the political interests of those who hold power and that respond to and shape their perceptions of their current situations. In the People's Republic of China (PRC), for example, students are taught that China endured a century of humiliation at the hands of the Western powers.

> The "century of humiliation" has been a central part of the P.R.C.'s founding mythology, of which the short version is this: Long the world's pre-eminent civilization, China fell behind the superior technology of the West over the centuries, an imbalance that finally came to a head with the loss in the Opium Wars. This began the most tumultuous century in the country's—or *any* country's—history, one that featured an incessant series of wars, occupations, and revolutions and one that did not end until the victory of the Communist Party in China's 1945–49 civil war.[20]

Students learn that China regained its position as a global power, enhanced its wealth, and won the respect of the world through the efforts of the Chinese Communist Party that has been firmly in control for more than 70 years. Some might see a linkage between this bold story of an again strong and powerful China and the willingness of the PRC to assert its aggressive claims of sovereignty in the South China Sea. China has been seizing shoals and small islands and building military bases and air strips in waters that are also claimed by other nations and that the United State insists is open water that should be navigable by all.[21]

You may be wondering if all attempts at reasoned discourse are futile. However, it is important to recognize that people can and do critique and evaluate the quality of the stories they hear and tell. When comparing the rival stories that compete for acceptance as people explain themselves and express their convictions, one can gain insight into the underlying differences in culture, values, political conditions, and experiences that shape human life. Narrative arguments are rational arguments, and we can learn a great deal about how people reason through stories. Knowing more about the narrative reasoning process will help learn to tell better—that is, more convincing, credible, and compassionate—stories.

THE NARRATIVE PARADIGM

We are exposed to hundreds of different stories in any given week. We hear stories in conversations with friends and family members, we hear them on news broadcasts, we watch them unfold in television programs or films, and we read them in books, magazines, newspapers, or blog posts.

How do we determine which stories are true and should guide our lives—and which are not true and should be dismissed? One criterion that we can apply is to determine whether the stories were intended as fictions. However, the line between real and fictional accounts often becomes blurred. Some fictions come to be accepted as truths and are especially useful in shaping our lives and helping us make sense of our experiences. Perhaps one of the best-known examples of a work of fiction that was taken as truth was Harriet Beecher Stowe's classic novel *Uncle Tom's Cabin*, a story about the experience of slavery told through the eyes of a slave family. This book had a tremendous impact on public attitudes toward slavery and came to be accepted as fact, despite its fictional characters. Indeed, the book was sometimes credited with having so inflamed abolitionist attitudes that it may have sparked the Civil War. Upon meeting Harriet Beecher Stowe, President Lincoln is purported to have said: "So this is the little lady who made this great war."[22]

One reason why it is sometimes difficult to distinguish between fictional narratives and historically accurate narratives is that those who produce creative content draw the subjects for their stories from real world events. One of your authors has become a huge fan of the long running mini-series *Homeland*, which involves multiple layers of conspiracy stories focused on terrorist plots that are discovered—and sometimes perpetrated—by CIA intelligence officers. Although the show is intended as fiction, its use of conspiracy as a repetitive storyline aligns with the perception of many people that things do not merely happen by chance—the forces of powerful but deeply secretive conspirators are often at work. Given the popularity of conspiracy narratives in Hollywood entertainment, should it surprise us that many people accept increasingly bizarre conspiracy theories? A 2019 study found that the acceptance of conspiracy theories is "not simply restricted to a fringe population. At least 50% of Americans believe in at least one conspiracy theory, ranging from the idea that the 9/11 attacks were fake to the belief that former President Barack Obama was not born in the U.S."[23] The same study found that over 29% of the population believed there was a "Deep State" working against President Donald Trump, and 19% believe that the government used chemicals to control the population.[24] The *Los Angeles Times* reported:

> A fringe theory that President Trump is at war with a global cabal of powerful, Satan-worshiping elites who control the world and run a child sex ring has shifted over the last three years from anonymous message boards to Trump rallies to the 2020 ballot. More than 60 current and former congressional candidates have promoted or embraced the unfounded QAnon theory, according to a count by Media Matters, a left-leaning research site that tracks conservative media.[25]

It is worth noting that the QAnon conspiracy theory links political elites, wealthy corporate executives, and Hollywood celebrities. Specifically, "The QAnon conspiracy theory is founded on the belief that the world is run by a powerful group of evil politicians and celebrities including the Clintons, the Obamas, the Bushes, George Soros and Hollywood celebrities including Oprah Winfrey and Tom Hanks."[26] The link between these supposed conspirators and a ring of powerful, secretive pedophiles has already led to a very dangerous encounter.

> Less than a year before Q started posting, the unfounded Pizzagate theory took off. On Dec. 4, 2016, Edgar Maddison Welch drove from his home in North Carolina to the Comet Ping Pong pizzeria in Washington, D.C., where he was convinced children were being held captive as part of a sex trafficking ring organized by Democrats and Hillary Clinton. Welch fired shots from an AR-15 semiautomatic rifle into a locked door. When he realized there was no evidence of a trafficking ring, he left his weapons in the store, walked out and was arrested. No one was harmed, and Welch was sentenced to four years in prison in June 2017.[27]

It is not just fringe conspiracy theories such as this one that have the potential to cost people their lives, however, as has been shown with regard to the COVID-19 virus.

A recent Pew Research poll reported that "most Americans (71%) have heard of a conspiracy theory circulating widely online that alleges that powerful people intentionally planned the coronavirus outbreak. And a quarter of U.S. adults see at least some truth in it—including 5% who say it is definitely true and 20% who say it is probably true."[28] The poll goes on to report that educational attainment is a big factor in who believes this conspiracy. Of those with a high school diploma or less, 48% believe it is true. Partisanship is also a factor, with 34% of Republicans and independents who lean to the GOP believing the conspiracy compared to only 18% of Democrats and those who lean Democrat believing it.[29] Finally, there is another aspect of the conspiracy that claims the death toll from COVID-19 had been inflated in order to cost Trump reelection. Where people get their news was a strong predictor of belief in this conspiracy. "The number of Americans who believe the death toll is inflated is highest among those who get their news from Fox News (61%) and Republicans (59%), while only 9% of Democrats and 7% of those getting their news from CNN and MSNBC believe the same."[30] Most researchers, by the way, argue the opposite, and believe that the COVID death toll is undercounted.[31]

We claimed earlier that the belief in COVID-19 conspiracy theories could cost lives. Another Pew Research Study found that "Democrats and Democratic-leaning independents are about twice as likely as Republicans and Republican leaners to say that masks should be worn always (63% vs. 29%). Republicans are much more likely than Democrats to say that masks should rarely or never be worn (23% vs. 4%)."[32] Studies also reported that those who did not believe that the virus was a serious threat were more likely to go out to bars and restaurants, more likely to socialize with friends and relatives, and more likely to feel comfortable visiting a grocery store.[33] Engaging in these activities without practicing social distancing increases the potential to spread the virus. Similarly, the decision to take the vaccines to prevent COVID-19 also fell along partisan political lines. In May 2021, for example, "The 20 states with the highest rates of residents who have received at least one vaccine dose all went to Joe Biden in last year's presidential election, while 19 of the 21 states with the lowest vaccination rates supported Donald Trump.[34]

So, the natural question is: how do we help people choose stories that are likely true and refute or offer counternarratives to stories that mislead and possibly endanger them? People will accept stories as true if those stories account for their experience. Walter Fisher has argued that people reason through narratives. He referred to this mode of reasoning as the narrative paradigm, which he summarized as follows:

> (1) Humans are . . . storytellers. (2) The paradigmatic mode of human decision making and communication is "good reasons," which vary in form among situations, genres, and media of communication. (3) The production and practice of good reasons are ruled by matters of history, biography, culture and character. . . . (4) Rationality is determined by the nature of persons as narrative beings—their inherent awareness of narrative probability, what constitutes a coherent story, and constant habit of testing narrative fidelity, whether or not the stories they experience ring true with the stories they know to be true in their lives. . . . (5) The world as we know it is a set of stories that must be chosen among in order for us to live life in a process of continual re-creation.[35]

Fisher claims that human reasoning need not be bound to argumentative prose or to clear-cut inferential or implicative structures. It is typically achieved through the stories that people tell. Viewed from this perspective, virtually all arguments can be understood and evaluated as stories. One of the most noteworthy aspects of Fisher's theory of argument is its assumption that ordinary people who are untrained in argumentation techniques are capable of resolving complex problems because they reason through narrative structures. For purposes of clarification, we will look at both the testing of rationality and the criteria for evaluating "good reasons" that Fisher mentions.

People first assess arguments by evaluating their ***narrative probability***. This concept refers to whether a story seems coherent. Is the argumentative structure of the story satisfying and complete? Does the chronology of events seem credible and convincing? Does the story account for the material facts of the situation in a satisfying manner? How do the primary characters in the story acquire their dramatic motivation? Do the heroes behave in ways that are appropriately heroic? Do the villains behave as villains are expected to behave? Are the actions of the characters reliable? Do their actions fit the plot that has been developed in the narrative structure? Are behaviors consistent with the values attributed to the characters by the plot?

In our earlier discussion we mentioned that former Secretary of State Hillary Clinton likened Russian President Vladimir Putin to Adolf Hitler and speculated that "he had no soul." The test of narrative probability encourages arguers to question whether Putin lives up to their expectations for a villain. Was the Russian strongman acting like the tyrant when he was accused of arresting, poisoning, and murdering his political enemies?[36] Or was he a patriotic leader taking the expected steps to protect the security of his nation and to counter intervention and espionage against it by the United States and other nations? Did Putin cynically invade Ukraine to steal and annex its territory? Or was he reclaiming traditional Russian territory and acting to protect Russian people living there? Did Putin plot and actively intervene in the 2016 U.S. presidential election by hacking into the Democratic National Committee's computers and publishing secret emails and by disseminating false news narratives? Or, should he be taken at his word, as President Trump said he did, when he denied that Russia had participated in any of these activities?[37] Should we worry that Putin plotted again to intervene in the 2020 presidential election? Or should we consider such threats mere distractions that were planted by "deep state" conspirators to discredit President Trump's 2016 victory and prevent his reelection?[38]

Many stories depend upon the credibility and good character of the key actors in the narratives. Actors seek to win our trust and support by emphasizing that they share our values. Political candidates, for example, frequently build their entire campaigns on the premise that they are people of good character. Some will remember the case of former Congressman Anthony Weiner (D-NY). Weiner was married to Huma Abedin, a long-time aide to Secretary of State Hillary Clinton. Unfortunately, Weiner used his wife's laptop to send inappropriate and sexually provocative images and messages to a 15-year-old girl. It was not the first time that Weiner had been caught sending lewd images, but the use of his wife's computer brought this case to the attention of the FBI. "During the investigation, the F.B.I. found emails belonging to Ms. Abedin on Mr. Weiner's laptop. The discovery led the F.B.I. director at the time, James Comey, to announce the bureau was reopening its inquiry into Mrs. Clinton's handling of official emails—an investigation that Mrs. Clinton has partly blamed for her election loss."[39] Weiner's criminal conduct became an issue in the closing days of the campaign and raised new suspicions about Clinton's character. In addition, it completely shattered what was left of Weiner's already damaged reputation. His wife filed for divorce, he was convicted and sentenced to prison, and he must register as a sex offender for the rest of his life.[40]

Character and integrity are important resources that are essential to one's power and credibility as a storyteller. Consider the case of Brian Williams, the former news anchor on *NBC Nightly News*. Over many years Williams told different versions of a story in which he claimed to have been in a military helicopter in 2003 when covering the war in Iraq. Williams claimed that the helicopter was struck by fire and forced to land. The pilot and crew that flew the helicopter on which Williams was a passenger remembered the situation differently, claiming there was no fire and the helicopter was not forced to the ground. Indeed, they claimed that they did not arrive until 30 minutes after an attack that forced other helicopters to land. Williams eventually apologized for an honest mistake—a product of "the fog of memory." Others saw Williams's story as a deliberate attempt to inflate the significance of his own role in the war. Critics argued that his deceptions, and his woefully inadequate explanation and apology, undermined his credibility and represented "an unmitigated disaster for NBC" because "an anchor's No. 1 requirement is that he or she has credibility. If we don't believe what an anchor tells us, what's the point?"[41] NBC suspended Williams for six months and then reassigned him to MSNBC, a much less glamorous position.

People like stories that do not leave loose ends untied. We prefer stories that offer resolution and satisfy our need to understand rapidly developing and complex issues and events. For example, have you ever watched a film that left you dissatisfied because the plot did not hang together very well? Although audiences enjoy films with surprise endings, the best of such films are carefully planned so when they are finished, the audience can look back and discover the clues that were available all along. Our interest in compelling and satisfying stories is no less intense outside of books or films. Most Americans, for instance, do not want to be dragged into a war in the Middle East until they are convinced that the conflict is unavoidable, the objectives are moral and justified, and the prospects for victory are sufficiently high that they will outweigh the costs.

The second test of stories, **narrative fidelity**, concerns whether a story represents accurate assertions about social reality.[42] This dimension of narrative reasoning is firmly rooted in the human capacity for making judgments about issues of value. Fisher argued that people make their decisions in accordance with the values they hold. They also want to determine if the "facts" revealed to them in the stories they encounter are indeed facts, if they are reliable and relevant, and whether they have been taken out of context.

People thus consider the degree to which any new story seems consistent with the stories they have heard before and have already accepted as true. The "Hussein as Hitler" story, for example, fared well in a test of narrative fidelity for many people. This was not a story, however, without some very obvious flaws. First, as mentioned above, Iraq was not Nazi Germany and Hussein's forces, unlike Hitler's, were no match for the U.S. forces. Second, Nazi Germany boasted a strong industrial base and very well-educated scientists, engineers, and other professionals as well as a very highly-skilled and well-trained industrial workforce. Third, for all his flaws, there was no evidence to suggest that Saddam Hussein was driven to achieve global conquest as Hitler had been. Still, many Americans likely came to believe that a negotiated settlement with Iraq was doomed to failure—just as attempts to make peace with Hitler had been. In addition, Hussein's willingness to bomb civilian targets in Israel, his killing of innocent women and children in his own nation, and his policies against any who opposed his regime suggested that he may have harbored the same blind hatreds and hostilities that Hitler did.[43]

As we have already mentioned, Fisher argued that the capacity for narrative argument is present in all humans because all of us are socialized and taught through stories. The power of this form of argument is often illustrated in the courtroom. Lance Bennett and Martha Feldman observed that jurors were able to make sense of complicated and sophisticated legal arguments when they evaluated such arguments as stories.[44] A prosecutor, for example, must fashion a structurally complete and internally consistent story that accounts for the evidence in the case.[45] Defense attorneys succeed if they can find a way to reveal flaws in the prosecutor's story. These flaws might involve such issues as evidentiary inconsistencies (including presenting new evidence that is important to the case yet fundamentally incompatible with the prosecutor's story) or the construction of a rival story that seems equally or more probable.

Human nature causes people to accept stories that fit their needs or further their interests. For example, a political candidate's story containing promises to fund increases in social programs while also decreasing taxes may appeal to a broad swath of voters because it promises benefits without pain. A rival story that says that the benefits will require an increase in taxes will be less appealing to many voters. Convincing people to reject the original story requires evidence that decreased taxes cannot fund increased social programs—the facts don't match the claim. We have argued that stories must meet the tests of narrative probability and fidelity, but sometimes people work hard to convince themselves that a story that serves their interests is true while one that does not is inaccurate.

The appeal of some stories, and the lack of appeal of other stories, is closely connected to the values and life experiences of people and of the cultures in which they live. Stories people tell and come to believe as probably true give form to their lives and thus help to shape their values and their self-conceptions. Fisher argued that people favor stories that confirm their sense of themselves. Stories that justify people's behaviors and motives, and make them feel important and worthwhile, have an easier time gaining public acceptance than do stories that impugn their self-image. People are more readily moved to action on the basis of stories that make such action and their own conduct seem appropriate and just. Skilled storytellers understand that people prefer stories that affirm their self-concept. For example, when political candidates go before groups like the American Legion or the Veterans of Foreign Wars, they appeal to the veterans' sense of pride in their patriotism, their love of country, and their feelings of camaraderie with fellow veterans.

A politician who wants to refute a story that we can increase spending on social programs and also lower taxes might stress the fact that the numbers have been "cooked" and that the result would be an increase in the budget deficit. Then this arguer could claim that the budget deficit might make it more expensive for the government to borrow money and to service the new debts that are incurred. The arguer could then suggest that our decision to live beyond our means today shifts our burdens onto the backs of our children. This appeal to the obligation that today's citizens have to future generations is persuasive because it addresses our desire to nurture and protect our offspring. The concern for the health and welfare of children is a natural human emotion, and thus a form of argument that will appeal to audiences across a wide span of time and a wide range of specific issues. More than 2,500 years ago, Aristotle wrote that happiness, justice, courage, fear, praise, sympathy, and empathy (among others) are common issues that are capable of influencing the opinions of listeners.[46] Listeners are more likely to be motivated to accept stories as probably true when those stories appeal to their values, emotions, sense of virtue, or instincts.

We should offer a caveat to the appeal of the politician's argument regarding the budget deficit. There are important differences between federal and family budgets. The most important difference is that federal governments can increase the amount of capital circulating, while families typically cannot change the volume of money coming into the family coffers. By increasing the amount of money, either by printing more money or by releasing it to banks to loan to those who are cash strapped, governments reduce the rate of interest and thus the cost of servicing debts. This story, about how debts and monetary policies achieve their desired goals, is more likely told and understood by trained economists than by ordinary citizens. In the past, this has been a position advocated by liberal economists.[47] The forced economic shutdown due to the COVID-19 pandemic in 2020 resulted in many politicians—although certainly not all—embracing this narrative to keep the economy active and businesses up and running.[48]

If all humans possess an almost instinctive ability to engage in narrative arguments—to tell stories and to evaluate and choose between the stories they are told—what need is there for a class in argumentation? The answer, we believe, lies in the fact that some people are better storytellers than others. The assumption we make is that by learning certain argumentative principles people can hone their storytelling skills and learn how to become better storytellers (advocates) and better critics of the stories that they are exposed to on a daily basis.

THE LIMITS OF ARGUMENT

One clear measure of a competent arguer is the ability to recognize when to argue and when to remain silent. Another measure is the ability to recognize a superior argument. A competent arguer knows when an adversary has presented arguments that are superior to his or her own. Learning when to argue and when not to argue will not only make you a more convincing advocate for the positions that you espouse but also will help you preserve your friendships. Although we will discuss the relationship between argumentation style and interpersonal relationships in greater detail in the last chapter, we discuss the issue briefly now because it is so important to developing the skills of effective argumentation.

We often find ourselves in conversations where someone makes a statement that we disagree with, but our disagreement is so trivial that we need to decide whether the relational tension that might result from a public disagreement is warranted. Sometimes arguments are not worth the effort because the issue about which we differ is not very significant. It may not seem worthwhile, for example, to argue that the color of a couch you admired in a furniture store was turquoise, if your friend insists it was teal. Obviously both turquoise and teal come in many different shades, and our ability to distinguish between them may be limited, as may be our ability to recall what we saw. Breaking into a full-fledged dispute over precisely what the color was is simply not worth the effort. The decision to argue (to engage in argument 2) over every trivial difference of opinion will impair your relationships with others. None of us choose as friends, lovers, or even close colleagues people with whom we find ourselves in constant disagreements over trivial issues. The tension level that results from such disputes can begin to undermine even otherwise healthy relationships.

Other arguments are not worth having because they do not concern questions that can be readily resolved through disputation, regardless of the relative skills of the competing arguers. For example, an argument over which college football team has gone to the Rose Bowl more often—the University of Southern California or Ohio State University—is not a dispute to be resolved through arguments (although similar arguments have certainly occupied the time of many sports fans!). This is an empirical question that can be answered with a simple internet search. If, however, the argument concerned which school had established the better football tradition, it would be resolvable only through argument. The nature of that issue requires the evaluation of argumentative claims. Evidence of Rose Bowl participation would be relevant but not sufficient to prove one football program's tradition superior to another. One might also be motivated to make and evaluate arguments about the appearance in other bowl games over the years, the respective strength of the conference and nonconference schedules, the quality of the coaches, consistency over a wide span of years, the number of Heisman trophies won, the number of former players who made it to the National Football League, the number of national titles earned, recent performance on the gridiron, the loyalty of their fans, and so on. All of these arguments and the empirical evidence that supported claims offered about them, might provide the grounds for developing beliefs about the relative merits of the two football powers.

Another type of argument that might not be worth making is an argument directed toward changing the mind of a genuinely and firmly committed ideologue. Some people hold beliefs so strongly that they are not open to critical reflection. Many arguments over the merits of particular religious philosophies fall in this category. Someone who is, for example, a committed Roman Catholic and who faithfully adheres to the teachings and philosophies of that faith is not likely to be very open to arguments about its flaws or errors. Such arguments would be especially difficult to accept if they came from someone outside of the faith. One might question both the arguer's knowledge of the religious teachings of Catholicism and the motives for seeking to discredit the faith.

Similarly, arguments between intensely committed political conservatives and equally committed political liberals are ineffectual because so little of their disagreement can be resolved through dispute and reasoning. For an effective argument exchange to occur, both parties must be open to arguments. They need not have suspended their beliefs and become what is known as *tabula rasa* or "blank slates," but they must be willing to confront the possibility that the beliefs they hold could be demonstrated to be wrong. Partisan advocates infrequently meet this condition.

Our goal is not to discourage you from forming strong opinions or from engaging in arguments with others who also hold such opinions. Instead, our point is that some assessment of the nature of the argumentative climate is important. Arguers need to make conscious decisions concerning whether participation in any given argument will serve their interests. They should ask themselves: Will having this argument damage my relationship with this person? Will the arguments we make really resolve the dispute? It is, of course, often difficult to predict the outcome of a disagreement or to determine in advance how it will affect our relationships. Nevertheless, sometimes we can predict quite accurately if we take the time to weigh the potential consequences of our words carefully and deliberately before we speak or write them. We believe arguers should choose their arguments carefully based on their sense of where each is likely to lead. We believe selectivity of arguments and situations, control of emotions, and thoughtful choices of argumentative strategy are all traits of effective arguers.

The Study of Argumentation

The information in this book will help you develop your reasoning and critical analysis skills. In the remaining chapters, we will consider the following topics:

- What issues are worth arguing over and what issues are beyond argument?
- How can arguers adjust their arguments to suit their audiences?
- What is the relationship between argumentation and critical thinking?
- What are the various forms of argument?
- What role does evidence play in argumentation?
- How do I best refute the arguments offered by others?
- How do visual images function and achieve their power as arguments?
- How do the forms and types of arguments that occur differ by context or situations?

The techniques for arguments do, of course, vary from situation to situation. We have taken the position that most arguers reason primarily from a narrative perspective and that most arguments are presented as stories. However, not all argumentative contexts or situations demand the same kind of stories. In fact, certain argument situations, and certain communities of arguers, have created their own standards for arguing. Thus, the arguments that are developed in the courtroom are substantially different from those developed in a legislative hearing, an academic debate, a classroom, a business meeting, a scientific conference, a religious conference, or a discussion between friends or family members. Learning the techniques for effective arguing therefore means developing one's sensitivity to the demands of a wide variety of different argumentative contexts.

One of the primary objectives of this text is to help you explore resources that may be useful to you as you develop arguments in a variety of contexts. We will consider how one finds, selects, and develops appropriate evidence; how this evidence is used to support the analysis and reasoning that strengthens claims; and how these arguments are best organized. We will also focus on techniques that will enable you to refute the arguments offered by others and to defend and rebuild your own arguments after they have been refuted. Finally, we will offer suggestions that will help you analyze your audience, enabling you to make the strongest possible case that might appeal to that audience given their background, experience, ideological commitments, and interests. By adapting your arguments to your audience, you can present a case that is not only well reasoned, well evidenced, and well organized but also more likely to convince those who will evaluate your arguments.

Summary

We believe all people have the capacity to argue and to evaluate arguments because people are by nature rational beings. The primary mode for the creation and evaluation of arguments is through storytelling, and our stories are tested through an evaluation of their narrative probability and narrative fidelity. Despite the fact that we all have the capacity for arguing, we can improve our argumentation skills by learning conventions and norms for arguing effectively in particular contexts—and by recognizing that some arguments will not be productive, will not result in agreement, may erode the quality of our relationships, and hence should be avoided.

KEY TERMS

narrative
narrative fidelity
narrative paradigm
narrative probability
stories
storytelling

ACTIVITIES

1. Think about your favorite Disney film from your childhood.
    a. Who is the hero of the story? Is the hero male or female? What ethnicity is the hero? What are the hero's personality characteristics and how did they impact the ability of the hero to fulfill his/her role?
    b. Who is the villain of the story? Is the villain male or female? What ethnicity is the villain? What are the villain's personality characteristics and how did they impact the ability of the villain to fulfill his/her role?
    c. What do the hero and the villain say about these types of characters?
    d. What was the moral lesson of the story?
    e. Did the film succeed in offering compelling narrative arguments for its moral lesson?
2. Make a list of what you think are the traditional values of U.S. culture. Now select a different culture or subculture. Make a list of what you believe to be the values of that culture. If you are not familiar with that culture you might ask someone from that culture to make a list and share it with you.
    a. Are there differences in the values of the two cultures?
    b. How are these differences manifested in behavior?
    c. Can you identify similarities in the values of the two cultures?
    d. Are these similarities manifested in similar behaviors?
3. Think about the last film that you saw.
    a. Were there points in the plot of the movie that did not seem to fit together?
    b. Were there subplots that were left unresolved?
    c. Did the characters act the way that you think characters in real situations would behave?
    d. How do these aspects of the story reflect Fisher's concepts of narrative probability and fidelity?
4. Pick a public issue from the headlines of a major newspaper. Discuss the issue with a classmate or a friend. Then analyze your discussion.
    a. Were there points on which you disagreed?
    b. Did you voice all such disagreements, or did you keep some to yourself?
    c. If you voiced all of your disagreements, what effect did this have on your discussion?
    d. If you kept some points of disagreement to yourself, why did you do this?

RECOMMENDED READINGS

Fisher, Walter R., "Clarifying the Narrative Paradigm," *Communication Monographs* 56 (1989): 55–58.

Fisher, Walter R., "Rationality and the Logic of Good Reasons," *Philosophy and Rhetoric* 13 (1980): 121–130.

Fisher, Walter R., "Toward a Logic of Good Reasons," *Quarterly Journal of Speech* 64 (1978): 376–384.

Hollihan, Thomas A., Patricia Riley, and Keith Freadhoff, "Arguing for Justice: An Analysis of Arguments in Small Claims Court," *The Journal of the American Forensic Association* 22 (1986): 187–195.

Jameson, Frederic, *The Political Unconscious: Narrative as a Socially Symbolic Act* (Ithaca, NY: Cornell University Press, 1981).

Rokeach, Milton, *Understanding Human Values: Individual and Societal* (New York: Free Press, 1979).

Tindale, Christopher, "Narratives and the Concept of Argument," in Paula Olmos Ed., *Narration as Argument*. Argumentation Library, vol 31 (Cham, Switzerland: Springer, 2017).

Wallace, Karl C., "The Substance of Rhetoric: Good Reasons," *Quarterly Journal of Speech* 49 (1963): 239–249.

ENDNOTES

[1] Krishnadey Calamur, "Crimea: A Gift to the Ukraine Becomes a Political Flashpoint," *NPR.org.*, February 27, 2014. https://www.npr.org/sections/parallels/2014/02/27/283481587/crimea-a-gift-to-ukraine-becomes-a-political-flash-point

[2] "Putin Opens 12-mile Bridge Between Crimea and Russian Mainland," *The Guardian*, May 15, 2018. https://www.theguardian.com/world/2018/may/15/putin-opens-bridge-between-crimea-and-russian-mainland

[3] Charlotte Alter, "Ukraine Orders Troops to Retreat from Crimea After Russia Annexes," *Time*, March 24, 2014. https://time.com/35319/ukraine-crimea-russia-retreat/

[4] Carol J. Williams, "Vladimir Putin: Russia's Human Tank," *Los Angeles Times,* March 26, 2014. https://www.latimes.com/world/europe/la-fg-russia-no-dissent-20140326-story.html

[5] Philip Rucker, "Hillary Clinton Says Putin's Actions 'Are Like What Hitler Did Back in the '30s,'" *Washington Post,* March 5, 2014. https://www.washingtonpost.com/news/post-politics/wp/2014/03/05/hillary-clinton-says-putins-action-are-like-what-hitler-did-back-in-the-30s/

[6] Josh Meyer, "DNC Email Hack: Why Vladimir Putin Hates Hillary Clinton," *NBC News,* July 26, 2016. https://www.nbcnews.com/news/us-news/why-putin-hates-hillary-clinton-n617236

[7] Ibid.

[8] James A. Baker III, "Why the U.S. Didn't March to Bagdad," *Los Angeles Times,* September 8, 1996. https://www.latimes.com/archives/la-xpm-1996-09-08-op-41778-story.html

[9] David Von Drehele and R. Jeffrey Smith, "U.S. Strikes Iraq for Plot to Kill Bush," *Washington Post,* June 27, 1993, p. A01.

[10] For an interesting and informative discussion of the narrative rationale offered to justify the invasion of Iraq in 2003 see: Richard N. Haas, *War of Necessity, War of Choice* (New York: Simon & Schuster, 2009). For the unique role that former Secretary of State Colin Powell played in winning support for the intervention on the basis of faulty intelligence information see: Robert Draper, "Colin Powell Still Wants Answers," *The New York Times,* July 17, 2020. https://www.nytimes.com/2020/07/16/magazine/colin-powell-iraq-war.html

[11] Ben Rhodes, "Inside the White House During the Syrian 'Red Line' Crisis," *The Atlantic,* June 3, 2018. https://www.theatlantic.com/international/archive/2018/06/inside-the-white-house-during-the-syrian-red-line-crisis/561887/

[12] Cited by James Fallows, "The Fifty-First State?" *The Atlantic,* November 2002, p. 53.

[13] Ibid., p. 53.

[14] Ibid., p. 54.

15. Adam Nossiter, "The Taliban Think They Have Won in Afghanistan, Peace Deal or Not," *The New York Times,* March 30, 2021. https://www.nytimes.com/2021/03/30/world/asia/taliban-victory-afghanistan.html
16. For example see: Adam Serwer, "Why Conservatives Want to Cancel the 1619 Project," *The Atlantic,* May 21, 2021. https://www.theatlantic.com/ideas/archive/2021/05/why-conservatives-want-cancel-1619-project/618952/
17. Stacy Pratt McDemott, "Lincoln & Race: The Great Emancipator Didn't Advocate Racial Equality. But Was He Racist?" National Public Radio, February 1, 2004. https://www.nprillinois.org/post/lincoln-race-great-emancipator-didnt-advocate-racial-equality-was-he-racist#stream/0
18. Rhea Mahbubani, "Pakistani Leader Imran Khan said Osama bin Laden Was Able to Hide in His Country because His Guerrilla Fighters were once regarded as 'Heroes,'" *Business Insider,* January 22, 2020. https://www.businessinsider.com/osama-bin-laden-perceived-as-a-hero-in-pakistan-2020-1
19. The argument for "American exceptionalism" is nicely developed by Robert J. McMahon, "By Helping Others We Help Ourselves," in Martin J. Medhurst and H. W. Brands, Eds., *Critical Reflections on the Cold War: Linking Rhetoric and History* (College Station: Texas A&M UP, 2000), 233–246.
20. Matt Schavenza, "How Humiliation Drove Modern Chinese History," *The Atlantic,* October 25, 2013. https://www.theatlantic.com/china/archive/2013/10/how-humiliation-drove-modern-chinese-history/280878/
21. James Holmes, "China Wants Ownership of the South China Sea. Here's Why that Can't Happen," *The National Interest,* July 17, 2020. https://nationalinterest.org/feature/china-wants-ownership-south-china-sea-heres-why-cant-happen-165070
22. There is no evidence that Abraham Lincoln ever read *Uncle Tom's Cabin* or that he ever saw the play focused on the book. Lincoln was, however, very much aware of the impact the book had on the American public. For a discussion of his conversation with the author Harriet Beecher Stowe, see Thomas F. Gossett, *Uncle Tom's Cabin and American Culture* (Dallas: Southern Methodist UP, 1985), 314–315.
23. Liberty Vittert, "Are Conspiracy Beliefs on the Rise?" *Livescience,* September 20, 2019. https://www.livescience.com/are-conspiracy-theory-beliefs-rising.html
24. Ibid.
25. Arit John, "Satanism and Sex Rings: How the QAnon Conspiracy Theory Has Taken Political Root," *Los Angeles Times,* July 15, 2020. https://www.latimes.com/politics/story/2020-07-15/qanon-conspiracy-theory-congressional-candidates
26. Ibid.
27. Ibid.
28. Katherine Schaeffer, "A Look at the Americans Who Believe There Is Some Truth to the Conspiracy Theory that COVID-19 Was Planned," *Pew Research Center,* July 24, 2020. https://www.pewresearch.org/fact-tank/2020/07/24/a-look-at-the-americans-who-believe-there-is-some-truth-to-the-conspiracy-theory-that-covid-19-was-planned/
29. Ibid.
30. Alison Durkee, "Nearly a Third of Americans Believe COVID-19 Death Toll Conspiracy Theory," *Forbes,* July 21, 2020. https://www.forbes.com/sites/alisondurkee/2020/07/21/nearly-a-third-of-americans-believe-covid-19-death-toll-conspiracy-theory/?sh=488414aa40ab
31. Ibid.
32. Pew Research Center, "Republicans, Democrats Move Even Further Apart in Coronavirus Concerns," June 25, 2020. https://www.pewresearch.org/politics/2020/06/25/republicans-democrats-move-even-further-apart-in-coronavirus-concerns/
33. Ibid.
34. Ryan Chatelaine, "State Vaccination Rates Falling Along Political Lines," *Spectrum News New York 1,* May 12, 2021. https://www.ny1.com/nyc/all-boroughs/health/2021/05/12/state-vaccination-rates-falling-along-political-party-lines
35. Walter R. Fisher, *Human Communication as Narration* (Columbia: University of South Carolina Press, 1987), 5.
36. David Fillipov, "Here Are 10 Critics of Vladimir Putin Who Died in Mysterious, Violent Ways," *Washington Post,* March 23, 2017. https://www.washingtonpost.com/news/worldviews/wp/2017/03/23/here-are-ten-critics-of-vladimir-putin-who-died-violently-or-in-suspicious-ways/
37. Julie Hirschfeld Davis, "Trump, at Putin's Side, Questions U.S. Intelligence on 2016 Election," *New York Times,* July 16, 2018. https://www.nytimes.com/2018/07/16/world/europe/trump-putin-election-intelligence.html

38 Adam Goldman, Julian E. Barnes, Maggie Haberman, and Nicholas Fandos, "Lawmakers Are Warned that Russia Is Meddling to Re-elect Trump," *The New York Times,* February 20, 2020. https://www.nytimes.com/2020/02/20/us/politics/russian-interference-trump-democrats.html

39 Michael Gold, "Anthony Weiner Released from Prison After Serving 18 Months for Sexting Teenager," *The New York Times,* May 14, 2019. https://www.nytimes.com/2019/05/14/nyregion/anthony-weiner-prison-release.html

40 Ibid.

41 Rem Rieder, "Brian Williams' Unmitigated Disaster," *USA Today,* February 5, 2015. https://www.usatoday.com/story/money/columnist/rieder/2015/02/05/brian-williams-unmitigated-disaster/22915325/

42 Fisher, 105.

43 For a discussion of these similarities and their argumentative power, see: Gerald F. Seib and Walter S. Mossberg, "Iraqi Missiles Hit Israel and U.S. Presses Air Attacks," *Wall Street Journal,* January 18, 1991, p. 1.

44 W. Lance Bennett and Martha S. Feldman, *Reconstructing Reality in the Courtroom,* 2nd ed. (New Orleans: Quid Pro Books, 2014).

45 Ibid.

46 *Rhetoric and Poetics of Aristotle,* trans. W. Rhys Roberts (New York: The Modern Library, 1954), see *Rhetoric,* Book 1.

47 Frances Coppola, "Governments Are Nothing Like Households," *Forbes,* April 20, 2018. https://www.forbes.com/sites/francescoppola/2018/04/30/governments-are-nothing-like-households/?sh=7c70223a54f8

48 Alan Rappeport and Jim Tankersley, "Monthly U.S. Budget Deficit Soared to Record $864 Billion in June," *The New York Times,* July 13, 2020. https://www.nytimes.com/2020/07/13/us/politics/budget-deficit-coronavirus.html

3

Audiences and Fields of Argument

Arguments are created for many different reasons, including attempts to change an opinion, influence someone's behavior, or justify one's own beliefs or actions. All arguments, however, regardless of their purpose, should be developed with an audience in mind. This is not to suggest that arguers are always aware of their audiences. The exchange of arguments, like many other human activities, sometimes becomes so reflexive that we do not take the time to think carefully through our argument strategies. One of the goals for this book is to help you to become more strategic in the arguments you choose to develop. To achieve this goal and to enhance the effectiveness of your arguments you need to think about the people who compose the audiences you want to influence with your arguments.

We have already established that people reason by assessing the quality of the competing claims they hear in rival stories. Some stories hold together better than others. Their plots are more compelling, their characters are given clear and distinctive roles to play, and they play them in accordance with our expectations. These stories are likely judged to have met the test of narrative probability. Likewise, some stories are especially believable and credible to us because they confirm and explain the prior experiences we have had in our lives. These stories ring true to us; because they correspond with our experiences, they lend a sense of predictability to our lives. When confronted with such a story we know how to respond because we have seen how such stories can be expected to turn out. These stories are judged to have narrative fidelity.

Arguers who want to prove that a story is credible must find a way to appeal to the values, experiences, and beliefs of their audiences. Arguers should construct stories that are coherent, complete, and satisfying. They should attempt to tell stories that are similar both in content and form to other stories that the people whom they are trying to convince have already heard and experienced. Stories are much more likely to be accepted as believable if they seem somewhat familiar to us. Arguers should also attempt to find ways to tell their stories so these narratives affirm the self-concept and self-interest of the person(s) whom they are trying to convince.

KNOWING YOUR AUDIENCE

One of the first challenges that you face as an arguer is to identify the *audience* for your arguments. Sometimes this is easy. For example, if you are having an argument with a close friend about how the two of you should spend your evening together, the target for your arguments is obvious. In other argument situations, however, identifying your audience is much more difficult. A salesperson who is showing a new car to a married couple, for example, might direct arguments about the car's features primarily to the husband on the assumption that men may be more knowledgeable about and interested in automotive features. If the wife will be the primary driver and is making the decision about what car to purchase, that strategy is a serious mistake. The salesperson's misdirected arguments—and the sexist attitudes that they reveal—could alienate the couple and result in a lost sale.

In complex argument situations, it may be difficult to identify the appropriate audience for your arguments. Candidates in political campaigns conduct expensive, complicated, and time-consuming public opinion polls to discover the values, beliefs, and interests of likely potential voters. Candidates must address the issues that voters believe are most important. Yet, there may be times in a campaign when candidates' personal political convictions and/or the ideology of their party might prompt them to create arguments that may not resonate very well with potential voters. There also may be instances, of course, where audience opinions change. For example, opposition to the Affordable Care Act (ACA), which many Republicans called "Obamacare," was a staple of conservative discourse in the 2012 and 2016 presidential election campaigns.

After he was elected, President Trump promised to "repeal and replace" Obamacare as soon as possible.[1] Senator John McCain (R-AZ), ill with terminal brain cancer, got out of his hospital bed to return to the Senate to vote against repealing the ACA. He was not confident that the GOP-led Senate would produce a replacement that did not deny coverage to many people who had signed up for medical coverage through the program. McCain was joined by two other Republican senators, Lisa Murkowski (AK) and Susan Collins (ME). All three drew Trump's ire.[2] Indeed, the GOP's persistent efforts to repeal the bill next moved onto the courts. The Trump Administration and 18 Republican state attorneys general asked the Supreme Court to strike down the ACA even though that would have meant that some 21 million people would become uninsured, and important protections would have ended.

> For example, allowing insurers to again discriminate based on health status would have jeopardized coverage for millions who could be charged more, denied coverage for certain diagnoses, or blocked from individual market coverage altogether—a particularly dire consequence in a pandemic. Eliminating ACA protections could have also let insurers charge higher premiums to women and people in certain occupations, reimpose pre-existing condition exclusions in employer coverage, and make premium tax credits nearly impossible to administer.[3]

In June 2021, the Supreme Court dismissed the case, the third rejection by the Court of a challenge to the ACA.[4] One might imagine that this decision disappointed most Republicans in office or running for election, but it probably did them a favor. Audience opinions had changed; opposition to the ACA was not as strong in the run-up to the 2020 election as it had been in the two previous elections. Most Republican candidates chose not to raise the issue in the midst of the worst global pandemic since the 1918 Spanish Flu.

Abstract arguments about whether the provision of health care should be a state or a federal issue were easier to present to voters before the enactment of the ACA. Arguments about taking away benefits that many constituents were now accustomed to—especially in the midst of the COVID-19 crisis—were much more difficult. Many of the 18 states that sued to repeal the ACA—led by Texas—were in the South and were home to many of the nation's poorest and most medically at-risk citizens. In 2021, these same states faced some of the highest numbers of infections, hospitalizations, and deaths from the coronavirus.[5]

Another challenge that political candidates or elected officials often face is that they must address arguments to political partisans who already share their ideology (reinforcing their support) as well as to undecided voters who may not share those opinions. To win the nomination of a political party, for instance, candidates must appeal to voters who are highly partisan and already committed to the values and beliefs that shape the agenda of their particular party. Voters in party primaries that determine the party's nominees are frequently much more partisan than those who vote in the general election, but they may still represent different wings of the same party. In the 2020 race for the Democratic nomination, for example, former Vice President Joe Biden was challenged by the need to try to move toward the more progressive wing of the party in order to attract those who had been strong supporters of candidates such as Bernie Sanders and Elizabeth Warren. As he did so, however, he risked alienating more moderate undecided, independent, and crossover voters who determine the outcome of most closely contested general elections. These voters tend not to be very partisan, are often not very interested in politics, do not pay as much attention to campaigns or issues, and tend to make their decisions about how they will vote—or even if they will vote—very late in a campaign. A vital part of the campaign promise for a candidate is identifying precisely who these undecided voters are and what issues are most likely to prompt their support (or to discourage them from voting for the opponent).

The techniques of modern public opinion polling permit political candidates to target their appeals toward very unique and specific clusters of potential voters. A candidate seeking to win the votes of suburbanites working in white-collar jobs will want to make very different arguments than a candidate seeking to win support from blue-collar residents of big cities. Candidates sometimes develop such sophisticated knowledge about their audiences that they construct appeals that are explicitly targeted toward very narrow audience segments. In local elections, for example, candidates may focus on winning the votes of teachers or public employees. Even if such voters might represent only a small portion of the electorate, their votes can swing an election. Candidates will also emphasize issues that cut across economic or social class concerns to reach out to voters who might share opinions on these issues. For example, a candidate might emphasize access to childcare, understanding that a substantial number of potential voters are single parents who must worry daily about balancing their responsibilities as wage earners with their responsibility to provide care for their children.

Assessing Your Audience

Although you will not likely know as much about the values and opinions of the audience you are trying to convince with your arguments as will a politician who has conducted polls, you should try to understand your audience as well as you can. One way to begin assessing your audience is by considering its demographic characteristics. Demographics are, of course, far from reliable predictors of the attitudes and values people hold. Indeed, these attributes may sometimes mislead arguers. Nonetheless, demographics is a good place to start thinking about the characteristics of your likely audience. Knowing demographic characteristics—age, social affiliations, gender, education, knowledge background and experience, and culture—is useful for a beginning assessment of your audience.

Age

Aristotle wrote *The Rhetoric* in the fourth century BCE. In the book, he discussed the differences between trying to persuade the young, the elderly, and those in the prime of life. Aristotle observed that young people were more likely to have volatile tempers, and they were also more concerned with pursuing victory and with proving their superiority over others. In contrast, he noted that older people were far less likely to have the emotional volatility of youth, but they were far more likely to be stubborn and set in their ways. Persons of middle age, however, those whom Aristotle described as being in their prime, typically did not have the extreme characteristics of those either younger or older than themselves.[6] One can surmise that Aristotle probably made these statements while he was himself in the prime of life! While Aristotle's observations of how the attitudes and values of people change as they age might seem a bit simplistic and stereotypical today, his comments continue to have some validity.

Common wisdom suggests that age might have significant influence on the values that people hold and on how open they are to arguments suggesting alternative views. An audience composed of older persons may, for example, be more likely to hold conservative views on social issues than might an audience composed of younger persons. The Pew Research Center found in 2019 that,

> On a range of issues, from Donald Trump's presidency to the role of government to racial equality and climate change, the views of Gen Z—those ages 13 to 21 in 2018—mirror those of Millennials. In each of these realms, the two younger generations hold views that differ significantly from those of their older counterparts. In most cases, members of the Silent Generation are at the opposite end, and Baby Boomers and Gen Xers fall in between.[7]

For the purpose of this study, the Pew Research Center classified the generations as follows: Generation Z, born after 1996; Millennials, born 1981 to 1996; Generation X, born 1965–1980; Baby Boomers, born 1946–1964; and Silent Generation, born 1928–1945.[8]

The younger generations differ from the previous generations in several respects, but this study found that differences were especially significant on the topic of race relations.

> When it comes to views on race, the two younger generations are more likely than older generations to say that blacks are treated less fairly than whites in the United States today. And they are much more likely than their elders to approve of NFL players kneeling during the national anthem as a sign of protest.
>
> The younger generations are also more accepting of some of the ways in which American society is changing. Majorities among Gen Z and the Millennial generation say increasing racial and ethnic diversity in the U.S. is a good thing for society, while older generations are less convinced of this. And they're more likely to have a positive view of interracial and same-sex marriage than their older counterparts.[9]

As might be expected, the study found that there were also sharp differences by age in attitudes regarding whether or not society should do more to recognize gender fluidity.

> When it comes to how accepting society in general is of people who don't identify as either a man or a woman, the views of Gen Zers and Millennials differ from those of older generations. Roughly half of Gen Zers (50%) and Millennials (47%) think that society is not accepting enough. Smaller shares of Gen Xers (39%), Boomers (36%) and those in the Silent Generation (32%) say the same.
>
> A plurality of the Silent Generation (41%) say society is too accepting of people who don't identify as a man or woman. Across all generations, roughly a quarter say society's acceptance level is about right.[10]

As you must already expect, younger people are also far more likely to be supportive of gay rights and gay marriage than are older people.

> Today, members of Generation Z are just as likely as Millennials to say allowing gay and lesbian couples to marry has been a good thing for the country (48% of Gen Zers and 47% of Millennials hold this view). One-third of Gen Xers say this is a good thing for the country, as do 27% of Baby Boomers. Members of the Silent Generation are the least enthusiastic (18% say this is a good thing).
>
> Relatively few Gen Zers or Millennials (15%) say same-sex marriage is a bad thing for society. Boomers and Silents are much more likely to view this change negatively (32% and 43%, respectively, say this is a bad thing). Across generations, about four-in-ten say allowing gays and lesbians to marry hasn't made much of a difference for the U.S.[11]

Because audiences are most likely to be concerned about issues that directly affect them, young persons might be especially concerned with issues such as the availability of federal funds to help them finance their education, student loan forgiveness, or finding a job after they graduate. Middle-aged people might be especially concerned with housing prices, interest rates, and access to day care or the quality of the local schools and the condition and availability of local parks and recreation programs. Older people might be more concerned with issues such as the cost of medical care, the sufficiency of their pensions and social security checks, crime and public safety, and the cost of their property taxes.

An especially interesting example of an issue that has different impacts on people depending upon their age is interest rates. The young are delighted when interest rates are low. Lower rates make it easier to borrow money to attend college, buy a car, or purchase or furnish a home. Older people are less likely to be negotiating new loans to buy property. Indeed, many retired citizens live off the income from their investments. Extended periods of time with low interest rates means elderly investors will get a much smaller return on their investments. Thus, economic conditions that greatly benefit one age group can pose serious problems for another.

U.S. political candidates generally spend significantly more time discussing issues that are of concern to elderly and middle-aged voters than issues that are of concern to younger people. Politicians have learned that young people are less likely to vote than older citizens. The corollary, as many studies have suggested, is that the avoidance of issues that might interest, concern, and motivate young voters further discourages their political participation, diminishing their interest in politics and decreasing their sense of political empowerment.[12] Neglecting any segment of your audience when advancing arguments can thus have consequences that may go beyond your likelihood of achieving a successful outcome in any single situation. It may leave behind a residue of attitudes and opinions that inhibit your ability to be effective in future situations.

In the Democratic presidential primary race in 2020 the division of younger and older voters was especially clear. Younger voters enthusiastically supported Senator Bernie Sanders (VT) and especially liked his advocacy of free college for all and a national health insurance program. Although younger voters attended his rallies during the first few primaries that winnowed the field of candidates, they did not turn out in high numbers to vote for Sanders. Instead, older voters continued their customary voting habits, and they cast their ballots for former Vice President Joe Biden. Aware that his path to the nomination meant convincing more of these older voters to support him, Biden avoided the very progressive policy positions on free college and national health insurance; instead, he promised instead more moderate policies, including some student loan forgiveness, more federal assistance for college financial aid, and reforms to expand the coverage of the ACA. Once he secured the nomination, however, it was important that Biden reach out to younger voters to persuade them to vote in the general election; hence there were some efforts to take more progressive positions.[13]

Social Affiliations

People belong to a variety of groups, and their memberships may provide some insight into their attitudes and values. People join groups because they enjoy certain types of interactions or recreational activities, because groups reflect their cultural or occupational interests, or because they are interested in certain topics, issues, and problems. Most people are socialized to acquire many of the values, attitudes, and beliefs of those with whom they spend their time. People often become more like those with whom they interact.

Obviously, you can learn something about people if you determine what political party they belong to, if they are religious or not, what church they might attend, and the civic, occupational, or recreational groups to which they belong. A member of the National Rifle Association probably would have very different values and opinions than a member of the Sierra Club, even though both groups may have an interest in the preservation of wetlands. People who are drawn to membership in the Jaycees or the local Chamber of Commerce will likely acquire attitudes about their communities, about the importance of civic identity, and about the political issues that concern these associations. Membership in a union, a professional association, or a veteran's organization might also influence people's public attitudes and opinions.

Knowledge about the group affiliations of people who compose your audience will help you create arguments that are more likely to resonate. The affiliations may also reveal that you are attempting to appeal to an audience that already agrees with you—or that even your best arguments are unlikely to gain support.

Gender

While it might be difficult to ascertain people's values on the basis of their gender identity, gender often influences our values and attitudes and the degree to which certain arguments appeal to us. For example, an audience composed primarily of men might be more responsive to football or other sports examples than might an audience of women. On the other hand, an audience of women might be expected to be more interested in arguments focused on women's rights.

Women are more likely than men to have experienced gender discrimination. Consequently, they are more likely to be sensitive to arguments about it. Perhaps gender identification might matter most to people who identify as trans. The Transgender Law Center is an activist group that promotes legal protection and anti-discrimination laws. It states:

> Transgender and gender non-conforming people often face discrimination in their day-to-day lives. That includes discrimination and mistreatment when accessing public accommodations, obtaining housing, and seeking employment. Many members of the transgender and gender non-conforming ("TGNC") community have displayed strength and courage in speaking out against and challenging this unjust discrimination.[14]

People who are transgendered, or those who have transgendered people in their families or among their circle of friends, are going to be more aware, and often more sensitive, to transgender experiences, difficulties, and challenges.

In December 2010, Congress repealed the "don't ask, don't tell" (DADT) policy. The 1994 policy had removed the ban on service by LGBTQ individuals instituted after World War II, but soldiers were prohibited from discussing their sexual orientation—and thousands were discharged for doing so until the 2010 legislation ended the policy in September 2011. In 2016, President Obama issued an executive order overturning the military's long-standing ban on openly transgender service members. In July 2017, President Trump sent out three tweets announcing his intention to overturn this policy and to once again disallow transgendered personnel from service. In 2019, that new policy went into effect, albeit amidst a flurry of lawsuits attempting to block it. In 2020, a study conducted by the Department of Defense found that about 66 percent of active-duty soldiers, sailors, air personnel, and Marines were supportive of serving alongside transgendered personnel. The claims that such service would be unsettling to discipline were not supported by the evidence; once transgender personnel were allowed to serve, they were accepted.[15] On January 25, 2021, just days after his inauguration, President Joe Biden issued an executive order enabling transgender individuals to serve openly in the U.S. military.[16]

Attitudes regarding gender discrimination, gay and trans rights, sexual harassment, and sexual violence are changing. However, these issues may continue to be very divisive, and audiences will hold very strong and often very different opinions about the issues. Consider the recent Supreme Court confirmation battle waged to secure a seat on the court for Associate Justice Brett Kavanaugh. In July 2018, President Trump nominated Judge Kavanaugh to fill the seat that was vacated by Justice Anthony Kennedy. In September 2018, the Senate began confirmation hearings to consider the nomination. The *Washington Post* published a letter by Christine Blasey Ford, a California psychology professor who claimed that Kavanaugh attempted to rape her at a house party when they were both teenagers. Ford said that she originally sent the letter to Senator Diane Feinstein (D-CA), but that she did not intend it to be made public. When the letter was leaked to the media, however, Ford decided to come forward. Kavanaugh denied that the incident ever took place. A few days later the *New Yorker* magazine published a second complaint, this time an allegation that Kavanaugh exposed himself to another woman at a dorm party while he was a student at Yale University. Both Ford and Kavanaugh testified at the confirmation hearings. As might be expected given the deep polarization in our country, the Democrats and Republicans on the committee were deeply divided on the nomination. The division went beyond party difference, however, as the Republican caucus was composed primarily of men, and the Democratic caucus was much more gender diverse. Although Kavanaugh was eventually confirmed (50–48), the nomination process revealed the depth of the chasm separating the two political parties and the differences of opinion that many people have regarding the degree to which a man should be held accountable for his past behavior whether the facts are proven or not.[17]

The so-called "gender gap" has persisted in U.S. politics for many years. Public opinion polls have revealed with some consistency that women are more concerned with social issues such as education, health, retirement security, and public welfare. Men, on the other hand, are more likely to be concerned about the state of the economy, crime, and foreign policy. As journalist Derek Thompson noted,

> Perhaps because the Democratic Party has become reliant on winning female votes, its policies are attuned to women's priorities. Women are more likely to live below the poverty threshold and rely on food stamps and other welfare services—part of a global phenomenon known as "the feminization of poverty." This fact may make them more receptive to Democrats' relatively consistent promises to expand the welfare state. As the *Washington Post* columnist Catherine Rampell writes, women are also more likely to work or be employed in government and government-regulated sectors, such as education and health care. It stands to reason that these employment trends make women less likely to vote for a Republican Party that has, for four decades, consistently promised to slash taxes and shrink government.[18]

As we have already mentioned, the gender gap is also evidenced by the congressional delegations. In 2020, 101 women held seats in the House of Representatives and 26 women held seats in the Senate. Of the total, 105 are Democrats and 22 are Republicans.[19]

Education and Knowledge

Arguers must adapt their arguments to the educational and intellectual level of their audiences. Not only might persons of different educational backgrounds harbor different attitudes and values but they also might process arguments differently. The more sophisticated and educated an audience is, the greater the probability that its members will be able to follow and to evaluate complex arguments. In fact, more sophisticated and educated audiences are more likely to demand such arguments, to want to see evidence and analytical reasoning, and to be more skeptical about solely emotional appeals.

Those who share knowledge about a subject also share the ability to communicate in the jargon of that discipline. Thus, an audience composed of physicians will use more sophisticated terms to argue about alternative treatments for patients with the COVID-19 virus than the general public would use. Arguers should also recognize the fact that certain educational experiences might predispose people toward certain beliefs. An audience composed of chemists, for example, would be more inclined to place their faith in scientific research as a means to solve social problems than might an audience composed of musicians. Even a shared appreciation of the scientific method might not be sufficient to facilitate shared understanding, however. For example, an audience of nuclear engineers is more likely to favor the continued development of nuclear power than would an audience composed of biologists.

Climate change illustrates a gap in understanding between scientists and many members of the public regarding whether human activities are responsible for global warming. Almost all scientists now believe that climate change is occurring, that humans have contributed to it, that it is happening much more rapidly than previously understood, and that it will have serious consequences for humankind; yet only 17% of people in the United States know that this scientific consensus exists. Fully 24% think, despite the strong evidence to the contrary, that fewer than half of scientists believe that human-caused climate change is occurring.[20]

A Pew Research study looked at opinion differences between the public and scientists on a number of issues, including genetically modified foods, animal research, childhood vaccines, climate change, nuclear power plants, and offshore drilling. The largest difference of opinion was for genetically modified food.

> A majority of the general public (57%) says that genetically modified (GM) foods are generally *unsafe* to eat, while 37% says such foods are safe; by contrast, 88% of AAAS [American Association for the Advancement of Science] scientists say GM foods are generally safe. The gap between citizens and scientists in seeing GM foods as safe is 51 percentage points.[21]

Research indicated that those who distrusted the safety of such foods were less likely to have significant knowledge about genetically modified organisms (GMOs), were more skeptical about scientists generally, and were more inclined to accept conspiracies as true. The study also found, however, that with more education, this skepticism could be reduced and that it was possible to change attitudes on the topic.[22]

Background and Experience

The background and experience of audience members exert tremendous influence on their attitudes and values. An audience member who experienced the death of a friend or family member because of a drunk driver, for example, may believe strongly in the necessity of tightening controls on those who drink and drive. People who have not experienced such a loss may believe current laws are sufficient. Likewise, the attitudes of parents raising a rebellious teenager might be more sympathetic to the parents of a gang member than the attitudes of parents raising a docile and well-adjusted teenager. In both cases, audience members may be guided to empathize with people whose experiences differ. Specific examples personalize abstract statistics.

People screen the arguments and the stories they hear through their own experiences. The more knowledge you have about the experiences of your audience members, the more effective you can be in structuring how you present your ideas. People naturally favor stories that elevate their self-worth. We have a natural resistance to stories that make us personally responsible for negative consequences or outcomes. For example, Thomas Hollihan and Patricia Riley discovered that the parents of delinquent children resisted arguments that blamed their parenting practices or personal problems (e.g., alcoholism or failed marriages) for the behavior of their children. They were, on the other hand, quite willing to blame their children's delinquency on the inadequacy of the public schools, on their children's friends, on the images of youth conveyed by the mass media, on the police, or even on their children's delinquent nature.[23] Therefore, in addition to knowing about the experiences of audience members, you need to consider how they see themselves as actors in their own life stories.

Culture

Another especially important factor that influences how people evaluate arguments is their culture. Socialization is the process of acquiring the shared norms, behaviors, values, beliefs, and expectations of a culture. Immersed in cultural traditions from birth, people may not recognize the influence of culture on their opinions, values, and actions. For instance, people raised in the U.S. culture generally have very different values, attitudes, and opinions from individuals raised in the Middle East, Asia, or even Europe. We often see the effects of cultural differences when people immigrate to the United States. People from different cultures may clash with their neighbors over such issues as child rearing, religious practices, style of dress, and so forth. Sometimes there are also tensions between generations. Parents who have come to the United States from abroad bring their cultural traditions with them. However, their children, who are exposed to the U.S. culture at school, through interactions with peers, and through the media see the world very differently. Given the tremendous differences in their native environments, religious beliefs, forms of government, family traditions, and political systems, it should come as no surprise that people from different cultures experience and evaluate arguments differently.

Research has suggested, for example, that Chinese arguers use very different strategies and argumentation styles than do Westerners. Chinese arguers are more likely to mask their emotions; they use silences to indicate disagreement; and they are far less likely to display their negative feelings.[24] Westerners frequently misunderstand/misinterpret Chinese communication. Westerners assume that the absence of direct disagreement and the lengthy silences mean the Chinese arguers agree with them—when, in fact, they may not. Chinese cultural and communication practices have been heavily influenced by Confucian principles. As Nancy Pine argued, Confucius celebrated a way of life that emphasizes: "Everyone is expected to behave with respect and kindness. Individuality and striving for uniqueness are not high on the list of prized attributes. People are viewed in relation to how they treat others, not for their independent ideas."[25] Bringing attention to yourself by openly disagreeing with or vociferously arguing with others, or even by directly stating your opinions, is therefore inconsistent with Chinese cultural norms and ideals.

Arguers should be aware that people from different cultures are more and more frequently coming into contact with each other. The great cities of the world—for instance London, Paris, Amsterdam, Rome, Hong Kong, New York, and Los Angeles—are becoming increasingly diverse. In addition, new global economic forces are changing the way nations and their citizens conduct business. People no longer live in isolation. Creating public policies that maintain social harmony requires that arguers be sensitive to differences in culture.

People Evaluate Arguments Differently

As previously stated, we believe people evaluate arguments in accordance with the principles of storytelling. Unique backgrounds, experiences, interests, affiliations, and cultures affect the evaluation of stories. If arguments must appeal to such a wide range of viewpoints, what is an arguer to do? How can you ever learn enough about your audience to be able to tailor your arguments to suit them? Furthermore, how can you avoid alienating some people in an effort to appeal to others? The Belgian philosopher and legal theorist Chaim Perelman and his colleague L. Olbrechts-Tyteca, observed:

Argumentation aimed exclusively at a particular audience has the drawback that the speaker, by the very fact of adapting to the values of his [sic] listeners, might rely on arguments that are foreign or even directly opposed to what is acceptable to persons other than those he is presently addressing.[26]

Perelman and Olbrechts-Tyteca suggested that arguers direct their appeals to a ***universal audience***. This universal audience does not exist; it is created in the mind of the arguer. Using an abstract audience as a reference point for evaluating arguments helps an individual tailor arguments for a broad range of potential audience members. Perelman and Olbrechts-Tyteca stressed that "argumentation addressed to a universal audience must convince the reader that the reasons adduced are of a compelling character, that they are self-evident, and possess an absolute and timeless validity, independent of local or historical contingencies."[27] To create arguments for this universal audience, one should strive for claims that will appeal to all reasoning persons. Although not an easy task, this is an appropriate goal for arguers to pursue. So how should an arguer proceed?

Perelman and Olbrechts-Tyteca emphasized that one should develop arguments that make use of ***objective facts*** that are knowable and uncontested. Such objective facts can be used to assert ***obvious truths***, generalizations that are commonly shared and understood. Perelman and Olbrechts-Tyteca acknowledged the difficulty in finding such readily agreed upon "facts" and "truths" when they observed that there are significant differences in this regard. They argued, "Everyone constitutes the universal audience from what he [sic] knows of his fellow men, in such a way as to transcend the few oppositions he is aware of. Each individual, each culture, has thus its own conception of the universal audience."[28] Consequently, the universal audience is a construction of the arguer—a self-conscious test that the arguer should submit any argument to in order to make it as strong as possible. Perelman and Olbrechts-Tyteca also recognized that, on rare occasions, there might be audience members who do not recognize the "objective facts" or "obvious truths" present in the arguments you create. To some extent they felt it would be legitimate to dismiss this recalcitrant few as stupid or abnormal. The danger in this is that you may find yourself making arguments designed to persuade fewer and fewer people, because you have relegated as stupid all those who do not agree with you and see the world as you see it.

Although the conception of the universal audience does not eliminate all challenges in adopting arguments to different viewpoints, it does lead to the creation of arguments that appeal to the largest number of people. Arguers should be aware of the need to create arguments that will convince the broader universal audience in addition to the unique interests, concerns, and beliefs of their particular audiences. Arguers need to search continually for objective facts and obvious truths because the very process of argumentative investigation can strengthen arguments and help create stronger cases.

THE PRINCIPLE OF PRESENCE

Perelman and Olbrechts-Tyteca also proposed that arguers consider the concept of ***presence***. From all possible arguments, an arguer must select those that will be most compelling to the audience. This selection process gives presence to some arguments and relegates others to the background—much like highlighting directs attention to some lines in a textbook as important and implying that unhighlighted lines are less significant.

Perelman and Olbrechts-Tyteca suggested that the simplest way to give an argument presence is through repetition. If a particular argument is important to your overall case, it should be repeated often, either in the same speech or in several speeches. In the 2016 presidential campaign, for example, Republicans continued to refer to Hillary Clinton's emails to remind voters that she had used a private email server; doing so showed questionable judgment and put national security at risk.[29] Democrats countered by reminding voters that Donald Trump stated he could grab women by their genitalia because "When you're a star, they let you do it. You can do anything."[30] Both sides were trying to argue, with very different issue framing, that the other party's candidate was unfit to serve as president.

Perelman and Olbrechts-Tyteca observed that an arguer can further accentuate important arguments or passages in oral presentations by the tone of voice used, by increasing one's volume, or by pausing just before uttering them.[31] Successful speakers often find they can increase the presence that a particular argument may have by the use of gestures, facial expressions, and other nonverbal cues.

Even if you have created your arguments for a universal audience, it is advisable to find a way to make those arguments uniquely appealing to the particular audience you are addressing. We have already detailed the ways in which different people might be expected to have different responses to the arguments they encounter. How then do you create arguments that have universal appeal but that also elicit your particular audience's attention to and concern for the issues you are presenting?

In essence, presence suggests concern for the stylistic dimensions of creating and communicating your arguments. In most instances, it is not helpful to communicate with your audience in such a way that you appear preachy or judgmental. Be sensitive to the feedback your audience provides by watching for signs of confusion or misunderstanding, head shakes, frowns, or other responses that might signal a failure to communicate your message.

Arguers should also attempt to pique the interests of their audiences, to provoke their sympathy or their feelings of empathy, and to construct arguments so audiences really feel them. Perelman and Olbrechts-Tyteca illustrated the concept of presence with a Chinese proverb: "A king sees an ox on its way to sacrifice. He is moved to pity for it and orders that a sheep be used in its place. He confesses he did so because he could see the ox, but not the sheep."[32]

A rescue mission that aids the homeless in Los Angeles sends out mailings to potential donors to raise funds to support their efforts. Although most of the recipients of the aid are men who suffer from mental illness or substance abuse, the mission's solicitations often emphasize the plight of homeless children. The mission thus creates greater presence to the problem of homelessness and probably gains more in donations. It is easier to evoke sympathy and concern when the emphasis is on children. We do want to be clear that we are not suggesting that the solicitations are deceptive. Indeed, to avoid "compassion fatigue" charities are often advised to focus on individuals suffering loss rather than on the large numbers of people suffering and to take advantage of potential donors' emotions in appealing for donations.[33]

As an arguer, your goal should be to develop arguments and a style of presentation that will make the issues you raise seem uniquely important to your audience. During the 2020 presidential campaign, for example, President Trump sought reelection on the argument that his administration had produced strong economic growth and record-setting low rates of unemployment, until it was undermined by the COVID-19 pandemic. He promised a quick, "V-shaped" recovery once the disease was behind us. The president also warned that if the Democrats returned to power there would be an escalation of crime and violence in U.S. cities, and that he was the "law and order" president. His opponent, former Vice President Biden, on the other hand, emphasized that the only people who had genuinely profited when the economy was booming was the top 1%, and that ordinary citizens never gained significant ground. Biden claimed that Trump's failure to contain the virus resulted in the suffering of ordinary Americans. This suffering included higher rates of illness and mortality, evictions, and job losses. As to the violence that Trump claimed would occur, Biden argued that violent crime rates were increasing during the Trump administration due to the poverty and desperate conditions many people experienced and that race relations in the United States were worsening due to Trump's divisive public statements.

The two candidates were appealing to different constellations of potential voters—and giving greater presence to different claims. Identifying which arguments will have presence for your audience and finding ways to present your arguments in a style that maximizes their importance requires knowledge of your audience and of the techniques for presenting arguments. As mentioned previously, candidates make extensive use of public opinion polls to learn more about their audiences. In addition, they frequently test their appeals and argument strategies with focus groups. Although such strategies are unavailable to most people, they demonstrate the importance of adjusting ideas and arguments to listeners.

ARGUMENT FIELDS

Philosopher Stephen Toulmin developed another view of how people construct and evaluate arguments. Trained as a logician, Toulmin became increasingly frustrated with the limitations of formal logic. He felt that the principles of formal logic were useful but did not reflect how people actually reasoned when making everyday decisions. Logicians believed that logical models were the most appropriate means for rationally arriving at conclusions and that the requirements for a rational argument did not change from one context to another. Toulmin argued, however, that different situations or contexts—which he referred to as *fields*—demanded different standards for arguments. As Toulmin and his coauthors Richard Rieke and Alan Janik declared:

> The trains of reasoning that it is appropriate to use vary from situation to situation. As we move from the lunch counter to the executive conference table, from the science laboratory to the law courts, the "forum" of discussion changes profoundly. The kind of involvement that the participants have with the outcome of the reasoning is entirely different in the different situations and so also will be the ways in which possible outcomes of the argument are tested and judged.[34]

Arguments can be considered to be in the same field when the data and conclusions are of essentially the same logical type. They will be in different fields when the data and conclusions are markedly different or in a case where the same data lead to different conclusions.[35]

To understand Toulmin's view of argumentation theory, it is important to determine what he meant by *fields*. Toulmin viewed the term *fields* and the term *disciplines* as roughly synonymous. His claim was that physicists argue similarly because they share training in physics. Likewise, attorneys argue in a similar fashion, members of the clergy share an argumentation style, as do historians, physicians, engineers, and so on. These disciplinary boundaries are not always formal or predictive. For example, physicists might be expected to argue in a similar fashion to engineers, biologists, and chemists because the scientific method underlies their shared fields.

Complications can occur because people are often members of several different argument fields simultaneously. Someone may be, for example, both a fundamentalist Christian and a scientist. As a Christian, this person might be encouraged to accept the biblical account of the creation of the universe as outlined in the Book of Genesis. As a scientist, on the other hand, this person might be inclined to accept Charles Darwin's theory of evolution. In such a situation, the person who belongs to the incompatible fields is continually forced to reconcile the tensions that may occur between them—and also to decide from situation to situation which field's argument standards to apply.

Other argumentation theorists have suggested it would be useful to consider argument fields from a broader perspective than that of disciplines. Charles Arthur Willard suggested fields should be seen as sociological entities. Willard said fields encompass terms such as "groups," "organizations," "frameworks," and "relationships," particularly when these entities share a "constellation of practices."[36]

Willard claimed that the practices of any field are consensually developed as members reach agreements regarding how their day-to-day work proceeds. Thus, chemists forge appropriate techniques for resolving disputes in the field of chemistry as they conduct their daily work. Likewise, accountants discuss their daily challenges and responsibilities, and then they propose appropriate means for addressing the problems they share. They continually hone the standards and practices of their profession. There may be times when there are arguments within a field and even across fields about what should be the appropriate standards. Accountants for example, frequently intersect with attorneys, judges, and those who pass laws.

One interesting illustration of such a confrontation of conflicting standards was the 2001 controversy involving the Enron Corporation and its accounting practices. Arthur Andersen, was one of the largest and best-known accounting firms in the United States, and its accountants conducted the audit of Enron. These accountants declared that it was "normal accounting practice" to destroy the records of the audit and to shred documents. The attorneys, representing both the government and private investors, argued that the destruction of the audit records was tantamount to the destruction of evidence in a court action and therefore constituted a criminal act. The dispute that resulted concerned whether or not the destruction of such records did indeed constitute accepted practice within the field of accounting (an intra-field dispute). Assuming it did, the dispute would focus on whether or not the practices of the legal field should be given primary consideration over those of accounting once a court action had been filed (an inter-field dispute). Ultimately, Enron and many of its top corporate executives were convicted of fraud, and the venerable Arthur Andersen accounting firm was essentially forced out of business.[37]

Willard acknowledged that although some fields may take a body of knowledge for granted, most fields actively attempt to perfect and improve the knowledge in the field.[38] Thus, for example, chefs argue about the best way to prepare a soufflé, orthopedic surgeons argue about the best way to treat a ruptured disc, hairdressers argue about the best way to color hair so it looks natural, accountants argue about the best way to conduct audits, and so forth. Willard also stressed that even the decision to participate in a particular field (which may on some occasions be an unconscious choice) may constrain the participants' ways of thinking about and approaching problems. To participate in the discussions within a field usually entails surrendering a certain amount of personal freedom because one views the world from the perspective of that field. Consequently, the attorney is always seeing problems from the perspective of questions of law, the scientist from the perspective of scientific inquiry, and the artist from an aesthetic perspective.[39]

Just as their audiences are composed of persons who represent fields or perspectives, arguers themselves represent particular fields and perspectives. Awareness of the implications of field theory should help you become more aware of the degree to which your experiences, beliefs, training, and membership in certain groups or organizations influence your argumentative techniques.

A few arguments may be so compelling that they meet the requirements for argumentative proof in all fields. Toulmin called these arguments *field-invariant*.[40] For example, most of us would accept as true the claim that parents who love their children want to protect them from harm. This claim could be considered field-invariant. Even a claim that seems as clear-cut as this one, however, may not always be true. The Branch Davidians offer a chilling illustration; the religious cult was depicted in *Waco*, a TV mini-series.[41]

In 1993, members of the Branch Davidians, including many parents and children ranging in age from infants to teenagers lived in a compound outside of Waco, Texas. When agents of the Bureau of Alcohol, Tobacco, and Firearms tried to serve a search warrant to investigate claims that the group was dealing in illegal guns, the cultists opened fire on the federal agents, killing several of them. The FBI then surrounded the compound; for 51 days the agency tried to convince the occupants to surrender—or at least to send the children out of the compound so they would not be injured. Finally, the government agents decided to fire tear gas into the compound to force the occupants to leave. Suddenly the building burst into flames. It is still under dispute whether the federal agents inadvertently sparked the fire or if the people inside deliberately set fire to the compound. What is known, however, is the flames consumed almost 100 persons, including 24 children, 17 of whom were under the age of ten.[42]

It was extremely difficult for most people around the world to understand how parents could intentionally put their children at such risk, or perhaps even cause their death. Those of us who do not participate in the Branch Davidians' argument field may feel that these parents did not love their children deeply enough to save them.[43] To members of this religious community, however, the decision to perish in the fire may have seemed very rational, and the taking of the children's lives might have been an expression of love for them. In their minds, the fiery end to this siege may have confirmed a biblical prophecy that fire would consume the earth and that the true believers in Christ would find their way to heaven.[44] Thus, for the Branch Davidians, fiery Armageddon represented not the end of their children's lives but the promise of a new beginning in heaven.

Sadly, this situation of parents putting their children to death to secure them a place in the afterlife has become even more common today as suicide bombers sometimes sacrifice themselves and their children in order to punish "nonbelievers" and to create a sense of public terror to achieve their personal or movement objectives. Even the argument that parents who love their children want to protect them is found to be *field-dependent* rather than field invariant.[45]

By field-dependent, Toulmin, Rieke, and Janik meant those argumentative proofs that potentially varied from one field to another. Think of what constitutes evidence. In a courtroom there are very strict rules about what kind of testimony can be considered as evidence. For example, hearsay is testimony by a witness of what another person said to a different person. With some strict exceptions, hearsay evidence is not permitted in a courtroom. However, in an interpersonal situation, you might treat your friend's account of what they overheard someone else say as evidence. You would be using a different field dependent standard than the one for the legal profession.

The standard of what constitutes a compelling argument or tentative truth can also vary. As noted above, nearly all scientists concur on the human contribution to climate change. Such agreement functions as a consensus and, unless new information is found to unsettle that agreement, scientists will proceed as if that matter is pretty much settled. What constitutes tentative truth in a court is the decision by a judge or jury. Such decisions are based on the preponderance of evidence in a civil trial or the higher standard of beyond a reasonable doubt in a criminal case.

Arguers should be sensitive to the requirements for establishing claims in the argument field in which they are participating and create arguments that will satisfy their audience by meeting the standards of that particular field. When dealing with people from different argument fields, or when it is difficult to determine what field's standards should be applied, it is desirable to create arguments that will appeal to people in as many different fields as possible. In a sense, this is the pursuit of arguments that appeal to the universal audience.

Another task that arguers sometimes face is the need to translate arguments from one field to another. Frequently this process means creating stories that appeal to people from different fields. As an illustration of this process we might cite the case of a scientist who is attempting to find scientific explanations for biblical stories. For example, an astronomer might speculate on any events in the heavens on the night Christ was born that could explain the story about the three wise men following the path of a star to find the newborn baby.

Summary

When forming arguments, if possible, arguers should carefully consider the values and attitudes of their audiences. The audience's demographic factors may provide insight into their interests, needs, and experiences. Arguers should also attempt to emphasize and give greater presence to those aspects of their arguments that are most likely to appeal to their listeners. In addition, arguers should recognize that people respond differently to arguments and often use different standards for evaluating arguments based on the fields in which they participate. Although it may be impossible to convince all your listeners, your goal should be the creation of arguments that will appeal to a universal audience of reasoning persons.

Key Terms

audience	fields	presence
field-dependent	objective facts	universal audience
field-invariant	obvious truths	

ACTIVITIES

1. To practice analyzing an audience, conduct a demographic analysis of your class.
   a. What is the age span of your class? What is the average age of your class?
   b. What are the social affiliations of the class members?
   c. What is the educational background of your class? What are students' majors?
   d. What are the cultural perspectives of your classmates?
2. Select a recent public controversy. Based on the information gleaned above, assume that your classmates compose your audience for arguments that you would make about this controversy. How will your classmates view the controversy? Answer the following questions:
   a. Would your classmates' views change if they were older? Were their views different when they were younger?
   b. Would your classmates' views change if they had different social affiliations?
   c. Would your classmates' views change if they had less education? If they pursued different majors?
   d. Would your classmates' views change if they were from a different culture?
3. Take a position on the public controversy identified in the preceding exercise. Now imagine supporting your position with two different audiences. If the only difference you know about the two audiences is that they differ in age, how might you adapt your arguments to gain the adherence of each of these two audiences? Repeat this for each of the audience variables identified in this chapter.
4. Listen to an argument interaction by, for instance, listening to a radio talk show, watching a talk show on television or online, attending a public meeting of local government, or observing your friends engaging in an argument. Now analyze the interaction.
   a. List the objective facts (those facts that are knowable and uncontested by the disputants).
   b. List the obvious truths (those generalizations that are commonly shared and understood).
   c. What facts and truths were contested? Were these points of disagreement resolved? If so, how were they resolved? If not, how might they have been resolved?
5. To learn more about the nature of argument fields, attend a meeting of your local city council and observe a criminal trial proceeding.
   a. What are the differences, if any, in what constitutes acceptable evidence in the two fields of argument?
   b. How do the participants introduce facts?
   c. How do the participants challenge the facts introduced by another participant?
   d. Are their controls on who may speak or on what they can say?

RECOMMENDED READINGS

Crosswhite, James, "Universality in Rhetoric: Perelman's Universal Audience," *Philosophy and Rhetoric* 22 (1989): 157–172.

Dean, Farmer J., "Scholarly Communities and the Discipline of the Communication Discipline," *Southern Communication Journal* 63 (1998): 169–173.

Frank, David, "The New Rhetoric, Judaism, and Post-Enlightenment Thought: The Cultural Origins of Perelmanian Philosophy," *Quarterly Journal of Speech* 83 (1997): 311–331.

Goodnight, G. Thomas, "The Personal, Technical, and Public Spheres of Argument: A Speculative Inquiry into the Arts of Public Deliberation," *Argumentation and Advocacy* 48 (2012): 198–210.

Groff, Richard and Wendy Winn, "Presencing 'Communion' in Chaim Perelman's *New Rhetoric*," *Philosophy & Rhetoric* 39 (2006): 45–71.

Gross, Alan, "A Theory of the Rhetorical Audience: Reflections on Chaim Perelman," *Quarterly Journal of Speech* 85 (1999): 203–211.

Prosise, Theodore O. and Greg R. Miller, "Argument Fields as Arenas of Discursive Struggle," *Argumentation and Advocacy* 32 (1996): 111–129.

Rowland, Robert C., "Purpose, Argument Fields, and Theoretical Justification," *Argumentation* 22 (2008): 235–250.

Schiappa, Edward, "Defining Marriage in California: An Analysis of Public and Technical Argument," *Argumentation and Advocacy* 48 (2012): 216–230.

Toulmin, Stephen E., *Human Understanding* (Princeton: Princeton University Press, 1972).

Toulmin, Stephen E., Richard Rieke, and Allan Janik, *An Introduction to Reasoning*, 2nd ed. (New York: Macmillan, 1984).

ENDNOTES

[1] Maggie Haberman and Robert Pear, "Trump Tells Congress to Repeal and Replace Obamacare Law 'Very Quickly,'" *The New York Times,* January 10, 2017. https://www.nytimes.com/2017/01/10/us/repeal-affordable-care-act-donald-trump.html

[2] Robert Pear and Thomas Kaplan, "Senate Rejects Slimmed-Down Obamacare Repeal as McCain Votes No," *The New York Times,* July 27, 2017. https://www.nytimes.com/2017/07/27/us/politics/obamacare-partial-repeal-senate-republicans-revolt.html

[3] "Suit Challenging ACA Legally Suspect but Threatens Loss of Coverage for Tens of Millions," *Center on Budget and Policy Priorities,* July 20, 2021. https://www.cbpp.org/research/health/aca-survives-legal-challenge-protecting-coverage-for-tens-of-millions

[4] "What Does the Supreme Court ACA Decision Mean?" *The National Law Review,* 11, #193, June 18, 2021. https://www.natlawreview.com/article/affordable-care-act-survives-supreme-court-challenge-what-happens-next

[5] Ibid.

[6] *Rhetoric and Politics of Aristotle*, trans. W. Rhys Roberts (New York: The Modern Library, 1954), 121–126.

[7] Kim Parker, Nikki Graf, and Ruth Igielnik, "Generation Z Looks a Lot Like Millennials on Key Social and Political Issues," *Pew Research Center,* January 17, 2019. https://www.pewresearch.org/social-trends/2019/01/17/generation-z-looks-a-lot-like-millennials-on-key-social-and-political-issues/

[8] Ibid.

[9] Ibid.

[10] Ibid.

[11] Ibid.

[12] John Holbein, "Why So Few Young Americans Vote," *The Conversation,* March 11, 2020. https://theconversation.com/why-so-few-young-americans-vote-132649. Also, Sydney Ember, "Young Voters Could Make a Difference. Will They?" *The New York Times,* November 2, 2018. https://www.nytimes.com/2018/11/02/us/politics/young-voters-midterms.html. Thomas A. Hollihan, *Uncivil Wars: Political Campaigns in a Media Age,* 2nd ed. (New York: Bedford St. Martins, 2009), 307–308.

[13] Susan Milligan, "Young Voters Love Bernie. Just Not Enough." *U.S. News and World Report,* March 11, 2020. https://www.usnews.com/news/elections/articles/2020-03-11/young-voters-love-bernie-sanders-but-older-voters-gave-joe-biden-the-win

[14] "Trans and Gender Nonconforming People Speak Out: Stories of Discrimination," *Transgender Law Center,* 2020. https://transgenderlawcenter.org/legal/discrimination-stories

[15] Meghan Meyers, "Two-Thirds of Troops Support Allowing Transgender Service Members in the Military, Pentagon Study Says," *Military Times,* February 27, 2020. https://www.militarytimes.com/news/

your-military/2020/02/27/two-thirds-of-troops-support-allowing-transgender-service-members-in-the-military-pentagon-study-finds/

16 https://www.whitehouse.gov/briefing room/presidential-actions/2021/01/25/executive-order-on-enabling-all-qualified-americans-to-serve-their-country-in-uniform/

17 "Brett Kavanaugh Fast Facts," *CNN,* March 5, 2020. https://www.cnn.com/2018/07/16/us/brett-kavanaugh-fast-facts/index.html

18 Derek Thompson, "Why Women Vote for Democrats," *The Atlantic,* February 9, 2020. https://www.theatlantic.com/ideas/archive/2020/02/how-women-became-democratic-partisans/606274/

19 "Women in the U.S. Congress 2020," *Center for American Women and Politics,* Rutgers Eagleton Institute of Politics, 2020. https://cawp.rutgers.edu/women-us-congress-2020

20 Eugene Linden, "How Scientists Got Climate Change So Wrong," *The New York Times,* November 8, 2019. https://www.nytimes.com/2019/11/08/opinion/sunday/science-climate-change.html

21 "Public and Scientists' Views on Science and Society," *Pew Research Center,* January 29, 2015. https://www.pewresearch.org/science/2015/01/29/public-and-scientists-views-on-science-and-society/

22 Brandon R. McFadden, "Examining the Gap Between Science and Public Opinion about Genetically Modified Food and Global Warming," *PLoS One,* 11(11) 2016: e0166140. https://journals.plos.org/plosone/article?id=10.1371/journal.pone.0166140

23 Thomas A. Hollihan and Patricia Riley, "The Rhetorical Power of a Compelling Story: A Critique of a 'Toughlove' Parental Support Group," *Communication Quarterly,* 35 (1987): 13–25.

24 Michael J. Cody, Wen-Shu Lee, and Edward Yi Chao, "Telling Lies: Correlates of Deception among Chinese," in J. P. Forgans and J. M. Innes, Eds., *Recent Advances in Social Psychology an International Perspective* (North Holland: Elsevier Science Publishers, 1989), 359–368.

25 Nancy Pine, *Educating Young Giants: What Kids Learn and Don't Learn in China and America* (New York: Palgrave Macmillan, 2012), pp. 37–38.

26 Chaim Perelman and L. Olbrechts-Tyteca, *The New Rhetoric* (Notre Dame, IN: The University of Notre Dame Press, 1969), p. 31.

27 Ibid., p. 32.

28 Ibid., p. 33.

29 Dana Milbank, "Our Nation Is in a Free Fall. But Sure, Let's Talk about Hillary's Emails Again," *Washington Post,* August 5, 2020. https://www.washingtonpost.com/opinions/2020/08/05/how-do-we-handle-5-million-covid-19-cases-us-talk-about-hillarys-emails/

30 Dara Lynn and Dylan Matthews, "When You're a Star, They Let You Do It. You Can Do Anything," *Vox.* October 7, 2016. https://www.vox.com/2016/10/7/13206364/vox-sentences-trump-sexual-assault

31 Perelman and Olbrechts-Tyteca, p. 144.

32 Ibid., p. 116.

33 Summer Allen, "Ten Ways to Encourage People to Give More," *Greater Good Magazine,* November 27, 2017. https://greatergood.berkeley.edu/article/item/ten_ways_to_encourage_people_to_give_more

34 Stephen E. Toulmin, Richard Rieke, and Alan Janik, *An Introduction to Reasoning,* 2nd ed. (New York: MacMillan, 1984), 8.

35 Stephen E. Toulmin, *The Uses of Argument* (Cambridge: Cambridge University Press, 1958), 7.

36 Charles Arthur Willard, "Argument Fields," in J. Robert Cox and Charles Arthur Willard, Eds., *Advances in Argumentation Theory and Research* (Carbondale: Southern Illinois University Press, 1982), 30.

37 Troy Segal, "Enron Scandal: The Fall of a Wall Street Darling," *Investopedia,* May 4, 2020. https://www.investopedia.com/updates/enron-scandal-summary/

38 Willard, p. 30.

39 Willard, p. 38.

40 Toulmin, p. 36.

41 Sophie Gilbert, "*Waco* Skims a Very American Tragedy," *The Atlantic,* January 24, 2018. https://www.theatlantic.com/entertainment/archive/2018/01/waco-paramount-david-koresh/551330/

42 J. Michael Kennedy, "Waco Cultists Perish in Blaze: FBI Calls It a Mass Suicide," *Los Angeles Times,* April 20, 1993. https://www.latimes.com/archives/la-xpm-1993-04-20-mn-25025-story.html

43 For a discussion of public reactions to the tragedy in Waco, see J. Michael Kennedy and Lianne Hart, "In the Eye of the Cult Firestorm," *Los Angeles Times,* April 20, 1993. https://www.latimes.com/archives/la-xpm-1993-04-20-mn-25027-story.html

44 Ibid.

45 Toulmin, p. 38.

4

The Language of Argument

In the previous chapter we discussed how strategic arguers analyze their audience(s) and the argument context so that they may adapt their arguments and increase their effectiveness. In this chapter, our goal is to demonstrate how language enhances your ability to create arguments that audiences find compelling. We begin by discussing the importance of language in argumentation, move on to consider how language influences the components of a good story, and then conclude by examining a special type of argument: metaphor.

UNDERSTANDING LANGUAGE

The symbols we use to make sense of our experiences are rich with meaning. They reflect our thoughts and values, and they direct us how to act. A label, or more appropriately, language, is a template that constrains what we think and what we know.

Language Defined

Language is a shared symbol system. This rather simple statement has profound implications for the study of argument. First, language is symbolic. In chapter 1 we defined *symbols* as special types of signs that call attention to significances: they relate to what has been perceived; they point to, indicate, or denote something other than themselves. Because symbols relate to what has been perceived, they are, as Kenneth Burke argued, a partial reflection of reality. Furthermore, because we choose which words will represent the thing perceived, our choices reflect our values. Therefore, symbols are also a deflection of reality.[1] By this Burke means that language intervenes between the thing (also known as the subject) and the arguer, and this intervention is not benign. Rather, language has an *epistemic function*; that is, the language we learn and employ shapes and constrains our understanding of what constitutes reality. What is real to us is what we express linguistically. Our language influences both *how* we create meaning and *what* we choose to make sense of in our daily lives.[2]

Meanings do not, of course, inhere in language. We may call the object speakers stand on when delivering a speech a podium, but we also know that many other speakers using our same shared English language might refer to it as a lectern. We also know that if this same object were found in a church it would be called by still another name, a pulpit. The various symbols and meanings facilitate linguistically rich understandings. For example, a reporter could declare that the president used his office as a pulpit in a speech about the need to improve the living conditions and opportunities for poor people living in the United States. The use of the term *pulpit* suggests the president spoke in a style exhorting us to action, similar to the way a preacher might call out our moral responsibilities in a church.

Although such linguistic choices give texture, complexity, and added power to our rhetorical and argumentative interactions, the fact is that all of the terms themselves are arbitrary. We could have called the podium a *smerl* and the pulpit a *worquel*. The words have meaning only to the extent that everyone using the shared symbols of the language system has agreed to give them the same meaning. The groups agreeing to a meaning may be as large as a culture or as small as a clique that creates its own lingo: surfers, bikers, skateboarders, gamblers, and the like.

A culture's agreed-upon word meanings are usually detailed in a dictionary—but, of course, most of us have never read an entire dictionary. When one does consult a dictionary, one often finds multiple definitions for a single word. The multiplicity may be the cause of misunderstandings about what a speaker meant or what a listener comprehended.

Consider for a moment the word *stump*. Among the definitions are: a "part of the tree trunk left protruding from the ground after a tree has fallen or been felled"; "a part, as of a branch, limb, or tooth, remaining after the main part has been cut away"; "an artificial leg"; a "short, thickset person"; a "a place or an occasion used for political or campaign oratory"; "to stub a toe or foot"; or "to cause to be at a loss, baffle."[3] Thus, if we use the term *stump* in a sentence, and you do not know which usage we intended, we have *stumped* you!

How then do we make sense of the words that others use? One answer is that the symbols we share are governed by the *system* of language, which is often referred to as the grammar. The rules of language use help us to ascertain which of the various meanings of a word is intended. The principle of linguistic context permits a single word to be used in a multitude of ways. In fact, as I.A. Richards wrote, "Most words, as they pass from context to context, change their meanings, and in many different ways. It is their duty and their service to do so."[4] Understanding the rules of grammar enables us to make sense of the context and assign meaning to the words. Thus, if a reporter declared on the evening news that "Governor Newsom traveled up and down the State of California *stumping* for a tax increase to balance the budget," you would presume that he was using oratory to urge voters to agree with his proposed policy alternative and not that he was moving about the state attempting to baffle voters about his intentions with regard to his economic policies.

Understanding definitions is only part of how we make sense of words. Dictionaries provide only the **denotative meaning**, that is, the content level of the word. They generally do not include value judgments that are often embedded in words, and they certainly cannot convey individual feelings—the **connotative meaning** of a word.

Think for a moment about the term *mother*. One definition is "a woman who gives birth to a child." But the dictionary also acknowledges a mother as "a woman whose egg unites with a sperm, producing an embryo"; "a woman who adopts a child"; "a woman who raises a child," and "a woman who holds a position of authority or responsibility similar to that of a mother," as well as "maternal love and tenderness."[5] Which sense of the term did you think of initially? Perhaps none of these dictionary definitions capture your meaning for this term. Were your experiences with your own mother positive? If so, then the word *mother* probably evokes a warm sense of security, fond memories, and love. For individuals who may have had unhappy relationships with their mothers—perhaps a mother who was neglectful, abusive, or overly controlling—the word *mother* may awaken ambivalent or even negative feelings.

The term *mother* may also be adapted to fit the needs and/or values and even cultural ideology of different families. For example, former Vice President Mike Pence, who is known to be very religious and to hold culturally conservative values, refers to his wife Karen as "mother."[6] President Joe Biden was a widower raising two sons after the tragic death of his wife and daughter in a car accident. When he married Jill, the family made the choice to refer to the first wife and natural mother of the boys as "Mommy" and to call Jill "Mom" to distinguish them from each other and to signal that both had a special, unique, and continuing role to play in family life.[7] When exhorting his people to prepare for the first Gulf War, Saddam Hussein declared that the coming conflict would be "the mother of all battles."[8] He was not promising a "loving" war, he was referencing a confrontation that would be so fierce and intense that it would be the equivalent of the primal or first war that defines the very essence of the human experience in conflict. Context helps us select the appropriate denotative meaning. Individuals may have very different connotative meanings for words, which can lead to misunderstandings despite general agreement on denotative meanings.

Abstraction

That a speaker and a listener might speak the same language does not mean arguers and audiences always understand each other. One reason for the failure to achieve shared understanding arises from the principle of **abstraction**. The word *pen* is more specific and concrete than *writing instrument*. The more abstract the term, the more meanings it conveys—and the more opportunity for confusion or obfuscation. Sometimes though, we must recognize that it is the specific and concrete term that has the rhetorical and argumentative power and not the more abstract term. Thus, for example, the declaration: "the *pen* is mightier than the sword" may communicate a greater sense of power than the declaration: "the *writing instrument* is mightier than the sword." It may also have much greater impact than the more contemporary declaration: "the *word processor* is mightier than the sword." The phrase "the *internet* is mightier than the sword," however, may leave room for argument!

Confusion can arise when someone who is developing arguments to advocate a position uses language that is more abstract than necessary. This lack of precision can lead an audience to believe they understand an advocate when they do not. Unscrupulous or perhaps just careless advocates sometimes intentionally take advantage of imprecise language to mislead audiences.[9] Sometimes political figures on either the left or the right make misleading claims that seem to be more than the accidental use of abstract or unclear language. For example, President Obama misled the public when he claimed when advocating for the Affordable Care Act that "if you like your plan you can keep it." In fact, once the new program was in place, many pre-existing health care plans were eliminated because they did not meet the coverage requirements of the new law. For instance, they might not have offered coverage for mental health care. In many cases, the elimination of these "bare bones" policies meant that people would, in fact, need to pay more for the new coverage.[10] President Trump left us many examples of misleading or outright deceptive claims. Perhaps his most noteworthy was that Mexico would pay for his wall on the southern border,[11] a claim that he made frequently. Mexico didn't pay; in fact, Trump threatened to shut down the federal government in December 2018 if Congress did not provide $5 billion to fund his border wall.[12] He also claimed that China paid the tariffs that he imposed on their exports during the trade war that he initiated. Again, they didn't. The tariffs were instead paid by U.S. companies and consumers who purchased the Chinese goods.[13]

There are instances, however, where candidates or elected officials use terms that may not be so much deceptive or misleading as they are ambiguous, giving audiences the ability to make of them whatever they wish. As an example, former President George W. Bush's declared that he was a "compassionate conservative." Individual voters responding to this message were invited to assign whatever meanings they saw as appropriate to each of the two terms. They were also free to determine which of these terms they believed should receive the greatest emphasis—*compassionate* or *conservative*. Candidates also use vague declarations. A claim to "eliminate waste in government" can appeal to voters with very different notions regarding what spending is essential and what is deemed wasteful, given their different interests, concerns, and values. Agricultural subsidies may seem very wasteful to urbanites, for example, but may be seen as critical to the survival of family farms and to those who make their living on the soil. In recent years, we have also seen candidates make use of the phrase "family values" in their argumentative appeals. Few explicitly define what they mean, allowing voters to assign meaning that fits their value hierarchy.

Understanding the utility of ambiguity, the skilled advocate chooses words carefully. If the advocate wants the audience to have a more precise understanding, the advocate uses more precise language. If the opposite is desired, then more abstract language is employed. In that our goal is to emphasize the use of arguments that will enable people to make informed, deliberate, and rational choices, we would strongly urge you to use language that is precise, not misleading or deceptive.

Advocates who wish to enhance understanding should not only select more concrete language but also develop argument strategies that include the use of redundancy, repetition of key claims, and the restatement of positions in alternative ways. Listeners often do not hear what is being said the first time and benefit from having arguments repeated. When repeating arguments, it is more effective not to use the exact same words, which can be annoying. People may disregard or in extreme cases mock verbatim repetition. In the 2016 presidential campaign, candidate Donald Trump invoked China in his public statements about the imbalance of foreign trade so frequently that a popular YouTube video circulated that featured him repeating "China" over and over with different vocal intonations and inflections.[14]

In the next section, we consider how audiences evaluate arguments. Because the meanings we assign to phenomena vary depending on the language used, the specific depiction of characters, scenes, and events can be crucial to how audiences reach an understanding. How audiences understand arguments, in turn, influences whether they will grant adherence to the claims advanced.

LANGUAGE AND GOOD STORIES

One of the foundational assumptions of the narrative approach to argumentation that we employ in this text is that all arguments are conveyed through the use of stories. There are three central elements to any story—characters, scenes, and events. We will now consider how language influences each in turn.

Depicting the Characters in Stories

Central to the narrative perspective is the belief that all humans are social actors. As such, they assume roles, create images, and act to sustain those impressions. They are *characters* in the stories of social life. Daniel Nimmo explained: "The dramatistic viewpoint regards all social relationships as dramatic action. A person in a social drama . . . performs in accordance with the image he [sic] wants to leave on his audience."[15] There are two components to the characters in stories: roles and character types.

A *role* is a set of assumptions about how an individual should act based on their position, occupation, behavior, and status. We don't expect teachers and students, doctors and patients, parents and children to behave the same way. What behavior we do expect of them is influenced, to an extent, by the roles the individuals are playing. We judge people's effectiveness at least in part by how well they fulfill our expectations for their roles. Your professor, for example, should be friendly with you but will probably not become your best friend, a role that could undermine effectiveness as an educator. A "too close" relationship between a student and a professor may diminish the student's respect for the professor and make it awkward for the professor to provide honest and necessary feedback about the student's academic progress. Such a relationship between a student and a professor can also create problems because other students may perceive special treatment or better grades than merited.

Judges provide another example of our expectations for how people fulfill roles. We expect that judges will be confident, fair, impartial, and knowledgeable about the law. We would not feel comfortable having our legal dispute resolved by a judge who seemed tentative, uncertain, and uninformed about legal issues—or who seemed to have decided against us before hearing all the facts in the case. Indeed, judges who do not fulfill our expectations for their role because they make too many judicial errors, are reversed too often on appeal, or openly express their prejudices from the bench may not only be removed from office but could also, in highly unusual cases, find themselves disbarred.

Another constraint upon how characters fulfill their role in dramas is their *character type*. Orrin Klapp concluded there are three major social types: heroes, villains, and fools.[16] Klapp argued Americans are guided by the desire to emulate positive social types and to avoid negative ones. Thus, social types serve as models for how we should behave. Although Klapp's focus was on American character models, we would contend that other cultures probably pursue these same social types, although there will almost certainly be culture-specific expectations. In many Asian cultures, for example, individuals are encouraged not to stand out from the group—contrasted with Western values that prize individuality.

One important way to understand the role of characters in stories is to think about different character types as "an organized set of actional tendencies."[17] Because certain character types tend to act in characteristic ways, we develop expectations. If characters do not behave as we expect them to, we may question the accuracy of their presentation. Kenneth Burke described this phenomenon as satisfying our desire for the fulfillment of "form." He described form as "creation of an appetite in the mind of the auditor and the adequate satisfying of that appetite."[18]

Consider for a moment the character types heroes, villains, and victims. Dramatic plots involve actors in each of these roles. Within each character type we can imagine alternative ways in which the role might be enacted. For example, heroes can be willing or reluctant. They can demonstrate their heroism through the power of their intellect, their raw courage, their moral character, or their physical strength and prowess. Heroes can be glib or taciturn.

In the 1939 film *Mr. Smith Goes to Washington*, Jimmy Stewart plays a shy individual upon whom the role of hero is thrust. He is sent to Congress to represent his state and is immediately uncomfortable in his role as a senator. He is depicted as such an outsider in a capital dominated by cynical professional politicians and highly paid lobbyists that he is the subject of mockery. Yet, his straightforward values, naïve genius, and fundamental moral character are attributes that contribute to the role of the bashful hero. His greatness stems from his simplicity. Through his honesty, determination, and willingness to adhere to his own moral compass, he exposes and brings down the forces of corruption. As the audience watches Mr. Smith confront these evil forces, they identify with his simple values and are enabled to feel just a bit heroic themselves. The narrative appeal of the ordinary outsider as the solution to the failed and corrupt political system can be reanimated by candidates proclaiming that never having held political office is a unique qualification for election rather than a shortfall.

Another interesting example of a naïve film hero was Forrest Gump played by Tom Hanks in the 1994 film of the same name. Forrest is allowed to emerge as a hero even though he is depicted as mentally challenged and is not especially courageous or physically strong (although he runs with incredible speed and stamina and excels at table tennis). Forrest's heroism emerges through a combination of good fortune and moral innocence. Indeed, his greatest appeal is that he is not corrupted by the dominant values of an era that might have tainted the judgments and the essential "goodness" of his contemporaries. Forrest grows up in the segregated South but evidences no bigotry. He loves his childhood sweetheart with a love so pure he immediately forgives her for her failings and inadequacies. What Forrest is, more than anything else, is fiercely loyal to those around him. As audiences watch Forrest live through the experience of many of the key events and controversies of the time, they are given reason to reconsider their own attitudes and value priorities.

Compare the heroic characters of Mr. Smith and Forrest Gump with the roles often played by Dwayne Johnson, "The Rock," in many of his films. Johnson's heroism does not emanate from his intellect or from his naïve wisdom. His strength is almost purely physical. With violence instead of words, Johnson rights the wrongs of the world and thereby brings evil to its knees. As a protagonist, Johnson does not give audiences much reason for introspection or self-evaluation. His focus is on action, not wisdom, and on quick reactions, not careful reflection.

Just as heroic characters may take alternative forms, so too do villains. Klapp differentiated, for example, between villains who symbolize a threat to the social order and those who use that order to accomplish their evil deeds. The desperado, outlaw, or gangster may use violence to cause harm; typically, these roles are antithetical to social order. When the outlaws ride into town, all kinds of terrible things can happen. Think of Bonnie and Clyde or Al Capone. If all, or even most, humans acted this way there would be no social order, only anarchy.

The authoritarian dictator, or the manipulator, on the other hand, may adhere to an established social order, but it may be an order that has been manipulated to meet the character's need for power. Such a dictator can achieve control of the military by rewarding generals and key troops—and then use the military to exert control over people who might be inclined to challenge the power of the state. Soon the police, judges, and key business leaders can all be enlisted in support of a corrupt state machine pursuing strategies to maintain and expand the dictator's hold on power. The result may be a denial of fundamental human freedoms and democracy, or even the elimination of individuals deemed to be enemies of the state. Through all the suffering, however, the order of the state is preserved. Although several authoritarian dictators could be cited as typifying this form of villainy, one who immediately comes to mind is Kim Jong-un, the third-generation despot in the Kim family to preside over North Korea. Kim effectively stifles public dissent, controls all forms of media, imprisons all potential adversaries (including family members), executes possible rivals for power (including his uncle and his half-brother), and plunges his nation into dire poverty and famines as he spends his nation's meager resources to pursue a nuclear arsenal.[19]

Finally, victims may be of various sorts. Some are innocent and unsuspecting, while others may be willing martyrs. Still others bring ruin upon themselves because they are unwary, ignorant, or uninvolved. People might be expected to feel greater sympathy for victims who are depicted as innocent and naïve and, therefore, unprepared for the damage inflicted upon them. Likewise, we have greater sympathy for victims with whom we can identify because they are like us in some way. During the COVID-19 pandemic we have seen some very interesting and sometimes deeply moving narratives of victimhood. For example, stories about health care workers becoming infected and passing away, stories of whole families decimated by the disease, and stories of nursing homes where the disease takes many of our most vulnerable people. We have also seen some isolated coverage of a different character, however, stories of people who publicly belittled the significance or threat of the disease or people who claimed that it is "their right" to refuse to wear a face mask who become ill and succumb to the disease or spread the disease to others. Victims of this latter sort not only may earn less sympathy but also are sometimes mocked on social media platforms.

Successful arguers understand the importance of character types and depict the actors in the social dramas they describe accordingly. President Ronald Reagan, for example, almost completely reframed the public discussion about the civil war in Nicaragua in the early 1980s when he began to call the guerrilla soldiers—who had previously been referred to as the "contras"—"freedom fighters."[20] This reframing may have helped transform the public's negative images into something more favorable. With this softening of attitudes, Reagan could more actively support efforts against the ruling regime.

If the contras were truly freedom fighters, the United States had no choice but to support their efforts. To abandon freedom fighters would be to abandon freedom itself. Freedom fighters, much like our own patriotic founders, are heroic personae, and heroes require and merit our support—especially when they are battling a common enemy. Reagan declared they were waging war against the forces of global communism. Despite Reagan's successful efforts to reframe the dispute, his administration had difficulty sustaining public support for U.S. intervention in the war. Evidence emerged that the contra "freedom fighters" illegally mined the harbors, blew up schools and roads, trafficked in illegal drugs, and plotted assassinations of leftist clerics. In addition, there were explicit claims that they raped, tortured, and murdered ordinary citizens.[21] Such actions failed to live up to the expectations we would have for heroes, and this had the effect of diminishing the appeal of Reagan's story and support for his efforts to intervene in the conflict.[22]

As we discussed in chapter 2, both presidents named George Bush declared Iraq's strongman ruler Saddam Hussein a despicable villain in their speeches calling for military intervention against Iraq. George H. W. Bush sought support for military action to expel Hussein's forces after Iraq intervened in neighboring Kuwait in the first gulf war. George W. Bush argued that Iraq possessed weapons of mass destruction (weapons that were never found) and that Saddam Hussein represented an existential threat to peace in the region. While Saddam Hussein and his forces were cast in this narrative as villainous actors, the U.S. forces that were to be sent to topple his outlaw regime were cast as liberators bringing democratic freedoms to the region. Sadly, the moral clarity of this narrative began to crumble after photographs surfaced inside a prison where Saddam Hussein had detained and tortured the opponents of his regime, a prison that was now used by U.S. military.

> Most of the prisoners . . . there were several thousand, including women and teenagers—were civilians, many of whom had been picked up in random military sweeps and at highway checkpoints. They fell into three loosely defined categories: common criminals; security detainees suspected of "crimes against the coalition"; and a small number of suspected "high-value" leaders of the insurgency against the coalition forces.[23]

The photographs taken on the cell phone cameras of the U.S. soldiers responsible for guarding the detainees reached media outlets and were released to the public. In the photographs, the soldiers seemed especially proud of their achievements, but the photos were devastating to the narrative that the U.S. forces were somehow morally superior to Saddam Hussein's henchmen. As the noted journalist Seymour Hersh wrote:

> The photographs tell it all. In one, Private England, a cigarette dangling from her mouth, is giving a jaunty thumbs-up sign and pointing at the genitals of a young Iraqi, who is naked except for a sandbag over his head, as he masturbates. Three other hooded and naked Iraqi prisoners are shown, hands reflexively crossed over their genitals. A fifth prisoner has his hands at his sides. In another, England stands arm in arm with Specialist Graner; both are grinning and giving the thumbs-up behind a cluster of perhaps seven naked Iraqis, knees bent, piled clumsily on top of each other in a pyramid. There is another photograph of a cluster of naked prisoners, again piled in a pyramid. Near them stands Graner, smiling, his arms crossed; a woman soldier stands in front of him, bending over, and she, too, is smiling. Then, there is another cluster of hooded bodies, with a female soldier standing in front, taking photographs. Yet another photograph shows a kneeling, naked, unhooded male prisoner, head momentarily turned away from the camera, posed to make it appear that he is performing oral sex on another male prisoner, who is naked and hooded.
>   Such dehumanization is unacceptable in any culture, but it is especially so in the Arab world. Homosexual acts are against Islamic law and it is humiliating for men to be naked in front of other men, Bernard Haykel, a professor of Middle Eastern studies at New York University, explained. "Being put on top of each other and forced to masturbate, being naked in front of each other—it's all a form of torture," Haykel said.[24]

In chapter 10 of this text we will focus on the power of visual images, and these were some of the most powerful and instantly repelling images ever witnessed.

Indeed, they persist to this day; they can be found easily through an internet search of images of the Iraq war. This case serves as a reminder that controlling the narrative is essential to controlling the public's understanding of events. With the abuse depicted in these images, the United States lost control of the narrative that it was a highly moral actor sending heroic soldiers to build a new democracy in Iraq. Sadly, the U.S. reputation continues to suffer, especially in the Arab world, because we undermined our own story.

Depicting the Scene in Stories

In addition to presenting the actors in terms of the character types they play in the story, arguers also construct images of the *scene*. Scene refers to what is transpiring on the stage. In public argumentative dramas, scene may include the immediate context surrounding events—for example, the Abu Ghraib prison discussed above; a larger international scene—for example, the Iraq war in the context of a great power competition between nations; or even a broad sweep of history—for example, the intervention in Iraq in the context of thousands of years of tension between the primarily Christian West and the Muslim peoples of the Middle East. An arguer selects what elements of the scene are given presence and how they are presented to support the claims made.

We might consider the events in Hong Kong as an example of alternative narrative constructions of the scene. When the United Kingdom agreed to return Hong Kong to China in 1997, China stated that Hong Kong would retain its independence and its way of life under a principle of "one country, two systems." Specifically, Article 5 of the Basic Law stated that China's "socialist system and policies" shall not be observed in Hong Kong, and "the previous capitalist system and way of life shall remain unchanged for 50 years".[25] However, many in Hong Kong, and especially young people, argue that the Beijing government is increasingly impatient and that it is "tightening [its] grip on their city, from the detention of booksellers by mainland security agents to the expulsion of a foreign journalist, the jailing of young activists, sweeping legal interpretations by Beijing on city matters, and curbs on electoral freedom."[26] The Hong Kong government, which is firmly under the control of Beijing, proposed an extradition bill in 2019 allowing Hong Kong authorities to detain and transfer suspects wanted in territories with which it had no formal extradition agreements, including the People's Republic of China.[27]

Hundreds of thousands of protesters took to the streets to oppose the law. They believed that it would be used to arrest and extradite to the mainland individuals advocating greater freedom and democracy in Hong Kong and that those arrested would be denied the legal protections and freedoms in the courts controlled by the Communist regime that they were entitled to under the Hong Kong Basic Law. In the face of the massive and crippling public protests that brought large swaths of the city to a halt, the Hong Kong government announced that it would "suspend" efforts to pass the extradition bill. It did not, however, commit to not attempting to pass it or similar laws in the future.[28]

Faced with an unresponsive and intransigent local government that was subservient to the hostile and authoritarian regime in Beijing, the protests continued into 2020. "In the months that followed, protesters filled the city's streets, broke into the local legislature and vandalized it, staged sit-ins at the airport, and turned a university campus into a fiery battleground."[29] The Beijing state-controlled media intensified its coverage of the protests and the disruption occurring in Hong Kong, describing a scene of chaos and violence, especially focusing on the violence directed against police and the claim that ordinary Hong Kong workers were unable to get to their jobs because businesses and traffic were disrupted. China had long called the protests "a color revolution"—a term that refers to the civil protests that led to the break-up of the former Soviet Union—and dismissed the protesters as "thugs" and as "separatists" seeking to turn Hong Kong into an "independent or semi-independent political entity."[30] As the protests persisted, the Beijing government escalated its rhetoric and described the protests as a "political virus" and said that the city would not calm down until this "poisonous," "violent," and "recklessly demented force" was eliminated.[31] Rather than describing a scene in Hong Kong where the protests were emerging as a result of a young generation of Hong Kong residents expressing rising levels of frustration and anxiety about their future under authoritarian rule, China attributed the protests to "the Black Hand" of U.S. involvement in fomenting the disorder. As evidence," Beijing-backed media outlets circulated a photo of Julie Eadeh, the political unit chief of the U.S. consulate general in Hong Kong, meeting in a hotel lobby with prominent members of the opposition, including 22-year-old Joshua Wong, a key figure in protests that rocked Hong Kong five years ago."[32]

In response, to this chaotic and disruptive scene, now characterized not as an internal protest but as an international conspiracy to divide China, Beijing pushed through a new national security bill that took effect on June 30, 2020, an hour before the twenty-third anniversary of the city's hand-over to China from British rule. The new law was much more draconian than the proposed 2019 version that sparked the initial protests. The new law allows China to exert unprecedented control over life in Hong Kong. The BBC reported that the new law contained the following key provisions (emphases in original text):

- Crimes of secession, subversion, terrorism and collusion with foreign forces are punishable by a *maximum sentence of life in prison*.
- *Damaging public transport* facilities can be considered *terrorism*.
- Those found guilty will not be allowed to stand for public office.
- Companies can be fined if convicted under the law.
- *Beijing will establish a new security office in Hong Kong*, with its own law enforcement personnel—neither of which are under the local authority's jurisdiction.
- This office can send *some cases to be tried in mainland China*—but Beijing has said it will only have that power over a "tiny number" of cases.
- In addition, *Hong Kong will have to establish its own national security commission to enforce the laws, with a Beijing-appointed adviser*.
- *Hong Kong's chief executive will have the power to appoint judges to hear national security cases*, raising fears about judicial autonomy.
- Importantly, *Beijing will have power over how the law should be interpreted*, not any Hong Kong judicial or policy body. If the law conflicts with any Hong Kong law, the Beijing law takes priority.
- Some *trials will be heard behind closed doors*.
- People suspected of breaking the law can be *wire-tapped and put under surveillance*.

- Management of foreign non-governmental organizations and news agencies will be strengthened.

- The *law will also apply to non-permanent residents* and people "*from outside [Hong Kong] who are not permanent residents of Hong Kong.*"[33]

In Great Britain and the United States, the scene in Hong Kong was depicted very differently. Media coverage in these nations described Hong Kong as a city whose public was dismayed that the Beijing government was breaking its promise to allow Hong Kong to retain its democratic freedoms and autonomous legal system until 2047. Within a month of the passage of the new national security law, the British government announced that it would rescind its extradition act with Hong Kong and restrict the access of the Chinese electronics giant Huawei to the U.K. markets.[34] The United States took even harsher actions in response to the new law. Not only did it also cancel its extradition treaty with Hong Kong but it also declared that since Hong Kong no longer enjoyed meaningful independence from China it was no longer entitled to the "special status" that it long enjoyed with the United States. This would mean that Hong Kong would now be treated the same way as was the rest of China with regard to trade and travel restrictions, banking regulations, access to restricted U.S. technologies, etc.[35]

Once a scene is understood and explained, it imposes demands for the types of actions that are legitimate, or even required, in response. It also sets expectations for the conduct of the actors who will be assigned roles in response to this scene. The gap between China and the West in understanding the events in Hong Kong was truly profound.

Depicting the Events in Stories

The third element of a story is the *events,* or the actions engaged in by the various characters. As with the first two components of a good story, the language one uses in this aspect of the argument is important. Change the important terms, and you change the argument. Returning to the Hong Kong example, the West typically described the events in Hong Kong as "pro-democracy protests," as "demonstrations," or as anti-government protest actions."[36] The media in China, however, referred to the protestors as "separatists," "trouble makers," and as "violent terrorists," guided by "meddling foreign forces."[37] What was the consequence of this dramatically different depiction of the events? In China, the government made efforts to arrest and prosecute protestors under the new national security law, while in the West, there were attempts to honor the protesters by awarding them the Nobel Peace Prize, a move that the Beijing government vociferously protested.[38]

An important historical example of the power of stories in the construction of events was provided by the attempt to impeach and remove President Bill Clinton from office. On February 11, 1994, Paula Jones, a low-level former employee of the state government of Arkansas, held a news conference and declared that the then governor of the state Clinton, had summoned her to his hotel room in Little Rock. She then claimed that the governor then lowered his trousers to demand oral sex. Clinton immediately denied the story, and Jones filed suit for sexual harassment. Settlement talks began between attorneys for both parties but broke down when Clinton refused to admit responsibility. Nonetheless, the parties were reported not to be very far apart, and the prospects for a settlement were promising. Jones became upset, however, when she learned Clinton's attorneys were making disparaging remarks about her to the press. She decided to fire her attorney and then retained as counsel a firm with a long history of involvement with conservative causes. This firm pursued the matter aggressively and filed a subpoena demanding a deposition from the president. Although Clinton sought to postpone his testimony until after he left the presidency, the Supreme Court denied his request and ruled that he submit to a civil deposition. Jones's attorneys were permitted to ask the president, under oath, whether he had engaged in sexual relations with other women whose careers he could influence. Clinton testified, under oath, that he had not. One of the women whose name arose in the questioning was that of a young White House intern, Monica Lewinsky.[39]

Lewinsky had confided in a friend, Linda Tripp, another White House employee who had been hired by the Bush administration and retained by the Clinton administration, that she and President Clinton had been sexually intimate. Tripp notified the office of Kenneth Star, the special prosecutor investigating allegations of financial improprieties committed by the Clintons in Arkansas. Starr summoned Lewinsky to a meeting to determine whether he could prove that the president had perjured himself during his testimony in the Jones case. Lewinsky refused to wear a wire, as the special prosecutor wished, but she did ultimately cooperate with the investigation in order to escape prosecution for perjury herself. Clinton's problems worsened when Lewinsky reported she still had in her possession a blue dress that she claimed was stained with Clinton's semen. Starr secured the dress, and then requested a blood sample from Clinton for DNA testing. The DNA tests confirmed that the semen stain was the president's, and Clinton's denials under oath of sexual intimacies with staff members were proven to be lies.[40]

Special Prosecutor Starr referred this new evidence to the Judiciary Committee of the House of Representatives. With Republican members supporting the resolution and Democrat members opposing it, the committee recommended that President Clinton be impeached and removed from office for perjury. The full House of Representatives, again voting largely along party lines, agreed and passed two articles of impeachment, which were then forwarded to the Senate for trial. Public opinion polls consistently revealed that the U.S. public did not support the attempt to remove the president from office, and the articles of impeachment failed when Republicans could not convince more than 55 senators (67 were needed to convict) to vote for either of the impeachment resolutions.[41]

To many conservatives, President Clinton was a morally loathsome and contemptible figure who was completely unfit to serve in the office of the presidency. These people saw the original complaint by Paula Jones as evidence of his immorality and personal corruption. Their distrust and dislike for the president were fueled by the additional stories that he had engaged in sleazy sexual contact with Monica Lewinsky, a girl who was the age of his daughter. These sordid events were more than ample justification to turn the president out of office.

Many others, however, viewed President Clinton as much a victim as a perpetrator in this sorry episode. Many of these people found Jones's story unconvincing, and the events she described as unlikely to have occurred. Furthermore, they thought Lewinsky and her friend Linda Tripp were the true villains in this episode—Lewinsky because she seemed to have intentionally sought to seduce the president and Tripp because she breached her friend's confidence when she told the office of the special prosecutor. Many believed that Clinton's poor judgment and his infidelity to his wife were not grounds for impeachment or removal from office.

These events were thus given very different meanings in the competing stories that played out in the press. To some storytellers the events revealed Clinton's deep moral failing and his lack of respect for the law and for the office of the presidency, justifying his immediate removal from office. Other storytellers conceded that the president had erred, but they argued these events in no way justified his impeachment and that almost everyone lies about sex. That these events were criminalized and blown out of proportion as they were, they believed, was due to the political ambitions and blind hatred of the conservatives for the Clintons. Public opinion polls revealed that the actions of Kenneth Starr were especially condemned by many citizens as having more to do with his political goals than with the pursuit of justice. Ultimately public opinion polls revealed that most people did not support the removal of the president from office, and the impeachment effort failed.[42]

Although public opinion polls showed that the public did not support President Clinton's removal from office, many analysts and experts who evaluated the results of the 2000 presidential election suggested that the question of Bill Clinton's character mattered a great deal to the voters and that the negative perceptions of Clinton damaged Vice President Gore in the race against George W. Bush.[43] The impeachment drama also undermined Clinton's own legacy, particularly now in the "Me Too" era marked by greater sensitivity to sexual harassment and to the degree to which power differences may corrupt even consensual relationships.[44] Some also argued that Bill Clinton's impeachment, and indeed his long history of sexual relationships with other women, led to persistent negative opinions of his wife, Hillary Clinton, in the 2016 presidential race.[45]

Naming

To illustrate the importance of naming, we begin with a brief introduction to the difficulties of discussion or argument when a problem or injustice has not yet been named. If words are not available to describe a problem adequately, the possibilities for finding a resolution diminish. If language doesn't exist to discuss an experience, individuals may know that something is wrong but may not be able to describe their experience so that others understand. Naming a problem is particularly difficult for marginalized groups who often feel disadvantaged by the dominant language. "When language expands to encompass and express the perceptions and experiences of marginalized group members, they have more possibilities available for naming their experiences."[46]

> The term *sexual harassment* illustrates how a problem cannot be talked about until words are invented to describe it. Although the phrase *sexual harassment* is an accepted and widely used phrase today, the problem of sexual harassment could not be adequately acknowledged and addressed until there was a label for it. Lin Farley is credited with coining the term after teaching a class, Women and Work, at Cornell University. In class discussions, she noticed a pattern among her women students—they had either quit or been fired from a job because they were made uncomfortable by and/or had refused men's sexual advances. In 1975, Farley was asked to testify before the New York City Human Rights Commission Hearings on Women and Work. As part of her testimony, she used the term *sexual harassment* to describe "unwanted sexual advances against women employees by male supervisors, bosses, foremen or managers." A reporter heard Farley's remarks and incor-

porated the term into an article published in the *New York Times*, which then put the phrase into national circulation. Today, *sexual harassment* is standard language in the antidiscriminatory policies of corporations, government agencies, and educational institutions. Until there was a label for the problem, however, sexual harassment was a phenomenon that was generally not seen, not discussed, and consequently not addressed.[47]

The choice of words in argument is vitally important. Linguistic relativity explains how the act of naming affects how something is viewed. The Sapir-Whorf hypothesis argues that the language available to individuals influences how they perceive and experience the world.

> Kenneth Burke extends the notion that language is a filter through which reality is perceived. He suggests that language provides particular frames of reference or ways of looking that he calls terministic screens. In other words, the terms chosen to describe something focus attention in one direction rather than another.[48]

Naming directs perceptions and behavior.

There is great power in the names we give things. During the summer of 2020, incidents of police violence in several U.S. cities, but especially in Minneapolis, Louisville, and Kenosha (WI), resulted in national protests under the banner Black Lives Matter. When some of these peaceful protests spun out of control and began to morph into violence and vandalism, President Trump turned to Twitter to condemn the violence and to mobilize his supporters into action to counter the violence. For example, "in a tweet, Trump shared a video of the pro-Trump caravan driving into Portland (OR) and labeled its members 'GREAT PATRIOTS!' In another tweet, he referred to protesters in Washington, D.C., as 'Disgraceful Anarchists' and said, 'We are watching them closely.'"[49] The tweets became especially controversial when a 17-year-old Trump supporter and militia member traveled from his home in Illinois to Kenosha and killed two protesters and injured another; a Trump supporter went into Portland to engage in a counter-protest and was shot and killed. Trump's rival in the 2020 presidential campaign, Vice President Joe Biden immediately condemned Trump's tweets.

> As a country, we must condemn the incitement of hate and resentment that led to this deadly clash . . . What does President Trump think will happen when he continues to insist on fanning the flames of hate and division in our society and using the politics of fear to whip up his supporters? He is recklessly encouraging violence.[50]

Biden further declared that "The job of a president is to lower the temperature . . . and all of us are less safe because Donald Trump can't do the job of the American president."[51]

In responding to Biden's claim that Trump's discourse was not healing and was further deepening the divide in the United States, Mark Meadows, Trump's Chief of Staff declared on *Meet the Press*: "You know, you want to talk about Donald Trump's America. Most of Donald Trump's America is peaceful. . . . It is a Democrat-led city in Portland that we're talking about this morning who just yesterday denied help once again from the federal government."[52] Chuck Todd, the host of the program responded to Meadows's comments by asking if Trump believes he doesn't have "responsibility of governing and leading the entire country?"[53] These exchanges clearly reveal the power of naming—and indeed the power of word choice and language.

In recent years, cities around the world have been subjected to attacks by suicide bombers or armed terrorists. To most of us, these attackers are vile terrorists; their actions represent a core capacity for unthinkable evil. No political objectives and no injustices warrant the slaughter of innocent civilians. Yet to people who have shared the experience of poverty and oppression, these terrorists are heroic freedom fighters; after death they are celebrated as martyrs to a cause whose significance and purpose justifies such sacrifice. From this perspective, the victims in these killings are not innocent civilians—they are representatives of the unjust political regimes that have perpetuated conditions of poverty and oppression and prevented the full embrace of religious law and authority. Those who sympathize may see the deaths as unfortunate collateral damage justified because violence is the only alternative for people who lack the power for political solutions and the resources for conventional forms of warfare.

Terrorist or freedom fighter, murderer or martyr, wanton slaughter of innocents or justified military action—what is the significance of the names applied? Think for a moment of the mental pictures conjured up by these symbols. Embedded within each of these terms are multiple images that guide people in the formation of attitudes about the acts themselves and about the motives of the individuals responsible for them. The particular symbols people select to describe these attacks give insight into the experiences, attitudes, values, and ideological positions of those who have selected one name over another. Likewise, the exposure to the different names colors the response to the violent acts.

The televised images of these tragedies are remarkably similar and consistent from one news report to the next. We see images of the site of the violence (for example the smoking wreckage of the now desecrated interior of a church). We see pictures of bleeding victims and mangled bodies, and we hear the piercing screams of people lamenting their losses. We hear the wailing sirens and see the images of the speeding ambulances. We see images of the bleeding victims who survived the attacks. We see the grieving families and friends of the deceased—mournful tears for the victims and sometimes celebrations for the heroic acts of the martyrs. Despite the similarities in the images that are broadcast on different television networks, the language used to describe the events and the names given to the bombers and their victims may differ significantly. Each network employs language to account for and explain the visual images. The language used to describe events determines how the behavior is interpreted and establishes the context in which the arguments are presented. Thus, the voice-over language that accompany the images on CNN may be substantially different from that of Al Jazeera—the Middle Eastern network, or CCTV—the Chinese network, or RT—Russia Today.

The Middle Eastern region known as the Holy Land is sacred to Muslims, Christians, and Jews. For more than 70 years, the area has suffered prolonged violence and open warfare over conflicting claims of Jewish and Arab national movements. Disputes between Israel and Palestinians have thwarted efforts to create a Palestinian state on the West Bank of the River Jordan and the Gaza Strip on the Mediterranean coast. Two major parties have dominated Palestinian politics since 2006. The Fatah-led Palestinian Authority governs the West Bank, and Hamas governs the Gaza Strip. Hamas does not recognize Israeli sovereignty. There have been constant skirmishes and three major confrontations between Hamas and the Israelis. The war that began in December 2008 lasted 22 days; the 2014 war lasted 50 days. The 2021 war lasted 11 days, ending with a fragile cease-fire.[54]

The Palestinian cause has been verbally, and to an extent materially, supported by its Arab neighbors in the region, including Israel's arch-enemy Iran. Whether or not the Hamas or the Israeli actions in the conflict are justified depends on the source of the arguments presented. The Israelis claim that their actions are intended only to quell the violence, stop the attacks on Israel, and save lives.[55] *The New York Times* summarized Israel's long-term strategy as an effort "to deter Hamas" and "destroy enough of the group's weaponry to secure an extra few years of what some Israelis describe as 'quiet.'"[56] Those who oppose the Israeli actions, such as Yousef Munayyer, a Washington-based analyst and human rights advocate, believe "The very calculus that Israel uses to judge its military success is illegitimate . . . Israelis often refer to this callously as 'mowing the lawn,' periodic maintenance it has to do by bombing one of the world's most densely populated spots, which it also holds under a blockade. . . . There is no morality in a war whose repetition is preplanned."[57]

The Palestinians in 2021 launched 3,350 bombs at civilian targets in Israel and killed 12 Israelis.[58] More than 230 Palestinians were killed in Gaza, including 65 children. In addition, Israeli air strikes "devastated civilian infrastructure, wrecked sewage systems and water pipes, damaged at least 17 hospitals and clinics, severely damaged or destroyed about 1,000 buildings and suspended operations at Gaza's only coronavirus testing laboratory."[59] Both Israel and Hamas were accused of committing war crimes.

> Civilians are paying an especially high price in the latest bout of violence between Israel and Hamas in the Gaza Strip, raising urgent questions about how the laws of war apply to the conflagration: which military actions are legal, what war crimes are being committed and who, if anyone, will ever be held to account.
>
> Both sides appear to be violating those laws, experts said: Hamas has fired more than 3,000 rockets toward Israeli cities and towns, a clear war crime. And Israel, although it says it takes measures to avoid civilian casualties, has subjected Gaza to such an intense bombardment, killing families and flattening buildings, that it likely constitutes a disproportionate use of force—also a war crime.[60]

The Palestinians insist that Israel turned Gaza into a virtual prison and that their lives are so desperate that they have no choice but to continue to fight so that the world understands the depth of suffering they endure on a daily basis.[61] The economy of Gaza has been described over many years as "in ruins," unemployment is soaring, the Hamas government has been unable to provide even basic services to the citizens as a result of Israel's blockade.[62] Israel's Prime Minister Netanyahu defended his government's military strikes and incursions into Gaza. He asserted that the International Criminal Court (ICC) investigation into whether Israel had committed war crimes was a case of "pure anti-Semitism."[63] Netanyahu argued that it was not a war crime "when democratic Israel defends itself against terrorists who murder our children, [and] rocket our cities."[64] He further complained that the ICC "refuses to investigate brutal dictatorships like Iran and Syria who commit horrific atrocities almost daily". . . [and vowed Israel would] "fight this perversion of justice with all our might!"[65]

The ongoing Israeli-Palestinian conflict is thus as much an information war as it is a kinetic war. The disputants used public arguments to explain their positions, justify their strategies, and legitimize the morality of their actions for their domestic audiences, for their opponents in the conflict, and for other people and governments around the world. In this long-standing tragic conflict, you can observe the power of naming and language—and the significant impact on lives.

Metaphor

Savvy arguers have also learned that there are special forms of argument that can enhance the appeal of a claim. One illustration is the use of *metaphor*. You probably learned all about metaphors, similes, and other figures of speech in English classes. They are often referred to as ornaments of language. Saying a classmate "roars like a lion" (simile) and is "bullheaded" (metaphor) communicates information about that classmate in a manner that is more creative than merely saying the classmate is very loud and strong-willed. (Of course, these examples are clichés that you should probably avoid!) Metaphor is, however, a very useful and highly influential form of argumentation, and thus it has value beyond being ornamental language.

An *ornamental metaphor* asks audiences to see that phenomenon A has some characteristics that resemble phenomenon B. If we say, "Peter is as strong as an ox," we are only comparing one aspect of Peter—his strength—with one aspect of the ox—its strength. No one would surmise that Peter walks on four legs, pulls carts behind him, and has a tail suitable for making soup. The point of the comparison is figurative only—Peter certainly does not have the actual equivalent strength of an ox. Some metaphors, however, are intended literally. A recent example is when people referred to the Russian President Vladimir Putin as "Vlad the Poisoner." The name is intended to remind people of "Vlad the Impaler," the fifteenth century ruler of Transylvania (what is now Romania). This Vlad was said to have invited his political adversaries to a banquet where he stabbed them to death and then impaled their bodies on stakes. Some claim that Bram Stoker based the fictional character Dracula on Vlad.[66] The metaphor is literal given that Putin is said to use poisons to assassinate his political opponents.[67] An *argumentative metaphor* contends that phenomenon A should be seen as phenomenon B. An argumentative metaphor is a powerful tool for influencing how we make sense of the world.

Jason Wingard, president of Temple University in Philadelphia, wrote an op-ed in 2021 advising that universities embrace their position as a force for rigorous debate and balanced discourse—especially during a time when political polarization has divided the country. As campuses attempted to reopen after a year of lockdowns, many of the culture wars roiling communities and families heightened tensions on campus threatening higher education's core value of critical, evidence-based thinking. The conflict over mask wearing and vaccines joined dissension over gun rights, abortion, Black Lives Matter, critical race theory, transgender rights, the Israel-Palestine conflict, white supremacy, and climate change.

> Consider a seemingly intractable subject: the Israel-Palestine conflict. There is so much history, passion and personal investment in this heated issue that civil conversations are frequently impossible, never mind being over before they start.
>
> These non-conversations often spill into the social media meat grinder, leading to public outcry and demands to fire faculty or expel an offending student.
>
> What if the response to a Jewish student group and a pro-Palestinian student group getting into a shouting match in a public space on campus was not just to issue a banal statement condemning incivility? What if the response was not just to try and thread a nonexistent needle of neutrality?[68]

Note the metaphors in the quotation: social media meat grinder and thread a needle. Do they advance Wingard's premise? Note the effective use of language in urging colleges and universities not to hide from difficult issues but to be the vehicle for understanding differing views and opening minds." What if, in fulfilling its promise as a place for education and personal growth, a university tackled a thorny, intractable problem by applying a thoughtful, strategic process as a goal in its own right?"[69] He states that an effective institutional response is not to hide from difficult issues but to foster open dialogue grounded in facts. The intent is not to decide who is wrong or right but to empower everyone with an interest to question positions—including their own—or perhaps to question the language of how the question is posed.

> Higher education is the last bastion of hope for this type of civil debate. If universities are to survive and reestablish their valued position, they must fully leverage the power of convening, and aggressively encourage active, bipartisan discourse in pursuit of learning that will ultimately preserve the institution, and advance a peaceful and productive society.[70]

A metaphor thus acts as a template for interpreting new information. Viewing A as B limits, shapes, and constrains our understanding of A. We come to "know" A (in the above case Vladimir Putin) with respect to what we "know" about B (an evil villainous character), and the values embodied in B are transferred to A through this sense-making process. Those who accept the assessment of President Putin as a ruthless leader who cold-bloodedly assassinates his adversaries would be invited to interpret Russia's actions within a narrative frame of evil versus good. Such a dramatic structure would also demand that our nation act appropriately to counter any threat that Russia might pose to our democracy or our way of life. Even those occasions where Russia acted charitably or morally might be viewed with suspicion because storytellers understand that evil people cannot be trusted and likely have ulterior motives. Evidence of President Putin's intentions to undermine the United States was provided by concerted efforts to circulate misinformation and meddling in the 2016 and 2020 presidential elections.[71]

Another example of a metaphor that achieved great persuasive power is a statement attributed to former Chinese Communist leader Deng Xiaoping: "It doesn't matter whether a cat is black or white as long as it catches mice."[72] In China, party leaders were expected to demonstrate absolute loyalty to Communist Party orthodoxy. Deng's metaphor stressed that faithful adherence to Marxist (or Maoist) principles were less important to solving China's political and economic problems than the pursuit of pragmatic policies that would invigorate the Chinese economy, attract foreign investment, and raise the standard of living of the Chinese people.

The power of this metaphor cannot be fully appreciated unless one understands a bit more about Deng's life and his political struggles. Deng studied Marxist theory in Paris during the 1920s. He participated in the "Long March" (1934–1935) and became a key ally of Mao Zedong. He was elected to the Central Committee of the Communist Party in 1945, where he served until 1966 when he was removed from office during the Cultural Revolution for not being sufficiently "pure" in his adherence to Mao's teachings. He returned to power as the vice premier of China in 1973, only to be purged again in 1976 following the death of a key political ally, Zhou Enlai. In 1977, Deng gained control of the Chinese government after the death of Mao and the arrest of the members of the "Gang of Four" who had led the Cultural Revolution.[73]

Deng's metaphor had been cited as a reason for purging him during the Cultural Revolution, but it was also a reason to resurrect him as others in the party came to understand the need to modernize China's economic system. The metaphor continues to play an important role in Chinese politics today. Deng died in 1997, but his legacy is marked by political leaders who argue for still more reforms to respond to the widening gaps between urban and coastal Chinese who are acquiring new sources of wealth and power and the rural Chinese peasants who are lagging further and further behind. Finally, Deng's legacy and metaphor are also a resource for Chinese activists seeking political as well as economic reforms. His metaphor reduces the objectives of governmental economic planning to very simple and easily understood pragmatic goals that, because of their simplicity, are much more difficult to refute. Furthermore, his metaphor clearly appeals to an accepted form of storytelling that strongly resonates within the Chinese culture. Even though some today express doubts that he made the statement in this exact way, the statement persists as a very powerful argumentative metaphor.[74]

Unlike the figurative or ornamental metaphor, in which only one characteristic of A is seen in terms of B, the argumentative metaphor views all of A as B. This gives the metaphor a ***generative capability***. That is, if we know some of the characteristics of A in terms of B, we can infer (or generate) other characteristics. This makes the metaphor a powerful argumentative tool, for it enables us to evoke in an audience a deep, intense response, simply by noting a superficial connection between A and B. As an example, George Lakoff and Mark Johnson wrote that Americans conceive of argument as war.[75] This can be seen in the language that is commonly used to describe arguments.

"Your claims are indefensible."

"He attacked my argument point by point."

"I demolished their arguments."

"I have never won an argument with her."

"She preempted my arguments."

The generative power of the war metaphor can be seen in how we prepare for and actually engage in arguments, as well as in the personal stake we sometimes feel in the arguments we advance. If our position is defeated, we might feel personally vanquished. These are some of the consequences of seeing arguments in terms of war. If you can come up with other similarities between how we argue and how we wage war, then you've proven the generative capability of the argumentative metaphor.

Argumentative metaphors and analogies, which we discuss more fully in chapter 6, are not the same. Both entail comparisons and both have generative functions, but the literal analogy compares cases of phenomena that are materially similar. Metaphors, like the figurative analogy, compare cases that are materially dissimilar.

When citizens expressed their fears that the war in Afghanistan might become another Vietnam, they were arguing analogically. Both were cases of military intervention in a foreign nation. Respondents could counter such arguments by claiming that the analogy was false because military objectives were substantially different in Afghanistan, or because the desert landscape was very different from the jungles of Vietnam. On the other hand, if someone argues homelessness is a plague that is sweeping the nation, the arguer is not literally claiming that homelessness is a contagious disease, only that it is useful to conceive of one in terms of the significance of the other.

Summary

In this chapter we considered the ways advocates can use alternative language strategies to increase the effectiveness of their arguments. Language shapes understanding. Therefore, advocates should judiciously and wisely select the language that will best communicate their positions. We discussed the qualities of language, looked at how good stories utilize language, and considered a specific type of argument tool, the metaphor.

Key Terms

abstraction
characters
character type
connotative meaning
denotative meaning
events
language
   epistemic function of

metaphor
   argumentative
   generative capability of
   ornamental
role
scene

Activities

1. In this chapter we discussed language and indicated that each culture or subculture creates its own way of talking about the things it considers important. For example, think about your favorite kind of music. How do you describe it? What label do you use for music that you consider good? How do you label music you consider bad? Now select a subculture with which you are familiar. List some of the unique language that culture employs and provide a definition of these terms. If you are unfamiliar with the language of a subculture, you may need to interview someone to complete this exercise.

2. Provide your own definition for each of the following terms and indicate whether the term evokes positive feelings for you or negative ones. Now ask a friend or classmate to do the same. Are there differences? Discuss the source of the similarities and differences.

freedom	welfare	marriage	charity
government	retirement	children	religion

3. Select and read an op-ed from a newspaper or website. Then answer the following questions about its narrative form.

    a. Who are the heroes?

    b. Who are the villains?

    c. Who are the victims?

    d. What qualities does the author assign to these characters in their representative roles?

    e. In what actions do each of these actors engage?

    f. How does the author describe the scene?

4. Throughout the day, you enact many roles. Think about your day and list the roles you fill (for instance: student, parent, child, worker, sibling, friend). Choose two of these roles and consider how they influence your behavior.

   a. Are some behaviors acceptable in one role but not in the other?

   b. Are there differences in the amount of power you have in the two roles?

   c. Are there differences in whether or how you express your feelings in the two roles?

   d. Do others respond differently to you when you enact the different roles? For example, are you more likely to be listened to in one role than in the other?

5. Try to discover the influence of metaphors in your life. If you work, think about your place of employment and how your boss talks about it. Does your boss talk about the workers as part of a team? Is a sports metaphor being invoked? If your boss uses military terminology, then perhaps the metaphor is intended to evoke military efficiency. List examples of the metaphors your employer uses. What do these metaphors reveal about how your boss wants employees to act? If you have the good fortune of not having to work, then analyze the metaphors in a different context or environment. Perhaps you belong to a team or a club, or a fraternity or sorority, or a church. What metaphors are used in the setting you choose?

RECOMMENDED READINGS

Anderson, Karrin Vasby, "Hillary Rodham Clinton as 'Madonna': The Role of Metaphor and Oxymoron in Image Restoration," *Women's Studies in Communication* 25 (2002): 1–24.

Hollihan, Thomas A. and Patricia Riley, "The Rhetorical Power of a Compelling Story: A Critique of a 'Toughlove' Parental Support Group," *Communication Quarterly* 35 (1987): 13–25.

Howe, James, "Argument Is Argument: An Essay on Conceptual Metaphor and Verbal Dispute," *Metaphor and Symbol* 23 (2007): 1–23.

Klumpp, James F., "Argumentative Ecology," *Argumentation and Advocacy* 45 (2009): 183–197.

Lakoff, George and Mark Johnson, *Metaphors We Live By* (Chicago: University of Chicago Press, 1980, 2003).

Olmos, Paula (Ed.), *Narration as Argument* (Cham, Switzerland: Springer International, 2017).

Osborne, Michael, "Archetypal Metaphor in Rhetoric: The Light-Dark Family," *Quarterly Journal of Speech* 53 (1967): 121–131.

Poppel, Lotte van, "The Study of Metaphor in Argumentation Theory," *Argumentation* (2020). https://doi.org/10.1007/s10503-020-09523-1.

Steen, G. J., "Deliberate Metaphor Theory: Basic Assumptions, Main Tenets, Urgent Issues," *Intercultural Pragmatics* 14 (2017): 1–24.

Xu, C. and Y. Wu, "Metaphors in the Perspective of Argumentation," *Journal of Pragmatics* 62 (2014): 68–76.

ENDNOTES

[1] Kenneth Burke, *Language as Symbolic Action: Essays on Life, Literature, and Method* (Berkeley: University of California Press, 1966), 45.

[2] See for example, Suzanne K. Langer, *Philosophy in a New Key: A Study of the Symbolism of Reason, Rite, and Art,* 3rd ed. (Cambridge: Harvard University Press, 1957). An excellent discussion of the epistemic function of rhetoric was offered by Richard A. Cherwitz and James W. Hikins, *Communication and Knowledge: An Investigation in Rhetorical Epistemology* (Columbia: University of South Carolina Press, 1986).

[3] *American Heritage Dictionary,* 5th ed. (Boston: Mariner Books, 2018).

[4] I.A. Richards, *The Philosophy of Rhetoric* (London: Oxford University Press, 1936/1981), 11.

[5] *American Heritage Dictionary.*

6. John Kruzel, "Does Mike Pence Call His Wife 'Mother'?" *PolitiFact.* March 27, 2018. https://www.politifact.com/article/2018/mar/27/does-mike-pence-call-his-wife-mother/
7. Carol Lozada, "From Jill to Mom: Inside Jill Biden's Relationship with Beau and Hunter," *The Washington Post,* June 4, 2015. https://www.washingtonpost.com/news/book-party/wp/2015/06/04/from-jill-to-mom-inside-jill-bidens-relationship-with-beau-and-hunter/
8. Dominic Tierney, "'The Mother of All Battles': Twenty Years Later," *The Atlantic,* February 28, 2011. https://www.theatlantic.com/national/archive/2011/02/the-mother-of-all-battles-20-years-later/71804/
9. Fareed Al-Hindawi and Nesaem Al-Aadili, "The Pragmatics of Deception in American Presidential Electoral Speeches," *International Journal of English Linguistics* 7 (July 29, 2017). DO- 10.5539/ijel.v7n5p207.
10. Angie Drobnic Holan, "Lie of the Year: 'If you Like Your Plan You Can Keep It.'" *PolitiFact,* December 12, 2013. https://www.politifact.com/article/2013/dec/12/lie-year-if-you-like-your-health-care-plan-keep-it/
11. Erin Corbett, "Trump Has Said Mexico Will Pay for Wall at Least 20 Times Since 2015," *Fortune,* December 13, 2018. https://fortune.com/2018/12/13/trump-mexico-border-wall/
12. Ibid.
13. Howard Gleckman, "China Trade War: What Is a Tariff and Who Pays It?" *Forbes,* September 25, 2018. https://www.forbes.com/sites/howardgleckman/2018/09/25/what-is-a-tariff-and-who-pays-it/#48a1dd4c137b
14. "Donald Trump Says 'China.'" August 28, 2015. https://www.youtube.com/watch?v=RDrfE9I8_hs
15. Daniel Nimmo, "The Drama, Illusion, and Reality of Political Images," in James E. Combs and Michael W. Mansfield, Eds., *Drama in Life: The Uses of Communication in Society* (New York: Hastings, 1976), 261.
16. Orrin E. Klapp, *Heroes, Villains, and Fools: The Changing American Character* (New York: Routledge, 2014).
17. Walter R. Fisher, *Human Communication as Narration: Toward a Philosophy of Reason, Value, and Action* (Columbia: University of South Carolina Press, 1987), 47.
18. Kenneth Burke, *Counter-statement* (Berkeley: University of California Press, 1931, rpt. 1968), 31.
19. Anna Fifield, *The Great Successor: The Divinely Perfect Destiny of Brilliant Comrade Kim Jong-un* (New York: Public Affairs, 2019).
20. Ronald Reagan, "Excerpts from Reagan's Address on Aid to Contras and the Democratic Reply," *The New York Times,* February 3, 1988, p. A10.
21. Doyle McManus, "Rights Groups Accuse Contras: Atrocities in Nicaragua Against Civilians Charged," *Los Angeles Times,* March 8, 1985. https://www.latimes.com/archives/la-xpm-1985-03-08-mn-32283-story.html
22. Because President Reagan was unsuccessful in convincing the public and Congress to support direct military assistance for the contras, he permitted members of his administration to devise a clandestine strategy to provide such aid. Colonel Oliver North solicited support from U.S. allies around the world, but especially from the Middle East, to donate weapons and ammunition directly to the rebels. He also arranged the sale of weapons donated by these allies to Iran, and then diverted the profits to the Nicaraguan rebels. This was in violation of U.S. law, and resulted in criminal indictments against North, Secretary of Defense Caspar Weinberger, and others. President Reagan was personally damaged by the disclosure of these violations of law that were the subject of extensive congressional investigations and lengthy court proceedings. For an excellent discussion see: *United States v. Oliver L. North*, U.S. Criminal Case #88-0800-02 GAG.
23. Seymour M. Hersh, "Torture at Abu Ghraib," *The New Yorker,* April 30, 2004. https://www.newyorker.com/magazine/2004/05/10/torture-at-abu-ghraib
24. Ibid.
25. Greg Torode and James Pomfret, "Explainer: Hong Kong's 'Borrowed Time'—Worry about 2047 Hangs Over Protests," *Reuters,* August 23, 2019. https://www.reuters.com/article/us-hongkong-protests-explainer/explainer-hong-kongs-borrowed-time-worry-about-2047-hangs-over-protests-idUSKCN1VD0S6
26. Ibid.
27. Mike Ives, "What Is Hong Kong's Extradition Bill?" *The New York Times,* June 10, 2019. https://www.nytimes.com/2019/06/10/world/asia/hong-kong-extradition-bill.html
28. Ibid.
29. Austin Ramzy and Mike Ives, "Hong Kong Protests, One Year Later," *The New York Times,* June 9, 2020. https://www.nytimes.com/2020/06/09/world/asia/hong-kong-protests-one-year-later.html
30. "Beijing Intensified Condemnation of Hong Kong Protests," *Time,* September 3, 2019. https://time.com/5667184/beijing-reaction-hong-kong-protests-hkmao/
31. Helen Davidson, "China Calls Hong Kong Protesters a 'Political Virus,'" *The Guardian,* May 6, 2020. https://www.theguardian.com/world/2020/may/06/china-calls-hong-kong-protesters-a-political-virus

[32] Eva Dou, Natasha Kahn, and Wenxin Fan, "China Claims U.S. 'Black Hand' Is Behind Hong Kong Protests," *Wall Street Journal*, August 9, 2019. https://www.wsj.com/articles/china-claims-u-s-black-hand-is-behind-hong-kong-protests-11565356245

[33] "Hong Kong Security Law: What Is It? And Is It Worrying?" *BBC News*, June 30, 2020. https://www.bbc.com/news/world-asia-china-52765838

[34] Stephen Castle, "UK Suspends Extradition Treaty with Hong Kong Over Security Law," *The New York Times*, July 20, 2020. https://www.nytimes.com/2020/07/20/world/asia/extradition-treaty-hong-kong.html

[35] "The President's Executive Order on Hong Kong Normalization," *The White House*, July 14, 2020. https://trumpwhitehouse.archives.gov/presidential-actions/presidents-executive-order-hong-kong-normalization/

[36] Jessie Yeung, "The Hong Kong Protests, Explained," *CNN*, December 20, 2019. https://www.cnn.com/2019/11/15/asia/hong-kong-protests-explainer-intl-hnk-scli/index.html

[37] Amy Qin, "Hong Kong Protests China's Tightening Grip: An Explainer," *The New York Times*, May 27, 2020. https://www.nytimes.com/2020/05/27/world/asia/why-are-hong-kong-protesters.html

[38] "China Warns Norway Against Peace Prize for Hong Kong Protestors," *Bloomberg News*, August 27, 2020. https://www.bloomberg.com/news/articles/2020-08-28/china-warns-norway-against-peace-prize-for-hong-kong-protesters

[39] "Special Section: Long Road to Impeachment, Pathway to Peril," *Los Angeles Times*, January 31, 1999. https://www.latimes.com/archives/la-xpm-1999-jan-31-mn-3627-story.html

[40] "An Affair of State," *Time*, September 21, 1998.

[41] R. A. Serrano and M. Lacey, "Clinton Acquitted: Votes Fall Far Short of Conviction," *Los Angeles Times*, February 13, 1999, p. A1.

[42] David A. Graham and Cullen Murphy, "Bill Clinton's Impeachment: The Inside Story," *The Atlantic*, December 2018. https://www.theatlantic.com/magazine/archive/2018/12/clinton-impeachment/573940/

[43] David Leonhardt, "The Clinton Legacy: Impeachment Hurts the President," *The New York Times*, October 13, 2019. https://www.nytimes.com/2019/10/13/opinion/impeachment-clinton.html

[44] Patrick Andelic, "Unlike Most Former Presidents Bill Clinton Is Becoming Increasingly Unpopular," *Quartz*, January 18, 2018. https://qz.com/1182889/bill-clintons-declining-legacy-monica-lewinsky-impeachment-metoo-and-trump/

[45] See for example, Nick Bryant, "U.S. Election: The Man Hurting Clinton in Her Fight with Trump," *BBC News*, 31 May 2016. https://www.bbc.com/news/election-us-2016-36412809 Also: Lydia Saad, "Trump and Clinton Finish with Historically Poor Images," *Gallup*. November 8, 2016. https://news.gallup.com/poll/197231/trump-clinton-finish-historically-poor-images.aspx

[46] Karen Foss, Sonja Foss, and Alena Ruggerio, *Feminism in Practice: Communication Strategies for Making Change* (Long Grove, IL: Waveland Press, 2022), 94

[47] Ibid., pp. 94–95.

[48] Ibid., p. 95.

[49] Allan Smith, "Trump Praises Right-Wing Supporters, Rails Against Protesters After Unrest in Portland," *NBC News*, August 30, 2020. https://www.nbcnews.com/politics/donald-trump/trump-rails-against-protesters-following-unrest-portland-n1238808

[50] Ibid.

[51] Ibid.

[52] Ibid.

[53] Justine Coleman, "Meadows: 'Most of Donald Trump's America Is Peaceful,'" *The Hill*, August 30, 2020. https://thehill.com/homenews/sunday-talk-shows/514323-meadows-most-of-trumps-america-is-peaceful

[54] Dan Bilefsky, "What Drove the Israel-Gaza Conflict?" *The New York Times*, September 30, 2021. https://www.nytimes.com/article/israel-gaza-what-we-know.htm

[55] Isabel Kershner and Ben Hubbard, "Israel Says Its Forces Did Not Kill Palestinians Sheltering at U.N. School," *The New York Times*, July 28, 2014, p. A6.

[56] Patrick Kingsley and Ronen Bergman, "Israel's Military Inflicted a Heavy Toll, But Did It Achieve Its Aim?" *The New York Times*, May 21, 2021. https://www.nytimes.com/2021/05/21/world/middleeast/israel-gaza-war-ceasefire.html

[57] Ibid.

[58] "Biden Voices Support for Cease-Fire in Israeli-Palestinian Conflict," *The New York Times*, May 21, 2021. https://www.nytimes.com/live/2021/05/17/world/israel-gaza-updates

[59] Ibid.

60. Declan Walsh, "When Fighting Erupts Between Israel and Hamas the Question of War Crimes Follows," *The New York Times,* May 19, 2021. https://www.nytimes.com/2021/05/16/world/middleeast/israel-gaza-hamas-civilian-casualties.html
61. Jodi Rudoren and Ben Hubbard, "Despite Gains, Hamas Sees a Fight for Its Existence and Presses Ahead," *The New York Times,* July 28, 2014, p. A6.
62. "With Gaza in Ruins, Hamas Faces Palestinian Elections as Rulers Not Resistors," *The Times of Israel,* February 3, 2021. https://www.timesofisrael.com/with-gaza-in-ruins-hamas-faces-palestinian-elections-as-rulers-not-resistors/
63. "Netanyahu: An ICC Investigation of Israel Would Be 'Pure Anti-Semitism,'" *The Times of Israel,* February 6, 2021. https://www.timesofisrael.com/netanyahu-an-icc-investigation-of-israel-would-be-pure-anti-semitism/
64. Ibid.
65. Ibid.
66. Marc Lallanilla, "The Real Dracula: Vlad the Impaler," *Live Science,* September 14, 2017. https://www.livescience.com/40843-real-dracula-vlad-the-impaler.html
67. Laurence Peter, "Navalny and Russia's Arsenal of Exotic Poisons," *BBC News,* August 26, 2020. https://www.bbc.com/news/world-europe-53907761
68. Jason Wingard, "Colleges Can Lead Hot-Button Issues by Pushing Critical Thinking." *Chicago Tribune,* October 18, 2021, p. 12.
69. Ibid.
70. Ibid.
71. Jane Mayer, "How Russia Helped Swing the Election for Trump," *The New Yorker,* September 24, 2018. https://www.newyorker.com/magazine/2018/10/01/how-russia-helped-to-swing-the-election-for-trump. Also, Julian Barnes, "Russia Continues Interfering in Election to Try to Help Trump, U.S. Intelligence Says," *New York Times,* August 7, 2020. https://www.nytimes.com/2020/08/07/us/politics/russia-china-trump-biden-election-interference.html
72. Mark Buckle, "Black Cat, White Cat . . . ," *China Daily,* August 2, 2018. http://www.chinadaily.com.cn/a/201808/02/WS5b728ae4a310add14f385b4a.html
73. For an excellent study of Deng Xiaoping see: Ezra F. Vogel, *Deng Xiaoping and the Transformation of China* (Cambridge, MA: Belknap Press, 2011).
74. Ibid.
75. George Lakoff and Mark Johnson, *Metaphors We Live By* (Chicago: University of Chicago Press, 1980, 2003).

Argumentation and Critical Thinking

In the preceding chapters we focused on argumentation as a form of storytelling. We emphasized that people are natural storytellers and that they are able to create and test competing stories. Although this is true of all people, some people are more gifted arguers than others. People have different argumentation talents. Some are more articulate than others, some use more vivid examples, some have better vocabularies, some have better memories, some think on their feet more quickly, and some have a better capacity for refuting the claims made by others.

You can enhance your arguing skills if you understand some of the techniques for creating reasoned arguments. Different argument fields often demand different argumentation styles, strategies, and techniques. In addition, several analytical techniques are available to help you improve the quality of your claims and to assure a more systematic analysis of the arguments that you encounter. Our objective in this chapter is to enhance your critical thinking skills—to sharpen your analytical abilities—so that you create better arguments, evaluate others' arguments more carefully, and, ultimately, make better decisions. This chapter will explore alternative principles for the evaluation of propositions, suggest how arguers can make strategic decisions regarding how best to express their arguments and their disagreement with others' arguments, and discuss some alternative methods for the analysis of arguments.

In this chapter, we focus on argumentation as a set of principles that can be learned, rather than as a naturally occurring human activity. We continue to believe that humans are by nature storytellers and that arguments are primarily created and understood through stories. In fact, the theories we will discuss can be understood as a unique style of storytelling that is especially appropriate for evaluating argumentative propositions. The information learned in this chapter will help you become more effective arguers in meetings, when writing papers or reports, in formal debates, or at rare but important occasions such as a visit to traffic court or small-claims court.

PROPOSITIONS

A natural starting point for any argumentative interaction is an investigation of the proposition under dispute. A *proposition* is a statement that expresses the subject of the dispute. The degree of formality in the actual wording of a proposition will vary depending on the formality of the setting.

In a casual conversational setting, for example, the proposition might be stated very simply and informally: "I think we should go to the movies," or an opposing proposition: "we always end up at the movies; I think we should go hear some live music." As the setting becomes more formal, however, there will be a more careful statement of the proposition. For example, a curriculum committee meeting is likely to follow parliamentary procedure. A participant would probably be required to state the proposition as a formal motion: "I move that all students be required to take a class in argumentation." In a court of law, the proposition would most likely be stated even more formally: "The State contends that the accused, Michael Smith, did commit a second-degree sexual assault, which is a felony according to Section 364A of the criminal statute." In an academic debate, the proposition would also be stated formally:

> Resolved: That the federal government should guarantee that all citizens in the United States have access to a comprehensive program of dental care.

There are several benefits to formally stating or expressing a proposition for argument, even in an informal interaction. First, a formally stated proposition clearly establishes the issues that are in dispute. In casual interactions arguments may rage even when the participants lack a clear understanding of precisely what they are disputing. For example, in the informal argument cited above, one person is arguing that they should go to a movie while the other is arguing that they should go to hear live music. The dispute, however, may have less to do with the specific entertainment planned for the evening than with the underlying tensions in the relationship. Thus, the claim, "We always end up at the movies, I think we should go hear some live music," might really be a disguised version of a different proposition: "You always get to decide what we will do when we go out. I think that I should have the opportunity to decide this time." If the disputants were to clearly state their actual propositions, they might discover the precise cause for their disagreement and thus reach a resolution sooner.

Second, a formally stated proposition divides the ground between the disputants. The advocate of a required course in argumentation might be facing someone who believes there should be a foreign language requirement. Another advocate could believe that students taught to argue more effectively might become more disagreeable. Someone else might believe that students should not be saddled with specific requirements but instead should have the freedom to design their own programs of study. Explicit statements of the proposition help the participants gain a clear understanding of the specific points of contention.

Third, explicitly stated propositions help disputants see what might result from the completion of an argument. For example, if the legal proposition mentioned earlier is proven true, and Mr. Smith is found guilty of the charge of sexual assault, he can expect to face the state's penalty for this crime. If, on the other hand, his defense attorney is able to establish that Smith could not have committed the alleged act or that the act Smith did commit was of a very different character than that which the prosecution alleged—namely that it did not fit the requirements of the state's charge of second-degree sexual assault—Smith will be acquitted.

Finally, a formally stated proposition helps to facilitate a clear argumentative *clash*—a sharply focused disagreement between rival positions. The proposition lays out the issues that are disputed, directs the advocates in how to develop their arguments, and reveals the issues likely to be used to support the opposing cases.

Types of Propositions

There are three different types of propositions, each appropriate to the particular types of issues that may be in dispute.

Propositions of Fact

Whenever there are disagreements about factual statements, a ***proposition of fact*** is in dispute. Consider two friends arguing about the hottest place in the United States. The statement, "Death Valley is the hottest place in the country," is a proposition of fact. The rival proposition, "Houston is the hottest place in the country," is also a proposition of fact. While propositions of this type readily lend themselves to argument, they are also typically resolvable through empirical evidence. For our example, the National Weather Service keeps records of the daily temperatures and average temperatures of reporting stations around the United States. Even with this data, there might still be room for interpretation and disagreement. One advocate could contend that the annual average daily temperature in Houston is the best data to support the claim that Houston is the hottest place in the country. The other advocate might argue that the hottest single day on record is the best data, and Death Valley hit a high of 130 degrees Fahrenheit one day during the summer of 2020. Still another advocate might argue that decade-long averages are the best evidence. Someone else might maintain that the use of "comfort indexes" that include such factors as humidity or average wind speed should be considered.

As anyone who has ever engaged in such an argument knows, the possibilities for contention are only as limited as the creative energies of the arguers. Before such disputes can be proved or disproved by accessing factual evidence, the parties must agree on the meaning of the key terms. Only after the advocates agree on the definition of "the hottest place in the country" can the dispute be resolved by consulting the appropriate reference.

Legal disputes are typically stated as propositions of fact, and almost all focus on issues that have already occurred (except for court injunctions to prevent something from occurring). The jury deciding defendant Smith's guilt or innocence in the sexual assault example must determine whether the offense occurred and, if it did, then consider whether it meets the legal definition for the charge and whether Smith perpetrated the attack.

Arguers sometimes differ over propositions of future fact, although such arguments are always speculative in nature and therefore do not lend themselves to tidy resolution. We could assert, for example, that at some point during your lifetime you will see the election of the first woman president of the United States. A claim of future fact is certainly arguable. The resolution of such an argument, however, rests on the arguers' prognostications about the changing political landscape in the United States and its future consequences and not on verifiable material evidence.

Propositions of Value

Closely related to propositions of fact are ***propositions of value***. The primary difference between the two types of propositions is that factual propositions hinge upon potentially objectifiable evidence, but value propositions can be resolved only on the basis of the opinions and beliefs of the arguers and their audiences. The claim, "the Boston Celtics have the most NBA championships," is a proposition of fact. It may be proven or disproven by consulting a reputable sports information source. The claim, "The Boston Celtics are the best team in the NBA" is a proposition of value. The proposition can only be decided based on the arguers' conception of what the term "best" means. A team's win-loss record could certainly be one consideration, but so might other key factors: the team's record in the playoffs, the number of championship titles, the quality of the other teams in the division in which they compete, the quality of key players or of the bench, the quality of the coach—and, perhaps most important, where the arguers reside. Incidentally, in 2021 the Boston Celtics and the Los Angeles Lakers were tied, with each team having won 17 NBA titles. Any arguments about which team is the best are likely to be both prolonged and spirited.

Because propositions of value focus on subjective beliefs and judgments, they seem impossible to resolve through reasoned argument—and we feel that we have no alternative but to fight over them. We are often eager to avoid engaging in value disputes for this very reason. Disputes have raged for generations over such value propositions as "abortion is morally wrong," "capital punishment is morally justified," and "our obligation to protect the First Amendment outweighs our concerns about pornography." In any complex, multicultural, and diverse society we can expect that values will be hotly contested.

To analyze value propositions effectively, ask yourself the following questions.

1. What are the foundations for the value under dispute? Is the value expressed in civil, religious, or natural law? If so, is it consistently expressed across these contexts?
2. How closely is the value adhered to and by how many persons? What sorts of people ascribe to this value? Have they particular expertise in the subject under dispute?
3. How important is this value in the hierarchy of values? People are influenced by many values, how central is this value?
4. Is the value absolute? Are there situations in which this value is set aside? For example, most of us believe that killing is morally wrong, yet the Supreme Court has repeatedly upheld the state's right to execute convicted murderers when certain criteria are met. What criteria, if any, must be met for this particular value to be suspended?
5. How might an advocate establish the criteria that justify upholding a proposition that goes against a widely held value? Are these criteria formally established (as in the case of legal burdens that must be met), or are they informally agreed upon?

Some value differences are so fundamental that they cannot be easily minimized or overcome even through systematic analysis. As a result, the outcome of many human value disputes is that individuals engaged in such arguments may simply agree to disagree.

Propositions of Policy

A *proposition of policy* is a statement outlining a course of action that the advocate believes should be taken. It usually entails both an action and the agent who ought to do the action. Such a statement can range from the informal ("We (agent) should go to the movies tonight (action)") to the complex ("Resolved: That the federal government should guarantee that all citizens in the United States have access to a comprehensive program of dental care"). Propositions of policy imply such value judgments as movies are a worthwhile way to spend one's time or access to dental care is a right that government should guarantee to all its citizenry. These propositions may also imply such factual judgments as we have time to see a movie because we have no previous commitments or not all citizens currently receive dental care.

Propositions of policy always concern the future, and they typically state that a certain policy change should occur. The best-formulated propositions of policy are those that specify the precise change that should occur and who should be the agent of that change. The following are examples of well-formulated policy propositions.

Resolved: That the State of Hawaii should legalize casino gambling.

Resolved: That the NCAA should no longer sponsor tackle football as a collegiate sport.

Resolved: That the federal government should legalize the cultivation, sale, and possession of marijuana by any person over the age of 18.

If our goal is to produce the fairest and best argumentation on an issue, then we should strive to create explicitly and carefully worded propositions. A precisely worded proposition is easier for arguers to dispute. Recall our earlier definition of *clash*: a sharply focused disagreement between rival positions. To facilitate clash on an issue, a proposition should be worded so that it leaves ground on both sides. A very narrowly worded proposition might not make for very effective clash and might also fail to result in successful or effective public policy.

Resolved: That the federal government should fund a program to provide polio vaccines for all Hopi Indian children residing in Arizona.

There are two problems with this proposition. First, it is difficult to justify federal action for a program limited to Hopi children. An advocate who opposed this proposition could make the case that the public health department of the state of Arizona would be a better agent for this action since it is responsible for other vaccination programs and is closer to the people involved. Using Arizona instead of the federal government would be an effective argument against the adoption of this particular proposition or, at the very least, an argument for rewriting the scope of the proposition.

Second, this proposition severely limits the ground of those who would advocate for its adoption. Why fund a program for only one disease rather than a program to vaccinate children for many childhood diseases? Children who are not receiving polio vaccinations may also not be receiving the necessary vaccinations to prevent a wide array of other diseases as well, such as measles, mumps, rubella, diphtheria, tetanus, HPV, and COVID-19. Would it not be more efficient and productive to fund a program that would systematically vaccinate children against many of these diseases at the same time? Thus, a more effective proposition would be:

Resolved: That the United States government should fund a program to provide immunizations against contagious diseases for all children living in poverty.

This wording does a better job of dividing ground to enhance clash on the issue. It focuses on the problem in such a way that makes it easier for the advocates to find materials to support their arguments, and it would probably lead to more effective and responsible health management policies. There may be times when a narrowly worded proposition is warranted—for example, when advocates already have extensive expertise and knowledge on the subject or when a preliminary investigation has already narrowed the range of policy alternatives. However,—in most cases a broader proposition facilitates better clash on the issues.

The Techniques for Analyzing Propositions

Once the proposition to be disputed has been created or discovered, it is time to begin the process of *analysis*. Arguments in support of or against a proposition are created through analysis. This process is the most interesting and creative dimension of the argumentative enterprise. In his theory of rhetoric, Aristotle referred to the process of analysis as **invention**—meaning the invention of arguments to support the position that you want your listeners to accept. As you are aware, both weak and strong arguments can be advanced in support for almost any proposition. Your task as an advocate is to create the best arguments that you can and to create those arguments that will appeal to your audience. In short, you must invent arguments that cast your claims into stories that your audience finds appealing and believable given their experiences and values.

Defining Key Terms

The first step in the analysis of a proposition is to define the key terms. To illustrate, let's return to the proposition that we just created.

> Resolved: That the United States government should fund a program to provide immunizations against contagious diseases for all children living in poverty.

There are several important terms that must be defined for this proposition to be understood.

- "United States government": the federal government—not state or local governments and not private industry or insurance companies
- "fund": to create the monetary support for, but not necessarily to administer or operate
- "a program": an ongoing effort, as opposed to a one-time only event
- "immunizations against contagious diseases": prophylactic injections to prevent people from becoming infected with a wide range of diseases, including polio, tuberculosis, diphtheria, influenza, measles, tetanus, chicken pox, the human papilloma virus, and SARS-COV-2.
- "children living in poverty": children under the age of 18 from families whose incomes fall below the federal poverty standard

The foregoing examples are suggested only to illustrate reasonable interpretations of the key terms in this proposition. Different disputants would almost certainly choose to define some of these terms differently in order to stake out the ground they wish to argue. For example, an advocate could use a very narrow definition of "children living in poverty" to try to limit the discussion only to the medical problems routinely faced by children in rural America. The advocate's opponent, however, would then be entitled to argue that it is unreasonable to focus only on rural children and to exclude urban children. Another advocate could attempt to use a more expansive definition. Thus, for example, this advocate could seek to provide access to vaccines to children whose family income is not below the poverty line but who may not have private health insurance or access to other medical assistance programs. Such a strategy might expand the benefits of the program to cover more recipients and thus prevent more diseases. It would also increase the cost of the program, which could lay the groundwork for reasons that such a program would be undesirable.

Another strategy an advocate might use to narrow the proposition "immunizations against contagious diseases" would be to focus the arguments on the need for children to receive measles vaccinations. An opponent then might argue that it is unreasonable to limit the discussion to only one disease when the explicit wording in the propositions is "diseases."

In most argument situations, arguers do not formally define their terms. Instead, they usually recall the contexts or stories in which they have previously heard such terms used. Definitions are, in other words, shaped by popular usage. Terms acquire their meanings from their use in conversation, and these accepted usages give us our commonsense notions of what terms mean. In some cases, however, arguers may need to define their terms more systematically and can consult a number of different sources in order to do this. They can consult a dictionary, although dictionaries typically offer several alternative definitions in descending order of commonalty, and many of these will not be equally acceptable to all audiences. Arguers can also consult specialized sources in the relevant literature of the field. On a topic about medical care, for example, they can consult the journals and periodicals of the medical profession; on issues of law they can consult a legal dictionary or legal periodicals; on an issue pertaining to education policy they can consult journals in the field of education; and so forth.

Definitions may themselves frequently become the subject for further argument. If during the course of an argument your adversary challenges your definitions of the key terms of a proposition, it is helpful to cite the source of your definitions and to argue their reasonableness and appropriateness by providing examples drawn from relevant literatures.

Establishing the Point of Clash

Once you have defined the key terms in the proposition, you need to decide what issues you wish to advance—where you will choose to draw your point of clash. This is known as establishing your point of *stasis*, or the place where you choose to differ with the arguments developed by your opponent.

Turning back to our argument about immunization policy, an advocate for a federal program to provide immunization for poor children might stress the severity of the debilitating effects of childhood illnesses, including the number of lives lost to diseases that could have been prevented. The advocate would also want to argue that many children now go without vaccinations because their parents lack the financial means to provide adequate medical care. This would be a logical and appropriate point of stasis. Those who wish to oppose the proposition might contend that almost all children who need vaccinations currently receive them either through existing public assistance programs at the state or local level or through private insurance. They might also argue that a large and unwieldy federal program might only increase the government bureaucracy and not be the best way to help children. In addition, opponents to the plan to provide vaccinations to all children might argue that the reason many children fail to receive vaccines today is that an anti-vax movement has developed, and it is scaring many parents away from having their children immunized. Further government efforts might deepen conspiracy narratives that are already circulating—and would reinforce anxieties and make the problem worse.

Hermagoras—a Greek philosopher, rhetorical theorist, and teacher of rhetoric who lived during the second century BCE—developed a checklist for determining where to draw stasis. He developed his stasis theory to explain the major points of disagreement in the courts, suggesting four levels for considering claims.[1]

1. **Conjecturing about a fact.** This involved whether a crime had been committed. What are the facts of the case? Did person X kill person Y?
2. **Definition.** How should the killing of Y by X be defined? Does the action of X fall within the category of homicide or murder?
3. **Quality.** What was the motivation for X killing Y? Were there any justifications? U.S. courts, for example, recognize self-defense under some circumstances as a reasonable justification for taking another person's life.
4. **Objection.** Is there a basis to object to the trial? Was the trial conducted properly or should the trial have been held in some other court?[2]

Other rhetorical theorists, including Cicero, applied Hermagoras's theory of stasis to policy arguments in addition to legal arguments. The following illustrates the levels of stasis applied to a policy dispute.

1. **Conjecturing about a fact.** The arguer establishes or disputes a material claim. The advocate arguing for or against the claim that "significant numbers of poor children are not vaccinated and suffer diseases because their parents cannot pay for required medical care" is conjecturing about a fact.
2. **Definition.** The arguer contends that while a material fact may be true, it is not described or defined precisely as it should be. For example, an advocate might admit that significant numbers of poor children are not vaccinated but also argue that this is not because there are no programs available to provide vaccinations. Instead, the advocate might assert that children fail to receive vaccinations because their parents do not take advantage of the existing programs. Perhaps they lack awareness of the importance of vaccinations, perhaps they are unaware of programs to provide them, perhaps they lack transportation, perhaps they have religious or cultural objections to modern medicines, or perhaps they have accepted conspiracy theories about vaccines and believe injections might cause rather than prevent illness.
3. **Quality.** The arguer asserts that, although the material facts might be true and although the material evidence is correct, other aspects influencing the material quality of the claims might lead to different interpretations. An advocate arguing from quality might admit that poor children are not vaccinated and that there are inadequate programs to provide for vaccinations but contend that the failure to vaccinate is not a significant factor in the children's health. Instead, they might argue that poverty itself leads to poor health by detailing the consequences of poverty that can affect health: food insufficiency, poor diet, substandard housing, low birth-weight babies, drug or alcohol addicted parents, and so on.

4. **Objection.** This is a decision to draw stasis at the level of interpretation. An advocate who draws stasis here might concede that poor children are not vaccinated and suffer disease as a result, that the problem results from a lack of government programs to provide health care, and that the failure to vaccinate is responsible for a significant number of deaths of these children. The advocate might contend, however, that the health statistics are not reliable, and many of these children may have perished from other diseases for which no immunizations were available.

As is clear from the examples that we have provided, these levels of stasis are presented in descending order of their strength or power. Consequently, it is better to be able to argue at the level of fact than it is to be compelled to argue at the level of definition. Both are stronger arguments than those directed at the issue of quality, and the weakest type of argument is one that relies on objection. Because Hermagoras was fundamentally concerned with inventing arguments, he focused almost exclusively on the quality of the logical claims that arguers made. He stressed that appropriate logical techniques could be learned and taught to others.

Whether you argue in support of a proposition or in opposition to it, you must decide where and how to draw your point of stasis. The decision is an important one. Having developed the primary argument strategy that defines your case—your central story, it is difficult to change your mind and dart off in some different direction. There is no substitute for careful planning and preparation when developing your arguments.

Stock Issues

One approach to assist arguers in the analysis of policy propositions is the use of *stock issues* that recur throughout history. These issues consistently draw the attention of arguers and audiences. Many argumentation theorists adhere to the perspective, originally developed by John Dewey in 1910, that thinking (and thus decision making) follows five logically distinct steps: (1) recognition of a felt difficulty, (2) location and definition of the difficulty, (3) suggestion of a possible solution, (4) development by reasoning of the consequences of the solution, (5) further observation and experiment leading to the acceptance or rejection of the solution.[3] Dewey's claim that policy changes most often occur in response to the location of a felt difficulty, or the identification of a problem in existing policy, led to the formulation of the stock issues perspective. Based on Dewey's reflective thinking model, Lee Hultzen further developed and added a clear explanatory framework for the stock issues perspective.[4] The stock issues involve a consideration of the ill, the blame, the cure, and the cost. We will discuss each in turn.

ILL. The stock issue of an *ill* challenges the advocate to analyze the proposition by considering the inadequacies or problems in the existing system. Turning again to our earlier example, when the advocate demonstrates that poor children are contracting infectious diseases, especially when these diseases might have been prevented by vaccines, they are demonstrating the existence of an ill—a flaw—in current health care policy.

The identified ill must also be shown to be significant. An advocate can demonstrate two different types of significance. One type is quantitative significance—that large numbers of children are affected. The other type of significance is qualitative significance—that those affected are harmed in a serious way. In our example, perhaps children miss days of school and fall behind their classmates, perhaps they suffer grievously, perhaps they are permanently disabled, or they may even die. To develop a strong case in justifying the seriousness of a flaw in an existing policy, an advocate would want to demonstrate both quantitative and qualitative significance. Doing so enhances the impact and power of their arguments. Meanwhile, it is the task of the opposing advocate to undercut the significance by demonstrating that few people suffer from the supposed ill and/or that those who do suffer may suffer only minimally.

BLAME. When considering the stock issue of *blame*, the advocate attempts to assign responsibility for the existence of an ill. In a policy dispute, an arguer claims that an established policy should be changed to address and eliminate a currently existing harm or ill or to prevent an impending harm or ill. To succeed, the advocate must prove that current policy (the status quo—the way things now stand) is inadequate and fails to achieve its stated purpose. In most cases, the arguer identifies a problem that is inherent in the present system. *Inherency* suggests that the problem will certainly repeat itself unless the current policy is changed. Inherency is significant because policy makers would not concern themselves with ills that would probably repair themselves if left alone.

There are three types of inherent ills. The first is called *structural inherency*. A program may be said to have structural inherency if its inadequacy results from a flaw in its design or from a structure that includes barriers to the desired course of action. The ill of our country not having an immunization program for children living in poverty might be shown to have structural inherency if the advocate points out that there is currently no single government agency responsible for providing medical services to poor children. The current structure is a patchwork of medical programs operating at the federal, state, and local levels, supplemented by inadequate private charities and private health insurance. As a result, many poor children may slip through the cracks and not receive the necessary immunizations that might protect them against devastating diseases.

A second type of inherency is *attitudinal inherency*. An ill may be said to result from attitudinal inherency if the advocate can demonstrate that while there may be a policy in place to correct the ill, that policy is undermined by the attitudes or values either of the people who administer it or the people whom it is intended to serve. For example, even if a program to provide immunizations to poor children were to exist, it might fail to provide the necessary vaccinations. An advocate might argue that although we have programs intended to provide medical care for the poor, these programs are flawed because they have a crisis orientation. Children receive medical care when they are grievously ill, often in an overcrowded emergency room at a public hospital, but they do not always receive the preventive care that might have decreased or even eliminated the risk of the disease. The inconvenience created by the scarcity of facilities available to serve the poor—perhaps the long distances that must be traversed or the long wait times required before one is seen by a health care provider—prevent people from seeking care except in the most dire emergencies. The advocate can point to attitudes on the part of the patients themselves (e.g., fear of needles), their parents (e.g., anxiety about modern medical practices, techniques, or therapies), the health care providers (e.g., a lack of caring or compassion for their patients), or program administrators (e.g., a focus on providing crisis care) as possible attitudes that prevent current policies from being effective. Some of these attitudinal barriers might be longstanding, such as the anxiety about vaccines being linked to autism despite the lack of credible medical evidence to support such a claim.[5] Other attitudinal barriers may be short-lived and may develop in response to a unique moment in time. Many people resisted taking the vaccines developed to control the COVID-19 pandemic, and many people put off visiting the emergency room when they faced very serious medical problems, because they feared they might contract the coronavirus.[6]

Structural inherency is typically more compelling than attitudinal inherency, because it supports the claim that a policy change is needed to remedy the structural deficiencies that led to the existence of the ills. Essentially, governmental actors *cannot* solve a problem if there is structural inherency. If attitudinal inherency is claimed, current governmental actors could solve the problem but they *will not*. It is better if the advocate can demonstrate that these attitudes result from characteristics of the existing policy that are themselves caused by the structures. If the attitudes are caused by the structures, then amending the structures might in and of itself lead to a change in attitudes. If the attitudes are not a result of the structures, however, and merely reside in the people, it is more difficult for an advocate to demonstrate that these attitudes can be changed and thus that the underlying problem can be resolved through a policy change. For example, it is unlikely that an advocate can easily overcome children's fear of needles. To the extent that children do not receive vaccines today because they fear needles, it is not likely that a comprehensive plan will overcome this fear. A counter-advocate may be able to argue, however, that many of the new generation of vaccines can be given orally or with almost pain-free technology devices. On the other hand, if the primary attitudinal barrier argued is the crisis orientation of program administrators, it might be resolvable. The crisis orientation more than likely results from a shortage of funds, a lack of staff, and a lack of emphasis on preventive care. A new federal program would likely be able to develop the resources and the education and training programs to overcome these challenges and change these attitudes.

The third type of inherency exists when current policy makers have not yet considered or addressed the problem, and the advocate of change argues that they should. This is called *existential inherency*. In 2001, at the height of the post-9/11 terrorism scare, some advocates contended that the United States should begin a smallpox immunization program for adults. The smallpox disease had been considered eliminated but fears surfaced that terrorists could produce it in a laboratory and then weaponize it. The Bush administration decided that only select health care workers would be immunized so that these individuals could assist the sick without contracting the disease if there were a smallpox outbreak. The potential ill resulted from a deficiency in the status quo, but there was no policy that caused the problem and no attitude that prevented the ill from being addressed; rather the problem was new and had not been considered before. A similar situation occurred in 2020 as national policy makers discussed how they would spur the development of new vaccines and assure that all Americans could be vaccinated against COVID-19. Existential inherency addresses new and previously unforeseen problems.

The primary purpose for analyzing a policy proposition from the perspective of the stock issue of blame is to focus attention on the specific deficiencies in existing policy that might be remedied through the adoption of new polices—policies that are outlined in the wording of the proposition that is being argued.

CURE.   Once the advocate has identified an ill and placed blame for its existence on the deficiencies of current policies, it is time to propose a *cure.* The cure is the new policy that the advocate believes will remedy the ill. The proposed cure should be developed to address the specific ill that has been outlined and to overcome the inherent factors blamed for the creation of the ill.

If the inherency is structural, the cure should include the creation of a new structure that replaces, remedies, or modifies the structures that are now in place. In the case of the inoculation program for children in poverty, the cure might be a program funded by the federal government that requires all children to receive vaccinations. A bureaucracy to staff the program might be established and a means to locate and treat the children created. This policy would address the structural deficits by, for example, creating a new agency responsible for vaccinating people against communicable diseases.

If the identified inherency is attitudinal, the proposed cure must correct the blighted attitudes blamed for the existence of the problem. For instance, if the inherency is that parents do not take advantage of existing medical assistance programs and do not seek vaccinations for their children, then the advocate must propose a policy that changes parental behavior. An advocate might propose health education and awareness programs for parents to educate them about the importance of vaccinations and other preventive health measures.

The greatest challenge to the advocate who proposes a new policy is to argue in a convincing manner that this new policy will remedy the specific ills cited and that it will also overcome the inherency barriers claimed as flaws in existing policy. There is no merit in changing policies if doing so will not remedy the problems plaguing the status quo.

COST. The final stock issue is *cost*. While the previous stock issues were discussed primarily from the perspective of the advocate favoring a policy change (although touching on how issues that surface also guide the selection of arguments by advocates opposing a policy change), the stock issue of cost is approached from the perspective of the arguer who wants to refute the need for policy change. This stock issue asks the arguer to consider what the likely costs of the proposed policy change might be. The issue could focus on the monetary costs of the proposed policy. How much would it cost to undertake the new health initiatives that are outlined above? Certainly, comprehensive national health insurance has long been favored by many policy makers, but it has not been adopted due in part to arguments about its costs and also because some worry about giving the federal government so much influence over medical care. This controversy was well illustrated in the congressional and public debates over the Affordable Care Act. It was also an issue in the 2020 Democratic presidential primaries when some candidates, particularly Senator Bernie Sanders (VT), favored a "single-payer" plan and others, including Vice President Joe Biden (DE), opposed it. Given the size of our current national budget deficit, the many other pressing social problems that our society faces (homelessness, deteriorating schools, crumbling highways and bridges, confronting climate change, and the need to stimulate the economy in the wake of the COVID-19 pandemic), and the reluctance of citizens to pay higher taxes, is this proposal the best way to spend scarce public funds? An advocate should not simply ask this question, of course, but should argue that this either is, or is not, the way to spend money and that a program to provide vaccinations for children either will or will not produce sufficient benefits to justify these costs.

Another way to think about the costs is to consider the disadvantages that might result from the adoption of a new policy. An arguer could assert, for example, that there is actually a certain amount of danger from inoculations and that some people might actually contract diseases or suffer illness as a result of adverse reactions to the vaccines. These are difficult arguments to make given that research is quite conclusive that vaccinations save lives. However, the arguments could diminish some of the opposing advocate's quantitative significance about lives saved by demonstrating that some lives would be lost to the vaccinations themselves.

When considering the issue of the costs of new policies, advocates should allow their creative energies to direct them, and they should consider a wide range of potential outcomes from a change in policy. The fact that a program such as the one proposed might be costly, for example, might allow an advocate to develop arguments about the implications of these costs: the government is so short of money that money spent for one program will almost certainly mean less for funding other programs. Spending more money on health might prevent increased spending on education, and without improvements to our schools and educational outcomes, children might be locked into lives in poverty.

An advocate might also argue that there are too few laboratories to produce the needed vaccines. Encouraging pharmaceutical companies to gear up to produce more vaccines for the childhood illnesses mentioned above would divert their attention and resources from focusing on producing the even more urgently needed vaccine against COVID-19. Indeed, an advocate could also argue that the long-term health of the world's citizenry would be far better served by a program that focused on the prevention of infectious diseases perhaps as yet unknown but likely to develop. Perhaps the COVID-19 pandemic could have been averted if our medical researchers and pharmaceutical companies had heeded warnings from decades earlier about conditions in South China where many very poor people live "cheek by jowl and in close proximity to pigs and poultry," and where deadly cross-species viral mutations were already known to occur.[7]

Decision Calculus

Arguers who use stock issues as starting points for the analysis of propositions should be mindful of the ***decision calculus*** that will be applied to the arguments they develop. A decision calculus can best be summarized as:

Ill (significance of harm)
    Mitigated by: Cure (degree to which new policy reduces ill)
        Less: Cost (problems or disadvantages of new policy)
            Equal: Benefits of policy change

The stock issues perspective is a tool that guides arguers in the application of cost-benefit analysis to a study of policy issues. Like all other tools of analysis, its effectiveness depends on the person using it. The advocate who is thorough, creative, and thoughtful in the application of the stock issues perspective will create better arguments than will the advocate who is sloppy, indifferent, or uncreative. Another consideration is that this approach strongly values the quantification of argument claims. The concept of costs and benefits emphasizes the importance of empirical verifications of arguments.

Certain intangible dimensions of arguments that go beyond their empirical significance might have a dramatic effect on listeners. In the example about vaccinations, an advocate would want to keep in mind that we have been arguing about children—children who are exposed to serious and preventable diseases; children who may suffer and die from these diseases. Cold calculations about the costs of policy change may not sufficiently account for the personal loss, grief, and suffering endured when a family loses a child who might have been saved had they received the appropriate vaccination. Arguers should constantly keep in mind the moral, ethical, and philosophical values tied to policy deliberations that sometimes do not lend themselves to objective or quantifiable measures.

An arguer who chooses to utilize cost-benefit analysis should also remember that arguments must still be adapted to their audiences, and listeners respond to arguments by evaluating them as stories. The stories of suffering children can be very compelling—despite an effective presentation of the high costs of a program of prevention and treatment.

Systems Analysis

An alternative approach for the analysis of propositions, especially propositions of policy, is provided by general systems theory and the method known as *systems analysis*. A system may be defined as "an assembly of objects all of which are related to one another by some form of regular interaction or interdependence so that the assembly can be viewed as an organic or organized whole."[8] When applying the principles of systems theory in propositional analysis, the advocate attempts to identify, study, and evaluate the constituent parts of the system in order to determine their effectiveness.

There are several important underlying assumptions that must be understood before systems theory can be applied. First, systems theory presumes that the constituent parts (often called components) of a system are interdependent. That is, if one component in a system is changed, one might expect the change to influence the performance of the other components.

Second, systems are characterized by an ordered sequence of events. Because systems (both naturally occurring ones, such as the human body, and created ones, such as a university) are designed to achieve some purpose, their components parts must all function in accordance with their established purpose. When one or more components fail to carry out their assigned functions, the entire system may begin to falter. A problem with your liver, for example, might lower your resistance to disease and jeopardize your life. Similarly, a university might have a very strong faculty and outstanding students, but if the curriculum is poorly conceived or poorly designed students might not be taught the courses and subject material essential to a solid educational foundation.

Third, a system's components are connected to and controlled by each other. Because systems are often extremely complex, they must contain procedures for communication and control that keep the system operating and in a state of balance. Thus, a system might begin to falter because a component is not performing its assigned function or because the networks of communication and control intended to link the components to each other are failing.

Fourth, systems entail both a structure and a set of processes.[9] The processes that the system must carry out determine the structure of a system; likewise, the processes of the different components in a system are determined by the structures that are present. Thus, if the structures are inadequate for the processes that need to be performed, those structures must be changed. If the processes underway do not reflect the maximum utilization of the capabilities of the structures, the processes should be changed. An illustration might be the changes in systems that must occur as organizations become larger and/or more complex. A small business, for example, may operate effectively with somewhat informal accounting and administrative processes. As the business grows larger, a more rigorous and formal set of procedures may be better suited to the opportunities and challenges of the new business environment. Many companies fail because the entrepreneurial skills that enabled someone to start a business are very different from the administrative and managerial supervisory skill sets necessary to keep a larger entity prospering.

Systems theory is applied to describe the operations of an existing system; it can also be utilized to evaluate the effectiveness of that system and to compare it to other possible alternative systems. Because systems theory is a tool of analysis, it benefits an advocate only if it is artfully and creatively applied to the study of a proposition.

A Model for Systems Analysis[10]

Functions	Terms	Definitions
Description	Components	the discrete, unique or constituent parts that compose the system
	Relationships	the identity that exists between two or more components; the action of a system—that is, the nature/characteristics of the activity between two or more things
	Goals	the stated or operational objectives, designs, aims, or intentions of the people interacting with the environment; the critical decision-making process designed to achieve these goals
Evaluation	Effects	the assessment, fulfillment, accomplishment, impression, or outcome of a system as a result of certain goals; an evaluation of the elements of the system as measured against the goals of the system

A Systems Analysis of a Policy Proposition. An advocate who chooses to use systems theory to analyze a policy proposition should first describe the components of the existing system and their relationship to each other and then evaluate them in terms of their effectiveness in meeting their goals. To illustrate the process, we will suggest steps for analyzing the following proposition.

> Resolved: That the federal government should establish a program to promote sex education, birth control information, and access to contraceptives in clinics in all public secondary schools in the United States.

The advocate should first detail the components of the system that currently provide sex education and contraceptives to teenagers. This advocate would likely find that many different organizations, with very different objectives, provide information and services. The components of such a system may include the following.

- **Existing clinics in public schools.** A few schools might have precisely the type of clinics that the advocate would like to see developed at all public schools throughout the nation. Advocates can frequently research and locate such "demonstration" projects and argue for the expansion of a network of such programs. In the case of this topic, such clinics might provide teenagers with information on preventing pregnancies and avoiding sexually transmitted diseases; they might even provide staff capable of conducting medical examinations for students who may not have access to suitable health care. These clinics could serve as pilot projects to illustrate the benefits of school-based programs. Currently, however, these programs would likely be limited in number and able to serve only a small fraction of the total number of teens in the United States.

- **Sex education classes in public schools.** More schools might have classes that provide information about contraceptives, the prevention of sexually transmitted diseases, and even information about dating, child-rearing, and parental responsibility, but they would not be able to provide students with contraceptives or with physical examinations. Although such classes might produce some of the benefits the advocate seeks, they would not likely exist in all schools and would not be available for all students. They also, of course, would not assure actual access to the contraceptives or the desirable level of medical services.

- **Planned Parenthood and/or other nongovernmental organizations.** In many communities, schools do not provide sex education, contraceptive information, or information about sexually transmitted diseases. Organizations like Planned Parenthood may be available to fill in the gaps. Many such organizations offer free or low-cost medical examinations for students who cannot access such services through other means. The challenge, of course, is in making students aware of the existence of such services and also in helping them overcome barriers, such as lack of transportation to get them to such programs. It may be awkward for many young women, for example, to announce to a parent that they need a ride to the local Planned Parenthood office so that they can get a prescription for oral contraceptives. Thus, access to such services through a community organization is not necessarily equivalent to access in one's public school.

- **Churches and religious groups.** Many communities have sex education programs sponsored by churches, religious organizations, or religious support groups. Such programs may provide very useful information to teens but will often focus on trying to prevent them from becoming sexually active, rather than explicitly dealing with such issues as preventing pregnancies or recognizing or preventing sexually transmitted diseases. Such programs may also close off certain kinds of choices for teens. For example, programs that attempt to persuade teens that terminating pregnancy is a sin and therefore should never be considered may then fail to address many associated problems or issues that teens might face.

- **Parents, friends, and others.** For some teenagers there may be no access to information about sex from organized and professional external sources. These students may, as a result, get their information from parents or other relatives, their friends, or even from strangers. Since many parents feel uncomfortable discussing sex with their children and may not want to believe that their children are sexually active, they may put off the discussion until it is too late to prevent a pregnancy or a sexually transmitted disease. Furthermore, such sources may provide teenagers with incomplete or even inaccurate information.

- **The media.** Many teenagers will turn to the media, including social media, for information about their sexual health. Those who actively look for such information and have the ability to identify reliable sources may find very useful information online or in books, magazines, or documentaries. For many others, however, sources will be limited to entertainment media, which may provide misleading or inaccurate information.

After identifying the different components of the system that provide information and services to teenagers, the advocate can begin to assess how these different components function in relationship to each other. One will likely find, for instance, that only a small number of teenagers have access to the kind of comprehensive education and services that school-based clinics can provide. Perhaps sex education programs exist at some schools, but they are not in all schools. Urban teens may have access to nongovernmental organizations, such as Planned Parenthood, but these organizations may not be available to teens living in rural areas. Others will not know about the availability of such services or will have transportation problems or other barriers that prevent them from accessing the programs. Consequently, the advocate might learn that most teenagers get most of their information about sex from their parents or their friends, and they must utilize their own initiatives to get access to contraceptives.

An analysis of the goals of the present system would also help inform the advocate. For example, the goal of many current sex education programs, and the focus of much of the instruction provided to teenagers, is to prevent them from becoming sexually active. Many parents and religious groups, for example, do not tell children much about sex beyond preaching the merits of abstinence. The advocate can critique the system, however, by establishing that many teenagers do become sexually active despite this instruction, and thus they badly need information that will help them prevent pregnancy and disease. The advocate might find that the goals of the present system limit its effectiveness in solving the problems society faces. A teenager who is getting a strong dose of preaching about the importance of sexual abstinence from their parents and church may not be inclined to turn to these same sources of information with a question about the most effective means of preventing pregnancy or about how to recognize the symptoms of an STD. Yet, for many students, there may be few alternative sources of information available.

Through an analysis of the effects of the current system, the advocate can identify the problems left unresolved by the existing policies and programs offering sex education programs to individual communities, school districts, and parents. Although the rate of teen pregnancy has dropped in recent years, it remains stubbornly high, especially in lower income families.[11] Further, although the teen pregnancy rate is declining in the United States, it is still among the highest in the developed world.[12] The Centers for Disease Control estimates people between the ages of 15 and 24 account for one half of the STDs in the country each year. Many STDs are undetected, resulting in infected individuals infecting others; the diseases have very serious health consequences, even leading to death.[13] It is also well known that many teens struggle to understand and come to terms with their sexual orientation and gender identity. LGBTQ youth are at a far greater risk for suicide than their peers.[14] Access to sex education programs and health clinics in public schools may prevent some of these tragic outcomes. Given these findings, it may well be time to propose a more comprehensive program to address these issues.

The final task for the advocate is to utilize systems theory in designing an alternative to the current system. In this step the advocate proposes to solve the problems in the current system by creating a new system. The school-based clinics mentioned earlier might be seen as the most effective way to provide information and health services because they are easily accessible to students and meet them on their own turf.

Those who defend the current system and reject the resolution can also use systems theory. Often advocates can argue that the system functions well as currently designed or that only minor alterations in the existing system would effectively address the few problems that may be identified. For example, they could argue that the current programs could be expanded, that mass media could be used more fully to get information out to teens who do not receive information in school or from other programs or sources, or even that other new and creative means could be created to reach young people. For example, we could create a contest for the best video created by young people to teach other young people about safe sex. This video could then be shared online.

An advocate for the current system might argue that a change in the system could prove counterproductive and could worsen the problems. For example, one could argue that an attempt to create a federal program to provide sex education and clinics in public schools could result in a public backlash. Conservative or very religious parents could voice strong objections to a government mandate creating high school clinics or a standardized sex education curriculum in public schools. They could withdraw their children and either home school them or enroll them in private or religious schools. Such a backlash might result in less sex education for many students and thus perhaps even greater numbers of unwanted teen pregnancies and STDs. Another argument could claim that access to contraceptives and information about sex might lower the students' resistance to peer pressures to become sexually active. Consequently, the new program would increase the likelihood that children will engage in sexual relations at a younger age. Other advocates could assert that no contraceptive is 100 percent effective, that some risk of pregnancy or disease would still exist, and that sexual activity at a younger age can create emotional or physical problems, resulting in individuals making other unwise decisions, such as consuming drugs or alcohol.

THE BENEFITS IN APPLYING SYSTEMS THEORY. While the traditional theory of stock issues presumes that change occurs only when there is some recognizable need, "felt difficulty," or ill, systems theory suggests that change is always occurring and must be managed in the best way possible. It presumes that minor policy corrections are inevitable and desirable. Consequently, some have argued that systems theory is a more effective way to evaluate policy arguments in contemporary society.[15]

Another benefit of systems theory is that it more accurately reflects the increasing complexity of modern life. Many layers of government (state, local, and federal regulatory agencies) combined with multinational and/or nongovernmental organizations (e.g., the World Trade Organization, the International Monetary Fund, etc.) create policies that can affect our lives. It is useful to employ a tool of analysis that reflects this complexity and the characteristics of contemporary decision-making structures.

Both stock issues theory and systems theory are best understood as tools of analysis. They are useful because they guide advocates as well as critics in the careful and thoughtful consideration of arguments.

SUMMARY

This chapter considered the different types of propositions that may be argued: propositions of fact, propositions of value, and propositions of policy. It also discussed the importance of defining the key terms of any proposition and the process of analysis. The chapter offered suggestions for how advocates should select the point of stasis (or the point of clash) in an argument, and it discussed two perspectives for propositional analysis: stock issues theory and systems theory.

KEY TERMS

analysis	invention	stock issues
clash	propositions	blame
decision calculus	of fact	cost
inherency	of policy	cure
attitudinal	of value	ill
existential	stasis	systems analysis
structural	status quo	

ACTIVITIES

1. As practice in writing propositions, select controversies reported in local or national news sites. Try to identify the main point of stasis for each controversy. Phrase these differences as propositions of fact, value, or policy, depending on the nature of the disagreement.

2. Recall the last time that you and a significant other (friend, parent, roommate, etc.) got into an argument. Looking back, what was the issue that caused the dispute? Try to phrase it as a proposition (fact, value, or policy).

3. Examine the following propositions and identify whether each is a proposition of fact, value, or policy:
   a. The weather today is nice.
   b. The high temperature today was 74 degrees.
   c. If you do not wear a jacket this evening you will be cold.
   d. You should wear a jacket this evening.
   e. Parents should require their children to bring jackets to school on chilly days.
   f. Failing to wear a jacket on a chilly day can cause illness.
   g. Protective outerwear keeps a person warm.

4. Select a public controversy and analyze how the key terms in the controversy might be defined. Note the differences, if any, in the alternative definitions and consider how the differences may influence the argument process. Consult each of the following as appropriate:
   a. Your own personal definition.
   b. A popular dictionary definition.
   c. A specialized dictionary definition from the appropriate field (for example, from a legal, medical, scientific, or technical dictionary).
   d. How advocates who are engaged in the controversy define the key terms.

5. Select an essay or article in which an advocate is calling for a change (for example an editorial or op-ed). Then examine the way the advocate identifies the ill, places the blame, and proposes a cure. Were all three of the stock issues presented? Did the advocate also discuss the potential arguments about costs?

Recommended Readings

Asen, Robert, "Deliberation and Trust," *Argumentation and Advocacy* 50 (2013): 2–17.

Hoppman, Michael J., "A Modern Theory of Stasis," *Philosophy and Rhetoric* 47 (2014): 273–296.

John, Peter, "Theories of Policy Change and Variation Reconsidered: A Prospectus for the Political Economy of Public Policy," *Policy Sciences* 51 (2018): 1–16.

Klumpp, James F., "Argumentative Ecology," *Argumentation and Advocacy* 45 (2009): 183–197.

Klumpp, James F., Bernard L. Brock, James W. Chesebro, and John F. Cragan, "Implications of a Systems Model of Analysis on Argumentation Theory," *Journal of the American Forensic Association* 11 (1974): 1–7.

Lichtman, Allan J., "Competing Models of the Debate Process," *Journal of the American Forensic Association* 22 (1986): 147–151.

Rowland, Robert C., "The Battle for Health Care Reform and the Liberal Public Sphere," in Frans H. van Eemeren and Bart Garssen, Eds., *Exploring Argumentative Contexts* (Amsterdam: Johns Benjamins Publishing Company, 2012), 269–288.

Endnotes

[1] For a more complete discussion of the principle of stasis see Ray Nadeau, "Some Aristotelian and Stoic Influences on the Theory of Stasis," *Speech Monographs* 26 (1959): 248. See also, George Kennedy, *The Art of Persuasion in Greece* (Princeton: Princeton University Press, 1963), 303–309.

[2] George A. Kennedy, *A New History of Classical Rhetoric* (Princeton: Princeton University Press, 1994).

[3] John Dewey, *How We Think,* (Boston: Heath, 1910).

[4] Lee S. Hultzen, "Status in Deliberative Analysis," in Donald C. Bryant, Ed., *The Rhetorical Idiom* (New York: Cornell University Press, 1958), 97–123.

[5] Rosanna Xia and Rong-Gong Lin II, "Disneyland Measles Outbreak: Infected Woman Took Two Flights Before Diagnosis," *Los Angeles Times,* January 13, 2015. https://www.latimes.com/socal/daily-pilot/news/la-me-ln-disneyland-measles-20150113-story.html

[6] Becky Upham, "COVID-19 Is Scaring People Away from Doctor's Offices and Hospitals," *Everyday Health,* July 20, 2020. https://www.everydayhealth.com/coronavirus/covid-19-fears-are-causing-americans-to-avoid-doctors-offices-and-ers/

[7] "China's Chernobyl?" *The Economist,* April 26-May 2, 2003, 9–10.

[8] Bernard L. Brock, James W. Chesebro, John F. Cragan, and James F. Klumpp, *Public Policy Decision Making: Systems Analysis and Comparative Advantages Debate* (New York: Harper and Row, 1973), 27.

[9] Ibid., pp. 27–29.

[10] Ibid., p. 50.

[11] Gretchen Livingston and Deja Thomas, "Why Is the U.S. Teen Birth Rate Falling?" *Pew Research Center,* August 2, 2019. https://www.pewresearch.org/fact-tank/2019/08/02/why-is-the-teen-birth-rate-falling/

[12] Amanda Holpuch, "U.S. Teenage Birth Rates Fall Again but Still Among the Highest in Developed World," *The Guardian,* September 28, 2016. https://www.theguardian.com/us-news/2016/sep/28/us-teenage-birth-rates-fall-again

[13] "STDs in Adolescents and Young Adults," Centers for Disease Control, 2021. https://www.cdc.gov/std/life-stages-populations/stdfact-teens.htm

[14] "Sexual Orientation, Gender, and Attempted Suicide among Adolescent Inpatients," Suicide Prevention Resource Center, November 30, 2018. https://www.sprc.org/news/sexual-orientation-gender-attempted-suicide-among-adolescent-inpatients

[15] For example, see: Adam A. Anyebe, "A Overview of Approaches to the Study of Public Policy," *International Journal of Political Science* 4 (2018): 8–17. https://www.arcjournals.org/pdfs/ijps/v4-i1/2.pdf

6

Types of Arguments

Humans are natural arguers—we have an affinity for making, using, and evaluating arguments. Despite this natural proclivity for arguing, however, we benefit from learning the basic components of arguments. This knowledge enables decision makers to dissect and evaluate argumentative claims more systematically. Learning argumentation principles also enables arguers to construct stronger arguments. In this chapter we discuss the reasoning process and consider arguments as complete logical claims.

From a logical perspective, arguments are considered rational when they correspond with accepted standards of reasoning. The reasoning process involves three separate elements. First, you must identify the data or grounds that will be used to develop your claim. Second, you must reason from the data through logical induction or deduction. Third, you must offer a claim or conclusion that builds upon the data and constitutes a new and original insight. This chapter focuses primarily on the second step, the inductive and deductive reasoning process.

Inductive reasoning argues from specific cases to more general conclusions. ***Deductive reasoning*** is essentially the opposite process; it moves from overall theories or generally accepted principles to conclusions about specific cases. Both inductive and deductive arguments occur frequently and naturally. They are typically embedded in the stories people tell to make decisions, resolve disputes, or identify solutions to problems. Both forms of reasoning can be equally compelling and persuasive, and neither form is preferred over the other. Arguers create inductive or deductive arguments in response to the problems they face, using the method most suited to the arguments they are creating.

INDUCTIVE ARGUMENTS

In a situation where you have information about a number of specific cases but you lack an understanding of the factors that might unite those cases into a general theory or principle, you can utilize the inductive reasoning process to seek conclusions. There are three types of arguments you may utilize to reason inductively.

Argument by Example

An ***argument by example*** examines one or more cases within a specific class and reasons that if these cases have certain common features then other, as yet unknown, cases in that class will also have the features. All arguments by example are based on generalizations from known cases to unknown ones. Here are some examples:

- Susan Jones, Yi Chen, and Leticia Watt are members of the Delta Delta Delta sorority, and they are all on the dean's list. Tri-Delts are good students.
- My friends Javier, Diane, and Lynn were communication majors, and they got into really good law schools. Communication must be a good pre-law major.
- The last time I sought help from the Advising Office I got passed around from one person to another. No one knew the answers to my questions. That department is incompetent.
- A Chinese company announced in 2020 that it would build a lithium battery recycling plant in Mexico instead of the US.[1] Earlier, American environmental regulations also resulted in lead battery recycling plants moving to Mexico.[2] Environmental regulations cost Americans employment opportunities.

As you can see from the illustrations above, the process of arguing on the basis of examples is familiar and common. Not all arguments from example are strong or convincing, however, and several tests of these arguments can and should be applied.

The first test is *sufficiency* of examples. Are there a significant or sufficient number of examples offered to support the claim? Obviously, there is a great danger in arguing from a very limited number of examples to a more general conclusion. All of the arguments offered above might be challenged on the basis of the sufficiency of the examples cited. The arguer who reasons from only a limited number of cases risks drawing conclusions that may not be true for other cases. For example, there may be 70 young women in the Delta Delta Delta sorority. Knowing that three of them (about four percent) are very good students is not sufficient to provide much confidence that the other 67 are equally successful in the classroom.

A second test is *typicality*. Are the examples cited typical of the category or class about which the arguer is trying to generalize? Because one individual asked questions that the staff members in the Advising Office were unable to answer does not necessarily suggest that this office is typically unable to answer students' questions. Perhaps these questions were truly extraordinary and rare. They might have been questions that the staff had never encountered before, such as an inquiry about the acceptance of transfer units from an unknown university. Another possibility is that the specific advisors to whom this student spoke were new to their positions and not yet sufficiently well trained to answer such questions. Perhaps other advisors, who might have been busy assisting other students, would have been able to answer the student's questions. In order to determine if this experience is typical, you might consider your own experience with the staff in this office. You might also consider the previous stories you have heard about this office from other students.

The third test is *accounting for counterexamples*. Are negative examples or rival stories accounted for in the argument? For example, Javier, Diane, and Lynn may have had great success in qualifying for admission to very competitive law schools, yet there are certainly many other communication majors who probably failed to gain admission to any law schools during that same admission cycle. Should you not also consider these cases? Also, of course, students majoring in other academic disciplines were applying for admission to law school. How well did they fare on gaining admission? Certainly, this might be useful information in any evaluation of the related merits of different undergraduate majors with regard to law school admissions.

The final test of arguments by example is *relevance*. Are the cited examples relevant to the claim being advanced? Many factors might, for example, influence a company's decision to shift their operations overseas. Increased environmental safety or worker safety regulations might indeed be factors in these decisions, but companies might also be seeking to benefit from lower wage rates, transportation variables, ready access to foreign suppliers or markets, or the desire to collocate different parts of their company such as design, engineering, manufacturing, and marketing.

Arguments from examples to a generalization that move too quickly or without a sufficient rationale may be labeled a *hasty generalization*. A hasty generalization is a logical *fallacy*—a flaw in the reasoning process. An advocate who commits a hasty generalization has potentially reasoned fallaciously, and the generalization that is the claim should be examined more closely.

Arguments by Analogy

An ***argument by analogy*** strives to identify similarities between cases that on the surface seem dissimilar in order to permit an inference to be drawn. Analogies are typically literary and creative devices that appeal to the listener's experiences and beliefs, and they are often used to embellish our stories. There are two types of analogies: literal and figurative.

A *literal analogy* is a statement drawing a direct comparison between two or more cases. The following are examples of literal analogies.

- In business circles there is a new awareness of customer service. It is time for professors to begin thinking of students as the customers of the university.
- Students who want an education only to prepare them for careers are like apprentices attaching themselves to carpenters. That is not what a liberal education should achieve.
- Gorbachev, Yeltsin, and Putin, the leaders who have led Russia since its transition from the communist regime, were charged with trying to create democratic institutions. They faced the same kinds of problems that Thomas Jefferson, Benjamin Franklin, and our other founders faced more than two centuries ago.

A *figurative analogy* is a statement that makes comparisons between classes that are materially dissimilar from each other but that are nonetheless suggestive of each other in some characteristic or manner. The following are examples of figurative analogies.

- The builders and developers have attacked the undeveloped hillsides of the city like hungry locusts.
- Many senators responded angrily to the bill limiting their income from outside sources. They are like drug addicts demanding their daily fix.
- The Iowa presidential caucuses are like a beauty contest for all the candidates who want to gain their party's nomination.

Both literal and figurative analogies are especially compelling types of arguments in that they correspond to people's ability to create stories and to test those stories when they argue. There is an important dramatic element to an effective analogy, for it creates a vivid picture in the minds of the audience. Consequently, analogies readily lend themselves to the tests of narrative probability and fidelity that we have already discussed in great detail.

In addition to these narrative tests, however, asking two questions can also test analogies. First, *are the compared cases alike in some meaningful way?* Is it really useful, for example, to think of students as customers? Customers are typically passive consumers who expect the businesses they patronize to wait on them. Students, on the other hand, should be active participants in the learning process. Education is not something that can be done for you; it is something that students must largely do for themselves. Thus, while this analogy might appeal to students, it is not likely to appeal to many other listeners—and especially not to the professors to whom it may be directed!

Second, *are the compared characteristics accurately described?* For example, the candidates who march through Iowa campaigning for support in the Iowa presidential caucuses are expected to meet thousands of voters in gatherings large and small, to give countless "stump" speeches and media interviews, and to lay out their political agenda and qualifications for the presidency. These processes may strongly advantage candidates who can raise large amounts of campaign contributions as well as those who may already be well-known to the voters. Although these caucuses may not constitute an ideal form of deliberative democracy, the claim that they are merely a beauty pageant for contenders seems unfair and less than persuasive. In the 2020 Democratic presidential campaign, for example, Pete Buttigieg (the previously little-known mayor of South Bend, Indiana) emerged as a serious candidate after he won the pledged-delegate count in the caucuses. The results took so long to be finalized, however, that Buttigieg did not get the campaign "bounce" that an Iowa winner frequently gains, and he failed to go on and secure the Democratic nomination after former Vice President Joe Biden handily won the South Carolina primary.

An advocate who compares apples with oranges may be said to have committed a logical fallacy called *false reasoning by analogy*. If you encounter such advocacy you should demand more information before granting adherence to such an argument.

Arguments from Causal Correlation

An even more sophisticated form of inductive reasoning is the ***argument from causal correlation***. This type of argument examines specific cases, classes of cases, or both in order to identify an actual relationship or correlation between them. Most research in the scientific tradition adheres to the principles of the inductive causal correlation argument or its deductive cousin, the causal generalization, discussed in the next section.

The following examples might help you identify arguments from causal correlation.

- Children who are exposed to excess levels of lead, either from eating paint chips, from air pollution, or from lead water pipes (as happened in Flint, Michigan) often suffer serious brain deficiencies and learning disabilities.
- Excessive exposure to violence on television or in video games leads to a willingness to accept violence as appropriate behavior and decreases people's sense of revulsion toward violence in real life.
- People today are given so many different antibiotics to combat infections that they are increasingly becoming inured to them. All too often the result is the development of resistant strains of diseases that are much more difficult to cure.

There are several tests of causal correlation that enable an arguer to assess this type of argument. The first is the *consistency of the correlation*. For example, do all (or even most) people who watch violent television shows or who play violent video games become more accepting of violence? Do people who are more inclined toward pacifism watch a lesser amount of television violence? These questions are designed as tests of causal correlation such as those that were first proposed by John Stuart Mill, an English philosopher and logician. Mill asserted that causal correlations could be tested on the basis of three canons that assessed the strength of the associations being claimed. The questions posed above all assess what Mill described as *concomitant variation*.[3] This test says that if increased exposure to violence is claimed to increase one's acceptance of violence, then decreased exposure to violence should also mean a decreased acceptance of violence. Mill believed that there should be a predictable pattern and relationship between a cause and its alleged effect.

Mill also asserted that discovering whether the *method of agreement* between the cases was the same could test the consistency between cause and effect. He thus claimed, "If two or more instances of the phenomenon under investigation have only one circumstance in common, the circumstances in which alone all the instances agree is the cause (or effect) of the given phenomenon."[4] Turning again to the argument about violence on television and in video games and the effect on behavior, an arguer would seek to determine if the subjects in the argument were alike in their video habits and in their proclivity toward violence but dissimilar in other respects such as social status, income, children living in single parent homes, neighborhoods, and/or lifestyle. This inquiry might lead one to conclude that exposure to violence on television and in video games was or was not a more important factor in shaping attitudes and behaviors regarding violence than the other factors studied.

Finally, according to Mill, considering whether the *method of difference* between the cases compared is consistent can test the congruence between cause and effect. "If, for example, the instance where the phenomenon under investigation occurs and that instance where it does not occur have every circumstance in common except one, that one occurring only in the former, then the circumstance in which alone the two cases differ is the effect, or the cause of the phenomenon."[5] Returning again to our test case, one might cite an example of two boys who both grow up in a violent inner-city neighborhood, in single-parent homes, and with a single parent who is abusive and alcoholic. One child commits a violent felony and is sent to prison. The other becomes an ordained minister and community leader. The argument about the relationship between video violence and real-life violence would be supported if the arguer could establish that the minister's parent did not own a television set. Consequently he was seldom exposed to the video violence that was the other boy's constant companion. Although such an example would be very convincing, locating such specific evidence in the real world to establish causality would be rare indeed.

All three of Mill's canons—concomitant variation, method of agreement, and method of difference—are essentially subsumed under the first test of a causal correlation—the test of the consistency of the association between cause and effect.

A second test of a causal correlation argument asks about the *strength* of the correlation: *Is the alleged association a strong one?* This is often an empirical test. There are, for example, many children who watch violence on television and in video games who do not become violent adults. What percentage of those who see violent programs do become violent? How much violence did these children see? Is there some point up to which watching violence may not be harmful but beyond which it is? Is there a certain age at which violent television programs become either more or less dangerous? All of these questions investigate the degree to which the statistical association between watching violent television programs and committing violent acts can be predicted.

A third test of a causal correlation asks: Does the movement of cause to effect follow a *regular and predictable* time sequence? For example, if one argues that children who are exposed to higher levels of lead suffer learning disabilities as a result, one should be able to argue definitively about the length of time it takes for the exposure to cause the harmful effect. Does it take hours, weeks, days, or months for the symptoms to manifest themselves? Furthermore, how long do the symptoms persist? Does the damage from lead poisoning correct itself over time, or is the damage permanent?

Research into the AIDS virus demonstrated the importance of carefully considering the time frame as a test of argument. Doctors now understand that AIDS is unlike most other diseases. First, it takes some time for medical tests to confirm that a patient has been exposed to the virus (perhaps as long as six months) because doctors can determine that patients are HIV-positive only after they begin to develop antibodies to fight the infection. Second, even after these antibodies appear, most patients will continue to be healthy for many months or even many years before beginning to develop symptoms of the disease. Finally, even after patients develop symptoms of an HIV-infection, it may be another extended period before their condition is identifiable as full-blown AIDS. In the early years of AIDS research, doctors assumed that patients who had been infected but showed no symptoms would probably be able to fight the disease on their own. Early estimates based on this reasoning predicted that only 10 percent of those infected with the virus would succumb to the disease. As more and more patients became ill, doctors were forced to keep increasing their estimates—20 percent, then 30 percent, and so on. Ultimately, the doctors conducting AIDS research realized that virtually all HIV-positive patients would eventually contract AIDS (the last phase of HIV-infection) unless they had access to a rigorous program of state-of-the-art drugs to manage their viral loads. As a result, the lag time from exposure to the onset of the disease has been not only extended but also fundamentally reconsidered. Only with this new realization of the ways in which the disease progressed (the cause) was the severity of the global AIDS epidemic understood (the effect).

The final test of causal correlation is *coherence*. It asks: Is the alleged association between cause and effect coherent? Essentially this asks the arguer to offer a persuasive explanation for the relationship between cause and effect. For example, many years ago in San Francisco an enraged city supervisor named Dan White murdered Mayor George Moscone and a fellow supervisor named Harvey Britt. The defense attorney claimed during the trial that White committed the murder because he was addicted to and binging on junk food. This junk food, the attorney reasoned, produced such a "sugar-high" that the murderer could not be held responsible for his actions. This so-called "Twinkie defense" won wide attention from the media but was criticized by nutritional experts as largely spurious. These experts argued that while there might be some association between physical behavior and diet, there is no coherent explanation to support an association between a willingness to commit violent acts and one's diet.

It is surprisingly common for individuals to confuse the sequence of events with a belief in cause and effect. In the Middle Ages, villagers whose crops withered in the field blamed the dead crops on the actions of individuals. The result was to ostracize those who were different, or sometimes to label them as witches and burn them at the stake. These tendencies did not die with the Enlightenment. Even today we look for the cause of an incomprehensible event. When school shootings occur, the cause is sometimes attributed to exposure to certain types of music, to video games, to violence on television, to certain websites, or to the existence of cliques at the school that caused the shooter to feel alone and isolated. The shooter most likely suffers from some form of mental illness, and there is little probability of identifying a cause to prevent similar tragic acts. Nonetheless, we search for rational causes for abhorrent effects.

Confusing the "sequence of events" with "cause and effect" is called the *post hoc ergo propter hoc* **fallacy**. It literally means "after this, therefore because of this." Sometimes we commit this fallacy purposefully—for example claiming that it rained because we forgot our umbrella or washed our car. However, arguments that attribute causality without adequate rationale should be questioned. We should seek additional information, lest we be guilty of committing the *post hoc* fallacy.

Now that we have introduced the three primary forms of inductive arguments, it is time to consider the different forms in which deductive arguments occur.

DEDUCTIVE ARGUMENTS

In deductive arguments one generalizes from theories or principles believed to be true to claims about individual cases. There are two types of deductive arguments.

Arguments from Sign

An *argument from sign* relies on the presence of certain attributes observable in a specific case to prove that it can be related to a generalization that is assumed to be true. When using this form of argument, one identifies certain characteristics or signs and then seeks to account for them by tying them to a conclusion or claim. Consider the following examples.

- The lack of respect for other people's property—the graffiti and vandalism, as well as the increased number of violent incidents—are signs that many American youth lack values.
- Bob is suffering from fever, sore throat, a cough, headache, and fatigue. These are signs he has contracted COVID-19.
- The students were hunched over their desks in apt concentration, and the quiet in the room was almost deafening. These signs indicated that the students were taking their required competency examinations very seriously.

There are three separate tests that can be used in the evaluation of a sign argument. First, *regularity*: Are the cited signs regularly indicators of the general theory being cited? The symptoms cited in the example about COVID-19, for example, might also be symptoms for other medical conditions. It could, for example, be influenza or mononucleosis. A doctor would need to rule out other conditions and to perform a test before diagnosing COVID-19.

Second, *sufficiency*: are there a sufficient number of signs present to support the conclusions offered? The students who are hunched over their desks taking their examinations, for example, might simply be exhausted from a night of intense partying and might not be concentrating on their tests after all. One might want to determine whether there are other signs that the students took the examination seriously. For instance, did they study for the test? And, how well did they score?

Third, are *contradictory signs* accounted for? If signs that are inconsistent with the generalization are present, have they been carefully considered? With regard to the argument about COVID-19, for example, it may be that Bob has been socially isolated, has not been exposed to anyone infected with the coronavirus, and that when tested he shows no antibodies for the disease. This combination of factors would likely cause his doctors to doubt that his symptoms alone meant that he was infected with this highly contagious disease.

Those advocates who would have us move too quickly from a limited number of signs are guilty of the fallacy of *false reasoning by sign*. If we suspect that this might be the case, it would be to our benefit to examine the argument more closely. A specific type of false reasoning by sign is called ***guilt by association***. If an advocate attacks a person because of the people with whom the person is friendly, for example, the advocate would be casting aspersions where none might be logically warranted. Just because someone hangs out with bad people is not sufficient evidence that the person is of bad character, and it would be a logical fallacy to act as if it did. In Los Angeles, for example, the police department for many years went to court to get injunctions that were intended to prevent people who were suspected of belonging to local street gangs from congregating together on street corners or in public parks. The American Civil Liberties Union filed a lawsuit against this practice, however, and convinced an appeals court to prohibit the issuing of such injunctions. As the *Los Angeles Times* reported: "The court clearly recognizes the way the city of Los Angeles has been enforcing gang injunctions over decades violates due process in a way that makes it likely they will place people on gang injunctions who may not be gang members."[6]

Arguments from Causal Generalization

The second type of deductive argument is the ***argument from causal generalization***. Causal generalization is the direct counterpart of causal correlation that we have already discussed. While causal correlation argues inductively from specific cases to identify a connection between these cases, causal generalization argues deductively from some general principles that are assumed to be true to judgments about specific cases. The following are examples of causal generalizations.

- It is well known that Hepatitis C is transmitted by exposure to the blood of an infected person. This frequently occurs when drug addicts share hypodermic needles. Mark was an intravenous drug user, which probably accounts for his infection.
- Steven is bound to abuse his children because he was himself abused as a child.
- It is unwise to raise the minimum wage. Every time the minimum wage is increased employers lay off some workers.

There are three tests of arguments from causal generalization. First, is the cause that is identified sufficient to produce the effect? This is the test of *sufficiency*. The fact that Steven was abused as a child might influence his parenting style, for example, but there are many persons who were abused as children who are very good parents and who do not abuse their children. As a result, one can question whether being a victim of childhood abuse is sufficient to predict abusive behavior as a parent.

Second, are there unanticipated *effects* linked to the cause? Perhaps Steven has such negative recollections of his childhood experiences that he will be especially motivated to avoid such behaviors with his children. He might become a parent who is exceptionally sensitive and kind to his own children precisely because his parents were not sensitive and kind to him.

Third, can *intervening factors* preclude the expected relationship between cause and effect? In some cases, an adjustment upwards of the minimum wage will stimulate economic growth by putting more purchasing power into the hands of consumers. Minimum wage workers are likely to spend their earnings on products and services that will grow the broader economy and generate higher profits for local businesses.

Fallaciously reasoning from a known generalization to a specific case is called the fallacy of *false reasoning by causal generalization.* As with the other fallacies introduced in this chapter, you should seek additional information if you suspect that an advocate is reasoning falsely before accepting that the specific case fits the generalization.

THE DEDUCTIVE SYLLOGISM

We can test all deductive arguments, whether they are arguments from signs or from causal generalizations, by phrasing them in syllogistic form and then examining their structural properties. A *syllogism* is a formal, logical type of reasoning. A syllogism consists of three statements. The *major premise* states a generalization: *All humans are mortal.* The *minor premise* relates a specific case or class to the generalization: *Socrates is a human.* And the *conclusion* is deduced from the two premises: *Socrates is mortal.*

The example about Socrates is what is known as a *categorical syllogism*—one that makes a statement about all cases within a given category. The major premise asserts a generalization that prescribes the category, the minor premise locates a specific case being argued within that category, and the conclusion is the deductive judgment that presents itself when these two premises are rationally or logically evaluated. The categorical syllogism is thus a very straightforward and simple deductive judgment. The following is another example of a categorical syllogism.

Major Premise   All Christians believe in God.
Minor Premise   Fred is a Christian.
Conclusion   Fred believes in God.

Analyzing deductive arguments as syllogisms enables an arguer to assess their validity quickly. (A *valid* syllogism is one that meets the required characteristics of argumentative form.) As we will discuss in detail later, logical validity is not the same as material truth. A syllogism that is not true may be valid, and an invalid syllogism may be materially true. Nonetheless, tests of logical validity are very useful to arguers and are easy to learn because they are often intuitive.

First, a valid categorical syllogism must in its major premise so define the category in question that it can be determined for certain that the specific case cited in the minor premise will fall within it. In the most recent example, the category defined "*all* Christians" is so clear that once the minor premise labels Fred as a Christian we can immediately conclude that he believes in God. If, for example, the major premise had asserted only that *some* Christians believe in God, it would have been impossible for us, based on the information provided in the syllogism, to know whether or not Fred fell within that group.

Second, no term can be found in the conclusion that is not found in one of the premises. For example:

Major Premise All tennis players are athletic.
Minor Premise Jim is a tennis player.
Conclusion Susan is athletic.

This syllogism cannot be presumed valid because the specific case Susan is not specified in either the major or the minor premise. We do not know from the information provided in this syllogism whether Susan is a tennis player or not. Thus, her specific case cannot be deduced from a generalization about tennis players.

Third, the major and minor premises cannot both be negative statements. If both statements offer negative judgments, it is impossible to derive a positive conclusion about a specific case based on the information provided in the syllogism.

Major Premise No Republicans favor tax increases.
Minor Premise Senator Jones is no Republican.
Conclusion (Who knows?)

Fourth, whenever the major or minor premise is a negative statement the conclusion must also be a negative statement.

Major Premise No Democrats favor cuts in social programs.
Minor Premise Senator Williams is a Democrat.
Conclusion Senator Williams does not favor cuts in social programs.

You have probably discovered by now that most of these categorical syllogisms are fairly easy to evaluate. In order to further guide your assessments of the validity of a syllogism, you can construct what is known as a Venn diagram (named for its creator, the nineteenth-century mathematician John Venn). In a Venn diagram one takes the broadest category, which is established in the major premise, and draws it in a large circle. One then takes the more specific term of the minor premise and draws it in a smaller circle. Finally, one takes the particular case to be categorized and draws it in the smallest circle. The Venn diagram for our "all Christians" example follows.

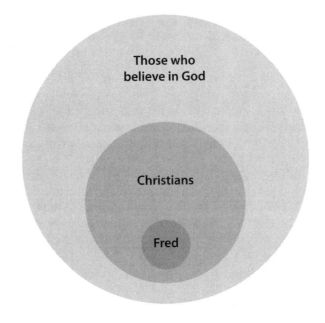

The Venn diagram reveals that this is a valid syllogism because the three circles are located within each other. We can thus visually determine that Fred, as a Christian, falls within the category of those who believe in God.

A Venn diagram can also reveal the invalidity of a syllogism, as illustrated by our example in which both the major and minor premises were negative.

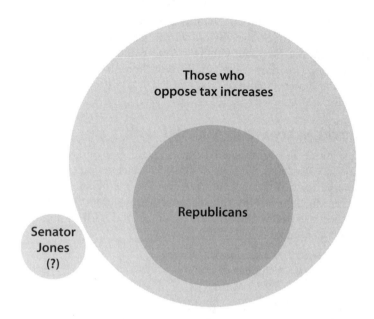

Because, in this case, we cannot place the term we are seeking to define (Senator Jones) within the circles representing the two proposed defining characteristics, this Venn diagram reveals that the syllogism does not meet the requirements of formal validity.

The Conditional Syllogism

A conditional syllogism might best be described as an "if/then" syllogism. This type of syllogism asserts that if a particular thing occurs, then some other particular thing will follow.

Major Premise   If students study, they get better grades.
Minor Premise   The students will study.
Conclusion   The students will get better grades.

The antecedent, or "if" premise, sets up the reasoning process that makes the syllogism function. If the consequent, or minor premise, affirms the antecedent, the syllogism is presumed valid. However, if the consequent denies the antecedent, the syllogism cannot be presumed valid:

Major Premise   If students study, they get better grades.
Minor Premise   The students will not study.
Conclusion   The students will get better grades.

This syllogism is not valid because the consequent does not meet the conditions specified in the antecedent.

The Disjunctive Syllogism

A disjunctive syllogism contains premises that are essentially "either/or" statements.

Major Premise   The university must either raise tuition or cut faculty and programs.
Minor Premise   The university is unwilling to make cuts.
Conclusion   Therefore tuition must be increased.

The disjunctive syllogism may be judged valid when the major premise includes all of the possible alternatives, thereby allowing a conclusion to be drawn through the process of elimination. Frequently there are more alternatives than are provided for in the major premise. This flaw is less a failure of the syllogistic reasoning, however, than it is a test of the material truth or falsity of the syllogistic claim. This leads us to the next issue for discussion.

Structural Validity versus Material Truth

The evaluation of syllogistic form is useful as a demonstration of explicit logical deduction. By applying the tests of syllogistic reasoning, an arguer can readily determine whether or not a conclusion argued in a syllogism is valid. The same tests are not effective in determining the material truth underlying the argumentative claim, however, because material truths are assumed in the formation of premises. Consider the following example.

Major Premise   All cats have three legs.
Minor Premise   Felix is a cat.
Conclusion   Felix has three legs.

The syllogism is valid. It meets all the tests of a categorical syllogism. Obviously, however, the syllogism is not materially true since we know that cats have four, not three, legs. The test of whether or not a syllogism is *sound* is a test of validity and not a test of whether or not the premises are materially true. The arguer who wishes to test a syllogism needs to remember that a syllogism's being valid does not make it true. The truth or falsity of a syllogism must also be evaluated by an examination of the material truth of the premises and the degree to which the claims offered in the premises are verifiable.

THE TOULMIN MODEL

Another approach to viewing arguments is the *Toulmin model* of argument.[7] (Chapter 3 introduced Stephen Toulmin's argumentation theory in the discussion of argument fields.) Few artifacts of argument exhibit all of the elements of the Toulmin model, and abstracting an argument from its social context in order to diagram it risks distorting and oversimplifying it. However, the Toulmin model is a useful tool for understanding the components of argument, and it provides valuable insight into the reasoning process that arguers use. Once you understand the elements of an argument, you can critically evaluate each one in turn. In that way the Toulmin model can also help you create arguments to refute another argument. There are six components in the Toulmin model.

Claim: conclusion of the argument; the statement the advocate wishes the audience to believe
Grounds: foundation or basis for the claim; the support
Warrant: reasoning that authorizes the inferential leap from the grounds to the claim

Backing: support for the warrant
Modality: degree of certainty with which the advocate makes the claim
Rebuttal: exceptions that might be offered to the claim

Before discussing each of these elements in greater detail we will examine an entire argument and diagram it.

Megan: The Dodgers will probably win the National League Pennant this year. (claim)
Sean: What are you basing this claim on? (request for grounds)
Megan: They have the best pitching (grounds)
Sean: Maybe, but how does the fact that they have the best pitching lead you to believe that they will win the pennant? (request for warrant)
Megan: The team with the best pitching usually wins. (warrant)
Sean: Is there any proof that the team with the best pitching usually wins? (request for backing of the warrant)
Megan: Well, that is what has happened over the last few years. (backing)
Sean: How sure are you that they will win? Do you want to bet on it? (request for modality)
Megan: Well, I did say probably, so I don't want to bet too much. (modality)
Sean: Well, you seem pretty confident. Why don't you make a nice big wager?
Megan: There is always the possibility that the Dodgers will have a lot of injuries. (rebuttal)

Following the Toulmin model, this argument would be diagrammed in this way:

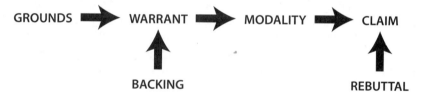

Claims

The first component of an argument is the *claim*. The claim is the statement that the arguer seeks to convince the audience to accept. Claims may be made in the past, present, or future tense. The following are examples of claims.

- It is time for you to start working on your term paper.
- The economy will go into a deep recession next spring.
- We should probably give more foreign aid to the people of Afghanistan.

Each of these claims is a declarative statement that expresses the advocate's belief. Claims are not always expressed in declarative statements, however. "Won't deficit spending come back to haunt us?" is another way of asserting that it *will* come back to haunt us. There are several different types of claims that can be argued.

Claims of fact: potentially verifiable assertions about the nature of things.
- 764,427 Americans died of COVID-19 by November 16, 2021.
- The number of high school dropouts is increasing.
- Millions of Americans have no health insurance.

Claims of value: indications of preference or judgment. Often values are predicated on facts, but they also contain value judgments.

- It is wrong for people to put others at risk for COVID-19 because they refuse to wear masks or be vaccinated.
- The large number of dropouts is evidence that our school systems are failing.
- It is unacceptable that some persons continue to be denied access to health care because they cannot afford it.

Claims of policy: assertions that something should be done. They are easily identified because they contain words like *should* or *ought* or imply should or ought.

- We should make sure that we have a systematic national policy in place to end the current pandemic and to prevent the next one.
- We should revise our school curriculums to encourage students to stay in school so they can earn their diplomas.
- The federal government ought to close the gaps in the Affordable Care Act and create a single-payer program of national health insurance.

The first objective in analyzing a claim is to determine whether it is a claim of fact, value, or policy. Once you have identified the claim and categorized it, you can determine whether you wish to challenge it.

Sometimes the type of claim is not readily apparent. This may occur because an argument is poorly developed and expressed. Often advocates themselves are not sure precisely what they are arguing. On other occasions, advocates are reluctant to explicitly state their claims. For example, they may have a hidden agenda. In such situations you must infer from the information available to you what the advocate is claiming. This inference process is, of course, subject to great error, so the advocates who wish to be clearly understood should explicitly state their claims.

Grounds

"What are you basing your claim on?" is a question about the ***grounds,*** or foundational assumptions, underlying your argument—the evidence you offer in support of your claim. The grounds may include examples or signs from which you generalize. Evidence should consist of such things as factual statements, statistical proof, the statement of accepted principles, and testimony. Each type of evidence can be subjected to tests evaluating its quality. The grounds for arguments and the appropriate tests of evidence will be discussed in far greater detail in chapter 7.

Warrants and Backing

The next two elements of the Toulmin model are called the ***warrant*** and the ***backing.*** Just as a judge may issue a warrant authorizing the police to conduct a search of a suspect's dwelling, a warrant authorizes an advocate to make a claim based on the grounds provided. A warrant is the reasoning that permits an inferential leap; it works like a bridge connecting the grounds to the claim.

Backing refers to the support for the warrant. If a warrant has backing, there is reason to believe that the warrant is legitimate. In essence, a warrant is a secondary claim. The backing for the warrant is thus the grounds for this secondary claim. There are several different types of warrants, which correspond to the different forms of reasoning we discussed in the beginning of this chapter. One can reason warrants from examples, analogies, signs, and causal correlations or generalizations. In addition, an arguer can use warrants that are drawn from authority (this claim is true because a significant, respected, and qualified source says it is true) or from principle (this argument is true because it depends upon a principle that virtually everyone would accept as true).

Earlier in this chapter we discussed the tests to which arguments from example, analogy, causality, and signs could be subjected. There are also tests to evaluate arguments from authority and principle. Arguments from authority depend on the quality of the authority cited, and arguments from principle depend on the principles being readily accepted and likely held by your audience. These tests for arguments from authority and principle will be considered more fully in chapters 7 and 9.

Modality

The fifth element of the Toulmin model is called the ***modality*** and refers to the degree of certainty the advocate has that the claim is true. Words like *probably, possibly, might,* or *may* are illustrations of modal qualifiers. The absence of a modal qualifier in an argument makes a claim unequivocal—that is, certain.

Consider the following adverbs and adverbial phrases. Which of these communicate the greatest certainty and which conveys the least certainty?

| very possibly | it would seem | presumably |
| apparently | certainly | quite likely |

When attempting to discern the modality of an argument artifact you must be careful not to confuse those adverbs that modify other elements of the argument with those that modify the certainty of the claim. Modality refers only to those that modify the claim. For example, an advocate could argue "I definitely smell smoke, so it is likely there is a fire." The modality of this argument is expressed by the word *likely* not *definitely*.

Modal qualifiers are a very important element of the argument model. Claims that are absolute, about which the arguer is certain, leave no room for doubt. The grounds must be equally certain. By diagramming an argument and identifying whether a modal qualifier is present and its relationship to the grounds, you can begin to assess both the merits and the possible weaknesses of the argument.

Rebuttal

The final component of the Toulmin model is called the ***rebuttal.*** The rebuttal refers to exceptions, cases in which the claim would not be true. Understanding the nature of rebuttals, and being able to identify them, is important to the evaluation of arguments for two reasons. First, some advocates admit to rebuttals when presenting their arguments. For example, an advocate could argue that current deficit spending by the federal government has significantly drained capital resources (grounds) and that unless new sources of capital are discovered (rebuttal), continued deficit spending will bankrupt the economy (claim). In this case, the advocate has admitted that there could be an intervening factor that would deny the validity of the claim. If an advocate admits to a rebuttal, a critical audience can consider the possibility that this rebuttal will negate the claim. If the outcome suggested in the rebuttal actually appears probable, the arguer will not likely win adherence to his or her argumentative claim. It is noteworthy that this type of argument is frequently offered in the United States Congress. The Republicans call for significant tax cuts even in the face of an ever-growing federal budget deficit because they believe that these cuts will stimulate the economy and ultimately lead to enhanced federal revenues. This argument was also offered by Democrats during the COVID-19 pandemic, when Democrats argued that growing the budget deficit in order to put stimulus checks into the hands of citizens and businesses would help keep the economy afloat during the long government-imposed shutdowns and prevent a recession from turning into a depression.

Rebuttals are also important to opponents of an argument because they highlight a potential point for refutation. Since there may be an exception to almost any argument that makes the claim invalid, critical thinkers should draw upon their own knowledge and experience to identify and create rebuttals. Giving presence to the role of rebuttals in arguments thus facilitates critical analysis.

SUMMARY

This chapter considered arguments as complete logical claims and focused on the ways that such claims can be constructed and analyzed. Two primary modes of argument, inductive and deductive claims, were discussed. Inductive arguments can be developed from example, analogy, or causal correlation. Deductive arguments can be developed from signs or from causal generalization. Each type of argument can be tested, critically assessed, and responded to as is appropriate. We focused on the deductive syllogism as a formal test of argumentative reasoning. Principles for constructing and evaluating syllogisms were specified. Finally, the chapter discussed the utility of the Toulmin model as a means for arguers to develop and analyze the component parts of argumentative claims.

KEY TERMS

deductive reasoning
    argument from causal generalization
    argument from sign
fallacy
    false reasoning by analogy
    false reasoning by causal generalization
    false reasoning by hasty generalization
    false reasoning by sign
    post hoc ergo propter hoc
guilt by association
inductive reasoning
    argument by analogy
    argument by example
    argument from causal correlation

syllogism
    conclusions
    major premise
    minor premise
Toulmin model
    backing
    claim
    grounds
    modality
    rebuttal
    warrant

ACTIVITIES

1. Find an opinion essay in a newspaper or online. Select a major argument advanced in the essay. Identify what type of argument it is and apply the appropriate tests of reasoning provided in this chapter. Do you find the reasoning sufficient to support the primary claim(s)?

2. President Trump claimed that the 2020 presidential election was stolen from him and that if all legal ballots were counted, he would have been reelected. What types of arguments did he offer in support of this claim? Did these arguments meet the tests outlined in this chapter?

3. Construct a categorical syllogism that is both structurally valid and sound.

4. Find a song and try to diagram it using the Toulmin model. What is the claim advanced by the songwriter? What grounds does the advocate provide as a basis for the claim? Is there a warrant provided? What type of reasoning does the warrant employ? If the warrant is not explicit, can you provide it? Are any other elements of the Toulmin model included in the advocacy?

5. There was a robust debate during the COVID-19 pandemic about the benefits of wearing face masks and whether proclamations that masks were necessary infringed on individual liberty. Look back to media coverage of this controversy and identify the types of arguments offered, assess their quality and sufficiency, and offer an evaluation of which arguments you believe were strong and weak.

RECOMMENDED READINGS

Bruschke, John, "Argument and Evidence Evaluation: A Call for Scholars to Engage Contemporary Public Debates," *Argumentation and Advocacy* 49 (2012): 59–75.

Eemeren, Frans H. van, "How Should One Respond to Fallacious Moves," *Argumentation and Advocacy* 45 (2009): 198–206.

Inch, Edward S. and Kristin H. Tudor, *Critical Thinking and Communication: The Use of Reason in Argument*, 7th ed. (Englewood Cliffs, NJ: Pearson, 2014).

Innocenti, Beth, "Countering Questionable Tactics By Crying Foul," *Argumentation and Advocacy* 47 (2011): 178–188.

Rieke, Richard D., Malcolm O. Sillars, and Tarla Rai Peterson, *Argumentation and Critical Decision Making*, 8th ed. (Englewood Cliffs, NJ: Pearson, 2013).

Rybacki, Karyn C. and Donald J. Rybacki, *Advocacy and Opposition: An Introduction to Argumentation*, 7th ed. (Englewood Cliffs, NJ: Pearson, 2012).

Simosi, Maria, "Using Toulmin's Framework for the Analysis of Everyday Argumentation: Some Methodological Considerations," *Argumentation* 17 (2003): 185–203.

Vasilyeva, Alena L., "The Treatment of Fallacies in Argumentative Situations During Mediation Sessions," *Argumentation and Advocacy* 46 (2010): 173–192.

Willard, Charles Arthur, "On the Utility of Descriptive Diagrams for the Analysis and Criticism of Arguments," *Communication Monographs* 43 (1976): 308–320.

Zarefsky, David, *The Practice of Argumentation* (New York: Cambridge University Press, 2019).

Endnotes

1. Ann Deslandes, "Ganfeng Announces Lithium Battery Recycling Plant in Mexico," *Diagolo Chino,* December 2, 2020. https://dialogochino.net/en/climate-energy/38594-ganfeng-announces-lithium-battery-recycling-plant-in-mexico/
2. Tim Johnson, "Lead-Battery Recycling Has Moved to Mexico," *The Seattle Times,* March 25, 2013. https://www.seattletimes.com/nation-world/lead-battery-recycling-has-moved-to-mexico/
3. John Stuart Mill, *System of Logic* (New York: Harper & Brothers, 1904), 288–291.
4. Ibid., p. 280.
5. Ibid.
6. James Queally, "Los Angeles Barred from Enforcing Nearly All Gang Injunctions, Federal Judge Rules," *Los Angeles Times,* March 15, 2018. https://www.latimes.com/local/lanow/la-me-ln-gang-injunction-court-order-20180315-story.html
7. This model of argument was originally discussed in the book, Stephen E. Toulmin, *The Uses of Argument* (Cambridge: Cambridge University Press, 1958). It was later modified and it is the modified model that is used here. See Stephen E. Toulmin, Richard Rieke, and Allan Janik, *Introduction to Reasoning* (New York: MacMillan, 1978).

7

The Grounds for Argument

Humans around the world have begun to ponder the consequences of their actions on the biosphere. One result of this environmental focus is an ongoing debate about climate change. One side paints a bleak picture. Humanity's heavy reliance on burning fossil fuels is releasing large amounts of carbon dioxide into the atmosphere. The result is the greenhouse effect: carbon dioxide traps the earth's heat, causing the planet to gradually become warmer. This, advocates contend, will melt the polar ice caps, cause severe weather effects, and lead to the loss of key species, human famine, population migrations, and wars over resources. The economic losses will be unparalleled, but they will not be distributed evenly. For example, tens of millions of people will lose their homes and land in Bangladesh, and places such as the Republic of the Maldives (an island nation in the Indian Ocean) will completely disappear beneath the water. These advocates claim that we should take immediate and expensive steps to fundamentally change our lifestyles to reduce the use of fossil fuels. Representative Alexandria Ocasio-Cortez of New York and Senator Edward J. Markey of Massachusetts, both Democrats, have introduced a bill in Congress called "The Green New Deal," which would "wean the United States from fossil fuels and curb planet-warming greenhouse gas emissions across the economy. It also aims to guarantee new high-paying jobs in clean energy industries."[1]

The other side tells a different story. Current evidence does not support significant actions to discourage fossil fuel use, and such actions would slow the growth of the economy, increase unemployment, drive up the costs of goods and services, and result in an intrusive system of government regulations. These advocates argue that a focus on economic development will better serve global interests and that the data available to us now are insufficient to support the arguments that human activity has impacted the changing climate. "Republicans have cast the Green New Deal as a socialist takeover and say it is evidence that Democrats are far from the mainstream on energy issues."[2]

These conflicting narratives have persisted over many years and have been exploited by political partisans—and thus they will prove very difficult to change. The debate originated in the early 2000s when the United States Environmental Protection Agency scientists issued a report about global warming that was critical of government actions to respond to the problem. The scientists called for more draconian and costly policy solutions similar to those proposed in the Green New Deal. The Bush administration objected to the language of the report and subjected it to careful editing that softened both the language and the suggested policy alternatives. This resulted in a fierce battle about government attempting to censor scientists that spilled out onto the front pages of the nation's newspapers.[3] The controversy has by no means diminished since that time, as many climate change skeptics have even begun to criticize the wisdom, methods, and motivations of the scientists. This controversy has starkly revealed the differences in the positions between those who view global warming as an imminent crisis and those who believe that we can simply turn up the air conditioning. Some have gone on to argue that consultants working to safeguard corporate interests have intentionally orchestrated the attacks on the scientists.[4]

The stasis of the dispute between these two views is in what should be done immediately. Each side is now closer than they were two decades ago to finding agreement that global warming is occurring, that it is undesirable, and that if it were certain that human activity was responsible for it, policy changes might be desirable. However, they disagree about the nature of evidence used as the foundation for their claims. This dispute illustrates how disagreements over the facts can be at the center of a long-standing and intense debate.

The question asks the advocate to identify and state the grounds or evidence supporting their argument. Whether the argument is inductive or deductive, **grounds** serve as the evidence, support, or foundation for the claim. According to Aristotle, the basis for a claim may be one of two types.[5] If support for the claim depends on the reasoning, analysis, inspiration, or creativity of the advocate, it is considered an ***artistic proof***. If support for the claim comes from someone else—quotations, ideas, numbers, or examples from outside sources—it is considered ***inartistic proof***. Contemporary practice is to cite inartistic proof using an agreed upon style manual such as APA or MLA. Both types of evidence may include premises, examples, statistics, and testimony.

Aristotle identified three types of artistic proofs. He thought that audiences could be persuaded by the logic employed by an advocate. He called this form of proof ***logos***. Audiences also could be persuaded, or they would be more receptive to the logical appeals of the advocate, through an arousal of the emotions of the audience. This he called ***pathos***. Finally, Aristotle believed that sometimes audiences are persuaded just because they feel the advocate possesses practical wisdom, is virtuous, and has good intentions. This is called ***ethos***.

In this chapter we focus on the support or grounds advocates use for their claims. We will identify the types of grounds used by advocates, present the tests critical consumers of argument typically employ to assess the validity of grounds, and suggest ways advocates might choose supporting data that will increase the likelihood they will gain adherence to their claims.

PREMISES

All evidence acts as the premise or starting point of a claim. As a premise, grounds function as an established point of agreement between advocates and their audiences. A *premise* therefore is a point accepted without the requirement of additional support.

The premises an advocate can use to support a claim are based on two types of knowledge: personal knowledge and cultural knowledge.[6] ***Personal knowledge*** is that which we know to be true because we have firsthand experience with it. Personal knowledge is an artistic proof.

We know that fire is hot, ice is cold, rain is wet, and so on because our senses provide us this information. We had to learn the labels, but the senses give us basic data that is easily recognizable because we have experienced these sensations previously. Personal knowledge extends beyond such sensory data, however, and thus supplies premises. We know that snow may appear beautiful when it falls from the sky but also that it can be heavy to shovel off of our sidewalk and that it can also be treacherous to drivers. We know the economy is failing us when times are tough because we may be unemployed, because we know others who are unemployed, or because we are given cause to worry that we, like the others around us, might soon lose our jobs. We believe such things because we have experienced them and witnessed others who are close to us experience them. When an advocate uses a premise that taps into our personal knowledge, we are likely to find fidelity in the argument because the premise rings true with experiences we know to be true.

There are other things we believe to be true that we have not experienced ourselves. We may hold these views because we are part of a culture. This **cultural knowledge** may consist of shared values or shared truths. It may be explicit—codified into rules, principles, or laws—or it may be tacitly derived from our behavior. It is contained in the stories we tell about ourselves, who we are, where we have been, and where we are going. Cultures are defined by the stories that are told about them—both by the people who live with them and by the outsiders who confront them. Cultures are thus created and maintained through communication.[7]

In our culture we teach a multitude of stories to our children: accounts of the Pilgrims crossing the stormy seas of the Atlantic on the crowded and tiny Mayflower, narratives about the suffering of the Continental Army soldiers under the command of General George Washington at Valley Forge, reports of President Abraham Lincoln speaking at Gettysburg, tales of Teddy Roosevelt and his troops charging up San Juan Hill, accounts of President John F. Kennedy's speech in Berlin, narratives about the heroic firefighters climbing up the stairs of the doomed World Trade Center towers to rescue people trapped inside. All these stories reveal something about what it means culturally to be American. It is through the telling and retelling of these stories that we inculcate American values in our youth. And these values and "truths" about our public experiences may constitute the premises advocates use in their arguments. As an example, the heroism and the deaths of the New York City firefighters on September 11, 2001, might be cited as an argument to pay first responders better salaries, as an argument about the contributions immigrants make in U.S. culture (many of the firefighters were "ethnic" Americans), as an argument for better disaster planning, or even as an argument against the construction of new high-rise buildings.

Another way a culture reinforces its shared knowledge is through rituals. **Rituals** are behavior patterns so often repeated that the participants know them by heart and expect them to be performed at precise times. From who sits where at a family meal to the inauguration of a president to the taking of an oath before offering testimony in a courtroom, many of our cultural practices are scripted by ritual.[8] One of the most painful and poignant moments for many Americans during the COVID-19 pandemic was the unhappy decision to forgo their traditional Thanksgiving celebrations with family and friends to avoid spreading the virus. It required a concerted campaign by public health officials, political leaders, and media personalities to convince people to give up their ritual celebrations in 2020 to safeguard the health of their loved ones and to assure their participation in future celebrations.

When you successfully complete your college degree you will be invited to participate in a commencement ritual. Participants will be suitably garbed in the vestments of the academic community. You will probably wear a black robe and a strange flat hat with a tassel hanging from it. Likewise, the faculty members and senior academic administrators of the campus will wear their robes often accompanied by colorful hoods signifying the disciplines and universities where they earned their doctoral degrees. These robes may be traced back to the universities established in the Middle Ages. Indeed, in Germany when student protestors during the 1960s and 1970s expressed their rage against the conservatism and elitism of the university culture, they demanded many reforms. One of the first and most visible things they sought to change was the wearing of academic robes by university faculty and students. The slogan was "The stink of a thousand years comes from beneath those robes." It became a rallying cry for the student protestors, and today German graduates are among the few in world who do not wear traditional academic garb on their graduation day. Of course, the very reason that the German protestors opposed the gowns—that they signified cultural elitism—may be why so many Americans enjoy the day. Wearing the graduation gown, marching in the procession, hearing your name called out, receiving a diploma, and the highly formulaic and usually forgettable speech—because so many commencement speakers focus on their own accomplishments—are all ritualized activities that honor the achievements of the graduates and that welcome them into the ranks of the educated elite. It is through such rituals that universities, families, and cultures communicate their faith in the values of discipline, education, and intellectual development. As we learned in 2020 and 2021 during the pandemic, Zoom commencement celebrations were no match for the traditional rituals.

Symbols are yet another way a society teaches its values. Visit any state or national capital and you will undoubtedly see great monuments and halls devoted to governance. Must the chief executives of states reside in stately mansions such as the White House? Is it necessary to construct huge buildings with impressive rotundas, pillars, and lofty ceilings? No, those ornaments are not necessary. They are the vestiges of monarchical tradition, and they are perpetuated to communicate the importance and seriousness of the business conducted in them. Such buildings are also intended to honor the significance and importance of the persons who work in those buildings. One of the many enjoyable things to do on a visit to Washington, DC, is to tour the neighborhoods where other nations maintain their embassies. Even small and poor nations typically try to acquire impressive buildings to provide space for their diplomats to work and to represent the interests of their governments in the United States. The buildings, in some sense, serve as images of the importance, substance, and solidity of the political system and the nationalistic cultures that they represent.

Shared premises enjoy ***presumption*** with audiences. That is, audiences tend to believe these premises until convinced otherwise. The concept behind presumption is that most people, most of the time, are comfortable with the way things are. We generally are apprehensive about the unknown. We stick to familiar beliefs, values, and policies until sufficient reasons are presented to convince us that they should be changed. (The topic of presumption will be discussed in greater detail in chapter 11).

Advocates can build arguments on shared premises by invoking them through their own support for their claims (artistic proofs) or by citing evidence that calls on shared premises (inartistic proofs). For example, most of us have little personal experience with governmental censorship. But just because we have not actually been arrested for something we have said or for a message that we posted to our website does not diminish the fervor with which we support freedom of speech. In this political culture, unlike some other political cultures with histories of authoritarian leadership, we cherish the right to express our views freely. Consequently, advocates who argue against attempts to censor the lyrics of popular music or against attempts to restrict free speech on the internet can draw on this shared premise.

Where can an advocate look to discover shared premises? A good source might be the adages or proverbs that we all know. Here is a short list; you undoubtedly can add other examples.

> Good triumphs over evil.
> Experience is the best teacher.
> Love conquers all.
> Hope for the best, but prepare for the worst.
> Good things come to those who wait.
> Haste makes waste.
> A penny saved is a penny earned.
> Good fences make good neighbors.

The slogans or manifestos that we profess faith in are another source of premises. Look, for example, to the articulation of beliefs in the Declaration of Independence and the Constitution. They express our collective political and cultural commitments to equality, liberty, the freedoms of speech and religion, due process; the freedom to pursue happiness, property rights, and the rule of law. All these beliefs provide important sources for the premises of arguments. Note, however, that often these freedoms conflict with each other. Thus, for example, freedom and equality may often be in conflict. Some advocates may place greater emphasis on the freedom to follow their own religious beliefs than on others' rights to be treated equally. Thus, some may claim that since they believe homosexuality is a sin they should not be expected to prepare and sell a wedding cake to a gay couple. Gay citizens, on the other hand, understandably claim that they are entitled to live as they wish and that they should have access to all goods, services, and accommodations without fear of discrimination. Thus, although audiences may generally grant adherence to shared premises, arguments predicated on accepted premises will not necessarily win automatic agreement. Critical consumers of arguments and advocates constructing discourse will have to evaluate the use of the premises in the support of individual claims. We identify three tests of the use of premises.

Testing Premises: Shared Premises

First, the premise employed by an advocate must be shared by the audience. While the definition of a premise presumes agreement, beliefs are not static. Some things that we believe now, we may have once rejected. People once scoffed at the idea that the Earth was round and that it revolved around the sun. But we need not go back that far into history to find examples of beliefs that have dramatically changed. Consider, for example, public attitudes toward acceptance of gay marriage. A Pew Survey found that in 2001 only 35% of Americans polled supported same sex marriage; by 2019, fully 61% supported it.[9]

In the United States, attitudes on many topics change as people age. A longitudinal study over many decades conducted by scholars from the University of Chicago, for example, found that age is an important influence on political beliefs in the United States.

> Research suggests that there is a neglected dimension of polarization, one driven by age: younger people are disproportionately liberal, and then drift steadily to the right, becoming just as disproportionately conservative by retirement age.
>
> "We can say, with a great deal of confidence, that people get more conservative when they get older—and a lot more," says Chicago Booth's Sam Peltzman, who conducted the research. "It's not just a little bit. It's a pretty big change over their lifetime."
>
> Though some people form their political beliefs early in life and stick with them, most of us follow a predictable and durable pattern: our political beliefs steadily become more conservative as we age, no matter what generation we belong to or what era we grew up in, the research finds.[10]

Peltzman also observed that he thought young people today were probably no more liberal than young people had been over the past 50 years. He believes the pattern that has persisted across forty years of data will continue. By the time today's liberals turn 45, many of them (although of course not all) will have become conservative.[11]

Another difficulty with assuming that all audiences share the same premises arises from the increasing impact of different cultures. As a result of population migrations, the ease of communication, access to travel, and the impact of a global economy, we are experiencing changes that many have referred to as the "globalization" of our planet.[12] Due to globalization, we can no longer presume that the people whom we are trying to convince share the same cultural premises that we hold dear. Cultural premises themselves are now a source for disagreement and argument.[13] Some conservatives have argued that the U.S. educational system now fails to teach the essential core values of Western culture. They argue that because our school children no longer read the same great classic books in their literature classes or learn about the important Western philosophers and their theories, they are not taught the principles that will enable us to sustain our political culture. Students today, they lament, are taught that all cultures are equally valuable. As a result, they fear that our children will grow to become adults who do not share the same value system.[14]

Others have called for even greater inclusion of great books, philosophers, and the teaching of the values of non-Western cultures. They argue that U.S. school children should be expected to have a deeper knowledge of Eastern cultures or the cultures of the Southern hemisphere. Teaching from a multicultural perspective, they argue, validates the experiences of minority students and makes all citizens more sensitive to the differences between people.[15] Knowledge of diverse cultures is also important today, of course, given the likelihood that almost all Americans will find employment in culturally diverse workplaces.[16]

The continuing debate in higher education over the teaching of cultural perspectives reveals the difficulties in assuming that all audiences share the same premises. There may be differences between and within audiences because the persons composing them collectively or individually represent different cultures.

Testing Premises: Contradictory Premises

A second concern with the use of premises as grounds for a claim is that there are sometimes contradictions and conflicting claims under consideration. Bromides reflect U.S. values; they also reveal the tension between competing wisdoms. Consider the belief that you should "Look before you leap" versus "He who hesitates is lost." Similarly, is it "Absence makes the heart grow fonder" or "Out of sight, out of mind"?

On a more serious level, Walter Fisher argues that one of the unifying elements in U.S. culture is what is known as the American dream.[17] Even though most citizens could tell you about the American dream and what it means to them, Fisher argued that the American dream is actually derived from two frequently contradictory beliefs. The first is the belief in the United States as a land of opportunity. The opportunity to achieve unlimited material success is a fundamental cornerstone of capitalism. Hundreds of thousands of immigrants came to the United States, often at the cost of great sacrifice and danger, to realize this aspect of the American dream. According to this dream, hard work in the United States will be rewarded. The children of blue-collar workers can gain a university education and secure professional careers, and anyone can save their money and ultimately purchase their own home. This is the materialistic dimension of the American dream. The second dimension is that the United States is the land of equal opportunity. Regardless of race, ethnic identity, religion, gender, age, or sexual preference, this aspect of the dream affords the promise of equal protection under law. This is the moralistic aspect of the American dream.

There are times when the materialistic and the moralistic elements of the dream are in opposition. For example, some argue that affirmative action programs are moralistic attempts to redress inequities at the price of impinging on the materialistic endeavors of those who are not in the protected classes. The steps taken to counter the history of racial discrimination and minorities' lack of access to adequate education means that non-protected students, who may by some measures be better qualified than minority students, may be denied spots in first-tier universities or professional schools. The 2003 Supreme Court case that reviewed the affirmative action remedies undertaken at the University of Michigan revealed the profound disagreement among the justices over the conflicting elements of the American dream. Ultimately, the Court held that affirmative action was permissible but also that such a remedy to past racial discrimination will be short-lived and no longer necessary in approximately 25 years.[18] The disagreement over affirmative action in college admissions was so intense, however, that neither the Court nor the voters waited 25 years to revisit the issue. Several states, including California and Michigan, eliminated racial preferences in university admissions via ballot initiatives. In April 2014, the Court:

> Upheld a Michigan constitutional amendment that bans affirmative action in admissions to the state's public universities. The 6-to-2 ruling effectively endorsed similar measures in seven other states. It may also encourage more states to enact measures banning the use of race in admissions or to consider race-neutral alternatives to ensure diversity.[19]

The controversy over racial preferences in college admissions continues. In 2020, the Department of Justice (under the control of Attorney General William Barr and during the last months of the Trump administration) brought a federal complaint against Yale University, alleging that the Ivy League school discriminated against Asian-American and white applicants in its systematic attempts to increase the opportunities for African American and Mexican American students to gain admission to Yale.[20] The Biden Administration subsequently dropped this lawsuit.[21]

It often seems that the most hotly contested contemporary disputes have contradictory premises at their core. As an example, we can cite the controversy over the need to protect the citizens of the United States from the threats of terrorism versus the rights of our citizens to be free from unwarranted intrusions into their private lives. In the wake of the September 11 tragedy, the government passed legislation known as the Patriot and Homeland Security Acts. Both bills dramatically increased the power of government agencies to conduct surveillance on citizens via telephone taps, access to email records, access to banking and financial transactions, and even access to confidential health information. Those who favored the legislation insisted that the government's obligation to protect "life, liberty, and the pursuit of happiness" meant a clear responsibility to protect our lives from those who would seek to kill us or otherwise damage our safety and security. Those who opposed these bills, however, argued that the real and potential losses of liberty and privacy from such bills would chill dissent, undermine our democracy, and provide the clearest evidence that the terrorists who were intent on destroying U.S. democracy had in fact succeeded.[22] When Edward Snowden, an employee working as a contractor for the National Security Agency, revealed the extent of government surveillance conducted on American citizens without a warrant or specific authorization, many of those same people who had expressed strong support for the Patriot Act expressed their horror at precisely how far government agents had gone to snoop on people who were suspected of no crimes.[23] A robust debate continues to this day as to whether or not Edward Snowden was a "whistle-blower" who deserves to be protected and even rewarded for stealing and disclosing documents or whether he should be subjected to criminal prosecution for violating the law and creating a threat to national security by jeopardizing our intelligence gathering efforts. Unwilling to risk an arrest and trial that could send him to federal prison for years, Snowden fled to Russia. In November 2020, he applied for Russian citizenship.[24]

Testing Premises: Public vs. Private Beliefs

Finally, there are often discrepancies between our public and private beliefs. The values that a culture shares are not always exemplified in the actions of the individuals who comprise a culture. As a society, we abhor racism and bigotry—yet it would be naïve to think that the United States has no racists or bigots. The recent rise of white power groups provides strong evidence that racism and bigotry continue in the U.S.[25] The progress of our contemporary society may have succeeded in partially purging public language and antisocial behavior, but many of the hostile attitudes toward people who are of another race persist. Social actors may have learned acceptable code words with which to express their prejudice. An audience that privately rejects a publicly shared belief is not likely to find appeals to such beliefs compelling. There are cases, by the way, where people find themselves in trouble, not necessarily for the beliefs that they hold but for violating the social rules and disclosing those beliefs. The disclosure brings critical attention to a subject that others would prefer not be so illuminated.

For example, Senator Strom Thurmond experienced a long and remarkable career as a governor and then senator from South Carolina. A staunch segregationist, Thurmond left the Democratic Party to run for president in 1948 as a "Dixiecrat" on an anti-civil rights platform. Eventually, Senator Thurmond became a Republican and continued to serve the people of South Carolina until his retirement from the senate in 2002 at the age of 100. On Senator Thurmond's retirement from the senate, then Republican Senate Majority Leader Trent Lott was effusive in his praise. "I want to say this about my state [Mississippi]: When Strom Thurmond ran for president, we voted for him. We're proud of it. And if the rest of the country had followed our lead, we wouldn't have had all these problems over all these years, either."[26]

Although Senator Lott quickly apologized for his statement and made clear that he was just trying to celebrate Senator Thurmond's long life and service to the nation and not his segregationist platform, the apology was not sufficient to satisfy his critics who did not agree that the accomplishments in the area of civil rights should be referred to as the accumulated "problems over all these years." Senator Lott had himself long opposed virtually all civil rights legislation, but he had previously phrased his opposition in appropriate legalistic policy language. In this public statement, however, he let his guard down. As a result, many believed he revealed his racism. After President George W. Bush weighed in on the controversy, Senator Lott was forced to step down from the post of majority leader.

A similar controversy, but absent the apology, surrounded President Trump's comments following a "Unite the Right" rally that was held in Charlottesville, Virginia, in August of 2017. White nationalists held the protest in an effort to persuade the city to reverse its decision to remove a statue of Confederate General Robert E. Lee. Rally participants chanted anti-Semitic, Nazi-associated phrases, including the declaration, "the Jews will not replace us," and clashed with counter-protesters. A car driven by a right-wing supporter backed into a crowd of counter-protesters killing a woman and injuring several others. Even though the perpetrator was ultimately convicted of murder, President Trump refused to condemn the white supremacists, instead saying: "There were very fine people on both sides." Trump's comments were condemned by many, but he refused to retract them, declaring: "If you look at what I said, you will see that that question was answered perfectly." Trump then went on to praise Robert E. Lee as "a great general," despite the fact that he led the confederate troops in an insurrection against the United States and in an effort to defend slavery.[27] The controversy over his remarks dogged Trump throughout the remainder of his presidency.

Advocates confronting uncertain situations should take pains to support the premises they employ and to use language that is consistent with those premises. Simply stating what one believes to be a widely shared premise may not be enough. Providing real support for a premise and then using that premise as the foundation for the next claim advanced is a preferred way to organize an argument.

EXAMPLES

Examples are specific instances or occurrences of a given phenomenon. They may be detailed or cursory. The advocate may use an example from personal experience (artistic proof) or provide an example from another source (inartistic proof). In chapter 6 we identified the inductive process of using examples to reason to a generalization. In that chapter we discussed four tests for reasoning from examples.

1. Are there a sufficient number of examples offered to support the claim?
2. Are the examples that are selected typical of the category or class to which the arguer is trying to generalize?
3. Are negative examples sufficiently accounted for in the argument?
4. Are the examples that are cited relevant to the claim being advanced?

In addition to these tests, we would admonish advocates to provide whatever details are necessary to gain the audience's adherence. On the one hand, listing several specific examples may enhance the validity of the claim for a given audience. On the other hand, providing fewer but detailed examples (also called *extended illustrations*) can give power to a claim by making it more memorable and by arousing the audience's emotions.

Consider the effect of briefly listing the names of five students who have died in alcohol-related automobile accidents. The use of these examples may be a sufficient basis for a claim that students should not drink and drive, but providing an extended illustration of how one student lost her life may have the same persuasive effect. In addition, hearing the details of the accident may enable the audience to visualize the events, which may stir empathy for the individual. Presenting additional information about the effect of her death on her parents, siblings, and friends may further humanize—and strengthen—the argument by prompting people to recognize the devastating impact that the loss of their own lives would have on people they love.

During the COVID-19 pandemic, for example, newspapers often chose to devote a page or two to identify the people who had lost their lives to the virus. Such coverage went beyond just providing their names, age, and work-life or careers. These stories discussed what they meant to their families, gave insight into their hobbies or quirks, talked about their battle against the disease, and helped readers understand that the lives sacrificed were not merely numbers on a page but rather flesh and blood human beings who will be missed.[28]

Advocates can also bolster the audience's faith in the examples by drawing them from sources the advocate considers credible (inartistic proof). In this way they combine examples and testimony. Some advocates even attempt to emulate statistical methodologies and select examples randomly from the set of possible examples.

STATISTICS

Multiple examples may enhance the likelihood of their acceptance, but time constraints may limit the number of specific cases that may be presented. As a result, advocates may choose to present statistics instead.

Statistics are numeric expressions of examples. There are two basic types of statistics: descriptive and inferential. ***Descriptive statistics*** are numeric representations that present the entire set of instances of a phenomenon. When advocates present, for example, the number of COVID-19 deaths worldwide since the pandemic began, they describe the entire population of victims. Similarly, statistics about the total number of U.S. soldiers killed in the Iraq War, the number of handgun deaths each year, the number of lives lost to opioid overdoses, or the number of motorcyclists who lose their lives in traffic accidents summarize the available data on the deaths that occurred.

Inferential statistics are numeric representations that attempt to infer the properties of a population from inspection of a sample drawn from that population. The advocate who cites public opinion polls reaches conclusions about the general public using the data from the sample. The inferential data is based on a presumably representative sample that was selected. The pollster infers that the views presented by people in the sample accurately represent the views of the entire public.

Testing Statistics: Methods of Gathering

Both kinds of statistics are useful as proof, and both have potential weaknesses. Whether advocates are presenting their own statistics or those from other sources, meeting certain tests enhances the likelihood that critical audiences will find the data convincing.

First, it may be important to know how the statistics were gathered. Understanding the methodology employed in counting the cases may reveal weaknesses in the evidence. One technique for gathering statistics relies on individuals reporting instances of the phenomenon. This method can lead to misleading statistics, due to what is called reporting bias. If there is a motivation to make the numbers look "good," by having fewer cases or by having more cases, it can result in unreliable statistics. For instance, if there are disincentives for reporting instances of the phenomenon, it can result in artificially low numbers of cases or *underreporting*. For example, how much child abuse was there in the United States last year? Law enforcement and social service agencies compile the number of cases reported to them, but are all instances reported? Unfortunately, many abused children do not come forward, and most abusers, their partners, and their relatives are reluctant to report the abuse. School teachers, school nurses, and pediatricians are required by law to report suspected cases of abuse, but are the official counts of abused children an accurate reflection of the actual number of cases of abuse? Obviously not, since underreporting is inevitable. Thus, the true number of abused children is certainly far larger than the official statistics indicate. This underreporting was almost certainly worse than normal during 2020. The COVID-19 pandemic closed many schools around the country, decreasing the contact with outsiders who could potentially notice the bruises or other signs of abuse on children left in the care of harried parents and caregivers who were overly stressed and perhaps facing financial ruin and eviction because they lost their jobs.[29]

There is also evidence to suggest that when the COVID-19 pandemic was first detected in Wuhan, China, local government officials there deliberately underreported the number of cases. Leaked documents revealed that "officials in the Hubei province, where the virus is believed to have originated, failed to report thousands of new daily cases. On February 10—when China reported 2,478 new cases—officials privately recorded 5,918 new cases, more than double the published figure."[30] The underreporting of the cases may have occurred due to bureaucratic hurdles, a lack of trust between local and central government officials, and the fact that local authorities were slow in getting a handle on the seriousness of the disease and how it spread. The central government in Beijing eventually issued a public warning that it was essential that all local governments become more transparent in reporting all new coronavirus cases and deaths to Beijing.[31] The failure to institute such transparency sooner did have consequences, however. Had the news of the serious threat posed by the new virus been shared more completely and quickly, it is possible that other nations around the world would have reacted more urgently to prevent the global pandemic.

There may also be incentives for *overreporting* cases of a phenomenon. During the Vietnam War, U.S. soldiers were told to report the number of enemy soldiers they killed in action. The system was created for monitoring areas with the most enemy activity and making sure military resources flowed to those areas. Unfortunately, however, individual field commanders saw these statistics as an invitation to inflate the numbers of enemy killed both to attract resources and as evidence of their effectiveness. Critics argued that the military's desire to show that the United States was winning the war resulted in exaggerated body counts. Thus, when the statistical method is used to collect individuals' reports, the motive of those doing the reporting must be considered.

In addition to problems with underreporting and overreporting, some statistics are simply **not gathered**. The summer of 2020 brought the nation's attention to actions by the police that resulted in the deaths of Blacks. The 1994 Violent Crime Control and Law Enforcement Act required that the attorneys general "acquire data about the use of excessive force by law enforcement officers" and for the Justice Department to publish an annual summary, which has not been done.[32] The FBI collects statistics on justifiable homicides by the police and on arrest-related deaths, but the statistics are unreliable because they are based on voluntary self-reporting by police departments. There is no requirement that fatal shootings by police be reported to a national clearinghouse. In 2015, journalists at *The Guardian* and *The Washington Post* began tracking the number of civilians shot and killed by police.[33] The *Post* found that FBI numbers undercounted deaths from police shootings by more than half. Through September 2021, the *Post* has documented more than 5,000 fatal shootings by studying news accounts, social media postings, and police reports.

Similarly, before they were asked to dispense COVID-19 vaccinations, pharmacists across the nation reported being overworked and worried that medical mistakes could cost lives.[34] Yet, we cannot really compare pharmaceutical errors across the years to see if there are more errors now than in the past because the reporting of errors is voluntary. There is no required, systematic reporting of such problems.[35]

It is not just public agencies such as child welfare, the police, or the Pentagon that under- and overreport statistical measures. Many people when asked how much they exercise or how long they studied to prepare for a test tend to overreport their activity levels. The point is, it would be a good idea to be somewhat skeptical of statistics if the people gathering them have a motive to misrepresent them.

Inferential statistics rely on descriptions of a subset of the population and then infer that what is true of the sample is also true of the entire population. The method by which this subset is selected is consequently very important. The sample must be representative of its parent group, or else any general conclusions drawn will not be valid. Thus, most researchers use random samples. A ***random sample*** is defined as a sample in which each element of the larger group has an equal and independent probability of being selected.

Let's assume we wanted to discover how the students of a particular university felt their student body president was doing in office. We could question all of the students enrolled in the university (a descriptive statistic). This would clearly be the best method because it would account for the opinion of every student. It would also, of course, be a very difficult method because it would involve a very large number of opinions, and some students might not be located or might not respond to the survey. A more likely method then would be to randomly poll students in such a way as to assure that all students have an equal chance of being included in the study.

One technique for assuring an equal chance to be questioned is ***simple random sampling***. Researchers using this method employ a random numbers table—a list of numbers randomly generated by a computer. For example, by assigning all of the students on campus a number, we could then use the random numbers table to survey a predetermined number of students. If the number of students in our sample is sufficiently large, we are relatively certain we will have a sample that roughly mirrors the opinions of the student body.

A second way researchers generate random samples is by using an ***interval sampling*** system. With interval sampling we might construct our sample of students by including every twentieth student on the roster. As we randomly determine where to start choosing the students, each student will have an equal chance of participating.

Equality of participation, however, does not guarantee that we will have a representative distribution of graduate students, undergraduate students, part-time students, international students, males or females, and so forth. To make sure that such groups are included in numbers proportionate to their size, we could use a modification of the random and interval procedures called ***stratified sampling.*** Instead of sampling from the entire student population, stratified sampling divides the population into specified groups to be included in the sample. Once the population has been stratified, we could select students from each stratum using either the simple random number technique or the interval technique. The size of each stratum as a percentage of the total population determines the number of students selected from each group.

Polls are a specific type of inferential statistics. Professional pollsters and researchers employ sophisticated sampling techniques to assure the reliability of their results. When they report their findings, they usually identify the ***margin of error*** as well. Gallup polls of voter preference during presidential campaigns, for example, will acknowledge that their statistics could be off by 2, 3, or 4 percent. Thus, if a poll reports a margin of error plus or minus 3 percent, a candidate that a poll shows as having the support of 52 percent of the electorate may actually have the support of as few as 49 percent of the electorate or as many as 55 percent. Obviously, that is a significant difference. Polls that do not reveal their margin of error should be viewed with suspicion.

Respondents who change their minds or who do not vote further complicate presidential preference polls. A poll is, after all, only a snapshot in time, and public opinion in the United States is profoundly evanescent. As a result, pollsters search for ways to measure the intensity of support for a particular candidate. They generally ask respondents how likely they are to vote in the next election. Historically, only 15 to 27 percent of eligible voters cast ballots in local elections.[36] In contrast, the 2020 presidential election had the best turnout in more than 50 years, as approximately 62 percent of eligible voters cast ballots.[37] Although it is great to see that more voters are participating in our elections, it is noteworthy that more than a third of our citizens did not vote. Predicting who will and who will not cast a ballot remains a challenge for pollsters. The accuracy of the presidential polls in 2016 and 2020 was somewhat diminished from previous years because the pollsters had difficulty securing a reliable sample of likely voters. The Pew Research Center, for example, reported that securing an adequate representation of likely Republican voters has become more difficult. "Survey participation has long been linked to individuals' levels of education and social trust. Now that the GOP is doing better attracting voters with lower levels of education and, according to some analysts, doing better than in the past attracting low trust adults, Republican participation in surveys is waning, increasing reliance on weighting as a corrective."[38]

One should also be wary that many surveys that appear to be carefully constructed public opinion polls are not. For example, many periodicals and websites will survey and report the opinions of their readers. The use of such polls as evidence of what the population believes is profoundly unreliable, however, because the survey participants are self-selected. Only those who read the periodicals or go to the websites are asked to respond to the questions—and only those who are highly motivated to express their opinions are likely to exert the effort to respond. Thus, the conclusions drawn in such surveys suffer from self-selection bias and may bear little resemblance to the opinions of the overall population.

Similarly, internet polls have become increasingly popular on television and radio shows. Many television networks report poll results nightly. In the past, some networks have asked viewers for instance, to offer their opinions about who won the presidential debates. Yet, only those with access to the internet, who watched the show, and who bothered to take the time to respond, are included in such polls. Special interest groups, such as political parties, activist groups, or lobbying groups (e.g., the National Rifle Association or Moveon.org) have actively coordinated how their members will participate in the internet polls. Naturally, excessive participation by any segment of the population distorts poll results.

The results of such polls are thus not scientific because they do not approximate the views of the overall population. Broadcasters often mention this, yet they continue to cite the results of these polls—sometimes treating the results as legitimate news stories. If the results are essentially meaningless, we wonder why they bother. Perhaps it is because they believe that their audiences enjoy participating in such polls and that conducting them makes their broadcasts more interactive and builds viewer loyalty. It is unfortunate, however, that such polls often mislead the public.

Testing Statistics: Defining Categories

In addition to potential problems that might arise with the ways in which the statistics are gathered, there is a second and equally significant issue of how research categories are defined. If the categories are not exact or precise, the counts of the numbers of cases falling within each category will be inexact.

When researchers assign particular occurrences to categories, they often must make judgments about those occurrences. Sometimes the categories are forthright—"alive" or "dead" would be such categories. Yet, there are often gray areas that make categorization difficult. For example, "employed" or "unemployed" appear to be fairly discreet categories requiring little interpretation by the researcher, but appearances can be misleading. If you are on a payroll and your salary is reported to the government, you are clearly someone who will be classified as employed. If you have been laid off and you are collecting unemployment compensation, which requires that you be actively looking for a job, you will be classified as unemployed. There are multiple other categories, however: unemployment compensation could have expired; someone could have quit looking for a job because they were discouraged at not being able to find one; another person may not actively look for a job but would accept a position that accommodates a school schedule; another person picks up "odd jobs" for a day or so at a time as they become available. In all of these situations, the individual is not easily categorized as either "employed" or "unemployed"—none of these situations matches how the government chooses to define "unemployed."

As another example, we all know that there are many instances of sexual harassment in the workplace. But how many cases are there? Experts, victims, and perpetrators may hold very different interpretations of what constitutes harassment. Some people would see harassment in behaviors that others might see as only minor flirtations or boorish behavior. Given the differences, how does one count the number of cases? Some studies cite the number of grievances or complaints filed, but that does not address unreported cases go or unsubstantiated complaints. So how many cases of sexual harassment occur in the workplace? The statistics and estimates, as might be expected, vary widely and may be a topic for spirited arguments.

Testing Statistics: The Time Frame

The third test of statistics relates to *time frame*. The point at which one begins and ends a time period under statistical analysis can directly influence what the statistics will reveal. At the beginning of this chapter we discussed the issue of climate change. Some argue that the climate is significantly warming, while others suggest that it might not be and that we are only witnessing temperature variations that are within the range of previous annual averages. Some argued, for example, that the Northern Hemisphere experienced cooling from the 1940s to the 1970s.[39] Advocates who either began or ended their statistical analysis by drawing evidence focused on those decades might succeed in convincing an uncritical audience that the Earth's climate was actually cooling. But researchers who look at longer periods of time, for example studying temperature averages over the last century, might find ample evidence to support the theories of global warming.

In chapter 6, we discussed the time frame issue with regard to the AIDS crisis. When the AIDS epidemic first surfaced, some medical experts mistakenly believed that only some HIV patients would develop full-blown AIDS. This occurred because it can take many years before the disease ultimately claims its victims. Then, after some of the new drug therapies to treat AIDS were introduced, there were others who claimed that AIDS could be managed and need no longer be considered a-fatal disease. A functional cure describes a process through which HIV could be kept in check without using antiretroviral drugs. A functional cure could be described as a permanent remission in which the virus could not cause illness even if traces of the virus remained in the body—in contrast to a vaccine that would fully eliminate HIV from the body. Françoise Barré-Sinoussi, the Nobel Prize laureate and co-discoverer of HIV, in 2014 voiced the opinion that a functional cure could be reached but specified no time frame. Noted HIV researcher Bruce Walker in 2021 suggests that a functional cure is unlikely and that vast gaps in understanding about HIV remain.[40]

Historically Americans have had faith in science and in scientific methods, although this faith is now waning for at least some individuals. Typically, statistical data is very compelling evidence, but many audiences understand that statistics can also be used to mislead—captured in the adage "There are lies, damned lies, and statistics." Skilled advocates recognize that, although susceptible to distortion, statistics remain compelling argumentative tools. They do not hesitate to use them or to provide as much detail as possible about the methods used to gather and categorize the data, as well as the time frame of the analysis. Combining statistics with specific examples can make for a compelling argument for many audiences.

Testing Statistics: Abusing Percentages

Some statistics are not particularly helpful until they are put into a context. Knowing how many aggravated assaults occurred in Plano, Texas, in 2020 (230) does not help us to know if Plano is a safe or dangerous city until we compare that number with the population (285,190).[41] The number of assaults per 1,000 inhabitants (.08 in Plano) is a figure that permits meaningful comparisons with national data. In 2020, there were 2.9 aggravated assaults per 1,000 people in the United States.[42] The comparison provides a basis for individuals to decide whether Plano is safe or dangerous.

Crime statistics are informative but can also mislead because so many measures can be combined or omitted without sufficient explanation. For example, advocates might cite data that overlooks or misrepresents the distinction between violent and nonviolent crimes, or between city, suburban and rural crime rates. There are also, of course, different types of dangerous crimes such as murders, assaults, rapes, robberies, etc. People's impressions of large cities are also influenced by narratives about dangerousness. Chicago, for example, is often characterized as a dangerous city because of the number of homicides. However, it was not in the top 25 most violent cities in 2020. The following cities, in order, were described as the five most dangerous: Memphis, Detroit, St. Louis, Little Rock, and South Bend.[43] Do any of the entries surprise you?

Similarly, percentages are not meaningful unless the base number is also known. So, for example, a 10 percent increase in the cost of tuition at one university could be fewer dollars than a 5 percent increase in tuition at another university. If the previous year's tuition was $50,000 at one institution, a 5 percent increase would be $2,500. If the previous year's tuition at another institution was $12,000, a 10 percent increase would be $1,200. If an advocate made an argument that referenced only the percentage increases, the grounds would be misleading because the base numbers are so different. Those who evaluate argumentative claims must be wary of simplistic comparisons of such statistics.

TESTIMONY

There is a fourth type of grounds utilized by advocates. ***Testimony*** consists of observations and judgments by the advocate or sources cited by the advocate. Testimony may be descriptive or interpretive. ***Descriptive testimony*** refers to the observation of supposedly factual (verifiable) information. ***Interpretive testimony*** involves making judgments or drawing inferences from the facts in discussion. In each case a similar set of tests can be applied.

Before accepting an advocate's arguments, critical audiences evaluate the credibility of the advocate and of the authorities cited by the advocate. ***Credibility*** refers to the audience's assessment of the competence and trustworthiness of the source. This is a contemporary interpretation of what Aristotle called ethos (mentioned at the beginning of the chapter). It is important to emphasize that sources do not possess credibility; rather, audiences attribute varying levels of credibility to them. Thus, a source may be quite credible to one audience and wholly lacking in credibility to another. An arguer could attempt to support an argument, for example, by citing a statement by conservative commentator Sean Hannity. The source may have credibility for conservative listeners, but for a liberal audience the mere mention of Hannity's name might be akin to waving a red cape in front of a bull. Not only would the liberal audience be unlikely to find Mr. Hannity a credible source but also the choice of that particular source would diminish the arguer's credibility as well.

Testing Testimony: Competence

As mentioned above, the first dimension of credibility is ***competence***. There are three ways to think about competence.

First, ***capability*** refers to whether the source of the testimony was able to form the observation. Have you ever heard someone claim to have seen something when the person could not have done so? Did you doubt the veracity of their claim? If so, you applied the test of capability. In a courtroom, a witness might testify he heard someone verbally threaten a victim. If, however, it can be established that the witness was not even in the room at the time, then he could not be presumed capable of having heard the threat. If it is established that he was in the room but it was a very noisy and he was very far from the exchange, his capability of hearing what was said could be questioned.

Correspondence is a second test of competence. Does what the advocate stated accurately correspond to the historical record? Descriptions of facts are potentially verifiable, and one of the benefits of smart phones and tablets is the nearly instant ability to ascertain if a statement of fact is accurate or not. Certainly, advocates sometimes make claims that do not correspond with any available evidence. Perhaps no example is more poignant than President Trump's insistence that he won the 2020 election and that only a huge conspiracy kept him from gaining a second term. Susan Glasser wrote about the 46-minute address that Trump posted to Facebook on December 2, almost a month after the election.

> One of Trump's biggest obsessions is with a voting-machine company known as Dominion. Trump and his lawyers claim that Dominion, although it is owned by a New York-based private-equity firm, was somehow in league with the deceased dictator of Venezuela, Hugo Chávez, in a fantastical plot to steal the Presidency. In his speech, Trump explained that "we have a company that's very suspect," and that "with a turn of a dial, with a change of a chip," his votes could disappear on its systems, which are so confusing that "nobody understands" how they work, "including in many cases the people that run them." Trump elaborated that the company had given many donations to Democrats, that its "glitches" were numerous, and it was only "the tip of the iceberg" of wrongdoing. He even suggested that the Dominion machines were secretly controlled from overseas. How? Who knows? Here's his quote in full: "And, frankly, when you look at who's running the company, who's in charge, who owns it, which we don't know—where are the votes counted, which we think are counted in foreign countries, not in the United States."[44]

Neither the president, nor Rudy Giuliani his personal attorney, nor his Attorney General William Barr, nor FBI Director Christopher Wray, nor his director of cyber-security Christopher Krebs who oversaw the elections offered any substantiation for these wild claims, but the president continued to circulate them.[45] Dominion eventually sued Rudy Giuliani and Sidney Powell, both attorneys for Trump, and the FOX News Network for "making demonstrably false claims" and for "defamation that damaged the company's reputation" in circulating the "disinformation campaign." The lawsuit seeks damages of $1.3 billion. At this time, the lawsuit is still pending in the courts, and the company's attorneys have said more suits could be forthcoming, including against Trump himself.[46] In June 2021, Rudy Giuliani lost his license to practice law in New York when a New York court ruled that he "made demonstrably false and misleading statements" in public and in court while fighting the results of the 2020 election on behalf of President Trump.[47]

Sadly, this continuing drip of conspiracy messages and misinformation did have the effect of decreasing trust and confidence in our elections and in the democratic process. Polls suggested that as many as 70 to 80 percent of Republicans believed that something was amiss in the election results. Although this may be primarily a reflection of political partisanship and polarization rather than genuine conviction, there is a clear danger that it could have lasting consequences.[48] One consequence is that many states under Republican control took a series of measures under the guise of eliminating potential fraudulent voting that will make it much more difficult for people, especially poor people and people of color, to cast ballots in future elections.[49]

Source ability is a third measure of competence. Ability may be the result of education, training, or life experience. Most Americans believe, for example, that trained physicians have more ability to diagnose illnesses than do witch doctors. Why? Because anyone can claim to be a witch doctor, but physicians are required to complete years of specialized education and training. Does the fact that a physician finished a rigorous program of formal education guarantee that the physician will be correct and the witch doctor will be wrong? Not necessarily, but most American audiences will likely find testimony provided by a physician more credible than that provided by a witch doctor. Of course, physicians may know less than witch doctors about the effectiveness of some herbal medicines found in nature.

This last point reminds us of the importance of the concept of *field dependence* and competence. Experts are only authoritative in their own fields. One of the more controversial figures in the COVID-19 pandemic was Dr. Scott Atlas, an advisor to President Trump, a FOX News commentator, and a Fellow at the Hoover Institute, a conservative think-tank affiliated with Stanford University. Atlas achieved significant influence in the White House by articulating views that were closely aligned with Trump's, even though his remarks were frequently at odds with those of the leadership of the Centers for Disease Control and epidemiologists/public health experts such as Dr. Deborah Birx and Dr. Anthony Fauci. For example, Atlas declared that schools should be reopened, sports should be resumed, and that face masks were not necessary. He criticized the coronavirus restrictions issued by state governors and urged residents to "rise up" against them. His statements were deemed so controversial that a group of faculty members from Stanford University urged the university to condemn his misleading statements because "His actions have undermined and threatened public health even as countless lives have been lost to COVID-19."[50] It is noteworthy that Dr. Atlas was trained as a radiologist and not as an epidemiologist. Had he not strayed so far from his lane of expertise, he might not have become such a controversial figure forced to resign his post.

Celebrities testifying outside of their fields pose an interesting illustration of this issue of competence. If, for example, Tiger Woods is used in a testimonial advertisement to talk about the benefits of a particular brand of golf ball or golf clubs, we might afford him credibility. If, however, Tiger Woods is asked to give a testimonial advertisement for a particular brand of automobile, should he be accorded greater competence or credibility than any other figure? Interestingly, such questions may also loom in contemporary political discussions. Many Hollywood celebrities hold strong partisan political opinions. Should their beliefs and convictions be accorded any more credibility than your own beliefs? Does success on the screen or at the box office translate into evidence of issue knowledge or political wisdom or judgment?

Competence need not require extensive training. Life experiences can make people experts within a given field. If we wanted to know what it was like to be homeless in America, for instance, we might consult scholars who had written on the subject. We might also find that the testimony of a homeless person would not only be more authoritative but it might also have greater impact and spark far more empathy and compassion in audiences. One might even try to live as a homeless person for a period of time to experience what it is like to sleep on the sidewalk. It is important to understand, though, that a personal experiment with homelessness does not truly replicate the experiences of the homeless. The experiment will end, and the advocate will return home to resume a life far different from that of a truly homeless person.

Testing Testimony: Trustworthiness

Another dimension of credibility is *trustworthiness*, which is an audience's assessment of the integrity of the source. Source integrity concerns the source's motives. Is the source willing to report his or her observations and judgments fairly? Sometimes sources have something to gain from what they report. This may influence what they say, causing source bias.

When Congress holds hearings before enacting legislation, they invite experts to present their views on the issue at hand. If the issue is, for example, automobile safety, experts from the automobile manufacturing companies will be called to testify. Their statements, however, will reflect corporate interests. Thus, Congress may also call for testimony from insurance companies, consumer groups, and independent scientific researchers. While their testimony might also reflect personal agendas, the net effect is that Congressional representatives hear a variety of conflicting views, which they can evaluate to make up their minds regarding how they will vote on proposed legislation.

Testimony of advocates or their sources that contain self-serving statements or bias is less reliable than testimony that seems not to be motivated by personal needs or bias. In fact, many audiences consider *reluctant testimony*, testimony given grudgingly because it does not serve the motives of the source, as the most reliable kind. Individuals who step forward and admit misdoings are generally considered more credible, for example, than those who admit culpability for something only after they have been confronted with incontrovertible evidence.

Evidence that demonstrates *internal consistency*—free from self-contradiction—is usually considered more reliable than testimony containing contradictions. For example, the police often use internal consistency to evaluate the integrity of a suspect. If a suspect changes details when retelling a story, the police will consider the inconsistency as evidence of duplicity. Parents have learned to apply the same tests. If they think their children may be lying, they may ask them to repeat their stories to see if the retelling reveals some flaw or error.

The ability of advocates to provide several concurring sources is likely to encourage an audience toward a positive evaluation of the argument. This demonstration of *external consistency*—showing that the testimony is consistent with the testimony of others—strengthens the credibility of each cited source, since none of them are alone in their observations. Corroboration by other experts increases the trustworthiness of the evidence.

Verifiability is another component of trustworthiness. Sources that cannot be verified because they are neither available nor properly identified are not likely to be given much credibility. In the legal field, hearsay evidence (testimony given by witnesses concerning what they heard others say) is, with few exceptions, considered inadmissible because, in part, the statements are not verifiable and the opposing side has no opportunity to challenge them.

A final test of the trustworthiness of testimony is *recency*. Some advocates and audiences assume that the date of testimony is critical to its value. But the importance of recency depends on the nature of the testimony and the issue under consideration. Some evidence is outdated almost as soon as it is presented. For example, consider the win-loss record of your favorite major league baseball team. You need to know the team's record on the day you are using it as evidence because it will likely change the next day. Other testimony seems perpetually valuable. For example, quotations from Aristotle generalizing about the principles of persuasion and argumentation are still relevant today. The test of recency is most usefully applied when the advocate or the audience is asked to consider whether anything has happened between the date of the evidence and when it is used to support an argument that might make that testimony invalid. If nothing has changed in a significant way, then the observations offered in the testimony are sufficiently recent to be relevant to deciding the issue under consideration.

On some issues, of course, events change very quickly, making recency an especially important concern. Scientific, technical, medical, or economic issues are very dynamic, and an arguer has an especially important responsibility to present recent testimony. Issues involving moral, ethical, or philosophical testimony are probably less dependent on recency because these issues are less dynamic and less driven by events.

An interesting question about recency involves historical testimony. As we know, new histories are written every day. Is the history of the Civil War written by the soldiers, statesmen, or citizens who may actually have experienced the conflict more reliable than a history of the Civil War written by contemporary academics plowing back through the archives? Certainly, an argument could be made for the value of both histories. The firsthand accounts would be informative and would create a real sense of the emotion and tenor of the times. On the other hand, would such writers be able to judge the events with detachment, or might they instead present their own conduct in the most favorable light? Contemporary scholars are temporally removed from the events that occurred during the Civil War. Would they be likely to apply today's standards of behavior and morality to such events, perhaps doing a disservice to our genuine understanding of the times? Indeed, differences of opinion over the value of recency may prompt important arguments. Consider contemporary confrontations about Civil War memorials or the names of buildings on college campuses.

Of course, there are other issues that may affect the credibility of testimony. Research reveals that audiences are likely to view speakers whose arguments are well organized more favorably than those whose presentations seem scattered or disorganized. Thus, the clarity of a presentation, the structure of the text, and the degree to which an audience can reason along with the source will all influence the effectiveness of the message. Also, testimony that uses strong, dynamic, and active language communicates that the source has confidence in what is claimed. This also influences how testimony is perceived by audiences.

Testimony delivered by advocates who demonstrate care and concern about their audiences and about their audience's well-being will also be accorded more trust. Advocates who care about and respect their audiences do not try to seduce or coerce them through arguments. Instead, such arguers have nothing to hide. They are explicit and clear, and they allow the best evidence to be revealed and evaluated. Arguers who try to mislead, deceive, or play games with their audiences on one issue may find themselves embroiled in a credibility damaging controversy that spills out into other issues. President George W. Bush and former Secretary of State Colin Powell were accused by many to have misrepresented the case for the Second Gulf War in Iraq by falsely claiming that there was verifiable evidence that Iraq possessed weapons of mass destruction.[51] Of course, some would argue that telling the truth meant more to audiences two decades ago than it does today.[52] We would hope that respect for truth telling is renewed over the next few years.

The Intersectionality of Testimony and Examples or Statistics

With the exception of premises (which arguers might assume are shared by audiences and therefore remain unstated), advocates typically introduce the grounds for an argumentative claim. If an arguer provides an example, whether the person making the argument created the example (an artistic proof) or cited someone else (an inartistic proof), the tests of both example and testimony come into play. Similarly, if an advocate provides statistics, the tests of statistics and testimony are relevant. To be effective before a critical consumer of argument, testimony involving examples must pass both sets of tests. The same is true for testimony that draws upon statistical claims.

The Delivery of Testimony

Research has long supported the fact that audiences are more inclined to grant adherence to claims advanced by advocates who are perceived as likable and dynamic. If advocates seem personable and friendly, audiences may make allowances for them and grant them greater credibility than they might otherwise. Also, if audiences see an advocate as similar to them—sharing their interests and concerns—they will be more likely to accept the advocate's statements as credible.[53] Think about how you respond to your friends' statements or arguments as opposed to those of people you hardly know or, worse yet, dislike. We tend to find the claims of those whom we like more compelling.

Finally, advocates who are excited about their claims and animated in their presentation send us cues that suggest they believe in their arguments. These dimensions of a speaker's sincerity reinforce perceptions of integrity. Of course, we are generally suspicious of those who attempt to conceal the weakness of their arguments by resorting to an artificially dynamic delivery. Consider, for example, the overly polished, smooth-talking salesperson. Dynamism must be measured so that it does not boomerang and become counterproductive.

SUMMARY

In this chapter we have considered the grounds used by advocates when they make claims. We identified four specific types of grounds, premises, examples, statistics, and testimony. We pointed out that each type of evidence is subject to tests to determine the likelihood that critical audiences will accept or reject it. Critical decision makers will consider the grounds presented before they render a judgment on the advocacy of others. Advocates seeking to maximize the effectiveness of their arguments will consider what kinds of grounds are most likely to sway their audience.

KEY TERMS

artistic proof	logos	ritual
competence	margin of error	statistics
capability	overreporting	descriptive
correspondence	pathos	inferential
source ability	personal knowledge	symbols
credibility	premise	testimony
cultural knowledge	presumption	descriptive
ethos	random sample	interpretive
examples	interval sampling	time frame
external consistency	simple random sampling	trustworthiness
grounds	stratified sampling	underreporting
inartistic proof	recency	verifiability
internal consistency	reluctant testimony	

ACTIVITIES

1. Examine an argumentative artifact. Once you have ascertained the claim, determine whether the grounds provided are artistic, inartistic, or both. Next, identify the kinds of grounds that are presented: premises, examples, statistics, or testimony. Then apply the appropriate tests to determine whether you find the grounds convincing.

2. Find a public opinion poll in a newspaper or online. Examine the polling sample, the questions asked, and the definitions of the statistical categories. Does the statistical evidence pass the appropriate tests?

3. Examine a speech by a public figure. Identify the types of data the speaker employed and apply the appropriate tests to determine whether or not you find the evidence compelling.

4. Look through a popular magazine and locate three advertisements. What kinds of grounds do the advertisers utilize? Apply the appropriate tests to determine whether you find the grounds compelling.

5. Select a public controversy of interest to you. Take a position on this controversy and then find grounds drawn from each of the four types to support your position.

RECOMMENDED READINGS

Aristotle, *The Rhetoric and The Poetics of Aristotle,* trans. W. Rhys Roberts and Ingram Bywater (New York: The Modern Library, 1954, 1984).

Best, Joel, *Damned Lies and Statistics: Untangling Numbers from the Media, Politicians, and Activists,* Updated ed. (Berkeley: University of California Press, 2012).

Bruschke, John, "Argument and Evidence Evaluation: A Call for Scholars to Engage Contemporary Public Debates," *Argumentation and Advocacy* 49 (2012): 59–75.

Inch, Edward S. and Kristin H. Tudor, *Critical Thinking and Communication: The Use of Reason in Argument,* 7th ed. (Englewood Cliffs, NJ: Pearson, 2014).

Rieke, Richard D., Malcolm O. Sillars, and Tarla Rai Peterson, *Argumentation and Critical Decision Making,* 8th ed. (Englewood Cliffs, NJ: Pearson, 2013).

Rybacki, Karyn C. and Donald J. Rybacki, *Advocacy and Opposition: An Introduction to Argumentation,* 7th ed. (Englewood Cliffs, NJ: Pearson, 2012).

Schiappa, Edward and John P. Nordin, *Argumentation: Keeping Faith with Reason* (Boston: Pearson, 2014).
Walton, Douglas, *Methods of Argumentation* (New York: Cambridge University Press, 2013).
Zarefsky, David, *The Practice of Argumentation* (New York: Cambridge University Press, 2019).
Zarefsky, David, *Rhetorical Perspectives on Argumentation* (Switzerland: Springer International, 2014).

ENDNOTES

[1] Lisa Friedman, "What Is the Green New Deal?" *The New York Times,* February 21, 2019. https://www.nytimes.com/2019/02/21/climate/green-new-deal-questions-answers.html

[2] Ibid.

[3] For example, see Andrew C. Revkin and Katharine Q. Seelye, "Report by the E.P.A. Leaves Out Data in Climate Change," *The New York Times,* June 19, 2003.

[4] Robin McKie, "Attacks Paid for By Big Business are 'Driving Science into a Dark Era,'" *The Guardian,* February 18, 2012. https://www.theguardian.com/science/2012/feb/19/science-scepticism-usdomesticpolicy

[5] *The Rhetoric of Aristotle,* trans. Lane Cooper (Englewood Cliffs, NJ: Prentice-Hall, 1932), 8.

[6] To learn more about how theorists have distinguished between personal and cultural knowledge, see: Michael Polanyi, *Personal Knowledge: Towards a Post-Critical Philosophy,* Enlarged ed. (Chicago: University of Chicago Press, 2015); and Lloyd F. Bitzer, "Rhetoric and Public Knowledge," in Don M. Burks, Ed., *Rhetoric, Philosophy, and Literature* (West Lafayette, IN: Purdue University Press, 1978), 67–93.

[7] For an interesting discussion of this topic, see Clifford Geertz, *The Interpretation of Cultures* (New York: Basic Books, 1973).

[8] For interesting discussions of the importance of rituals, see: Mircea Eliade, *The Myth of the Eternal Return: Cosmos and History* (Princeton: Princeton University Press, 2015); and Joseph Campbell, *Myths We Live By* (New York: Bantam Books, 1972).

[9] "Changing Attitudes on Same-Sex Marriage," *Pew Research Center,* May 14, 2019. https://www.pewforum.org/fact-sheet/changing-attitudes-on-gay-marriage/

[10] Sarah Kuta, "There are Two Americas and Age Is the Divider," *Chicago Booth Review,* June 9, 2020. https://review.chicagobooth.edu/economics/2020/article/there-are-two-americas-and-age-divider

[11] Ibid.

[12] "Globalization," *Stanford Encyclopedia of Philosophy,* June 21, 2002, updated November 5, 2018. https://plato.stanford.edu/entries/globalization/

[13] Hatice Kavaslaan, Annette Hohenberger, Hilmi Demir, Simon Hall, and Mike Oaksford, "Cross-Cultural Differences in Informal Argumentation: Norms, Inductive Biases and Evidentiality," *Journal of Cognition and Culture* 18 (2018): 358–389. https://brill.com/view/journals/jocc/18/3-4/article-p358_7.xml?language=en

[14] Two prominent conservative academics who advanced such claims are: Alan Bloom, *The Closing of the American Mind,* 25th anniversary ed. (New York: Simon and Schuster, 1987, 2012); and E. D. Hirsch, *Cultural Literacy: What Every American Needs to Know* (Boston: Houghton Mifflin, 1987).

[15] For an excellent discussion of the value of multicultural education see: Dana L. Powell and Robert G. Powell, *Classroom Communication and Diversity: Enhancing Instructional Practice,* 3rd ed. (New York: Routledge, 2016).

[16] Sabrina G. Anwah, "What Does Diversity Mean to Small Businesses?" *The Balance,* February 8, 2021. https://www.thebalance.com/cultural-diversity-3306201

[17] Walter R. Fisher, "Reaffirmation and Subversion of the American Dream," *Quarterly Journal of Speech* 59 (1973): 160–167.

[18] Peter Schmidt, "Supreme Court Upholds Affirmative Action in College Admissions," *Chronicle of Higher Education,* June 23, 2003.

[19] Adam Liptak, "Court Backs Michigan on Affirmative Action," *New York Times,* April 22, 2014. https://www.nytimes.com/2014/04/23/us/supreme-court-michigan-affirmative-action-ban.html

[20] Anemona Hartocollis, "Justice Dept. Accuses Yale of Discrimination in the Application Process," *The New York Times,* August 13, 2020. https://www.nytimes.com/2020/08/13/us/yale-discrimination.html

[21] Rachel Treisman, "Justice Department Drops Race Discrimination Lawsuit Against Yale University," *NPR.* February 3, 2021. https://www.npr.org/2021/02/03/963666724/justice-department-drops-race-discrimination-lawsuit-against-yale-university

[22] For an excellent discussion of the conflicting opinions see: Richard C. Leone and Greg Anrig, Jr., Eds., *The War on Our Freedoms: Civil Liberties in an Age of Terrorism* (New York: Public Affairs, 2003).

23. Ewen Macaskill and Gabriel Dance, "NSA Files Decoded: What the Revelations Mean to You," *The Guardian*, November 1, 2013. https://www.theguardian.com/world/interactive/2013/nov/01/snowden-nsa-files-surveillance-revelations-decoded
24. William Adkins, "Edward Snowden Seeks Russian Citizenship," *Politico,* November 2, 2020. https://www.politico.eu/article/edward-snowden-seeks-russia-citizenship/
25. Ramtin Arablouei and Rund Abdelfathah, "Throughline: The Rise of the Modern White Power Movement," *NPR*, January 25, 2021. https://www.npr.org/2021/01/25/960253858/throughline-the-rise-of-the-modern-white-power-movement
26. Carl Hulse, "Lott's Praise for Thurmond Echoed His Words of 1980." *The New York Times,* December 11, 2002, sec. A, p. 24.
27. Jordyn Phelps, "Trump Defends 2017 'Very Fine People' Comments, Calls Robert E. Lee 'a Great General,'" *ABC News,* April 26, 2019. https://abcnews.go.com/Politics/trump-defends-2017-fine-people-comments-calls-robert/story?id=62653478
28. For a background on the coverage see: "Those We've Lost," *The New York Times,* November 30, 2020. https://www.nytimes.com/interactive/2020/obituaries/people-died-coronavirus-obituaries.html
29. Sanchari Sinha Dutta, "250,000 Cases of Child Abuse or Neglect May Have Gone Unreported in U.S. COVID Pandemic," *News: Medical Life Sciences,* November 12, 2020. https://www.news-medical.net/news/20201112/250000-cases-of-child-abuse-or-neglect-may-have-gone-unreported-in-US-COVID-pandemic.aspx
30. Thomas Colson, "Leaked Documents Reveal China Severely Underreported Coronavirus Cases as the Pandemic Spread," *Business Insider,* December 1, 2020. https://www.businessinsider.com/china-underreported-covid-19-infections-cnn-report-2020-12
31. Nectar Gan, "China's Premier Warns Local Officials Not to Hide New Coronavirus Infections," *CNN,* March 25, 2020. https://www.cnn.com/2020/03/25/asia/china-coronavirus-li-keqiang-intl-hnk/index.html
32. James Bovard, "Police Killings Have Been Federally Neglected for Years," *USA Today,* June 11, 2020. https://www.usatoday.com/story/opinion/2020/06/11/george-floyd-police-killings-violence-neglected-federally-column/5320501002/
33. *The Guardian* tracked the number of deaths from police shootings in 2015 and 2016. See https://www.theguardian.com/us-news/series/counted-us-police-killings. The *Washington Post* continues to maintain its Fatal Force database, September 30, 2021. https://www.washingtonpost.com/graphics/investigations/police-shootings-database/
34. Adel Kaplan, Vicky Nguyen, and Mary Godie, "Overworked, Understaffed: Pharmacists Say Industry in Crisis Puts Patient Safety at Risk," *NBC News,* March 16, 2021. https://www.nbcnews.com/health/health-care/overworked-understaffed-pharmacists-say-industry-crisis-puts-patient-safety-risk-n1261151
35. "Medication Errors Related to CDER-Regulated Drug Products," FDA, September 8, 2021. https://www.fda.gov/drugs/drug-safety-and-availability/medication-errors-related-cder-regulated-drug-products
36. Jan Brennan, "Increasing Voter Turnout in Local Elections," National Civic League 109 (Spring 2020). https://www.nationalcivicleague.org/national-civic-review/issue/spring-2020-volume-109-number-1/?popup=true
37. Nicholas Riccardi, "Referendum on Trump Shatters Turnout Records," *AP,* November 9, 2020. https://apnews.com/article/referendum-on-trump-shatter-voter-record-c5c61a8d280123a1d340a3f633077800
38. Courtney Kennedy, Jesse L. Lopez, Scott Keeter, Arnold Lau, Nick Hatley, and Nick Bertoni, "Confronting 2016 and 2020 Polling Limitations," *Pew Research Center,* April 8, 2021. https://www.pewresearch.org/methods/2021/04/08/confronting-2016-and-2020-polling-limitations/
39. "The Discovery of Global Warming: The Modern Temperature Trend," August 2021. https://history.aip.org/climate/20ctrend.htm
40. Dennis Sifris and James Myre, "How Close Are We to a Functional Cure for HIV?" Verywell Health, May 21, 2021. https://www.verywellhealth.com/how-close-are-we-to-a-functional-cure-for-hiv-49618
41. "Plano Police Department: Summary and Crime Comparison Year End Report 2011 through 2020." https://cintinc.com/wp-content/uploads/2021/03/Neutralizr-Crime-Summary-Comparison-Report.pdf
42. Rachel E. Morgan and Alexandra Thompson, "Criminal Victimization, 2020," Bureau of Justice Statistics, October 2021.
43. George Hunter and Hayley Harding, "Detroit Remains Nation's Most Violent Big City FBI Statistics Show." *Detroit News.* https://www.detroitnews.com/story/news/local/michigan/2021/09/27/detroit-most-violent-big-us-cities-fbi-uniform-crime-report-2020/5883984001/
44. Susan B. Glasser, "President Trump Is Acting Crazy, So Why Are We Shrugging It Off?" *The New Yorker,* December 3, 2020. https://www.newyorker.com/news/letter-from-trumps-washington/the-president-is-acting-crazy-so-why-are-we-shrugging-it-off

45. Michael D. Shear, "Trump Delivers 46-Minute Diatribe on the 'Rigged Election' from the White House," *The New York Times,* November 2, 2020. https://www.nytimes.com/2020/12/02/us/politics/trump-election-video.html
46. Nick Corasaniti, "Rudy Giuliani Sued by Dominion Voting Systems for False Election Claims," *The New York Times,* January 25, 2021. https://www.nytimes.com/2021/01/25/us/politics/rudy-giuliani-dominion-trump.html
47. Nicole Hong, William K. Rashbaum, and Ben Protess, "Giuliani's Law License Is Suspended Over Trump Election Lies," *The New York Times,* June 24, 2021. https://www.nytimes.com/2021/06/24/nyregion/giuliani-law-license-suspended-trump.html
48. Emily Badger, "Most Republicans Say They Doubt the Election, How Many Really Mean It?" *The New York Times,* November 30, 2020. https://www.nytimes.com/2020/11/30/upshot/republican-voters-election-doubts.html
49. Amy Gardner, Kate Rabinowitz, and Harry Stevens, "Voting Laws Proposed by Republicans in 43 States Would Limit Voter Access," *Washington Post,* March 11, 2021. https://www.washingtonpost.com/politics/interactive/2021/voting-restrictions-republicans-states/
50. Kaitlin Collins, Jim Acosta, and Devin Cole, "Dr. Scott Atlas Resigns from Trump Administration," *CNN,* December 1, 2020. https://www.cnn.com/2020/11/30/politics/scott-atlas-resigns-trump-administration-coronavirus-task-force/index.html
51. For example, see Ariana Huffington, "If His Words Are His Bond We're in a Bind," *Los Angeles Times,* July 16, 2003.
52. Glenn Kessler, Salvador Rizzo, and Meg Kelly, "President Trump Has Made More than 20,000 False or Misleading Claims," *Washington Post,* July 13, 2020. https://www.washingtonpost.com/politics/2020/07/13/president-trump-has-made-more-than-20000-false-or-misleading-claims/
53. David K. Berlo, James B. Lemert, and Robert J. Mertz, "Dimensions for Evaluating the Acceptability of Message Sources," *Public Opinion Quarterly* 33 (1970): 56–76.

8

Building Arguments

You are engaged in a conversation with a classmate who makes a claim with which you intensely disagree. The problem is that you are not sure why you are adamantly opposed to the claim. How can you express your disagreement convincingly? This and many other argumentative situations you will encounter require that you investigate the sources of your beliefs so you can create compelling arguments to convince others to share your views. This process requires research to identify grounds for your argumentative starting points, careful analysis, and effective organization.

In this chapter we will describe the research process, give some suggestions as to where to locate sources, help you assess the quality, reliability, and truthfulness of alternative sources of information, and discuss how you can organize your research results to increase the likelihood that your arguments will gain the adherence of your audiences.

DEFINING RESEARCH

The first step in any research project is to determine the general and specific purpose of the project. Typically, the general purpose of a research project is to persuade or inform. The specific topic might be to persuade an audience (either orally or through written arguments), for example, to reduce corporate tax rates or call for a greater focus on environmental sustainability.

Once the general and specific purposes are determined, you have to decide if you need more information than you already possess. As we have already explained, rational arguments contain three basic elements: the grounds used as the basis or premise to develop a claim; the reasoning that justifies the inferential leap from grounds to claim; and the claim itself, which is the conclusions drawn from the grounds and reasoning. The grounds refer to the foundation or support for the claim the advocate wishes the audience to accept (see chapter 6). Like a house, an argument is only as solid as its foundation. Thus, it is imperative that you provide grounds that will appeal to your audience. But where do you find the data for these grounds?

The best answer is: from our life experiences. We argue based on what we know—what we have read, heard, studied, and lived. That is why U.S. universities generally emphasize a liberal arts education—so students can draw from a variety of perspectives. As an advocate you should always use what you know as the basis for your claims. Take advantage of the preparation time spent developing your arguments to expand your storehouse of information—read! Be an informed citizen and you will become both a better advocate and a better consumer of arguments.

No matter how well read you are or how many interesting personal experiences you have had, there will come a time when your current personal knowledge is insufficient to convince your audience of the claim you want to advance. In many cases, you will also discover that your life experiences may be contradicted by the life experiences of others. To make a convincing claim, you will need to look elsewhere for support. Perhaps you have been asked to give a formal presentation of your views. If you wish to demonstrate the comprehensive quality of your knowledge, and you are committed to being an ethical communicator, you will need facts and opinions drawn from other sources. Engaging in this process of inquiry to identify such material is what we consider to be argumentative *research*.

PLANNING THE RESEARCH PROCESS

Without ready access to information we would be forced to make decisions in a vacuum—with a significant chance that we would err or be misled. Once you have decided to supplement your knowledge and explore the ideas of others, you will need to decide where to begin. The available information can be overwhelming. Libraries, for example, resulted from a conscious effort to create informed citizens and to give people the opportunity to read widely to enhance their ability to reason about what is or is not true. Today the internet is another source of abundant information. Deciding which of the extensive sources available to use in developing your arguments—and which to dismiss—requires a *research plan* or strategy to determine what information you need and the best way to obtain it.

Our advice is to start with general sources and move to more specific ones as your research progresses. By *general sources* we mean those that will give you a broad understanding of all aspects of the issue under investigation. There are five benefits in starting with more general sources.

First, a broad overview of the topic gives you a foundation for understanding the particular perspectives of various sources. Authors write because they believe they have something to contribute to an ongoing conversation. Sometimes it is very clear what has prompted them to write, and sometimes their agenda is not clear and must be inferred by the reader. For example, authors may respond directly to arguments that have already been advanced by others, or they may anticipate and preempt arguments that they believe others might raise. You can understand why both types of information—after-the-fact and preemptive—would be very valuable to your research. You can also see how easily you might miss this information if you do not have a comprehensive understanding of the controversy. The result can be poor argumentation, or you may be compelled to return to and reread material that you neglected. Neither outcome is efficient or desirable.

A second benefit of starting with more general sources is that doing so will enable you to generate a list of topic headings and synonyms. This can be invaluable because when you consult indexes or search engines you may need to look under several different key words. A lack of familiarity with the overall picture can frustrate good-faith efforts to research a topic. We once assigned a group of students to research "ethos." They returned to class claiming that they found few materials in the library on what they had been told was a major element of public speaking. The students had searched only one term (ethos). When they expanded their search and looked for related topics (public speaking, oratory, source credibility, and Aristotle's rhetoric) they had much better results.

The broad understanding of the controversy yielded by general sources offers a third benefit in that it enables the researcher to select those lines of inquiry that seem most promising. There may be many reasons, for example, to support legislation limiting access to handguns in the United States. If you have less than ten minutes to convince an audience, however, it probably makes sense to limit the scope of your advocacy to a couple of positions. That means selecting the most compelling reason or reasons and building your case around them. Knowing your options early in the research process can save you a lot of time and can also make the time that you do invest in argument preparation more productive.

A fourth benefit is the discovery of potential critical responses to your advocacy. In order to gain the adherence of a critical audience, you will need to know the likely objections to your arguments. Researching only one side of a controversy may not prepare you adequately. Understanding the arguments from both sides in a dispute enables you to anticipate possible objections to your claims and to prepare responses to those refutations. Knowing how opponents of your position think also gives you the option of addressing their concerns during your advocacy. Perhaps members of your audience share the opposing perspective. Including refutations in your presentation addresses those concerns before they are verbalized.

The fifth benefit of focusing on general sources in your initial research efforts is that they tend to be easier to read and comprehend than more specific and technical writings. General sources are written for lay audiences, and the terms used are typically defined and explained. Authors of more specific or technical writings, on the other hand, usually presume that their audience is knowledgeable about the basics of the issue and familiar with the jargon of the field. They may also write using language, style, and references that impede your comprehension. For example, contrast reading a newsmagazine article on the technical challenges that doctors may face when separating conjoined twins versus reading an essay on the same topic in the *New England Journal of Medicine*. Ultimately, of course, you may need and want to know about the contents in the journal article, but we would urge you not to start with more technical and advanced information. Start with sources that will provide you with a broad understanding of the controversy you are investigating and then move to more specific information as you acquire greater knowledge, familiarity with the issues and vocabulary, and a wider range of the different perspectives on the topic.

SOURCES OF INFORMATION

Interviewing Experts

Having decided that you wish to start with broader sources of information, the next question is: where do you find such information? A common first step in the research process is to begin by interviewing a knowledgeable expert on the subject. It is likely that faculty members on your campus are knowledgeable about the topic you want to investigate. They might make excellent subjects to interview. Representatives from public interest groups might also be good persons for you to interview as you begin your research efforts. If your topic is about a controversy in society, there might be many groups of citizen activists who will have literature advocating one side of the controversy or the other. Although interviewing members of a public interest group might be valuable, it might not be the first thing you want to do. You need to be on guard to assure that your interview subjects do not mislead you; they might see you as a target for their advocacy. In short, you may not yet know enough about the topic to critically evaluate the information that the advocate provides.

As with conducting research using books or internet searches, you should have a general knowledge of the topic or controversy before seeking more detailed information. If you ask your expert/subject to tell you everything they know about your topic, the expert may not know where to begin. Instead, your subject expects you to give guidance by asking the right questions. If you do not have enough background information and understanding of the issues in the controversy and of the different opinions on the topic, it will be tough for you to ask intelligent questions. As a result, you might end up wasting the expert's time. Even if the expert is generous with their time, the results may not be especially useful. Our advice is that you should not conduct interviews until you have done preliminary reading on your topic and have acquired sufficient background information and knowledge to assure that your questions will be both probative and productive to your research effort.

Another consideration is that statements made in personal interviews are frequently not accepted as valid by educated audiences. Since the advent of the printing press, the written word has enjoyed a prominent place in Western culture. Ideas that appear on the printed page are usually considered intrinsically superior to those delivered in oral speech. Neil Postman has argued that in the academic world the published word is given greater credence than the spoken word. He argues that this emphasis stems from the transitory nature of oral communication.

> What people say is assumed to be more casually uttered than what they write. The written word is assumed to have been reflected upon and revised by its author, reviewed by authorities and editors. It is easier to verify or refute, and it is invested with an impersonal and objective character. . .; that is to say, the written word endures, the spoken word disappears; and that is why writing is closer to the truth than speaking.[1]

This emphasis on the written word perhaps accounts for why so many of us are not particularly good at monitoring what we say. When the spoken word constituted the preferred form of communication, we were probably better at communicating orally. Now that the emphasis has shifted to the written word, we are better writers but possibly less effective at communicating orally.

Just as we may suffer discomfort when we hear our recorded voice or see ourselves on a video, it can be disquieting to see our spoken words written out in black and white. A frequent and understandable reaction to transcribed conversation is the desire to rephrase an utterance. In some cases, we deny that such words could have come out of our mouths, or we insist that the words are misleading without the accompaniment of the other words that we used to surround them and to provide the context of our thoughts. This may account for the frequency of the claim that reporters have misquoted their subjects when conducting interviews.

A final reason why educated audiences may assign less validity to statements made in personal interviews is the lack of verifiability. Published statements are potentially available to all and can be checked for accuracy and veracity. Personal interviews are not. Thus, we believe you should save the interviews until you have specific questions to ask. Even then, you should focus on asking experts questions for which their sources of information are published and accessible to others.

One expert that you ought to consider speaking with, however, is the reference librarian at your campus library. These individuals are committed to helping students research productively. They may know all sorts of helpful hints that they will happily share.

General Sources

Having postponed interviews until later in the research plan, you will still need to find general sources that provide you with a broad view of your topic. Most will turn to internet search engines, and most likely Google. It is important to keep in mind that Google is a profit-driven enterprise, however.

> When you use Google to search for anything from financial information to local weather, you're given a list of search results generated by Google's algorithm. The algorithm attempts to provide the most relevant results for your query, and, along with these results, you may find related suggested pages from a Google Ads advertiser.
> To gain the top spot in Google advertisements, advertisers have to outbid each other. Higher bids move up the list while low bids may not even be displayed.
> Advertisers pay Google each time a visitor clicks on an advertisement. A click may be worth anywhere from a few cents to over $50 for highly competitive search terms, including insurance, loans, and other financial services.[2]

Your Google search results will likely contain a mix of sites for you to consult: content from mainstream and alternative news sources, scholars and academic experts, journals, companies, foundations, interest groups, and advertisers. As an advocate or as a consumer of content gleaned from internet sources, you must become an active and discerning reader who is always prepared to critically evaluate the materials that you access.

We suggest that your information-seeking efforts be guided by the journalistic ethic. Reporters are generally taught to research and report both sides of a controversy. Presenting the competing views is considered balanced coverage. For our purposes that means you should begin with sources that report the controversy, rather than those that advocate a single, particular viewpoint. Mainstream sources such as *Time, Newsweek, The Atlantic,* or *The Economist* include articles from contributors who take diverse views; these publications tend to offer stories that present more than one perspective on an issue. Their stories also tend to be written in a style that is accessible to the lay reader. At this point in your research process, you are trying to gain a breadth of information in a quick and efficient way, and newsmagazine stories tend to be short. The same generally is true for articles in newspapers. After consulting magazines and newspapers, you may wish to move to articles that are a bit longer. Please be mindful too of the differences between articles that attempt to engage in objective reporting of facts, articles that offer news analysis (often labeled as such), and opinion essays and editorials.

The internet has provided relatively easy access to a wide array of outstanding newspapers and magazines, although paywalls may still prevent access to some stories. It is worth considering, however, that if you log in and access these websites through your college library you will likely be able to secure free access. We believe the best newspapers, which are able to devote the most resources to reporting on a wide array of topics, include *The New York Times, Los Angeles Times, Wall Street Journal, Washington Post, Chicago Tribune, Boston Globe,* and *The Christian Science Monitor.* We also turn frequently to *The Guardian*, published in the United Kingdom. Of course, for local issues and news coverage you should consult your local newspaper. With regard to other magazine sources, we often consult *Vanity Fair, The New Yorker, The New Republic, The Nation, The Weekly Standard, The National Review,* and *Mother Jones.* You will find significant differences in ideological perspective across this array of magazines.

On political issues and topics, there are also an array of digital news sources that you may want to consider. Such sources as *Politico, Axios, The Hill, Slate, Salon, BuzzFeedNews,* and *Reason.com*, to name just a few examples, introduce political issues and controversies with a lively and opinionated style of coverage. Do understand that some of these sources slant to the left and others to the right, however, so be prepared to critically evaluate the information that you access and also be prepared for the fact that some people whom you may be attempting to convince with your arguments and your evidence may be skeptical of information that you draw from some of these sources. Vanessa Otero, a patent attorney, created an interesting chart on the issue of media bias and slant in 2016 and has updated it several times.[3] Alarmed by the media landscape, she used her expertise in content analysis to create the chart. She notes that sources people categorize as news sources are actually dominated by opinion pieces. She considers the extremes on the Media Bias Chart® to be toxic and damaging to the country because they play to people's worst instincts, such as fear and tribalism.[4]

Specialized Sources

Once you have read what some general sources have to say about your topic, you will be ready to conduct a more focused search of ***specialized sources***. These publications contain essays that are targeted to audiences who want in-depth information about a specific topic related to a particular field and who typically have background knowledge in the field. Having already covered a number of general sources, you should now be familiar with the issues in the controversy and know some of the key terms and jargon. There are four reasons why it will be beneficial for you to continue your research by consulting specialized sources.

First, articles written for the general public often report the conclusions of experts in the field, but they seldom explore a controversy in great depth. While breadth means that a larger number of people know a little about the topic, to discover where truth resides or to find the material to gain the adherence of others you need to read more deeply so you can learn the rationale behind the conclusions drawn by the experts.

Second, as you gain more knowledge of your topic, you will discover the unstated assumptions of the experts. For example, we remember when it was widely reported that U.S. oil reserves would be exhausted in less than 75 years. This claim, of course, depended upon many different assumptions, such as consumption patterns, whether drilling would be allowed in areas contested by environmentalists (e.g., off the Florida or California coasts, or in Alaska), the amount of oil we purchased from foreign suppliers, the price of oil, and the technologies for extraction (that might make it physically and economically viable to remove oil that is harder to find and pull from the ground). We thus *may* deplete the U.S. oil reserves in 75 years, or even less if the SUV craze continues, but such a claim obviously rests on many assumptions that you as a researcher should understand if you are to become an effective advocate. It may be that the United States will have access to domestic oil for many generations to come, assuming of course that the price of oil remains sufficiently high to justify the cost of extracting it via a costly method of production such as fracking.

Third, additional research should uncover specific information necessary to support the arguments you wish to convey. General sources may give you most of the information that you need to justify your position but there may be gaps that need to be filled. For example, newsmagazines may provide basic information about the importance of childhood immunization programs, but they may not provide the details necessary for a compelling argument. Consulting journals devoted to public health could yield statistics on the efficacy of immunizations, examples of the consequences of failing to immunize children, or the procedures necessary to fully protect youngsters.

The most important benefit of consulting specialized sources of information is the opportunity to discover more about your topic than you might think you need. Have you heard the saying "a little knowledge is a dangerous thing"? This adage refers to cases in which individuals assume that having some knowledge of a topic means they know the entire truth, when, in fact, they may only know a small part of it. Then, on that basis, they enter into a discussion and leap to an incorrect conclusion that has a negative effect on themselves or others. Achieving a more thorough grasp of the subject by conducting more focused research should help you avoid sounding like you think you know it all when you don't.

Once you have decided to pursue the lines of research indicated by your general reading, you need to pinpoint what types of sources to consult and where to go to find them. We will present two types of specialized sources—this does not suggest that there are no others. However, these two types should provide a good start on most topics.

SOURCES FOR SPECIFIC DISCIPLINES. In any academic discipline, scholars are expected to contribute to the understanding of the field by publishing the results of their research in professional journals. These articles are not written for the general public but for readers familiar with the jargon of the field and with the issues and controversies important to that field. **Google Scholar** is a specialized search engine that enables you to search across an array of academic disciplines for journal articles, theses, dissertations, and academic books. You can also consult **ResearchGate**, which is a European search engine providing access to international publications, or **JSTOR**, which indexes past research articles. If the topic you are researching involves scientific questions, you may choose to search **Web of Science** or **Science Direct**. If it is a medical topic, you might search **PubMed**. If it is a legal topic, you should consider a search using **LexisNexis** to find legal journal articles, law review articles, past court cases, and even stories published in the media.

There are also a wide variety of popular magazines that publish in-depth articles and editorials on various topics. For example, such magazines as *Science, National Geographic, Psychology Today,* and *Wired,* to name only a few, are not necessarily written in the same style and with the same degree of scholarly rigor as are most academic journals, but they nonetheless offer more detailed and thorough coverage of subjects within their sphere of influence than do other sources. Sometimes the references provided in such articles can be used to find specialized sources replete with useful information. Thus, the more specialized popular magazines can prove to be very useful as research resources to support your arguments.

GOVERNMENT SOURCES. The United States Congress holds hearings on almost every topic that is identified as a matter of national concern or where there will be a demand for legislative policy action. At these hearings, experts from both sides of the controversy present sworn statements and answer questions from members of Congress. The experts usually testify as advocates in favor of, or in opposition to, proposed federal legislation. Consequently, the statements from these sources contain practically everything an advocate would need to construct convincing arguments. Similarly, congressional committees, independent agencies, cabinet departments, federal commissions, and a host of other agencies produce reports that are available via the internet to the public.

To locate government publications you can consult usa.gov/, which is an online guide to government information and services. This website offers links to all three branches of the federal government, to some local and state government websites, and even to some of the websites of foreign nations. The Library of Congress Catalog is the access point for the Library's collection and includes a link to an extensive e-resources online catalog.

Congress also prints a record of the debates that take place on the floor of the House and Senate. *The Congressional Record* is indexed to help you find useful information. Since senators and representatives can revise and extend their remarks, and even insert documents for the record, you can find a tremendous wealth of helpful research information in the *Congressional Record*.

Of course, some controversies that interest you may be more prominent in local discussions than in national discussions. Your state may publish information about their legislative or governmental proceedings. Consult your reference librarian for additional information about how to locate such information for your state.

The Internet

The internet has transformed how people communicate, establish and maintain interpersonal relationships, share their opinions, gather news and information, engage in political activity, and seek entertainment. Many will forever recall an entire academic year that was conducted via the online meeting platform known as Zoom. Although most of the contributions of the internet have been positive, we have also witnessed a darker side to many aspects of digital online communications.

A global network of libraries and a vast array of news sources, research articles, conference presentations, blogs, and videos are now easily and immediately accessible online. Arguers in the past often had difficulty finding information to support their claims, especially if they lived in rural areas or small towns without access to a good research library and a world-class newspaper. The problem today is more likely that researchers find too much information and that they are unable to wade through it all to make good choices about what evidence will prove most useful. The other challenge, of course, is that for many people "information is information" regardless of the source. These users are unable or unwilling to expend the energy necessary to critically engage the evidence they discover and to assess the quality of the claims offered and the credibility of the source. Academics for many years have discussed the importance of media literacy—the ability to analyze and evaluate media messages critically for accuracy, credibility, and evidence of bias. Learning how to use media wisely is more important now than ever before to avoid being misled by spurious, deceptive, and inaccurate claims shared on the internet.

As we noted earlier, the easiest way to research a topic is to conduct an online search. The Google search engine is now so dominant that "to Google" has become an accepted verb. We will identify four challenges to keep in mind when conducting your search.

First, not all websites have equal power, standing, respect, or editorial quality. Certainly, as already argued in this chapter, many excellent sources of information are accessible online, but ascertaining the accuracy and reliability of information on the web can be problematic. Major newspapers, broadcast news networks, magazines, academic journals, professional organizations, and individual experts maintain websites that are profoundly useful to researchers. You must remember, however, that it is easy to create a website and post information there. A website that looks official and reliable can be produced in someone's basement. If you do not know the reliability of the source you are consulting, you should be skeptical about the information you discover on the web. Many websites exert very little, if any, editorial control over the information that is posted on the site. Many blogs, for example, have no restrictions on the content placed on them. Similarly, those using the platform Twitter can post and share random, unresearched, and inaccurate thoughts. A very significant problem that surfaced in 2021 was the extensive appearance of misinformation regarding the COVID vaccines that appeared on social media platforms. The misinformation that circulated primarily on conservative social media platforms and cable TV networks falsely characterized the vaccines as dangerous, ineffective, unconstitutional, and even as a nefarious federal plot. As a result, fully 47% of Republicans in one poll indicated that they would not be vaccinated, even as new variants of the disease were ravaging the country and claiming unvaccinated victims.[5]

Platforms have been very reluctant to play the role of content moderators, and so inaccuracies go unchecked. In January 2021, Facebook, Twitter, and YouTube took the unprecedented step of banning President Donald Trump from their platforms after his misleading claims that he had won the 2020 presidential election in a "landslide" provoked an insurrection that caused his supporters to swarm the Capital in a violent effort to halt the counting of the electoral votes certified by the states.[6] Five people died in the insurrection, which led to President Trump being impeached by the House of Representatives. Trump became the first president to have been impeached twice.[7] While it is noteworthy that this extreme crisis and the tragedy that resulted provided sufficient motivation for these platforms to actively suppress misleading and dangerously deceptive content, this rare intervention does not suggest that they will continue to monitor content. The responsibility to carefully and systematically assess the content discovered on the web still rests with those citing information gleaned from web sources.

Second, we have already noted in this chapter that the printed word is generally considered more compelling because it goes through an editorial process and because it is potentially verifiable. Websites may or may not use a similar editorial review process. It is common, for example, for academics to post lectures, working papers, and conference presentations on their websites. Such papers may prove very useful, and some of them will constitute outstanding work that represents "state of the art" research on any given topic at that point in time. Yet, most of them will not have been through the kind of rigorous editorial review that is required of essays published in leading journals. As a result, errors in this work may go undetected, and the work will not have benefited from helpful editorial critiques by other experts in the field. In addition, internet materials often lack permanence; what is accessible today on the web may be gone tomorrow. That means revisiting or verifying information may be impossible or at least very difficult. We have already encouraged advocates searching for evidence drawn from academic sources to make use of Google Scholar, a feature on the popular search engine that specifically focuses on scholarly journals and presentations that have gone through an editorial review process.

Third, almost anyone can call themselves an organization or a group when producing online content; therefore, audiences may give less credibility to material accessed on the web that did not come from recognized outlets. For instance, declaring, "according to www.aboutviolence.org" (a site we invented) is not as credible as saying "according to an editorial in *The New York Times*." If your audience does not perceive the source of the information that you present as credible, then you have gained little by drawing upon that source. If a website provides the name of the primary source of information, you would be better off looking up and citing that source. Primary sources tend to be seen as more reliable than secondary sources—especially when you do not know the credibility of the secondary source.

Fourth, as we all have become aware, much of the information accessed online is either deliberately or inadvertently inaccurate and misleading. Some people or organizations may mislead in the pursuit of gaining "clicks" or attention that can be monetized.[8] Others may deliberately distort, mislead, or deceive people for strategic political gain or for some other nefarious purpose. Here we might cite the example of the fake conspiracy narratives that were shared online by those who followed the posts of QAnon, a set of conspiracy theories including the belief that President Trump was a messianic warrior battling "deep-state" Satanists and that Democrats were part of a global network of pedophiles. As preposterous as these posts were, they gained the support of thousands of disgruntled and angry supporters and greatly contributed to the radicalization of the fringes of the Republican Party and even to the political violence at the U.S. Capitol on January 6, 2021.[9]

People are especially susceptible to misleading information that aligns with beliefs that they already hold dear. As a safeguard, take the time and energy to interrogate information to determine its accuracy even if it seems plausible when you first encounter it.[10]

Another disinformation technique that is proving especially difficult to counter is what is known as a "deepfake"—fraudulent visual images, fake digital video clips, and sham sound clips created by technologies that use artificial intelligence algorithms to produce images/sounds that seem real. Sometimes the objective is pornographic. For example, a celebrity's face is digitally appended to another person's body engaged in a lurid pornographic act. On other occasions a public or political figure is shown as either doing or saying something that seems outrageous or inflammatory. Due to the nature and speed of online communications, such images may travel very quickly and may be profoundly difficult to counter.[11] Those who study intergroup relations, for example, are very concerned that deepfake images or video clips could be used to spark or intensify racist prejudices. Deepfakes showing cases of police violence, for instance, could inflame the passions of protestors and could even be used by a foreign government intent on destabilizing the United States. Although it may be relatively easy to detect some deepfakes, those that are created using the most sophisticated software and powerful graphics cards are much more difficult to detect.[12] Fortunately, government-funded researchers and new technology companies are working to develop ever more sophisticated programs to detect and remove deepfakes.

The next section reviews strategies to assess the accuracy and quality of internet accessed information to help you avoid being deceived yourself and to prevent you from unintentionally deceiving others.

Identifying Misinformation Online

In searching for information, or when simply encountering information online, you should first consider the source. Did the information come from a reliable publication or outlet? Once you have identified the source, you might want to see if it appears on the media bias chart discussed above (endnote #3 provides a link to the chart). This will give you some guidance as to whether or not the source that you are evaluating is advancing some political or ideological interests.

Second, did the information that you encountered seem particularly shocking or provocative to you? Did it make you angry? In contrast, did it make you feel especially happy? Remember that website algorithms can direct messages to you that align with your previous internet habits, interests, and opinions. If you have clicked on previous posts or conducted searches on similar topics, the algorithms use that information to make it more likely that you will see future posts that will capture your attention, hold your interest, and keep you engaged. Be suspicious and skeptical about posts that incite extreme emotional responses.

Third, did the information that you encountered seem likely to be true. Apply the tests of narrative storytelling. Did the post seem internally consistent? Did it account for the material facts in a coherent manner? Did the post seem likely true in that it was similar to other stories that you have previously heard and know to be materially true? Remember that things that seem too good to be true are usually not true—and just as likely, things that seem too shocking to be true are also seldom true, no matter how they might engage your interest and attention. If the narrative reasoning does not detect a flaw, you might do additional investigation. Turn to fact-checking sites such as FactCheck.org or Snopes.com to see whether or not they can confirm the information that you have discovered online. If the claim that you have encountered has been made by a political candidate or elected official, you can also look it up on the site known as PolitiFact.com. You might also Google the topic to see if multiple reliable sources confirm the accuracy of the claims.

Fourth, was a specific source identified for the claim offered? Often web posts will offer claims without naming the source for the findings or offering information about the source's credentials, education, knowledge, or capability to render such an opinion. During the height of the COVID-19 crisis, for example, President Trump was reported to be taking advice from Dr. Scott Atlas, a Fellow of the Hoover Institute at Stanford University. One hears Hoover Fellow, Stanford, and the title Dr., and one naturally presumes a highly qualified and respected expert. (Recall the discussion of field dependence in chapter 7.) The advice that Atlas provided, however, both to Trump personally and to the public in multiple media appearances, frequently contradicted the advice offered by the Coronavirus Task Force, the Centers for Disease Control, the National Institutes of Health, and the nation's most renowned virologists and epidemiologists. Further research into Atlas's qualifications would have quickly revealed that while he was indeed a medical doctor with a Stanford appointment, his specialty was radiology and MRIs. He clearly was not the best source for information on the global pandemic.[13]

Fifth, was the post well-written and did it have proper grammar? Frequently, misleading information is hastily written by someone who is not a native English-speaker and by someone who is merely trying to capture web-clicks for profit. Such posts will often contain spelling errors, the mistaken use of words such as "there, they're, or their," "were or where," "then or than," etc. Most legitimate sources carefully proofread and have copy editors to go over their work before it is printed. Be a bit of a grammar sleuth to check out the likely truthfulness of a claim you find online.

Sixth, was the post a meme? Memes such as visual images of smiling cats, cuddly puppies, or cartoon characters, etc., may quickly catch our attention, draw our interest, make us chuckle, or provoke feelings of fondness or hostility. Such memes may also cause people to let down their guard, however. As a result, individuals may be less likely to rigorously test the information in the meme, making it more likely that they will be seduced by misinformation.[14]

The sharing of misleading information on social media platforms can have very significant consequences. A strong case can be made, for example, that the exchange of false or misleading posts about corrupt voting machines, lost or stolen ballots, and dead people casting ballots in the 2020 presidential election contributed to the persistent beliefs among many registered Republicans that Joe Biden was not the legitimate winner of the election. This belief persisted despite the fact that no credible evidence to support these claims was ever offered in a court of law and that such claims were dismissed in 61 separate lawsuits, many thrown out by judges who had been appointed by President Trump.[15] Despite the absence of evidence, however, social media sites in the weeks following the election and leading up to the counting of the electoral votes by Congress were replete with posts urging Trump supporters to travel to Washington, DC. On the morning of January 6, 2021, Trump addressed the assembled crowd in the morning and urged them to march to the Capitol to "fight like hell" and to "stop the steal." He also declared: "And we fight. We fight like hell. And if you don't fight like hell, you're not going to have a country anymore."[16] The combination of Trump's fiery call to action and the sustained internet misinformation campaign helped to radicalize the crowd, turning at least some citizens on the fringes of the political movement to become a violent mob that overtook the Capitol and engaged in pitched battles with police officers resulting in at least five deaths.[17]

It is one of the greatest challenges of a democracy in the digital era that citizens acquire the critical and analytical skills to evaluate the information that they are exposed to online so that they are not personally misled and misinformed—and so they do not share false information and thus mislead others.

Books

In addition to periodicals, government documents, and digital information gleaned online, researchers often turn to books. Books published on the controversy that you are researching may be very helpful to you. We have listed books last, however, because there are problems with focusing your research effort on books.

First, reading books can be very time-consuming. Although comprehensive research necessitates reading deeply and broadly on a subject, most of us lack the time to be as thorough as we would like to be. We thus need to obtain the greatest possible return for the time we invest. Because of their length, books may not have the same efficiency as other sources of information for a research report or class presentation. Second, a book will generally offer you the perspective of only one author. The same time invested in reading journal articles or other periodicals, for example, will likely offer a number of different perspectives and viewpoints.

In addition, it can take a long time for a manuscript to evolve into a published book. For some controversies, especially those focused on historical events, this is not a problem. However, recency of information is critical when researching current events or some scientific or technical issues. By the time a book reaches the public, it may already be out of date regarding some issues. A book about digital media, for example, may be out of date before it makes it to the shelves in the library because changes in online communication occur so quickly.

While books are one source of being fully informed on the topic that you are investigating, do not turn to them too early in the research process and do not make them the only focus of your research.

How to Record the Evidence

Having located an article, essay, news story, or book that contains information to develop support for your arguments, you next need to document the source using a citation system.[18] If you are writing a scholarly essay or college paper you will need to familiarize yourself with the requirements of the particular style manual that you are expected to follow. It is very frustrating, and requires significant extra time, if you have to go back to the original source materials because you neglected to write down all the information necessary for the citation. We recommend that you record the following five components:

1. **Author's name.** The first thing to record is the author's complete name. Some style manuals require that you provide only the author's last name and the initials of their first and middle names (e.g., APA); others require that you use the full name in your citation. If you do not know for sure which manual you will eventually use, it is always best to record the full name so that you have it if you need it.

   What do you do if there is no author identified? This is frequently the case with newspaper or magazine articles, pamphlets, or blog posts. The source that produced the information—the newspaper, magazine, group that produced the pamphlet or blog post, etc.—should be considered the author. This also applies to articles written by unidentified staff writers. The publications are, in a sense, the "author" of the information.

2. **Author's qualifications.** None of the official style manuals that we have mentioned require, or even permit, the inclusion of the author's qualifications in the reference section. These citation systems make no judgment about the quality or the competence of the sources that the advocate chooses to cite. Audiences, however, do evaluate and are often heavily influenced by the quality, training, reputation, and competence of the sources that an advocate uses. Advocates who cite sources that the audience views favorably (that is, sources that the audiences find to be especially credible) benefit from a "halo effect." If a source that the audience considers trustworthy and competent supports your

argument, it makes your argument *and you* look better. Of course, the reverse is also true. Consequently, it is important that you record the author's qualifications. Doing so can then help you choose from among the different sources you have identified to support your arguments. You cite those you believe will be most likely to strengthen the appeal of your claims in the eyes of your audience. If you are arguing about immunizations for children, for instance, a statement supporting your position from an epidemiologist from the Centers for Disease Control will have far greater credibility than a statement quoting an article written by a staff writer for the *Omaha World Herald*. (No offense to the *Omaha World Herald* intended.)

Occasionally, you will not know the qualifications of an author, and the material you are referencing does not provide the information. Chances are good that you can learn more about the author by undertaking a quick Google search. Many experts post biographical information, often including their academic or scholarly resumes, on the web.

Once you record the qualifications for the sources you intend to use, be sure to use them in the text of your advocacy. This is especially useful if you are presenting a persuasive speech. Your audience may not know that your sources are experts unless you tell them. Therefore, it is to your advantage to include enough information about the authors of your sources so your audience learns about their many accomplishments when you cite their words, ideas, or research.

3. **Source information.** Style manuals require that you provide enough information about the source so that members of your audience can locate the articles, essays, or books themselves. For a book, this necessitates the full title and the name of the publisher. APA no longer requires place of publication, but other style manuals do. For an article, you will need the title of the article, and the name and volume as well as the date of the periodical. For a website, you will need the name of the site and its URL (its web address). Most style manuals no longer require the date that you accessed the website, but you might want to record the information in case you need to reference it.

If you are citing unusual sources such as pamphlets, sound recordings, translated materials, edited volumes, TV programs, videos, speeches, personal interviews, and so forth be sure to consult the style manual you are using so that you list all the information required.

4. **Date.** In chapter 7, we discussed the test of evidence called *recency*. We argued that the date of the material is not as important as what has transpired since the material was written. Thus, some very recent data are already outdated, while other evidence will always be considered relevant. For the citation, you must record the specific date that the material you cited was produced. The date is required by all style manuals and is necessary if someone is to locate the original source that you cited. Some websites do not provide a date; in the citation, you record this as n.d. As mentioned above, you should also document the date you accessed the information. The date you located the material on the web might help another researcher locate it in a web database archive.

You may influence audiences favorably by mentioning the date of the material you are using to support your arguments. Audiences may be greatly impressed if your evidence is very recent, particularly if recency is critical for your topic.

5. **Page number.** If you intend to quote an author directly, style manuals require that you provide the specific page number where the passage appeared in the original source. In addition, the style manual may require that your list of references includes the beginning and ending page numbers for articles in journals or for chapters in edited books. Thus, it is very important that you develop the habit of recording this information in your research notes.

WHAT TO LOOK FOR WHEN RESEARCHING

You have been busily researching your topic and have located many great sources that will help you support the arguments you wish to develop. You have also carefully recorded the source information. Now you are reading the materials that you located in order to determine what to write down in your notes. How do you determine what information is going to prove relevant to your arguments? This is a difficult question. Experience will prove to be your best teacher, but we can offer some suggestions.

What Is Necessary to Gain Adherence

We have previously discussed the role of *stasis* and *stock issues* in argumentation (chapter 5). Think about the issues that must be addressed and where there will likely be disagreement with the claims that you wish to advance. To illustrate this, we will consider the deliberative arguments that develop in an instance of policy analysis.

Remember that the first stock issue in traditional policy analysis concerned the existence of a problem or the identification of an *ill*. Locating and demonstrating the existence of an ill—or refuting the existence of an ill that has been argued by your opponent—generates several questions.

- How many people are affected by the problem?
- How are they affected?
- To what extent are they affected?
- What are the likely consequences of these effects?

Such questions get at the heart of the stock issue of ill. If you are trying to convince an audience that the status quo needs to be changed, you will want to show them the nature and extent of the problem. After all, there is no sense in changing the status quo if the problem is not a significant one. Evidence that directly answers such questions as those listed above should be recorded.

The second stock issue is *blame*. This issue concerns the cause of the problem and why our current policies may be inadequate. The following questions help analyze blame.

- What is the main cause of the problem?
- Why are other potential causes less important?
- What is the status quo policy toward this problem?
- If there is a policy, why is this policy inadequate?
- Why have presumably "good" people tolerated the existence of this problem?
- Can the status quo policy be saved with minor changes?

The third stock issue is *cure*. This deals with whether the proposal would solve or ameliorate the problem. Questions like the following are relevant to cure.

- What specifically should the agent of change do?
- Who should initiate the change in order to secure the best results?
- What proof is there that a new policy will work better than the status quo?
- Has the proposed new policy been tried elsewhere? With what results?
- Would the new policy meet with likely resistance? How might such resistance be overcome?

Finally, consider the stock issue of *cost*. Remember, this issue asks the question, "Are there any disadvantages to the proposal that might outweigh the advantages?" Search for and record evidence that addresses questions such as the following.

- Will the proposed solution cause any new problems?
- Will the proposed solution exacerbate any existing problems?
- Will the proposed solution delay some other desired outcome?
- Is the proposal ethical?
- What is the likelihood that there will be some other unintended consequences?
- How much will the proposed solution cost, and what sacrifices will be required to cover those costs?

Recalling the requirements of the various stock issues will help guide your research and help you discover how to support your arguments effectively. Now you need to consider how to make your arguments as convincing and compelling as possible.

What Is Likely to Gain Adherence

In order to create arguments that are as effective and convincing as possible, you need to think about the audience that you will address and the argumentation field in which your arguments will be considered. Merely having the relevant facts may not be enough to assure that you have made a convincing case, since facts are subject to interpretation. You must not only secure the evidence necessary to gain adherence but you must also make sure it is likely to persuade your audience to embrace your perspective or beliefs. From a narrative perspective, this means finding evidence that helps you frame your story in such a way that the actors, the events and the scene you describe are vivid, compelling, and align with your audience's worldviews.

If, for example, your story depicts government public servants as loyal, competent, conscientious, and even heroic, you must find evidence that supports these characterizations. If, on the other hand, your story depicts government public servants as inattentive, uncaring, insensitive, incompetent, or even malicious, then evidence that supports these views is required. Sometimes such stories are complex and contain elements of both. When Trump supporters stormed the Capitol in an attempt to stop the counting of electoral votes, for example, there was evidence that some Capitol police officers performed heroically and even sacrificed their lives to protect the Capitol. There was also evidence that suggested that other officers may have posed for selfies with the invaders and perhaps even directed them toward the chambers where congressional representatives were meeting.[19] To argue that the officers were either heroic or complicit with the violent mob would almost certainly provoke refutation with counterexamples.

Similarly, the data you use as the foundation for your portrayal of the events and of the scene should reflect and support the narrative construction that you are creating. Quotations can be particularly effective, for the language of the authority may embody the label you wish to depict. Returning to the example of the riot in the Capitol, a reporter described one scene: "A vague air of confusion hovers over these insurrectionists: soldiers waiting for direction from a leader who long ago fled the battlefield. Lies have led them here—gaudy fantasies about an election stolen and a birthright robbed—and they seem, now that they have reached the inner sanctum of American government, unsure how to proceed with their victory."[20] Another account of the insurrections began: "Dozens of video clips posted to social media on Wednesday captured the image of outnumbered D.C. law enforcement officers apparently being overwhelmed by waves of pro-Trump rioters, who swarmed police barricades, sprayed chemical agents, smashed windows, and entered the U.S. Capitol building by brute force. It was the first time since the War of 1812 that the building was breached."[21] Similarly, you can make your arguments by looking for quotations that characterize the actors in your narratives.

In addition, remember the importance of *examples* and *analogies*, which we discussed in chapter 6. Not only do these serve as proof, they also make the argument more comprehensible to your audience. Consequently, it is useful to record examples and analogies you find compelling. You will probably convey them in your own words, so it won't be necessary to record them verbatim, but you will wish to acknowledge the source of this information. To do so will enhance your credibility and also protect you from the charge that you may have plagiarized the work or words of others.

When we discussed examples, we noted that a single example might not be found typical of the set of other possible examples. Even a few examples might lead to a hasty generalization. *Statistics,* the numeric expression of examples, reduce the likelihood of such errors. Record statistics that show the extent of the point that you are trying to make. Remember that statistics alone are rather cold and might not move an audience; therefore, it is useful to combine them with examples. Examine your readings to see if there are statistics and examples that you can combine to make more compelling arguments. The combinations helps you illustrate your claims and also clarify them. Keep in mind that with statistics it is often desirable to tell an audience how the statistics were gathered and by whom, so be sure to record this information.

Authoritative opinions can also be compelling. Examine what experts have said. A concise quotation that directly supports a point that you are trying to make can be very effective, especially if the audience is likely to respect the source as an authority who is well qualified and free from bias. Thus, as a reminder, it is important to record the qualifications of your sources.

Be careful when recording quotations that you also include more information than just the author's conclusions. The reasoning the author uses to develop an argument is as important as the conclusion reached. Audiences may find the reasoning compelling even in those cases where they might reject a one sentence conclusion from the same author. After all, the reasoning reveals the author's analysis and argumentation. Merely quoting the author's concluding claim assumes that the audience will be convinced by the author's credibility alone. Perhaps they will, but a knowledgeable advocate takes the precaution of including the author's reasons for advancing the claim.

Finally, when selecting data to record, be sure to consider the tests of data that we presented in chapter 7. Audiences and opposing arguers will be far more likely to listen respectfully and even to grant adherence to data that passes those rigorous tests.

In summary, we think the best advice is to think about the kind of claims that you will need to advance to make your arguments convincing. Then, go out and find the data that proves your claims are well founded.

Organizing Your Advocacy

Even the best arguments will fail if an audience cannot understand or make sense of them. That is why it is important that you construct your advocacy carefully. Part of this certainly entails making lucid and succinct claims. It also entails discovering relevant and convincing evidence. But even good arguments must be well organized if they are to convince audiences.

Exactly how you choose to organize your arguments will depend on several factors: the occasion, the audience, your subject, and your personal communication style. Each of these factors constrains advocates, and thus each will be discussed in turn.

The Occasion

Some occasions, circumstances, or situations lend themselves to structured arguments—others do not. Clearly, in the middle of an interpersonal discussion, it might be awkward and inappropriate to launch into an extended monologue advocating a specific point of view. Even in public speaking situations, which lend themselves to prepared addresses, there may be times when pointed advocacy is considered inappropriate. For example, we recently heard a commencement speaker who received distinctly mixed reviews. Rather than focusing his remarks on the achievements of the graduating class or the ceremonial occasion, he devoted his time to arguing for a change in the way the city was administered. He might have been successful in making city governance a focus for his speech that day had he, for example, talked about the role that the graduates and those of their generation could play in making political reforms. However, he seemed to misunderstand the occasion. As a result, he made arguments that seemed to be promoting himself as a future mayoral candidate. His words failed to meet the demands of the situation or to respond to the expectations of his audience.

Two academic theorists have had much to say about the nature of the rhetorical situation and the expectations of audiences. Lloyd Bitzer argued that a rhetorical situation not only invited utterance but it also invited a particular kind of utterance, an utterance that genuinely met the audience's expectations and fit the situation.[22] A similar view was developed by Kenneth Burke, who declared that appropriate rhetoric must meet the expectations of form (see chapter 4). Many of you will someday be asked to give a toast to celebrate the wedding of a close friend. There are ceremonial expectations for the toast. It is typically not the best time to talk in detail about the previous boyfriends or girlfriends that either of the newly married couple experienced, nor is it time to talk about how many marriages fail and end in divorce. Emphasizing either topic would likely not please many members of your audience.

The Audience

Audiences do not approach argumentative situations as blank slates. They bring to each new argumentative encounter a host of experiences, values, attitudes, and beliefs. Even those who are willing to suspend their judgment and give a full and impartial hearing to arguments do so from within the perspective of the value framework and the narrative experiences that have defined their lives. Advocates need to assess these perspectives to organize their arguments effectively.

The audience will also reveal something about the *field* of argumentation. We have already explained (see chapter 3) that the assumptions about the nature and tests of arguments vary from field to field. The types of arguments expected or even demanded in one field may not be accepted in another. Thus, the advocate must take into consideration the field of argument embraced by the audience.

The Subject

We have identified three different types of propositions that arguers might be called upon to support: *fact, value,* and *policy.* Each type of claim will lend itself to different organizational patterns. Questions of fact are organized into main points, each of which constitutes the reasons why an advocate believes some statement of fact to be correct or not.

Value questions usually involve setting criteria for the evaluation of an argument in support of or against some value judgment. For example, an advocate who claimed that Chadwick Boseman was the best male actor in 2020 would be required to offer two lines of argument: the first would involve establishing the criteria for selecting the best actor; and the second would demonstrate that Boseman met these criteria better than did other actors. The argument could turn on many factors such as awards received, critical reviews, box office success, the demands/challenges of performances, personal preferences/tastes, and perhaps the ability to perform under adverse circumstances. For example, Boseman turned in an outstanding performance in the film *Ma Rainey's Black Bottom* even though he was facing terminal colon cancer and died before the film's release in 2020.

Finally, there are questions of policy. There are four ways policy advocates typically organize their advocacy. Each reflects a pattern of reasoning. The first method is called the ***needs*** (or stock issues) ***case***. As you are aware, this entails organizing your arguments around the stock issues ill, blame, cure, and cost. This approach works most effectively when the advocate can clearly demonstrate that there is a significant and compelling problem; the advocate can identify who or what is responsible for the problem (where to place the blame); and the advocate can offer an effective solution. An obese U.S. population might be identified as a leading problem to explain the rise in diabetes. Changing dining habits may be identified as the preferred solution to remedy the problem. Altering how the purveyors of fast foods market their products may be identified as a way to change people's dining habits and thus reduce their calorie intake and likelihood of developing diabetes.

A second organizational format, which stems from systems analysis, is called the ***comparative advantage case***. In this approach, advocates present their policy proposal and then compare the status quo (what exists now) to what would exist after the introduction of alternative policy measures. The advocate's goal is to demonstrate that the alternative policies would likely prove desirable compared to current policies. This organizational approach might be most effective when there are not significant and readily identifiable ills in the present system. An advocate can convincingly argue that changing the system would be an improvement. An obese U.S. population may again be cited as the problem contributing to diabetes. Changing dining habits by teaching people to make better food choices may solve the problem. Educating people about nutrition, empty calories, and good meal planning may help solve or reduce the problem. Coaching people to eat healthier meals and providing simple-to-use recipes could contribute to reducing obesity. Providing accurate, easy to read labels on foods and encouraging people to consume more vegetables and less sugar or corn syrup sweetened processed food could help people lose weight.

A third approach is a variant of the comparative advantage case called the ***goals case***. With this approach, the advocate attempts to convince the audience that they share a commitment to a particular goal (helping people to lead long and healthy lives, for example). If the advocate can convince the audience that the proposal has a better chance of achieving that goal than does the status quo alone, then the audience will more likely find the case compelling.

A fourth organizational pattern used by policy advocates is called the ***criteria case***. When audiences agree that a problem exists (or when the advocate successfully convinces them that a problem exists) but they disagree as to what to do about the problem, the advocate may choose to present and defend specific criteria to guide them to the appropriate course of action. The criteria may be fairly self-evident: the new policy should be reasonably inexpensive, easily administered, and likely to be successful. Or, if necessary, the criterial could be very detailed and complicated. For example, policies to reduce obesity and decrease the incidence of diabetes could focus on: educating consumers about better food choices, reducing the cost and increasing access to healthier foods, setting limits on portion sizes, controlling the content of food advertisements, better food labeling, addressing the challenge of "food deserts" (neighborhoods where residents have fewer stores selling vegetables and fresh produce than are available in more advantaged neighborhoods). An advocate first establishes criteria and then presents the policy that best meets the criteria. This organizational pattern entails three main points: a review of the existing problem, the presentation of criteria to judge the scope of the problem and potential solutions, and the application of the criteria to the specific policy (or policies) proposed.

In all four of the organizational patterns, the advocate must tell the story of the way things are (the status quo) and the way things might be if the proposal were in place. Both depictions are necessary and challenge the advocate to create arguments that will gain the adherence, fully or partially, of their audience.

SUMMARY

In this chapter we have argued that research is important to the argumentation process, and we have attempted to equip you with the basic skills of research to support sound claims. We began by defining the research process and urged you to construct a research plan. We then recommended that you begin with general sources and move on to more specialized materials. Next, we considered what you should research and how to go about conducting research. We then discussed recording all the elements required for the citations of sources. We offered advice on what to consider and what you must prove in your arguments to gain the adherence of your audience. The final section of the chapter focused on how best to organize your claims.

Key Terms

comparative advantages case
criteria case
general sources
goals case
needs case
research
research plan
specialized sources

Activities

1. Select a controversy that you wish to research. Construct a research plan. Be sure to indicate what sources you will consult for each step of the plan, identifying your intentions to conduct both general and specific research.

2. Make a list of key terms and synonyms that you will use to conduct a survey of the controversy that you have selected.

3. Find an article, book, or essay relevant to your research using each of the following.
   a. The electronic search system in your college library
   b. Google
   c. Google Scholar
   d. A legal or government index
   e. The Web of Science

4. Record the full source citation and text of a quotation drawn from each of the sources that you found in question three.

5. Find a policy argument presented in an argument artifact and attempt to reorganize the advocacy using the four policy organization formats provided in this chapter: needs case, comparative advantage case, goals case, and criteria case.

Recommended Readings

Bogenschneider, Karen and Thomas J. Corbett, *Evidence-Based Policymaking: Insights from Policy-Minded Researchers and Research-Minded Policymakers* (New York: Routledge, 2010).

Bruschke, John, "Argument and Evidence Evaluation: A Call for Scholars to Engage Contemporary Public Debates," *Argumentation and Advocacy* 49 (2012): 59–75.

Chesebro, James W., "Beyond the Orthodox: The Criteria Case," *Journal of the American Forensic Association* 7 (1971): 208–215.

Chesebro, James W., "The Comparative Advantages Case," *Journal of the American Forensic Association* 5 (1968): 57–63.

Committee on the Use of Social Science Knowledge in Public Policy, *Using Science as Evidence in Public Policy* (Washington: National Research Council, 2012).

Greener, Ian and Brent Greve (Eds.), *Evidence and Evaluation in Social Policy* (Malden, MA: John Wiley and Sons, 2014).

Han, Bing and Edward L. Fink, "How Do Statistical and Narrative Evidence Affect Persuasion? The Role of Evidentiary Features," *Argumentation and Advocacy* 49 (2012): 39–58.

Lewinski, John D., Bruce R. Metzler, and Peter L. Settle, "The Goal Case Affirmative: An Alternative Approach to Academic Debate," *Journal of the American Forensic Association* 9 (1973): 458–463.

Macagno, Fabrizio, "Argument Relevance and Structure: Assessing and Developing Students' Uses of Evidence," *International Journal of Educational Research* 79 (2016): 180–194.

Zarefsky, David, "The Traditional Case-Comparative Advantage Case Dichotomy: Another Look," *Journal of the American Forensic Association* 6 (1969): 12–20.

Endnotes

[1] Neil Postman, *Amusing Ourselves to Death: Public Discourse in the Age of Show Business* (New York: Penguin, 1985), 21.

[2] Eric Rosenberg, "How Google Makes Money," Investopedia, June 23, 2020. https://www.investopedia.com/articles/investing/020515/business-google.asp

[3] "Intro to the Media Bias Chart®," Ad Fontes Media, September 2021. https://adfontesmedia.com/intro-to-the-media-bias-chart/

[4] Shawn Langlois, "How Biased Is Your News Source? You Probably Won't Agree with This Chart." Marketwatch, April 21, 2018.

[5] Lisa Lerer, "How Republican Vaccine Opposition Got to This Point," *The New York Times*, September 12, 2021. https://www.nytimes.com/2021/07/17/us/politics/coronavirus-vaccines-republicans.html

[6] Brian Contreras, "Internet Speech's Future After Trump," *Los Angeles Times*, January 13, 2021, p. A8.

[7] Nicholas Fandos, "Trump Impeached for Inciting Insurrection," *The New York Times*, January 13, 2021. https://www.nytimes.com/2021/01/13/us/politics/trump-impeached.html

[8] Daniel Funke, Susan Benkelman, and Cristina Tardaguila, "Factually: How Misinformation Makes Money," American Press Institute, September 26, 2019. https://www.americanpressinstitute.org/fact-checking-project/factually-newsletter/factually-how-misinformation-makes-money/

[9] Drew Harwell, Isaac Stanley-Becker, Razzan Nakhlawi, and Craig Timberg, "QAnon Reshaped Trump's Party and Radicalized Believers. The Capitol Siege May Be Just the Start," *Washington Post*, January 13, 2021. https://www.washingtonpost.com/technology/2021/01/13/qanon-capitol-siege-trump/

[10] For an interesting discussion of the power of precognitive reasoning see: Milton Lodge and Charles S. Taber, *The Rationalizing Voter* (New York: Cambridge University Press, 2013), especially chapters 1 and 7.

[11] Ian Sample, "What Are Deepfakes and How Can You Spot Them?" *The Guardian*, January 13, 2020. https://www.theguardian.com/technology/2020/jan/13/what-are-deepfakes-and-how-can-you-spot-them

[12] Ibid.

[13] Vanessa Romo, "Dr. Scott Atlas, Coronavirus Adviser to Trump, Resigns," NPR, November 30, 2020. https://www.npr.org/2020/11/30/940376041/dr-scott-atlas-special-coronavirus-adviser-to-trump-resigns

[14] Ofra Klein, "Misleading Memes: The Effects of Deceptive Visuals of the British National Party," *PArtecipazione e COnflitto, The Open Journal of Sociopolitical Studies,* March 15, 2020. https://cadmus.eui.eu/bitstream/handle/1814/67311/Misleading_memes.pdf?sequence=1&isAllowed=y

[15] William Cummings, Joey Garrison, and Jim Sergent, "By the Numbers: President Donald Trump's Failed Efforts to Overturn the Election," *USA Today*, January 6, 2021. https://www.usatoday.com/in-depth/news/politics/elections/2021/01/06/trumps-failed-efforts-overturn-election-numbers/4130307001/

[16] Associated Press, "Transcript of Trump's Speech at Rally Before U.S. Capitol Riot," *US News and World Report*, January 13, 2021. https://www.usnews.com/news/politics/articles/2021-01-13/transcript-of-trumps-speech-at-rally-before-us-capitol-riot

[17] Elizabeth Dwoskin, "Facebook's Sandberg Deflected Blame for Capitol Riot, but New Evidence Shows How Platform Played Role," *Washington Post*, January 13, 2021. https://www.washingtonpost.com/technology/2021/01/13/facebook-role-in-capitol-protest/

[18] MLA (Modern Language Association), APA (American Psychological Association), Turabian (developed by Kate Turabian), and Chicago Manual of Style (developed by researchers and editors at the University of Chicago) are all organized style systems. Your instructor in this class or others will likely assign one of these citation systems for your use. Most are available in software programs to accompany your word processing program. All are also available for consultation online, in reference libraries, or in book form (available for purchase in your campus bookstore or online). What is most important is that you faithfully and consistently follow the guidelines in the style manual you select.

[19] Holly Honderich, "Eugene Goodman Hailed for Guiding Mitt Romney to Safety," BBC News, February 11, 2021. https://www.bbc.com/news/world-us-canada-55623752

[20] Megan Garber, "When the Mob Reached the Chamber," *The Atlantic*, January 7, 2021. https://www.theatlantic.com/culture/archive/2021/01/capitol-when-mob-entered-chamber-pictures-tourists/617586/

[21] W. J. Hennigan and Vera Bergengruen, "Insurrectionists Openly Planned for Weeks to Storm the Capitol. Why Were Police So Easily Overwhelmed?" *Time*, January 7, 2021. https://time.com/5927215/capitol-hill-police-riots-unprepared/

[22] Lloyd F. Bitzer, "The Rhetorical Situation," *Philosophy and Rhetoric* 1 (1968): 1–14.

9

Refuting Arguments

We have all, from time to time, found ourselves inclined to disagree with a statement that was uttered by someone else. We might be engaged in a discussion around a conference table or kitchen table, or we could be in a classroom, living room, boardroom or even a bedroom. When such a moment of disagreement occurs, we must decide whether or not we should voice our disagreement. Is the disagreement worth pursuing? Would we be better served to keep silent? If we continually express disagreement with the claims of others, they may decide we are argumentative and that assessment may lead them to reduce their communication with us. Nevertheless, if we conclude that it is worthwhile to express our disagreement, we then have to consider how we might best formulate and present our arguments. Unfortunately, even the best arguments we can muster to support our convictions might not be adequate to convince others to agree with our views. They may be persuaded, however, if in addition to presenting our own views we simultaneously point out the weaknesses in their claims. This process is called *refutation*.

Even when we are not engaged in direct conversations with other advocates, we may automatically—and almost instinctively—subject the arguments offered by others to the refutational process. Why? Because it is natural for us to evaluate critically the claims that others offer for our consideration. Humans are not sheep that can be led wherever or whenever another person wishes to lead them. Humans have agency. We have choice over our actions and naturally evaluate the claims advanced by others because we have learned that uncritical acceptance of advocacy directed our way can lead to undesirable consequences. So, we scrutinize the messages we receive. Some we accept; others we reject. Understanding the refutation process will enable you to evaluate more carefully the arguments you personally encounter and will give you the tools to identify why you reject a claim, should you decide to verbalize your objections.

In this chapter we will first define the refutation process. Then we will systematically guide you through the steps necessary to critically evaluate an argument, formulate a response, and verbally present your refutation.

THE REFUTATION PROCESS DEFINED

To refute an argument is to deny its validity and refuse to agree with it. The *refutation process*, therefore, is a series of actions culminating in the denial of an argument advanced by another. It is not simply attacking another's argument; instead, it is figuring out an appropriate strategy to develop and organize a response to another's claim. Refutation may be in response to written or oral arguments. In this discussion, however we will primarily focus on refutation aimed at oral arguments. We believe that the refutation of an oral argument involves four steps:

1. Listening in a focused way
2. Critically evaluating the arguments
3. Formulating a response
4. Presenting that response

Focused Listening (Step One)

Listening versus Hearing

Have you ever had a conversation where you remember hearing the other person speak but you cannot recall what was actually said? Almost certainly you have. Odds are good that this has happened in a classroom. You were hearing a lecture, but you were not really tuned into what was being said. This is a case where you were hearing but not listening. Hearing is passive. We have little or no control over it. Surely at some time or another you have been stuck in a car or a small room where someone has played annoying music. Try as you might, blocking out the noise is almost impossible. We cannot choose not to hear. In contrast, listening is active. It requires concentration or focus. This applies in reading too. If you find yourself rereading something because you do not remember what you just read, it could be because you lost your concentration. There are several reasons why people may be considered poor listeners.

Factors Affecting Listening

SELECTIVE EXPOSURE. We all tend to seek out discourse (in either written or oral forms) with which we agree and to avoid discourse with which we do not agree. It is more cognitively comforting when we discover that our already held opinions are reinforced by others. In contrast, it is cognitively discomforting to encounter contrary information. Samuel Popkin has described people as "cognitive misers"—they do not work harder to make decisions than is necessary, and they are willing to take reasoning shortcuts in order to confirm their existing beliefs.[1] Consequently, many people avoid exposing themselves to messages that they believe will be contrary to their existing beliefs. For example, liberals for the most part avoid tuning into Sean Hannity, and conservatives avoid listening to Rachel Maddow.

DISTORTION. It is often unsettling to be exposed to messages with which we strongly disagree. Since we prefer not to be unsettled, our minds may help us by distorting the message into something we find more palatable. We may also distort messages because we anticipate the rest of a message before hearing it in its entirety. Did you notice that the word *in* was repeated in the prior sentence? Some readers will have skipped right over the repeated word because they anticipated the end of the sentence. We can distort advocates' arguments the same way—by thinking we know what they are going to say prior to their saying it.

INTRAPERSONAL ARGUMENTS. Another common human reaction when hearing something is that we turn our attention away from the discourse to an internal discussion in our minds. When we argue with ourselves or focus on what we are going to say instead of attending to the comments being offered by someone else, we are not doing a very good job of listening.

EXTERNALITIES. Distractions can also prevent us from being good listeners. Noise draws our attention away from what is being said. Many different things can constitute such noise. For example, it could be a whirring fan in the background, or freeway noise, or the annoying couple behind talking loudly all through a film. But you can also think of noise in a different sense. Noise can be your smartphone that distracts you and pulls you away from the conversation, enticing you to browse websites or text friends. It can be the attractive person who walks by and attracts your attention. It can be the smell of the potato chips that the person sitting next to you is eating in class. Any external factor that draws your attention may diminish your ability to be an effective listener. Beware the bright and shiny objects when listening!

INTERNALITIES. Just as external factors can interfere with your perception of messages, internal factors can also distract you. If you feel ill that day, perhaps you have a headache or an upset stomach, you will not be a good listener. If you did not get a restful sleep, you will not be as effective as a listener. If you are upset about something, it might distract you and cause you not to be a good listener. Sometimes the person who is arguing with you will, intentionally or unintentionally, manage to hit your "hot buttons"—those sensitive, psychological points that upset you or cause you to unravel. Relatives, and especially siblings, often are adept at hitting those buttons, and they seem to know just what to say to get us riled up—a skill no doubt derived from years of practice! But when we react emotionally to these triggers, we lose our ability to listen effectively.

So, the first step in effective listening is to attend to the discourse so you can comprehend it and understand exactly what it is that the advocate is arguing. But active listening is only half of the task of being an effective listener. You also have to develop your critical ear. A critical ear is one that is listening intently in order to identify the potential flaws or weaknesses in the arguments advanced by other advocates.

CRITICALLY EVALUATING ARGUMENTS (STEP TWO)

In this text, we have attempted to teach you to be skeptical of the advocacy efforts of others. Many of the issues presented in this book come together in the refutation process. Listening actively is a good start, but it is only a start. The product of active listening is accurate reception of the other person's argumentation—correctly hearing what the other person has said. But you still need to evaluate the messages that you received.

Determining What the Advocate Is Arguing

You should begin your evaluation by trying to determine what it is that the other person is arguing. Sometimes this is not as easy as it sounds. Some advocates just do not argue well. As a result, they can be very difficult to follow. Others may deliberately try to conceal their objectives. The intentional attempt to disguise or conceal one's real argument may be considered *obfuscation*. There are at least two reasons why an advocate might resort to obfuscation: to be kind or to be tricky.

Advocates may deliberately use language that is not explicit because they wish to shield the listener from unnecessary pain or discomfort. Often this is accomplished through the use of euphemisms. A *euphemism* is a mild or inoffensive term that can be used in place of language that might offend or suggest something unpleasant. A friend of ours provided an interesting example. She taught her three-year-old son that when he went to dinner at someone else's house and was served a food he did not like, he should tell the host or hostess that it was "interesting." All seemed to be going well. The child was served a cooked vegetable. Without prompting, he declared it to be "interesting." Then he brightly looked up and told the hostess: "When I say something is interesting, that means I don't like it!" The child had sort of mastered the art of using a euphemism. What he had not yet learned is that euphemisms generally work best if you leave it to the listener to decode their meaning.

There are many examples, such as the one above, where language is used euphemistically to achieve relatively benign purposes. Think of the language used to refer to someone who is dying: people pass away, they go to a better place, they leave this earth, they move on, or they go to sleep. Such terms are intended to soften the impact of declaring that someone is dead.

Cultures also have many names given for what individuals do in bathrooms. Some printable examples include: powdering one's nose, going to the john, freshening up, and answering the call of nature. Indeed, the entire process of using the proper term to excuse yourself from a group so that you can perform natural bodily functions that everyone else in the group also has to perform is part of a cultural ritual.

At other times language may be used perniciously to confuse or conceal. This type of language is called *doublespeak*. The use of doublespeak is especially common in times of war. Prisoners of war, for example, might be called "detainees" rather than prisoners. Innocent civilians who are killed might be referred to as "collateral damage." Indeed, the weapons of war themselves may be referred to as "patriot missiles," "smart bombs," "peacekeepers," or "Minutemen." Such names are important because they symbolically distance us from the acts of violence that may be conducted in our name when we go to war.[2] Doublespeak is the strategic use of language to conceal meaning. "Taxes" become "revenue enhancements." Workers are not "laid off," they are "transitioned," "retrenched," or they accept "voluntary severance."

There are at least two specific ways in which language can conceal.

AMBIGUITY. When advocates deliberately employ language that is overly broad or unclear, they are utilizing *ambiguity*. Such a situation may result in our having only a vague understanding of what it is that they are actually advocating. Politicians who wish to avoid alienating public support for their decisions often speak so vaguely that what they say is almost indecipherable. George W. Bush and members of his administration, when speaking to the public, said that many of the prisoners detained at Guantanamo Bay went through a process of "enhanced interrogation"—rather than saying they were tortured. As another example, politicians talk about support for "family values." But what does that expression really mean? Does it mean opposition to abortion rights? Does it mean support for paid family leave to take care of sick relatives? Does it mean after-school programs for children? Does it mean welfare reform programs that make it more difficult for unwed mothers to move out on their own and get their own apartments? Does it mean censoring films or TV programs to prevent children from viewing material deemed inappropriate to their development? Does it mean encouraging "stay at home" moms? Does it mean subsidized day care centers? Does it mean taking a position either in favor of or in opposition to same-sex marriages? Obviously, the term "family values" can mean many different things to many different people, some of which seem to advance a liberal political agenda and others a conservative agenda.

EQUIVOCATION. Allowing the same stance to take on two different meanings at different times is *equivocation.* For example, political candidates may equivocate so that different audiences assign different meanings to roughly the same words. In this fashion, they try to ensure that potential voters are not alienated by the positions taken. As an illustration, during the 2008 presidential campaign candidate Barack Obama criticized his primary opponents (then) Senator Hillary Clinton and (then) Senator John Edwards for accepting "special interest" campaign donations, referring specifically to contributions from labor unions. Later, deciding to pursue money from unions himself, he characterized unions "as the representatives of working people," and declared that he was "thrilled" by their support.[3]

The issue of allowing undocumented immigrants access to drivers' licenses has similarly created challenges over many decades for Democratic political candidates who sought to win the votes of minorities without losing the support of moderate or conservative voters who wanted the government to pursue more strict limitations on immigration. For example, former Governor Gray Davis of California frequently proclaimed that he was "tough" on crime. During his reelection campaign in 2002 he declared his opposition to legislation that would permit undocumented immigrants to get drivers' licenses. One year later, faced with the prospect of a recall election, Governor Davis announced his enthusiastic support for a bill that would permit the undocumented to get drivers' licenses. Now he argued that if the Department of Motor Vehicles' files contained photographs, thumbprints, and addresses of the undocumented it would be easier to find those who were suspected of committing crimes. Again, this position was offered as evidence that the governor was "tough" on crime. The governor's office also issued a statement declaring that the governor had not changed his mind in response to the upcoming recall election or because the bill was endorsed by organized labor (a constituency that was very important to his campaign).[4] Opponents of the bill complained that the governor's change of mind illustrated that he was "willing to sacrifice the very lives of law-abiding Americans and legal residents in exchange for [Latinx] votes to stay in office." The sponsor of the bill argued that it showed that the governor recognized "that on national security and national traffic safety issues, this is good policy."[5] Hillary Clinton, a U.S. senator from New York at the time, similarly allowed her position to change on the drivers' license issue, only she moved toward a more conservative position. Clinton expressed support for a plan issued by (then) Governor Eliot Spitzer to offer undocumented immigrants in New York access to drivers' licenses in October 2007. Yet, only a month later during a televised primary debate in Nevada "she replied with a simple 'No' when asked if she approved the drivers' license idea in the absence of comprehensive immigration reform."[6] As of 2020, only fifteen states in the United States permitted undocumented immigrants to acquire drivers' licenses. The consequences were made clear during the COVID-19 pandemic. As NPR reported:

> Hailed as heroes during the pandemic, essential workers have cared for the elderly in nursing homes and kept food supplies moving from farms to supermarkets. But thousands of these workers are also undocumented immigrants facing this choice to keep their jobs: ride a crowded bus or drive without license.[7]

Riding a crowded bus clearly increased the risk of exposure to COVID-19, and it was also clear that "immigrant communities experience disproportionately higher rates of deaths" from the disease. Thus, the issue of giving undocumented workers access to drivers' licenses became even more urgent.[8]

In many political campaigns, candidate equivocations are often called out as "flip-flops." Candidates are criticized for changing their positions on issues, usually for political gain. It is not well known by many today, but as Governor of California, Ronald Reagan in 1967 signed one of the most liberal abortion laws in the nation. Yet later, as a candidate for president, he declared himself a "pro-life" and "anti-abortion" candidate, expressing views that appealed to and mobilized social conservatives in the GOP.[9] Barack Obama consistently expressed support for public funding for presidential campaigns and promised that he would accept public funding in 2008. Taking the federal funds, however, would have limited his campaign spending to $84.1 million. When it became clear that he could raise significantly more than that amount, and that he could outspend his Republican opponent Senator John McCain, Obama changed his mind and rejected the public funds. A McCain campaign spokesperson, as could be expected, quickly condemned the inconsistency.

> Today, Barack Obama has revealed himself to be just another typical politician who will do and say whatever is most expedient for Barack Obama. . . . The true test of a candidate for president is whether he will stand on principle and keep his word to the American people. Barack Obama has failed that test today, and his reversal of his promise to participate in the public finance system undermines his call for a new type of politics.[10]

Voters often react badly to candidates who equivocate ("flip-flop) on their previously expressed positions, as political scientists Michael Tomz and Robert Van Houweling explain.

> Without penalties for repositioning, politicians would have little incentive to speak honestly. They could say almost anything during campaigns, knowing that voters would excuse them for reneging on commitments. Under such circumstances voters would find it extremely difficult to learn who represents their views. Advertisements, speeches, and policy manifestos would amount to cheap talk, rather than reliable cues about the policies that candidates would pursue in office. Thus, representative democracy may not function well unless voters apply at least some penalties against politicians who deviate from their promises.[11]

But, Tomz and Van Houweling also conceded that the views of politicians and public opinion on issues do evolve over time. Thus, it is not only reasonable for candidates and elected officials to change their minds but it is also understandable and arguably even desirable that they do so on some issues.

> If voters react negatively to repositioning, they could deter leaders from adapting to shifts in public opinion or the arrival of new policy-relevant information. The existence of penalties for repositioning could also contribute to polarization and legislative gridlock.[12]

In short, there is no easy answer for assessing the meaning, importance, and significance of a political candidate or elected official's equivocation or flip-flopping. Each case should be evaluated based on individual circumstances and merits. It is further complicated because some advocates who equivocate may use language that purposely confuses or hides their real motivations. In such cases, it may be necessary to ask questions of the advocate and read between the lines. You should also look for cues in the information that is available to you. Can you glean anything from your knowledge of the context for the argument? How about from your knowledge of the advocate? Do other messages that emerge at the same time shed light on what might motivate the advocate? Such analysis is an important way to critically evaluate arguments in order to better understand the advocate's intentions and goals.

Evaluating the Reasoning

We have previously discussed the reasoning process (chapter 6) and the data used to support claims (chapter 7). These are the starting points for the critical assessment of ideas that is central to the refutation process.

In chapter 6 we presented different forms of inductive and deductive reasoning. The first step in evaluating the reasoning employed by the advocate is to determine what kind of reasoning is being used and to apply the appropriate tests for that type of reasoning. Recall the discussions in chapter 6 of the tests for reasoning from examples, analogies, causal correlations, sign, and causal generalizations. If the reasoning appears to pass those tests, you should then consider the additional tests of arguments presented below. An argument that uses flawed reasoning may be considered *fallacious*, and the tests below are known as *fallacies of reasoning*.

Argument scholars have identified many examples of fallacies. Audiences in each field determine whether to grant adherence to a story or not, but it is useful to understand and to recognize different types of fallacies. We present three categories of fallacies and offer several illustrations of each.

FALLACIES OF IRRELEVANT REASONING. Some advocates base their claims on what most argument scholars consider irrelevant reasons. We identify seven.

1. **Ad populum.** If an advocate attempts to prove a claim by arguing that most people agree with that claim, the advocate is committing the ***ad populum*** (appealing to the people) fallacy. For example, poll data may indicate that the majority of Americans believe that public schools fail to do a good job in educating students. Yet, for an advocate to offer this poll data as proof that public schools are failing may be fallacious. The majority could be wrong. It is much more important to know why people believe that the schools are failing. What are their reasons? When these reasons for the public opinions are presented, they can be examined as could any other reasons. Simply because a majority believes something is true does not make it correct. Majorities once believed the world was flat, that slavery was morally acceptable, and that kings were divinely chosen. Contemporary audiences know the reasons why these beliefs are incorrect and would not give them even a moment's consideration.

2. **Ad hominem.** We recall hearing a friend providing dietary advice to a colleague. The colleague later rejected the advice. He justified dismissing the generally sound advice about avoiding certain types of fats because the friend who

provided it to him was himself overweight. Does the friend's weight invalidate his argument? If an advocate argues that an idea should be rejected because there is something wrong with the person presenting it—not something wrong with the idea—they are engaging in ***ad hominem*** (attacking the person). Even the worst person—someone who lacks good character and good judgment—can have a good idea. You should argue about the merits of the claim that is offered and not the qualities of the source. This can be tricky, of course, as we are not arguing that as an advocate you should ignore the credibility of a source or the integrity of an advocate. We do believe, however, that advocates should never presume that it is sufficient to refute an argument only by attacking its source.

3. **Appeal to pity.** On rare occasions the only basis for a claim will be a statement intended to provoke pity. When the claim calls for compassion, pity may be a relevant reason. For example, audiences might be moved to act on the basis of an argument that produces pity for children who could be denied life-saving medicines or surgery because their parents lack the means to pay for treatment. On the other hand, a student who attempts to petition a teacher for a higher grade on an examination on the basis of an ***appeal to pity*** is not making a very strong claim.

4. **Appeal to fear.** The threat "your money or your life" relies on fear to convince people to agree to hand over their cash. Such ***appeals to fear*** do not provide real choice, and thus they are not really reasons offered to win agreement—even if they are sometimes successful in gaining compliance.

5. **Tu quoque.** Defending one's actions by pointing out that others acted in a similar fashion is not really an appropriate or sufficient defense (***tu quoque*** means you're another). Thus, if you are pulled over for speeding, a judge will not likely be persuaded by a defense that says others were also speeding so it is unfair for you to have been the one detained. The fact that others also were violating the speed limit does not invalidate the charge against you. This form of fallacy is sometimes referred to as "whataboutism." It is a strategy to distract someone by essentially calling them hypocritical for being concerned about one issue while overlooking another. Following the insurrection at the U.S. Capitol on January 6, 2021, for example, some arguers sought to defend the rioters by comparing them to Black Lives Matter protesters during the summer months of 2020. That some of those earlier protests led to violence and property damage does not diminish the significance of the violence sparked by the unique threat of attempting to halt the tallying of the electoral votes in a presidential election.

6. **Appeal to tradition.** Because something has always been done a particular way may or may not be a good reason to continue to do it that way. Determining whether it is appropriate to do something in the way it has customarily been done requires an evaluation of the reasons. For example, a congressional representative argued that the United States should hold elections on Saturdays instead of Tuesdays in order to increase voter turnout. He reasoned that since more people were off work on Saturdays, they would be more likely to cast their vote. Another representative, who opposed increasing voter turnout (probably because his own candidacy and perhaps his party was advantaged by

lower turnout), argued that the United States has always voted on Tuesdays and thus always should do so. Although there may be other good reasons not to change the day on which Americans cast their ballots, merely invoking an *appeal to tradition* is probably an insufficient reason not to consider alternatives.

7. **Slippery slope.** If you have ever started down an ice-covered hill, you have experienced how difficult it is to stop your momentum. As you gain momentum, you run the risks of not stopping and/or becoming injured. When an advocate objects to something not because it is itself undesirable but because it may eventually lead to something else that is undesirable, the advocate is employing the *slippery slope* tactic. For example, some conservatives have opposed extending legal immigration status to young people who were brought to the United States as children because they believe doing so rewards illegal behavior (in this case, not the behavior of the children who would be granted legal status but the behavior of parents or guardians) and thereby encourage others to come to the United States illegally. One can almost always take an action that may be desirable without causing other undesirable outcomes to follow. Granting legal status to youngsters who may have no memory of ever having lived anywhere except the United States and who may not even be conversant in the language of their native country does not prevent the government of the United States from continuing to strictly enforce immigration laws for those yet to arrive in the United States. Linking a justifiable outcome with the potential for an objectionable result is not a convincing reason to reject the proposal.

FALLACIES OF MISCASTING THE ISSUE. Sometimes advocates commit errors in reasoning by casting the dispute in fallacious terms. We present three such fallacies.

1. **Fallacy of composition.** The *fallacy of composition* is committed when an advocate argues that what is true of the parts is also true of the whole. For example, we recently heard someone argue that the faculties of the state university system were creative in dealing with problems and thus the budget cuts that were being proposed would not be devastating to students. The fact that faculties are capable of making do with less, however commendable that may be, does not suggest that the entire university system would be creative or that individual students would not suffer from cuts that decreased the number of classes available to them, increased the average class sizes, and shrunk the budgets for library acquisitions and student aid.

2. **Fallacy of division.** This fallacy is the reverse of the fallacy of composition. The advocate who claims that what is true of the whole must be true of the individual parts is committing the *fallacy of division*. For example, a U.S. Army unit serving in Iraq was accused of badly mistreating Iraqi civilians who had been arrested as suspected terrorists. The military commander responded to the complaint by asserting that the case must not be true because the U.S. military was committed to discipline and to treating prisoners in accordance with the established laws of war. It may, of course, be true that institutionally the military is committed to discipline and to protecting the rights of detainees, but this does not mean that all individual soldiers are similarly committed to honoring these laws of war. Thus, such an assertion does not deny that this case of alleged abuse may have occurred.

3. **Fallacy of false dichotomy.** Life is rarely all black or all white. There often are gray areas. An advocate who casts an argument in either/or terms may be committing a *fallacy of false dichotomy*. On September 20, 2001, President George W. Bush declared a "war on terrorism" and asserted that nations could decide to be either "with us or with the terrorists."[13] Many Americans seemed to take the president at his word. When our long-time allies, the French, German, and Canadian governments, declined to support U.S. military intervention in Iraq there were loud public protests and expressions of opposition to their disloyalty. Indeed, at least for a time, tourism to these nations declined and there were attempts to boycott purchasing goods from them. The argument that opposition to a U.S. incursion into Iraq constituted support for terrorism was not very well reasoned or compelling, at least if viewed from a perspective less infused with patriotic emotion.

FALLACIES OF MISDIRECTING THE ISSUE. The final category of fallacies concerns those occasions when advocates avoid proving their claims by distracting the audience.

1. **Shifting the burden of proof.** Instead of proving their own claim, some advocates challenge audiences to disprove the claim. "There is no end to the universe, and I challenge you to prove that there is!" Perhaps the claim is true, but the advocate who advances the claim has the responsibility to prove it. There is no obligation to refute an unproven claim. An advocate who challenges an audience to do so is *shifting the burden of proof*.

2. **Begging the question.** An advocate who essentially restates his or her claim and offers it as the only reason in support of the claim is guilty of *begging the question*. "I think I should have received an A on this paper," said a student. When asked why, the student said, "Because it is an A paper." The student's reason is the same as the claim. The argument has thus not been advanced or supported. The student could have given some data or offered some well-reasoned arguments—the paper was thorough, the topic was important, it was well-researched, it was carefully organized, it was clear, it was coherent, it was well-written, and it offered compelling arguments. There must be reasons to support of the claim—not just a repetition of the claim.

3. **Straw man fallacy.** It is not difficult to knock over a man constructed from straw. Nor is it especially difficult to refute an opponent's argument if you get to present their claim in an unfair fashion. Some advocates, for example, have repeatedly attacked arguments in favor of reforming the health-care delivery system in the United States by labeling such proposals as attempts to offer socialized medicine. Then they attack socialism. These advocates often fail to argue how the proposed policies equate with "socialized medicine." They often fail to provide specific reasons why socialized medicine would be undesirable. They may even fail to delineate specific objections to the new proposal. As a result, they fail to refute the merits of the arguments for the new systems. They have attacked a straw man in order to divert attention from a substantive analysis of the actual proposal. This form of reasoning constitutes a *straw man fallacy*.

4. **Red herring.** A *red herring fallacy* is an attempt to distract someone from attending to an argument by urging them to attend to something else. A stu-

dent of one of your authors submitted a paper that was taken word-for-word from a paper submitted by a student at another university and posted to the internet. When the student was confronted about the plagiarism, she did not attempt to offer a defense. Instead she offered a teary explanation about all of the financial sacrifices that her parents had made to pay her tuition and room and board at an expensive private university. Yes, her actions will no doubt disappoint her parents, and we felt bad for them because she would suffer the financial cost of having to retake the class. In addition, she would face other severe sanctions imposed by the university. Sadly, however, disappointing her parents was not a compelling defense for her ethical lapse.

In each of the foregoing fallacies the reasoning offered is flawed. As a result, the argument is a ***non sequitur***, which means that the conclusion does not follow from the claim.

Once you have subjected the reasoning offered in support of a claim to critical scrutiny, it is time to turn your attention to the advocate's narrative and to the grounds or evidence offered.

Evaluating the Narrative and the Grounds

In chapter 4 we considered how advocates use language to construct their arguments. We specifically discussed the elements of a narrative: actors, scene, and events. With each, we discussed what constituted effective argument. As the audience of another's argument you should also carefully examine these depictions. Analyze how the advocate depicts these narrative elements. Are the characterizations fitting? Are they consistent? Are there alternative and more appropriate constructions? Similarly, if the advocate employs a metaphor, the critical consumer will want to evaluate whether this particular metaphor is appropriate. Are there weaknesses in the comparisons it makes?

In chapter 8 we presented four types of data that advocates use to support their arguments: premises, examples, statistics, and testimony. We also identified ways in which you can test the data to see whether audiences will consider them compelling. Now we will discuss strategies for refuting data.

FORMULATING A RESPONSE (STEP THREE)

Once you have discovered what it is that an advocate has said and evaluated the discourse to determine whether the argument is faulty or not, you must determine how you wish to respond. If the argument is not faulty, you may find that you actually agree with it. If, on the other hand, you find you still disagree with an argument, you must decide on the most appropriate manner to express that disagreement.

Sometimes the best response to an argument is to offer no response at all. In some cases, an opposing advocate's argument may be so weak that it falls on its face and does not even merit a response. On other occasions, the price that you might pay by engaging in an argument may be too great. Individuals who continually find fault with the advocacy advanced by others are considered argumentative. Most people prefer not to associate with argumentative people. Thus, we urge you to choose your arguments carefully. Once you do decide to refute an argument, you must develop a strategy that best expresses your opposition and that best discovers and exposes the weaknesses or flaws in the opposing arguments.

Strategy

Your first decision at this point is to determine which of your opponent's arguments you believe to be most vulnerable. It is likely that not all of your adversary's arguments are faulty. Even if they were, you might not wish to spend the time and energy required to attack them all. Your choice of which arguments you will oppose will vary from situation to situation, with the nature of the arguments advanced, and in response to your insights about the audience for your claims.

If you are engaging in interpersonal argument, then you may have little time to present your views before you are interrupted. In such circumstances, you would probably be wise to decide what the most critical point is and start there. If you are engaging in an audience debate, you may have more time and you may be able to advance a number of objections. So, consider the situation you are in when choosing your strategy.

You should also consider the nature of the dispute. Is this a disagreement over a claim of fact, value, or policy? The stock issues for each kind of dispute are fairly well established (see chapter 5), and you may choose which of these you wish to dispute. Policy advocates, for example, must convince neutral audiences that there is a problem with the status quo, that the current policies cannot solve that problem, that the proposed policy will solve that problem, and that there are not significant disadvantages to the new proposal. If you are attempting to refute a policy argument using this approach you can choose which of these stock issues you will address. You need not refute them all. There is no reason to adopt a new policy if the existing problems that have been identified are really not all that significant (ill), if the new policy that has been advocated (cure) will not likely solve the ill(s), or if the current mechanisms already in place will ultimately be able to remedy the problem (blame). Selecting the point of stasis is an important element in your strategic planning.

Finally, take into consideration the values and beliefs of the audience. The field of argument determines the standards for what constitutes good evidence. Arguments that might work in a legal context (accusations of hearsay evidence, for example) might be irrelevant in interpersonal argument situations. Further, the values of the audience will certainly influence the arguments you choose for your refutation. You may believe that capital punishment is immoral but if you know your audience does not share the belief you will construct your arguments accordingly.

Tactics

Having decided what arguments you wish to refute, you must now go about the business of refutation. You will continue to face some strategic choices that could influence the effectiveness of your arguments.

REFUTATION BY DENIAL. Sometimes an advocate seems completely wrong. He or she makes a statement that you believe cannot be supported. As an illustration, we cite the claim that one of our students made: "There are absolutely no significant ideological differences between Democrats and Republicans." If you believe that someone has made a statement that cannot be supported, you are justified in selecting a strategy of denial. This entails attempting to prove that the claim(s) offered by that advocate is (are) erroneous. Such a strategy will, in all likelihood, necessitate that you have evidentiary material that supports your opposite conclusion. But such supporting material alone may not be sufficient. Your opponents and your audience should not be left with contradictory arguments without also having a basis for determining which conclusion is the better one.

To be successful in *refutation by denial* you must be able to account for why the two conclusions conflict and why the conclusion that you prefer is indeed the more compelling one. Perhaps you can point out how the opposing advocate has made erroneous assumptions, or perhaps you can demonstrate that the evidence that you present in support of your argument is stronger than that offered by your opponent. In some cases you may discover that the argument advanced by the other advocate contradicts a claim that the advocate previously offered. It certainly strengthens your argument if you can offer a convincing case for deciding why the view that you are espousing is superior. For the example mentioned above, you might want to select two or three very concrete issues that illustrate the significant differences between the ideological commitments of the Democratic and Republican parties. Consider as examples the numerous executive orders that President Trump signed to unravel policies created by President Obama on issues such as immigration, environmental regulations, oil and gas leases, the rights of transgendered people to serve in the military, etc. Once President Biden took office, he issued a similar spate of executive orders overturning those issued by Trump and returning to many of the policies of the Obama era.

REFUTATION BY MITIGATION. The effect of *refutation by mitigation* is to minimize the impact of the advocacy you wish to undermine. Perhaps the other advocate has, in your mind, exaggerated the claims that he or she has offered or overstated the breadth or significance of a problem. Maybe the reasoning offered is dubious, the characterizations are spurious, or the evidence that has been provided is questionable. In any case, it is doubtful that these arguments alone will convince the advocate or an undecided audience that the advocate is completely wrong. At best such refutation will diminish the strength of the advocate's claims, but some probative argumentative force will probably remain. Thus, the strategy of mitigation must be used in conjunction with other arguments. An arguer could claim, for example, that we are witnessing the impact of global climate change in the increased number of wildfires and the damage to communities in the West. Another arguer could try to mitigate this argument by arguing for far stricter building codes in areas where residential tracts border wilderness areas.

REFUTATION BY ADDITIONAL CONSIDERATION. The opposing advocate may also offer arguments that you find both logically correct and convincing, in which case it may not be possible for you to either deny or mitigate the advocate's position. This does not leave you without recourse, however, for you might still be able to identify ways in which the advocate's reasoning may be incomplete. We consider two possibilities that employ *refutation by additional consideration*.

Reducing the Argument to Absurdity. The Latin term for *reducing to absurdity* is *reductio ad absurdum*. With this tactic you attempt to take the opposing advocate's reasoning to its logical conclusion, hoping to reveal how it is flawed. Consider one of the arguments that has been advanced for the legalization of cocaine: laws forbidding the use and sale of drugs have been ineffective. You might oppose this argument by noting that the assumption of this claim is that if a law cannot be enforced it should be abandoned. Indeed then, any law that has been frequently violated is a law that might, by this standard, be abandoned. Should this reasoning then logically extend to laws against speeding, drunk driving, assault, or even murder? Many people fail to pay their legally required taxes. Should the government simply stop enforcing the tax code? Examining the advocate's reasoning this closely may illustrate the faulty assumption of the argument—that the inability to adequately enforce a law means that the behavior it prohibits should be legalized.

Turning the Tables. It is possible that the advocate is correct, as far as the reasoning goes, but the consequences he or she opposes are actually desirable. In academic debate this type of argument—*turning the tables*—is called a turnaround. It simply means taking a negative position and turning it into a positive, or taking a positive position and demonstrating how it is really a negative one. Suppose an advocate argues that some policy might have adverse consequences for the U.S. economy. For example, an advocate might claim that a ban on fracking and on oil leases in the Alaskan wilderness would lead to escalating and unstable oil prices that could damage the prospects for long-term economic growth. The opposing advocate, however, could argue that gasoline prices in the United States are actually too low—much lower, for example, than the prices paid by Europeans. These low prices, it could then be argued, have encouraged wasteful practices such as people driving to work alone, the purchase of gas guzzling sport utility vehicles, and the use of energy inefficient appliances. Higher oil prices, on the other hand might lead to greater conservation methods, might spur the transition to more electric and zero-emission vehicles, might encourage the development and use of mass transit, and might help address the existential crisis of climate change. An advocate might also argue that higher oil prices might cause our economy to grow at a slower but more sustainable rate that would actually improve economic conditions over the long term.

Preparation for Refutation

Deciding on the strategy and tactics that you wish to use will be much easier if you have had the opportunity to prepare for the refutation process. While preparation is unlikely in the case of interpersonal arguments, it is possible to be prepared in more formal situations, that is in fields like debate, in academic or scientific disputes, or in legal disputes. In such situations, you should anticipate what your opponent might argue and prepare for different contingencies and then consider the stock issues that need to be addressed. Gather your supporting materials ahead of time. These materials may be prepared in the form of briefs (sometimes called blocks) of arguments.

Briefs are a series of arguments, claims, and the requisite supporting evidence and/or analysis organized to support a specific point of clash. A well-prepared advocate prepares for a variety of different contingencies and probably has many more briefed arguments than they would use in a particular dispute. For example, attorneys anticipate which witnesses the opposition might call and outline the questions that they intend to ask. They even anticipate the cross-examination conducted by the other side and the questions likely to be asked so that they are prepared to follow up when given an opportunity to redirect questions to that witness. Likewise, debaters anticipate the arguments their opponents will raise, prepare responses, and in some cases anticipate what the opponents will say to those responses and prepare extension briefs to answer those points.

— **SAMPLE BRIEF** —

If you want to argue that "fish-farming" or what is sometimes known as aquaculture might resolve the world's hunger, an opponent could argue that fish-farming damages the environment. In anticipation of such arguments, you might develop a brief to refute these claims.

Responses to "fish-farming" or aquaculture damages the environment:

1. **All forms of agriculture potentially damage the environment.**
   "Environmental Impacts of Agricultural Modifications," *National Geographic*, 2021.[14]
   Global climate change is destabilizing many of the natural processes that make modern agriculture possible. Yet modern agriculture itself is also partly responsible for the crisis in sustainability. Many of the techniques and modifications on which farmers rely to boost output also harm the environment.

2. **Modern agriculture is a primary cause of the environmental crisis.**
   "Agriculture and the Environment: Changing Pressures, Solutions and Trade-offs" World Agriculture: Towards 2015/2030, Food and Agriculture Organization of the UN, 2021.[15]
   Agriculture places a serious burden on the environment in the process of providing humanity with food and fibers. It is the largest consumer of water and the main source of nitrate pollution of groundwater and surface water, as well as the principal source of ammonia pollution. It is a major contributor to the phosphate pollution of waterways (OECD, 2001a) and to the release of the powerful greenhouse gases (GHGs) methane and nitrous oxide into the atmosphere (IPCC, 2001a).

3. **The meat industry is greatest cause of damage from the agriculture sector.**
   Brad Plumer, "The Meat Business, a Big Contributor to Climate Change, Faces Major Tests," *The New York Times*, April 17, 2020.[16]
   Cattle have an outsized environmental impact largely because they belch up methane, a potent planet-warming gas. Studies have found that beef production creates roughly four to eight times the emissions from pork, chicken, or egg production per gram of protein, and all have a larger climate-change footprint than plant-based proteins like soy or beans.

4. **Environmentally sustainable fish-farming is possible.**
   Jonah van Beijnen and Gregg Yan, "Six Tips to Make Your Fish Farm More Environmentally Sustainable," *The Fish Site*, March 25, 2020.[17]
   "Fortunately, many of today's forward-looking aquaculture operators have the technology, the knowhow and the heart to take increasing responsibility for reducing the environmental impacts of their businesses. . . . [we offer] six tips which have not only helped to improve the environmental sustainability of numerous aquaculture operations, but have also been shown—perhaps more surprisingly—to improve their financial performance too, creating a win-win situation for both people and nature."
   1. Choose the right species.
   2. Select a suitable farm site.
   3. Farm design and layout to treat and reuse water.
   4. Manage feeding practices.
   5. Minimize chemicals and veterinary drugs.
   6. Plant native vegetation.

   "Through these six tips, we hope to help today's generation of forward-thinking fish farmers produce more seafood sustainably. Knowing you're doing your part to alleviate food security while protecting the environment? Now that's good for both the gut and the heart."

(continued)

5. **Fish-farming protects wild species.**
   Brian Barth, "Is Fish-Farming Sustainable," *Modern Farmer,* March 31, 2015.[18]
   "One inherently sustainable aspect of aquaculture is that it doesn't depend on wild species, removing the issue of over-harvesting from the sustainable seafood equation."

6. **Aquaculture can feed the world's poor and starving citizens.**
   "Scientists Call for Global Policymakers to Treat 'Fish as Food' to Help Solve World Hunger," *Environmental Defense Fund,* January 19, 2021.[19]
   "We are urging the international development community not only to see fish as food, but to recognize fish as a nutrient-rich food that can make a difference for the well-being of the world's poor and vulnerable."
   "Scientists Call for Global Policymakers to Treat 'Fish as Food' to Help Solve World Hunger," *Environmental Defense Fund,* January 19, 2021.
   "By refocusing on nutrition, in addition to the many other benefits fisheries provide, we're amplifying a call to action for governments, international development organizations and society more broadly to invest in the sustainability of capture fisheries and aquaculture."

7. **Aquaculture leads to economic growth and pulls people out of poverty.**
   John Kruskal, "Aquaculture May Reduce Rural Poverty, Income Inequality," *Chicago Policy Review,* February 18, 2019.[20]
   Land used for aquaculture is more economically productive than land used for farming, yielding 4.7 times the revenue of a farm plot of the same size. The model also revealed that aquaculture creates more demand for labor, requiring an average of 94 days of labor per acre per year, compared with 24 days for cropland. In addition, the researchers found that fish farming generates significant positive spillover effects in rural economies, raising the average incomes of nearby community members who do not own their own ponds.

8. **Aquaculture can help reverse climate change.**
   "Climate Change Mitigation Strategies," Food and Agriculture Organization of the UN, 2021.[21]
   Many capture fisheries and their supporting ecosystems have been poorly managed and the economic losses due to overfishing, pollution, and habitat loss are estimated to exceed $50 billion per year. Improved governance, innovative technologies, and more responsible practices can generate increased and sustainable benefits from fisheries. Currently there are more fossil fuel consuming fishing vessels operating than necessary to catch the available fish resources efficiently. Reducing the fleet overcapacity will not only help rebuild fish stocks and sustain global catches but also can substantially reduce carbon emissions from the sector.

Presenting Your Response (Step Four)

Only when you have completed the first three steps are you ready to present your arguments. We will now discuss two processes for refuting an advocate's arguments: declarative refutation and refutation by questioning.

Declarative Refutation

The first refutation process involves the systematic assertion of one's objections to an argument. In a well-organized, thorough, carefully reasoned manner, one "declares" a series of criticisms or beliefs that counter the opponent's arguments. There are four steps to presenting your declarative refutation arguments.

1. **Identify the point to be refuted.** You must tell the advocate and the audience what argument you wish to refute. Is it a specific point or subpoint offered by the other advocate? Are you grouping a number of points together and responding to them collectively? Or, are you responding to the essence of their entire case?

2. **Label and signpost your refutation.** What is the essence of the point you want to make? Try to state your argument succinctly. For example, note the way the arguments are labeled in the sample brief provided below. This is the claim that you intend to offer in response to the advocate's argument and this is what you want the opposing advocate and your audience to remember, so clarity is vitally important. If there are several points to your refutation, you need to enumerate them to help your audience identify them and keep them in mind.

3. **Support the refutation.** You have already labeled your argument; now you must fully develop it. What is your reasoning? What supporting evidence (premises, examples, statistics, or testimony) can you present to support your claim?

4. **Show the impact of the refutation(s).** What effect do your arguments have on the entire dispute? Did you win this particular argument? Did you at least mitigate or diminish the other advocate's claims? What must the advocate do in order to answer your refutation? If indeed you do believe that you have convinced your audience that you won this point, what effect does your having won this particular argument exchange have on the other issues that are under dispute? Do not trust the advocate or your audience to resolve these questions on their own. They may see the outcome of the controversy differently than you do. You must provide the criteria for positively evaluating your arguments.

These four steps should be repeated for each point that you wish to refute. Your refutation is considered effective if you have convinced a neutral listener of the merits of your position.

Refutation by Questioning

Asking questions is an important part of almost all argumentative interactions. In academic debate and the law, the process by which one refutes another through the use of questioning is known as ***direct examination*** or ***cross examination***. Each of these fields has specialized guidelines for the process. We will present some general orientations that apply to all contexts in which arguers use questioning.

The chance to question an opponent can be very inviting. Some individuals get swept up in the process, however, and engage in tactics that undermine their credibility and likability. We encourage you to remember the golden rule and to treat the person you are questioning in the manner in which you would want to be treated yourself. Do not badger. Ask questions in a way that they can be answered and in a way that does not unfairly bias the answer (e.g., when did you stop beating your wife?). Finally, make sure that you allow the other advocate time to answer the question. Do not cut off or interrupt the advocate.

Questioning can serve three important purposes. It permits you to clarify what an opponent has argued, to provide an argument so you can expose potential weak points, and to highlight those weaknesses of which you might already be aware. This latter purpose can be very useful for setting up arguments you will make later. It is unlikely that your opponents will concede their arguments during questioning, so concession is not a purpose that should motivate your strategy in developing or selecting your questions or in the style of your interaction.

Just as declarative refutation has several steps that you should follow, so too does questioning.

1. **Identify the point about which you wish to question your opponent.** Don't merely ask questions out of thin air. Something that your opponent has said has prompted you to want an answer to your question. Tell your opponent and any audience what that point was.

2. **Ask your question succinctly.** Try be brief. Questioning time is best not used for lengthy speeches. The most effective questions are those that are both direct and specific. Avoid asking compound questions or questions that require elaborate preparation; they take too long to set up and may in fact cause you to be interrupted. You should also avoid asking *loaded questions*. Loaded questions direct your opponent as to how to respond, for example: "Do you support wasting millions of dollars for new manned space missions?" No one would answer that question affirmatively. But if your opponent favors space research, they will not simply take such a question lying down. They will object to your phrasing, and you will likely find that you have lost ground with your audience.

3. **Ask follow-up questions.** Only occasionally will one question accomplish all that you wish to achieve. Listen to the answer and probe it. Try to uncover its unspoken assumptions. Probe as well the characterizations and the reasoning that are implicit in the answer.

4. **Move on.** When you have accomplished what you wanted to accomplish, you should not continue to ask questions about that point. Just as moving on too quickly by not asking an appropriate follow-up question can prevent you from exposing the potential weaknesses in an argument, dwelling too long on a point with unnecessary and/or unproductive questions can undercut your effectiveness, distract your listeners, and waste time.

5. **Use the information you acquire.** The information you glean from questioning can help you construct subsequent arguments. In some argumentative contexts, such as academic debate, cross-examination is only effective if the answers are used to develop arguments that are made in subsequent speeches.

Whether you present your refutation declaratively or through questioning, you will reap the rewards of your thoroughness if you have chosen your strategy and tactics well and communicated your refutation clearly.

SUMMARY

In this chapter we have considered the process of refutation. We defined the refutation process as a series of actions culminating in the denial of the argument advanced by another. This process included four specific steps: focused listening, the critical evaluation of an argument, the formulation of a response, and the presentation of your points of refutation. It is our belief that carefully thinking about refutation from a strategic perspective benefits both individuals who wish to refute someone else's claims and individuals who want to become critical consumers of arguments.

KEY TERMS

ad hominem	loaded question
ad populum	non-sequitur
ambiguity	obfuscation
appeal to fear	red herring
appeal to pity	reducing to absurdity
appeal to tradition	refutation by additional consideration
begging the question	refutation by denial
cross examination	refutation by mitigation
direct examination	refutation process
doublespeak	shifting the burden of proof
equivocation	slippery slope
euphemism	straw man fallacy
fallacy of composition	tu quoque
fallacy of division	turning the tables
fallacy of false dichotomy	

ACTIVITIES

1. Listen to two or more individuals engaged in an argument on a radio or television program. Try to find indications of flawed listening, and then identify which of the factors affecting listening provides the best explanation for the failure.

2. Assess your own listening behavior. Listen to an individual engaged in public advocacy on a talk show. As you listen, apply the five factors that affect listening to your listening behavior.

3. Construct an example for each of the different types of fallacies of reasoning presented in the text.

4. Select a public controversy that interests you and take a position on one side of the controversy. Identify a claim made by the opposition. Now construct a brief refuting that opponents claim similar to the one we provided in the sample on the merits of fish-farming.

5. Have a friend or classmate help you practice your questioning techniques. First, reread the section of the text on questioning. Then have your colleague take a position on a public controversy and ask questions about that position. Be sure to follow the golden rule.

RECOMMENDED READINGS

Babitsky, Steven and James Mangraviti, *Cross-Examination: The Comprehensive Guide for Experts* (Falmouth, MA: Seak, 2003).

Bennett, Bo, *Logically Fallacious: The Ultimate Collection of Over 300 Logical Fallacies* (Sudbury, MA: Archieboy Holdings, 2021).

Chichi, Graciela Marta, "The Greek Roots of the Ad Hominem Argument," *Argumentation* 16 (2002): 333–349.

Dudczak, Craig A., "Direct Refutation in Propositions of Policy: A Viable Alternative," *Journal of the American Forensic Association* 16 (1980): 232–235.

Eemeren, Frans H. van, and Peter Houtlosser, "How Should One Respond to Fallacious Moves," *Argumentation and Advocacy,* 45 (2009): 198–206.

Hansen, Hans Vilhelm, "The Straw Thing of Fallacy Theory: The Standard Definition of Fallacy," *Argumentation* 16 (2002): 133–156.

Kimball, Robert H., "Moral and Logical Perspectives on Appealing to Pity," *Argumentation,* 15 (2001): 331–349.

Paul, Richard and Linda Elder, *Fallacies: The Art of Mental Trickery and Manipulation* (Thinkers Guide Library, Tomales, CA: Foundation for Critical Thinking, 2014).

Ribiero, Henrique Jales, *Systematic Approaches to Argument by Analogy* (Heidelberg: Springer, 2014).

Van Vleet, Jacob, *Informal Logical Fallacies: A Brief Guide* (Lanham, MD: University Press of America, 2011).

Vasilyeva, Alena L., "The Treatment of Fallacies in Argumentative Situations During Mediation Sessions," *Argumentation and Advocacy* 46 (2010): 173–192.

Walton, Douglas, "Why Fallacies Appear to Be Better Arguments than They Are," *Informal Logic* 30 (2010): 159–184.

Wellman, Francis L., *The Art of Cross Examination,* 4th ed. (New York: Touchstone Books, 1997).

Wohlwrapp, Harald R., *The Concept of Argument: A Philosophical Foundation,* trans. Tim Personn (Doredrecht: Springer, 2014).

Endnotes

[1] Samuel Popkin, *The Reasoning Voter,* 2nd ed. (Chicago: University of Chicago Press, 1994).

[2] For an excellent analysis of the power of language and naming in war, see: Charles Kauffman, "Names and Weapons," *Communication Monographs* 56 (1989): 273–285.

[3] Michael Dobbs, "Top Ten Democratic Flip-Flops," *Washington Post,* February 25, 2008. http://voices.washingtonpost.com/fact-checker/2008/02/dem_flipflops.html

[4] Carl Ingram, "License Bill Draws Mixed Response," *Los Angeles Times,* July 29, 2003 p. B1.

[5] Ibid.

[6] Ibid.

[7] Chris Burrell, "Pandemic Renews Debate Over Drivers' Licenses for Undocumented Workers," *NPR.* November 27, 2020. https://www.npr.org/2020/11/27/938936451/pandemic-renews-debate-over-drivers-licenses-for-undocumented-workers

[8] Ibid.

[9] John Terbush, "12 Huge Presidential Campaign Flip-Flops," *Business Insider,* October 10, 2011. https://www.businessinsider.com/any-way-the-wind-blows-12-epic-flip-flops-from-presidential-campaigns-2011-9

[10] Fredreka Schouten, "Obama Opts Out of Campaign Finance System," *ABC News,* June 19, 2008. https://abcnews.go.com/Politics/story?id=5206643&page=1

[11] Michel Tomz and Robert Van Houweling, "Political Repositioning: Detailed Synopsis, July 2012." https://tomz.people.stanford.edu/sites/g/files/sbiybj4711/f/tomzvanhouweling_politicalrepositioning.pdf

[12] Ibid.

[13] George W. Bush, Address Before a Joint Session of the Congress on the United States Response to the Terrorist Attacks of September 11. September 20, 2001. https://www.govinfo.gov/content/pkg/WCPD-2001-09-24/pdf/WCPD-2001-09-24-Pg1347.pdf

[14] "Environmental Impact of Agricultural Modifications," *National Geographic,* 2021. https://www.nationalgeographic.org/article/environmental-impacts-agricultural-modifications/

[15] "Agriculture and the Environment: Changing Pressures, Solutions and Trade-Offs," World Agriculture: Towards 2015/2030, Food and Agriculture Organization, 2021. http://www.fao.org/3/y4252e/y4252e14.htm

[16] Brad Plumer, "The Meat Business, a Big Contributor to Climate Change, Faces Major Tests," *The New York Times,* April 17, 2020. https://www.nytimes.com/2020/04/17/climate/meat-industry-climate-impact.html

17. Jonah van Beijnen and Gregg Yan, "Six Tips to Make Your Fish Farm More Environmentally Sustainable," *The Fish Site,* March 25, 2020. https://thefishsite.com/articles/six-tips-to-make-your-fish-farm-more-environmentally-sustainable
18. Brian Barth, "Is Fish-Farming Sustainable," *Modern Farmer,* March 31, 2015. http://modernfarmer.com/2015/03/dear-modern-farmer-is-fish-farming-sustainable
19. "Scientists Call for Global Policymakers to Treat 'Fish as Food' to Help Solve World Hunger," *Environmental Defense Fund,* January 19, 2021. https://www.edf.org/media/scientists-call-global-policymakers-treat-fish-food-help-solve-world-hunger
20. John Kruskal, "Aquaculture May Reduce Rural Poverty, Income Inequality," *Chicago Policy Review,* February 18, 2019. https://chicagopolicyreview.org/2019/02/18/aquaculture-may-reduce-rural-poverty-income-inequality/
21. "Climate Change Mitigation Strategies," Food and Agriculture Organization of the UN, 2021. http://www.fao.org/fishery/topic/166280/en

10

Visual Argument

During the long, brutal, and devastating course of the civil war in Syria, approximately 5.6 million refugees fled from the fighting. Many sought to make their way to the countries of the European Union in the hope that they could create new lives for themselves and their children. The world witnessed this parade of misery over many months. Indeed, there were so many images of suffering that they were numbing and overwhelming. How could one respond to a crisis of such a massive scope? The nations of Europe largely closed their borders to the refugees and refused for the most part to accept them for resettlement. They came by land, and they came by boat, and most ended up in cold, wet, crowded, and wholly inhumane squalid refugee camps.

But then, in September 2015, one image circulated around the globe that changed the public's opinion and awareness of the Syrian tragedy and suffering. As a result of that image, a sense of deep sympathy and compassion for the refugees began to soften many hearts. The image was captured by a Reuters photographer, and the accompanying story explained:

> An image of a drowned toddler washed up on the beach in one of Turkey's prime tourist resorts swept across social media on Wednesday after at least 12 presumed Syrian refugees died trying to reach the Greek island of Kos.
>
> The picture showed a little boy wearing a bright red t-shirt and shorts lying face-down in the surf on a beach near the resort town of Bodrum. In a second image, a grim-faced policeman carries the body away.
>
> Turkish media identified the boy as 3-year-old Aylan Kurdi, whose 5-year-old brother died on the same boat. Media reports said he was from the north Syrian town of Kobani near the Turkish border, scene of heavy fighting between Islamic State insurgents and Kurdish regional forces a few months ago.
>
> The hashtag "KiyiyaVuranInsanlik"—"humanity washed ashore"—became the top trending topic on Twitter. In the first few hours after the accident, the image had been retweeted thousands of times.[1]

The image is painful and difficult to see. Indeed, it is one of the most heartbreaking images that we have ever seen. We apologize to those of you who will be made uncomfortable by seeing it, but we cannot fully explain its power without sharing it with you.

198 Chapter Ten

Across Europe the public reacted with horror at the image. The heads of state in the United Kingdom, Germany, France, Spain, and other EU member nations suddenly declared their willingness to accept for resettlement at least some Syrian refugees.[2] What was it about this image of the drowned child that provoked such a dramatic shift in public opinion and public policy? We believe that it was because this image contracted the scope of public suffering to a loss that almost all of us could personally share, experience, and grieve. Almost everyone who saw this image was reminded of a toddler in their own lives and of the joy of a three-year-old only beginning to live a life filled with promise and wonder. They were also reminded that earlier in the day a parent or relative had carefully selected clothes and dressed that child for a journey to a new and safer place—a place beyond the terror of war, a place that promised a new beginning and new opportunities. Yes, the journey was fraught with risk, but the reward of a peaceful life justified the risk. The image was a jarring, visceral reminder of the fragility of human dreams and of human life. This image made the tragedy of the Syrian refugee crisis fully human and created a far more urgent call to find solutions to end the suffering, misery, and death.

On June 25, 2019, a very similar image appeared in American newspapers. *The New York Times* published the picture below taken by Julia Le Duc of the Associated Press.[3] The image captured the great risk immigrants take in trying to cross our border. The reaction in the United States was quite similar to the European reaction in 2015. Images of death, especially the death of children, can and do evoke sympathy and outrage in many audiences.

Scholars of communication have long recognized the importance of visual elements of the communication process. Gestures, facial expressions, eye contact, and posture are nonverbal aspects of spoken communication that can affect an audience's assessment of a speaker. The old adage, "look me in the eyes and say that" comes from the belief that liars have difficulty sustaining direct eye contact. Psychologists are trained to look for nonverbal behaviors that "leak out" and contradict what a patient is saying and that help others detect attempts to deceive.[4]

Thus, visual aspects of the communication process can be important to perceptions of honesty, sincerity, and veracity. In this chapter we focus on how visual elements can be used in the construction of arguments, or indeed how visuals may in and of themselves function as arguments. Scholars have discovered that visual images often are more compelling and produce more deeply felt and visceral reactions than do words alone.[5] Of course, images do not typically appear alone; they are usually accompanied by textual discourse. It is thus misleading to assess the power of images without also considering these texts.[6] As Mitchell argued "visual images are often 'read' using text, text is usually accompanied by associative images, and more often than not, text and images are presented together. What exists thus is the 'imagetext,' which is constituted by 'complex intersections' of representation and discourse."[7]

There are, however, cases where visual texts consist only of images and not of words. At least one powerful example is the film *Samsara,* a nonnarrative documentary that consists of a series of visual images of natural wonders, of humans in nature, and of human society acting upon and altering nature's rhythms.[8] The film includes many hauntingly beautiful, a few starkly ugly, and even a few deeply disturbing images that have a lingering argumentative and persuasive power. Because the film invites viewers to construct their own meanings of the importance of the individual images, however, and because human nature encourages viewers to seek to create a unifying and coherent message, the film serves as an excellent illustration of how a visual text can lead to and shape a lively discussion. One of our suggested learning activities in this chapter is that you should watch the film with friends, perhaps even as a shared class experience, and then discuss its meaning. We believe that the images in this film are argumentative, even though the viewer must create the narrative text. Watch the film and make your own judgment as to whether you agree.

In today's hypermediated digital era, photographs, cartoons, charts, graphs, and video clips circulate instantaneously and have significantly altered the communication landscape. In this chapter we explore visual images as evidence to support other arguments and as arguments in their own essence. We hope to help you understand how visual arguments may impact your personal judgments and also how you might make use of them to convince others. We will also discuss some criteria for judging the "truth" claims regarding visual arguments, especially given how easy it may be to manipulate images through editing and/or "photo-shopping" using digital technologies.

Physical Images

Many scholars have studied how physical images are used as arguments. Advertisers have long understood that attractive physical images capture viewers' attention and draw them in for a closer look at whatever products or services they might be selling. You have no doubt seen hundreds of thousands of images of attractive men and women selling clothing, beverages, cars, fast food, mobile phones, etc. Travel advertisers understand that eyeballs are more likely drawn to images of beautiful young people cavorting in skimpy bathing suits on the beach than they are to images of middle-aged tourists with sagging bodies, even though anyone who has taken a luxury cruise or stayed in an expensive resort will confirm that most of the bodies lounging about the pool deck would probably look better if they left more to the imagination! The advertisers assume that consumers and/or travelers want to see themselves—or a younger version of themselves—in such ads and come to believe that buying these products and/or traveling to these destinations will enable them to create or perhaps rediscover a life filled with greater excitement and pleasure.

Visual images of bodies can also be used to support other types of arguments. We have already mentioned in chapter 3 that advertisements seeking donations for homeless shelters make use of images of needy families and mothers with children more frequently than they do images of single men, even though the largest number of homeless are single men with addictions or suffering from mental illness. Images of children, however, naturally provoke greater sympathy. The images of bodies can also be used to manipulate opinions regarding not just the desirability of certain body types but also to shape arguments about health and wellness. Many have claimed, for example, that the constant exposure to reed-thin fashion models and actresses has led to unhealthy notions about what constitutes an ideal body shape. As a result, many people suffer from eating disorders because they develop an unrealistic sense of their own body image or of the idealized body. The French government even went so far as to consider legislation that would "prohibit modeling agencies from hiring dangerously thin models," and that would require that "retouched photos of models be clearly labeled."[9] In response to the public expressions of concern regarding anorexia, there have been websites created by women with anorexia who see their condition as a "lifestyle" choice. Some of these websites include images of beautiful and scantily clad very thin women and proclaim, "Thou shall not eat, without feeling guilty."[10] Such contrasting visual images, sometimes with accompanying texts, challenge viewers' assumptions about health, beauty, desirability, and free speech—as some advocates have sought to take such websites down because they see them as profoundly dangerous to young women suffering from serious eating disorders.

Idealized body images and health concerns also influence judgments about people deemed obese. There is an obesity epidemic in the United States. In 2020, 12 states had obesity rates 35 percent or higher compared to 3 states in 2014. In 2012, no state had an obesity rate above 35 percent; in 1985, no state had an obesity rate higher than 15.[11] This dramatic increase in obesity has terrible health consequences, including increased risk of heart disease and diabetes. Visual images of obese adults and children are frequently used to shame, ridicule, or cajole people into healthier eating habits. The juxtaposition of images of thin, average, and obese individuals is a particularly impactful way of drawing attention to the obese body and contrasting it with the more commonly presumed physically desirable body and with the healthy body.[12] The negative impact of these images and the public ridicule has provoked a "fat acceptance" movement.[13]

Physical images or objects can be used in multiple ways in arguments. Visual argument scholars David Birdsell and Leo Groarke advise that an image functions as a visual flag "when it is used to attract attention to a message conveyed to some audience."[14] When Iraqis cast votes for the first time in the post-Saddam Hussein era, they put their fingers in an ink well to distinguish between those who had already cast their ballots and those who had not. Many Iraqis proudly displayed their ink-stained fingers as proof that democracy had arrived. No translation was necessary because the image transcended linguistic barriers. The images of ink-stained fingers was evidence of the claim that Iraq was now a democracy. The images thus drew attention to the newly democratic nation of Iraq in much the same way as would an image of a patriot waving his or her nation's flag.

The use of objects as visual images can also demonstrate or buttress arguments made orally. During the COVID-19 pandemic, one hotly contested image became the face mask. While the doctors and scientists of the CDC reminded citizens that wearing appropriate masks could be the most effective personal action that they could take to protect themselves and others from contracting the deadly virus, some conservatives characterized mask mandates as an attack on people's autonomy and personal freedom.[15] Images of people wearing or choosing not to wear masks were commonly circulated. Below is an image of Vice President Mike Pence, who declined to wear a mask during a tour of a Mayo Clinic medical facility that mandated that face masks be worn.[16]

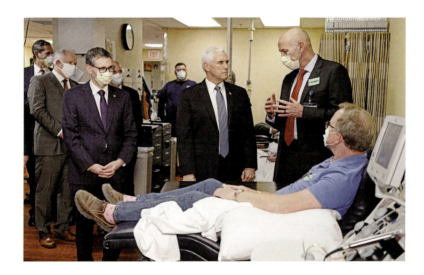

Masks also became a canvas for expressing political messages and ideological commitments. The image on page 202 is of Representative Marjorie Taylor Green (R-GA), who was removed from her congressional committees. In social media posts and videos made before she was elected to Congress, Greene, a freshman from Georgia, embraced a slew of far-right conspiracy theories, including questioning whether deadly school shootings had been staged and whether a plane really hit the Pentagon on 9/11. A sup-

porter of the fantastical QAnon conspiracy theory, she also shared videos with anti-Semitic and anti-Muslim sentiment, and expressed support for violence against Democratic leaders in Congress.[17]

In addition to visual images such as those that we have shown you thus far, advocates frequently turn to graphs, tables, charts, and other data visualization to offer support for claims and also to show the relationships among many different factors in complex situations. There are countless very creative examples of presenting data. One of first scholars to make use of sophisticated computer-assisted visualization techniques was the late Hans Rosling, a Swedish public health researcher who gave impressive lectures about the relationship between rising incomes, development, and life expectancy. YouTube has one of his visualizations (https://www.youtube.com/watch?v=jbkSRLYSojo).[18]

Visual images are also often used to evoke strong and compelling arguments celebrating heroism, sacrifice, and cultural memories. Think for example of the way in which we honor the service of veterans of war with statues, monuments, paintings, or photographs of them charging into battle—swords drawn, engaged in hand-to-hand combat, or planting a flag under enemy fire. Joe Rosenthal's historic photograph of Americans raising the flag atop Mount Suribachi at Iwo Jima, Japan, in World War II was the inspiration for the Marine Corps War Memorial.

Joe Rosenthal's historic photograph of Americans raising the flag atop Mount Suribachi at Iwo Jima, Japan, in World War II, from which the Marine Corps War Memorial was sculpted.

Flags are often especially potent argumentative symbols. Heated debates and even violence have been inspired, for example, by protesters who have sought to make their political points by setting the U.S. flag afire or by otherwise desecrating it to protest what they see as unjust actions or policies. A bitterly divided U.S. Supreme Court upheld the right of protesters to burn the flag as an expression of their free speech rights, but the act remains contentious.

There also remains a persistent controversy regarding the Confederate Battle Flag from the Civil War. Although many white Southerners have proudly displayed the flag and claimed that it was a way to honor their Southern heritage, African Americans have long regarded it as a bitter reminder of the era of slavery and racial violence. Heated debates occurred in several Southern states regarding whether or not the "stars and bars" should be removed from their state flags. The controversy over the confederate flag emerged again during the Capitol insurrection on January 6, 2021, when one of the marauders who broke into the Capitol was photographed carrying the Confederate Battle Flag through the Rotunda—something, of course, that Confederate soldiers never managed to achieve during the Civil War.

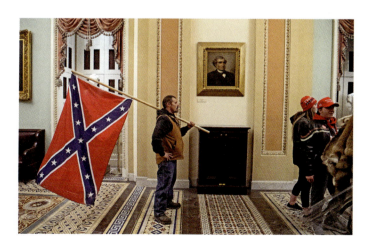

Another especially moving example of the power of visual images is military cemeteries, that are often designed in such a manner as to uniquely honor the service of the war dead and veterans who are buried together. The uniformity of the grave markers, the straight columns, and the accompanying flags, all convey elements of the visual argument and allow those who gaze upon such images to contemplate the discipline, sense of order, and rich history of military service and of loss.

Arlington National Cemetery.

Argumentation scholars have studied military cemeteries and memorials to assess the impact of visual elements on how cultures create shared memories and how those memorials further communicate foreign policy objectives. For example, William Balthrop and Carole Blair studied the cemeteries that the United States developed in Europe to honor the U.S. soldiers who lost their lives on the battlefields of World War I, paying special attention to the aesthetic choices made in the commemorative design of the grounds and statues.[19] Still other argumentation scholars have studied the visual impact of the Vietnam Veterans Memorial on the National Mall in Washington, D.C. because it was such a novel and unusual way to honor the dead from that highly contested and unpopular war.[20] Rather than present the war via statues celebrating heroic actions of our soldiers, the memorial consists of a stone wall carved into the ground with the names of the dead engraved onto its surface. The dead are not separated by their rank or listed alphabetically; rather, they are listed in chronological order by the date of their death. New names are added to the wall as veterans of the Vietnam war die from causes that are determined related to injuries they experienced in combat.

When the Vietnam Veterans Memorial was first proposed, many veteran groups protested its nontraditional form and argued that more traditional representational statues depicting soldiers carrying their weapons be added to the site. After the wall was completed, however, most were stunned by its impact. The engraved names of so many lives lost (58, 318) gave size and scope to the totality of sacrifice in service of the country. The individual names gave families, friends, and fellow soldiers the opportunity to remember and honor their loved ones. Indeed, very soon after the wall was completed, people began to leave items behind to honor their loved one's memory. These included such things as stuffed animals, balls, bats, gloves, roller skates, photographs, and much more. These items further communicated that the loss was not abstract but instead deeply personal, thus deepening the scars of the conflict. The demands for more traditional statues persisted, however, and two years after the wall was completed, a flagpole and the Three Servicemen Statue were added to the memorial on Veteran's Day 1984. The three soldiers—one African American, one Hispanic, and one Caucasian—represent the diversity of soldiers who served in Vietnam. The soldiers face the wall. Nine years later, the Vietnam Women's Memorial was added—a statue depicting three women caring for a fallen soldier.

Blair, Jeppeson, and Pucci analyzed the Vietnam Veterans Memorial and concluded that its unique combination of traditional and nontraditional forms results in

The Vietnam Veterans Memorial.

The Three Servicemen Statue.

many arguments rather than just one. They posit that "Rather than telling the story, it tells multiple stories."[21] Different audiences, they contend, come away with different messages: "The Memorial both comforts and refuses to comfort. It both provides closure and denies it. It does not offer a unitary message but multiple and conflicting ones."[22] Visual arguments are subject to even greater varieties of interpretation by the audience than linguistic arguments.

A similar visual memorial device that many of you may have seen is the AIDS Quilt. When people began dying of AIDS in the early 1980s, the heartbreaking deaths were sometimes compounded by shame associated with the disease. Many of its earliest victims were not open about their sexuality; succumbing to what was first considered a "gay cancer" was, in some instances, an embarrassment to their families. Government and the medical and scientific communities were slow to respond to the crisis of the new disease. Many believed the slow pace was because a marginalized and even stigmatized population was dying. In 1985, it was proposed that individuals who had died from the disease might be honored with a quilt panel that captured their interests, hobbies, passions, or commitments. These panels could then be stitched together into a mosaic of panels that both individualized the sense of loss and gave insight into the size and scope of the tragic disease. The quilt could also be moved from city to city so that public audiences could learn more about the disease—and in the process become more sympathetic to those suffering, more supportive of federal research funding for a cure, and ultimately more supportive of gay rights. The quilt functioned as an especially influential visual argument in changing public opinion regarding the disease.[23]

The AIDS Memorial Quilt filling the National Mall.

Visual representations—photographs, drawings, paintings, videos, films, memes, and other visual media—include any depictions representing actual objects, people, or events. Such representations may not only constitute powerful visual arguments but as we have already argued, they sometimes shake the world. To many followers of Islam, it is sacrilegious to depict Muhammad in a photograph or an illustration. Yet some publications, especially in Europe, deliberately challenged this belief. In 2006, a Danish newspaper published several cartoons mocking the Prophet as a terrorist. The cartoons circulated through cyberspace, were reprinted in several newspapers in the Islamic world, and led to violent street protests and the deaths of several demonstrators.[24] The cartoons were deemed so offensive and controversial that most newspapers in the United States chose not to reprint them, even though they devoted significant coverage to the protests.

Despite the violent reaction, however, a satirical and arguably antireligious weekly publication in France, *Charlie Hebdo*, continued to print cartoons mocking the Prophet Mohammad as well as other religious and political leaders. The Hebdo offices were firebombed in 2011. The violence continued. In January 2015 two brothers, self-identified as members of al Qaeda in the Arabian Peninsula, attacked the Hebdo offices. Twelve people including the newspaper's editor were killed, and 11 others were wounded. Two days later five more people were killed and another 11 were wounded in an attack at a supermarket in a predominantly Jewish neighborhood in Paris.[25] The violence sparked an intense display of the cultural and ideological gaps between the East and West, as protests occurred in Paris and other European and American cities with activists marching in support of free speech. "Je suis Charlie" ("I am Charlie") became a rallying cry around the world. Approximately two million people, including 40 heads of state, marched in the streets of Paris to show solidarity with the French people and to support secular values and free speech.

Visual representations of police violence have also sparked significant and sometimes violent reactions. The beating of Rodney King by Los Angeles police officers was captured on videotape in 1991—one of the first videotaped instances of police abuse.[26] In 2014, the deaths of Eric Garner in New York and Laquan McDonald in Chicago were captured on video. In 2016 the girlfriend of Philando Castile live streamed video of his lifeless body in the driver's seat after he was killed by a police officer. One day earlier a bystander used a smartphone to record two police officers causing the death of Alton Sterling in Louisiana and posted the video online. None of these videos sparked the global outrage that occurred after the death of George Floyd on May 25, 2020.

Deeply disturbing bystander videos of brutal police behavior in the Floyd case quickly went viral. Four Minneapolis Police Department officers responded to a call that Floyd had passed a counterfeit bill in a convenience store. Finding the suspect sitting in a car nearby, they ordered him to exit and submit to an arrest. When Floyd resisted the police, officer Derek Chauvin knelt on Floyd's neck for a full 9 minutes and 29 seconds. Floyd can be heard calling out to his mother for help and declaring that he was unable to breathe.[27] As noted above, the viral footage was not the first to document police brutality, but its impact was notably more pronounced. Experts attributed the difference to the length of the video and its very graphic nature. Communication professor Allissa Richardson, author of *Bearing Witness While Black: African Americans, Smartphones, and the New Protest #Journalism*, commented that gunshots are immediately traumatic but people then look away, "This video transfixed people because of the callous nature of the killing coupled with the brazen nature of the police, who knew they were being filmed and still did it anyway."[28]

Protests erupted in cities across the United States. Although most of the protests were peaceful, some did turn both to violence and property crime as rage and frustration boiled over at yet another atrocity committed by the police against people of color. The contrasting images of the peaceful protests and the looting and violence were used by both progressive and conservative activists to support their claims regarding the meaning of the protest actions.

The protests over Floyd's murder became an issue in the 2020 presidential campaign, especially after President Trump ordered that peaceful protesters in front of the

White House be cleared from the area with tear gas so that he could cross the street for a photo opportunity standing in front of a boarded-up church holding a bible. The President seemed to want to communicate to his base supporters, and conceivably also to suburban independent voters, that he was a man of faith who would keep the peace and preserve and protect their property even in the face of violent protests. Forcibly clearing the area of protesters received harsh criticism from many current and retired military leaders. For example, former Secretary of Defense Robert Gates commented: "I think it's just a reality that this president has not seen it as one of his priorities to try and bring people together, either in general or in response to terrible events, whether it's the pandemic or the response to George Floyd's death."[29] General Mark Milley, the current Chairman of the Joint Chiefs of Staff, expressed his regret at having participated in the photo opportunity. Such public protests by mili-

tary leaders are rare indeed and likely outweighed any potential advantages that Trump's campaign may have hoped to achieve from the photo op's intended symbolism.[30]

Perhaps some of the most significant visual images of the past few decades have been the images connected with the global war on terror. Adversaries make use of conflicting images to conduct a rhetorical and argumentative skirmish. In 2002, the U.S. Department of Defense released a series of visual images of the detainees held in Guantanamo Bay prison camp on the island of Cuba. The intended communication to the American people and to America's adversaries overseas seemed to be that the United States had captured the perpetrators of terror, that they were being held in a secure location, and that this should serve as a message to those who might contemplate future attacks.

To many in the Islamic world, however, these images communicated something very different. Although the Department of Defense may have been seeking to communicate that the United States was meting out a harsh justice, many saw such images as evidence of the intent to humiliate and even torture these prisoners. Thus, it should not surprise anyone that a few years later the terrorist warriors representing ISIS (the Islamic State in Syria) began to utilize very similar visual messages. Indeed, before executing their prisoners on the battlefield, the ISIS warriors dressed them in similar orange jumpsuits and then broadcast the images around the world to attract the maximum amount of press coverage.

The willingness to put heinous war crimes on full public display seemed to signal an entirely new strategy in an era dominated by digital media. We want to remind readers of the need to assess not just what visual images seem to mean from your perspective but also what they might mean to others. It is possible that powerful visual images might be weaponized against you by your adversaries. The ISIS warriors were likely convinced that sharing these horrific acts of violence with the world would frighten and intimidate their enemies plus win new converts to their movement. Indeed, this may have been the result for some who viewed these videos. Most people around the world, however, reacted with anger and condemnation. As we have already argued, visual representations often evoke much stronger reactions than words alone.

THE POWER OF IMAGES

All humans can visualize. Such visualizations might appear in dreams or in our thoughts. We can make sense of the past and present and reflect upon and imagine what the future will entail. Visualizations have powerful influence. Few of us can imagine a more terrible death than a beheading or by being burned alive. These terrible images command attention. Visual communication scholar Rick Williams posits that the majority of information that the brain processes is visual. Williams goes so far as to argue that visual cognition is preconscious. That is, we may react to visual information without cognitive reflection.

> Simply put, visual cognition operates on preconscious levels to process visual information into knowledge that motivates behavior before the conscious processes of the neocortex receive or understand the information. I call this prerational, predominantly preconscious cognitive ability *intuitive intelligence* because intuitive means to attain knowledge through cognition without the use of reason.
>
> I believe that *visual intelligence* is the primary intuitive intelligence because the majority of information that the brain processes is visual and most other intelligences also employ significant visual cognition.[31]

Neil Postman offered still another explanation for why visualizations hold such power. Drawing upon the work of Marshal McLuhan, Postman contended that with the spread of literacy, humans moved from storytelling (an oral tradition) to a literary tradition where the written word enjoyed primacy. Rationality in an oral world is based on the tests of a good narrative. Rationality in a literate world is based on reason and reasoning. Most importantly, Postman contended that television, and we would now add the internet, changed the paradigmatic mode of communication to the visual. This resulted in changes to how we evaluate arguments, giving primacy to the visual.[32]

It is important to again emphasize that different visual images work differently for different people. Images, even those accompanied by texts, are often subject to multiple interpretations shaped by the historical experiences, cultures, worldviews, and current concerns of individuals. The lack of specificity in the meaning of an image permits the receiver to decode the message as it makes sense to them. This means that the very same image can have different meaning for different people.

Look at the image on the left. Surely you have seen it. For many, it means OK—that all is well. But now this symbol is also being used by white power extremists.[33]

One of the authors participated in a workshop for economic development officers sponsored by the World Bank that included participants from around the world. As a part of the lesson, he shared the two images below and asked those in attendance to discuss them. When asked to describe the photo of the children playing soccer, participants from more economically affluent nations focused almost exclusively, and sympathetically, on the fact that the children were playing soccer barefoot. Participants coming from less developed and less affluent nations, however, focused on several facts: the children had the liberty to play games and were not compelled to work; they wore matching jerseys; they played with a real ball rather than rags tied together with string. Indeed, many of these respondents fondly remembered their childhoods of playing ball barefoot.

When asked about the crowded freeway, participants from developed nations focused on the soul-killing traffic jam that wasted hours of peoples' lives and on the damage to the environment by all of the automobile exhaust and miles of concrete ribbon making up the freeway system. Participants from developing nations, on the other hand, talked about the incredible display of wealth with so many citizens driving in personal automobiles and the huge investment in highway infrastructure. They also commented on how impressed they were that cars were traveling in an orderly fashion in their own lanes and adhering to traffic laws—something that is profoundly rare in many parts of the world.[34]

On the left is an iconic photograph of a sailor kissing a dental assistant in Times Square on V-J (Victory over Japan) Day, August 14, 1945. Most Americans recognize the behavior as a spontaneous reaction to the end of World War II. The photograph is usually not accompanied by text to explain its meaning. What argument do you think the image offers?

Cultural studies scholar Stuart Hall has studied visual images extensively. He reveals that visualizations may be decoded from three perspectives.[35] First, there is the ***dominant reading*** of the visual text. Hall argues that images represent a society's preferred way of viewing the world. Hall would probably argue that decoding the iconic photograph as a celebratory moment of U.S. triumph reinforces the dominant and hegemonic way of viewing the world. A very different view of the same photograph is that it celebrates militarism and chauvinism. The male is, after all, grabbing and kissing a woman that he presumably doesn't even know. Hall might call such a reading of the photograph an ***oppositional reading***. From such a perspective, a viewer would recognize but reject the dominant interpretation. The third perspective available to the viewer is ***negotiated reading***. From this vantage point, the viewer accepts some of the hegemonic meanings but also recognizes some exceptions. In this case, the viewer might celebrate the peace that comes with the end of war but reject the sexist male chauvinism revealed by the kiss. If, as Hall argues, there are multiple interpretations for a single visualization, then a critical consumer of visual images needs to be cognizant of the possibility that others see the image differently.

TESTS OF VISUAL ARGUMENTS

Throughout this text we have asked you to approach the arguments you encounter with a healthy dose of skepticism. We urge you to become a critical consumer of arguments by testing the grounds and the reasoning to determine whether or not to give your assent. The same is true for visual arguments. We believe that there are several questions that you should ask with regard to the visual arguments you encounter.

1. Is the visual image accurate?

Is the figure, body, object, or event faithfully and accurately depicted. Does the image truthfully represent reality? The image below quickly circulated online in the wake of the 9/11 terrorist attack. The image was reported to be a tourist standing atop the World Trade Center, as the plane was about to crash into it. Careful sleuthing,

however, revealed several problems with the accuracy of the image. Skeptics noted that it was the wrong model of plane and approaching from the wrong direction. The outside observation tower was not accessible at the time of the crash. It was a very warm morning, yet the man is shown in winter clothing. Eventually it was revealed that the photo was taken years earlier and then "photoshopped" to intentionally mislead.[36]

Sometimes, of course, the manipulations occur more for artistic than for substantive reasons—but this is not to say that the manipulations do not mislead. For example, in February 1982 *National Geographic* published a cover showing two pyramids behind some figures and camels. In response to a flurry of letters, the magazine admitted that it had squeezed the pyramids together to fit the magazine's vertical format. The photograph was not accurate.[37] In 1982 such photographic manipulation was rare; as digital technology improved, photo manipulation has become common. By 2015, the World Press Photo Awards committee reported that it had disqualified 20 percent of its contest finalists because the images were either "intentionally manipulated or post-processed carelessly."[38]

> It seems some photographers can't resist the temptation to aesthetically enhance their images during post-processing either by removing small details to "clean up" an image, or sometimes by excessive toning that constitutes a material change to the image. Both types of retouching clearly compromise the integrity of the image.[39]

At the end of June 1994, two national news magazines chose the mug shot of O. J. Simpson for their covers. Many critics argued that *Time* had darkened Simpson's image so that he would appear more sinister and to invoke stereotypes about African American criminality. *Newsweek* ran the mug shot without alteration. The magazines appeared side by side on newsstands. The readily apparent differences prompted spirited discussions about race and media objectivity.[40]

Photoshopping is now so common that photos, for example of celebrity actresses or fashion models, are routinely retouched and often slenderized, perhaps further sending a message of the "ideal" body that tyrannizes young women and arguably contributes to eating disorders. British actress Keira Knightley posed nude in a 2014 issue of

Interview magazine. Knightley demanded a "no Photoshop" clause in the agreement so that she could show her fans what she really looks like. "I think women's bodies are a battleground," stated Knightley, "and photography is partly to blame."[41]

Many instances of digital photo manipulation have little consequence and are merely created to amuse. In other cases, however, the manipulations can become very dangerous. Consider the potential implications of a manipulated image such as the one below in a conspiracy saturated media environment. Or consider the damage that could be done to a politician (or to anyone) if a digitally altered image of that person circulated showing them having sexual relations with a minor or being present at a murder scene. Putting someone's face on someone else's body in a graphic video is one example of a deepfake (see chapter 8). Famed American director Jordan Peele created a public service announcement in 2018 to show how easy it is to make his own face morph into an image of Barack Obama. He hoped to warn Americans not to believe everything they see on the internet.[42] Given the rapid speed with which images travel on social media platforms, learning how to detect manipulated images so that you are not deceived by them and do not inadvertently share them and deceive others is an important test of new media literacy.

2. Is the visual image relevant?

Just as advocates sometimes cite grounds that are not really relevant to the claim being made (see chapter 8), physical and representational visualizations must also be relevant to the claim being advanced. If the claim is that unions are hostile to management, an image of a fat union boss with buckets of money is probably neither accurate nor relevant. If an advertising campaign is seeking to sell a power drill, then placing the drill in the hands of an attractive woman may capture the male gaze but will not offer much substantive or relevant information as to why this particular product is better than competing products.

3. Does the visual image provoke appropriate emotional reactions?

As we have noted earlier, visualizations often evoke emotional reactions. In fact, visualizations can overwhelm rational thought. American courts recognize this. Consequently, they sometimes limit the amount of visual evidence so as to not inflame a jury. According to federal rules, evidence should be excluded from a trial if it is deemed more inflammatory or graphic than probative. As you examine images, you should ask yourself if you are being emotionally manipulated by the inclusion of the image or by the selection of a particular image rather than some other image. This often happens in news coverage of crimes. Editors, for example, take advantage of people's assumptions about race differences and criminal activity by selecting images that either focus on the race of the suspects or the victims of criminal activity. Should the crime be considered more heinous because the victim is a beautiful young woman? Research suggests that many people are more sympathetic when crime victims are attractive. They are also more sympathetic when victims are white rather than from minority populations. Minority defendants are more likely to be convicted and harshly sentenced than are white defendants, and jurors are more likely to be sympathetic to the police in confrontations with minority suspects.[43]

Visual images of criminals stalking quiet, comfortable suburban neighborhoods are often used in advertisements for products and services such as home security alarms and private guard services, for example. The images provoke fear, which is reinforced through films and television entertainment programs that depict home invasions as frequent occurrences—despite the number of home invasions that occur in the United States each year being quite small. You should be critical of the power of such images to stoke fear and anxiety.

Summary

In this chapter we introduced the idea that visualizations can be used as grounds for a verbal claim or as complete arguments. We are barraged on a daily basis with visual arguments. Some are created deliberately to try to shape our opinions. Others may not have been intended to influence us, but we nonetheless interpret them in such a way that they animate our beliefs and understandings. We suggested two general types of visualizations—physical and representational—and explained why visualizations might be more powerful than verbally expressed claims. Finally, we offered some tests of visualizations to consider when deciding whether to utilize particular visuals in support of your arguments or to accept such arguments as proof in support of someone else's claim.

Key Terms

dominant reading
negotiated reading
oppositional reading
visual representation

ACTIVITIES

1. Watch the film *Samsara* either alone, or we would suggest, with friends or classmates. What were the primary arguments offered in the film? What do you believe the filmmaker intended to communicate? What do you think might have been some of the unintended consequences of the selection of particular themes or images? If you watched with others, what differences were discovered?

2. Go to the website *The Living Room Candidate*. This site contains television commercials developed for presidential campaigns from 1952 through today. How did the use of visual images in these campaigns change over time? How did these images give insight into individual candidates? Which visuals did you think were most effective and why?

3. Search for visual arguments in contemporary newspapers or magazines. Which visuals do you find most influential? Most ineffective? Most informative? Most emotionally provocative? Most offensive? Why?

4. Systematically watch local TV news. Identify those news video clips that you think were most effective in helping the reporters communicate their stories. What news topics led to the creation of the most useful videos?

5. Spend a week looking at the front page of a newspaper. Over the course of that week what photographs appeared above the fold? What topics generated the photos? What people were captured most frequently in photographs? What were the aesthetic characteristics of those photographs?

6. Search the internet for memes. Examine those memes and suggest the meanings that they convey. Which memes did you see most frequently? What issues, characters, events, or opinions were communicated in the most frequently shared memes?

RECOMMENDED READINGS

Birdsell, David S. and Leo Groarke, "Toward a Theory of Visual Argument," *Argumentation and Advocacy* 33 (1996): 1–10.

Edwards, J., "Echoes of Camelot: How Images Construct Cultural Memory Through Rhetorical Framing," in C. Hill and M. Helmers, Eds., *Defining Visual Rhetorics* (Mahwah, NJ: Lawrence Erlbaum, 2004) 179–194.

Finnegan, Cara, "Darkening O.J.: Visual Argument in Controversy," in Thomas Hollihan, Ed., *Argument at Century's End: Reflecting on the Past and Envisioning the Future* (Annandale, VA: National Communication Association, 2000), 235–243.

Groarke, Leo and Catherine H. Palczewski, "Navigating the Visual Turn in Argument," *Argumentation and Advocacy* 52 (2016): 217–235.

Hahner, Leslie A., "The Riot Kiss: Framing Memes as Visual Argument," *Argumentation and Advocacy* 49 (2013): 151–166.

Harriman, Robert and John Lucaites, "Performing Civic Identity: The Iconic Photograph of the Flag Raising at Iwo Jima," *Quarterly Journal of Speech* 88 (2002): 363–392.

Lake, Randall and Barbara Pickering, "Argumentation, the Visual, and the Possibility of Refutation: An Exploration," *Argumentation* 12 (1998): 79–93.

Landau, Jamie, "Women Will Get Cancer: Visual and Verbal Presence (and Absence) in a Pharmaceutical Advertising Campaign about HPV," *Argumentation and Advocacy* 48 (2011): 39–54.

Pineda, Richard and S. Sowards, "Flag Waving as Visual Argument: 2006 Immigration Demonstrations and Cultural Citizenship," *Argumentation and Advocacy* 43 (2007): 164–174.

ENDNOTES

[1] "Troubling Image of Drowned Boy Captivates, Horrifies," *Reuters*, September 2, 2015. https://www.reuters.com/article/us-europe-migrants-turkey/troubling-image-of-drowned-boy-captivates-horrifies-idUSKCN0R20IJ20150902

[2] "Europe Migrant Crisis: World Leaders React to Images of Drowned Toddler Washed up on Turkish Beach," *ABC Australia News*, September 3, 2015. https://www.abc.net.au/news/2015-09-04/world-leaders-react-to-dramatic-images-of-drowned-toddler/6748652

[3] Azam Ahmed and Kirk Semple, "Photo of Drowned Migrants Captures Pathos of Those Who Risk It All," *New York Times*, June 25, 2019, https://www.nytimes.com/2019/06/25/us/father-daughter-border-drowning-picture-mexico.html

[4] Paul Eckman and Wallace V. Freisman, "Nonverbal Leakage and Clues to Deception," *Psychiatry: The Journal for the Study of Interpersonal Processes* 32 (1969): 88.

[5] See for example: Cara Finnegan, *Picturing Poverty: Print Culture and FSA Photographs* (Washington: Smithsonian Books, 2003). Also, Sonja K. Foss, "A Rhetorical Schema for the Evaluation of Visual Imagery," *Communication Studies* 45 (1994): 213–224.

[6] W.J.T. Mitchell, *Picture Theory* (Chicago: University of Chicago Press, 1994).

[7] Ibid., p. 327.

[8] *Samsara* was directed by Ron Fricke and filmed over five years in 25 different countries. The film debuted in 2011 at the Toronto International Film Festival and was released to art-house theaters in 2012. The film achieved significant critical acclaim and provoked a great deal of public attention because it included images of controversial subject matter including meat processing plants, sex toys, prison scenes, etc. The trailer of the film is available at https://www.youtube.com/watch?v=qp967YAAdNk. The entire film is often available on Amazon Prime.

[9] Allysa J. Rubin, "French Bill on Anorexia and Models Passes a Test," *New York Times*, April 4, 2015, p. A4.

[10] Robin E. Jensen, "The Eating Disordered Lifestyle: Imagetexts and the Performance of Similitude," *Argumentation and Advocacy* 42 (2005): 1–18.

[11] *The State of Obesity 2020: Better Policies for a Healthier America*, Trust for America's Health, 2020. https://www.tfah.org/report-details/state-of-obesity-2020/

[12] Emma Frances Bloomfield and Angeline Sangalang, "Juxtaposition as Visual Argument: Health Rhetoric in *Super Size Me* and *Fat Head*," *Argumentation and Advocacy* 50 (2014): 141–156.

[13] Adwoa A. Afful and Rose Ricciardelli, "Shaping the Online Fat Acceptance Movement: Talking About Body Image and Beauty Standards," *Journal of Gender Studies* 24 (2015): 1–20.

[14] David S. Birdsell and Leo Groarke, "Outlines of a Visual Theory of Argumentation," *Argumentation and Advocacy* 43 (2007): 104.

[15] Bill Hutchinson, "Incomprehensible: Confrontations Over Masks Erupt Amid COVID-19 Crisis," *ABC News*, May 7, 2020. https://abcnews.go.com/US/incomprehensible-confrontations-masks-erupt-amid-covid-19-crisis/story?id=70494577

[16] Jane C. Timm and Dareh Gregorian, "'Dangerous and Disrespectful': Doctors Tear Into Pence's Maskless Hospital Visit," *NBC News*, April 29, 2020. https://www.nbcnews.com/politics/white-house/dangerous-disrespectful-doctors-tear-pence-s-mask-less-hospital-visit-n1195611

[17] Grace Segers, "Marjorie Taylor Greene Removed from House Committee Assignments," *CBS News*, February 5, 2021. https://www.cbsnews.com/news/house-votes-to-remove-gop-rep-greene-from-committees/

[18] See: "Hans Rosling's 200 Countries, 200 Years, 4 Minutes—The Joy of Stats," *BBC 4*, November 26, 2010. https://www.youtube.com/watch?v=jbkSRLYSojo

[19] V. William Balthrop and Carole Blair, "'LaFayette, We Are Here!' Why Did the United States Commemorate Its World War I Dead in Europe?" in Randall A. Lake, Ed., *Recovering Argument* (New York: Routledge, 2018), 3–15.

[20] Peter Erenhaus, "The Vietnam Veterans Memorial: An Invitation to Argument," *Argumentation and Advocacy* 25 (1988): 54–64.

[21] Carole Blair, Martha S. Jeppeson, and Enrico Pucci, Jr., "Public Memorializing in Postmodernity: The Vietnam Veterans Memorial as Prototype," *Quarterly Journal of Speech* 77 (1991): 279.

[22] Ibid., p. 281.

[23] Marita Sturken, *Tangled Memories: The Vietnam War, the AIDS Epidemic, and the Politics of Remembering*. (Berkeley: University of California Press, 1997).

[24] Craig S. Smith and Ian Fisher, "Temperatures Rise Over Cartoons Mocking Muhammad," *The New York Times*, February 3, 2006. https://www.nytimes.com/2006/02/03/international/europe/03cartoons.html

25. "Charlie Hebdo Attack: Three Days of Terror," *BBC News*, January 14, 2015. http://www.bbc.com/news/world-europe-30708237
26. Reha Kansara, "Black Lives Matter: Can Viral Videos Stop Police Brutality?" BBC Trending, July 6, 2020. https://www.bbc.com/news/blogs-trending-53239723
27. Nicholas Bogel-Burroughs, "Prosecutors Say Derek Chauvin Knelt on George Floyd for 9 Minutes 29 Seconds, Longer than Initially Reported," *New York Times*, March 30, 2021. https://www.nytimes.com/2021/03/30/us/derek-chauvin-george-floyd-kneel-9-minutes-29-seconds.html
28. Quoted in Kansara.
29. David Welna, "Gen. Mark Milley Says Accompanying Trump to Church Photo-Op Was a Mistake," NPR, June 11, 2020. https://www.npr.org/sections/live-updates-protests-for-racial-justice/2020/06/11/875019346/gen-mark-milley-says-accompanying-trump-to-church-photo-op-was-a-mistake
30. Helene Cooper, "General Milley Apologizes for Trump Photo Op Role," *The New York Times*, June 11, 2020. https://www.nytimes.com/2020/06/11/us/politics/trump-milley-military-protests-lafayette-square.html
31. Rick Williams, "Theorizing Visual Intelligence Practices, Development, and Methodologies for Visual Communication," in Diane S. Hope, Ed., *Visual Communication: Perception, Rhetoric & Technology* (New York: Hampton Press, 2006), 31–56.
32. Neil Postman, *Amusing Ourselves to Death* (New York: Penguin, 1985).
33. Bobby Allyn, "The 'OK' Hand Gesture Is Now Listed As A Symbol of Hate," *NPR.org*, September 26, 2019, https://www.npr.org/2019/09/26/764728163/the-ok-hand-gesture-is-now-listed-as-a-symbol-of-hate
34. This image was photoshopped and is fake. The original photo was of the 405 Freeway in Los Angeles, but the photograph was digitally manipulated to add lanes and cars. It is worth noting that in the many times the author used the photograph as a teaching example, not knowing himself that it was fake, no one ever challenged its authenticity. See: "When Photoshop Is So Good It's Bad." https://www.bricoleurbanism.org/whimsicality/when-photoshop-is-so-good-its-bad/
35. Stuart Hall, *Encoding and Decoding in the Television Discourse* (Birmingham, UK: Centre for Cultural Studies, University of Birmingham, 1973), 507–517.
36. "9/11 Tourist Guy: Know Your Meme," http://knowyourmeme.com/memes/911-tourist-guy
37. Heather Perlberg, "Photoshop Blunders: Manipulated Reality," *Bloomberg Business*, April 26, 2012.
38. Ye Ming and Olivier Laurent, "World Press Photo Disqualifies 20% of Its Contest Finalists," *Time*, February 12, 2015. http://time.com/3706626/world-press-photo-processing-manipulation-disqualified/
39. Ibid.
40. "O.J.'s Darkened Mug Shot," *The Museum of Hoaxes*, accessed July 24, 2015. http://hoaxes.org/photo_database/image/darkened_mug_shot
41. Eliana Dockterman, "Keira Knightley Posed Topless to Protest Photoshopping," *Time*, November 5, 2014. http://time.com/3559286/keira-knightley-topless-photoshop/
42. Aja Romano, "Jordan Peele's Simulated Obama PSA Is a Double-Edged Warning Against Fake News," *Vox*, April 18, 2018, https://www.vox.com/2018/4/18/17252410/jordan-peele-obama-deepfake-buzzfeed
43. For example, see: Jon Hurwitz and Mark Peffley, "Explaining the Great Racial Divide: Perceptions of Fairness in the U.S. Criminal Justice System," *The Journal of Politics* 67 (2005): 762–783.

PART II

ARGUMENTATION IN SPECIALIZED FIELDS

The remaining chapters will focus on argumentation in selected specialized fields. As we have already discussed, the norms and practices that characterize argumentation differ according to context. You will likely not find yourself arguing the same way in an ordinary conversation between friends as you might in an academic debate, as a candidate in a political campaign, in a court of law, or at work in a business or organizational setting. The requirements for establishing acceptable proof, the style of presentation, and the criteria for evaluating knowledge claims are substantially different in each case.

The fields selected for discussion in the following chapters are intended to reflect some of the differences found when one argues in alternative settings. The selection is representative rather than exhaustive. We do not claim that these chapters will identify or represent all of the important dissimilarities found in different argument fields—in fact, we could have selected other fields for discussion. We chose these fields because they are substantially distinct from one other and because it is likely that you will come into contact with each of them at some point during your lives.

Chapters 11 and 12 address academic debate. Chapter 11 introduces the rudiments of debate as a field, and chapter 12 gives you a glimpse of some of the more complex theoretical issues that emerge in debate competitions. Many teachers of argumentation assign debates as class requirements because these contests provide an outstanding way to teach students the practical skills of argumentation and to get them thinking on their feet. Academic debate was first developed as a model of what reasoned argumentation should look like. It is a competitive activity designed to teach the skills of research, case building, refutation, and oral argumentation. We encourage you to read these chapters and to try your hand at debating. It is an enjoyable experience and an outstanding way to expand your mind.

Chapter 13 focuses on the arguments that surface in politics and political campaigns. These arguments fix our attention on the vital political issues of the day and involve all of us as citizens and, we hope, as voters. Political arguments shape our public life and organize our collective energies. These arguments represent the very fabric of our system of pluralistic democracy. Warts and all, the political campaign practices of today represent the culmination of more than 200 years of experimentation in representative democracy and electoral politics. This chapter should interest all of you and should help you to fulfill your responsibilities as citizens in a democratic nation.

Chapter 14 considers the argumentation that takes place in our courts. These arguments, directly or indirectly, involve all of us. Some of you may become litigants, others may experience careers as attorneys or judges, and many more of you will serve as jurors. All of us are affected by the argumentation that takes place in our courts because the courts reflect our social values, resolve our most significant public controversies, and create what passes for justice in our frenzied contemporary society.

Chapter 15 examines argumentation in business and organizations. This chapter is included because almost all of you will someday find yourselves working in an organization. Your effectiveness in achieving your career goals may be very much influenced by how well you can represent your ideas through both spoken and written arguments. Although we would caution all readers that organizations differ and that the specific requirements for arguing in any particular organization may be unique to that organization, we believe that there are general characteristics of arguments created in business and organizational settings. Learning and mastering these characteristics will help you become a much more effective organizational member.

Finally, chapter 16 discusses arguing in interpersonal relationships. This chapter also affects all of us as we engage in creating, managing, nurturing, and sometimes disengaging or terminating interpersonal relationships. The method for managing disagreements or conflicts in interpersonal relationships is argumentation. Our goal is to make you a more effective, sensitive, and strategic arguer in these interactions—in short, to help you win friends and influence people!

Academic Debate Overview

Academic debate is a special field of argumentation distinguished by the problems it addresses and the methods used to evaluate disputes. Each year thousands of high school and college students participate in debate. Some do so in the classroom; others represent their schools in competition against students from other institutions. There are several types of debate. Although each has its own rules and terminology, they share some theoretical orientations. In this chapter we provide an overview of academic debate; in the next chapter we examine the most popular types of debate in which college students engage.

THE DEBATE ORIENTATION

We have approached argumentation as part of the natural process of life—a way of making sense of our world and negotiating our understandings with others. Our intent has not been to teach you how to win arguments; rather, we have given you the tools to reach your own decisions and to construct your own advocacy. We have also contended that through argument you can discover the best conception of probable truth.

Academic debate is a somewhat different proposition. It is a laboratory for practicing the skills of argumentation. Students are frequently assigned to debate both sides of a controversy. Their arguments do not necessarily reflect their opinions or their best conception of truth. Rather, debaters offer the best arguments they can find for the position on a topic that they have been tasked to defend. Although it is hoped that debaters will emerge with a more informed position on the issues they debate (and thus a better understanding of where the truth might lie on those issues), the focus of debate is competitive. As a result, the more truthful arguments may not emerge as the most successful arguments. The intent of debate is to have fun, refine your argument skills in a structured and rule-governed environment, get some feedback and critiques from those who serve as your audience or judges, and—if your skills are up to the challenge—to win.

Although there is widespread agreement within the argumentation community as to the value of academic debate, there are a number of different debate formats that emphasize different debating skills. Consequently, if you will be involved in academic debating, your instructor or coach will likely give specific instructions regarding what you should expect and how you should prepare.

The Resolution

The focus of any debate is the proposition. The proposition is a statement that expresses the subject of the dispute. In academic debate the proposition is called the *resolution.* Because debate is a formal setting for argument, the resolution is explicitly worded prior to the debate. It may be a proposition of fact, value, or policy. It is obviously less rewarding to debate a proposition that can be easily proven true or untrue. Because a debate may essentially be finished if someone produces definitive physical or empirical evidence, as can happen with a proposition of fact, most contest debates utilize either value or policy resolutions. We briefly discuss debates of fact, but value and policy debates will be the focus of this chapter and the next.

The purpose of the resolution is twofold. First, it announces to all participants the topic of the debate. This gives both teams an equal opportunity to prepare for the contest. Second, it divides the ground for the two teams and thus delineates their argumentative tasks and responsibilities.

Affirmative Burdens

Almost all debates divide the propositional ground into those who favor the resolution, the *affirmative* (in parliamentary-style debate this is called the government), and those who oppose the resolution, the *negative* (called the opposition in parliamentary debate).

In that the resolution typically proposes a change from currently held beliefs, values, or policies, the affirmatives are also known as the advocates of change. The affirmative's burden is to convince the audience and/or the judge assigned to render a decision that the resolution is truthful, correct, or desirable. To do so, they must explain what they believe the resolution means and then present sound reasons in support of the resolution.

Negative Burdens

The resolution also conveys certain argumentative obligations to those who say "no" or who oppose the resolution. These individuals, known as the negative team, have the *burden of rejoinder.* This is the obligation to disagree with or refute the affirmative position. Implicit within this burden is the obligation to clash (discussed in detail in chapter 5) with the arguments presented by the affirmative. Clash refers to responding directly to the arguments the affirmative advanced. Often this is done point by point. Sometimes negatives group arguments and respond to the group of affirmative arguments. Either way, effective advocacy demands that the negative develop a strategy to refute the affirmative's arguments. As a representative of the current belief, the negative is not required to persuade the audience that the resolution is false; the negative is merely obliged to rebut the story advanced by the affirmative. Negative debaters may show that the affirmative's narrative lacks probability or fidelity. This may be best accomplished by presenting a competing narrative. If a competing story better accounts for the facts, it will seem likely that the affirmative's narrative is not true.

Presumption and the Burden of Proof

Although all arguers must provide support for their arguments, affirmative debaters have the *burden of proof* to show the resolution is true. This necessitates that they present and defend a ***prima facie case***: a narrative that, on its first presentation prior to any refutation, would meet the burdens necessary to persuade a reasonable audience that the resolution is true.

Affirmatives have the burden of proof because they must overcome ***presumption***. In the field of law, this principle assumes that an individual is innocent until proven guilty. In academic debate, we presume that current beliefs are justified until there is a good and sufficient reason for a change. In most debates, presumption resides with the negative and against the resolution.

Assume the resolution for an academic debate is *Resolved: that the United States should significantly strengthen its trade restrictions on imports coming from China*. Both teams would know that the affirmative team would be calling for the imposition of stronger trade restrictions by the United States, and the negative team would be obliged to rebut the imposition of such new trade restrictions. The burden of proof would be placed upon the affirmative, for the affirmative is advocating a change in policy. Presumption would be against such a change. Both teams would also know that the debate would focus on U.S.-China trade policies. This would enable them to investigate the relevant literature to discover and prepare for the issues likely to figure in this debate.

THREE TYPES OF ACADEMIC DEBATING

Fact Debates

Sometimes debates focus on questions of fact. Typically, this involves giving some descriptive characteristic to a referent. Is today (referent) Tuesday (descriptive characteristic)? Did Russia hack into U.S. government computers? Does access to a handgun for self-protection increase the risk of death or injury when confronted by a criminal? To each of these questions, there is a yes or no answer. Either today is Tuesday or it is some other day of the week. Either Russia hacked into the computers or it did not. Either access to a handgun makes one safer or it doesn't. There is no judgment about a value in any of these questions, nor is there a recommended course of action (a policy judgment). The outcome of such debates would merely establish the facts that are in dispute.

Addressing questions of fact requires a greater focus on the "terms" within the resolution than does addressing resolutions of value or policy. This results from the importance of determining the attributes of the important terms. What makes a chair a chair? There are certain characteristics that distinguish a chair from a bench or a stool. Consider the resolution: *Resolved: That the novel coronavirus SARS-CoV-2 (COVID-19) was accidentally released from a research laboratory in Wuhan, China*. The debate would focus on how viruses can infect humans. Debaters would likely contrast narratives about accidental releases from a lab with deliberate releases as well as how viruses can cross over from animal species to humans. Such a resolution is contrary to the current scientific consensus. The affirmative would have the burden of proof while the negative would enjoy presumption.

Value Debates

In ***value debates*** the affirmative asks the audience to agree to a judgment stated in the resolution. There are two components to this resolution: a value object and a value judgment. For example, the topic may be *Resolved: that the Pledge of Allegiance is inappropriate private expression in public schools.* In this case, the value object is the Pledge of Allegiance and the value judgment is that reciting the pledge in public schools is "inappropriate." To support this resolution the affirmative would need to present a value criterion for determining how to judge what is "inappropriate" and by implication what is "appropriate." This would, of course, constitute a value judgment. Whether the Pledge of Allegiance is deemed "inappropriate" would depend on the values linked to the words "appropriate" and "inappropriate." For example, an affirmative might argue that expression in public schools that supports religion is "inappropriate." The underlying value would therefore be the separation of church and state, and the public school would be argued to be an extension of the state. The affirmative would need to be able to defend this criterion and would then need to contend that reciting the Pledge of Allegiance constitutes support for religion because the Pledge includes the term "under God." This provides the negative with the opportunity to clash with the criteria presented by the affirmative as well as with the specific example as to whether the Pledge of Allegiance does actually support religion. Winning either argument would spell victory for the negative.

Policy Debates

In *policy debate* the affirmative team is generally asked to present a specific proposal or plan to implement the change called for in the resolution. For example, during the 2020-2021 school year, high school students debated the topic: *Resolved: The United States federal government should enact substantial criminal justice reform in the United States in one or more of the following: forensic science, policing, sentencing.* The affirmative would present a plan that detailed how they think the United States ought to substantially change some aspect of the criminal justice system. For example, they might focus on the arrest and prosecution of persons charged with the possession and sale of narcotics. To justify such a change, the affirmative would need to prove that the current policies are not working well (by identifying an existing ill in the current system and by assigning blame or responsibility for the existence of that ill) and that a different strategy for the arrest and prosecution of those suspected of narcotics violations would result in a superior policy (a proposed cure). Most affirmatives would compare a narrative of the status quo (the current policies in this area) with a narrative of the status quo as modified by the affirmative plan. They would argue that the status quo + plan is significantly better than the status quo alone. The negative would be called upon to refute this viewpoint. Since the current system enjoys presumption, negatives do not have to prove that the status quo is better than the status quo + plan. They merely have to argue that the proposed change would not be better. A "tie" goes to the negative because of the principle of presumption already discussed.

FORMAT

Most academic debates are conducted in a format in which two-member teams face each other, although other formats of debate also exist. For example, one-on-one debate, known as Lincoln-Douglas debate, is also common. The nature of speeches, the speaker order, and the time limits of each speech are referred to as the ***debate format***. The specific formats used in each type of debate will be presented in the next chapter.

The Order of Speaking

While there is some variety in the specifics, all common debate formats share some traits. The most important shared trait is that the format is designed to provide balanced competition; neither side is given a unique advantage by the format. Another is that the proponent of change—the affirmative—both initiates and concludes the debate. This is the case because the affirmative generally has the burden of proof. In the first speech, the affirmative defines the terms and establishes the grounds of the debate. If the affirmative did not speak first, there would be nothing for the negative to negate. The affirmative also gets to present the last speech in the debate. The rationale is that the affirmative must convince the audience that the present policies or beliefs are problematic, and this burden of proof is challenging. The advantage of speaking first and last is offset by the fact that the negative team always retains presumption.

Other speeches in the debate alternate between affirmative and negative speakers. The one exception is that in order to have the affirmative start and end the debate it is necessary to have two consecutive negative speeches at some point. This is called the *negative block* and is generally considered a significant advantage, because the negative gets to hold the attention of the audience or judge for a significant amount of time.

Constructive Speeches

Each participant in a four-person academic debate presents a ***constructive speech***. In this speech you can present any arguments you consider relevant. This is the opportunity to construct the positions you believe should be the focus of the debate. It is also the occasion for presenting your initial responses to the positions developed by the opposition.

Rebuttal Speeches

Each participant in a four-person academic debate also presents a ***rebuttal***. In this speech you will rebuild your initial constructive positions and extend your attacks on the opposition. Because rebuttal speeches take place in the latter part of the debate, debaters are prohibited from initiating new arguments. You can extend your own arguments and refute the arguments developed by your opponents. You are permitted to provide further evidence and analysis to support the arguments that you initiated in your constructive speeches but cannot start a brand-new argument.

For example, consider the trade topic illustration we used earlier. If the negatives had not discussed in their constructive speeches the possibility that China would respond to new trade restrictions on Chinese goods bound for the United States by implementing their own restrictions on American goods coming into China, it would be too late to bring this up in rebuttals. If this is an important argument to the negative's case, it should be introduced in one of the negative's constructive speeches and not saved for the rebuttals when the affirmative might not have time to respond to it. The requirement that arguments be first introduced in the constructive speeches helps encourage a more complete and careful examination and consideration of these positions. The prohibition against introducing new arguments in rebuttals also prevents the affirmative from coming up with new reasons to support their policy in their final rebuttal, when the negative would have no opportunity to respond.

Rebuttal speeches are shorter than constructive speeches. This means that speakers must adapt to the rebuttal situation. Sometimes this means offering a much briefer and thus less complete explanation of your arguments. Sometimes it means choosing which arguments you need to discuss and dropping others. It is important to remember, however, that if you do not discuss an argument in your last rebuttal, it is likely that the audience or the judge will not consider this argument when deciding who won the debate.

The final rebuttal provides the speakers the last opportunity to convince the audience or the judge why you believe your arguments are better than those offered by your opponents and why you believe you have won the debate. This means that you should explain which of your arguments are superior and why those arguments are sufficient to overcome the arguments offered by your opponents. Putting the arguments presented in the debate together into a coherent story that can be readily understood and evaluated by your hearers is at this point a very effective strategy.

Cross-Examination

Most debate formats incorporate question periods. In debate this is called *cross-examination* (once again parliamentary debate is different, and those differences will be discussed in chapter 12). Each debater asks questions of, and is questioned by, the opposition. The individual asking the questions is naturally called the *questioner*. The debater who has just now concluded a constructive speech and is now being questioned is called the witness.

You may decide to use this time to clarify what the opposition has argued. While this may be necessary because, after all, one cannot refute what one has not heard, it is not the most effective use of cross-examination time. Asking questions that probe an opponent's argument can be a more profitable use of this time. Arguments and evidence often are predicated on unproven assumptions. Discovering these assumptions may permit you to dispense with arguments in a very expeditious fashion. Also, if you know what the weaknesses of an opponent's arguments are, it can be useful to highlight these weaknesses during the questioning period and before you develop and present the arguments in your next speech. The strategy permits you to reference the admissions gleaned in your cross-examination.

We discussed the art of argumentative questioning in depth in chapter 9, but debate cross-examination is a little different. In most contexts, argument is regulated by the norms of polite conversation. If you are abusive or uncooperative, people will probably stop interacting with you. Two rules govern the cross-examination expected of debaters, and they are quite strict.

First, the questioner controls the cross-examination period. If you are the questioner, you get to ask the questions—the witness does not. You can also politely interrupt the witness if you feel the need. This may happen because you think you have the answer you need or because the witness is not answering the question you asked. But you may not badger the witness or demand yes-or-no answers. Some questions cannot be adequately answered with a "yes" or "no," so it is unfair to make such a request. You are not permitted to assert a new argument during cross-examination, even if you intended to give the witness a chance to respond. Arguments and evidence must be presented during a speech.

Second, witnesses must cooperate as fully as possible. This means that if you are the witness you should answer the questions as clearly and as succinctly as possible. You should not attempt to stall or obfuscate. Nor are you permitted to read new evidence. Of course, you are permitted to refer to the evidence you presented in your speech, and you may be asked by the questioner to reread evidence that you just presented in your speech.

Time Limits

Each team receives an equal amount of speaking and cross-examination time. This is another attempt to maintain the competitive balance of the activity. These time limits are strictly enforced, and when your speaking time has expired, you must end your speech.

Now that you have an idea of how a debate operates, we can discuss in greater detail the types of debate arguments typically advanced.

THE NATURE OF DEBATE ARGUMENTS

As one might expect, most of the arguments advanced in debate focus on the reasons why the audience should accept or reject the resolution. These are called *substantive arguments*. There are some arguments, however, that may precede the substantive ones.

Procedural Arguments

Procedural arguments are those that must be resolved prior to the consideration of substantive issues. These arguments are customarily initiated in the first two speeches (first affirmative constructive or first negative constructive). The most important procedural argument is topicality. We will also discuss criteria arguments that are used in value debating.

TOPICALITY ARGUMENTS. We have already noted that the affirmative burden is to prove the resolution. The affirmative therefore has the right to define the key terms of the resolution. But the affirmative must do so in a non-abusive manner. If the arguments presented by the affirmative deal with something other than the resolution, the affirmative will not have proven the resolution true. A negative argument alleging that the affirmative has strayed from proving the resolution is called a *topicality argument*.

Typically, the affirmative first defines the key terms of the resolution and then develops the arguments supporting the resolution. In policy debate the plan proposed by the affirmative, or the policy change under consideration, is the focus of the topicality question. If the plan were topical, that is, if the proposed plan does what the topic calls for, the advantages that flow from the plan would prove the resolution true. If the plan is not topical, the advantages would not be relevant, and they would not serve as reasons why the resolution should be implemented. For example, if the affirmative defined trade restrictions as tariffs and quotas, the plan must specify how U.S. tariffs and quotas would be modified. The advantages of such a policy change must then be shown to flow from these modifications.

In value debate there is no plan. Thus, a different determination of topicality is used. With value resolutions the issue of topicality focuses on the relationship between the definitions and the arguments advanced by the affirmative in support of the resolution. Let's consider, for example, the resolution *Resolved: that the welfare system exacerbates the problems of the urban poor.* The affirmative might choose to define the key terms: *welfare system, exacerbates, problems,* and the *urban poor.* The affirmatives would then present reasons why they think the resolution is true. If they argued that public schools do not adequately prepare the urban poor for careers, and the negative team did not think that schools should be considered elements of the welfare system, the negative could issue a topicality argument.

Although topicality is an affirmative burden, it is generally presumed that an affirmative will present a topical case. Thus, it is generally the first negative speaker who initiates a topicality argument if one is considered warranted.

CRITERIA ARGUMENTS. In both fact and value debates there is a special kind of definition presented—an argument about the criteria to be applied in judging the resolution. With propositions of fact, affirmatives must present *criteria* for the key terms. This means determining those defining attributes that separate one object from another, for example, a just war from an unjust war. Similarly, in value debates, the affirmative must present a value that focuses on the coherence of the decision-making process. It is the affirmative's right and obligation to present reasonable criteria to help in rendering a judgment about what value to use in determining the truth of the proposition. You will recall that in the value proposition about the "Pledge of Allegiance," we suggested that one criterion might be an argument about which team best meets the long-accepted principle from the United States Constitution that there should be a separation of church and state.

Negative speakers can respond to affirmative criteria arguments by accepting or rejecting them. If they accept the affirmative criteria, then the audience will use them as a filter to evaluate the arguments presented in the debate. Therefore, in a value debate, if both teams agree that the preservation of life is paramount, the audiences will look first to determine whether the affirmative or the negative arguments best uphold this value. Arguments that address other values, such as the protection of human rights, would not flow through the accepted criteria and should therefore not enter the debate. Since the affirmative can select their criteria, and since this selection often provides a strategic benefit, many negatives choose to clash with the criteria that have been proposed by the affirmative. To do so, the negative must give reasons why the affirmative criteria are not acceptable and then present *counter-criteria* that they believe are better than those presented by the affirmative.

Regardless of whether the criteria used in evaluating the outcome of the debate are presented by the affirmative or the negative, they should be defined and the rationality behind their selection should be presented and defended. The team that does the better job of debating about criteria will convince the audience to use their criteria for evaluating the debate.

Substantive Arguments

While topicality and criteria arguments are both potentially decisive, most debates focus on the substantive arguments that remain. In a substantive debate on matters of value, the focus may be only on what is happening at the current moment or the status quo. In a substantive debate on a question of policy the affirmative is called upon to envision and depict two worlds: the world of the status quo and that of the status quo plus the plan. We will consider each in turn.

SUBSTANTIVE ISSUES IN VALUE DEBATES. Once the criteria analysis has been presented, affirmatives in a value debate must show that the status quo should be negatively evaluated. This is usually accomplished through the presentation of a story that demonstrates the validity of the value judgment. For example, in arguing that the welfare system exacerbates the problems of the urban poor, an affirmative could present the principle of independence as the value to look to when determining the truth of the resolution. Then in their arguments they would need to show that the welfare system frustrates the achievement of this value of independence by the urban poor. This would probably entail the presentation of several ways in which the welfare system fosters a culture of dependence. The relationship between the procedural and the substantive issues in a value debate should now be clear. The substantive elements of the case demonstrate the failings of the present system with regard to the value criteria advocated in the debate.

In responding to the substantive issues presented by the affirmative, the negative would challenge the story presented. The negative would look to the motives and behaviors attributed to the actors in the affirmative's story. Are those on welfare dependent? Do they seek independence but are frustrated by their attempts to get off the welfare rolls by some policies of the welfare system? Are there counter-causalities, such as discrimination, poor education, lack of jobs, inadequate access to childcare, that are more likely causes of or at least contributing factors to welfare dependence?

In addition, most negatives present arguments against the value criteria. An argument of this type is often called a ***value objection***. This is an argument that says embracing the value favored by the affirmative would have adverse consequences. For example, some affirmative values focus on the rights of individuals. The negative could argue that basing decisions on individual rights is a bad idea because individual rights reinforce the notion that individuals are more important than the group. This, some authorities contend, has adverse consequences on society. One might argue that our wasteful, throwaway, pollution-filled society is the result of elevating the individual above the group. Therefore, the negative could maintain that argumentative criteria that focus on individual rights should be rejected and that shared, or community rights and responsibilities, should be viewed as more important. If the affirmative loses the argument about individual rights that they have established as criteria for the evaluation of the arguments in the debate, they should lose the debate, as it is unlikely that they can win the arguments regarding the superiority of the value judgment presented in the topic without establishing their criteria. This would, in turn, permit the negative to argue that the affirmative failed to prove the resolution true. At the very least, this becomes another reason to support the superiority of the use of the negative's criteria instead of the criteria offered by the affirmative. We witnessed a substantive argument about the competition between individual rights and community or group interests in the recent controversy regarding whether or not people should be required to accept the COVID-19 vaccines.

The substantive arguments—including the clash over whether the status quo achieves the value criteria and the debate over the merits (including the potential harms or risks of harms outlined in the value objections)—are then evaluated alongside any procedural arguments that have been introduced into the debate. The judge formulates a decision as to whether the proposition has been affirmed or negated.

SUBSTANTIVE ISSUES IN POLICY DEBATES. In examining the status quo, the policy affirmative presents a story about the world as they see it. This entails describing the actors, the scene, and the events in narrative terms. In order to win, the affirmative must convince the audience that their proposed change would result in more advantages than would the decision to cling to current policies existing in the status quo.

Needs Case. Traditionally, affirmatives presented a world with problems that needed to be resolved. An affirmative story of this type is called a ***needs case*** (see chapter 8). Problems (the stock issue known as ill) identified must be significant and inherent to the status quo (the stock issue known as blame). If the ills of the status quo are insignificant, there would be no sense in enacting a new policy. If the problems are not inherent to the present system—that is, if we do not know the causes of the problems and why current policies are inadequate—then a new policy might not solve the problem. Finally, we must have good reason to predict that the proposal will actually solve the identified problems (the stock issue known as the cure). If the plan accrues no advantage, it should not be enacted.

The negative refutes a needs case by challenging the story told by the affirmative. They may do this by showing that there is not a significant problem (using denial or mitigation tactics) with the status quo (thus that no significant ills exist), or that the present system is solving the problems that have been identified or could solve these problems with minor adjustments that are typically referred to as minor repairs (this is thus related to the stock issue known as "blame"). The negative will often also choose to argue that the proposal advanced by the affirmative will not solve the problems that have been identified and thus it should not be adopted (this is the issue of "cure"). Most negatives will choose a mix of arguments that address the significance of the harms that have been identified, that propose minor repairs, and that also create doubts about the affirmative's ability to enact a cure. It is important to remember that to win the debate the negative does not have to win each and every one of the stock issues. The negative can conceivably win the debate by winning in a convincing way one of those stock issues or by otherwise demonstrating that the affirmative proposal will not yield significant advantages when compared to the status quo.

Comparative Advantage Case. It is common for debaters to construct narratives that merge the three stock issues (ill, blame, and cure) and present a ***comparative advantage case*** (see chapter 8). In such an approach, the affirmative presents a plan and argues that the advantages of the plan compare favorably to the status quo. Thus, there does not have to be a significant problem (ill) with the present system, just a significant advantage (cure) that results from enacting the plan. The question of blame becomes part of the solvency issue. If the plan compares favorably to the status quo, then the inherency burden has been met—unless the negative can show that the same inadequacies that thwarted the status quo efforts will also thwart the affirmative's proposal.

In order to refute a comparative advantage case, the first substantive decision the negative must make is how to respond to the affirmative's depiction of the status quo (the issues of ill and blame). Suppose the affirmative is claiming that health-care assistance programs for Syrian refugees are failing and that, as a result, thousands will die. They might specifically cite the potential for disastrous polio, cholera, and COVID-19 outbreaks to develop as a result of all of the violent political conflicts and the movements of vast numbers of refugees in the region. There are three potential responses to this claim. First, the negative can accept this depiction but clash with another aspect of the affirmative's case. This is risky because it grants the affirmative the point that the problem area that they address is significant. If their case shows even the potential to protect thousands of lives, they will have gained an important advantage in the debate.

Second, the negative can attempt to deny the depiction of the current situation. Perhaps there is evidence that, contrary to the affirmative's claim, health assistance programs are working, and the health of Syrian refugees is improving. Usually when teams are contending polar opposite positions, each side offers empirical evidence and the testimony of experts. Sometimes these differences are the result of conflicting definitions of important key terms, sometimes there is a difference in the time frame provided for the data used in the evidence, sometimes the qualifications or interests of the experts account for the divergence of opinion, and sometimes it is a matter of unstated assumptions behind the conclusions. There are certainly situations, for example, where experts are guided by their ideological and political convictions. These differences result in very different opinions about complex issues. The negative should try to figure out why their data or expert evidence differs from that offered by the affirmative, and they should also strive to explain why their evidence and thus their arguments are superior to what has been offered by the affirmative.

Third, the negative can attempt to minimize the significance of the affirmative's depiction of the conditions of the Syrian refugees. For example, it could be that the numbers presented by the affirmative represent a worst-case scenario; therefore, the loss of life will probably be significantly less than the affirmative has argued. Minimization of the significance of the affirmative case, however, is a strategy that must usually be accompanied by some other tactic. The negative is not likely to win by saying only that the problem in the status quo is not as significant as the affirmative depicts. An audience is likely to conclude that even if the negative wins their arguments, there are still sufficient problems in the status quo to warrant the adoption of the affirmative plan.

Solvency Attacks. The negative will often choose to refute the affirmative's depiction of the status quo while also attacking the affirmative's claim that their proposed plan would be superior to the status quo. First, the negative may try to deny that significant advantages will result from implementing the plan. Such arguments challenge the affirmative prediction that the proposed policy will solve the problems of the status quo, hence they are called *solvency attacks*.

There are several reasons why a plan may not accrue the advantages predicted by the affirmative. The negative must research the proposals to find out why they have not already been adopted. If the proposal is really likely to accrue significant benefits, a natural question to consider is: why have we not already adopted it? There are often good reasons, and these reasons may provide the negative with strong arguments against the proposed plan.

- *Sometimes the proposed plan would not be practical.* If one scholar or policy analyst has argued for a specific proposal, it is possible (perhaps even likely) that another has critiqued that proposal. If the plan is modeled after a policy in a foreign country, you should study the situation in that country and examine the policy to see how well it is actually performing. Advocates must be aware, however, that such comparisons are themselves subject to argumentative tests challenging advocates to compare the population demographics, national cultures, economic conditions, political institutions, educational levels, etc. If these other nations are too dissimilar from ours, the arguments will not likely survive close scrutiny.

- *Sometimes proposals are not adopted because special interests oppose them.* Debaters may be able to argue that the plan will not work because it is open to **circumvention**. In such a case you are arguing that people who have the will to thwart the new proposal will find a way to get around it. To construct a circumvention argument, you need to show that there is both a motive and the means for someone to get around the proposal. For example, during Prohibition people had the motive—the appetite for alcoholic beverages and the profits to be made from smuggling—and the means—home distilled beverages and illegal imports from Canada and Mexico under mob control—to circumvent the law. As a result, the policy was largely ineffective. If an affirmative suggests a similar prohibition, for instance on the sale of cigarettes or perhaps more stringent limits on political campaign contributions, the motive and means may exist for circumvention of these new policies as well.

A negative that fails to clash with an affirmative's solvency arguments ends up conceding solvency claims to the affirmative. This greatly enhances the appeal of the affirmative's case and also raises the threshold level that must be overcome in the construction of the stock issue of "cost."

Disadvantage Arguments. The stock issue of cost provides the negative with the opportunity to argue that even if the affirmative policy did produce some benefit or advantage over current policy, it has noteworthy drawbacks or costs that should be carefully considered and evaluated. Such a negative argument is called a ***disadvantage***. A disadvantage is typically related in the form of a story that says there will be undesirable consequences should the affirmative's policy be adopted. Disadvantages usually assume affirmative solvency, but the negative contention is that even if the plan were solvent, we would not want to do it because of its disadvantages.

There are several types of disadvantages. Each disadvantage is a story involving actors, events, and scenes. Debaters must be cognizant of how they depict the actors in their arguments. Inconsistency can destroy the validity of the story.

- *Sometimes proposed policy actions might create problems where none currently exist.* For example, you could argue that an affirmative case that prohibited the private ownership of handguns might leave the citizenry defenseless against home invasions by criminals or even against invasion by a foreign power. Or a negative could argue that the second amendment to the U.S. Constitution is considered so fundamentally important to many of our citizens that any attempt to tamper with it would lead to the formation of reactionary militia movements opposed to the government. This, one might argue, could also spawn the production of more incidents such as the bombing of the federal building in Oklahoma City or the attack on the U.S. Capitol that occurred on January 6, 2021.

- *The newly proposed affirmative policy might exacerbate existing problems.* Pollution is already a serious concern. The negative could argue that the affirmative plan that promises to increase employment opportunities dramatically and to spur economic growth in the United States would also result in increased energy consumption, expanded levels of pollution, accelerated global climate change, and perhaps a permanent alteration of the climate by melting the polar ice cap. This, in turn, could produce a kind of economic disaster previously unknown to humankind.

- *New policies also may be a step in an undesirable direction.* For example, an affirmative might argue in favor of a policy change that creates a constitutional amendment to ban same-sex marriage. The negative could counter argue such a policy by claiming that the United States of America has been moving for many years toward the creation of a more egalitarian nation. This is evidenced in the extension of voting rights and equality of opportunity for women, persons of different races and ethnic backgrounds; protections for the rights of the elderly and disabled; and recently in the extension of rights such as the permission of same-sex marriage and the right of gay and transgender people to serve in the military. An affirmative plan that sought to reverse the progress toward full equality for LGBTQ people would increase the likelihood that resistance to equal rights for all of these other different classes of persons would again become common. Thus, a desirable movement toward equality for all citizens would be undermined; because of this, the affirmative plan should be rejected.

- *Plans can be attacked on moral or philosophical grounds.* This necessitates developing a value justification. If you are arguing against a policy that calls for the death penalty for terrorists, you could oppose the plan on moral grounds. If so, you might argue that capital punishment is immoral, that civilized nations around the world have been abolishing state executions, and that the morality of a policy action is an important consideration that should not be ignored by decision makers.

Burdens. Regardless of the type of disadvantage, the negative must meet several burdens. First, the negative must demonstrate a clear *link* to the affirmative policy. This means that the negative must show that there is a clear causal connection between the affirmative plan and the disadvantage. Second, the disadvantage must be *unique*. To be unique, the affirmative plan must be the sole cause of the disadvantage. If many things can cause the disadvantage, you would have to show the unique increment in the disadvantage that the affirmative plan causes. Third, the negative must show the affirmative plan is sufficient to **cause** the disadvantage. There are two ways this may be accomplished.

- *Some disadvantages propose that the present system is on the* **brink,** *or precipice, of a disadvantage.* With this kind of argument, you need to contend that the affirmative action is enough to push us over the cliff. For example, perhaps the affirmative has proposed to build a high-speed rail system, such as those that exist in Western Europe, Japan, and China, to address transportation problems and to reduce the consumption of fossil fuels. The negative could argue that many cities in the U.S. West (e.g., Phoenix, Las Vegas, Los Angeles, Palm Springs, and San Diego) already face a very serious water shortage. The negative could then argue that access to high-speed rail transportation in the region would dramatically increase the building of housing in the desert and spur further increases in population as people moved out into desert communities but used the new trains to commute to jobs in Southern California where land and housing prices are prohibitively expensive. Then the negative might argue that this rapid development would greatly aggravate the water shortage, perhaps destroy the underground aquifer, and lead to an ecological catastrophe.

  The affirmative can deny the validity of the brink argument if they can show that alternative sources for water exist (perhaps desalinization of ocean water), can defend other strategies for limiting growth, or can establish that credible programs of water conservation can be developed. They might also be able to diminish the credibility of the brink argument by claiming that threats of impending doom have been issued for years, but despite those threats, and despite the continued rapid development of this region, the catastrophe has never materialized.

- *Other disadvantages are* **linear.** This means that each increment is undesirable. We know additional pollution would be harmful, so if the affirmative policy causes additional pollution it would seem to be a bad idea. With such disadvantages you may be required to show how much more pollution the affirmative would cause and the impact of this additional increment of pollution.

Finally, *time frame* may be critical. If the affirmative plan could cause a significant disadvantage before it accrues its advantage, that could be a reason to reject the proposal. If the achievable affirmative advantage has a shorter time frame than the eventual disadvantage, the audience may decide to accept the eventual risk of the disadvantage for the nearer term benefit of the affirmative proposal.

Affirmative Responses. The negative must be wary when presenting disadvantages because the affirmative has two options for response. One option is called a ***take out***. This is an argument that simply denies the chain of events in the story. Its name stems from the idea that if you take out one link in a chain, the chain falls apart. Similarly, if you break the sequence of events in the story the negative tells, you deny the validity of the story. For example, the negative story is that removing economic sanctions against Iran will anger Israel and make it more likely that Israel undertakes a military strike against Iranian nuclear facilities that would lead to a broader regional war. The affirmative could respond by agreeing that Israel would be angered by the removal of the sanctions but deny the likelihood that Israel would take military action or that the result would be a wider conflict in the Middle East.

The second kind of affirmative response to a disadvantage is particularly dangerous to the negative. Affirmatives may present arguments called ***turnarounds***. A turnaround is an argument that takes a disadvantage and turns it into an advantage for the affirmative. There are two ways that a disadvantage can be turned.

- *First, an affirmative may turn the link.* If a negative argues that implementing the UN's declaration on human rights is undesirable because it reinforces the domination of male leadership in the world, an affirmative may respond by claiming that, rather than reinforcing the patriarchy, the UN's declaration is a tool for enhancing the role of women in the world because it extends the protection of women to corners of the world where women are still viewed as male possessions. Thus, if patriarchy is a bad thing, it is more advantageous to implement the declaration than not to do so.

- *The second kind of turn is an impact turn.* For example, the negative argues that providing more foreign aid to Pakistan is disadvantageous because many in Pakistan do not trust the United States and are hostile to U.S. development workers. They then argue that an increase in aid and aid workers would lead to an escalation of political conflict and violence in Pakistan. An affirmative speaker could grant this scenario but claim that rather than a disadvantage, such civil unrest would be desirable because it could lead ultimately to a more democratic form of government and perhaps also diminish the power of fundamentalist war lords or terrorist networks. Thus, the impact, internal strife, is turned from an undesirable outcome to a desirable one.

Policy debaters are not particularly interested in determining the likelihood that their proposals will actually be enacted. Rather, they prefer to concentrate on the merits of the proposed policies. The wording of policy debate resolutions does not say that the policy *will* be enacted. Instead, such debate topics use words that indicate that a policy "should" or "ought" to be adopted. Raising doubts about whether or not the agent of action "would" do the action is called a **should-would** argument and is not considered relevant to a policy debate. As a result, you should not spend your time trying to determine whether Congress or the executive branch of government would actually enact the proposed affirmative policy. Instead, focus on whether the proposed policy should or should not be adopted based upon its desirability.

Flow Sheeting as Systematic Note Taking

When good students listen to lectures, they take notes so that they may return to this information later and study for examinations. Debaters must also take notes, but their notes do not have to be as complete because they will be using their notes in a few minutes. The system of note taking in debate is referred to as *flowing*. It is a very important part of the debate process. In order for debaters to be sure they have answered all of the arguments raised by their opponents, and to be sure they have extended all of their own, they must write down what people have said. They also must record their notes in a fashion that makes them easy to read while they speak. In addition, they must write their notes quickly enough that they succeed in recording everything important that their opponent argues. This is not an easy task, but it is an essential task.

Here are some tips that may make the process a little easier:

1. Use at least two legal pads. Draw lines that divide the paper horizontally into eight equal sections. You now have room to record the arguments advanced in each of the eight speeches of the debate. Do not worry about flowing cross-examination but be sure to listen attentively to it. One pad will be the *case flow*. The other will be the *off-case flow*. On the case flow, you will need to record the first affirmative and all of the arguments (both affirmative and negative) that deal directly with the affirmative case. On the off-case flow, you will record all of the procedural arguments, any solvency arguments about the plan's effectiveness in a policy debate, and any disadvantages or value objections.

2. When you record a speaker's arguments, do not cross the lines you drew on the flow pads. To avoid crossing the lines you will need to write very small, and you will need to abbreviate words and terminology.

3. Record the enumeration employed by a speaker. If a speaker says this is the "first argument," write down #1. If a speaker says "subpoint A" you should write that down too. We suggest that you might also circle the enumerated structure of the affirmative case as presented in the first affirmative constructive and all subsequent references to the affirmative case structure. That will make these numbers stand out. Then in later speeches when a debater says, "On their B subpoint I will have three responses," you can easily find the B subpoint on your flow.

4. Leave space between groups of arguments. Sometimes arguments expand as the debate develops, and you may want more room to record them. Leaving space also helps you to find the group of arguments quickly.

5. Use arrows and lines to show which argument applies to which. If the first negative speaker has offered three arguments against the IB2 subpoint of the first case, it helps to draw a line to that subpoint.

6. Record the number and claim of the argument. As you get better, you will be able to record the source citation and the essence of the evidence as well. If you miss something, ask your partner about it or ask about it during cross-examination.

7. Alternate the colors of the fine point pens you are using, one color for the affirmative arguments and another for the negative arguments. That way you can tell at a glance who said what.

8. Before it is your turn to speak, try to write down the arguments you intend to make. If you have your arguments on the flow pad, all you have to do is read your

flow from left to right. You will have, right in front of you, what your opponent said and what you plan to say. If you have been flowing correctly, you will be able to see how an argument unfolds during the course of a debate. You should be able to follow the argument across your paper, hence the term *flow paper*.

TRUNCATED SAMPLE FLOW*

Topic: Resolved that implementation of the United Nations' universal declaration of human rights is more important than preserving state sovereignty.

First Aff Const	First Neg Const	Second Aff Const
①Definitions UN- intern'l org implmt- fulfill UDHR- doc of HRts presrv- sustain st sov- legal concpt of governance	① OK	① granted
②Crit- HRts Ⓐ HRts prereq 4 civilization - humanity & progress tied to recog of HRts	② Ⓐ 1. must arise w/in -only when fought 4 are rts valued	② Ⓐ implmnt=assist & ed so = arise w/in
Ⓑ HRts O/w st sov - states trample HRts & that's bad	Ⓑ 1. only sov guar safety -purpose of sov to presrve st & Rts of people	Ⓑ 1. demo=guar too eg, USA 2. Rts more imprtnt fight to presrv Rts
Ⓘ UDHR protects Democracy Ⓐ UDHR respcts other views - when writ=respct 4 divrgnce	Ⓘ Ⓐ OK	Ⓘ Ⓐ granted
Ⓑ UDHR plants seeds of Demo - adopted by all to accpt demo goals Ⓒ Demo=freedom - demo protcts a variety of Rts	Ⓑ&Ⓒ Demo Bad 1. aid=dependency - aid fosters reliance 2. -! repression - aid—alignmnt of classes, presrvd w/repression	Ⓑ 1. nations do move away -eg, Korea 2. others ask for aid -many nations reqst aid 1. aid=rep past exmpls prove 2. UDHR solves rep - purpose=protct Rts

* This truncated sample flow only shows parts of the first three speeches of the debate.

Explanation of Truncated Sample Flow

The First Affirmative Constructive
Observation ① Definitions
UN—United Nations
Implmt—implement
UDHR—Universal Declaration of Human Rights
presrv—preserve
st sove—state sovereignty
Observation ② Crit-Criteria; HRts-Human Rights
 The affirmative is arguing that "more important" will be determined by examining which preserves human rights better, implementing the UDHR or state sovereignty
Subpoint ⓐ HRts prereq 4 civilization—Human Rights are a prerequisite for civilization
 evidence: humanity and the progress of humanity throughout history have been tied to a recognition of human rights
Subpoint ⓑ HRts o/w st sov—Human Rights outweighs state sovereignty
 evidence: nation states have trampled human rights and such abuse is not warranted

Contention ①. UDHR protects Democracy
Subpoint ⓐ UDHR respects other views
 evidence: when then UDHR was written it was written with a recognition of and respect for divergent viewpoints
Subpoint ⓑ UDHR plants seeds for Democracy
 evidence: the UDHR has been adopted by all of the members of the UN and that means they all accept the goals of a democracy
Subpoint ⓒ Democracy preserves freedom
 evidence: democracies are established to protect a variety of rights of their citizens

First Negative Constructive
Observation ① OK—we have no arguments with the definitions
Observation ②
Subpoint ⓐ
 claim: human rights must arise from within a nation
 evidence: only when people have fought to obtain them are rights valued by the people
Subpoint ⓑ
 claim: only state sovereignty guarantees the safety of the people
 evidence: the purpose of sovereignty is to preserve the state and the safety of the people and in doing so, it preserves the rights of the people
Contention ①
Subpoint ⓐ OK—we have no arguments with this subpoint

(continued)

Explanation of Truncated Sample Flow

Subpoint (B) and (C) are grouped together
   claim #1: foreign aid promotes dependency in the recipient nation
   evidence: a nation which receives aid from other nations becomes dependent on that aid
   claim #2: dependency leads to increased repression
   evidence: aid leads to class differentiation, the haves and the have nots. Those who administer the aid attempt to perpetuate their status through repression

The Second Affirmative Speech
Observation (1) the negative granted our definitions
   explanation: the definitions cannot be challenged in subsequent speeches
Observation (2)
Subpoint (A)
   claim: by implementation we mean assistance and education
   explanation: our definition of implement was to fulfill the UDHR through assistance and education, so the rights will arise from within the nation
Subpoint (B)
   claim #1: democracy guarantees safety too
   explanation: the United States is a democracy and it guarantees the rights of its citizens
   claim #2: Rights are more important
   explanation: democratic nations have gone to war to fight to preserve the rights of the people. This shows that rights are more important than safety
Contention (I)
Subpoint (A) The subpoint was granted by the negative
Subpoints (B) and (C)
First Negative Argument #1
   claim #1: many nations do move away from aid
   evidence: at one time South Korea received significant American aid. It has now become self-sufficient
   claim #2: Other nations ask for aid
   evidence: requests for foreign aid from the U.S. are significant
   explanation: other nations wouldn't request aid if it were so bad
First Negative Argument #2
   claim #1: aid does not lead to repression
   explanation: many nations have received aid without it leading to repression
   claim #2: UDHR solves repression
   evidence: the purpose of the UDHR is to protect those rights of individual recognized by the UN

In most situations you will need to respond to each argument or group of arguments raised by your opponents, even if only to say, "We grant that point to the other team." You will also want to extend your arguments, especially if your opponents had nothing to say about them. To extend an argument means to remind the audience/judge that this argument is still pertinent. On a flow sheet it means moving the argument to the next column. A good flow will enable you to do this.

Summary

In this chapter we examined the argument field of academic debate. We presented the theory and practice of fact, value, and policy debate. The debate format was identified, and both affirmative and negative burdens were generally considered. We then discussed the different kinds of procedural and substantive issues that can be raised. Finally, we introduced a technique of note taking known as flow sheeting.

Key Terms

affirmative
brink
burden of proof
burden of rejoinder
case flow
circumvention
comparative advantage case
constructive speech
counter-criteria
criteria
cross-examination
debate format
disadvantage
flowing
linear
link
needs case

negative
off-case flow
policy debate
presumption
prima facie case
procedural arguments
rebuttal
resolution
should-would argument solvency
substantive arguments
take out
time frame
topicality argument
turnaround
unique
value debate
value objection

Activities

1. Select a value or policy proposition and construct an affirmative case for it. Be sure that your case addresses the issues required by the type of resolution you choose.

2. Select a point of stasis in the resolution you have chosen and construct a negative brief that addresses this point. Be sure to include the enumerated claims, the full source citations, and the text of the data you intend to present in your brief.

3. Construct a disadvantage to implementing the change advocated by the affirmative. This should include the structure and data, including the full source citation, that support the specific claims offered in your argument.

4. Prepare an affirmative brief responding to one or both of the arguments you constructed in the two preceding exercises.
5. Search for and locate a video clip of a college debate online. Listen to the debate as it unfolds and practice taking a flow of that debate.

RECOMMENDED READINGS

Dalton, Philip and John B. Butler. *Public Policy Argumentation and Debate: A Practical Guide for Advocacy,* 2nd ed. New York: Peter Lang, 2021.

Freeley, Austin J. and David L. Steinberg. *Argumentation and Debate: Critical Thinking for Reasoned Decision Making.* 13th ed. Boston: Wadsworth, 2014.

Knapp, Trischa. *Elements of Parliamentary Debate: A Guide to Public Argument.* Boston: Pearson, 1999.

Meany, John and Kate Shuster. *Art, Argument, and Advocacy: Mastering Parliamentary Debate.* New York: International Debate Educational Association, 2002.

Patterson, J. W. and David Zarefsky. *Contemporary Debate.* Boston: Houghton Mifflin, 1983.

Pfau, Michael, David A. Thomas, and Walter Ulrich. *Debate and Argument: A Systems Approach to Advocacy.* Glenview, IL: Scott, Foresman, 1987.

Remland, Martin, Timothy J. Brown, Kay Neal, and Roger Davis Gatchett. *Argumentation and Debate: A Public Speaking Approach,* 2nd ed. Dubuque, IA: Kendall-Hunt, 2014.

Wolfson, Jonathan A. *The Great Debate: A Handbook for Public Policy Debate and Public Forum Debate.* Naperville, IL: Lightning Bolt Press, 2013.

12

Advanced Academic Debate

Academic debate is practiced in a variety of contexts: in-class debates, debates before public audiences, and intercollegiate debates, among others. In chapter 11 we presented the general information needed to participate in any of these contexts. But to keep the ideas manageable, we also skipped some of the thornier aspects of debate theory, and we treated debate as a general topic rather than focusing on the different types of debate that one may wish to try.

In this chapter we will delve more deeply into specific areas of debate not fully covered in the preceding chapter. The issues we discuss should prove useful to anyone wishing to gain additional insight into academic debate. We will also present the formats and general nature of debate that occur under the auspices of the National Debate Tournament Committee (often referred to as NDT style), the Cross-Examination Debate Association, the National Parliamentary Debate Association, and the National Forensics Association (primarily Lincoln-Douglas debate).

THE RESOLUTION

In chapter 11 we identified the resolution as the focus of debate and indicated that the affirmative is obligated to present a topical case. We also suggested that affirmatives present definitions of the key terms of the resolution. We think this is a good idea for beginning debaters. In policy debate tournament competitions, however, it is more common for experienced debaters to define their terms operationally.

Operational Definitions

When an affirmative uses *operational definitions*, the audience and the negative are expected to ascertain what the affirmative thinks a term means by looking at their plan or their arguments. In short, the definitions are not explicit but rather are implicit. For instance, if you want to know how an affirmative defines a key phrase in the resolution such as "substantially change its development assistance policies" you look at the policies the affirmative plan would modify. Only if such operational definitions are challenged by the negative (typically in the form of topicality attacks, a type of procedural argument also discussed in chapter 11) will the affirmative present formal definitions.

Constructing Topicality Arguments

In chapter 11 we explained how a negative that believes the affirmative is not debating the resolution fairly can present a topicality argument. This is the argument that seeks to convince the audience that the affirmative interpretation of the topic is illegitimate. Fortunately, policy topics are worded today with language that is often very specific, and thus topicality is not an issue in most debates. If you do choose to clash with the affirmative on the issue of topicality, you will need to know how such an argument is constructed. Usually a topicality argument has three components: standards, violation, and impact.

STANDARDS. The negative typically presents standards that they wish the judge or audience to use when evaluating the arguments regarding whether or not the affirmative case was topical. Many years ago in academic debate, all an affirmative needed to argue to defend the topicality of their case was that their interpretation of the resolution was "reasonable." But the claim that an interpretation is "reasonable" is slippery. What constitutes reasonability? How does one determine that an affirmative has crossed the line from reasonable to unreasonable? There is no way to establish what an individual judge or an assembled audience will consider to be reasonable. Consequently, most scholars of academic debate now agree that when there is a disagreement regarding what definition is superior, the *better definition* should be used. But this is still somewhat vague. How does one establish that one definition is better than another? This is where the concept of applying argumentative standards comes into play. There are a variety of means employed to determine the better definition. We will consider several common standards presented by negatives. These are also used by affirmatives as counter-standards.

Unique Meaning. This argument is premised on the assumption that each word has a *unique meaning.* This seems self-evident. Even Alice from the book *Alice in Wonderland* knew that we cannot make words mean whatever we want. Yet, debaters sometimes interpret the resolution in such a way as to render some words meaningless. For example, if the resolution calls for a change in *development assistance policies,* and the affirmative's interpretation of the topic is that all assistance policies are in essence developmental, then the affirmative has rendered the term *development* meaningless. A better definition preserves the unique meaning of each word of the resolution.

Precision. The *precision* standard argues that the more specific or concrete definitions are, the more they clearly mark the boundaries of what is topical and what is not topical. Arguing that *urban* refers to those who live in cities rather than those who live near such communities is more precise because it is easier to determine who lives in a city than it is to decide who lives near a community. Therefore, the better definition is that which more precisely defines the terms of the resolution.

Limiting and Breadth. The broader the resolution, the more latitude affirmatives have in locating ground for constructing a topical case. As a result, the negative will have to prepare for debates featuring a very broad range and large number of potential affirmative cases. Such a situation greatly increases the burden on negative teams to find evidence and to prepare arguments against these different cases. Consequently, affirmatives gain a tactical advantage if they can broaden the range. To offset this advantage, negatives sometimes argue that the *limiting definition* is the superior one because it establishes more manageable boundaries.

For example, if any public assistance program is considered to be a part of the welfare system, then the negative will have to be prepared for a wider range of cases than if the welfare system is defined more narrowly as only including income transfer policies. In the former case the negative might have to be prepared to refute cases focused on health care, housing assistance, nutritional support programs, educational programs, etc. If the narrower definition were used, the negative would only have to be prepared to oppose cases with a focus on cash assistance programs.

Thus, while negatives typically favor a limiting definition, affirmatives usually present the opposite view as their counter-standard; they generally argue for **breadth**. The view here is that broader topics are more challenging, less tedious or repetitious, and require more research. Affirmatives may argue that broader topics require debaters to learn more about the benefits or negative characteristics of alternative policy proposals. Advocates can argue that the better definition sets limits, or they can argue for breadth. Judges will choose the standard based on their assessment of the arguments presented.

Field Definitions. The *field definition* standard maintains that the better definition is one that would be commonly used by members of the field (or participants in the discipline) that is the focus of the resolution. The rationale behind this standard is the understanding that each field tends to bring its own meanings to the terms it employs. For example, the term "campaign" has a different meaning in a military context than in a political context. Since jargon varies from field to field, it would be better to use definitions from the appropriate field.

Context. I.A. Richards, among many others, has argued that a word gains its meaning from the *context* in which it is used.[1] Defining a word without considering the other words in the sentence will likely lead to error and will mislead your audience. Define *red* and *herring* separately and you will not likely come up with the same meaning as you would for *red herring*. As Richards wrote, "a word or phrase when isolated momentarily from its controlling neighbors is free to develop irrelevant sense which may beguile half the words to follow it."[2] Consequently, it makes sense to define words in the context of the terms that accompany them whenever it is possible.

These common definitional standards may be used selectively to advance particular argument strategies by affirmatives and negatives. Speakers choose a standard that supports the definition they wish to use in a given debate. If the definition they wish to read does not meet a particular standard, then that standard is not offered for consideration. Of course, as reasonable as each of these standards sounds, there are indictments of each, so debaters must be prepared to defend them.

Furthermore, just as there is an incentive for the affirmative to define the resolution broadly to create so many different cases that the negative cannot prepare to attack them all, so too is there an incentive for the negative to define the resolution narrowly so there are fewer possible cases. If the negative definition is so narrow that the affirmative may not have a reasonable chance to win, the affirmative will argue that this is an unfair standard.

Regardless of the standard or counter-standard presented, debaters must convince the judge or audience that their standard is superior and should be employed—or they must use the standard that has been advocated by their opponents.

Violation. The second component of a topicality argument is the **violation**. Once the negative has presented the standard they wish the audience to use, they must present their definition, state why they think this is a better definition (because it more closely adheres to the standards they have previously presented), and explain why they believe the affirmative violates this specific definition.

If the affirmative believes they *do* meet the definition advocated by the negative, they may accept the negative standard and respond to the arguments alleging that the affirmative case violates the definition of the topic.

Impact. Finally, negatives must indicate, as with all of their arguments, what *impact* their topicality argument has on the debate. In policy debate, topicality is a voting issue. This means that if the negative convinces the audience that the affirmative case is not topical, the negative wins. All other arguments then become irrelevant. Why? Because if the plan is not topical, no matter how advantageous it is, the advantages do not prove the resolution true.

In value debate the impact of a topicality argument depends on what part of the affirmative case is not topical. If, for example, an affirmative presents three ways in which the welfare system worsens the plight of the urban poor, and only one of these is not topical, many audiences will simply disregard the non-topical part of the case. What remains may still be sufficient to overcome the negative's value objections and win the debate for the affirmative.

Reverse Voting Issue. Some affirmatives argue that since the negative can win the debate with a topicality argument, negatives will be inclined to argue topicality even against cases that most debaters, judges, and audiences would consider topical. To discourage frivolous topicality arguments some debaters will argue that topicality should be a *reverse voting issue*. This means that if the negative loses the topicality argument, and the affirmative case is deemed within the terms of the resolution, that the negative should lose the debate. Virtually no argumentation theorists support this position, however, because it simply does not make much sense.

Use the court system as an analogy to consider this type of argument. Imagine a situation where an attorney argues before a judge that the court does not have appropriate jurisdiction to adjudicate some dispute and thus the charge should be dismissed. If the judge rules against the claim and decides that the court has jurisdiction the case is allowed to proceed. The judge does not say, however, that because the case can go forward that the attorney who argued for the motion to dismiss and failed should lose the case because of the unsuccessful jurisdictional claim.

In a sense, topicality represents a similar jurisdictional argument. The negative is saying that the terms of the resolution do not give the judge the power to consider the affirmative case because it advances a rationale outside the jurisdiction of the topic. A finding for the affirmative on the issue of topicality is not akin to a finding on the merits of their entire argument; it simply means that the debate should proceed. Also, implementing the "reverse voting issue standard" would make it too risky for negatives to argue topicality. This would give the affirmative even greater latitude to run cases of questionable topicality. But negatives must be prepared for the possibility that affirmatives will argue this position and must have their responses ready.

Hasty Generalizations

We have indicated that the affirmative burden is to prove the resolution true. But this claim glosses over a controversy in value debate. In policy debate it is commonly accepted that the resolution serves as a parameter for determining the range of cases that may be presented. As long as the case is topical, the case proves the resolution to be true. This approach is known as the ***parametric standard***. The resolution acts as a parameter, laying the boundaries for what is topical. All the affirmative must do is fall within the parameters to be considered topical and to prove the resolution true. There may be many cases that prove the resolution true, but the affirmative is required to present and defend only one such case. In value debate, this is not necessarily true.

Value resolutions tend to be generalizations. For example, "advertising degrades the quality of life" is an unqualified claim—a generalization. If the parametric approach to topicality is used with such a resolution, the affirmative need only select one example of advertising that degraded the quality of life and then offer up this example as proof of the truth of the resolution. Permitting affirmatives to argue only one example of the resolution results in at least two potentially significant advantages. First, they do not have to defend examples of the resolution that may be untrue. For instance, if some advertising degrades the quality of life and some does not, the affirmative could choose to present only an example of advertising that does degrade. Second, affirmatives can dismiss arguments that are not specific to the case that they present. Just as a policy debater can dismiss a disadvantage that does not link to the mandates identified in the affirmative plan, a value debater can dismiss an argument that does not respond to the specific claims offered by the affirmative to prove the resolution true. Such a strategy may, however, become more complicated in a real debate. For example, consider a case where the affirmative argues that advertising is annoying and encourages a wasteful consumer culture that degrades the environment and thus degrades the quality of life. The negative might reply, however, that there are other instances where advertising saves lives. As an example, they might cite advertisements for prescription drugs that make people aware of how to recognize the early symptoms of cancer and encourages them to consult a physician. Should a judge or audience consider the merits of both claims in assessing whether or not advertising degrades the quality of life?

In policy debate the focus of the debate is the plan. The plan is the operational definition of the resolution. The resolution calls for a change from the present system, and the plan identifies that change. If the plan is proved to be advantageous, the resolution is proved to be true. Value debate generally has no plan. In addition, argumentation proves a generalization to be true either by arguing at the level of the generalization or by arguing inductively from examples to a generalization. An affirmative may therefore present examples of the resolution and argue that what is true of the examples is true of the generalization; or an affirmative may argue the truth of the ***whole resolution***.

Affirmatives that argue by example cannot dismiss counterexamples such as the one offered above regarding prescription drug advertisements and the early detection of cancer. As we mentioned in chapter 5, generalizations established by examples must account for counterexamples. An affirmative that reasons by example may be charged with committing a hasty generalization. Permitting affirmatives to reason by example gives the negative at least two potential strategic advantages. First, negatives do not have to prepare for the specific affirmative examples presented; all they must do is present the same counterexamples and the same hasty generalization argument in every debate. We do not believe this would promote much learning. Second, it is nearly impossible to find a generalization that divides ground fairly yet does not have some counterexamples. If a single counterexample invalidates an unqualified generalization, then affirmatives would be unable to win.

If both the parametric standard and the inductive approach are flawed, what is the affirmative to do? The answer resides in whether the issue identified is **intrinsic to the resolution.** According to this view, there are certain qualities that are inherent to the value object.[3] The affirmative should identify these inherent qualities and argue that the value judgment is causally related to these intrinsic attributes. For example, are there certain qualities that are present in all advertising? Does the identified degradation by the affirmative stem from one such inherent quality? All advertising sells something such as a product, an idea, or a candidate. Is selling degrading? All advertising creates a need or desire on the part of a consumer. Does the creation of this appetite or desire necessarily degrade?

Some scholars contend that there is no suitable way to ascertain the intrinsic qualities of a value object. Consequently, they argue, the claim that the case area must be intrinsic is not an appropriate definitional standard.[4] There is no consensus at this point on the issue. As a result, many debates are still characterized by extensive arguments regarding the appropriate theoretical foundations to judge the burdens that affirmatives must meet to prove a value resolution true.

PLANS AND COUNTERPLANS

In chapter 11 we indicated that the affirmative in policy debate is called upon to articulate the details of the proposal enacting the change mandated by the resolution. Here we examine the role of plans in detail, as well as the negative's option of presenting their own proposal or counterplan. Value debate is arguably pre-policy, and the vast majority of debates remain at that level. Yet, some say it is possible to present quasi-policy proposals in a value debate. Plans are increasingly used in value debates for two reasons.

First, they can give affirmatives tactical advantages (any advance in debate theory that gives one team or another a tactical advantage will eventually be attempted). Plans permit affirmatives to focus the debate on those aspects of the topic that they consider especially relevant. For instance, the topic calling for a comparison between implementing the UN's Universal Declaration of Human Rights and preserving state sovereignty resulted in a fair number of affirmatives giving the details of the term *implementation* in something that strongly resembled and sometimes was actually called a plan. This permitted affirmatives to focus the debate on the process of implementation they selected and to dismiss methods of implementing the Universal Declaration of Human Rights that were less desirable.

Second, plans appear to be warranted by some topics. One way to reveal the inadequacies of the welfare system, for example, is to compare the current system with a modified system, presumably one modified by an affirmative plan. As a result, the following comments about plans and counterplans may be as relevant to value debaters as they are to policy debaters.

Plans

In order to clarify the change being advocated, the affirmative sometimes specifies the elements of the plan of action they support. The specificity of the resolution directly influences the level of detail required of a plan. In general, plans typically have five components.

1. **The agent.** In this plank of the plan, the affirmative identifies who will implement the plan. This may, for example, be the federal government or a specific agency of government, such as the Environmental Protection Agency, the Federal Communications Commission, the Department of Energy, etc.
2. **The mandates.** These are the specific actions called for in the plan. For example, if the affirmative wishes to change development assistance policies by significantly increasing or decreasing agricultural assistance programs, the details of these actions are presented in the plan mandates.
3. **Funding.** If the proposal necessitates the expenditure of monies, some affirmatives specify where that funding will come from. Others rely on the normal funding processes, such as the general revenues of the federal government.
4. **Enforcement.** Policies requiring enforcement may have those provisions identified in this plank of the plan. Enforcement planks may specify the agent responsible for enforcement and the penalties for violating the mandates of the plan.
5. **Intent.** To clarify the purpose of the proposal, the affirmative may elect to present a summary statement of the plan. This plank derives from the judicial process of examining legislative history in order to clarify the intent of legislation.

Affirmatives occasionally incorporate other components in their plans that preclude disadvantages and/or counterplans. These are called *plan spikes*. For example, the affirmative may avoid giving the negative a link to a disadvantage about the negative consequences of increased government spending by arguing that their plan will reduce government spending for something else, such as agricultural subsidies for tobacco farmers. Such plan spikes are controversial in that many such planks that neutralize disadvantages (and occasionally even result in the affirmative claim that they are accruing additional advantage—e.g., a reduction in the amount of tobacco grown and sold) do not constitute topical actions. Thus, the negative might choose to argue that a particular plan plank may yield a non-topical advantage.

Counterplans

Traditionally, presenting a *counterplan* was predicated on an explicit admission by the negative team that there was a problem in the status quo that could not be solved but that the affirmative plan should be rejected because there was a different and superior way to solve the problem. In contemporary debate, counterplans are sometimes introduced conditionally. The negative might choose to contest the need for a change and the solvency of the affirmative plan but say "if" the judge is convinced of the need for a change, a plan conditionally offered by the negative would be a superior solution.

In order for the counterplan to be a reason to reject the resolution, it must meet two standards: it must be non-topical and competitive. Usually the negative reads the counterplan (it is written just like a plan) and argues that it meets those standards. Most contemporary scholars believe that these requirements, like procedural arguments, must be presented in the first negative speech.

The negative can construct non-topical counterplans either by employing a non-topical agent of action or by advocating a non-topical action. Advocating a topical counterplan provides another rationale for accepting the truth of the resolution. Consequently, topical counterplans are not a reason to reject the resolution.

Competitiveness is a difficult issue. To be competitive, a counterplan must be a reason to reject the resolution. This is often understood to mean that to reject the resolution, counterplans, in addition to being non-topical, must be both mutually exclusive and net beneficial.[5]

For a plan and counterplan to have ***mutual exclusivity*** they must be unable to coexist.[6] For example, consider two mutually exclusive strategies that politicians have presented to close the federal deficit. One party wants to cut personal income taxes to spur the economy to generate more new jobs and more taxable income. Another party wants to raise personal income taxes to pay down the deficit. These two plans are competitive because they cannot coexist. No one can cut and raise the same taxes at the same time. On the other hand, we could simultaneously raise personal income taxes and cut corporate taxes. Since these two actions "could" coexist, they would not be mutually exclusive.

Some negatives abuse this standard by artificially creating mutual exclusivity. For example, some negatives include a counterplan plank that prohibits adopting both the affirmative plan and the negative counterplan. Others steal the same funding planks. These are arbitrary and artificial because they do not pertain to the substantive mandate planks of the counterplan. Similarly, arguments that the two plans are redundant and/or philosophically incompatible are not tests of whether the plans could coexist. They are arguments that the plans should not coexist, which more correctly fall into the net benefits test.

The ***net benefits standard*** says it is more advantageous to implement the counterplan than it is to implement the affirmative plan alone or both the affirmative plan and the counterplan. A counterplan that is net beneficial when compared to the affirmative plan does not in and of itself warrant rejecting the resolution. Suppose, for example, the affirmative plan is to establish national health insurance, and the affirmative says that this will save thousands of lives each year. If the negative were to counterplan with a foreign aid program that saves millions of lives each year, the counterplan would not be a reason to reject the resolution, for it would be possible to do both. In this example, the counterplan is not net beneficial when compared to the affirmative plan and the counterplan together. At first glance, this counterplan is also not mutually exclusive from the affirmative plan, since hypothetically the federal government could establish national health insurance and simultaneously substantially increase foreign aid. If, however, the negative can demonstrate that the federal government **should not** do both plans because doing both would destroy the economy, then the counterplan alone would be presumptively better than doing both. The affirmative would not be without arguments to refute this assumption, of course. They could argue, for example, that the U.S. government should emphasize meeting the needs of its own citizens first by offering them health insurance before sending aid overseas.

If the counterplan cannot coexist with the affirmative plan and should not coexist with the affirmative plan, then the counterplan is a reason to reject the resolution and it is therefore competitive. If the counterplan is also not topical, and produces greater advantages than the affirmative plan, the negative should win.

Permutations

In response to negative counterplans that artificially establish mutual exclusivity, affirmatives may initiate something called a ***permutation.*** This is a tactic whereby the affirmative illustrates the artificiality of the mutual exclusivity by proposing to amend their plan. For example, if the negative says it will use the same funding mechanism as the affirmative and therefore the two plans cannot coexist, the affirmative could illustrate that the funding mechanism is an artificial competitiveness. They could amend the affirmative plan by identifying a different source of funding, perhaps by rewriting their funding mechanisms in order to reveal the artificial nature and the lack of clash in the counterplan's mandates.[7]

Fiat

In debate, *fiat* refers to the assumption that if the affirmative can demonstrate that a proposal *should* be adopted, we can assume that sensible policy makers would adopt it through normal means. If the agent of action is the United States federal government, then "normal means" refer to the democratic processes typically followed when legislation is enacted. To dispute whether the plan *would* be enacted, rather than *should* be enacted, is called a ***should/would argument*** and is generally dismissed.

The enactment of legislation is no guarantee, however, that the legislation will solve the problem identified or result in the advantages claimed. If, for example, adverse attitudes preclude the status quo from accruing the advantages now, the enforcement of the new legislation may be thwarted by the same pernicious attitudes. Fiat is no magic wand. It does not automatically overcome attitudes. It only implements the legislation.

An understanding of fiat is necessary to avoid or point out situations of fiat abuse. We have heard both plans and counterplans that abuse fiat. One plan called for the nations of the world to eliminate their militaries. The team then argued that the United Nations should then form its own military force. The UN would then be the only entity with access to military force. Needless to say, the plan was advantageous when compared to the status quo where almost every nation has its own military and conflicts between nations are common. Could this plan be implemented through normal means? What are the "normal means" by which the nations of the world abolish their militaries? We believe the plan was an abuse of fiat because it attempted to "set aside" and avoid debate over precisely those issues that an advocate would need to refute to evaluate the merits of the affirmative's case.

THINKING STRATEGICALLY

Since debate is an intellectual contest, it is important that you approach it that way. Some debaters have better tactical skills than others—perhaps they can speak more succinctly or more rapidly, or they have more or better evidence. They may simply have more experience than you. Some of these advantages can be minimized through strategic planning and anticipating how the debate may unfold and preparing accordingly.

Controlling the Ground

The affirmative has an advantage in that they get to start and end the debate. Starting the debate means selecting how they want to go about proving the truth of the resolution. This is their ground. Anyone familiar with sports will confirm that there is often a home court advantage. The same is true of academic debate. As much as possible, the affirmative will want the debate to unfold according to their terms. In policy debate, they will construct the plan and case so that the focus is on the issues that they think they are most likely to win. Similarly, in value debate experienced debaters are very adept at presenting criteria that advantage them and make it less likely they will lose the debate.

Some negatives are skilled at capturing the ground. If the negative presents several off-case arguments, the focus of the debate can shift from the affirmative case to the off-case. The off-case is the negative's turf. They get to select, from all of the possible off-case arguments, those they feel they are best able to win. Arguing one's own issues should be an advantage for the negative.

Planning for the End of the Debate

What do you think will be the telling issue or evidence at the end of the debate? If you think in terms of how the audience will eventually make sense of the debate, it may help you decide how or when to present an argument.

When you first begin to debate, it is difficult enough to come up with what you can say in your constructive speech. As you gain experience, you will start to think in terms of what your opponent will say in response to your arguments, and then what you will say about your opponent's arguments. Good chess players think several moves ahead. So, too, do good debaters. In fact, just as chess players lay traps for their opponents or divert their attention from their real objectives, so do debaters. Anticipating what an opponent will say in response to your argument enables you to decide, in advance of the debate, what to say to defeat that response. If you cannot beat the response, perhaps you should not make the argument in the first place.

Winning in Rebuttals

Advanced debaters often attempt to narrow the debate to a limited number of issues in the final rebuttals. This means selecting those issues or arguments a team is most likely to win. The negative often has several arguments that they can choose to extend in the final rebuttal: case arguments, procedural arguments, a counterplan, and/or several disadvantages. Because of time constraints, however, it may be difficult to cover all of them. As a result, many negatives grant answers that destroy the reasoning of a disadvantage or ignore an argument in their final rebuttal. This essentially removes these arguments from the decision-making calculus. It also permits affirmatives to more fully explain and extend the remaining arguments.

The art of deciding what to go for in the last rebuttal is central to understanding what argumentation is about and is also a place where your skills in reasoning, analysis, and refutation meet up with your ability to analyze and persuade your judge or audience.

Maximizing Your Strengths

Some basketball teams walk the ball up the court. Others run it. Some football teams run the ball on almost every down, others pass the ball on most downs. Why? Because most teams are able to identify their strengths, and they try to take advantage of them when developing a game plan. In determining their strategies, teams develop plays that permit them to capitalize on their best resources. Think about your strengths in debate. Are you good at explaining arguments? Do you speak quickly? Do you have a knack for finding compelling evidence? Discover your strengths and weaknesses and then construct your strategy accordingly.

We have known debaters who were prepared for almost any arguments an opponent might introduce. Such debaters maximized their strengths by constructing a broad affirmative case. But we have also coached teams whose strength was dealing with a limited number of arguments. Such debaters were better off with a case that invited fewer arguments but that permitted them to explain their positions more fully.

Specialized Debate Formats

Throughout this and the previous chapter we have focused on the most common formats for engaging in academic debate. Here we introduce some of the specifics of the various types of debate.

National Debate Tournament and Cross-Examination Debate Association

The oldest intercollegiate debate association is the *National Debate Tournament (NDT)*. The first tournament was held at the United States Military Academy at West Point in 1947. Every year since that first tournament, the best debate teams from across that nation have competed against each other to qualify for the national tournament. NDT teams debate policy topics at invitational tournaments that are hosted by different colleges and universities from September until April. Teams may qualify for the NDT either on the basis of their outstanding performance at these invitational tournaments (what is known as an "at-large" bid) or by winning one of the bids to NDT by doing well in their district-qualifying tournaments.

In 1971, the *Cross-Examination Debate Association (CEDA)* was created as an alternative to NDT debate. The original motivation for the creation of CEDA was to create a form of debate where students used a more persuasive and communicative delivery style, where they spoke more slowly, and where debates could be more easily understood by untrained audiences. For many years CEDA operated as a completely separate entity. Frequently it used value resolutions and, in an effort to decrease the importance of evidence and increase the focus on persuasive communication, the CEDA debate resolution changed mid-season so that debaters were challenged to undertake research on a second topic. Several years ago, however, the two organizations enjoyed a rapprochement, and now they share the same resolution throughout the year. They each hold a national championship tournament, but there now seems to be very little difference between the style and form of debate sponsored by each organization.

FORMAT. The following is the format for an NDT/CEDA debate.

9 minutes	First Affirmative constructive
3 minutes	negative speaker cross-examination of the First Affirmative speaker
9 minutes	First Negative constructive
3 minutes	affirmative speaker cross-examination of the First Negative speaker
9 minutes	Second Affirmative constructive
3 minutes	negative speaker cross-examination of the Second Affirmative constructive
9 minutes	Second Negative constructive
3 minutes	affirmative speaker cross-examination of the Second Negative speaker
6 minutes	First Negative rebuttal

6 minutes   First Affirmative rebuttal
6 minutes   Second Negative rebuttal
6 minutes   Second Affirmative rebuttal

Each speaker thus gives a constructive speech, each speaker cross-examines a speaker from the other team, and each speaker is asked questions in cross-examination.[8] The affirmative both initiates and concludes the debate. As is the case in almost all debate formats, both sides get the same amount of time to speak.

PREPARATION TIME.   Each team also receives a total of ten minutes of ***alternative use time***. The debaters use this time to prepare for their next speech. It is time that they can use to discuss strategy, find the evidence they wish to present, and prepare the notes they will use when they speak. Judges or timekeepers typically are responsible for keeping track of this time.

THE RESOLUTION AND EVIDENCE.   By vote of its membership, an NDT/CEDA resolution is chosen in the summer and used throughout the year. This permits debaters a great deal of time to delve deeply into the literature on the resolution in the pursuit of evidence to support the arguments that they will make. In recent years the NDT/CEDA has moved to more specific wording of its resolutions in an attempt to decrease the breadth of cases for which students must prepare. For example, the 2020–2021 national debate topic was: Resolved: The United States Federal Government should reduce its alliance commitments with Japan, the Republic of Korea, North Atlantic Treaty Organization member states, and/or the Republic of the Philippines by at least substantially limiting the conditions under which its defense pact can be activated.

As is apparent, this topic still included the possibility that affirmatives could focus on one or many different nations and could advocate a wide range of different policy proposals. The research and evidentiary demands for debaters who hope to compete at the most advanced levels of debate are significant.

The National Forensic Association's Lincoln-Douglas Debate

Most policy debating in postsecondary education involves competition by teams composed of two persons. Nevertheless, there is increasing opportunity for one-on-one debate. This style of debate is known as ***Lincoln-Douglas or L-D Debate***. It is named after the historic debates between Abraham Lincoln and Stephen Douglas. The sponsoring organization for most L-D Debate in the United States is the National Forensic Association. The NFA was founded in 1971 to promote individual events (public speaking contests such as persuasive and informative speaking, extemporaneous and impromptu speaking, after-dinner speaking, rhetorical criticism, oral interpretation of prose and poetry, etc.) and to crown national champions in these events. In 1990, the NFA expanded its competition to include L-D Debate.

Lincoln-Douglas Debate is a variation of NDT/CEDA debate. It uses policy topics. The stock issues of ill, blame, cure, and cost tend to be the focus of the adjudication of the contests. There are, however, some substantive differences. In addition to being one-against-one debates, L-D is somewhat more oriented toward persuasive speaking. NDT and CEDA both permit, some would say encourage, speaking at a very fast rate—speeches are delivered at rates that are often very difficult for those who are not familiar with contemporary debating to comprehend. Debaters use this strategy to introduce as many arguments as physically possible into the contest in the hope that they can overwhelm their opponents. Jargon and gamesmanship are also encouraged by the lack of rules and the willingness to allow debaters to challenge norms during NDT and CEDA debate rounds. L-D Debate specifies in its rules that speaking too quickly is "antithetical to the purpose and intent of this event."[9]

FORMAT. In Lincoln-Douglas Debate, as with team debate, the affirmative speaks first and last; both speakers question and are questioned during cross-examination periods. Typical time limits for NFA L-D Debate are:

6 minutes	Affirmative constructive
3 minutes	cross-examination by negative
7 minutes	Negative constructive
3 minutes	cross-examination by affirmative
6 minutes	Affirmative rebuttal
6 minutes	Negative rebuttal
3 minutes	Affirmative rebuttal
4 minutes	prep time per debater

The affirmative speaker cannot introduce new arguments in the rebuttals, nor can the negative speaker. This rule is true in all forms of academic debate.

THE RESOLUTION AND EVIDENCE. Members of the National Forensic Association select the topic, usually a policy resolution, during the summer, and it is used throughout the year. Claims need to be proved, but the reliance on evidence is balanced by the need to persuade the judge, which results in the amount of evidence matching what would be used in a well-supported persuasive speech. The first time a source is cited, the debater must provide a full-source citation. The resolution for the 2020–2021 season was: Resolved: The United States federal government should implement immigration reform that removes substantial statutory restrictions on legal immigration into the United States.

JUDGES. Unlike NDT/CEDA tournaments, L-D Debate is held in conjunction with Individual Events (IE) tournaments. Frequently debaters are also participants in other such events. Judges for L-D also serve as judges for the IE competitions. That means that the judges frequently have limited experience in coaching and judging debate. This is also by design. The result is that debaters must talk to the judges as if they are reasonable people but lack expertise in debate. This also minimizes jargon and increases the emphasis on communicating effectively.

National Parliamentary Debate Association

Most forms of intercollegiate debate emphasize argument to such an extent that public speaking skills are too frequently neglected. This is not the case in ***parliamentary debate***. Such debate rewards wit and rhetorical skill. It is loosely modeled after the kind of debating that occurs in the British House of Parliament. While there are several types of parliamentary debate, we will focus on that sponsored by the National Parliamentary Debate Association (NPDA). NPDA began in 1993 and is now one of the largest debate associations in the nation. You will note many similarities between parliamentary debate and the other forms of debate previously examined, but you will also note some significant differences.

THE RESOLUTION. In traditional intercollegiate team debate, a resolution is announced and the same resolution is used for a year, semester, or at minimum a tournament. In parliamentary debate, the resolution changes each round. Fifteen minutes (plus walking time) before a debate is scheduled to begin, the topic is announced. This results in debates that call upon the general knowledge of the participants rather than on pre-competition research. In fact, inartistic proofs cannot be introduced into the debate. Debaters can consult any written materials they brought to the tournament, but they cannot cite these sources during the debate. This results in a truly contemporaneous quality to the debate. Robert Trapp, one of the founders of the NPDA, considers its extemporaneous nature to be one of the primary differences between parliamentary debate and NDT/CEDA.[10]

Parliamentary debate resolutions may be fact, value, or policy propositions. They may also be metaphorical. Metaphorical resolutions require interpretation or translation by the debaters. At a recent tournament, students debated the resolution: "This House would rather be in than out." While some debaters undoubtedly took the topic literally and argued the pros and cons of trying to fit in, others might focus on very complex and significant policy issues, such as whether the United States should seek membership with the other signers of the Comprehensive Test Ban Treaty, the Land Mine Treaty, the World Court of Justice, or the Trans Pacific Partnership.

THE AUDIENCE. The principle distinction, and the reason that speaking skill is rewarded, stems from the audience perspective. The format of parliamentary debate is accessible to public audiences. Parliamentary debaters are expected to offer informed, reasoned, extemporaneous arguments that are enjoyable and educational. Coaches who judge parliamentary debate typically approach judging as nonexperts. The debaters, understanding this, avoid jargon and talk to the judges as if a larger public audience were present.

FORMAT. Another difference is that debaters are not referred to as affirmatives and negatives; rather they are known generally as the proponents and opponents of the resolution. Each debater is given a role in the format used at most tournaments:

7 minutes	First Proposition Constructive speaker
8 minutes	First Opposition Constructive speaker
8 minutes	Second Proposition Constructive speaker
8 minutes	Second Opposition Constructive speaker
4 minutes	Opposition Rebuttal by First speaker
5 minutes	Proposition Rebuttal by First speaker

Parliamentary debate does not permit preparation or alternate use time. Debaters must go to the podium and begin their speech as quickly as possible after the previous debater has concluded speaking.

Points of Information, Privilege, and Order

While other debate formats set aside time for asking and answering questions, there is no predetermined time for cross-examination. Instead, debaters can stand up and ask for the floor at any time during a constructive speech—except during the first and last minute of the speech, which is protected time. The debater currently speaking can yield for a *Point of Information (POI)* or indicate that they are not willing to yield at this time. If the speaker yields, the questioner can ask a question or make a short statement. The clock does not stop during the POI.

In addition, debaters can rise for a *Point of Personal Privilege (PPP)* and a *Point of Order (POO)*. A Point of Personal Privilege is raised if the debater believes that their words have been grievously misconstrued or if the debater believes that the opponent has personally insulted them. It is a serious charge and must not be raised for a minor transgression. "Debaters may be penalized for raising spurious points of personal privilege."[11] A Point of Order is raised if a debater thinks that another debater has violated the rules of parliamentary debate. The clock is stopped for both PPPs and POOs and the judge rules immediately.

Even when not seeking the floor, the other debaters need not sit quietly. Heckling in parliamentary debate is perfectly acceptable. Usually such commentary is limited to a "well said" encouragement to a teammate, or a "shame shame" to the opposition if the speaker mischaracterizes an argument. But heckling can go further. According to Theodore Scheckels and Annette Warfield, "A heckle is a brief, witty, and somewhat substantive remark hurled at the speaker so that everyone can hear it."[12] The purpose of such heckling is often refutation; it helps to call attention to what one side may see as a weak or preposterous argument offered by their opponents. A good parliamentary speaker masters the art of responding to the heckling with a witty retort and then proceeding without any sign of having been ruffled. Keeping a firm check on one's temper when faced with heckling is often an important test of one's ability to engage in this form of debating.

SUMMARY

In this chapter, we focused on additional aspects of the resolution, including topicality, hasty generalizations, and the parametric standard. We also considered the nature and functions of plans and counterplans. Moving beyond specific tactics employed in debates, we offered advice as to how debaters can think strategically. Finally, we considered three increasingly popular forms of intercollegiate debate: NDT/CEDA, L-D Debate, and NPDA. Some of the issues we addressed are controversial and are the subject of arguments in these debates. We encourage you to experiment with the different formats and types of arguments.

KEY TERMS

alternate use time
better definition
breadth
competitiveness
context
counterplan
Cross-Examination
  Debate Association (CEDA)
fiat
field definition
impact
intrinsic
limiting definition
Lincoln-Douglas Debate (LD)
mutual exclusivity
National Debate Tournament (NDT)

net benefits standard
operational definitions
parametric standard
parliamentary debate
permutation
plan spikes
Point of Information (POI)
Point of Order (POO)
Point of Personal Privilege (PPP)
precision
reverse voting issue
should/would argument
standards
unique meaning
violation
whole resolution

ACTIVITIES

1. Construct an affirmative case outline and a plan in support of the following policy debate topic. Resolved: That the United States should eliminate all forms of foreign aid and assistance to Pakistan.

2. Construct a negative case brief to refute the case that you have just created regarding assistance to Pakistan.

3. Construct a counterplan to the case created regarding aid to Pakistan. Remember that your counterplan must be non-topical and also that you must identify advantages that flow from the counterplan and that go beyond the advantages claimed by the affirmative case.

4. Search the web for video clips of intercollegiate debates. Find a debate in which topicality is offered as a voting issue. Assess the quality of the topicality arguments and/or defenses to the claims offered by the debaters.

5. Create a case in support of the value resolution: This House believes that the use of drones is morally justified in the war on terror. Remember to create the criteria as to why this value should be affirmed.

6. Now create a negative case in opposition to the value resolution above. What counter-criteria might you advance?

RECOMMENDED READING

Edwards, Richard E., *Competitive Debate: The Official Guide* (New York: Penguin Press, 2008).

Herbeck, Dale and John P. Katsulas, "The Affirmative Topicality Burden: Any Reasonable Example of the Resolution," *Journal of the American Forensic Association* 21 (1985): 133–145.

Herbeck, Dale, John P. Katsulas, and Karla K. Leeper, "The Locus of Debate Controversy Reexamined: Implications for Counterplan Theory," *Argumentation and Advocacy* 25 (1989): 150–164.

Johnson, Steven L., *Winning Debates: A Guide to Debating in the Style of the World Championships* (New York: International Debate Education Association, 2009).

Keenan, Claudia J., "Intercollegiate Debate: Reflecting American Culture, 1900-1930," *Argumentation and Advocacy* 46 (2009): 79–97.

Knapp, Trischa, *Elements of Parliamentary Debate: A Guide to Public Argument* (Boston: Pearson, 1999).

Madsen, Arnie, "General Systems Theory and Counterplan Competition," *Argumentation and Advocacy* 26 (1989): 71–82.

Madsen, Arnie and Allan D. Louden, "The Jurisdiction/Topicality Analogy," *Argumentation and Advocacy* 26 (1990): 151–154.

Meany, John and Kate Shuster, *Art, Argument, and Advocacy: Mastering Parliamentary Debate* (Harrisburg: International Debate Educational Association, 2002).

Murphy, Thomas L., "Assessing the Jurisdictional Model of Topicality," *Argumentation and Advocacy* 26 (1990): 145–150.

Perkins, Dallas, "Counterplans and Paradigms," *Argumentation and Advocacy* 25 (1989): 140–149.

ENDNOTES

[1] I. A. Richards, *The Philosophy of Rhetoric* (London: Oxford University Press, 1936).

[2] Ibid., p. 55.

[3] Kenneth Bahm, "Intrinsic Justification: Meaning and Method," *CEDA Yearbook* 9 (1988): 23–29; and David M. Berube, "Hasty Generalization Revisited, Part One: On Being Representative Examples," *CEDA Yearbook* 10 (1989): 43–53.

4 Bill Hill and Richard W. Leeman, "On Not Using Intrinsic Justification in Debate," *Argumentation and Advocacy* 26 (1990): 133–144.

5 These are the classic determinants used to evaluate counterplans introduced by Allan J. Lichtman and Daniel M. Rohrer, "A General Theory of the Counterplan," *Journal of the American Forensic Association* 12 (1975): 70–79.

6 Kevin Baaske, "The Counterplan: A Reevaluation of the Competitiveness Standard," Western Speech Communication Association, 1985.

7 For a thorough discussion of permutations, see Dale A. Herbeck, "A Permutation Standard of Competitiveness," *Journal of the American Forensic Association* 22 (1985): 12–19.

8 It is considered permissible for affirmative teams, although it is not common, to assign the first affirmative speaker the role of second affirmative rebuttal speaker, and the second affirmative speaker the role of first affirmative rebuttal speaker.

9 See the NFA L-D rules at https://www.dropbox.com/s/wucmhz25hkyav85/LDNFABYLAWSAPPROVEDAT2014NFA.pdf?dl=0

10 Robert Trapp, "Parliamentary Debate," National Parliamentary Debate Association, original publication 1995.

11 NPDA Rules. National Parliamentary Debate Association, October 2018. https://www.parlidebate.org/npda-rules

12 Theodore F. Scheckels and Annette C. Warfield, "Parliamentary Debate: A Description and Justification," *Argumentation and Advocacy* 27 (1990): 88.

13

Argumentation in Politics
Campaigns and Debates

As a presidential candidate in 2020, former Vice President Joseph Biden promised that he would search for bipartisan solutions to America's problems and that he was ready to reach across the aisle to engage Republicans in his policy proposals. His many years of experience in the Senate had helped him understand how to compromise, and the collegial relationships that he had formed with Mitch McConnell and other Republicans over many years would help change the culture of Washington.[1] Yet, within a few weeks of his inauguration, it had become apparent that while President Biden might discover that many of his policy proposals were popular across the political spectrum, the current political culture did not make it easy for elected officials to come together to pass legislation. For example, polls suggested that upwards of 75 percent of the U.S. voters supported Biden's massive stimulus bill to address the needs of those suffering due to the COVID-19 pandemic, including 61 percent of Republicans, yet the legislation passed both the House and Senate without a single Republican voting to support it.[2] Republicans who might be inclined to vote with the Democrats to pass Biden's legislative proposals feared that such a vote might mobilize the most committed conservative party activists and result in a primary challenge from the right.

One respected polling firm summarized the political polarization as follows.

> The studies we've conducted at Pew Research Center over the past few years illustrate the increasingly stark disagreement between Democrats and Republicans on the economy, racial justice, climate change, law enforcement, international engagement and a long list of other issues. The 2020 presidential election further highlighted these deep-seated divides. Supporters of Biden and Donald Trump believe the differences between them are about more than just politics and policies. A month before the election, roughly eight-in-ten registered voters in both camps said their differences with the other side were about core American values, and roughly nine-in-ten—again in both camps—worried that a victory by the other would lead to "lasting harm to the United States."[3]

Conducting rational deliberative political arguments in the face of such an intensely polarized electorate is, to say the least, profoundly difficult. It is not simply issues of ideology or of policy preferences that are dividing people; rather, it is their understanding of what constitutes the facts themselves. One illustration of such deep differences was evidenced in public reactions to the COVID-19 pandemic.

> In a Pew Research Center study conducted before the pandemic, Americans were more ideologically divided than any of the 19 other publics [from other nations around the world] surveyed when asked how much trust they have in scientists and whether scientists make decisions solely based on facts. These fissures have pervaded nearly every aspect of the public and policy response to the crisis over the course of the year. Democrats and Republicans differ over mask wearing, contact tracing, how well public health officials are dealing with the crisis, whether to get a vaccine once one is available, and whether life will remain changed in a major way after the pandemic. For Biden supporters, the coronavirus outbreak was a central issue in the election—in an October [2020] poll, 82% said it was very important to their vote. Among Trump supporters, it was easily the least significant among six issues tested on the survey: Just 24% said it was very important.[4]

Why has the United States become so deeply polarized? Experts argue that our media system, particularly cable news media outlets that tailor their programming to attract partisan voters, are significantly to blame.[5] In addition, many people get much of their political information from social media platforms such as Facebook and Twitter, where they exchange information accessed from friends with whom they are likely to share political beliefs and convictions—and where they will seldom be exposed to information from different perspectives. This creates an "echo chamber" effect that strongly reinforces existing beliefs and does not challenge people to question their beliefs.[6] Researchers Milton Lodge and Charles Taber also found significant evidence that "affective and cognitive reactions to external events are triggered unconsciously, followed spontaneously by the spreading of activation through associative pathways which link thoughts to feelings, so that very early events, even those that remain invisible to conscious awareness, set the direction for all subsequent processing."[7] In short, much of our information processing, including that of political information, is automatic and unconscious. To improve critical thinking, we believe that people must become more aware of their subconscious biases and opinions and more open to discovering the foundations of their beliefs.

Others have argued that our political identities have been defined by cultural, historical, regional, religious, and racial divides. A system based on identity can be exploited by candidates to mobilize voters. It is far easier to play to political differences than it is to build political community and to facilitate citizens working together to confront common problems.[8] Still others declare that the polarization is more intense in the United States due to the fact that our president is ultimately selected not by a popular vote of our citizens but instead by the Electoral College, which makes it profoundly difficult, if not impossible, for a third-party candidate to gain the presidency. The result has been the preservation of our two-party system.

> America's relatively rigid, two-party electoral system stands apart by collapsing a wide range of legitimate social and political debates into a singular battle line that can make our differences appear even larger than they may actually be. And when the balance of support for these political parties is close enough for either to gain near-term electoral advantage—as it has in the U.S. for more than a quarter century—the competition becomes cutthroat and politics begins to feel zero-sum, where one side's gain is inherently the other's loss. Finding common cause—even to fight a common enemy in the public health and economic threat posed by the coronavirus—has eluded us.[9]

Perhaps one of the most important and most cynical examples of zero-sum and cutthroat politics today has been the reactions to the closely contested 2020 presidential election. President Trump refused to accept the results of the election and claimed that the election had been "stolen" from him. Although the courts found no evidence of significant voter fraud, millions of Trump's voters were convinced that their votes had somehow gone uncounted and that ineligible votes were cast for the Democrats. Indeed, 76 percent of Republicans told Quinnipiac University pollsters that they believed "there was widespread fraud in the 2020 election."[10] Many Republican donors also believed the election was stolen. As a result, the GOP began to raise money to pressure state legislatures to pass laws restricting access to voting. States that Trump lost but where Republicans controlled the governorships and legislatures (including Arizona, Georgia, Pennsylvania, and Wisconsin) took steps to make it more difficult to vote. Strategies included restricting early voting, limiting access to vote by mail, eliminating Sunday voting (that was especially effective in getting African American voters to the polls), eliminating ballot harvesting (third parties collect mail-in ballots and drop them at polling places), purging voter rolls of those who haven't voted recently, and requiring proof of identification.[11] These changes were justified by the claimed need to ensure the integrity of the voting system even though there was scant evidence of fraud in past elections. Sadly, it seems that political polarization has deepened to such an extent that democracy itself is under siege and the voting rights of many citizens, especially underrepresented minorities, are endangered.[12]

We see the current crisis of political polarization as an urgent warning call to rehabilitate deliberative political argumentation so that our citizens and their elected officials can begin to reason together to reach solutions to our most urgent political problems. We also believe that a healthy democracy needs liberal, conservative, and independent voices presenting a wide array of competing viewpoints, values, and policy proposals for our consideration. Healthy and respectful public political disputes in which advocates offer and refute each other's claims and support their arguments with both evidence and analysis are an avenue to better solutions to our problems.

In this chapter we explore, from a narrative perspective, the elements on which candidates focus to gain the attention, adherence, and support of voters. Because so many voters get their information about politics from the media, candidates work to project the proper image and to display character traits that exhibit and command respect. We will examine how candidates use meaningful achievements and events from the past and the present in their stories about values and dreams to attract voters. We also look at the form and structure of political arguments and debates. The communication that shapes the pragmatic politics of legislation and governance in the United States is fundamentally argumentative in character.

ISSUES AND VOTERS

People in general, and especially people as voters, are attuned to issues that directly impact their lives and situations. Thus, farmers are predictably drawn to candidates who support policies that are helpful to agricultural producers, those who work in the oil or coal industries are deeply suspicious of candidates whom they perceive as too focused on addressing the problems of climate change, small business owners favor candidates who will likely vote to enhance the profitability of their businesses, recent college graduates will support candidates who favor student loan forgiveness, and those who expect to inherit wealth will favor candidates who will reduce inheritance taxes, etc. In addition to courting constituencies such as these, however, political candidates also seek to appeal to voters who hold strong positions on other key political issues that are uniquely important to specific voter groups. Thus, religious voters may be so focused on the issue of abortion that they will cast their votes based on the single issue of limiting access to abortion. Other single-issue voters may similarly decide their votes on such issues as gun rights, the environment, or LGBTQ rights, etc. Candidates strive to develop positions on these especially divisive issues that will win them more votes than they will lose. Obviously a strongly pro-life voter is unlikely to vote for a strongly pro-choice candidate.

Although candidates attempt to appeal to particular interests held by voters, they must also try to avoid appearing so beholden to special interest or single-issue voters that they ignore the broader interests of other constituencies. In addition, candidates must attempt to create images, public personas, and stories that are consistent. A candidate who emphasizes certain issues to build support with a particular constituency also attempts to appeal to other voters with similar interests. Candidates develop ideological constituencies to preserve a sense of harmony and predictability in the stories that they tell. The stories that the candidates share, and the issue positions that the candidates take, also reflect the historical positions of their political party, of course. Thus, in the United States the Democratic Party is more likely to favor social service programs, increasing the minimum wage, public health and welfare programs, more environmental protections, more regulation of firearms, etc. The Republican Party is more likely to favor lower taxes, leaving the issue of the minimum wage up to the states, private rather than public spending on health care, relaxed environmental regulations, open carry firearms laws, etc. Although voters may switch their allegiances and vote for candidates from both political parties, and although more voters are now declaring themselves "independent," most voters find themselves more aligned with the overall ideological perspective of one party or the other. They may be registered as an independent, but they "lean" either to the Democratic or the Republican positions and governing philosophy.[13]

In chapter 7, we discussed Walter Fisher's explanation of the power of the "American Dream" metaphor, in which he argued that there were two elements of this dream. The first he called the *materialistic myth*. Stories emphasizing this myth focused on economic issues, material well-being, prosperity, and the drive to improve one's life and the lives of family members through the acquisition of material wealth. Voters are all concerned about the state of the economy, job security, the promise of the future, the ability to provide for their family members, and securing their own retirement incomes. The materialistic myth drives such shared cultural values as our beliefs in the work ethic, self-reliance, individual initiative, inventiveness and ingenuity, and the aspiration to own a home and achieve an education.[14] Think about all the potential political arguments and stories that flow from the values connected to the materialistic myth.

The second myth Fisher calls the *moralistic myth*. This myth celebrates the principles of equality, justice, unity, collective responsibility, and concern for our fellow citizens. While the materialistic myth stresses that government should stay out of our way so we can take care of ourselves and "do our own thing," the moralistic myth says that government has a responsibility to protect the weak and less fortunate and to elevate the spirit of humankind.

Fisher argued that virtually all individuals have some allegiance to both of these myths and that both of them shape our values, our political identities, the political culture, and the argumentative appeals that candidates make to voters.[15] Perhaps the most resourceful effort to fuse the two myths was when George W. Bush was a candidate for the presidency and he declared that he was a "compassionate conservative." As a "conservative," he expressed his conviction in self-reliance and individual effort and ingenuity with minimal government intrusion. As a person who is "compassionate," however, he claimed to also be committed to look out for those who are less fortunate and who need governmental assistance. Although many liberal critics at the time complained that Bush's rhetoric was short on specifics (see the discussion of ambiguity in chapter 4), it obviously won support from a substantial number of people, and he was elected to the presidency in 2000.

An ongoing political dispute that magnifies the contest between the materialistic and moralistic myths involves the rights of undocumented immigrants. Most Democrats in Congress would extend opportunities—such as the right to work, attend school, receive financial aid, and a path toward citizenship—to people who were brought to the United States illegally as children and who have spent many years in this country. Legislation first introduced in 2001 but never enacted was entitled The DREAM Act (Development, Relief, and Education for Alien Minors); undocumented youth became the poster children for immigration reform, referred to as Dreamers.[16] The Democrats argue that many Dreamers have no recollection of their native country and thus that the moral response is to fully welcome them into our communities and our country. In addition, the Democrats argue that if these immigrants are given full access to educational opportunities and employment in the United States, they can improve their material conditions. Immigration reform thus would reduce the number of poor and disadvantaged people.

Most Republicans in Congress, on the other hand, argue that granting such rights would not be an appropriate moral response because it would reward people who broke the law in entering our country illegally and that it might encourage others to do the same. Furthermore, they argue that these new waves of immigrants would depress wages in the United States, increase the cost of education and health care, and take jobs that would otherwise be available to U.S. citizens. Thus, they claim that immigration reform would depress our economic growth.

Recognizing that he faced deep Republican opposition to immigration reform, President Obama took executive action (DACA—Deferred Action for Childhood Arrivals) that exempted young people from deportation if they had arrived in the United States before they turned 16 and made them eligible for work permits.[17] Republicans in the House of Representatives made revoking these protections their first substantive action of 2015, even though their bill failed to pass in the Senate where Democrats pledged a filibuster to keep it from coming to a vote, and Obama pledged a veto should such legislation ever reach his desk.[18]

The issue further escalated during the 2016 presidential campaign when candidate Donald Trump pledged to send all 11 million undocumented immigrants residing in the United States back to their home country and also committed to building a wall along the entire U.S.-Mexico border to prevent future illegal crossings.[19] Once he was elected to office, Trump began building his border wall and attempting to end DACA protection. When Democrats refused to provide funds for the border wall, Trump sought to bargain by offering to once again extend protection to Dreamers in exchange for a commitment to pay for the wall. The Democrats refused, however, to accept this deal, leaving the Dreamers vulnerable to possible expulsion and leaving them unable to access some documents and benefits.[20] Several federal court rulings prevented Trump from completely terminating DACA.[21] On January 20, 2021, President Biden on his very first day in office issued new executive orders halting construction on the border wall and renewing the protections that Obama had extended to Dreamers.[22] The uncertainty intensified on July 16, 2021, when a U.S. District Court judge in Texas ruled that the original executive action by Obama was unconstitutional and that the program could not be legal unless it was passed by Congress where it faced continuing and stiff opposition from Republicans who would filibuster it in the Senate. The issue is now all but certain to go to the U.S. Supreme Court.[23]

VOTER ATTITUDES

People complain about politics and politicians for being inconsistent as well as for a variety of other reasons. Some believe that politicians do not really listen to them or represent their interests. Young voters, for instance, complain that politicians do not focus on the issues that are important to young people but instead spend most of their time talking about programs that matter to older people, such as Social Security or Medicare. It is not surprising that politicians do not spend much of their time talking about the issues that are important to young people because older people constitute the most reliable voters in most elections. Why should politicians spend their energy talking about issues that are important to young people if they are unlikely to vote? Others lament that regardless of whom they vote for, things never seem to change. Still others protest that candidates seem so dependent on special interest groups and large campaign contributions that they ignore the needs of their constituents.

Many have argued that President Donald Trump was elected to office because voters had become so disgusted by politics that they were willing to embrace an outsider, with no political experience, who promised to break the established order.[24] Throughout his presidency, however, Trump remained a deeply polarizing political figure. His highest polling number for those who approved of his job as president reached 47 percent in October 2018, and his lowest was 38 percent in October 2017. His average over his four years in office was 43 percent.[25] For the first seven months, President Joe Biden had approval ratings ranging from 51 to 55 percent and disapproval ratings from 34 to 43 percent. By the end of August, the approval/disapproval percentages were both 47; at the end of October 2021 he had a 43 percent job approval rating, and 51 percent disapproved of his performance in office.[26]

It is not just the support, or lack thereof, for the president that displays the depth of frustration and polarization in the United States. For many years, polls have reported that the public had little respect for members of Congress. Most congressional representatives and members of the Senate easily gain reelection. While voters may support their elected representatives, they have very little respect for Congress as an institution. In December 2020, fully 82 percent of those surveyed disapproved and only 15 percent approved of the work of Congress. The numbers showed a marked improvement by March 2021 although remaining negative: 61 percent disapproved and 36 percent approved of Congress. That approval rating declined in the next six months; by September 2021 approval was at 27 percent and disapproval at 69 percent.[27]

Despite the polarization and cynicism characterizing contemporary politics, however, there is some reason for optimism. The historical low point for voter participation was in the 2014 midterm elections. In the 25 states that held statewide primaries for both parties, only 14.8 percent of eligible voters cast ballots.[28] The results of a March 2015 primary election in the city of Los Angeles were even worse—only 8.6 percent of eligible voters bothered to cast their ballots.[29] Perhaps it was the polarization and passion of the Trump presidency that helped turn things around; turnout soared in the 2020 presidential election. Almost two-thirds of eligible voters cast ballots.

> Nationwide, presidential election turnout was about 7 percentage points higher than in 2016. . . . Turnout was the highest since at least 1980, the earliest year in our analysis, and possibly much longer. The rise in turnout was fueled in part by the bitter fight between incumbent President Donald Trump and challenger Joe Biden. A pre-election survey found a record share of registered voters (83%) saying it "really matter[ed]" who won. But another big factor was the dramatic steps many states took to expand mail balloting and early voting because of the COVID-19 pandemic.[30]

Despite the uptick in voting, however, "the U.S. still lags behind most of its developed nation peers when it comes to electoral participation. Out of 35 members of the Organization for Economic Cooperation and Development for which estimates of voting age population were available, U.S. turnout ranked an underwhelming 24th."[31]

The uptick in voter participation was celebrated by most experts as a good outcome. It demonstrated that citizens felt a high-level of political engagement, felt that their participation really mattered, and saw the outcome as having high stakes. It is also arguable, however, that the 2020 election represented something dangerous to the future of U.S. democracy because the party allegiances and the urban-rural divides that drove turnout illustrate the lack of comity and depth of polarization in U.S. politics.[32] The election also resulted in a prolonged public discussion led by the losing candidate and his supporters that the election was "stolen" and the results were "fraudulent," despite the fact that no convincing evidence in support of such a claim was ever presented. A relatively convincing case can be made that polarization and cynicism were higher than ever in 2021.[33]

It is also worth noting that in response to the dramatic increase in voter participation, many Republican-controlled state legislatures sought to roll back the very reforms that had made it easier for people to vote and had thus contributed to the higher turnout. Not surprisingly, the states that took the most dramatic and controversial steps to make voting more difficult were the "swing" states that voted for Trump in 2016 but that voted for Biden in 2020. One of the most controversial bills was introduced in Georgia.

> The Georgia law would, among other things, require a photo ID to vote absentee by mail, cut the period to request an absentee ballot and place limits on ballot drop boxes. It would also give more control over election officials to the state Legislature.
> It would also make it illegal to hand out water to voters in line. In recent elections, Georgia voters, particularly those in Black neighborhoods, have waited many hours in line to vote.[34]

President Biden and national civil rights groups condemned the Georgia bill as a return to the Jim Crow era and voter suppression. "The coordinated effort to force this restrictive bill onto the people of Georgia is a devastating reminder that we have not yet moved beyond the dark history of voter suppression in this country."[35]

We believe that all of us have an interest in addressing the issue of political polarization, continuing to improve voter turnout, restoring confidence in election outcomes whether our side wins or is defeated, and assuring access to the voting booth for every eligible voter. As W. Lance Bennett argued: "Restoring public interest in government, trust in leadership, and commitment to a livable society . . . are essential steps toward real solutions for problems like crime, homelessness, drug abuse, education, economic revitalization, and other obstacles to the 'good life'."[36] The United States cannot serve as a democratic beacon to other nations around the world if we cannot get our own house in order and serve as a model of healthy, vibrant, deliberative democracy. Nurturing such democratic argument is the goal of this chapter.

Campaigns as Stories

As you might expect given the theoretical slant of this book, we see political campaigns as stories offering voters alternative depictions of the past, current moment, and of possible futures. Issues great and small give candidates opportunities to attempt to connect with voters and earn their support or to discourage them from supporting a rival candidate. In recent years, for example, some candidates demand stricter gun control laws to prevent mass shootings, while others express their unwavering commitment to the second amendment and the right of all citizens to openly carry assault rifles. Some candidates have argued for a path to citizenship for Dreamers, while others advocate for stricter enforcement of immigration laws. Some candidates favor greater acceptance for LGBTQ people, while others advocate for legislation that will "protect" women's sports by limiting participation to those athletes who were "assigned female at birth."[37] As you can easily discern from these examples, a wide chasm of ideological difference animates the stories told during our political campaigns. The narratives highlight stark contrasts and diverse futures for our society.

The most reliable voters, those who vote in almost every election, are also the most partisan voters. Their minds are seldom changed by campaigns. Tightly contested elections are, for the most part, decided by voters who are less partisan. They may vote in some elections but not others. They may change their political allegiances and cross party lines because they are motivated by an issue or two that they find really important or because they particularly like, or more commonly strongly dislike, a particular candidate. These voters are also less likely to be significantly engaged in following political news either from legacy print media sources or from TV broadcasts.[38] Indeed, many such voters report that they get a significant amount of their political information from entertainment programs such as *Saturday Night Live, The Daily Show, The Tonight Show,* etc.[39] Voters, regardless of their level of partisanship or their personal political convictions, are also heavily influenced by those around them—their family members, friends, and neighbors. This explains the increasingly stark political fault lines that are separating rural from urban voters, working class from white-collar voters, and voters from one ethnic group from voters from a different ethnic group. Research consistently finds today that political identity may matter more to many voters than issue positions.[40]

The U.S. electorate has also revealed itself to be quite volatile. The cleavage between the blue team and the red team at the national level is so deep and so evenly separating us that we have seen volatile shifts from one election to the next. Campaigns try to activate their likely voters and discourage opposing voters by spending vast amounts of money on political advertisements. Ads are a preferred way to reach undecided voters because, as noted above, these voters are often not actively seeking news and political information. They are best reached through a medium that is ubiquitous and difficult to avoid.[41] More than $1 billion was spent on political advertising in just thirteen swing states during the 2020 presidential election.[42] Indeed, political ads so thoroughly saturate the air waves in these states that many are now beginning to question whether they work or if they turn voters off and make them more cynical about politics and politicians.[43]

Because political advertising, especially on television, is expensive, candidates simplify their messages and present them in the briefest possible form. These ads are often negative in tone because research has suggested that it is easier to convince people who do not follow politics closely to vote against someone than it is to vote for someone.[44]

We have consistently reminded readers that the world is made up of competing stories, each vying for public acceptance. Election campaigns provide excellent opportunities to watch such competing stories develop and emerge. The stories revolve around characters and the images that place them in sharp relief and help voters discern differences. They also center around dissimilar issues, focus on distinct problems, offer alternative policy solutions, and prey upon our hopes and fears. Larry K. Smith, a former manager of a presidential and several senate campaigns has observed that "every campaign is a story about the candidate and the nation."[45]

Image

Mediated campaigns are also *image* campaigns, where candidates are evaluated on the basis of their public personalities. The focus on image emphasizes such attributes as a winning smile, an ability to project warmth and empathy, the skill to give a winning speech, and/or the capacity to project toughness. The candidates also make use of appealing family portraits—campaigns include images of their spouses, children, grandchildren, and even their pets. Multiple stories, for example, emphasized that the White House would once again be home to the first-family's pets when Biden assumed the presidency. The previous occupant had not possessed any pets, whereas the Biden family had two German shepherds named Champ and Major. Even more significantly, accounts emphasized that one of two dogs, Major, was a rescue animal from a Delaware animal shelter.[46] That the president of the United States was bringing a rescue pet into the White House was celebrated by many as evidence of Biden's virtue and literal love of the underdog. Major made still more news within the first couple of months of the new administration when he was reported to have caused minor injury, biting a staff member.[47] The White House announced the death of Champ on June 19, 2021. The loss further humanized the first couple, as the press release declared, "Wherever we were, he wanted to be, and everything was instantly better when he was next to us."[48]

Politics has been described as a "morality play," and candidate images are created rather than merely discovered.[49] The candidates, of course, contribute to the creation of their images in speeches and public statements, in media interviews, in video clips, and in still photographs. These images are further refined and publicly shared by campaign consultants and used in advertisements. Images acquire further power in the statements offered by the candidates' supporters and opponents. Images are circulated, refuted, or recast in media accounts of the campaign. Finally, images are invoked in the conversations that voters have with friends and family members.

Ronald Reagan spent most of his career as a Hollywood actor. He was born in central Illinois but carefully crafted an iconic western image of a cowboy. He was frequently depicted in photos and video clips enjoying his ranch near Santa Barbara, where he road horseback clad in blue jeans, western-style plaid shirts, a cowboy hat, and boots. The image of the cowboy has a rich historical basis in the U.S. popular imagination, of course. It reminds us of our independent streak, our love of open spaces, and of a people moving west to conquer a frontier and build new settlements. Barack Obama was born and mostly grew up in Hawaii. He was the son of an African father born in Kenya and a white mother who grew up in Kansas. He spent a portion of his youth living in Indonesia. Yet, in his campaign narratives he always emphasized the influence in his life of his maternal grandparents and how he was shaped by their "Kansas values." Donald Trump was the son of a wealthy New York real estate investor. He was gifted significant sums of money from his father throughout his life to underwrite his various investments. Despite the influx of money, however, several of these business ventures failed spectacularly and fell into bankruptcy. Nonetheless, he crafted an image as an ultra-wealthy, successful businessman. Finally, Joseph Biden grew up in a middle-class family; he experienced tremendous losses throughout his life. His first wife and daughter were killed in a car accident and his two young sons were injured. Years later, one of those sons, Beau Biden, lost his life to cancer. Biden spoke frequently of these losses, and the public saw an image of a man of great empathy for the suffering of others. Many believe that Biden's empathetic image was the perfect antidote to the perceived lack of empathy in his predecessor, especially in the midst of the COVID-19 pandemic.[50]

Many governors aspire to become president. How does a governor who served in state politics establish a political image that he or she is likely to be a capable leader on issues of foreign policy? One strategy often used is to take a highly visible trip to meet and interact with the heads of state in nations of special importance to U.S. foreign policy or to current issues in the news. For example, Governor Chris Christie of New Jersey, a candidate for the Republican presidential nomination in 2016, took such a trip to Mexico to discuss immigration and trade. The trip was intended to demonstrate that Christie had the gravitas to share the platform with Mexico's president.[51] Christie was not the only Republican presidential candidate who was racking up the frequent flyer miles. Senator Rand Paul spent time in Guatemala and former Senator Rick Santorum and former Governor Mike Huckabee took trips to Israel.[52]

Given the importance of candidate image rather than positions on issues, one might question what role argumentation plays in U.S. political campaigns. The answer, as you might expect given the focus of this book, is a very important one, as images and arguments are woven together to form coherent campaign narratives.

Character

An important element in the consideration of a candidate's image is *character*. Voters naturally hope for candidates whom they believe are honest, trustworthy, and competent. We want elected officials who will keep their promises and be true to their word. We anticipate that some of our readers are now shaking their heads in disbelief at this point. They are likely thinking about a recent president who was reckless with the truth, was elected despite a history of failed business ventures, and who also had no previous experience in elected office that might have suggested he could perform the job competently and manage a large staff. Note however, that we did not say that *character* was the *only* consideration that voters consider when casting their ballots. We already reported that this incumbent never won support from more than 47 percent of the populace, that his negative evaluations over his four years in office were 57.9 percent, and that many who disapproved of his performance in office did so because of concerns about his character.[53] And yet, more than 74 million people voted for him.[54]

In another sense, we would also argue that people often judge character by whether or not candidates see the world the way that they themselves see it. They search for candidates who share their stories, values, beliefs, and worldviews.[55] Many argue that the most ardent, committed, and hard-core Trump supporters stuck with the president despite his character flaws. They felt that they had long been ignored and their interests disregarded by other politicians, and they believed that the New York real estate magnate and reality-TV star shared their values, spoke their language, and gave them political voice.[56]

One strategy that many candidates attempt to use to identify with potential voters is to emphasize their humble origins. For example, President George W. Bush emphasized his childhood in Midland, Texas, far more than he talked about his attendance at an elite East Coast boarding school as a high school student or his college years at Yale University. His opponent in 2000, Vice President Al Gore, emphasized his summers working on the family farm in Carthage, Tennessee, and not his childhood living in the prestigious Mayflower Hotel in Washington, D.C., as the son of a prominent U.S. senator. Emphasizing simple, rural roots is not limited to presidential candidates. For example, Joni Ernst sponsored a television ad in her campaign for the U.S. Senate in 2014 in which she declared she truly understood the agrarian values of Iowa because she grew up on a hog farm and participated in the castration of pigs. She claimed the experience would give her the unique ability to "cut pork" (referring to pork barrel spending) as a senator in Washington.[57] Senator John Tester (D-MT), who is the only member of the Senate who remains an active farmer, never misses an opportunity to talk to reporters while he is dressed in bib-overalls and performing farm chores. How better to prove his genuine credentials as an ordinary citizen who gets his hands dirty and shares the public's values and problems?[58]

Candidates eager to emphasize the importance of their identity frequently write autobiographies to help shape their public images. Most of these books end up selling very few copies, but some have been quite successful—notably Senator John McCain's book that recounted his experience as a prisoner of war in Vietnam and Barack Obama's book detailing his relationship with his largely absent father.

Another strategy that has proven popular is the creation of a biographical video. Such videos are often a highlight of the party's nominating convention. One of the best examples that we have seen was the 1992 video that Bill Clinton used to introduce himself during the Democratic Convention. The video described how Clinton grew up poor in the village of Hope, Arkansas. It described how he lived in a lower-middle-class home with an outhouse in the backyard. He was forced to endure his stepfather's excessive drinking, violent mood swings, and physical and emotional abuse. Despite these hardships, however, Clinton's life was defined by his efforts to succeed. Through hard-work and the unyielding support of his loving mother, he graduated from

Georgetown University, became a Rhodes Scholar at Oxford University, and graduated from Yale Law School. Then, although he could have accepted a highly paid job in the East, he gave up this opportunity to return to his home state and build a career of public service. This compelling narrative conveyed to the public that Clinton was a simple person much like them—but also that he was intelligent, gifted, loyal, and ambitious. All of these qualities established his character and countered arguments that he might lack the experience, maturity, or wisdom required of the office.[59]

The issue of a candidate's character takes on strong moral dimensions. Early in the 1992 presidential campaign, Governor Clinton was accused of having an extramarital affair. Affairs are not uncommon; indeed, many voters have been unfaithful at some point in their lives. However, there is a desire to hold political candidates to a higher moral standard than ordinary citizens. So, who was Bill Clinton? Was he a philandering and unfaithful husband selfishly pursuing his own gratification outside of the bonds of marriage? Was he a slick politician who would do anything to get elected? Or was he the humble, honest, devoted man of the people suggested by the biographical film shown at the convention?

On December 19, 1998 during his second term in office, Clinton was impeached for perjury and obstruction of justice regarding an affair with a 21-year-old intern. He was acquitted (February 12, 1999) at the impeachment trial.

> As the impeachment process unfolded, Clinton's ratings in public opinion polls were at an all-time high, hovering at close to 70 percent. Most Americans gave Clinton low marks for character and honesty. But, they gave him high marks for performance and wanted him censured and condemned for his conduct, but not impeached and removed. Many viewed key Republican attackers as mean-spirited extremists willing to use a personal scandal for partisan goals. In the end, voters were happy with Clinton's handling of the White House, the economy, and most matters of public life.[60]

Some voters wanted Clinton removed from office because they believed him morally unfit and unsuited to govern. Others believed that his marital infidelity should be considered a private issue and that there is an important difference between morality in one's personal life and morality in public life.

The issue of infidelity and other forms of sexual impropriety as a disqualification for office remains unsettled decades later. Recently, it was revealed a president paid a huge settlement to a porn star to purchase her silence about a prior sexual relationship, a governor of New York resigned after eleven subordinate state employees accused him of sexual harassment, and a congressman from Florida was accused of having sexual relations with a 17-year-old-girl. Has our view of character revealed through sexual harassment and power dynamics changed? It remains to be seen if the culture has shifted in the era of #MeToo.

While many lament the emphasis on a candidate's character, we see this as an inevitable dimension of the storytelling that occurs in contemporary political campaigns. An important measure of a story's narrative probability is its ***characterological coherence***.[61] Three questions related to the candidate's character are useful in testing a political narrative: Is this candidate the person that he or she claims to be? Does this candidate's character suit the demands of the public office? And, can I trust that my interests and the public interests that I hold as most important will be served by the candidate's election to office? We think these are very relevant and important questions for voters to consider in casting their ballots.

Stories of History, the Present, and the Future

All political campaigns provide *historical narratives* to explain our past and how we happened to find ourselves in the circumstances we are in now. Thus, virtually any candidate's political rhetoric will emphasize those aspects of history that enrich and provide foundational support for the story that he or she wants potential voters to accept. Both Republican and Democratic candidates draw freely on the Founders of the American Republic for their inspirational messages about our political system. In addition, Republicans celebrate the achievements of the great Republican leaders from the past, and the Democrats celebrate the legacy of their great leaders. In fact, after an ex-president has been dead for many years, it even becomes possible for him to be claimed by politicians from the other party. Thus, both Democrats and Republicans may invoke the names of Abraham Lincoln, Theodore Roosevelt, Harry Truman, John F. Kennedy, or Ronald Reagan.

These nostalgic recollections for the great political leaders of the past are more than idle memorializing. These leaders represent the ideological history of the different political narratives that live on in U.S. politics. To invoke the name of Franklin Roosevelt is thus to invoke the New Deal dream of a proactive government dedicated to enriching the condition of the masses. To invoke the name of John Kennedy is to remember the optimism, vitality, and youthfulness of his administration and the deep sense of loss after his tragic assassination. To invoke the name of Ronald Reagan is to express nostalgia for a time of relative prosperity and pride that marked his administration. Certainly, all of these presidents faced stiff opposition during their administrations. Nonetheless, we often search for the achievements and moral lessons of a bygone era to set our political compass to guide present actions.

When we argue about the events of the Watergate scandal, the Vietnam or Afghanistan Wars, the Clinton or Trump impeachment dramas, or the insurrection at the Capitol on January 6, 2021, we are using historical events to shape our understanding of current conditions. We are creating historical accounts to solve contemporary problems. Did we fail in Vietnam or Afghanistan because we lacked the will to see the fight through to its end? The answer to this question can help us determine what course of action we should follow in other future conflicts. If the lesson of Vietnam is that we should avoid involving ourselves in civil wars in the support of unpopular dictators, we will presumably conduct our foreign policy very differently than if we tell a historical story that celebrates the moral justice of our involvement and only condemns the fact that we lacked the will to fight and win.

Historical stories thus provide material for interpreting present problems and choices and also in articulating *future narratives*. All political candidates emphasize that if they are elected, and their proposed policies are enacted into law, the world will be a better place and the quality of our lives will be improved. On important public issues, competing candidates will construct very different depictions of history, accounts of the present, and views of the future. The historical stories must, of course, account for the facts of history and thus cannot be mere fabrications to achieve a candidate's purposes.

Facts can be tricky, however, as we suggested during our discussion of evidence. Did the U.S. economy prosper during the Obama or Trump presidencies or not? It depends on who is telling the story and which facts will be selected for emphasis. Some storytellers will cite gains in the stock market or job growth; others will cite the growth of deficits or the loss of jobs as a result of the pandemic.

Likewise, stories of the present must account for life as we know it. For example, President Trump loved to discuss the spectacular decrease in unemployment during the first three years of his term of office but not the loss of jobs and increase in unemployment due to the forced shutdowns to halt the spread of the deadly virus. Trump supporters give him credit for the rapid development of the vaccines to conquer COVID-19. Trump's opponents blame him for the fact that the virus was allowed to worsen to the point that so many lives were sacrificed and that the sacrifices were most acutely experienced by our most vulnerable citizens. Some of the facts that people encounter are experienced directly and personally. Others are experienced only through their interactions with others or through media. For many months, for example, people were dismissive of the dangers of COVID because they did not personally know anyone who had become ill, needed hospitalization, or died. Media coverage to which people are exposed may also alter their evaluations. We know, for instance, that partisan cable news channels may slant their coverage and may not report stories that reflect badly on their preferred party and/or politicians.

Stories about the future are more flexible than stories about either the past or the present. Political candidates assert that the world will be a much more prosperous, harmonious, and pleasant place if they are elected to office. Arguments of this type are often overly optimistic, describing a world so perfect that its existence is unlikely. For example, we routinely hear presidential candidates claim that if they are elected we will have an America where every child has access to an excellent education, all families have health insurance, our streets are safe and free from the scourge of illegal drugs, everyone has access to a well-paying job, and our environment is protected. Yet, year after year, the same problems persist.

THE STRUCTURE AND FORM OF CAMPAIGN ARGUMENTS

Because political campaigns are essentially narrative in form, the arguments offered to the voters seldom resemble the more formal arguments that might be used in an academic debate, in a courtroom, or even in a business meeting. Consequently, political campaign arguments may have very loose rules of evidence, lax standards for evaluation, and perhaps intentional obfuscation of issues. There is a tendency in much political arguing, for example, to tell only partial truths—or at the very least to embellish and exaggerate the facts in support of one's position. Perhaps the most classic example was when Vice President Al Gore made himself the subject of ridicule during the 2000 presidential campaign when he claimed responsibility for the development of the internet. Although the vice president had indeed been a big supporter of developments in new communication technologies during his service in the U.S. Senate, this claim seemed so exaggerated that it lacked credibility and may actually have undermined Gore's presidential campaign.

While some level of exaggeration might be expected in politics, there can be a profound credibility gap if political candidates or elected officials seem willing to lie or to deceive the public. For example, both President George W. Bush and British Prime Minister Tony Blair were subjected to withering criticisms for having exaggerated the threats posed by Iraq's strongman ruler Saddam Hussein in order to justify a preemptive strike against Iraq. Both leaders argued for the war with rhetoric that linked Hussein's regime to the international battle against terrorism and by claiming that Iraq was developing weapons of mass destruction. When no such weapons were discovered, many complained that the case for war was trumped up (or in the British vernacular "sexed up") and that these were instead "weapons of mass deception."[62]

President Obama was harshly criticized for having promised "if you like your health care plan, you can keep your health care plan" under his new program, the Affordable Care Act. Once the Affordable Care Act was adopted, thousands found that their insurance providers canceled their current health plans. The companies claimed that they did so because those plans no longer met the requirements imposed by the new law (for example, many plans did not contain mental health care coverage). Those old plans were frequently replaced with new plans that were either more expensive or that had significantly higher deductibles. Obama's exaggerated claim became an issue in the 2012 presidential campaign when he sought election to a second term and lingered as an issue in the 2014 midterm elections.[63]

President Donald Trump was frequently accused by reporters of having told blatant lies as well as exaggerations. Indeed, the *Washington Post* reported that it kept a tally of the president's misstatements during his term in office; in a bold headline a few days after he left office, the newspaper declared that Trump lied 30,573 times.[64] The lies and exaggerations covered issues large and small, but the most remembered was probably the claim that Mexico would pay to build his proposed border wall. We believe that such extensive lying and exaggeration of claims is ultimately corrosive. If citizens are exposed to so many deceptive statements, we fear they will eventually distrust virtually everything political figures tell them and thus will lose interest in politics or actively participating in civic life.

Reputable media have a responsibility to record, research, and evaluate the arguments advanced by political candidates and elected officials to help the public judge the quality and veracity of their claims. When covering political campaigns, the media must do more than treat them as they would a horse race; they must focus on the issues and arguments advanced by the candidates. The voters, in turn, must act upon the information provided to them. People have to be encouraged to read newspaper accounts, listen to news broadcasts, and follow news stories online. In short, citizens in a democracy must expend the necessary energy to evaluate the arguments offered by political candidates and elected officials.

If voters become more attentive to the quality of arguments advanced, there is some hope that candidates will become less inclined to deliver simplistic, sophomoric arguments. As Roderick Hart declared, candidates need to focus less on how "audience predispositions can be exploited" and more on "how citizens' needs can be met."[65] Our political leaders speak for us, and they speak on behalf of our nation. They should be creating arguments that challenge us, stimulate us, and educate us. Doing so will motivate us to learn more about political issues, to take positions, and, of course, to vote. What elected officials should not be permitted to do is to massage our egos and to make vague promises to satisfy our self-interests—that is, by making only the arguments that their polling tells them we want to hear.

Political Debates

The one format for political argumentation celebrated for its promotion of rational and deliberative discussions of issues is the political debate. Political debates are praised because they provide an opportunity to observe the candidates in face-to-face interactions discussing the issues. Certainly these contests have value, but it may be misleading to refer to them as debates. They clearly are not the same as the formal academic debates that we discussed in previous chapters. They are also not the same as the type of debating that is routinely conducted in legislative chambers or parliament. Instead, what passes for a political debate in a U.S. election campaign is more like a joint press conference where more than one candidate is questioned before the same audience.

In most U.S. political debates, candidates respond to questions posed by a single reporter or a panel of reporters. In Town Hall debates, candidates respond to questions posed by audience members. In all such contests, the quality of the debates is in large part determined by the resourcefulness and creativity of the questioners. If, on the one hand, the candidates are asked tough and penetrating questions that expose their positions on issues and the potential gaps in their understanding and/or experience, then these contests can have terrific probative value for the electorate. If, on the other hand, the candidates are lobbed "easily fielded softballs" that permit them to mouth only platitudes—or to make use of their slogans or buzzwords from their campaign speeches and paid advertisements—then the debates are of far less value.

Indeed, political candidates and those who help them prepare for these debates have learned both from their personal experiences and from research studies that audiences seem not to listen to political debates very closely. This permits candidates to avoid answering the questions they are asked, to reinterpret the question to one that may lend itself to an answer more likely to help them advance their candidacies, to skirt the issues, or to deflect attention from their failure to answer the question with a criticism of their opponent. Sometimes vigilant reporters detect these "slips" and "dodges" and point out that a question was not answered, but sometimes they do not. Potential voters who are watching and listening to these debates should focus both on what is being said and on what is not being said so that they can learn as much as possible from these exchanges. The application of critical listening techniques will help make these debates much more useful to audiences in evaluating the candidates.

Research in political campaign debates has confirmed that substantial argumentative clash occurs frequently and that candidates use more evidence and display more analysis and refutation in debate speeches than in other forms of campaign discourse.[66] Research has also suggested, however, that many who view debates are not able to identify whether a candidate has offered either evidence or analysis to support his or her arguments. Viewers are, however, able to determine which candidate was more aggressive in the debate and which candidate was more defensive. As you might expect, candidates were helped in the evaluation of their performance by being perceived as aggressive, and they were harmed if they appeared overly defensive.[67] They often aggressively pursue their opponents in the debate, but they are usually averse to responding to the attacks made on them—perhaps because they lack the skills to do so or perhaps because they do not wish to appear defensive. The result is that many political debates contain a lot of histrionic mudslinging but little in the way of probing, constructive argumentation. The first of the 2020 presidential debates between Donald Trump and Joe Biden set a new low for this type of insult-focused debating.[68]

Another problem with contemporary political debates is that they have become mediated campaign events where the press and the voters focus less on the substance of the discussion than they do on the candidates' momentum in the campaign. The media and the public expend most of their energy trying to determine who *won* the debate and which candidate's campaign was most helped by his or her performance. There is far less emphasis on the issues discussed or on the differences between the positions of the candidates. The emphasis on winning has had interesting outcomes. Voters questioned immediately after hearing the media's analysis of the outcome of a debate may have different impressions of the contest than they would if they were questioned a few days later—after having had time to reflect on what the candidates said and after being exposed to additional discussions of the debate.

That voters' opinions are heavily influenced by media reports of the outcome of the debate, which has also resulted in the phenomenon known as the spin.[69] Each campaign sprinkles spokespersons throughout the hall to be available for press interviews following the debate. Not surprisingly, the task of each spokesperson is to help shape the narrative of how the debate is reported, seen, and understood by anyone who will listen. The campaign spinsters never admit that their own candidate was anything short of brilliant and insightful or that the opposing candidate managed to achieve anything in the debate. The process might be considered humorous if it did not go so far toward trivializing politics in the United States.

Another hallmark of contemporary political debates is the search for the most significant error, gaffe, slip, or misstatement. The media and public alike have become used to the notion that if one or the other candidate makes such a mistake, this is what should determine the outcome of the contest. In perhaps the most significant gaffe ever, President Gerald Ford declared in 1976 that Poland could not be considered under the domination of the Soviet Union. The remark seemed to be a misstatement, and the moderator gave Ford the opportunity to clarify what he meant. Instead of admitting his error, the president reaffirmed his conviction that Polish citizens would not consider themselves to be under Soviet domination. The post-debate press commentary focused almost exclusively on the remark, all but ignoring the rest of the debate.[70] This focus on identifying and punishing gaffes can distract public attention from the substantive issues in the debate.

Former Texas Governor Rick Perry went from being a serious contender to a source for laughter in a humiliating moment in a 2011 Republican presidential primary debate when he was unable to remember the name of the third federal agency that he intended to close if he were elected president.[71] The media pundits pounced on the gaffe, and video clips of the governor's awkward moment flooded the airwaves and traveled quickly across social media sites. The public quickly turned away from Perry, even though everyone alive had no doubt had similar—although significantly less public—moments when they could not come up with a name or an idea that was on the tip of their tongue only a moment before.

There have also been many controversies regarding the debate formats used and their consequences. Even the determination about which candidates should be invited to participate sparks controversy. In some years, the primary field of candidates has been so large that they have had to split the debates into two separate panels of contenders. There may be some advantage being on the stage with the more prominent candidates rather than being relegated to what appears to be the "undercard" debate. Standing on a stage with perhaps ten other candidates in a primary debate also creates challenges. It is difficult a candidate to stand out from the crowd, and some candidates are often denied equal speaking time. The debates are clearly easier for audiences to follow when the format pits only the two leading candidates against each other with only a minimum of intervention from other speakers, including reporters.

Candidates who are given an opportunity to make statements, address questions to each other, and respond to each other's arguments have a better likelihood of making their positions known on the issues, revealing their differences, and highlighting the choices for voters. Such debates are often criticized because they exclude minor party candidates, however. It is difficult, if not impossible, to please everyone.

In recent presidential elections, several different formats have been used. The candidates and their handlers usually negotiate the selection of a format for a given debate in consultation with the organization sponsoring the debate. Regardless of what format is selected or how well the individual arguers may perform in the contest, research suggests that audiences find debates informative.[72] Most studies, however, also suggest that viewers' partisan belief structures tend to influence their perceptions of the candidates' performances. In short, Republicans tend to think that the Republican candidate did the best job, and Democrats usually think that the Democratic candidate performed better.[73]

Summary

The quality of the issues and arguments advanced by political candidates to gain the support of voters has a profound effect on the vitality of the U.S. electoral process. As already mentioned, many Americans have grown cynical about politics and politicians, and our politics have become deeply polarized.

In order to restore public confidence and trust in our political leaders—and in an attempt to shape political deliberative practices that can help us solve our most vexing political problems—we need to strive to improve the substance and quality of political argumentation. Candidates need to demonstrate greater respect for the intellect and wisdom of the voters, and they need to be honest and forthcoming about their positions on the issues. Voters need to invest more energy in learning about the issues and the candidates' stands on them. They also need to consult reliable sources of information and not be trapped in their own echo chambers that expose them only to arguments that they already believe to be true. They especially need to interrogate conspiracy narratives and misleading and deceptive news stories. Only an informed and involved electorate can expect to have influence over its elected officials. Voters will not respect elected officials until they demonstrate their respect for the voters.

Key Terms

character
characterological coherence
future narratives
historical narratives
image
myths

Activities

1. Consider why many people do not bother to cast their ballots. Write a short essay presenting the reasons for this lack of participation and offering suggestions that would encourage more people to vote.
2. The U.S. electorate has become deeply polarized. Why do you think this has occurred? What remedies might address this problem?
3. Read the transcripts of the two convention acceptance speeches from 2020 by Donald Trump and Joe Biden in the appendix. How does each speech develop a narra-

tive? Who are the heroes, villains, and victims? How do the speeches depict the scene in the world at the time the speech was given? How do they imagine the future?

4. Summarize and critique the political advertising strategies used by the candidates in the 2020 presidential election. View twenty-one television ads for each party at The Living Room Candidate website (http://www.livingroomcandidate.org/commercials/2020). How did candidates make use of different strategies to influence audiences?

5. The 2020 presidential debate was remarkable because the attacks became so personal. Watch the debate (https://www.youtube.com/watch?v=wW1lY5jFNcQ) and offer a critique of the candidates' performances. What suggestions would you make to improve the contest?

Recommended Reading

Arceneaux, Kevin and Martin Johnson, *Changing Minds or Changing Channels? Partisan News in an Age of Choice* (Chicago: University of Chicago Press, 2013).

Hart, Roderick P., *Civic Hope: How Ordinary Americans Keep Democracy Alive* (Cambridge: Cambridge University Press, 2018).

Hollihan, Thomas A., *Uncivil Wars: Political Campaigns in a Media Age,* 2nd ed. (New York: Bedford/St. Martin's Press, 2009).

Iyengar, Shanto, *Media Politics: A Citizen's Guide,* 4th ed. (New York: Norton, 2019).

Levendusky, Matthew, *How Partisan Media Polarize America* (Chicago: University of Chicago Press, 2013).

Lodge, Milton and Charles S. Taber, *The Rationalizing Voter* (Cambridge: Cambridge University Press, 2013).

Perloff, Richard M., *The Dynamics of Political Communication: Media and Politics in a Digital Age,* 3rd ed. (New York: Routledge, 2022).

Endnotes

[1] Osita Nwinevu, "Biden's Bipartisan Dream Is Already Over," *The New Republic,* January 29, 2021. https://newrepublic.com/article/161150/biden-bipartisan-covid-relief-gop

[2] Matthew Brown, "COVID-19 Stimulus Package: Polls Find Strong U.S. Support for Relief," *USA Today,* March 10, 2021. https://www.usatoday.com/story/news/politics/2021/03/10/covid-19-stimulus-package-polls-find-strong-support-relief/6936053002/

[3] Michael Dimock and Richard Wike, "America Is Exceptional in the Nature of Its Political Divide," *The Pew Research Center,* November 13, 2020. https://www.pewresearch.org/fact-tank/2020/11/13/america-is-exceptional-in-the-nature-of-its-political-divide/

[4] Ibid.

[5] Matthew Levendusky, *How Partisan Media Polarize America* (Chicago: University of Chicago Press, 2013).

[6] Milton Lodge and Charles S. Taber, *The Rationalizing Voter* (New York: Cambridge University Press, 2013).

[7] Ibid., p. 18.

[8] Thomas A. Hollihan, *Uncivil Wars: Political Campaigns in a Media Age*, 2nd. ed. (New York: Bedford St. Martins, 2009).

[9] Dimock and Wike.

[10] Chris Cillizza, "Three Quarters of Republicans Believe a Lie about the 2020 Election," *CNN Politics,* February 4, 2021. https://www.cnn.com/2021/02/04/politics/2020-election-donald-trump-voter-fraud/index.html

[11] See for example, Jeremy W. Peters, "In Restricting Early Voting, the Right Sees a New 'Center of Gravity,'" *New York Times,* March 20, 2021, p. A11. See also, Eric Lutz, "Republicans Are Taking a Sledgehammer to Voting Rights," *Vanity Fair,* March 2, 2021. https://www.vanityfair.com/news/2021/03/republicans-are-taking-a-sledgehammer-to-voting-rights

12. David A. Graham, "The Republican Party Is Abandoning Democracy," *The Atlantic*, December 10, 2020. https://www.theatlantic.com/ideas/archive/2020/12/republican-party-abandoning-democracy/617359/
13. John Laloggia, "6 Facts about U.S. Political Independents," *Pew Research Center*, May 15, 2019. https://www.pewresearch.org/fact-tank/2019/05/15/facts-about-us-political-independents/
14. Walter R. Fisher, "Reaffirmation and Subversion of the American Dream," *Quarterly Journal of Speech* 59 (1973): 161–163.
15. Ibid.
16. Jesús A. Rodriguez, "The Supreme Court Case that Created the 'Dreamer' Narrative," *Politico Magazine*, October 31, 2021. https://www.politico.com/news/magazine/2021/10/31/dreamers-undocumented-youth-forever-children-516354
17. Ibid.
18. Jeremy W. Peters, "House Votes to Revoke Immigrants' Protections," *New York Times*, January 15, 2015, p. 1A.
19. Kathleen Hennessey, "Trump Plan: Make Immigrants Pay for 'Permanent Border Wall' and Deport Millions," *Los Angeles Times*, August 17, 2015. http://www.latimes.com/nation/politics/la-na-trump-immigration-20150817-story.html
20. Nick Miroff and David Nakamura, "Trump Makes a Prime-Time Case to Grant 'Dreamers' Legal Status, Build Border Wall," *Washington Post*, January 30, 2018. https://www.washingtonpost.com/powerpost/trump-makes-a-prime-time-case-to-legalize-dreamers-build-border-wall/2018/01/30/6defe102-05ca-11e8-b48c-b07fea957bd5_story.html
21. Miriam Jordan, "Judge Rules DACA Is Unlawful and Suspends Applications," *New York Times*, September 27, 2021. https://www.nytimes.com/2021/07/16/us/court-daca-dreamers.html
22. Rafael Carranza, Daniel Gonzales, and Yvonne Wingett Sanchez, "Biden Addresses Immigration, Pauses Border Wall Construction, and 'Fortifies' DACA," *AZCentral*, January 20, 2021. https://www.azcentral.com/story/news/politics/border-issues/2021/01/20/biden-pauses-border-wall-construction-issues-immigration-plan/4232792001/
23. Ellie Honig, "The 'Dreamer's Future in the US Is Endangered After Judge's Decision," *CNN*, July 19, 2021. https://www.cnn.com/2021/07/19/opinions/daca-federal-ruling-democrats-honig/index.html
24. For example, see: Matt Flegenheimer and Michael Barbaro, "Donald Trump Is Elected President in Stunning Repudiation of the Establishment," *New York Times*, November 9, 2016. https://www.nytimes.com/2016/11/09/us/politics/hillary-clinton-donald-trump-president.html
25. Nigel Chiwaya and Wen Si, "Donald Trump's Presidency Was a Roller Coaster, His Approval Ratings Were Not," *NBC News*. January 21, 2021. https://www.nbcnews.com/news/us-news/donald-trump-s-presidency-was-roller-coaster-his-approval-ratings-n1255360
26. "How Popular Is Joe Biden?" *538.com*. October 29, 2021. https://projects.fivethirtyeight.com/biden-approval-rating/
27. "Congress and the Public," *Gallup*, September 2021. https://news.gallup.com/poll/1600/congress-public.aspx
28. Cited by Joshua Holland, "Will Americans Set a New Record for Political Apathy in 2014?" *Moyers & Company*, July 23, 2014. https://billmoyers.com/2014/07/23/will-americans-set-a-new-record-for-political-apathy-in-2014/
29. Lydia O'Connor, "Dismal Doesn't Even Begin to Describe LA's Voter Turnout," *Huffington Post*, March 4, 2015. https://www.huffpost.com/entry/los-angeles-voter-turnout_n_6803574
30. Drew Desilver, "Turnout Soared in 2020 as Nearly Two-Thirds of Eligible Voters Cast Ballots for President," *Pew Research Center*, January 28, 2021. https://www.pewresearch.org/fact-tank/2021/01/28/turnout-soared-in-2020-as-nearly-two-thirds-of-eligible-u-s-voters-cast-ballots-for-president/
31. Ibid.
32. For a discussion, see Lee Drutman, "The High Turnout in 2020 Wasn't Good for American Democracy," *Washington Post*, February 10, 2021. https://www.washingtonpost.com/politics/2021/02/10/high-turnout-2020-wasnt-good-american-democracy/
33. Aaron Blake, "Trump's 'Big Lie' Was Bigger than Just a Stolen Election," *The Washington Post*, February 12, 2021. https://www.washingtonpost.com/politics/2021/02/12/trumps-big-lie-was-bigger-than-just-stolen-election/
34. Deborah Barfield Barry, "A New 'Jim Crow Era': Biden, Civil Rights Leaders Slam Georgia Election Reform," *USA Today*, March 26, 2021. https://www.usatoday.com/story/news/politics/2021/03/26/georgia-voting-bill-2021-biden-civil-rights-leaders-slam-new-leaw/7015324002/

35 Ibid.
36 W. Lance Bennett, *The Governing Crisis: Media, Money and Marketing in American Elections* (New York: St. Martin's Press, 1992), 2.
37 Lee Strubinger, "South Dakota Governor Bans Transgender Sports Through Executive Order," *NPR*, March 29, 2021. https://www.npr.org/2021/03/29/982474861/south-dakota-governor-bans-transgender-girls-from-sports-teams-by-executive-orde
38 Hollihan, *Uncivil Wars.*
39 Kristin D. Landreville, R. Lance Holbert, and Heather L. LaMarre, "The Influence of Late-Night Comedy Viewing on Political Talk: A Moderated Mediation Model," *The International Journal of Press/Politics* 15 (2010): 482–498.
40 Cameron Brick and Sander van der Linden, "How Identity, Not Issues, Explains the Partisan Divide," *Scientific American,* June 19, 2018. https://www.scientificamerican.com/article/how-identity-not-issues-explains-the-partisan-divide/
41 Hollihan, *Uncivil Wars,* see chapter 6.
42 Dominico Montanaro, "Presidential Campaign Ad Spending Crosses $1 Billion Mark in Key States," October 13, 2020. https://www.npr.org/2020/10/13/923427969/presidential-campaign-tv-ad-spending-crosses-1-billion-mark-in-key-states
43 Alexander Coppock, Seth J. Hill, Lynn Vavreck, "The Small Effects of Political Advertising Are Small Regardless of Context, Message, Sender, or Receiver: Evidence from 59 Real-time Randomized Experiments," *Science Advances* 6 (2020). https://www.science.org/doi/10.1126/sciadv.abc4046
44 Many of the best known studies on the impact of negative advertising were conducted by Steven Ansolabehere and Shanto Iyengar, *Going Negative: How Political Advertisements Shrink and Polarize the Electorate* (New York: Free Press, 1995).
45 Cited by Wendy Kaminer, "Crashing the Locker Room," *The Atlantic,* July 1992, p. 63.
46 "Champ, Major, and Other White House Pets," *BBC News,* January 25, 2021. https://www.bbc.com/news/election-us-2020-54871695
47 Kate Bennett, "Joe Biden's German Shepherd Has Aggressive Incident and Is Sent Back to Delaware," *CNN,* March 10, 2021. https://www.cnn.com/2021/03/08/politics/president-joe-biden-white-house-dogs/index.html. Do not be alarmed by the headline! Major's exile to Delaware was short-lived, and he soon returned to the White House and the family was reunited.
48 Elena Moore, "President Biden's Dog Champ Dies at Age 13," *NPR,* June 19, 2021. https://www.npr.org/2021/06/19/1008356025/champ-joe-biden-dog-dies-white-house-german-shepherd
49 Larry K. Smith, cited by Kaminer.
50 Peter Wehner, "Biden's Empathy Is What Matches Him to This Moment," *The Atlantic,* November 2, 2020. https://www.theatlantic.com/ideas/archive/2020/11/joe-bidens-superpower/616957/
51 "Chris Christie Seeks Global Platform with Mexico Trip," *New York Daily News,* September 3, 2014. https://www.nydailynews.com/news/politics/chris-christie-seeks-global-platform-mexico-trip-article-1.1925911
52 Ibid.
53 "How Popular Is Donald Trump?" *FiveThirtyEight*, January 20, 2021. https://projects.fivethirtyeight.com/trump-approval-ratings/
54 "U.S. Presidential Election Results 2020: Biden Wins," *NBC News,* February 8, 2021. https://www.nbcnews.com/politics/2020-elections/president-results
55 Bruce E. Gronbeck, "The Presidential Campaign Dramas of 1984," *Presidential Studies Quarterly* 15 (1985): 386-393.
56 "Why Hard-Core Trump Supporters Ignore His Lies," *The Conversation,* September 20, 2020. https://theconversation.com/why-hard-core-trump-supporters-ignore-his-lies-144650
57 Sean Sullivan, "Republican Ernst Draws on Experience Castrating Hogs in Iowa Senate Cable Ad," *Washington Post,* March 25, 2014. https://www.washingtonpost.com/news/post-politics/wp/2014/03/25/republican-ernst-draws-on-experience-castrating-hogs-in-iowa-senate-cable-ad/
58 Holly Michaels, "Tester, a Montana Farmer, Says D.C. Hasn't Changed His Values in Third Bid for Senate," *Independent Record,* August 26, 2018. https://helenair.com/news/state-and-regional/govt-and-politics/tester-a-montana-farmer-says-d-c-hasnt-changed-his-values-in-third-bid-for/article_1b4bf668-9cbe-5bab-9e28-df805c4d77a4.html
59 "The Man from Hope," 1992 [Reupload], *YouTube,* August 28, 2018. https://www.youtube.com/watch?v=MrujaQDlN28
60 Russell Riley, "The Clinton Impeachment and Its Fallout." Miller Center, University of Virginia, 2021. https://millercenter.org/the-presidency/impeachment/clinton-impeachment-and-its-fallout

61 Walter R. Fisher, *Human Communication as Narration: Toward a Philosophy of Reason, Value, and Action* (Columbia: University of South Carolina Press, 1987), 47.
62 See "Blair's Court," *The Economist*, August 30, 2003, 39–40. See also, "Saddam's Elusive Arsenal," *The Economist*, January 30, 2004. http://www.economist.com/node/2401533
63 D'Angelo Gore, "Fact Check: If You Like Your Health Plan, You Can Keep It." *USA Today*, November 11, 2013. https://www.usatoday.com/story/news/politics/2013/11/11/fact-check-keeping-your-health-plan/3500187/
64 Glenn Kessler, Salvador Rizzo, and Meg Kelly, "Trump's False or Misleading Claims Total 30,573 Over 4 Years," *Washington Post*, January 24, 2021. https://www.washingtonpost.com/politics/2021/01/24/trumps-false-or-misleading-claims-total-30573-over-four-years/
65 Roderick P. Hart, *The Sound of Leadership: Presidential Communication in the Modern Age* (Chicago: Chicago University Press, 1987), 200.
66 John W. Ellsworth, "Rationality and Campaigning: A Content Analysis of the 1960 Presidential Campaign Debates," *Western Political Quarterly* 18 (1965): 794–802.
67 For a discussion of this research see Hollihan, *Uncivil Wars*, 164–176. For a more general discussion of presidential debates see: Diana Carlin and Mitchell McKinney, Eds., *The 1992 Presidential Debates in Focus* (Westport, CT: Praeger, 1994). Also, Kathleen Hall Jamieson and David S. Birdsell, *Presidential Debates: The Challenge of Creating an Informed Electorate* (New York and Oxford: Oxford University Press, 1988).
68 "First 2020 Presidential Debate Between Donald Trump and Joe Biden," *YouTube*, September 29, 2020. https://www.youtube.com/watch?v=wW1lY5jFNcQ
69 G. Lang and K. Lang, "The Formation of Public Opinion: Direct and Mediated Effects of the First Debate," in G. Bishop, R. Meadow, and M. Jackson-Beeck, Eds., *The Presidential Debates* (New York: Praeger, 1978). See also, Arnie Madsen, "Partisan Commentary and the First 1988 Presidential Debate," *Argumentation and Advocacy* 27 (1991): 100–113.
70 "The Blooper Heard Around the World," *Time*, October 18, 1976, p. 16.
71 Arlette Saenz, "Rick Perry's Debate Lapse: 'Oops'—Can't Remember Department of Energy," *ABC News*, November 9, 2011. http://abcnews.go.com/blogs/politics/2011/11/rick-perrys-debate-lapse-oops-cant-remember-department-of-energy/
72 A. H. Miller and M. MacKuen, "Informing the Electorate: A National Study," in Sydney Kraus, Ed., *The Great Debates: Carter vs. Ford, 1976* (Bloomington: Indiana University Press, 1978), 269–297.
73 S. A. Shields and K. A. MacDowell, "Appropriate Emotions in Politics: Judgment of a Televised Debate," *Journal of Communication* 37 (1987): 78–89.

14

Argumentation and the Law

The most formalized and ritualized setting for the creation and evaluation of arguments is the courtroom. Our expectations for arguers are most carefully delineated in the resolution of legal disputes. To achieve success, disputants must carefully research the facts of their cases and the relevant statutes and laws; they must present their arguments in accordance with carefully constructed rules; the evidence they present should be probative without being unduly prejudicial; their arguments will be weighed by jurors who typify the values of the community; and the entire process is controlled by a trained and supposedly impartial judge. The U.S. legal system also allows for appeals. A litigant who loses a case may appeal the decision to a higher court if he or she can establish that there was an error in the first trial.

The United States is a very litigious society. Former Supreme Court Chief Justice Warren Burger warned almost four decades ago that America was "a society overrun by hordes of lawyers, hungry as locusts."[1] At that time, there were 450,000 attorneys in the United States. By 2020, the number had grown to 1.33 million.[2] There has, however, been a sharp decline in the number of law school enrollments. Technological developments such as computer-assisted data searches have supplanted the hours of painstaking library research that once occupied armies of young legal associates. Despite the recent decline in law school admissions, however, we assume that many students reading this book and studying argumentation will choose to pursue legal education. We also believe that knowledge about the law and about argumentation in legal settings will serve all students well.

The increasing complexity of modern society, the tremendous number of new regulations created since the 1960s, the fact that courts now recognize that defendants in criminal trials have a right to legal counsel, and the fact that there are simply more lawyers trying to make a living has led to crowded court calendars. The COVID-19 pandemic, which required a temporary pause in jury trials in most regions of the country, added to the problem. The court docket is so crowded in some U.S. cities that it can take more than five years for some cases to make it to trial.

There are essentially two types of cases before the courts: *civil* cases and *criminal* cases. In civil cases, litigants typically sue someone for financial damages that they believe they have sustained as a result of the other party's actions or negligence. You might earn civil damages if you paid to have a house built and the contractor did not complete all of the work, if a surgeon made a mistake and amputated your right leg when it was your left that had been injured, or if someone ran a red light and hit your car when you were legally driving through an intersection. Criminal cases are, of course, those wherein a defendant is charged with violating the established laws of the local, state, or federal government. In criminal cases, litigants are charged by the district attorney on behalf of all of the citizens in the jurisdiction where the laws were violated. In the recent case in Minneapolis, for example, a former police officer was convicted of three counts for the killing of George Floyd while attempting to subdue and arrest him. The specific charges were filed as "State of Minnesota vs. Derek Chauvin."[3]

Before discussing the importance of argumentation theory and argumentation principles in legal settings, we will briefly consider the organizational characteristics of the U.S. judicial system.

THE U.S. JUDICIAL SYSTEM

The United States has courts that are operated by local jurisdictions (such as cities, counties, and states) and courts that are operated by the federal government. Each state has primary responsibility for its own courts, and the decisions in one state do not impact court decisions in another state. The structure of court systems varies somewhat from state to state, but typically states will have municipal (sometimes called circuit) courts and/or superior courts. The municipal or circuit courts are generally reserved for minor criminal cases or civil cases in which the amount of damages is fairly small. These courts may be subdivided further into traffic courts (where traffic offenses are adjudicated), probate courts (where challenges to wills or estates are considered), domestic courts (where marital and child custody matters are resolved), small claims courts (which decide civil lawsuits not requiring attorneys), and petty crimes courts. More substantial and important cases are decided in district or superior courts. The latter typically cover greater territory and jurisdiction and are noteworthy because judges are appointed or elected and may have more stature in the community and the legal profession. Each state also has state appeals courts and a state supreme court to rule on cases that have been decided by lower courts.

The federal courts resolve violations of federal laws and focus particularly on interstate issues. These include: violations of laws on federal lands or in national parks, as well as offenses such as environmental pollution that crosses state boundaries, immigration violations, income tax evasion, trafficking in drugs, treason, kidnapping that crosses state boundaries, and unlawful flight from one state to another to avoid capture. The federal court system is composed of 94 district courts and 13 federal appellate courts. Decisions from any of these federal courts, or even decisions from any of the state courts, can ultimately be appealed all the way to the United States Supreme Court.

The crush of activity in both the state and federal court systems has given attorneys, judges, and litigants increased incentives to divert cases from the court docket. Only a very small percentage of the cases that are initially filed, either civil or criminal, actually end up going to trial. Civil cases can be extremely expensive, and the fees paid to lawyers can be more than the awards paid to the plaintiffs. Consequently, litigants are encouraged to reach a settlement before the trial begins. Only two percent of federal criminal cases go to trial.[4] There is no standardized record-keeping system covering state court systems, but individual jurisdictions report fewer than three percent of criminal dispositions are determined by a jury trial. Most criminal cases are settled by plea bargains; the defendant agrees to plead guilty to a lesser offense than the one originally charged. Simply because a case never goes to trial does not mean that argumentation plays an unimportant role. The outcome of bargaining and negotiation sessions to reach a settlement depend on the argumentative skills of the participants. Building and presenting as strong a case as possible in these settings increases the likelihood that the other side will agree to settle the case.

THE ASSUMPTIONS OF THE SYSTEM

The U.S. judicial system, which was modeled after the British system, is ***adversarial*** in nature. This model assumes that the best way to determine truth is to have litigants, each taking incompatible positions, present their best arguments in support of their cases and let an impartial third party evaluate the truthfulness of their arguments. Furthermore, this system assumes that untrained citizen jurors can best resolve even very technical legal arguments at the trial level. Different states have created different standards for when litigants are entitled to a trial by jury. Typically, all civil cases beyond a certain level of damages (which varies from state to state), all felony criminal trials, and many misdemeanor trials can be decided by citizen jury if the litigant demands one. Alternatively, a defendant can waive the right to a jury trial and have the case decided by a judge; such trials are known as "bench" trials.

Citizen Jurors

One might ask why our society has placed such faith in untrained citizen jurors. Certainly, the jury system is costly and troublesome. Citizens do not eagerly come forward and volunteer their time for jury duty. In many jurisdictions, it is a constant challenge for courts to find suitable jurors to fill all of the jury panels needed. Many citizens actively avoid jury service. People who can prove that they are the sole providers of care for children or the elderly or those whose work is essential to the community and cannot easily be replaced (such as teachers, doctors, police officers, or firefighters) often win exemption from jury service. In addition, those who are self-employed and might face financial hardship are frequently excused from jury service. Others who work for companies that will pay for a short term of jury service may be excused from longer, more complicated, and arguably more important cases. As a result, juries in the United States are often composed of older and retired persons, public employees, and blue-collar rather than professional persons.

Thus, jurors may lack the education and preparation required to analyze the facts of cases involving complex laws. In technically sophisticated areas such as medical malpractice, antitrust prosecutions, complex tort actions, financial fraud cases, patent infringement cases, and even many criminal prosecutions that rely on scientific evidence, jurors may have difficulty understanding the arguments presented. In such cases it might be desirable to have these decisions rendered by experts and not by citizen jurors. Instead of turning to experts, however, our system emphasizes the ability of ordinary citizens to make these complicated decisions. The reasons for this commitment to citizen jurors are numerous and varied.

First, there is a general belief that citizen jurors are capable of making good decisions. They are careful and conscientious in the verdicts that they render, and they take their responsibility seriously. Research has suggested that judges agree with the verdicts rendered by juries most of the time.[5]

Second, even though the entire court system is organized and structured to assure litigants impartial and fair verdicts that will resolve complex questions of fact, one benefit of the jury system is that jurors are by their very nature not dispassionate arbiters of fact. Jurors are an important part of our legal system precisely because they temper their judgments with emotions and because they reflect the values of their community. Their judgments are shaped by their sympathy and/or anger both for the victims or plaintiffs and for the defendants. In this sense, jurors reflect the public will. The presence of citizen jurors in the process reflects the wisdom and the will of the people themselves—protecting litigants from the potential capriciousness of the state and ensuring that the courts are not the instruments of existing state power and control.

A significant issue in jurisprudence is "juror nullification." If the facts of the case demonstrate that a defendant has broken the law, jurors should render a guilty verdict. However, jurors may believe the law is unjust and refuse to convict. Because a verdict of not guilty cannot be overturned and jurors cannot be punished for their verdicts, the laws in such cases are described as nullified. For example, fugitive slave laws in the 1850s compelled citizens to assist law enforcement in the apprehension of runaway slaves. Jurors would refuse to convict someone who had provided food or shelter to an escaped slave.[6] Jurors also nullified prohibition laws in the early twentieth century and drug laws more recently. Voters in 18 states have legalized marijuana for recreational use, and 36 states allow the use of marijuana for medical purposes. Federal laws, however, continue to prohibit the growth and distribution of cannabis and classify marijuana along with heroin and cocaine as a Schedule I drug with no medical benefit. When courts have prosecuted marijuana growers, distributors, and sellers, jurors have sometimes refused to find for the prosecution because they believe the laws are unjust.

Third, economically and racially diverse juries, drawn from the community, may help convince people that the judicial system is functioning fairly for all members of that community. Such was the case in the Derek Chauvin trial. The jury was composed of four Black, six white, and two multi-race individuals.[7] When Chauvin was convicted on all counts by this jury, many people saw the verdict as a step toward healing.[8] Conversely, if juries do not represent the diverse communities in which they live, their decisions may reinforce systematic oppression of ethnic and racial minorities. "When the voices of those who have been historically marginalized and silenced are missing from juries, implicit biases are reinforced to the detriment of those outside of hegemonic expectations."[9]

Fourth, the opportunity to serve on a jury provides a civic involvement that is unrivaled by any other experience in our society. Jurors learn about the legal system, feel themselves much more a part of their government, and are likely to be more committed to the protection and preservation of our important civic institutions. This civic participation is thus an essential public ritual that helps sustain the health and vitality of the U.S. democracy.

Dispute Resolution

Because the U.S. legal system involves untrained jurors in the decision-making process at the most critical junctures of cases, the courtroom becomes an interesting field for argumentative study and inquiry. As we have already discussed, different fields develop specific standards for argument evaluation based on the need to resolve unique problems and to make effective decisions within the objectives of that field. In legal matters, for example, the key challenge is to decide how to categorize events. Several kinds of questions (recall our discussion of stasis in chapter 5) help with categorization.

Some of these questions are factual: Did the alleged assault occur? Did the defendant commit the assault? Other questions may focus on the characteristics of the act. Even if it can be clearly established that an assault occurred and that the defendant committed the assault, one could still question the nature of the assault: Was this action taken in self-defense? What was the character of the situation, and did this situation have implications for the defendant's actions? Did the defendant simply lose control and strike without thinking? Or was the act planned in advance and coldly calculated?

There are also questions of *precedent* (relevant decisions in previous court cases). In classifying and categorizing events, legal arguers attempt to assure that similar actions will be dealt with in like fashion by the courts. If all people are truly viewed as equal under law, an assault by a white defendant on an African American victim should be dealt with in the same way as an assault by an African American assailant on a white victim. The courts consider legal precedent as well as statutory guidelines to assure that the law protects the interests of its different constituencies equally well and is applied to events in a predictable and patterned way.

The work of the courts is primarily intended to resolve factual disputes and to classify and categorize actions and behaviors. The propositions being disputed are, therefore, propositions of fact. The specific wordings of the propositions in dispute will be carefully framed to reflect the demands for legalistic precision. In criminal indictments, the proposition considered is a formal complaint—a charge in which the district attorney alleges that the named defendant broke a specific statute on a specific date. Because we presume people to be innocent until proven guilty, the ***burden of proof*** in such a complaint rests with the prosecution (or the plaintiff in a civil action), and the prosecutor's argument must be sufficient to overcome a ***reasonable doubt***. What constitutes reasonable doubt is of course a matter of argument. Most judges will advise jurors that it does not mean the resolution of *all* doubts but that a reasonable person would be inclined to find the evidence and the arguments presented by the prosecution sufficient proof that the complaint is true. One of your authors was recently called for jury duty and was read an official jury instruction that indicated the prosecution in a criminal trial in California must present a case that proves the defendant guilty beyond a reasonable doubt. A reasonable doubt was defined as proof that leaves one with an "abiding conviction that the charge is true."[10] It was suggested that an abiding conviction meant a jury would reach the same decision if they came back the next day, the next week, and so on.

The complaints filed in civil cases are somewhat less precise than in criminal cases but still demand that the specific allegation be explicitly understood and spelled out. If, for example, the plaintiff is claiming that the defendant caused her injury when he struck her with his car, the plaintiff's attorney will have to prove that the accident was the defendant's fault and that the resulting injury was sufficiently severe that the plaintiff should be compensated for actual losses and perhaps also for pain and suffering. While the standard for determining culpability in a criminal case is beyond a reasonable doubt, the standard for ascertaining responsibility in a civil case is the ***preponderance of evidence***. To meet this standard the plaintiff must persuade the adjudicator that the facts in support of the suit are probable—that is, better than fifty-fifty. A very slim margin in favor of one side or the other can determine the outcome.

One important difference between a criminal case and a civil case, however, is that in a criminal case the verdict is typically guilty or not guilty, with little opportunity to create a middle ground (although in some jurisdictions, and with some kinds of crimes, a defendant could be convicted of a lesser offense). In a civil case, verdicts quite often involve compromises. For example, defendants could argue for a reduction in the amount of damages; they could claim that while they shoulder some responsibility for the accident, there was also negligence by one or more of the other parties in the case. In civil cases, a verdict in favor of the plaintiff is followed by further deliberation to determine the amount of damages to be awarded. In determining the amount of the financial award, the jurors are asked to temper their findings with feeling for both the plaintiff and the defendant.

The Attorney-Client Relationship

Your attorney is your advocate in any legal case; thus, the role of an attorney is to be argumentative. In criminal cases the prosecutor is the "people's advocate," who reflects the community's will in having its laws enforced. From the time attorneys are first introduced to a client, they are gaining information, undertaking a critical analysis of that information, and beginning to construct a theory of the case.

In a civil case, clients hire an attorney either to file a cause of action against another person or because someone has filed a complaint against them. In a criminal case, a client hires an attorney (or one is assigned by the court) after a criminal complaint has been lodged. During the first meeting, the attorney seeks information to assess whether this is a winnable, or deserving, case. Attorneys rarely want to spend their own time or the court's time on a case that they probably cannot win. This is why a defense attorney will urge a settlement or plea bargain if the facts suggest that it is unlikely that an outright acquittal can be achieved for their client.

The initial attorney-client interview also provides the attorney and client an opportunity to begin to get to know and trust each other. Trust is an important dimension of the attorney-client relationship. In order to present the best arguments for a client, attorneys must trust that their clients have been honest and forthright with them. There is nothing worse than clients who lie to their attorneys and carefully constructed arguments are invalidated when the lies are exposed at trial.

THE ROLE OF ATTORNEYS IN PRETRIAL PHASES

Much of the work of an attorney is accomplished long before a case ever comes to trial. This stage is called the pretrial phase. It includes all the activities of investigators and attorneys prior to the opening gavel. Many cases are won or lost in the pretrial phase.

The Discovery Phase

Once an attorney decides to represent a client, the process of researching the facts of the case to locate and link the material evidence to the client's claims begins. This is called *discovery.* Discovery typically includes interviews with witnesses or interested parties, an examination of important documents that might prove or deny the case, and a review of law books for cases to illustrate the specific statutes in dispute and to find relevant case precedents.

The evidence that the attorneys assemble may take many forms: letters, contracts, legal documents, financial records, photographs, statements or affidavits from witnesses, and so on. Witnesses to be subpoenaed to testify in court are identified. Other witnesses are deposed. The depositions are statements given under oath and in the presence of a trained legal stenographer, which can be read at trial.

From this vast amount of information, the attorney begins to organize the facts into a case that supports the client's position. The case is organized so that the key issues on which the case might turn are highlighted and accessible for discussion and scrutiny. Naturally, attorneys construct their case so that facts helpful to their client are given greater attention and prominence in the presentation (recall the discussion in chapter 3 about giving presence to facts). Facts that may be harmful to their client are obscured or perhaps even obfuscated.

To gain knowledge about what answers will likely be given, attorneys should interview witnesses before a deposition is taken or the trial begins. Asking a question during cross-examination when the probable answer is unknown can derail a carefully constructed case. Attorneys should also prepare their witnesses in how to present their testimony during the trial. Jurors evaluate not only what a witness says but also the credibility of the witness. Preparing a witness to use effective verbal and nonverbal communication so that truthful testimony is clear and understandable bolsters an attorney's case. Exactly how far an ethical attorney can go in coaching witnesses is open to interpretation. There is a significant difference between advising witnesses about effective communication and influencing a witness to present misleading information. *Woodshedding* is the term used for telling a witness exactly what to say or unfairly prejudicing a witness. It is unethical and unlawful for an attorney to tell a witness to say something that is not true or to permit a witness to say something known to be inaccurate. That is called suborning perjury, and it is illegal.

Developing the Theory of the Case

When interviewing a client, an attorney should be thinking about a **theory of the case**—the underlying idea that unites legal principles to the factual background and ties the evidence into a coherent story that puts the client's position in the best possible light. The fact that human decision makers rely on stories in the creation and evaluation of arguments has already been established. Consequently, it should come as no surprise that courtroom arguments also emerge in the form of stories.

The stories that the attorneys tell, like all other stories that listeners evaluate, will be judged on the basis of their narrative probability and fidelity. With regard to narrative probability—whether the story is coherent—attorneys must consider questions such as the following. Is the structure of the story satisfying and complete? Does it account for the chronology of events? Does it account for the material evidence that has been revealed? Do the actors in these stories perform their roles and fulfill the expectations of their characters in a reasonable and convincing manner?

Defense attorneys attempt to convince jurors to sympathize with their clients. Prosecuting attorneys want jurors to empathize with the victim. Prosecutors portray defendants as reprehensible. Defense attorneys suggest ways in which the victim does not deserve sympathy. In the very public prosecution of the late musical superstar Michael Jackson, for example, the prosecution sought to convince jurors that the singer was a predator. They alleged he actively sought out children and systematically groomed them to fulfill his sexual desires—inviting them to his home and into his bed for overnight stays, sometimes offering them liquor to numb their inhibitions. The prosecution cast the victims as vulnerable and naïve. One, for example, was a young boy from a broken home suffering from cancer. The defense created a very different story about the singer. This story characterized Jackson as a caring, empathetic, and "childlike" waif himself—someone who deeply loved children, was very generous toward them, and would never do anything to cause injury or harm to a child. Indeed, the defense claimed that the charges were the result of sick and twisted minds incapable of understanding or appreciating the purity and goodness of Michael Jackson's character. The defense claimed that the real villains in the case were the parents and their greedy lawyers who made such spurious charges in the pursuit of financial gain. Michael Jackson was ultimately acquitted on four charges of child abuse after lurid testimony was heard in a trial that lasted three months.[11]

The second test of stories is that of narrative fidelity. Does the story seem likely to be true? Does it coincide with the stories that jurors have known or experienced in their own lives? Does it match the stories heard about the lives of friends or family members? Does it correspond to stories in the press? Does it conform to fictional accounts of characters that seem reasonable and lifelike? Returning to the Michael Jackson example, the jury had to consider whether it was credible that an adult male would invite children to share his bedroom and perhaps his bed and not have sexual gratification in mind. Does such a story seem believable given other stories the jurors have heard throughout their lives and have believed as probably true? Although the performer escaped conviction in a criminal trial, he paid approximately $23 million to settle a civil complaint that he sexually abused a young boy.[12]

Two researchers, Lance Bennett and Martha Feldman, observed criminal trials in the Superior Courts in King County (Seattle, Washington) for a year.

> In order to understand, take part in, and communicate about criminal trials, people transform the evidence introduced in trials into stories about the alleged criminal activities. The structural features of stories make it possible to perform various tests and comparisons that correspond to the official legal criteria for evaluating evidence (objectivity, reasonable doubt, and so on). The resulting interpretation of the action in a story can be judged according to the law that applies to the case.[13]

Bennett and Feldman discovered that attorneys presented their legal arguments in the form of stories and that stories provided the means by which jurors organized information, recollected that information, and systematically tested and evaluated information.[14]

As we have argued in earlier chapters, it is understandable that listeners make use of their capacity for telling and evaluating stories in their role as jurors because storytelling comes naturally to us. Bennett and Feldman described the benefit of the use of stories as a means of legal reasoning.

> Stories have implicit structures that enable people to make systematic comparisons between stories. Moreover, the structural form of a completely specified story alerts interpreters to descriptive information in a story that might be missing, and which, if filled in, could alter the significance of the action. The inadequate development of setting, character, means, or motive can, as any literature student knows, render a story's action ambiguous. In a novel or film, such ambiguity may be an aesthetic flaw. In a trial, it is grounds for reasonable doubt.[15]

The best stories are those that not only account for the evidence presented in the case but also are simple, relatively straightforward, and easy for jurors to follow. The more complex a story is, the greater the likelihood that the opposing counsel can find ways to poke holes in it and reveal its flaws. It is also helpful if attorneys create stories that they themselves find believable. Attorneys should try not to argue a case that they themselves do not find plausible. Doing so reveals their lack of faith in the case to the jurors and poorly represents the interests of their client.

Because the burden of proof is always placed on the plaintiff (or the prosecutor in a criminal case), it is especially important that the plaintiff present a unified, compelling, and forthright story. Complex plot twists and inconsistencies of almost any kind prove especially troublesome to the construction of a compelling case by the prosecutor or plaintiff because they enhance the likelihood that a defense attorney can introduce an element of doubt in the juror's minds.

It is best if the defense counsel can also present a unified defense story that clearly contrasts and is incompatible with the opponent's story but that also accounts for the material evidence that is presented. Unfortunately, it is often difficult for the defense to construct such a story. In such cases, the defense counsel might choose to present multiple stories, all of which compete with—and therefore cast doubt on—the prosecutor's or plaintiff's story. In some cases, the defense attorney might even decline to present any story at all, choosing instead to present only a refutational case. This strategy capitalizes on the fact that the prosecutor or plaintiff has the burden of proof and strives to demonstrate reasonable doubt by probing the potential weaknesses in the opponent's case. The defense is under no obligation to present a story, or evidence, or to call the defendant as a witness. However, because jurors have a strong preference for narrative reasoning, this is a less than ideal strategy for the defense to use. Jurors may create their own rival stories to challenge the stories presented by the prosecutor or the plaintiff's attorney. If they are unable to construct their own stories, and if the defense counsel has also failed to present such a story, a verdict against the defendant might be more likely.

The preparation of the case and the pretrial work that goes into the development of the case is every bit as important, if not more so, than the trial presentations. Given that very few cases even get to trial, most cases are won or lost during the pretrial investigations and the construction of the case arguments. The decision as to whether to take a case to trial is often the most important one that an attorney will make. It should be made only after careful consideration of the evidence, the appropriate legal statutes, and the development of a theory of the case.

Pretrial Motions

Not all the evidence acquired before a trial can be used in court. Sometimes, for example, there are questions about whether the evidence was gathered and maintained properly. In such situations, attorneys representing the two sides of the dispute engage in pretrial motions. Evidence obtained by the police without a proper warrant or without probable cause to initiate the investigation may be suppressed (excluded) by a judge. This is called the ***exclusionary rule***, and it is intended to deter the state from violating an individual's right to privacy. If illegally obtained evidence leads to additional evidence, that too is excluded as "fruit of the poisonous tree." Once seized, the state must maintain a "chain of custody" for any physical evidence. This means the state must be able to demonstrate that the evidence, as it moved from hand to hand, was always under someone's protection or locked up so that there is no possibility that the evidence was tampered with or permitted to degrade.

There are many additional types of pretrial motions—from a change of venue motion, to requests for separate trials for codefendants, to motions that argue that evidence is too inflammatory to be presented to a jury. Entire courses at law school are devoted to these matters. Regardless of their nature, pretrial motions must be argued effectively before a judge. The matter may be decided strictly on the basis of legal arguments or litigants may call witnesses to corroborate or support an argument. In both situations, finding and citing relevant prior court cases (precedents) that support one's advocacy is an Important component of this process.

Jury Selection

The selection of the jurors occurs before the trial begins. Attorneys seek jurors whom they believe will be more sympathetic to their case. The assumption of the jury system is that jurors are selected so they represent a cross section of the community and will thus constitute, for any defendant, a jury of one's peers. Consequently, jury panels should include persons with racial, ethnic, religious, economic, and gender attributes that are proportionate to those found in the general population. Jury pools are drawn from voter registrations lists, driver's license lists, tax rolls, and other public records in order to represent all segments of the community. Jury service is a legal responsibility; once called, jurors must serve unless officially excused. We have already discussed the issue of exclusion. As a reminder, jurors may be excused because of physical limitations (poor health, disabilities of hearing or sight, and the like), because they must care for others (children or elderly relatives, for instance), or even in some instances because of their professional responsibilities.

The lists of jurors are then gathered into pools in such a way as to reflect the desire to achieve balance. These pools are then slated for specific cases. Trial judges actually seat the juries on cases following a process known as *voir dire*. During the *voir dire* process, the attorneys (or, in some jurisdictions, the judge) direct questions to the potential jurors to probe for any potential biases. The questions can explore many dimensions of the potential juror's life: their occupation, political beliefs, religious beliefs, personal opinions, hobbies, relatives, reading habits, and so on. During *voir dire,* the attorney seeks to determine if the potential juror is likely to be sympathetic to the client and capable of rendering a verdict in the case. Attorneys also use the *voir dire process* to attempt to establish a relationship with the potential jurors, to make a good impression on the jury, and to begin to win their favor.

There are three types of challenges that can be made to prevent someone from being seated on a jury. First, there is a *challenge to the array*. This is a claim that the entire jury panel was selected in an inappropriate way. Such challenges are very infrequent in contemporary society because most court jurisdictions are very careful in the selection of jury panels. Years ago, however, jury panels were sometimes selected by means that did not assure that the balance of the community was represented. Minorities were often excluded from jury service. Occasionally people could even volunteer to serve on a particular jury. In such cases, the fairness of the jury might be undermined because a juror could hold strong opinions about the case or because jurors were inclined to be sympathetic to one of the parties in the case. Challenges to the array are unlimited in number, but they are rarely sustained by the judge because the procedure for selecting jury panels is usually routine.

A second type of challenge is a *for cause challenge*. In this kind of challenge, an attorney can argue to the judge that a particular juror should be excused because of the inability to be impartial. Someone who has been a victim of rape, for example, might be excused from jury service in a rape trial. Someone who had a close relative who was murdered may be excused from a jury in a murder trial. Close relatives of police officers might be excused from cases where there are charges of police misconduct. Any juror who already has an opinion on the outcome of the case or admits to having learned a great deal about the case through pretrial publicity might also be excluded from the jury for cause. Finally, any juror who admits to racial or ethnic prejudice might be dismissed from a jury for cause. The attorneys in a case have an unlimited number of challenges for cause, but the judge must evaluate and rule on each challenge.

The final type of challenge that can be raised is a *peremptory challenge.* Either attorney can raise these challenges for any reason whatsoever, and they are not required to disclose their reason. Attorneys may decide to eliminate potential jurors because of political views, religious beliefs that might affect judgment, too much or too little education, and so forth. The number of peremptory challenges available to each attorney is limited (and varies by jurisdiction), so they must be exercised very carefully.

The selection of the jury requires thoughtful analysis on the part of the attorney. Attorneys evaluate potential jurors by considering their appearance, expressions, and answers to direct questions. Defense attorneys often probe for jurors who are similar to their client in the case, while prosecutors or plaintiffs search for jurors who are similar to the victim. Conventional wisdom suggests that political liberals tend to favor the defense, while conservatives may favor the prosecution. Minorities may be predisposed to the defense, while Caucasians might be predisposed to the prosecution. While these are stereotypical assumptions, and there are certainly many exceptions, these views do guide attorneys as they select jurors.[16]

Many large law firms hire consultants who specialize in providing litigants with jury selection advice. The consultation is expensive, so typically only the well-heeled litigant can afford to purchase the expertise. Trial consultants may also test the story (or potential stories) planned for the client with focus groups or mock juries that resemble the jury pool. By presenting their cases before mock juries, attorneys may be able to discover which arguments work best, which type of juror is most likely to find in their favor, and even how best to present and organize the arguments in their case.

The pretrial process, while time consuming and potentially expensive, can easily influence the quality and nature of the evidence and arguments made in the courtroom. It can therefore be the difference between winning and losing the entire case.

THE ROLE OF ATTORNEYS IN THE TRIAL

Opening Statement

Once the jury panel is seated, the trial can begin. The prosecutor or the plaintiff begins the trial by presenting an opening statement. The opening statement provides the attorneys an opportunity to introduce their stories of the case briefly and to offer an explanation as to how the evidence will be drawn together to support the case.

The opening statement "should respect the human brain's need for a narrative. It should provide a story with a clear beginning, middle and end."[17] The story should organize the evidence and guide jurors' attention throughout the trial. When jurors retire to deliberate, they should be able to remember the story and the evidence that supported it. Jurors are attracted to stories that reflect their life experiences. If the story in the opening statement resonates with jurors, it influences their perceptions. They attend to and recall evidence that is consistent with their stories, and they forget or reject evidence that is inconsistent.

> Attorneys should recognize that a jury trial is as much a contest of stories as it is a contest of evidence. Jurors do not merely try facts; they tell stories about the facts. Jury selection, then, should be seen as selecting storytellers. Opening statements and closing arguments are opportunities for attorneys to tell stories about the case. Deliberations are jurors' time to trade and refine stories.[18]

The opening statement is probably the most important moment in the case, especially for the prosecution or the plaintiff (for the purpose of clarity, future references will be to the prosecutor or prosecution, and we will assume a criminal rather than civil action is being described). If the case does not immediately seem clear and comprehensible to jurors before the defense has had a chance to speak, it is unlikely that the case can be won. Most of the trial evidence will be presented through the testimony of different witnesses and may come out in a somewhat disorganized and chaotic manner. The opening statement provides a framework for jurors to use in pulling this evidence together. An effective opening statement should stay in their minds throughout the case and should go with them into the jury room. In short, the opening statement provides the prosecutor the opportunity to create the context for the presentation of all the ensuing evidence in the trial.

The defense counsel may waive the right to make an opening statement. Generally, however, the defense will make a brief opening statement if only to alert the jury that the prosecution has the burden to prove its case. Defense attorneys may choose not to make an opening statement if, for instance, they do not yet have a clear story of their own case, they plan a purely refutational case strategy, or they wish to wait to hear their opponent's case before they commit themselves to a particular argumentative strategy.

Direct Examination and Cross-Examination

Following the opening statements, the prosecution presents its case. The legal case is presented through the introduction of the physical evidence and the testimony of relevant witnesses. The evidence becomes the substance of the legal case and can consist of physical evidence (such as contracts, a murder weapon, blood evidence, the drugs seized, etc.) as well as testimony. The prosecutor builds a case through what is known as **direct examination.** Physical evidence such as documents, forensic evidence, and the like are presented through direct examination of a witness. After the prosecutor's questions elicit the relevant evidence from the witness, the defense attorney has the opportunity to ask questions. This is known as **cross-examination.** The process is reversed if the defense chooses to call witnesses. Testimony of a defense witness is elicited through direct examination, and the prosecution then has the opportunity to cross-examine that person. The direct examination and cross-examination portions of the trial are especially important to the trial's outcome. They are the means by which jurors hear the assembled evidence and also the challenges to that evidence.

Unlike on television, however, witnesses rarely melt under the withering questions of the attorneys. There are usually no profound surprises produced during these examinations. If the attorneys have done their pretrial homework, they have a very good idea as to what the witnesses will say in response to their questions. As mentioned previously, neither the prosecutor nor the defense attorney should risk asking a witness a question to which counsel does not already know the likely answer. Doing so could jeopardize the case.

Attorneys develop questions that put their cases in the best possible light and that minimize the credibility of the opponent's stories. Questions are best asked in a simple and straightforward manner and in such a way as to prevent the witnesses from providing lengthy answers. Such elaborations can confuse jurors or raise questions in their minds that would not otherwise occur. Attorneys also try not to antagonize witnesses, even the opponent's witnesses, because it may enhance the witnesses' appeal for the jurors and undermine the attorney's appeal, likability, and trustworthiness.

There are many issues that attorneys must consider in presenting the witnesses in support of their case. Who should be called? In what order should they be called? A primary consideration is how to keep the jury engaged and involved.

> The first witness should set the tone for your case. Maybe a family member who best articulates who the plaintiff was, before and after the injury. Maybe the expert witness with personality, persuasion and international credentials. Build the momentum through each witness's unique role in your story.[19]

In keeping with a good narrative, present the best witnesses at the beginning and end of the case and the weaker witnesses in the middle.

Some people, of course, are better witnesses than others. Ideally a witness should come across as a person of integrity and good moral character who will be believed and viewed sympathetically by the jury. Prosecutors, for example, often call "jailhouse snitches" to the stand to provide testimony against the accused; cell mates report what the defendant may have admitted about their complicity in the crime for which they are charged. Although such testimony can be especially damning to defendants, it is also likely that jurors will be skeptical. The testimony is provided by a witness who likely has a criminal record and who may have been motivated to testify because of a promise of a reduction in their own sentence. The credibility of any witness who might be seen as having a grudge against the defendant or who might benefit by providing testimony will be suspect.

A good witness is also someone who demonstrates a good memory, seems thoughtful and conscientious, provides clear and focused answers, and does not attempt to qualify every answer given. Some witnesses pose unique problems to attorneys, including problems of character (the snitch described above, the convicted felon, the philandering husband, the youth who demonstrates a willingness to fib, etc.), poor communication habits (long-windedness, an antagonistic style, an unpleasant personality, etc.), or certain limitations (for instance, age or infirmities). An attorney who calls such a witness takes a calculated risk as to how the witness will hold up under cross-examination and how the jury will perceive them.

Attorneys also need to consider whether there are weaknesses in the testimony of the witness. Should a potential problem be introduced by the side that called the witness or left to be discovered by the opposing counsel? The wise attorney is careful and conscientious in the construction of the case and weighs the different strategic elements of the case in deciding these issues.

The cross-examination of witnesses is also a great challenge for the attorneys. When examining witnesses whom one has called to testify, one has a good idea as to what the witness will say because the attorney has likely already interviewed them. When cross-examining witnesses who have been called by the other side, however, the situation is far more difficult. The attorney may have learned through pretrial disclosure what the witness is expected to testify about, but the courtroom sometimes provides the first opportunity to speak directly to the witness. It is dangerous to risk asking questions that may strengthen the opposing case by helping witnesses enhance their credibility with the jury. In conducting cross-examinations, the attorney must carefully study the depositions that were introduced and the material evidence that the witness may be presenting. In addition, the attorney should carefully structure and phrase all questions. This is no time for a hunting expedition. A good attorney knows when to stop questioning a witness, so as not to undercut the progress made with a line of questioning. Legal argument expert Ronald Matlon provided the following example of a defense attorney cross-examining a witness.

Q. Where were the defendant and the victim when the fight broke out?
A. In the middle of the field.
Q. Where were you?
A. On the edge of the field.
Q. What were you doing?
A. Bird-watching.
Q. Where were the birds?
A. In the trees.
Q. Where were the trees?
A. On the edge of the field.
Q. Were you looking at the birds?
A. Yes.
Q. So, your back was to the people fighting?
A. Yes.
Q. Well, if your back was to them, how can you say that the defendant bit off the victim's nose?
A. Well, I saw him spit it out.[20]

Attorneys should ask clear and direct questions. They should vary their inflection and pacing so that the examinations do not become monotonous for jurors; and they should always remember that they are working to win jurors over to their side of the case. Consequently, they should not appear to badger or treat the witness rudely, even if the witness is an undesirable character—they do not want the jury to begin to sympathize with the witness rather than with them. The most important thing that attorneys must remember in cross-examination, however, is they must have a strategy in mind. They must know what they hope to accomplish; they must prepare their questions in advance; and they must be able to use the questioning process to tell their story of the evidence and events.

There are some limits to the types of testimony that may be elicited. **Hearsay evidence**, for example, is rarely permitted. You might think that this rule exists because confidence in the testimony would be diminished if it has passed through more than one person. Think of the telephone game where a statement is passed from person to person. By the time it completes its trip around the room, it frequently bears little resemblance to the original statement. The main reason that hearsay evidence is excluded, however, goes back to the philosophy of our system of justice. A key element of that system is the right to confront one's accusers. If someone has evidence to give against a defendant, that person must come forward. The defendant has the right to hear what the person has to say, and the defendant has the right to subject that testimony to the rigors of cross-examination.

Another limitation on testimony is the prohibition against asking witnesses to offer expert opinions unless the witness has been qualified as an expert (credentials are offered and accepted by the court). Witnesses are generally asked only to testify to what they saw—not to speculate as to why someone did something. A psychologist or psychiatrist may be able to explain the motivation behind an act, but most of us are not qualified to render such judgments. The use of experts in courts is another practice that is increasing.

Summary Judgments

Once the prosecution has completed its case, the defense portion of the trial begins. Defense attorneys may make a motion asking the judge to dismiss the complaint on the grounds that the prosecution's case is insufficient to overcome a reasonable doubt—that the prosecution has failed to present a *prima facie* case (see chapter 11). Such motions, **summary judgments**, are usually dismissed by the judge. As already mentioned, court dockets are so crowded that very few frivolous cases make their way to trial. In rare circumstances—a key prosecution witness did not show up to testify or the defense counsel's cross-examination shredded the testimony of the prosecution's witnesses—the judge may grant a summary judgment. If granted, the trial ends and the complaint against the defendant is dismissed. More likely, however, the judge will rule that the prosecution has met the burden of overcoming reasonable doubt, and the defense will be instructed to present its case. The defense now has the opportunity to call to the stand and examine its own witnesses.

One question that defense attorneys must consider is whether or not to call the defendant to testify. Jurors naturally prefer to hear defendants speak on their own behalf—to tell their stories to clear their names. To put defendants on the stand, however, means that they will be subject to cross-examination by the prosecution. Many, if not most defense attorneys, decide that the risk is too great that the defendant will admit to information during cross-examination that damages the case and increases the risk of conviction. Thus, defendants usually plead their Fifth Amendment right not to testify. Judges instruct jurors, prior to the start of deliberations, not to take a refusal to testify as evidence of guilt.

Although the prosecution must show a crime was committed and that the defendant had the motive, opportunity, and means to commit the crime, the defense can win if it raises substantial doubt about just one of those issues. For example, the defense may be able to provide an alibi for the time during which the crime was committed. Or the defense may raise substantial doubt about the defendant's ability to commit the crime as described by the prosecution. Or the defense may raise the possibility that there are others who had a better motive, opportunity, or means to commit the crime.

Closing Arguments

Following the presentation of the defense case, the trial proceeds to the closing-arguments phase. The prosecution presents its closing argument first, then the defense, and the prosecution has the option to conclude the trial with a rebuttal. Closing arguments allow the attorneys to pull the evidence and testimony together and to again tell their stories. Attorneys cannot use these speeches to present new evidence to the court. The time for introducing evidence is now past. Rather, the attorneys must assemble the evidence presented, both pro and con, into a coherent narrative for the jury.

The prosecution obviously tries to tell as coherent and complete a story of the events as possible. Loose ends prove especially dangerous to the prosecutor's case, so there is an attempt to demonstrate that the narrative has probability and that it rings true with the way we know people act. The defense clearly wants to discredit this story, to find flaws in it that will convince the jury the defendant should not be found guilty.

Attorneys must be careful in closing arguments to faithfully recount the facts that were presented in the case. If the evidence is inaccurately described at this point, the opposing counsel will almost certainly object. The attorneys also must decide what the key facts are in their case and what facts they want to emphasize. They probably do not want to rehash all of the minor details. Finally, it is important that the attorneys attempt to predict the flaws in their own case and preempt arguments that either the opposing counsel or the jurors themselves might advance as they consider the evidence. The attorney who can predict the key turning points in the case and resolve jurors' uncertainties regarding those turning points will have a better chance of securing a favorable verdict.

Closing arguments also offer attorneys a final opportunity to win over the jurors with their communication skills. Attorneys attempt to communicate their competence, fairness, and thoroughness in presenting their cases. Often, they will resort to emotional appeals in their closing arguments in order to win sympathy and empathy for their clients or for the victims. If the attorneys made the right choices in jury selection, they should have created a panel that will be open to those arguments. They will now take full advantage of these sympathies and win the jurors over to their case. It is especially important that the closing argument be simple, straightforward, and easy to follow. Often the attorneys will draw upon analogies and metaphors. As discussed in previous chapters, these techniques are proven and effective storytelling devices.

Decision Making

Once the attorneys have presented their closing arguments, the judge will instruct the jurors as to their responsibilities, commonly known as the judge's charge to the jury. This portion of the trial is extremely important to the outcome. The judge creates the context in which the other information in the trial is to be considered. Judges direct the jurors about the law, about the admissibility of certain evidence, about their obligations in reviewing the relevant evidence, and about their burdens in delivering a fair and impartial verdict. Jurors are also reminded of the standards—beyond a reasonable doubt or the preponderance of evidence—they should apply in reaching a verdict. Some jurisdictions provide the judge with what are called *pattern instructions*. These instructions are standardized to fit the nature of the charge and to reflect the statutory rules of the particular jurisdiction. Standardized instructions, however, frequently do not address the needs of the specific case under review, so judges often add other guiding statements to these standardized instructions.

Once the judge has charged them, the jurors are sent to their chambers to deliberate and to reach a verdict. In the jury room, the competing stories told by the opposing counsels are subjected to close scrutiny. The jurors may ask to reread portions of trial testimony, examine the physical evidence again, and ask questions of the judge, which are relayed through the court's bailiff. Jurors should not have discussed with each other or anyone else their opinions of the case or the evidence prior to being sequestered in the jury room. Once the case is in the jurors' hands, the attorneys can have no further effect on the trial outcome. They can only wait along with the victims and the defendants for the verdict to be read.

When the jurors have reached their verdict, the participants in the case are reassembled in the courtroom, and the verdict is handed over to the bailiff and announced. The attorneys will often interview the jurors to discover why they ruled as they did and to try to learn more about why their case strategy either succeeded or failed to persuade the jurors.

SUMMARY

The law is an especially important focus for argumentation. Attorneys use their argumentation skills in virtually every dimension of their professional lives—from their initial conversations with their clients, to the negotiations and settlement conferences they conduct, to the depositions and fact-finding phase, and finally in the courtroom. Many of the principles of effective argumentation discussed in this text are on full display in the courtroom. Advocates rely on a storytelling argumentative approach, and jurors make their decisions based upon their judgments of who told the better story. Thus, a course in argumentation should help you to be a more effective juror if called. In this argument field, as in many others, the emphasis should be placed on careful research and preparation. A well-researched and reasoned case theory is more likely to win over the jury.

KEY TERMS

adversarial
burden of proof
civil
criminal
cross-examination

direct examination
discovery
exclusionary rule
hearsay evidence
precedent

preponderance of evidence
reasonable doubt
summary judgments
theory of the case

ACTIVITIES

1. Attend a criminal trial and observe the presentation of the opening arguments. Try to ascertain the theory of the case developed by each side. Evaluate the opening statements in terms of their narrative probability and narrative fidelity.

2. Observe a criminal trial during the examination and cross-examination phases. Which lawyer most successfully examined witnesses? Which lawyer seemed to stumble? Why? What attributes did the best witnesses exhibit? What attributes did the weaker witnesses exhibit?

3. Observe a criminal trial during the closing statements. Which side had the better arguments? Why?

4. We have elsewhere described the importance of symbols and rituals. The courtroom is replete with both. Which ones did you observe? Why were they significant? What did they communicate to the litigants?

5. Observe a jury trial and watch the jury for their nonverbal cues. What did you see? What seemed to prompt their responses?
6. Visit a small claims court and compare what transpires there with what went on in other courtrooms that you visited. How did the participation of untrained citizen advocates impact the proceedings? What accommodations did the court make as a result?

Recommended Readings

Beach, Wayne A., "Temporal Density in Courtroom Interaction: Constraints on the Recovery of Past Events in Legal Discourse," *Communication Monographs* 52 (1985): 1–18.

Benoit, William L., "Attorney Argumentation and Supreme Court Opinions," *Argumentation and Advocacy* 26 (1989): 22–38.

Bycel, Ben, H. Mitchell Caldwell, and Michael S. Lief, *Ladies and Gentlemen of the Jury: Greatest Closing Arguments in Modern Law* (New York: Scribner, 2000).

Feteris, Eveline T., *Fundamentals of Legal Argumentation: A Survey of Theories on the Justification of Judicial Decisions,* 2nd ed. (Dordrecht: Springer, 2017).

Hollihan, Thomas A., Patricia Riley, and Keith Freadhoff, "Arguing for Justice: An Analysis of Arguing in Small Claims Court," *Journal of the American Forensic Association* 22 (1986): 187–195.

Huhn, Wilson R., *Five Types of Legal Arguments,* 3rd ed. (Durham, NC: Carolina Academic Press, 2014).

Larson, Brian N., "Law's Enterprise: Argumentation Schemes and Legal Analogy," *University of Cincinnati Law Review* 87 (2019): 663–721.

Pakken, Henry and Giovanni Sartor, "Law and Logic: A Review from an Argumentation Perspective," *Artificial Intelligence* 227 (2015): 214–245.

Walton, Douglas, *Legal Argumentation and Evidence* (University Park: Penn State University Press, 2002).

Worthington, Debra L. and David G. Levasseur, "Charity and the American Jury: Exploring the Relationship between Plaintiff's Need-Based Arguments and Mock Juror Verdicts in Medical Malpractice Suits," *Argumentation and Advocacy* 39 (2002): 23–29.

Endnotes

[1] Cited by Jeff Jacoby, "US Legal Bubble Can't Pop Soon Enough," *Boston Globe,* May 9, 2014. https://www.bostonglobe.com/opinion/2014/05/09/the-lawyer-bubble-pops-not-moment-too-soon/qAYzQ823qpfi4GQl2OiPZM/story.html

[2] "Number of Lawyers in the United States from 2007–2020," *Statista,* August 2021. https://www.statista.com/statistics/740222/number-of-lawyers-us/

[3] Minnesota Judicial Branch-27-CR-20-12646: State vs. Derek Chauvin, https://mncourts.gov/StateofMinnesotavDerekChauvin

[4] John Gramlich, "Only 2% of Federal Criminal Defendants Go to Trial, and Most Who Do Are Found Guilty," Pew Research, June 11, 2019. https://www.pewresearch.org/fact-tank/2019/06/11/only-2-of-federal-criminal-defendants-go-to-trial-and-most-who-do-are-found-guilty/

[5] Anna Leigh Firth, "Here's How Often Trial Judges Disagree with a Jury's Verdict," *The National Judicial Council,* August 27, 2019. https://www.judges.org/news-and-info/heres-how-often-trial-judges-disagree-with-a-jurys-verdict/

[6] Jury Nullification. FindLaw, February 27, 2019. https://www.findlaw.com/criminal/criminal-procedure/jury-nullification.html

[7] Paul Walsh and Hannah Sayle, "Who Are the Jurors in the Derek Chauvin Trial?" *Star Tribune,* April 19, 2021. https://www.startribune.com/who-are-the-jurors-in-the-derek-chauvin-trial-for-the-killing-of-george-floyd-in-minneapolis/600037651/

8. Torey Van Oot and Nick Halter, "Toward Healing and Calm," *Axios*, April 20, 2021. https://www.axios.com/epicenter-for-change-25de5a92-a9e8-45c0-9d85-65cbefc68bcd.html
9. Nacente S. Seabury, "Diversity Matters: Confronting Implicit Bias with Jury Diversity," American Bar Association, August 28, 2016. https://www.americanbar.org/groups/litigation/committees/commercial-business/practice/2016/diversity-matters-confronting-implicit-bias-jury-diversity/
10. "CALCRIM No. 103. Reasonable Doubt," *Justia*, October 2020. https://www.justia.com/criminal/docs/calcrim/100/103/
11. John M. Broder and Nick Madigan, "Michael Jackson Cleared After 14-Week Child Molesting Trial," *New York Times*, June 14, 2005. https://www.nytimes.com/2005/06/14/us/michael-jackson-cleared-after-14week-child-molesting-trial.html. The case was also the subject of an award-winning documentary *Leaving Neverland* in 2019. https://www.youtube.com/watch?v=YJ_fdLQ2on4
12. Ben Sisario, "What We Know About Michael Jackson's History of Sexual Abuse Accusations," *The New York Times*, January 31, 2019. https://www.nytimes.com/2019/01/31/arts/music/michael-jackson-timeline-sexual-abuse-accusations.html
13. W. Lance Bennett and Martha S. Feldman, *Reconstructing Reality in the Courtroom: Justice and Judgment in American Culture*, 2nd ed. (New Orleans: Quid Pro Books, 2014), 4.
14. Ibid., pp. 4–9.
15. Ibid., p. 9.
16. For a discussion of the jury selection process see, for example, John F. Denove, "Everything You Wanted to Know About Voir Dire," *Advocate Magazine*, January, 2018. https://www.advocatemagazine.com/images/issues/2018/01-january/reprints/Denove_article.pdf
17. Drury Sherrod, "When It Comes to Jury Trials, Should You Tell a Story or Stick to the Facts?" *ABA Journal*, April 11, 2019. https://www.abajournal.com/voice/article/the-jury-trial-trying-facts-or-telling-stories
18. Ibid.
19. Pamela Pantages, "Storytelling at Trial: Beginning, a Middle and an End." *Advocate*, January 2019. https://www.advocatemagazine.com/article/2019-january/storytelling-at-trial-beginning-a-middle-and-an-end
20. Ronald J. Matlon, *Communication in the Legal Process* (New York: Holt, Rinehart and Winston, 1988), 236.

15

Argumentation in Business and Organizations

The principles of argumentation that we have discussed in this book are not theoretical abstractions to commit to memory, regurgitate on a final examination, and then forget. Instead, these are concepts that you will use—whether or not you are conscious of them—throughout your daily life. Although most of you will not participate in formal academic debates once you have finished this class, and some of you may never be asked to create or evaluate arguments in a courtroom, all of you will find yourselves creating arguments in your workplace. As members of business, governmental, academic, or professional organizations you will often be called upon to develop arguments in support of your positions. We have designed this chapter as a useful and pragmatic guide to help you prepare for your professional careers. We want to help you develop the skills necessary to achieve effective advocacy in the workplace.

This chapter will help you learn to analyze the kinds of issues that are significant in business and organizational settings and then to advocate your positions in a forceful and convincing manner. We will suggest how you should prepare your arguments, assess your audience, create and present your messages, defend your ideas, and follow up on your presentations. The goal is to help you learn how to promote your ideas—and yourself—in an organization. In chapter 1 we discussed the distinction between argument1, the claims people make, and argument2, interactions characterized by disagreement. In this chapter we will be considering both types of argument.

COMPETING INTERESTS IN ORGANIZATIONS

As is the case in other argumentative contexts, organizational arguers typically make use of narratives and evaluate arguments on the basis of their appeal as stories. In fact, many organizations have developed "company stories" that are often embedded within and integral to the formation of the *organizational culture* that defines the organization and distinguishes it from its competitors. Michael Watkins, a professor at IMD business school in Switzerland, argued that organizational cultures evolve over time in response to "situational pressures" and that they serve to prevent "wrong thinking" and "wrong people" from being hired or from taking command of organizations.[1]

Culture is a social control system. Here the focus is the role of culture in promoting and reinforcing "right" thinking and behaving and sanctioning "wrong" thinking and behaving. Key in this definition of culture is the idea of behavioral "norms" that must be upheld and associated social sanctions that are imposed on those who don't "stay within the lines." This view also focuses attention on how the evolution of the organization shaped the culture. That is, how have the existing norms promoted the survival of the organization in the past? Note: implicit in this evolutionary view is the idea that established cultures can become impediments to survival when there are substantial environmental changes.

The challenge, of course, is that organizational culture can also "attack agents of *needed* change," and this often poses real challenges to organizations that must adapt to thrive or even survive in new markets or situational contexts.[2]

The stories that carry and animate the organizational culture are influenced by the broader culture of the societies in which organizations conduct their operations. This is evident in the differences and tensions that exist for organizations conducting their enterprise in multiple local, regional, and national cultures. You may have experienced such differences, for example, when you have visited large national chain stories or fast food outlets in different parts of the world. While the success of such businesses is often derived from their predictable "sameness"—a Starbucks will be much the same in Seattle, New York, London, Beijing, or Tokyo—the need to accommodate to local tastes and sensibilities creates a challenge for organizations seeking to maintain a unified culture while also acknowledging and rewarding local interests.[3]

Organizations are composed of people with different levels and types of education, expertise, and experiences. Organization members also have different opinions, worldviews, goals, and often competing interests. Nevertheless, as organizational citizens they are bound together to perform tasks and to produce goods or services.[4] Members of organizational systems transform inputs into finished products or outputs. Communication among the members of the organization is necessary to accomplish tasks. Because of the differences mentioned above, organizational participants will at times find themselves in conflict. People differ about how best to do their jobs and how best to help their organization compete and prosper. Allowing appropriate space for the airing of such differences can resolve conflicts and help people deliberate and make decisions based on well-reasoned arguments.

In a large and complex business organization, for example, you may find many different divisions. The objectives, problems, goals, and interests of these different units may be a natural cause for disagreements that can be resolved through productive arguments. Thus, the cultures of organizations are never monolithic. Divisions compete for resources, attention, and rewards. For example, a business organization may have divisions for research and development, manufacturing, quality control, marketing and sales, accounting and financial affairs, customer service, human resources, and legal affairs. Even though the executives from these different divisions all work for the same company and should be pursuing enterprise objectives that work for the benefit of that company, their different tasks, responsibilities, backgrounds, specializations, and personalities often lead them to very different views of how their company should be run and what decision outcomes will best serve the company's interests.

- *Accounting and Financial Affairs Division.* Executives from this division are especially concerned with the company's bottom line, with the return on investments, with the return of value to shareholders, and (for publicly traded companies) with the performance of the company on the stock market. These executives are sometimes referred to disparagingly as the "bean counters." They want to improve income and reduce expenses. They worry about complying with accepted accounting and audit requirements and with securities and taxation laws. They tend to be protective of the company's assets and may be reluctant to commit funds for developing new products, expanding into new market areas, purchasing new plants or equipment, hiring more employees, or increasing employee compensation packages.

- *Research and Development (R&D) Division.* Executives from this division are charged with developing new products and improving current products. They are the company's dreamers and are always thinking about the future. In successful organizations, especially in rapidly changing industries, the people in this division must be highly creative. They seek funding for technology enhancements, cutting-edge facilities, highly expert employees, and innovative new materials and practices that they believe will help improve the company's ability to continue to achieve success. They may have less concern about what their recommendations will cost, how difficult these new products may be to produce, or even whether or not there is a market for them. One can easily identify companies that had a very strong presence in their industry but failed to keep up with new developments and either contracted or failed. One frequently cited example is Eastman Kodak. The company dominated the manufacture of cameras, film, and film processing for decades. When it failed to keep up with new developments in digital technology, it was forced into bankruptcy in 2012. Although the company continues to this day, it is a mere shell of its former self.[5]

- *Manufacturing Division.* Those who work in manufacturing are keenly aware of how difficult it is to produce new products. They may be reluctant to take on new product lines and eager to continue operating as they always have in order to get their current products out on schedule, keep a ready flow of spare parts available, and maintain a stable and sufficiently trained workforce. New products require development money, new training programs, and are often prone to performance problems. Manufacturing division executives frequently think that new products require access to resources to hire new employees, secure more floor space, and purchase new equipment—money that the "bean counters" are reluctant to provide them. For a recent example of a manufacturing division that had difficulty meeting its schedule and quality commitments one can consider the challenges that the pharmaceutical company Johnson and Johnson faced in delivering its highly touted single dose vaccine for the recent coronavirus pandemic.[6]

- *Quality Control Division.* Executives working in this part of the organization are charged with identifying potential problems in products, taking appropriate corrective actions, and assuring the highest standards of production. Because this division primarily acts to prevent an increase in costs rather than to produce new revenue sources, workers in this division tend to attract less attention and may have greater difficulty securing resources than those in divisions that either create and/or manufacture flashy new products. The importance of this division is often not realized until problems emerge, and then it is sometimes too late to avoid costly damage to the company's reputation. A recent example of such quality challenges would include the problems with the new software system installed on the Boeing 737 Max airliner. The new software led to two crashes, the loss of many lives, and a costly and reputation-damaging temporary grounding of the expensive new airplane.[7]

- *Marketing and Sales Division.* The executives from the marketing and sales division are concerned with selling the products. Consequently, they want to market the innovative and new products developed by the R & D division, but they also do not want to undermine the secure markets and market share of existing products. They want products and spare parts available on time, and they want reliable products that they are able to sell at the most competitive prices. These conflicting demands clearly put pressure on all of the other divisions but especially create headaches for the "bean counters" who are always focused on reducing costs and increasing profit margins.

- *Human Resources (HR) Division.* This division is responsible for recruiting, hiring, maintaining, and right sizing the employees that carry out the work of the company. All of the other divisions of the company depend on the ability to find and promote the right people for the different tasks that must be performed. Obviously, the company culture will be damaged if this division does not have a knack for identifying the right skill sets and personality types to propel the company toward excellence. In addition, this division must assure that company policies regarding issues such as discrimination, sexual harassment, and ethics and integrity are shared, taught, reinforced, and evaluated. The HR division must also address such issues as appropriate compensation, succession planning, promotions, and retirement programs. The most important predictor of employee job satisfaction is the relationship that employees have with their coworkers and immediate supervisors. These relationships are essential to the creation of a positive corporate culture. Walmart is an example of a company that suffered from devastatingly bad publicity regarding the abuse of its workers. It was reported that the discount chain locked its employees into its stores at night, prohibiting them from leaving the work site even if they were injured or faced some medical necessity.[8]

- *Customer Service Division.* Executives in this division are charged with keeping the company's customers satisfied and helping them learn to maximize the use of the products they have purchased. This division helps insure that warranties are met; replacement parts, maintenance services, and repairs are provided; and customer questions, concerns, and complaints receive timely and appropriate responses. Like the quality control division, customer service is often not a flashy part of the company. In many companies, it is a cost center that does not provide substantial new revenues. It is thus often a division that may be underappreciated until problems emerge. Recall how badly the Volkswagen and Audi brands were damaged when it was discovered that executives in the company intentionally installed "software in diesel engines that could detect when they were being tested, changing the performance accordingly to improve results. The German car giant has since admitted cheating emissions tests in the US."[9] The company faced steep fines imposed by different nations around the world, was forced to buy-back or compensate many owners of VW and Audi vehicles, and was challenged with the difficult task of rehabilitating its reputation and winning back the trust of its customers.

- *Legal Affairs Division.* The role of the legal department is to mitigate risk and prevent the company from being damaged in costly tort litigation or from facing fines or injunctions for failure to meet applicable legal requirements. One can imagine how busy the attorneys were in the VW and Audi example mentioned above. Executives in other divisions sometimes characterize the attorneys as operating in the "Land of No" because they so often subject new initiatives or business decisions that the other divisions may wish to pursue to roadblocks because of perceived legal risks. Avoiding costly litigation may mean keeping an eye on environmental issues (such as the disposal of hazardous waste), employment issues (such as discrimination or harassment), fulfillment of contract obligations (such as financial terms, delivery commitments, pricing terms, etc.), patent infringements, etc.

As should be apparent from the examples provided, complex organizations are made up of divisions whose interests, obligations, objectives, and problems often put them at odds with each other. A well-managed and successful company needs strong, effective, rational, and articulate executives. The leaders of each division must represent the unique interests and concerns of their division and of the employees within their units in discussions with the senior leadership team, especially with regard to business strategies and the allocation of resources. If any division is poorly led or does not make its interests known, the entire company might suffer. The examples that we have cited above of companies where certain divisions failed to secure the appropriate resources or to achieve their desired outcomes suggest that the argumentative, deliberative, accountability, and ethical cultures of these organizations were inadequate to propel them to success.

Please notice, however, that even if all of these divisions are led by strong and articulate advocates, each focused primarily on pursuing the interests of their business units, there will be conflicts regarding where new resources—new employees, investments in technology, dollars for the development of new products, processes or policies, time and money devoted to promotion, marketing, and advertising, etc.—should flow to maximize profits and help the company meet its goals. Often the interests of these divisions create conflicts and tensions. For example, audits are burdensome and often require significant time and attention that takes executives away from their core responsibilities; yet audits are essential to the success of the enterprise. Likewise, a major focus on customer service is very helpful to a company, but it may also be costly if it entails liberal policies on warranties, commitments to replace faulty products without charging the customers, and other goodwill practices that do not generate quantifiable benefits.

In our earlier discussion on fields of arguments (chapter 3) we discussed how different situations or contexts require different standards for argument. Executives who work in the various divisions of the company are often going to reflect different fields of expertise, educational and professional training; as a result, they draw on different forms of data and warrants to construct their arguments. The divisions mentioned above, for example, might draw upon engineers, chemists, material scientists, accountants, psychologists, communication experts, and attorneys to fill their ranks. Those who win promotion to the top leadership positions in organizations will likely make their way to the executive suite because companies identify in them the particular skill sets, experience, and expertise deemed especially important to that company.

Chief executive officers (CEOs) are hired and are often paid very generous salaries and healthy bonuses because they know how to make tough decisions and guide companies through deliberative management processes. In complex technical organizations, there are often specific jobs that are well beyond the expertise of the senior leadership team. To evaluate conflicting argument claims to prioritize certain issues and to direct scarce resources, successful leaders must learn good listening and analytical skills. Effective CEOs must also learn how to articulate a corporate strategic vision that helps their subordinates understand and contribute to the goals of maximizing the success of the organization. Certainly, some CEOs are more effective than others and make better decisions. CEOs are more likely to achieve success if they establish a healthy deliberative culture that rewards the creation of arguments that reflect the intertwined interests and priorities of the different parts of the organization.

Organizational conflicts are often productive and necessary.[10] Arguers in organizations should not assume that their colleagues already know the facts and understand their thinking. Instead, they should view their argumentation as an opportunity to enlighten and inform their colleagues. In addition, it is important that organizational arguers not see conflicts as zero-sum games with winners and losers. They should address conflicts using arguments to initiate an investigative process that enables decision makers to choose the best course of action. This means that advocates should avoid personality attacks or personalizing the arguments directed against them. Arguments should be seen as a natural and important part of an organization's daily activity.

Preparing Arguments to Meet Objectives

The first consideration in developing arguments in an organizational setting, as in any other setting, is to clarify your objectives. What do you hope to accomplish? People may argue for many reasons: to advance an issue they believe is especially important, to effect change in the way the organization conducts its business or operates, to secure resources for a new project or processes, to promote themselves or their work unit, or to defend themselves or their unit from attack or criticism. It is important for you to have a clear idea of precisely what your purpose is before you develop your arguments. If your ideas are unclear and your objectives are not well-defined and carefully considered, you risk undercutting your purpose. For instance, say you want to argue on behalf of a new innovation that reduces the layers of bureaucracy in order to streamline your company and help it operate more efficiently and profitably. This argument could backfire if the executives who must approve your proposal believe that their jobs or their authority reside in the layer of bureaucracy that you believe is bothersome and should be eliminated. Carefully consider what you hope to accomplish and how you intend to go about accomplishing it before going public with your arguments.

Carefully assess the accepted communication or argumentation style in your organization. Different organizations reflect very different communication cultures. Some are friendly, supportive, and informal. In such organizations, the chain of command may be more loosely followed and the executives may be open to interactions from subordinate employees. The style of interaction in such organizations tends to be relaxed. Our students who have gone on to careers in Silicon Valley technology companies often report that their organizations are defined by such cultures. Other organizations are very formal and require communication to flow along specific paths that conform to the organization's hierarchy. In such an organization, interactions might be tense, people may be closed and somewhat cautious in their interactions with one another, and there may be an emphasis on preserving an explicit chain of command. Such organizations may repress conflict and discourage open disagreements.

One of the authors of this text has served as a communication consultant for various U.S. Navy commands. The Navy has an organizational culture where information tends to flow downward much more easily than upward. In this type of culture, it is profoundly difficult to challenge the decisions or perspectives of the commanders. One of the consulting projects involved the reduction of mishaps that damaged assets (e.g., ships, aircraft, weapons systems, computing systems, etc.) and/or caused injuries or even deaths. Mishaps covered a broad range—from a burned hand in a galley, a fall from a ladder, to the loss of a ship, submarine, or aircraft. The command wanted to create "situational awareness" where sailors actively assessed the risks, benefits, and alternative ways of approaching tasks. For example, if a sailor was given an order to crawl under a stalled Humvee on a muddy roadside shoulder to make a minor repair, they should assess whether it was safe to do so and if proper tools (i.e., a jack and jack stands to stabilize the vehicle) were available and could be safely and appropriately used given the conditions. If the conditions were not deemed safe, the sailor should be able to explain this to the superior officer who gave the order, and an alternative strategy should be developed. Challenging authority in such a culture, however, is never easy and is usually disapproved. Consider another example—a helicopter is ordered to pick up troops wounded on a battlefield. Those in command must assess the situation and determine whether the risk of losing additional troops and the helicopter due to adverse weather conditions or live fire outweighs the prospects for the mission's success. These are difficult decisions and instances where passion may triumph over wise judgment.

Still other organizations are shaped by cultures that are highly contentious. In these organizations conflict not only might be very common but also accepted as the norm. People feel free to openly disagree with each other and perhaps even to show signs of bad temper and a willingness to mock and humiliate colleagues. Our students and colleagues who work in the entertainment industry in Los Angeles tell us that this is the norm for their organizations. Such an organizational culture was revealed in the hack of emails from the Sony corporation a few years ago. The emails revealed a corporate suite populated by executives who made crass, unkind, demeaning, and even sexist or racist remarks about colleagues and others with whom they worked.[11] We can only hope that this organization, and others like it, have improved their organizational culture as a result of the "Me Too" Movement.

You will need to determine the nature of the organization that you have joined and respond accordingly. We are not, of course, encouraging you to adopt the negative elements of the communication style of your organization—particularly not communication that demeans or humiliates others. Everything we know about successful organizations suggests that such practices diminish organizational effectiveness, suppress creativity, increase employee turnover, and expose members and the organization to lawsuits and public embarrassment. We are saying, however, that you should take care not to violate important communication standards and practices of the organization because doing so will likely diminish your effectiveness as an advocate and might create discomfort and problems for you and your coworkers.

It is important to assess the audience for your arguments. Consider who ultimately makes the decision about the issues you intend to address. Once you have determined the decision maker, you can evaluate what this person might be looking for when they ponder the alternatives presented. What issues are most likely of interest to this person? Do the job requirements or time and experience with the company suggest a particular perspective? Has the person worked at another company? Does academic training shape reactions? What values or goals seem to influence judgments and how do these values or goals align with your objectives and arguments? What do you think keeps this person up at night worrying? If you can understand this, you may be able to create a sense of urgency regarding the arguments you are advancing. This is sometimes referred to as finding a "burning platform" that requires action—hopefully action that aligns with the arguments you are advocating.

Often the audience for your arguments in an organizational setting is your immediate boss. Consequently, you should always consider how to make arguments that your boss will find persuasive. Keep in mind, one way for you to prosper in an organization is to make your boss look good, which can have positive consequences for you.[12] Remember, in crafting and presenting your arguments, your boss is an ordinary person with biases, fears, preoccupations, goals, strengths, weaknesses, and so forth. Too often bosses make poor decisions because they have been poorly trained, are ill prepared for their jobs, or because they fail to get good information either from superiors, subordinates, or both. Subordinates may distort information to protect their own interests or because they fear relaying bad news. Superiors may keep subordinates in the dark because of a lack of trust or respect for subordinates or to protect their own power.[13] Your task as an arguer is to identify your boss's interests and objectives, be aware of idiosyncrasies, and adapt your arguments and strategies accordingly.[14] You should make every attempt to supply your boss with the information, evidence, and analysis necessary to make the best possible decisions that will improve the prospects for the success of your organization.

SHAPING THE MESSAGE: DEVISING STRATEGIES

Once you have decided what your objectives are and considered the audience to whom your arguments will be addressed, it is appropriate for you to consider from what vantage point you are arguing. What is your position in the company? How much authority, credibility, and *power* do you really have? If you have just been hired at an entry position, you may find that your ideas about how the company ought to be restructured will not receive much consideration. If, on the other hand, you entered the organization in a position of authority, your opinions and expertise are a source of worth to the organization. As a result, it is more likely that you will find a willing audience to listen to your arguments. Careful consideration of your resources will help prevent you from overplaying your hand and getting yourself in trouble. It will also help you understand that you are in an uphill fight against someone who holds a lot more power and influence than you do. Create your argument strategies to accommodate your vantage point.

In addition to assessing your power in the organization you should begin to form *coalitions* for support.[15] Before brashly going to your boss, you should cultivate support for the positions you want to advance from peers and from other important people in your organization who can help enhance your position and lend credibility to it. They may also provide what are known as "prestige referrals" that are, in a sense, somewhat like endorsements in a political campaign. If other people do not support your ideas, their feedback enables you to reshape or bolster your arguments—or perhaps to reconsider their merit. The feedback will help you understand your organization's and your coworkers' beliefs so that you can prepare for future argumentative encounters.

There are some strategies that you can consider using if you find yourself at odds with a more powerful organizational advocate. You can seek out a mentor who might sponsor your position and also help protect you from the flak that your idea might create in the organization. Ideally your mentor is someone at least as powerful as your principal potential adversary or is someone who has the credibility and organizational stature to be respected in the organization. Second, when you present your suggestions to your boss, you can encourage your boss to take "ownership" and become an advocate for your ideas. One important way to do this is to convince your boss that your idea grew from your shared outlook.

You should always think very carefully about who is likely to resist your arguments. Whose ox will be gored by your proposal? Whose interests will be undercut? How might these potential adversaries either be persuaded to come over to your side or, failing that, be neutralized? How much power in the organization do your adversaries have and how entrenched are their views? Who will likely choose to ally themselves with you and who will ally with your adversaries in the event of a confrontation? What compromises or accommodations might you offer that will win over those individuals? It is certainly preferable not to face determined and powerful adversaries, so how can you avoid such situations?

You should plan strategies for presenting your arguments in a manner that discourages opposition without undercutting your objectives. For example, perhaps you wish to propose a solution to a problem that you have identified in your organization, but there will be active resistance to your proposals. You might consider presenting two alternative scenarios as potential solutions to the problem. The first scenario might be a conservative, inexpensive, and perhaps easily enacted one, but also one that can be demonstrably shown as inadequate to fully solve the problem. The second scenario, in contrast, might be complex and expensive, replete with "bells and whistles." Although this scenario would solve the problem, its cost and complexity might make it less than acceptable. After your superior has shot down these two scenarios, you can mention a third—the one you actually favored all along—as a compromise to the first two. Scenario three, which might not have received careful consideration if proposed initially or individually, might now seem like a very reasonable approach compared to the first two scenarios.

In creating your arguments, do not forget the importance of careful preparation. To succeed as an organizational advocate, you must do your homework. You should begin by reviewing previous arguments that have been made in your organization regarding the issue that you are addressing. When the issue has come up for discussion before, how did the advocates express their claims? What were the outcomes of those prior discussions? What happened as a result of the decisions reached following those conversations? Were those results positive or negative? What historical lessons should you and your supervisors learn from these prior discussions and the decisions that followed them? What circumstances or conditions have changed in the time since? How do these changes impact the current argumentative situation?

You must also be careful to tailor your arguments to the primary decision maker(s) whom you are addressing. Be mindful of our earlier discussion of field theory (chapter 3). People in different fields often evaluate arguments differently. If you are talking to engineers, you need to adapt to that argument field. If you are talking to psychologists, you want to adapt your arguments to the forms of reasoning in that field. You should also take care to assess the extent to which the audience you are addressing has prior knowledge, expertise, or understanding of the issues you are raising. Often you will have far greater expertise on the issue being discussed than will the person to whom you are appealing. Do not presume that the person fully knows what you know; try to adapt your arguments and your examples your audience's areas of expertise and experience.

This situation is especially common in today's complex organizations where work tasks often require narrowly trained specialists who understand the details of very technical subjects but who must report to senior executives who lack such specialized knowledge. Perhaps these executives came from another branch or division of the company, or perhaps the technological advances in the industry have occurred at a very rapid rate and have left the executives unprepared for the kinds of problems now being faced. In computer science, for example, it is increasingly common that graduates who recently received their degrees have much more technological expertise than managers with decades of experience in their fields. Regardless of the reason, managers often report that they lack the expertise possessed by the people whom they supervise. Making effective decisions in such complex, technical areas of organizations takes concerted effort by superiors and subordinates alike to create a collaborative communication culture that helps foster understanding and that respects the value of reasoned disagreement as much as it does consensus.

You should pay special attention to the use of technical language or insider *jargon* in the arguments you present. If your listeners do not share your technical vocabulary, they are not likely to follow your arguments. Often people are very reluctant to ask for explanations or definitions because they feel that doing so reveals how little they understand and that they will be seen as ignorant or uninformed.[16] Be careful, however, not to demean the intelligence, background, or experience of your audience. Nothing puts people off more quickly than believing that someone has talked down to them. Assess the background of your audience before you begin your presentation; adapt your language to that background; define any terms that may be unknown to your audience; and carefully assess the feedback you receive.[17]

You should also carefully consider the alternative formats available for sharing your arguments. Sometimes it is preferable to write an email or a memorandum advocating your position. Sometimes a phone call is better. At other times you may need to request a one-on-one meeting or perhaps a formal briefing. You can decide which form of communication is appropriate based on several factors.

1. How many people will have to be involved in the implementation of your ideas? The more people who need to be involved, the more interaction is probably needed to plan and discuss the proposal. If face-to-face meetings take place during the planning of the innovations, it may be easier to convince people to accept the innovations and less reason for criticisms later.[18]

2. How complex are the issues that you are trying to communicate? The more complex an idea is the more people will feel a need to discuss it in order to gain confidence that they fully understand it.

3. How many feathers will be ruffled by your arguments? This, of course, requires a consideration of organizational politics. How much resistance do you anticipate? If you do anticipate encountering resistance to your ideas, it is probably best to present them in a briefing meeting. A memorandum can be too conveniently ignored, and an email is too easily forwarded to others for comment, perhaps in the process widening and deepening potential opposition to your ideas. A phone call can be distorted or misrepresented when discussed with others. A briefing, on the other hand, permits you to explain your position in your own words so that all parties can hear for themselves what you are advocating.

If you decide to make a formal oral presentation, you should systematically prepare for it. Conduct your research, outline your objectives, and prepare your appropriate *visual aids*. Today, most business presentations include PowerPoint slides that can contain graphs, charts, tables, key points arranged as "bullets," photographs, video clips, or even sound effects. Do not become too enamored with artful visual presentations. Remember that the essence of your arguments has to be revealed in the language that you select. Too many slides, too many special effects, and too much movement across the screen—such as bullet points magically appearing one after another on a slide—can distract from the essence of your argument. The rule of thumb should be to keep your slides simple; do not overload them with so much text that your audience has difficulty reading it, cannot keep up with your oral speech, or find themselves reading your slides rather than listening to you speak. Also, do not read your slides word-for-word. This becomes very boring. The slides should contain brief key-word prompts to help catch and focus your audience's attention. The slides should not contain the entirety of your message. One familiar adage is that each slide should not have more words on it than you would put on a T-shirt.

Most people are not very good at taking notes. If you wish your audience to remember key facts or arguments from your talk, you should be prepared to provide them with notes. Some speakers actually give their PowerPoint slides as notes for people to take away with them. Be careful not to provide so much extensive reading material that your audience reads it while you are speaking and stops paying attention to you. Many people will flip through the material and read ahead of you, or they will occupy themselves by doodling on the document. None of these activities help them pay attention to your arguments. If you want to be assured that your audience pays attention to what you are saying, you should keep your handouts brief and pass them out section by section so that you have some control over when the audience begins to peruse them. You then invite your audience to write comments in the margins if they wish.

Too many organizational advocates are sloppy and careless in the preparation of their reports. Take care to organize your materials so that your arguments are clearly expressed and easy to follow. Make certain that you use font sizes and colors that stand out and are easy to follow. A slide with yellow text on a brown background can, for example, be very difficult to read. Slides that are easy to read on your computer screen may be very difficult to see in a brightly lit room. Plan accordingly and select contrasting colors. Be sure that you proofread to catch spelling errors, typos, and other mistakes that may distract from the content of your messages. If your listeners become preoccupied counting all the misspelled words in your materials, they likely will not listen closely to what you have said.

Remember also how important appearances are to public presentations. You should make every effort to be well dressed, polished, prepared, and professional in your demeanor. This will communicate your competence and seriousness of purpose and will help enhance the appeal of your messages.

THE ORAL PRESENTATION

Most oral presentations succeed or fail on the basis of the quality of the advance preparation. The more time and attention you devote to analyzing the issues, developing your arguments, assembling your evidence, structuring and writing your remarks, and practicing your delivery, the better your talk will be. There are a number of helpful tips to keep in mind.

1. Familiarize yourself with the setting for the talk. If it is a conference room or auditorium, you should visit it and make sure that you can arrange where you will stand, where your computer will be placed so that you can access the keyboard and refer to the slides to establish your key points, and where your visual aids will be projected. Make certain that the room contains all of the equipment you will need, such as an overhead projector and a screen or white wall. Locate the outlets, and make certain that you have all the appropriate adaptors to connect your computer to the power source. If you are not bringing a laptop, make sure that the computer in the room that you will use can access and display your material. Nothing can be more unnerving than to devote hours of preparation to a PowerPoint presentation that you cannot access or show for one reason or another. Similarly, we have all attended meetings that began 20 minutes late because the speaker could not connect all of the equipment and/or access and display their slides. Always plan to be able to deliver your talk without the use of technology—if your technology fails, you can still make your presentation.

2. Construct your talk so you tell your audience a story that has a beginning, a middle, and an end. This allows you to create a new scenario to explain how things will be different if your proposed ideas are accepted, to paint a future that contrasts with the status quo, and to compare your story with the rival stories that might be circulating. Also, preface your story with an overview that lays out your objectives so your audience can see where you are going. An axiom of such presentations is: tell them what you are going to say; say it; and then tell them what you said.

3. Consider preparing both long and short versions of your talk. Often presentations are scheduled in meetings at which several other people will also be speaking. If their talks run long, you might find that you have only 5 minutes in which to deliver your 15-minute long presentation. Do not try to present the same talk in 5 minutes that you created for a 15-minute time slot. You will leave your audience feeling rushed and confused. Instead, offer them a brief thumbnail sketch of the talk that you had planned to give and leave them wanting more. Then reschedule your talk for a later day when you have the time to make a more complete presentation.

4. Always try to keep your presentation brief. The most frequently heard criticism in business meetings is that they are too long. Determine how much background information your audience needs and give them just that much. Con-

fine your comments to those that are germane to your topic. Never talk for 25 minutes when a 10-minute talk will do the job. Remember, people in the workplace almost always feel busy and rushed. The time spent in meetings listening to presentations is time away from their desks and their other responsibilities. Try to be respectful of other people's very busy schedules.

5. Use humor. This does not mean you should try to be a comedian; no one expects you to keep them in stitches. But people do enjoy a bit of humor and do want to relax and enjoy your presentation. If you decide to tell a joke, make sure that it is not going to offend anyone. Never tell an off-color joke or one that references anyone's gender, ethnicity, religion, or social identity; such jokes only serve to embarrass those who tell them. Also, jokes work best when they are topically connected to the content of your speech. If you are not a good joke teller and cannot think of an appropriate joke that fits your topic, then do not attempt to tell a joke.

6. Make sure that you encourage questions and always try to leave time for questions. Answering questions gives you an opportunity to clarify your arguments, to respond to potential misunderstandings, and to get feedback on how your audience sees your arguments. Often arguers communicate verbally that they are willing to answer questions while simultaneously sending nonverbal cues that suggest that questions are not really welcome or encouraged. Be careful not to do this. Also, be careful not to communicate an impression that you believe a question from someone in the audience is stupid or ill informed—a hostile reception squelches questions. Avoid becoming defensive when asked a question that seems hostile to your position. Answer questions carefully and honestly. If you do not know the answer to a question that you are asked, admit your ignorance. It is far better to admit that you do not know the answer than to make something up that may be wrong and therefore discredit your entire presentation. The best response may be: "I do not know the answer to that question right now but allow me to do some research into it and report back to you." Having made such a commitment, be sure that you in fact do get back to the questioner with a response.

ENCOUNTERING RESISTANCE

Organization advocates often face *resistance* to their arguments. As we have already observed, organizations are composed of people with different opinions, interests, and objectives. There will likely be opposition to at least some of your arguments. However, if you have carefully researched and prepared your presentation, you may have anticipated this resistance and are prepared to respond to it. Here are some tips for dealing with resistance.

1. Stay calm. Opposition to your arguments is not the same as opposition to you as a person. It does not necessarily mean that the person who opposes you dislikes you, is out to get you, or wishes you to look bad. If you remain calm and cordial it is more likely that the disagreement remains professional and respectful. If you become antagonistic and personalize the opposition you can expect that your counterpart will respond in kind. It is generally better for you if it is your adversary who loses their temper and not you.

2. Clarify your position. Sometimes people oppose arguments because of what they think they are hearing rather than what was in fact said. As a result, you may find that mere clarification of your argument mitigates the opposition. If, however, the opposition is genuine, it still serves your interests and the interests of clarity to fully understand the nature of the disagreement and what prompted it.

    Be wary of cases in which your adversary offers a false or misleading reason for their opposition to your argument. In a public setting, people often are reluctant to state the true reasons for their objections to arguments (you may have heard this phenomenon referred to as someone having a *hidden agenda*) because they may fear that they will appear selfish, resistant to new ideas, or inflexible. In such situations you need to decide how direct you wish to be in your response. Do you confront someone with your belief that the person may be holding something back in the explanation of why they oppose your arguments? Or do you play along and just respond to the adversary's stated public objections and simply hope for the best? There is no single right answer to such a problem; it depends on the situation and the persons involved.

3. Be prepared to add new evidence or new analysis to support your arguments. Just as in an academic debate, you should anticipate the refutation that your arguments might face in a business or organizational context and prepare answers to your opponent's arguments and extensions to your own positions. Do not retreat to your original position and simply repeat your arguments when you are faced with opposition. Instead, add to your arguments to strengthen them and actively look for opportunities to identify the weaknesses and mistaken assumptions or missing proof in the arguments offered by your adversary. Remember that the key to effective advocacy is the ability to refute the counterarguments offered by your adversary.

    Think also about the power of storytelling as a means of communication. Be prepared to expand your storyline to include new characters or actions and alternative views of history or of future scenarios. Think about the power of a shared story. We have been in meetings in which we were surrounded by statistical data that clearly suggested what the appropriate course of action should be, only to have someone in the meeting say: "Let me tell you about the last time we attempted to do something similar . . ." Suddenly this narrative account of shared historical experience became a far more compelling reason to support an alternative course of action than was the previously offered statistical data.

4. When faced with what appears to be intractable opposition, try to minimize the differences between your positions and those taken by your opponent. Avoid dichotomies and either-or language. Look for ways to make accommodations and to adapt to others' views. If a *compromise* is possible and will not undercut your argument, you should offer to compromise. Many decision makers are uncomfortable with conflict and resist making decisions that force them to support one strong-willed advocate while thwarting the will of another. Instead, they prefer compromise and consensus. If you can find a way to compromise, your adversary might agree with the newly modified position. The more "buy in" you get for a decision the more likely it is that people will stand behind it and not turn on you when something goes wrong or something unexpected occurs.

5. Challenge your opponent to prepare and defend alternative positions. It is much easier to oppose and speak out against change than it is to develop and advocate alternatives. Try to force your opponent to present alternative proposals and then be prepared to refute those alternatives if you are so inclined. Focus the discussion on the comparisons between the alternative positions so the decision maker can weigh carefully the benefits and disadvantages of the competing alternatives in deciding the issue.

6. Be a graceful winner or loser. Organizations typically reward people who can get along with their peers and do not cause problems. Do not flaunt your successes over those whom you have vanquished and do not stew over your losses. Instead, learn how to take both your successes and your failures in stride. Assume that during the course of your career you will have both successes and failures along the way.

Follow-Up Activities

One of the more common problems in organizations is that people do not follow through after a decision has been reached. If you win support for your arguments or concessions to your positions, you should document what was decided and the commitments involved. Send a memorandum or email to the decision maker summarizing what you understood to be the results of the meeting, asking for a response to any portion of the communication that may not be accurate. Then keep a copy of that communication and any response in your files. It is amazing how often commitments are "forgotten"; however, they are much more difficult to forget if there is a written record.

Schedule any required follow-up meetings as quickly as possible to demonstrate your commitment to this new project or proposal and to keep it fresh in people's minds. Do not let it fall between the cracks, or people will likely remember that they agreed to do something but that it must not have been successful—not that it failed due to a lack of organizational effort to see it through.

Take whatever actions are required of you personally and carefully document all of your activities. Ideally you should write progress reports to your supervisors keeping them posted on your activities and demonstrating that you are making progress toward achieving whatever goals you may have set for yourself or had others set for you.

The Challenge of Working at a Distance

One of the most challenging aspects of organizational life today is that so much of our work is undertaken by people who seldom—and in some cases never—get to meet each other in face-to-face settings. Large organizations are conducting business across the globe, work teams are challenged to adjust to different cultural differences and across various time zones, and many organizations during the pandemic and subsequently have expected their employees to work remotely and communicate via new digital technologies such as meetings conducted via Zoom. Although we can be grateful for the many conveniences and efficiencies that result from these new developments, we must also note that they pose unique problems for organizational communication, employee engagement and satisfaction, and the development of an effective and shared organizational culture. The most obvious challenge is that the serendipitous encounters that employees may have with their coworkers—those interactions in the elevator, the break room, the hallways, etc.—are greatly diminished when everyone is working remotely. Such informal encounters enable employees to develop personal relationships and affinity for their colleagues. They can learn about each other's families, personal interests, hobbies, worries, etc. These encounters enable workers to understand each other better and perhaps also to have greater empathy and compassion for each other's unique characteristics, backgrounds, values, and burdens.[19]

If your workplace is increasingly conducting much of its daily activity remotely, you should acknowledge the communication that is not occurring serendipitously and seek to replace it with a concerted effort to actively share information, create opportunities for addressing the unique demands for information by those who may be more isolated than their peers, and create opportunities for either real or virtual encounters that facilitate getting to know each other better and understanding personal situations.[20] This is especially important to the conduct of effective arguments in organizations. Research has suggested that people may be far less likely to argue respectfully if they are conducting those arguments online and with people whom they are unlikely to meet or get to know personally.[21] Certainly, such conflicts are detrimental to organizational effectiveness and should be of concern to employers and their workforce.

Summary

Arguing in an organization is in many respects similar to arguing in any other context. Arguments are effective when presented in narrative form; arguments still need to be supported by evidence and analysis; careful preparation pays dividends; and arguments should account for the self-interests of the intended decision maker. The key difference in the organizational context is that the person whom you are trying to convince may also be the person who signs your paychecks. Consequently, in this context more than in almost any other, it is important that you not allow personal antagonisms to develop. A clear track record of thoughtful, highly polished, and professional argumentative presentations will be most helpful in convincing your superiors that you are indispensable to the organization and deserving of promotions.

Key Terms

coalitions
compromise
jargon
organizational culture
power
resistance
visual aids

Activities

1. Interview someone who holds a position in the profession you hope to enter when you have completed your education. How do they assess the organizational culture in their workplace? On what do they base this assessment? How does the organizational culture affect their daily life? Be sure to keep answers confidential.

2. Ask your instructors to reveal how they learned about the culture of their academic institution. Are there stories that are told to each new faculty member to introduce them to the culture? Are there rituals that identify the institution's values?

3. Draft a hypothetical memorandum in which you present arguments to your supervisors or bosses for a new initiative, new resources, or a new organizational policy (e.g., extending family leaves, support for employees to go back for more education, more flexible work hours, etc.). Be sure to consider the advice we presented in this chapter.

4. Ask a friend or classmate to engage in a role-playing exercise with you. Assume the roles of a subordinate and of a supervisor. Have the subordinate orally present arguments for obtaining resources or a raise and have the supervisor provide resistance to these arguments. Then reverse the roles.

RECOMMENDED READINGS

Eisenberg, Eric M., Angela Trethewey, Marianne LeGreco, and H. L. Goodall, Jr., *Organizational Communication: Balancing Creativity and Constraint,* 8th ed. (New York: Bedford-St. Martin's Press, 2017).

Ford, Debra J. and Mary F. Hoffman, *Organizational Rhetoric: Situations and Strategies* (Thousand Oaks, CA: Sage, 2010).

Heath, Chip and Dan Heath, *Made to Stick: Why Some Ideas Survive and Others Die* (New York: Random House, 2007).

Kramer, Michael W. and Ryan S. Bisel, *Organizational Communication: A Lifespan Approach,* 2nd ed. (Oxford: Oxford University Press, 2020).

Lewis, Steven and Rebecca Weintraub, *InCredible Communication: Uncover the Invaluable Art of Selling Yourself* (London: Bloomsbury Press, 2022).

Mumby, Dennis K. and Timothy R. Kuhn, *Organizational Communication: A Critical Introduction* (Thousand Oaks: Sage, 2019).

Nicotera, Anne, Ed. *Origins and Traditions of Organizational Communication: A Comprehensive Introduction to the Field* (London: Routledge, 2019).

Quintanilla, Kelly M. and Shawn T. Wahl, *Business and Professional Communication: Keys for Workplace Excellence,* 4th ed. (Thousand Oaks: Sage, 2020).

ENDNOTES

[1] Michael D. Watkins, "What Is Organizational Culture and Why Should We Care?" *Harvard Business Review,* May 15, 2013. https://hbr.org/2013/05/what-is-organizational-culture

[2] Ibid.

[3] Ibid.

[4] Charles Perrow, *Complex Organizations: A Critical Essay,* 3rd ed. (New York: Random House, 1986).

[5] Michael Zhang, "A Brief History of Kodak: The Rise and Fall of a Camera Giant," *PetaPixel,* June 14, 2018. https://petapixel.com/2018/06/14/a-brief-history-of-kodak-the-camera-giants-rise-and-fall/

[6] Sarah Owermohle, "Emergent Admits to Manufacturing Issues with J&J Vaccine," *Politico,* April 1, 2021. https://www.politico.com/news/2021/04/01/johnson-johnson-covid-vaccine-478859

[7] See Matthew Yglesias, "The Emerging Boeing 737 Max Scandal, Explained," *Vox,* March 29, 2019. https://www.vox.com/business-and-finance/2019/3/29/18281270/737-max-faa-scandal-explained

[8] "Suit: Walmart Locked Janitors into Stores," *NBC News,* February 3, 2004. https://www.nbcnews.com/id/wbna4146540

[9] Russell Hotten, "Volkswagen: The Scandal Explained," *BBC News,* December 10, 2015. https://www.bbc.com/news/business-34324772

[10] John Estafanous, "Why You Need Team Conflict and How to Make It Productive," *RallyBright,* October 23, 2018. https://www.rallybright.com/why-your-team-needs-conflict-and-how-to-make-it-productive

[11] Amanda Holpuch, "Sony Email Hack: What We've Learned about Greed, Racism, and Sexism," *The Guardian,* December 15, 2014. https://www.theguardian.com/technology/2014/dec/14/sony-pictures-email-hack-greed-racism-sexism

[12] James Thompson, *Organizations in Action* (New York: Transaction Publications, 2003).

13. Paul Krivonos, "Distortion of Subordinate to Superior Communication in Organizational Settings," *Central States Speech Journal* 33 (1982): 345–352.
14. John Gabarro and John Kotter, "Managing Your Boss," *Harvard Business Review* 58 (1980): 92–100.
15. Samuel B. Bacharach and Edward J. Lawler, *Power and Politics in Organizations* (San Francisco: Jossey-Bass, 1980), especially chapter 4.
16. Gary L. Kreps, *Organizational Communication: Theory and Practice,* 2nd ed. (Boston: Pearson Education, 1990).
17. Patricia Andrews and John Baird, Jr., *Communication for Business and the Professions,* 8th ed. (Long Grove, IL: Waveland Press, 2005).
18. Increased participation in organizational decision making also results in increased employee satisfaction and decreased levels of job stress. Eric M. Eisenberg, Angela Trethewey, Marianne LeGreco, and H. L. Goodall, Jr., *Organizational Communication: Balancing Creativity and Constraint,* 8th ed. (New York: Bedford-St. Martin's Press, 2017).
19. Rebecca Weintraub and Steven Lewis, "3 Ways to Encourage Informal Communication in a Hybrid Workplace," *FastCompany,* May 18, 2021. https://www.fastcompany.com/90634744/3-ways-to-encourage-informal-communication-in-a-hybrid-workplace?partner=newscred&utm_source=newscred&utm_medium=feed&utm_campaign=newscred+fastcompany&utm_content=newscred
20. Ibid.
21. Aron Wall, "Why Are Internet Discussions Less Polite?" *Undivided Looking,* May 21, 2015. http://www.wall.org/~aron/blog/why-are-internet-discussions-less-polite/

16

Argumentation in Interpersonal Relationships

Disagreements are common in human interactions. The better we get to know someone the easier it is for us to express our disagreements with them. Upon just meeting someone, most of us are too polite to engage in open disagreement. As we get to know people better, however, we become more comfortable interacting with them. As our comfort level increases, we become less self-aware about how we may be perceived; we allow more of our "real" self to appear, often making it easier for us to disagree and even express anger with others. A popular joke tells of a boy rushing home from school one day and asking his father: "Dad, did you know that in some cultures a boy and girl do not even know each other until they get married?" His dad replies, "Son, that is true in **every** culture."

Most of us are explicitly taught when we are young to make attempts to get along with others and to be agreeable. Part of the socialization experience of children emphasizes respect for the worth of others, the need to share, the importance of being polite, and the obligation to permit others to get their way. It is in this sense that children are actively taught not to disagree.[1] They are especially taught not to disagree with those who have more power or influence. Thus, children are told not to "sass back" to parents, caregivers, teachers, or others with power and control over them. Many theorists have commented that young girls are especially encouraged to be deferential to authority. As a result, adult women tend to be less aggressive in their communication styles and less comfortable in situations characterized by disagreement.[2]

Although we would argue that most humans are socialized to try to avoid arguing (in this context we are referring to argument2—communication interactions characterized by disagreement, which we discussed in chapter 1), there are nonetheless critics who complain that Western society in general (and U.S. society especially) is far too focused on argumentation. Linguistics professor and best-selling author Deborah Tannen described this tendency as "the argument culture" and lamented: "In the argument culture, criticism, attack, or opposition are the predominant if not the only ways of responding to people or ideas."[3] Tannen goes on to protest the fact that people in the West tend to approach almost any issue, problem, or public person in an adversarial way.[4] She is especially bothered by the way in which metaphors of war and the symbolic slaying of one's adversaries make their way into public discourse. In essence, Tannen offers a very compelling argument for dialogue instead of rhetorical argument. Her view, of course, is not new. Advocates for dialogue since the time of Plato have been making the case against arguments (ironically by making arguments). What Tannen seems most concerned about is not arguments per se, but a "toxic culture" that is characterized by media and political practices that emphasize intense public squabbles at the expense of deliberative conversations and dispassionate reasoning and analysis.[5] As you have read, however, the entire focus of this text has been on the creation of arguments that do not deteriorate into squabbles and on elevating the quality of arguments across a wide array of contexts from public and mass mediated interactions to interpersonal conversations.

Our view is that it is sometimes necessary and even desirable for people to find ways to express their differences of opinion through arguments. The goal of this chapter is to help you find ways to express disagreements without appearing disagreeable. We believe that disagreements should not always be viewed negatively and that often the expression of disagreement is essential to the effective analysis of problems and even to the development and maintenance of healthy interpersonal relationships. All relationships will at some time or other experience conflict. Learning some techniques for *conflict management* can lead to improved interpersonal relationships. Learning how to argue in a constructive fashion has also been shown to reduce stress, which may in turn improve your health and perhaps even lengthen your life.[6]

This chapter will focus on how arguments develop and shape interpersonal communication interactions. Our focus is primarily on the process of arguing and how this process can be conducted to enhance and enrich our relationships with others. The chapter will discuss the impact of arguing and conflict mediation strategies on relationships, a conversational theory of argument, the relationship of argument to self-esteem, and the importance of empathic listening.

ARGUING AND CONFLICT MEDIATION STRATEGIES

In interpersonal relationships, as in other argumentation contexts, people engage in storytelling. They test the quality of the claims that they hear by evaluating them as stories. One dimension of becoming an effective arguer in interpersonal conversation is learning to construct stories you believe to be true and to present them convincingly. Another dimension, however, is the ability to listen carefully and appreciatively to the stories told by others. Those with whom you find yourself disagreeing are probably just as convinced that their stories are correct as you are that your stories are accurate. The world is filled with opposing stories and with people who adhere to these differing stories. Awareness of the theory of storytelling should help you better understand why people adhere to rival stories and why many of the people with whom you will interact during the course of your life will not agree with you.

Disagreements are typically expressed through arguments, and people argue to achieve at least three objectives in interpersonal interactions. First, people argue to make decisions. When people have different opinions about what actions they should take, what values are most important, or even about factual claims, they usually attempt to resolve these differences through arguments.

Second, arguments provide a means to manage interpersonal conflict and to preserve the possibility of successful and rewarding future social interactions. The alternative to resolving conflict through arguments might be the use of coercion or force. Certainly, having too many arguments can damage interpersonal relationships—but so too can brawls! Also, some people actively avoid conflicts to such an extent that they fail to express themselves, which can undermine interpersonal relationships. One of the authors of this book remembers a conversation that he had several years ago with two close friends, a married couple. The couple explained with great pride that they never argued and enjoyed an almost perfect relationship. You can guess the outcome of this story. A few months after this conversation, the couple reported that they had decided to divorce. The divorce settlement, and the negotiation of a child custody and support agreement, resulted in a long, nasty, and drawn out courtroom battle that cost each of them tens of thousands of dollars. One might speculate that this couple would have been much better off had they learned how to argue in a productive and useful fashion earlier in their relationship.

Third, arguments are often about power in human relationships. Kenneth Burke wrote that people are "goaded by the spirit of hierarchy."[7] By this Burke meant that there is a certain hierarchical imperative that guides human symbolic action. All of us seek, in some way or another, to advance our place or standing in the hierarchy. All of us want to be affirmed. We naturally want to be perceived as knowledgeable, competent, intelligent, valuable, and experienced. We want to be seen as necessary and even as irreplaceable. We communicate these needs both implicitly and explicitly in the positions (arguments and claims) that we develop and defend. Although this hierarchical urge is certainly stronger in some persons than in others (and thus influences individual communicative choices differently), it is always a factor in human interactions.

Our goal should be to argue well not just in the strategic sense that we are making strong, convincing, and persuasive arguments but also in conducting our arguments in a socially productive and useful manner. Truly successful arguers learn to manage their disagreements so that discord does not destroy friendships, prevent them from working effectively with colleagues, or result in marital separation and/or divorce. Scholars have noted that many close friends and intimate couples argue about the same issues over and over again. These arguments are called "serial arguments," and they have the potential to damage the relationship unless the arguers can find a way to resolve the underlying source of the conflict.[8]

This chapter is intended to help you to understand the role that your *argument style* plays in shaping effective social interactions. We hope that by making you more aware of the ways in which arguments function in interpersonal interactions you will become more sensitive and self-monitoring in your argumentation habits as well as more tolerant of the argument styles and strategies employed by others. In short, we wish to help you create and preserve positive social relationships.

The noted argumentation scholar Wayne Brockriede stressed the importance of avoiding coercive and/or exploitive argument styles and urged arguers instead to employ positive and mutually reinforcing argument techniques:

> One does not pursue the art of being human by coercing others through superior power or by manipulating them by charm or deceit to gain adherence to propositions from powerless or naïve individuals. Instead, one seeks a dialogic acceptance of others as persons and develops a bilateral relationship by equalizing opportunities to express attitudes and intentions by enhancing everyone's capacity for arguing.[9]

Just as some people are more skilled than others in the strategic dimensions of arguing, likewise some people are more skilled than others in the interpersonal and social dimensions of argumentation. Some people are so shy and reticent about expressing their opinions and so eager to avoid conflict that they are unable or unwilling to assert themselves or to stand up for their opinions or beliefs. Often such people have good ideas, but their reluctance to speak up and argue for those opinions undermines their influence and prevents them from contributing to effective decision making. The danger is that these individuals may go meekly wherever they are led because they are unwilling to argue for their positions. They not only sacrifice negotiating their needs, but they also lose the opportunity to strengthen a relationship by working through disagreements and reaching mutually acceptable outcomes.

Other people are very forceful and dynamic, perhaps even overbearing, in stating their opinions and achieving their desired outcomes. If these individuals do not use positive argumentative techniques, they leave many bruised egos, damaged self-concepts, and embittered enemies. Sometimes these arguers fail to influence the outcomes of decisions or to convince others to adhere to their beliefs precisely because they do not use better argumentation strategies. As a result, their arguments never get a fair hearing. Certainly, some people argue badly; they engage in name-calling, coercion, bullying, misrepresentation, and deliberate distortions. Some fail to listen, refuse to acknowledge the worth of alternative points of view, and refuse to recognize when others have presented better arguments. We continue to believe, however, that arguers are capable of learning techniques that will enable them to make well-reasoned and civil arguments that facilitate making sound decisions and resolving conflicts.[10]

Effective interpersonal arguers also recognize that some arguments are not worth having—either because they are not winnable or because any win would incur too high a cost. People should learn how to disagree with others without destroying friendships or work relationships. In recent years, for example, the political polarization in the United States has become so great that many families have worried about the political disputes and arguments that might emerge over the dinner table at family celebrations of major holidays such as Thanksgiving. As a result, very helpful advice columns have been written to guide people as to how they might have productive political conversations with friends and relatives with whom they have deep and seemingly irresolvable political differences.[11] The COVID-19 pandemic introduced another problematic context. Many individuals expressed concerns about the difficulty of months of quarantine with family members who held decidedly different opinions about how to respond to the risk of contracting the virus and the risk of spreading it to others.[12] Many of you may have experienced such family tensions and conflict in response to both political differences and the COVID-19 quarantine.

We want to assure you, however, that it is entirely possible to disagree in a socially acceptable fashion—even about complex and polarizing topics and even under the duress of a forced lock-down. It means focusing on the issues and not the other person. It means telling stories emphasizing personal experiences, observations, and beliefs. It means learning how to avoid using emotionally charged language and terms that may be interpreted as demeaning or designed to provoke others to anger. For example, conversations about race are some of the most difficult conversations that many people have today. It is certainly not helpful to label someone a racist, even when you might be convinced that they are exhibiting this belief structure. Similarly, throwing around terms such as "white privilege" will likely produce a defensive reaction if individuals do not feel that they "personally are privileged, because they worked hard for everything they achieved." It is certainly the case that people may have legitimately earned their achievements, so how can you engage them to think about how others can similarly improve their lives? How do you establish the points of connection that will help them understand your viewpoints and the problems faced by those who may continue to suffer from the effects of systemic discrimination?

We suggest it requires learning how to listen carefully and creatively to identify points of agreement and shared underlying values. Voicing points of connection as well as points of disagreement strengthens the effectiveness of arguments. When points of agreement are emphasized, it is more difficult to focus on the disagreement. Learn how to control your emotions and remain calm and open to alternative ways of thinking. Try to understand why others hold the beliefs that they do. Engage them in conversations about their personal histories and experiences and then offer contrasting stories that reveal the challenges that others may face. Avoid condescension and strive to create a real dialogue. Be patient with others. Learn to recognize when those with whom you are arguing have begun to lose control of their emotions. When that happens, pause your presentation. Something such as the following provides some respite: "This conversation has clearly revealed the depth of our disagreement and contrasting opinions. But we also know of our genuine fondness for each other and that is not diminished. We do not have to resolve these differences today. There will be future opportunities to continue the conversation." These conversations are difficult, but our experience suggests that most people do grow over time if given the opportunity to do so and if exposed to gentle persuasion and consistent messaging, so don't give up the effort.

A CONVERSATIONAL THEORY OF ARGUMENT

Despite the fact that disagreements are inevitable in human social interactions, researchers who have studied everyday human conversations have generally found that most people try to avoid disagreements. In fact, Sally Jackson and Scott Jacobs argued that the very nature of our language system discourages disagreements. Their research demonstrated that arguments in everyday social conversations occur when one conversant or another violates an unstated but generally understood rule or convention in language. Specifically, Jackson and Jacobs introduced the concept of ***adjacency pairs*** to argumentation theory. These are linkages between types of statements that define their relationship to each other.[13] An adjacency pair might be said to exist when a first statement specifies or calls for a particular type of response. For example:

First paired-part	Second paired-part
request	grant/refusal
question	answer/refusal to answer
boast	appreciation/derision

In such adjacency pairs the first paired-part (or statement) establishes a "next turn" position in the conversation because it solicits or expects a particular second paired-part response. Conversational disagreement or arguments occur when a first statement is comprehensible but a *preferred* second paired-part (or response) is withheld.[14]

If, for example, a man asks the woman seated next to him for a date, he prefers to have his request met with acceptance. If, on the other hand, the woman responds that she has other plans, and therefore signals her refusal with a *dispreferred* (undesired) response, then he can choose to ask for another evening or mumble his regrets and slink away with as much of his pride intact as possible. On some occasions, hopefully rare, the woman may respond with an even more overtly dispreferred response. For example, she might say: "How can you even think to ask me out when you know that I have been seeing your best friend?" This response is not merely a refusal to the request, it is also an attack on the man's character, his loyalty, and his commitment to his friend. Her conversational turn has thus been directly confrontational, and it almost necessitates that he respond with a defense of some sort. He could say, for example, that he did not realize that she and his friend were still dating. Or, he too could say something that escalates the confrontation. For example, he could tell her that he knows that "his friend is just not that 'into' her." The response that he has offered is naturally going to call for a different type of response from her and a further escalation of tensions would likely occur.

Consider the following example of two baseball fans having an argument as another illustration of the process of conversational turn taking.

> Bob: The National League has always been tougher than the American League.
>
> Alexandra: No way. The American League has better hitting, look at how much higher the batting averages are.
>
> Bob: The hitting is better because they feast on all that American League pitching. Look at how many home runs they give up in the American League.
>
> Alexandra: Those home runs are because American League pitchers have to face designated hitters that can hit the long ball rather than other pitchers who can't even make contact with it.
>
> Bob: Still, the National League has historically done better in the All-Star Game.
>
> Alexandra: You're nuts! They got blown out this year, and they lost last year too.
>
> Bob: Oh, yeah. I guess the American League is getting more respectable.
>
> Alexandra: Wow, I can't believe you admitted even that much.

The above argument is typical of the kind of bantering in which friends engage. Most conversations like this one are good-natured and even enjoyable to the participants. The participants in the conversation are expressing their disagreement as evidenced by the fact that they responded at several turns with dispreferred responses rather than with preferred responses. In the end, however, Bob acknowledges the superiority or at least reasonableness of Alexandra's arguments, and Alexandra acknowledges a sense of satisfaction with her win and also with her continued good relationship with Bob. The conversation could, of course, have proceeded differently.

> Alexandra: You're nuts! They got blown out this year, and they lost last year too.
>
> Bob: Well that doesn't change my mind. I still think the National League is better.
>
> Alexandra: Well, you are entitled to your opinion. No one expects a San Francisco Giants fan to be rational.
>
> Bob: Well Giants fans are every bit as rational as New York Yankees fans.

In this example Bob refuses to acknowledge that Alexandra's arguments are powerful and declares that despite the facts and the quality of the opposing arguments he will not change his mind. This could, of course, lead to an even more negative interaction. Instead, however, Alexandra decides that she is too fond of Bob to permit this refusal to stand in the way of their friendship. Rather than escalating the disagreement, she avoids continuing conflict, makes an attempt at a joke, and defuses the situation. The conversation might, of course, have taken still a different turn.

> Bob: Well, that doesn't change my mind. I still think the National League is better.
>
> Alexandra: Well, surprise, surprise, you're too bullheaded to listen to reason.
>
> Bob: Oh sure, and you are always the reasonable one, aren't you? You think you know everything.
>
> Alexandra: Well, at least I follow the news, and as a result I know who wins and loses All-Star Games.
>
> Bob: Well, I am glad that you at least read the sports news. I am sure that the international news and op-ed pages are too difficult for you to comprehend.
>
> Alexandra: You can really be a jerk.
>
> Bob: And you are an idiot.

This last conversation is, as you can see, far less pleasant than the two that preceded it. Neither speaker is willing to acknowledge the worth of the other's arguments. Furthermore, the speakers in the heat of the disagreement do not see the need to maintain the friendship as sufficiently important to modify their argument strategies. Consequently, a friendly and pleasant social interaction is permitted to become a hostile and most unpleasant interaction. In this case, the interaction deteriorates into very juvenile personal attacks and name-calling; indeed, it illustrates the type of conversational turn taking that children are taught to avoid by parents and teachers. Such interactions, even among adults, are far too common. They are likely to occur when the conversational partners are tired, insecure, harboring deep-seated anger or resentment toward others, depressed, or have consumed enough alcohol to diminish their reasonableness and judgment. Such conversational degeneration may also occur because of unresolved serial arguments that define the interpersonal relationship.[15] It is not too difficult to imagine this conversation occurring over a holiday dinner table where the topic is not about baseball but instead about politics.

Jackson and Jacobs see conversational argument theory as a method for organizing our conversational activity and managing our social interactions.[16] William Benoit and Pamela Benoit, in their research on conversational arguments, suggest that arguments will be enacted when people realize that two conversational pairs are in opposition to each other and when they see the potential argument as worth the investment of time, energy, and risk. They also say arguments are terminated when someone capitulates, when consensus or compromise is reached, or when escapes are enacted (someone departs, someone chooses to remain silent, or someone shifts the topic).[17] In your holiday dinner arguments, the escape may occur when someone else suggests that perhaps it is time to clear the dinner plates and serve the dessert.

Arguments occur or do not occur because individual advocates decide whether to pursue their differences. Some people are very reluctant to engage in arguments. Even when they sense that they disagree with someone, they may decide an argument is not worth the investment or the risk. Disengagement may result when individuals dislike conflict, when they do not want to jeopardize their relationship with the other person, or when they lack confidence in their own position, knowledge, or argumentative skills. For example, it may be very wise to choose not to argue with a person who holds power over you (for example, your boss or your teacher). It may also be that people decide that pursuing an argument will be like "tilting at windmills" because it is unlikely that the other party in the disagreement will be open to a change of mind, even in the face of compelling reasons to reconsider positions. Think for example, about the futility of arguing with a Q-Anon conspiracy theorist on the internet.

Other people are, of course, very argumentative and are often not just willing but actually eager to engage in arguments and to pursue them with great intensity—even if doing so may prove futile, counterproductive, and perhaps politically unwise. Such people may lack the effective social judgment that is part of the self-monitoring process necessary for the maintenance of positive and rewarding social interactions.

Robert Trapp made the following observations about arguments in interpersonal relationships.

> Argument episodes begin when one or both participants perceive some kind of incompatibility. Sources of incompatibility range from attitudes to values, to behaviors.... Once arguers perceive an incompatibility of significant magnitude, they must decide whether or not to confront their partners. As long as the cost of confrontation appears to outweigh the cost of continued incompatibility, arguing is avoided.... Once arguers decide to confront each other, they need to develop the content of the arguments they will make and the strategies they will use. They must invent and edit the arguments and strategies they think will be most effective and appropriate in the situation. Since people can develop their arguments and strategies without conscious reflection, this process is frequently unconscious or mindless.[18]

Effective social arguers learn that argumentative requirements and norms differ from situation to situation. One might employ very different argumentative strategies in an argument with one's lover than with a coworker or with one's boss. Regardless of the context for the argument, however, arguers need to avoid expressing hostility and/or demeaning others in their interactions. The earlier discussion of Tannen's "argument culture" addressed the prevalence of such negative and hostile interpersonal interactions over dialogue and conversations using reasoning and analysis.[19]

Dominic Infante used the term ***verbal aggression*** to describe people who rely on character attacks, competence attacks, personal appearance attacks, insults, brutal teasing, ridicule, profanity, and threats in their argumentative interactions.[20] Infante believed that people rely on such aggressive and counterproductive argument techniques because of their psychopathology, their disdain for other people who hold different opinions, their social learning (the argument style practiced in their families when they were growing up), and because they lack the skills for effective argumentation.[21]

While awareness of argumentation techniques and strategies will not change people's personalities, cause them to be more understanding and loving, or make up for communication style characteristics shaped by their family upbringing, we can hope to achieve some improvement in interpersonal argumentation by teaching people better argumentation strategies and techniques. That is the goal of this text.

STRATEGIC DIMENSIONS OF CONVERSATIONAL ARGUMENT

One of the primary ways an arguer can avoid having disagreements disintegrate into episodes of verbal aggression is to focus on the issues and not the personalities or other attributes of their opponents. Arguers should approach an argument in a conversation strategically, just as they should an argument conducted in a more formal or structured setting.

First, arguers should consider the likelihood that a resolution can be achieved. Is this an argument that has a probability of being accepted? Is the goal to change the other person's mind? What might be the repercussions if the conversation disintegrates into an unpleasant exchange? How might having an argumentative disagreement affect your relationship with this person? Is this issue sufficiently important to merit argument? Based on your past experiences, how do you expect the other person to respond to an expression of disagreement? In formal debate situations or in a courtroom setting, winning is the goal; in interpersonal arguments one can "win" and still lose. What good is securing a victory in an argument if the person you have argued with sees you as a bully, threat, or enemy? If someone begins to distrust you or dislike you as a result of an argument, the outcome of the interaction might not be worth the cost.

Effective interpersonal arguers should find ways to reach compromise and accommodation with their opponents and avoid crushing them with a total victory. Are there ways to make the rival stories competing with each other for acceptance compatible? At a minimum, is there room for the stories to coexist with each other? Trying to adopt a win-win philosophy rather than an "I win and you lose" philosophy may help arguers improve the quality of the decisions they reach. A decision reached through consensus is far more likely to be embraced, accepted, enacted, and even defended from attack by others than is one that people feel has been forced on them. Obviously, it is not always possible to find agreement, to reach a compromise, or to obtain consensus. Some disputes (such as a dispute between an abortion rights advocate and a pro-life advocate) are so intractable that people are not willing to surrender any ground, and there is almost no space in which rival stories are permitted to coexist. Nevertheless, in many circumstances the pursuit of inclusive stories and compromises preserves positive social relationships and fosters a respect for the worth of alternative perspectives.

Second, once an arguer declares an argument to be worth waging, they should consider the source of the disagreement that has led to the conflict. Is the disagreement one that centers on differences in fundamental values? If so, this may limit the chances of reaching a resolution. It will also influence your strategies in shaping your claim and in responding to the claims advanced by the other person. Is the difference one of experience? If so, how can you help others understand your experiences and how they influenced your opinions, especially if the experiences of others have been different? Likewise, how can you become sensitive to others' experiences? Is there appropriate evidence that you can muster to support your arguments? What evidence might your adversary see as credible and compelling? What stories and views of the world do you share, and how can those shared stories and views be used as a resource? If you can determine the underlying cause for the differences being expressed, you might be in a better position to find a way to accommodate your story so it is not incompatible with your adversary's story.

Third, successful arguers must learn how to control their tempers. When we are angry, or when we have decided that we do not especially care for someone, it is difficult for us to separate emotions from the consideration of the issues in dispute. This is not to say that anger is not sometimes an understandable, legitimate, or even strategically useful device; it can be. But anger should be controlled and managed. If you are angry all the time, you get little if any strategic benefit from that anger—it no longer serves to punctuate extremely important situations where anger is a warranted response. On the other hand, if you rarely exhibit anger, getting angry might have a dramatic impact on a conversation. Even in such a case, however, the anger should be carefully controlled and calibrated, and it should be allowed to appear only rarely so it is viewed as out of character.

ARGUMENTATION AND SELF-ESTEEM

How people conduct themselves in interpersonal arguments says a great deal about how they conceive of themselves and of others. As we have already mentioned, our argument style may have been influenced by our formative interactions with our parents. For example, a child who grows up in a family in which conflict is expressed through very hostile and aggressive interactions, such as name-calling and demeaning personal attacks, might be more likely to continue behaving this way as an adult. Lacking role models to demonstrate more positive argumentative behaviors, it is understandable that people model the behaviors they witnessed in their own homes. There is evidence to suggest that the exposure to such high-conflict environments may impact how the brain begins to process and understand conflict.[22]

People who have been demeaned or devalued by others' negative and verbally aggressive argument techniques may already suffer from diminished *self-esteem*. They may have been bruised and battered for so long that they believe all of the disparaging things that have been said about them, and they may thus lack confidence in their own self-worth.[23] It is in such repetitive interactions—abuse decreasing self-esteem—that problems as severe as the battered spouse syndrome can develop.[24]

As Trapp has observed: "The way people argue carries important messages about their self-concepts, how they see each other, and how they see their relationship. Every argument episode is about some content, but in its shadow is a larger relational issue."[25] Some of these relational issues are revealed in how the argument patterns of our loving relationships may change over time. All of us probably know couples or have personally experienced relationships where there was careful monitoring of communication behavior during the formative stages of the relationship. Both people eagerly sought to please each other. They carefully watched what they said, and they attempted not to anger, provoke, or hurt the feelings of their partner. As the relationship progressed and matured (perhaps not until after they were engaged or married), their willingness to monitor and limit the potentially hurtful remarks in their conversations diminished. Now they are far more willing to say what they think, even at the risk of hurting their partner's feelings or disrupting their relationship.

To an extent, this new honesty might be a desirable development. If people feel more comfortable with the relationship, they are more willing to be themselves. If taken to the extreme, however, the unrestrained honesty may signal a serious deterioration of the loving relationship. People sometimes find that they are monitoring their comments less and saying what they really feel at the moment because they are becoming disinterested in the preservation of the relationship and thus less committed to making it work or even last. People feeling trapped in such deteriorating relationships may resort to bullying, name-calling, and other forms of abusive and insensitive communication. Brian Spitzberg and William Cupach have written extensively on such interaction styles and have referred to them as "the dark side of interpersonal communication."[26] In relationships that are characterized by unhealthy conflict, every negative argumentative interaction may signal a willingness to escalate confrontation and for people to become even more nasty and aggressive in the next interaction. If relationships continue to progress in this fashion, people will eventually discover that they have fallen out of love and no longer have the will or the energy to try to patch things up.

Arguers need to learn to express their feelings in such a way as to achieve their objectives in an argument. Do they want to change someone's opinion or behavior? Do they want to punish someone and hurt their feelings? Do they want to sabotage or terminate a relationship? Often arguers will maintain that they only wish to change someone's opinion, while they may subconsciously be attempting to undermine the relationship. Arguers also need to consider how their relationship partners are hearing and reacting to their arguments. We know that communication is a process and that even though we may intend to say one thing our listeners may understand us to be saying something else. Many dysfunctional relationships develop because people become careless in framing their arguments. As a result, they are misunderstood.

THE IMPORTANCE OF EMPATHIC LISTENING

Effective interpersonal arguers also need to develop their listening skills and especially their capacity for ***empathic listening***. It is often difficult in an argumentative situation—when we are producing extra adrenalin, our aggressive instincts are kicking in, when our energy level is high, and when our creative strategic senses are agitated—for us to listen at all, let alone engage in empathic listening. Yet the most effective interpersonal arguers are those who have precisely this capability. Instead of listening to others with a focus on refuting their ideas, empathic listeners search for genuine understanding of where their fellow arguers are coming from, what they are expressing in their stories, and the argument claims they are presenting. Empathic listeners are tolerant and patient; they allow others to develop their positions; and they give these positions careful consideration before forming their responses to them.

Empathic listeners are more likely to find ways to compromise because they are less likely to speak without thinking and thus to say things that they later regret. Empathic listeners allow themselves more time to weigh their responses to arguments. In their search for a larger and more complete and compelling narrative, empathic listeners carefully and strategically consider the arguments made by others. This type of listening can be hard work, especially when we are distracted. There are also listening barriers such as laziness, closed-mindedness, insincerity, and boredom.[27] Empathic listening requires extra effort, but it can be achieved—and it is worth the effort.[28]

SUMMARY

To become an effective interpersonal arguer, listen carefully to the other person's arguments to understand the larger narratives that characterize that person's sense of self, key values, and style of argumentation. Important principles include interpersonal skills of politeness, respect for others, and tolerance of alternative perspectives and worldviews. For most of us, this means working on developing good communication habits in all of our interactions. Some conversations will certainly go better than others, but by improving our interpersonal skills we can work toward resolving our argumentative deficiencies.

Our ability to argue effectively in interpersonal interactions is a measure of our ability to analyze the situation and context, avoid destructive interactions, and determine what techniques will lead to productive exchanges with others. The spouse who learns how to communicate love and respect while also expressing disagreements will make a better marriage partner. The boss who knows how to argue with subordinates while demonstrating respect for their opinions will make a better employer and will help create a more successful and creative company. Children who learn how to argue with their parents without communicating disrespect for them will continue to nurture and sustain an important caring relationship. Our ability to reason—to use symbols to create and evaluate the choices that are available to us—is our most important human capacity. It is a capacity that we should always be trying to develop and enhance as we work to create the good, harmonious, and rewarding lives that we all seek.

Indeed, the ability to conduct arguments effectively and successfully may actually save lives, as we were reminded in June 2021 when a 13-story luxury condominium building in Surfside, Florida collapsed and claimed the lives of 98 people. Media reports indicated that the condominium board, elected by the residents to set policy and maintain the tower, was warned in 2018 that the 40-year-old building needed serious structural repairs that might cost residents as much as $9 million. At the insistence of some of the residents, however, the board did not make the structural repairs and instead devoted its resources to cosmetic repairs such as remodeling public bathrooms in the building. Although some board members were convinced that the structural repairs were essential, a dysfunctional argument culture on the board and among the residents prevented the board from making the right decision. The conflict on the board led to the resignations of several board members who advocated on behalf of the costly structural repairs. They said they were not respected and were harassed by fellow residents.[29] The tragic loss of lives reveals the importance of creating and nurturing an effective argument ecology. If residents had been able to evaluate the assembled evidence and arguments critically, the structural threat could have been addressed. The collapse of the building led to a national conversation about how many other condominium buildings might be at risk of structural failure as a result of their design elements, shoddy construction materials, lack of maintenance, or the failure of their governing boards.[30] What was at stake in this argument went beyond the issue of what repairs or expenses should be prioritized. The underlying controversy was an age-old struggle between those who are primarily concerned about private rights in property and the desire to keep down costs and communal responsibility.[31] Even relatively ordinary arguments that occur in everyday settings can have life-altering consequences if individuals do not have the skills to listen effectively and to analyze the evidence in arguments rationally and dispassionately.

Key Terms

adjacency pairs
argument style
conflict management
empathic listening
self-esteem
verbal aggression

ACTIVITIES

1. Paraphrasing is a proven, effective means for improving your listening skills in interpersonal argument situations. Engage a friend or classmate in a discussion on a subject about which you disagree. After your friend speaks, you are not permitted to respond with your own ideas until you have paraphrased what your friend said. This paraphrase must be acceptable to your friend. Only after the paraphrase has been approved may you proceed with your ideas. In turn, your friend must paraphrase your ideas before speaking again, and you must approve that paraphrase before any response. While this process is arduous and cumbersome, it is effective in forcing us to listen carefully to each other.

2. In another exercise, communicators must label utterances and identify the preferred response before they are permitted to continue the conversation. Thus, if one person asks a question, the respondent would first identify the utterance as a question and then indicate the preferred paired-part that is an answer. The respondent could then answer as he or she wished. There is no requirement that the respondent provide the preferred paired-part because the purpose of the exercise is merely to reinforce the informal preferences that govern interpersonal argumentation—not to control the conversation.

3. Form three student argumentation triads. Two students participate in an interpersonal argument of their choice. The third student acts as an evaluator of the argumentative process. If the third student observes argument behaviors that violate the norms of effective interpersonal argumentation—for example, if an individual exhibits verbal aggressiveness—the student evaluator should interrupt the conversation and identify the norm that has been violated. The two student discussants cannot challenge the evaluator but must repair the conversation and proceed. After a predetermined amount of time, the role of student evaluator should be rotated. The process should continue until all three students have had an opportunity to serve as evaluator. The concluding segment of the exercise should involve all three students in a discussion of the norms that were violated. How did this affect the conduct of the argument and the relationships among the participants?

4. Have a classmate or a friend engage in an argumentative interaction with you. Select a topic on which the two of you disagree. After about 5 minutes of argumentation, switch sides. In other words, if you were pro, now you must be con. Try your best to present as reasonable a set of arguments for each side as possible. After another 5 minutes passes, you should conclude your discussion by trying to reach a mutually agreed upon resolution to the controversy. Does one side possess probable truth? Does the other? Or is truth found somewhere between the opposing positions? This exercise will help you practice becoming less dogmatic in your views.

RECOMMENDED READINGS

Asen, Robert, "Deliberation and Trust," *Argumentation and Advocacy* 50 (2013): 2–17.

Averbeck, Joshua M., "Comparisons of Ironic and Sarcastic Arguments in Terms of Appropriateness and Effectiveness in Personal Relationships," *Argumentation and Advocacy* 50 (2013): 47–57.

Canary, Daniel J. and Harry Weger, Jr., "Competence in Conflict Management," *The International Encyclopedia of Interpersonal Communication* (2015). https://doi.org/10.1002/9781118540190.wbeic246.

Hample, Dale, Pamela J. Benoit, Josh Houston, Gloria Purify, Vanessa Van Hyfte, and Cy Wardwell, "Naïve Theories of Argument: Avoiding Interpersonal Arguments or Cutting Them Short," *Argumentation and Advocacy* 35 (1999): 130–140.

Hample, Dale and Adam S. Richards, "Attachment Style, Serial Argument, and Taking Conflict Personally," *Journal of Argumentation in Context* 4 (2015): 63–86.

Jacobs, Scott and Sally Jackson, "Conversational Argument: A Discourse Analytic Approach," in J. Robert Cox and Charles Arthur Willard, Eds., *Advances in Argumentation Theory and Research* (Carbondale: Southern Illinois University Press, 1982), 205–237.

Johnson, Amy Janon, "A Functional Approach to Interpersonal Argument: Differences Between Public and Personal Issue Arguments," *Communication Reports* 22 (2009): 13–28.

Johnson, Amy Janon, Dale Hample, and Ioana A. Ciocenea, "Understanding Argumentation in Interpersonal Communication," *Communication Yearbook* 38 (2014): 145–173.

Weger, Harry Jr., "Associations among Romantic Attachment, Argumentativeness, and Verbal Aggressiveness in Romantic Relationships," *Argumentation and Advocacy* 43 (2006): 29–40.

Weger, Harry Jr. and Daniel J. Canary, "Conversational Argument in Close Relationships: A Case for Studying Argument Consequences," *Communication Methods and Measures* 4 (2010): 65–87.

ENDNOTES

[1] Barbara J. O'Keefe and Pamela J. Benoit, "Children's Arguments," in J. Robert Cox and Charles Arthur Willard, Eds., *Advances in Argumentation Theory and Research* (Carbondale: Southern Illinois University Press, 1982), 154–183.

[2] Deborah Tannen, *You Just Don't Understand: Women and Men in Conversation* (New York: Harper Collins, 1990).

[3] Deborah Tannen, *The Argument Culture: Stopping America's War of Words* (New York: Ballantine Books, 1999), 7.

[4] Ibid., p. 8.

[5] For a more thorough and complete response to Tannen's book see: James F. Klumpp, Patricia Riley, and Thomas A. Hollihan, "Beyond Dialogue: Linking the Public and Political Spheres," in Thomas A. Hollihan, Ed., *Argument at Century's End: Reflecting on the Past and Envisioning the Future* (Annandale, VA: National Communication Association, 2000), 361–368.

[6] Rachel M. Reznik, Michael E. Roloff, and Courtney Waite Miller, "Communication During Interpersonal Conflict: Implications for Stress Symptoms and Health," *Argumentation and Advocacy* 46 (2010): 193–213. Also, Rachel M. Reznik, Michael E. Roloff, and Courtney Waite Miller, "Components of Integrative Communication During Arguing: Implications for Stress Symptoms," *Argumentation and Advocacy* 48 (2012): 142–158.

[7] Kenneth Burke, *Language as Symbolic Action* (Berkeley: University of California Press, 1966), 15.

[8] Robert Trapp and Nancy Hoff, "A Model of Serial Argument in Interpersonal Relationships," *Journal of the American Forensic Association* 22 (1985): 1–11. Also, Amy Janan Johnson, Joshua M. Averbeck, Katherine M. Kelley, and Shr-Jie Liu, "When Serial Arguments Predict Harm: Examining the Influence of Argument Function, Perceived Resolvability, and Argumentativeness," *Argumentation and Advocacy* 47 (2011): 214–227.

[9] Wayne Brockriede, cited in *Perspectives on Argumentation: Essays in Honor of Wayne Brockriede*, Robert Trapp and Janice Schuetz, Eds. (Long Grove, IL: Waveland Press, 1990), 41.

[10] This view of argumentation is more fully developed in Klumpp, Riley, and Hollihan.

[11] See for example, Emily VanDerWerf, "Don't Avoid Politics This Holiday Season. Use These 5 Tips for Productive Conversations," *Vox*, November 23, 2016. https://www.vox.com/culture/2016/11/23/13708622/talking-to-family-about-politics-arguments

[12] See for example, Maria Puente, "Family Feud: Clashing Over Coronavirus Is the New Source of Household Tension, Fighting," *USA Today*, April 9, 2020. https://www.usatoday.com/story/entertainment/celebrities/2020/04/09/coronavirus-quarantine-fighting-causes-family-drama-amid-virus-fear/2955382001/

[13] Sally Jackson and Scott Jacobs, "Structure of Conversational Argument: Pragmatic Bases for the Enthymeme," *Quarterly Journal of Speech* 66 (1980): 251–265.
[14] Ibid., p. 253.
[15] K. L. Johnson and Michael E. Roloff, "Serial Arguing and Relational Quality: Determinants and Consequences of Perceived Resolvability," *Communication Research* 25 (1998): 327–343.
[16] Jackson and Jacobs, p. 255.
[17] William L. Benoit and Pamela J. Benoit, "Everyday Argument Practices of Naïve Social Actors," in Joseph W. Wenzel, Ed., *Argument and Critical Practices* (Annandale, VA: Speech Communication Association, 1987), 465–474.
[18] Robert Trapp, "Arguments in Interpersonal Relationships," in Robert Trapp and Janice Schuetz, Eds., *Perspectives on Argumentation: Essays in Honor of Wayne Brockriede* (Long Grove, IL: Waveland Press, 1990), 46–47.
[19] Tannen, *The Argument Culture,* especially pp. 8–9.
[20] Dominic Infante, *Arguing Constructively* (Long Grove, IL: Waveland Press, 1988), 24–27.
[21] Ibid., p. 21.
[22] Alice C. Schermerhorn, John E. Bates, Aina Puce, Dennis L. Molfese, "Neurophysiological Correlates of Children's Processing of Interparental Conflict Cues." *Journal of Family Psychology* (2015). doi: 10.1037/fam0000088.
[23] Jeffrey Bernstein, "4 Ways Parents Can Damage Their Children's Self-Esteem," *Psychology Today,* October 28, 2019. https://www.psychologytoday.com/us/blog/liking-the-child-you-love/201910/4-ways-parents-can-damage-their-childrens-self-esteem
[24] Joan Cordutsky, "True Equality for Battered Women: The Use of Self-Defense in Colorado," *Denver Law Review,* 70 (1992): 117–140. https://digitalcommons.du.edu/cgi/viewcontent.cgi?article=2318&context=dlr
[25] Trapp, p. 54.
[26] Brian H. Spitzberg and William R. Cupach, Eds. *The Dark Side of Interpersonal Communication,* 2nd ed. (Mahwah, NJ: Lawrence Erlbaum, 2008).
[27] Dan O'Hair, Gustav W. Friedrich, John M. Weiman, and Mary O. Weiman, *Competent Communication* (New York: St. Martin's Press, 1995), 228–274.
[28] H. Holley Humphrey, "Empathic Listening," *Northwest Compassionate Communication*, October 11, 2000. http://nwcompass.org/about-nvc/empathic-listening/
[29] Rene Rodriguez, "Before Condo Collapse in Surfside, Board Disputes Delayed Work," *Miami Herald,* July 1, 2021. https://www.miamiherald.com/news/local/community/miami-dade/miami-beach/article252505623.html
[30] Matthew Gordon Lasner, "The Surfside Tower Was Just Another Condo Building," *The Atlantic,* July 2, 2021. https://www.theatlantic.com/ideas/archive/2021/07/surfside-tower-was-just-another-condo-building/619348/
[31] Ibid.

Appendix A

Transcripts of Two Convention Acceptance Speeches, 2020

Joe Biden Acceptance Speech
Democratic National Convention August 20, 2020[1]

Good evening.

Ella Baker, a giant of the civil rights movement, left us with this wisdom: Give people light and they will find a way.

Give people light. Those are words for our time.

The current president has cloaked America in darkness for much too long. Too much anger. Too much fear. Too much division.

Here and now, I give you my word: If you entrust me with the presidency, I will draw on the best of us not the worst. I will be an ally of the light not of the darkness.

It's time for us, for we the people, to come together. For make no mistake. United we can, and will, overcome this season of darkness in America. We will choose hope over fear, facts over fiction, fairness over privilege.

I am a proud Democrat and I will be proud to carry the banner of our party into the general election. So, it is with great honor and humility that I accept this nomination for president of the United States of America.

But while I will be a Democratic candidate, I will be an American president. I will work as hard for those who didn't support me as I will for those who did.

That's the job of a president. To represent all of us, not just our base or our party. This is not a partisan moment. This must be an American moment.

It's a moment that calls for hope and light and love. Hope for our futures, light to see our way forward, and love for one another.

America isn't just a collection of clashing interests of red states or blue states.

We're so much bigger than that. We're so much better than that.

Nearly a century ago, Franklin Roosevelt pledged a New Deal in a time of massive unemployment, uncertainty, and fear. Stricken by disease, stricken by a virus, F.D.R. insisted that he would recover and prevail and he believed America could as well. And he did. And so can we.

This campaign isn't just about winning votes. It's about winning the heart, and yes, the soul of America. Winning it for the generous among us, not the selfish. Winning it for the workers who keep this country going, not just the privileged few at the top. Winning it for those communities who have known the injustice of the "knee on the neck." For all the young people who have known only an America of rising inequity and shrinking opportunity. They deserve to experience America's promise in full.

No generation ever knows what history will ask of it. All we can ever know is whether we'll be ready when that moment arrives. And now history has delivered us to one of the most difficult moments America has ever faced.

Four historic crises. All at the same time. A perfect storm. The worst pandemic in over 100 years. The worst economic crisis since the Great Depression. The most compelling call for racial justice since the '60s. And the undeniable realities and accelerating threats of climate change.

So, the question for us is simple: Are we ready? I believe we are. We must be.

All elections are important. But we know in our bones this one is more consequential.

America is at an inflection point. A time of real peril, but of extraordinary possibilities.

We can choose the path of becoming angrier, less hopeful and more divided. A path of shadow and suspicion. Or we can choose a different path, and together, take this chance to heal, to be reborn, to unite. A path of hope and light.

This is a life-changing election that will determine America's future for a very long time. Character is on the ballot. Compassion is on the ballot. Decency, science, democracy. They are all on the ballot. Who we are as a nation. What we stand for. And, most importantly, who we want to be. That's all on the ballot.

And the choice could not be clearer. No rhetoric is needed. Just judge this president on the facts: Five million Americans infected with COVID-19. More than 170,000 Americans have died. By far the worst performance of any nation on Earth. More than 50 million people have filed for unemployment this year. More than 10 million people are going to lose their health insurance this year. Nearly one in six small businesses have closed this year.

If this president is reelected we know what will happen. Cases and deaths will remain far too high. More mom-and-pop businesses will close their doors for good. Working families will struggle to get by, and yet, the wealthiest 1 percent will get tens of billions of dollars in new tax breaks.

And the assault on the Affordable Care Act will continue until it's destroyed, taking insurance away from more than 20 million people—including more than 15 million people on Medicaid—and getting rid of the protections that President Obama and I passed for people who suffer from a preexisting condition.

And speaking of President Obama, a man I was honored to serve alongside for eight years as vice president, let me take this moment to say something we don't say nearly enough: Thank you, Mr. President. You were a great president. A president our children could—and did—look up to.

No one will say that about the current occupant of the office. What we know about this president is if he's given four more years he will be what he's been the last four years: a president who takes no responsibility, refuses to lead, blames others, cozies up to dictators, and fans the flames of hate and division. He will wake up every day believing the job is all about him. Never about you.

Is that the America you want for you, your family, your children? I see a different America. One that is generous and strong. Selfless and humble. It's an America we can rebuild together.

As president, the first step I will take will be to get control of the virus that's ruined so many lives. Because I understand something this president doesn't. We will never get our economy back on track, we will never get our kids safely back to school, we will never have our lives back, until we deal with this virus.

The tragedy of where we are today is it didn't have to be this bad. Just look around. It's not this bad in Canada. Or Europe. Or Japan. Or almost anywhere else in the world.

The president keeps telling us the virus is going to disappear. He keeps waiting for a miracle. Well, I have news for him, no miracle is coming.

We lead the world in confirmed cases. We lead the world in deaths.

Our economy is in tatters, with Black, Latino, Asian American, and Native American communities bearing the brunt of it. And after all this time, the president still does not have a plan.

Well, I do. If I'm president on day one we'll implement the national strategy I've been laying out since March. We'll develop and deploy rapid tests with results available immediately.

We'll make the medical supplies and protective equipment our country needs. And we'll make them here in America. So we will never again be at the mercy of China and other foreign countries in order to protect our own people. We'll make sure our schools have the resources they need to be open, safe, and effective. We'll put the politics aside and take the muzzle off our experts so the public gets the information they need and deserve. The honest, unvarnished truth. They can deal with that. We'll have a national mandate to wear a mask—not as a burden, but to protect each other. It's a patriotic duty. In short, I will do what we should have done from the very beginning.

Our current president has failed in his most basic duty to this nation. He failed to protect us. He failed to protect America. And, my fellow Americans, that is unforgivable.

As president, I will make you this promise: I will protect America. I will defend us from every attack. Seen. And unseen. Always. Without exception. Every time.

Look, I understand it's hard to have hope right now. On this summer night, let me take a moment to speak to those of you who have lost the most. I know how it feels to lose someone you love. I know that deep black hole that opens up in your chest. That you feel your whole being is sucked into it. I know how mean and cruel and unfair life can be sometimes. But I've learned two things. First, your loved ones may have left this Earth but they never leave your heart. They will always be with you. And second, I found the best way through pain and loss and grief is to find purpose.

As God's children each of us have a purpose in our lives. And we have a great purpose as a nation: to open the doors of opportunity to all Americans. To save our democracy. To be a light to the world once again. To finally live up to and make real the words written in the sacred documents that founded this nation that all men and women are created equal. Endowed by their Creator with certain unalienable rights. Among them life, liberty and the pursuit of happiness.

You know, my dad was an honorable, decent man. He got knocked down a few times pretty hard, but always got up. He worked hard and built a great middle-class life for our family. He used to say, "Joey, I don't expect the government to solve my problems, but I expect it to understand them." And then he would say: "Joey, a job is about a lot more than a paycheck. It's about your dignity. It's about respect. It's about your place in your community. It's about looking your kids in the eye and say, honey, it's going to be O.K."

I've never forgotten those lessons. That's why my economic plan is all about jobs, dignity, respect and community. Together, we can, and we will, rebuild our economy. And when we do, we'll not only build it back, we'll build it back better. With modern roads, bridges, highways, broadband, ports and airports as a new foundation for economic growth. With pipes that transport clean water to every community. With five million new manufacturing and technology jobs so the future is made in America. With a health care system that lowers premiums, deductibles, and drug prices by building on the Affordable Care Act he's trying to rip away. With an education system that trains our people for the best jobs of the 21st century, where cost doesn't prevent young people from going to college, and student debt doesn't crush them when they get out. With child care and elder care that make it possible for parents to go to work and for the elderly to stay in their homes with dignity. With an immigration system that powers our economy and reflects our values. With newly empowered labor unions. With equal pay for women. With rising wages you can raise a family on. Yes, we're going to do more than praise our essential workers. We're finally going to pay them. We can, and we will, deal with climate change. It's not only a crisis, it's an enormous opportunity. An opportunity for America to lead the world in clean energy and create millions of new good-paying jobs in the process.

And we can pay for these investments by ending loopholes and the president's $1.3 trillion tax giveaway to the wealthiest 1 percent and the biggest, most profitable corporations, some of which pay no tax at all. Because we don't need a tax code that rewards wealth more than it rewards work. I'm not looking to punish anyone. Far from it. But it's long past time the wealthiest people and the biggest corporations in this country paid their fair share. For our seniors, Social Security is a sacred obligation, a sacred promise made. The current president is threatening to break that promise. He's proposing to eliminate the tax that pays for almost half of Social Security without any way of making up for that lost revenue, resulting in cuts.

I will not let that happen. If I'm your president, we're going to protect Social Security and Medicare. You have my word.

One of the most powerful voices we hear in the country today is from our young people. They're speaking to the inequity and injustice that has grown up in America. Economic injustice. Racial injustice. Environmental injustice. I hear their voices and if you listen, you can hear them too. And whether it's the existential threat posed by climate change, the daily fear of being gunned down in school, or the inability to get started in their first job—it will be the work of the next president to restore the promise of America to everyone.

I won't have to do it alone. Because I will have a great vice president at my side. Senator Kamala Harris. She is a powerful voice for this nation. Her story is the American story. She knows about all the obstacles thrown in the way of so many in our country. Women, Black women, Black Americans, South Asian Americans, immigrants, the left out and left behind. But she's overcome every obstacle she's ever faced. No one's been tougher on the big banks or the gun lobby. No one's been tougher in calling out this current administration for its extremism, its failure to follow the law, and its failure to simply tell the truth.

Kamala and I both draw strength from our families. For Kamala, it's Doug and their families. For me, it's Jill and ours. No man deserves one great love in his life. But I've known two. After losing my first wife in a car accident, Jill came into my life and put our family back together. She's an educator. A mom. A military mom. And an unstoppable force. If she puts her mind to it, just get out of the way. Because she's going to get it done. She was a great second lady and she will make a great first lady for this nation. She loves this country so much. And I will have the strength that can only come from family. Hunter, Ashley and all our grandchildren, my brothers, my sister. They give me courage and lift me up. And while he is no longer with us, Beau inspires me every day.

Beau served our nation in uniform. A decorated Iraq war veteran. So I take very personally the profound responsibility of serving as commander in chief.

I will be a president who will stand with our allies and friends. I will make it clear to our adversaries the days of cozying up to dictators are over. Under President Biden, America will not turn a blind eye to Russian bounties on the heads of American soldiers. Nor will I put up with foreign interference in our most sacred democratic exercise—voting.

I will stand always for our values of human rights and dignity. And I will work in common purpose for a more secure, peaceful, and prosperous world.

History has thrust one more urgent task on us. Will we be the generation that finally wipes the stain of racism from our national character? I believe we're up to it. I believe we're ready.

Just a week ago yesterday was the third anniversary of the events in Charlottesville. Remember seeing those neo-Nazis and Klansmen and white supremacists coming out of the fields with lighted torches? Veins bulging? Spewing the same anti-Semitic bile heard across Europe in the '30s? Remember the violent clash that ensued between those spreading hate and those with the courage to stand against it? Remember what the president said? There were quote, "very fine people on both sides."

It was a wake-up call for us as a country. And for me, a call to action. At that moment, I knew I'd have to run. My father taught us that silence was complicity. And I could not remain silent or complicit. At the time, I said we were in a battle for the soul of this nation. And we are.

One of the most important conversations I've had this entire campaign is with someone who is too young to vote. I met with 6-year old Gianna Floyd, a day before her daddy, George Floyd, was laid to rest. She is incredibly brave. I'll never forget. When I leaned down to speak with her, she looked into my eyes and said, "Daddy changed the world." Her words burrowed deep into my heart. Maybe George Floyd's murder was the breaking point. Maybe John Lewis's passing the inspiration. However it has come to be, America is ready to in John's words, to lay down "the heavy burdens of hate at last" and to do the hard work of rooting out our systemic racism.

America's history tells us that it has been in our darkest moments that we've made our greatest progress. That we've found the light. And in this dark moment, I believe we are poised to make great progress again. That we can find the light once more.

I have always believed you can define America in one word: possibilities. That in America, everyone, and I mean everyone, should be given the opportunity to go as far as their dreams and God-given ability will take them.

We can never lose that. In times as challenging as these, I believe there is only one way forward. As a united America. United in our pursuit of a more perfect union. United in our dreams of a better future for us and for our children. United in our determination to make the coming years bright. Are we ready? I believe we are.

This is a great nation. And we are a good and decent people. This is the United States of America. And there has never been anything we've been unable to accomplish when we've done it together.

The Irish poet Seamus Heaney once wrote:

> History says,
> Don't hope on this side of the grave,
> But then, once in a lifetime
> The longed-for tidal wave
> Of justice can rise up,
> And hope and history rhyme.

This is our moment to make hope and history rhyme. With passion and purpose, let us begin—you and I together, one nation, under God—united in our love for America and united in our love for each other. For love is more powerful than hate. Hope is more powerful than fear. Light is more powerful than dark.

This is our moment. This is our mission. May history be able to say that the end of this chapter of American darkness began here tonight as love and hope and light joined in the battle for the soul of the nation. And this is a battle that we, together, will win. I promise you.

Thank you. And may God bless you. And may God protect our troops.

Donald Trump Acceptance Speech
August 27, 2020[2]

Friends, delegates, and distinguished guests: I stand before you tonight honored by your support; proud of the extraordinary progress we have made together over the last four years; and brimming with confidence in the bright future we will build for America over the NEXT four years!

As we begin this evening, our thoughts are with the wonderful people who have just come through the wrath of Hurricane Laura. We are working closely with state and local officials in Texas, Louisiana, Arkansas, and Mississippi, sparing no effort to save lives. While the hurricane was fierce, one of the strongest to make landfall in 150 years, the casualties and damage were far less than thought possible only 24 hours ago. This is due to the great work of FEMA, law enforcement, and the individual states. I will be going this weekend. We are one national family, and we will always protect, love and care for each other.

Here tonight are the people who have made my journey possible, and filled my life with so much joy.

For her incredible service to our nation and its children, I want to thank our magnificent First Lady. I also want to thank my amazing daughter Ivanka for that introduction, and to all of my children and grandchildren—I love you more than words can express. I know my brother

Robert is looking down on us right now from Heaven. He was a great brother and was very proud of the job we are doing. Let us also take a moment to show our profound appreciation for a man who has always fought by our side, and stood up for our values—a man of deep faith and steadfast conviction: Vice President Mike Pence. Mike is joined by his beloved wife, a teacher and military mom, Karen Pence.

My fellow Americans, tonight, with a heart full of gratitude and boundless optimism, I proudly accept this nomination for President of the United States.

The Republican Party, the party of Abraham Lincoln, goes forward united, determined, and ready to welcome millions of Democrats, Independents, and anyone who believes in the GREATNESS of America and the righteous heart of the American People.

In a new term as President, we will again build the greatest economy in history—quickly returning to full employment, soaring incomes, and RECORD prosperity! We will DEFEND AMERICA against all threats, and protect America against all dangers. We will LEAD AMERICA into new frontiers of ambition and discovery, and we will reach for new heights of national achievement. We will rekindle new faith in our values, new pride in our history, and a new spirit of unity that can ONLY be realized through love for our country. Because we understand that America is NOT a land cloaked in darkness, America is the torch that enlightens the entire world.

Gathered here at our beautiful and majestic White House—known all over the world as the People's House—we cannot help but marvel at the miracle that is our Great American Story. This has been the home of larger-than-life figures like Teddy Roosevelt and Andrew Jackson who rallied Americans to bold visions of a bigger and brighter future. Within these walls lived tenacious generals like Presidents Grant and Eisenhower who led our soldiers in the cause of freedom. From these grounds, Thomas Jefferson sent Lewis and Clark on a daring expedition to cross a wild and uncharted continent. In the depths of a bloody Civil War, President Abraham Lincoln looked out these very windows upon a half-completed Washington Monument—and asked God, in His Providence, to save our union. Two weeks after Pearl Harbor, Franklin Delano Roosevelt welcomed Winston Churchill, and just inside, they set our people on a course to victory in the Second World War.

In recent months, our nation, and the entire planet, has been struck by a new and powerful invisible enemy. Like those brave Americans before us, we are meeting this challenge. We are delivering lifesaving therapies, and will produce a vaccine BEFORE the end of the year, or maybe even sooner! We will defeat THE VIRUS, end the pandemic, and emerge stronger than ever before.

What united generations past was an unshakable confidence in America's destiny, and an unbreakable faith in the American People. They knew that our country is blessed by God, and has a special purpose in this world. It is that conviction that inspired the formation of our union, our westward expansion, the abolition of slavery, the passage of civil rights, the space program, and the overthrow of fascism, tyranny and communism.

This towering American spirit has prevailed over every challenge, and lifted us to the summit of human endeavor.

And yet, despite all of our greatness as a nation, everything we have achieved is now endangered. This is the most important election in the history of our country. At no time before have voters faced a clearer choice between two parties, two visions, two philosophies, or two agendas.

This election will decide whether we SAVE the American Dream, or whether we allow a socialist agenda to DEMOLISH our cherished destiny.

It will decide whether we rapidly create millions of high paying jobs, or whether we crush our industries and send millions of these jobs overseas, as has foolishly been done for many decades.

Your vote will decide whether we protect law abiding Americans, or whether we give free reign to violent anarchists, agitators, and criminals who threaten our citizens.

And this election will decide whether we will defend the American Way of Life, or whether we allow a radical movement to completely dismantle and destroy it.

At the Democrat National Convention, Joe Biden and his party repeatedly assailed America as a land of racial, economic, and social injustice. So tonight, I ask you a very simple question: How can the Democrat Party ask to lead our country when it spends so much time tearing down our country?

In the left's backward view, they do not see America as the most free, just, and exceptional nation on earth. Instead, they see a wicked nation that must be punished for its sins.

Our opponents say that redemption for YOU can only come from giving power to THEM. This is a tired anthem spoken by every repressive movement throughout history.

But in this country, we don't look to career politicians for salvation. In America, we don't turn to government to restore our souls—we put our faith in Almighty God.

Joe Biden is not the savior of America's soul—he is the destroyer of America's Jobs, and if given the chance, he will be the destroyer of American Greatness.

For 47 years, Joe Biden took the donations of blue collar workers, gave them hugs and even kisses, and told them he felt their pain—and then he flew back to Washington and voted to ship their jobs to China and many other distant lands. Joe Biden spent his entire career outsourcing the dreams of American Workers, offshoring their jobs, opening their borders, and sending their sons and daughters to fight in endless foreign wars.

Four years ago, I ran for President because I could not watch this betrayal of our country any longer. I could not sit by as career politicians let other countries take advantage of us on trade, borders, foreign policy and national defense. Our NATO partners, as an example, were far behind in their defense payments. But at my strong urging, they agreed to pay $130 billion more a year. This will ultimately go to $400 billion. Secretary General Stoltenberg, who heads NATO, was amazed, and said that President Trump did what no one else was able to do.

From the moment I left my former life behind, and a good life it was, I have done nothing but fight for YOU.

I did what our political establishment never expected and could never forgive, breaking the cardinal rule of Washington Politics. I KEPT MY PROMISES.

Together, we have ended the rule of the failed political class—and they are desperate to get their power back by any means necessary. They are angry at me because instead of putting THEM FIRST, I put AMERICA FIRST!

Days after taking office, we shocked the Washington Establishment and withdrew from the last Administration's job-killing Trans Pacific Partnership. I then approved the Keystone XL and Dakota Access Pipelines, ended the unfair and costly Paris Climate Accord, and secured, for the first time, American Energy Independence. We passed record-setting tax and regulation cuts, at a rate nobody had ever seen before. Within three short years, we built the strongest economy in the history of the world.

Washington insiders asked me NOT to stand up to China—they pleaded with me to let China continue stealing our jobs, ripping us off, and robbing our country blind. But I kept my word to the American People. We took the toughest, boldest, strongest, and hardest hitting action against China in American History.

They said that it would be impossible to terminate and replace NAFTA—but again, they were wrong. Earlier this year, I ended the NAFTA nightmare and signed the brand new U.S. Mexico Canada Agreement into law. Now auto companies and others are building their plants and factories in America, not firing their employees and deserting us.

In perhaps no area did the Washington special interests try harder to stop us than on my policy of pro-American immigration. But I refused to back down—and today America's borders are more secure than EVER before. We ENDED catch-and-release, stopped asylum fraud, took down human traffickers who prey on women and children, and we have deported 20,000 Gang Members and 500,000 Criminal Aliens. We have already built 300 miles of Border Wall—and we are adding 10 new miles every single week. The Wall will soon be complete, and it is working beyond our wildest expectations.

We are joined this evening by members of the Border Patrol union, representing our country's courageous border agents. Thank you all.

When I learned that the Tennessee Valley Authority laid off hundreds of American Workers and forced them to train their lower-paid foreign replacements, I promptly removed the Chairman of the Board. And now, those talented American Workers have been RE-HIRED and are back providing power to Georgia, Alabama, Tennessee, Kentucky, Mississippi, North Carolina, and Virginia. They have their old jobs back, and some are here with us this evening. Please stand.

Last month, I took on Big Pharma and signed orders that will massively lower the cost of your prescription drugs, and to give critically ill patients access to lifesaving cures, we passed the decades long-awaited RIGHT TO TRY legislation. We also passed VA Accountability and VA Choice.

By the end of my first term, we will have approved more than 300 federal judges, including two great new Supreme Court Justices. To bring prosperity to our forgotten inner cities, we worked hard to pass historic criminal justice reform, prison reform, opportunity zones, the long-term funding of historically black colleges and universities, and, before the China Virus came in, produced the best unemployment numbers for African-Americans, Hispanic-Americans, and Asian-Americans ever recorded. I have done more for the African-American community than any president since Abraham Lincoln, our first Republican president. I have done more in three years for the black community than Joe Biden has done in 47 years—and when I'm reelected, the best is yet to come!

When I took office, the Middle East was in total chaos. ISIS was rampaging, Iran was on the rise, and the war in Afghanistan had no end in sight. I withdrew from the terrible, one-sided Iran Nuclear Deal. Unlike many presidents before me, I kept my promise, recognized Israel's true capital and moved our Embassy to Jerusalem. But not only did we talk about it as a future site, we got it built. Rather than spending $1 billion on a new building as planned, we took an already owned existing building in a better location, and opened it at a cost of less than $500,000. We also recognized Israeli sovereignty over the Golan Heights, and this month we achieved the first Middle East peace deal in 25 years. In addition, we obliterated 100 percent of the ISIS Caliphate, and killed its founder and leader Abu Bakr al-Baghdadi. Then, in a separate operation, we eliminated the world's number one terrorist, Qasem Soleimani.

Unlike previous administrations, I have kept America OUT of new wars—and our troops are coming home. We have spent nearly $2.5 trillion on completely rebuilding our military, which was very badly depleted when I took office. This includes three separate pay raises for our great warriors. We also launched the Space Force, the first new branch of the United States military since the Air Force was created almost 75 years ago.

We have spent the last four years reversing the damage Joe Biden inflicted over the last 47 years.

Biden's record is a shameful roll call of the most catastrophic betrayals and blunders in our lifetime. He has spent his entire career on the wrong side of history. Biden voted for the NAFTA disaster, the single worst trade deal ever enacted; he supported China's entry into the World Trade Organization, one of the greatest economic disasters of all time. After those Biden calamities, the United States lost 1 in 4 manufacturing jobs. The laid off workers in Michigan, Ohio, New Hampshire, Pennsylvania, and many other states didn't want Joe Biden's hollow words of empathy, they wanted their jobs back!

As Vice President, he supported the Trans Pacific Partnership which would have been a death sentence for the U.S. Auto Industry; he backed the horrendous South Korea trade deal, which took many jobs from our country. He repeatedly supported mass amnesty for illegal immigrants. He voted FOR the Iraq War; he opposed the mission to take out Osama bin Laden; he opposed killing Soleimani; he oversaw the rise of ISIS, and cheered the rise of China as "a positive development" for America and the world. That's why China supports Joe Biden and desperately wants him to win.

China would own our country if Joe Biden got elected. Unlike Biden, I will hold them fully accountable for the tragedy they caused.

In recent months, our nation, and the rest of the world, has been hit with a once-in-a-century pandemic that China allowed to spread around the globe. We are grateful to be joined tonight by several of our incredible nurses and first responders—please stand and accept our profound thanks. Many Americans have sadly lost friends and cherished loved ones to this horrible disease. As one nation, we mourn, we grieve, and we hold in our hearts forever the memories of all of those lives so tragically taken. In their honor, we will unite. In their memory, we will overcome.

When the China Virus hit, we launched the largest national mobilization since World War II. Invoking the Defense Production Act, we produced the world's largest supply of ventilators. Not a single American who has needed a ventilator has been denied a ventilator. We shipped hundreds of millions of masks, gloves and gowns to our front line healthcare workers. To protect our nation's seniors, we rushed supplies, testing kits, and personnel to nursing homes and long term care facilities. The Army Corps of Engineers built field hospitals, and the Navy deployed our great hospital ships.

We developed, from scratch, the largest and most advanced testing system in the world. America has tested more than every country in Europe put together, and more than every nation in the Western Hemisphere COMBINED. We have conducted 40 million more tests than the next closest nation.

We developed a wide array of effective treatments, including a powerful anti-body treatment known as Convalescent Plasma that will save thousands of lives. Thanks to advances we have pioneered, the fatality rate has been reduced by 80 percent since April.

The United States has among the lowest case fatality rates of any major country in the world. The European Union's case fatality rate is nearly three times higher than ours. Altogether, the nations of Europe have experienced a 30 percent greater increase in excess mortality than the United States.

We enacted the largest package of financial relief in American history. Thanks to our Paycheck Protection Program, we have saved or supported more than 50 million American jobs. As a result, we have seen the smallest economic contraction of any major western nation, and we are recovering much faster. Over the past three months, we have gained over 9 million jobs, a new record.

Unfortunately, from the beginning, our opponents have shown themselves capable of nothing but a partisan ability to criticize. When I took bold action to issue a travel ban on China, Joe Biden called it hysterical and xenophobic. If we had listened to Joe, hundreds of thousands more Americans would have died.

Instead of following the science, Joe Biden wants to inflict a painful shutdown on the entire country. His shutdown would inflict unthinkable and lasting harm on our nation's children, families, and citizens of all backgrounds.

The cost of the Biden shutdown would be measured in increased drug overdoses, depression, alcohol addiction, suicides, heart attacks, economic devastation and more. Joe Biden's plan is not a solution to the virus, but rather a surrender.

My Administration has a different approach. To save as many lives as possible, we are focusing on the science, the facts and the data. We are aggressively sheltering those at highest risk—especially the elderly—while allowing lower-risk Americans to safely return to work and school.

Most importantly, we are marshalling America's scientific genius to produce a vaccine in RECORD TIME. Under Operation Warp Speed, we have three different vaccines in the final stage of trials right now, years ahead of what has been achieved before. We are producing them in advance, so that hundreds of millions of doses will be quickly available.

We will have a safe and effective vaccine this year, and together we will crush the virus.

At the Democrat convention, you barely heard a word about their agenda. But that's not because they don't have one. It's because their agenda is the most extreme set of proposals ever put forward by a major party nominee. Joe Biden may claim he is an "ally of the Light," but when it comes to his agenda, Biden wants to keep you completely in the dark.

He has pledged a $4 trillion tax hike on almost all American families, which will totally collapse our rapidly improving economy and once again record stock markets. On the other hand, just as I did in my first term, I will cut taxes even further for hardworking moms and dads, not raise them. We will also provide tax credits to bring jobs out of China BACK to America—and we will impose tariffs on any company that leaves America to produce jobs overseas. We'll make sure our companies and jobs stay in our country, as I've already been doing. Joe Biden's agenda is Made in China. My agenda is MADE IN THE USA.

Biden has promised to abolish the production of American oil, coal, shale, and natural gas—laying waste to the economies of Pennsylvania, Ohio, Texas, North Dakota, Oklahoma, Colorado, and New Mexico. Millions of jobs will be lost, and energy prices will soar. These same policies led to crippling power outages in California just last week. How can Joe Biden claim to be an "ally of the Light" when his own party can't even keep the lights on?

Joe Biden's campaign has even published a 110-page policy platform co-authored with Far-Left Senator Bernie Sanders. The Biden-Bernie Manifesto calls for suspending ALL removals of illegal aliens, implementing nationwide Catch-and-Release; and providing illegal aliens with free taxpayer-funded lawyers. Joe Biden recently raised his hand on the debate stage and promised to give away YOUR healthcare dollars to illegal immigrants. He also supports deadly Sanctuary Cities that protect criminal aliens. He promised to end national security travel bans from Jihadist nations, and he pledged to increase refugee admissions by 700 percent. The Biden Plan would eliminate America's borders in the middle of a global pandemic.

Biden also vowed to oppose School Choice and close down Charter Schools, ripping away the ladder of opportunity for Black and Hispanic children.

In a second term, I will EXPAND charter schools and provide SCHOOL CHOICE to every family in America. And we will always treat our teachers with the tremendous respect they deserve.

Joe Biden claims he has empathy for the vulnerable—yet the party he leads supports the extreme late-term abortion of defenseless babies right up to the moment of BIRTH. Democrat leaders talk about moral decency, but they have no problem with stopping a baby's beating heart in the 9th month of pregnancy.

Democrat politicians refuse to protect innocent life, and then they lecture us about morality and saving America's soul? Tonight, we proudly declare that all children, born and unborn, have a GOD-GIVEN RIGHT TO LIFE.

During the Democrat Convention, the words "Under God" were removed from the Pledge of Allegiance—not once, but twice. The fact is, this is where they are coming from.

If the left gains power, they will demolish the suburbs, confiscate your guns, and appoint justices who will wipe away your Second Amendment and other Constitutional freedoms.

Biden is a Trojan horse for socialism. If Joe Biden doesn't have the strength to stand up to wild-eyed Marxists like Bernie Sanders and his fellow radicals, then how is he ever going to stand up FOR you?

The most dangerous aspect of the Biden Platform is the attack on public safety. The Biden-Bernie Manifesto calls for Abolishing cash bail, immediately releasing 400,000 criminals onto your streets and into your neighborhoods.

When asked if he supports cutting police funding, Joe Biden replied, "Yes, absolutely." When Congresswoman Ilhan Omar called the Minneapolis police department a cancer that is "rotten to the root," Biden wouldn't disavow her support and reject her endorsement—he proudly displayed it on his website.

Make no mistake, if you give power to Joe Biden, the radical left will Defund Police Departments all across America. They will pass federal legislation to reduce law enforcement nationwide. They will make every city look like Democrat-run Portland, Oregon. No one will be safe in Biden's America.

My administration will always stand with the men and women of law enforcement. Every day, police officers risk their lives to keep us safe, and every year, many sacrifice their lives in the line of duty.

One of these incredible Americans was Detective Miosotis Familia. She was part of a team of American Heroes called the NYPD or New York's Finest. Three years ago on Fourth of July weekend, Detective Familia was on duty in her vehicle when she was ambushed just after midnight and murdered by a monster who hated her purely for wearing the badge.

Detective Familia was a single mom—she'd recently asked for the night shift so she could spend more time with her kids. Two years ago, I stood in front of the U.S. Capitol alongside those children, and held their Grandmother's hand as they mourned their terrible loss and we honored Detective Familia's extraordinary life.

Detective Familia's three children are with us this evening. Genesis, Peter, and Delilah, we are so grateful to have you here tonight. I promise you that we will treasure your mom in our memories forever.

We must remember that the overwhelming majority of police officers in this country are noble, courageous and honorable. We have to give law enforcement, our police, back their power. They are afraid to act. They are afraid to lose their pension. They are afraid to lose their jobs, and by being afraid they are not able to do their jobs. And those who suffer most are the great people who they want so desperately to protect.

When there is police misconduct, the justice system must hold wrongdoers fully and completely accountable, and it will. But what we can never have in America—and must never allow—is MOB RULE. In the strongest possible terms, the Republican Party condemns the rioting, looting, arson and violence we have seen in Democrat-run cities like Kenosha, Minneapolis, Portland, Chicago, and New York.

There is violence and danger in the streets of many Democrat-run cities throughout America. This problem could easily be fixed if they wanted to. We must always have law and order. All federal crimes are being investigated, prosecuted, and punished to the fullest extent of the law.

When the anarchists started ripping down our statues and monuments, I signed an order, ten years in prison, and it all stopped.

During their convention, Joe Biden and his supporters remained completely silent about the rioters and criminals spreading mayhem in Democrat-Run Cities. In the face of left-wing anarchy and mayhem in Minneapolis, Chicago, and other cities, Joe Biden's campaign did not condemn it—they DONATED to it. At least 13 members of Joe Biden's campaign staff donated to a fund to bail out vandals, arsonists, looters, and rioters from jail.

Here tonight is the grieving family of retired police Captain David Dorn, a 38-year veteran of the St. Louis Police Department. In June, Captain Dorn was shot and killed as he tried to protect a store from rioters and looters. We are honored to be joined tonight by his wife Ann and beloved family members: Brian and Kielen. To each of you: we will never forget the heroic legacy of Captain David Dorn.

As long as I am President, I will defend the absolute right of every American citizen to live in security, dignity, and peace.

If the Democrat Party wants to stand with anarchists, agitators, rioters, looters, and flag-burners, that is up to them, but I, as your President, will not be a part of it. The Republican Party will remain the voice of the patriotic heroes who keep America Safe.

Last year, over 1,000 African-Americans were murdered as result of violent crime in just four Democrat-run cities. The top 10 most dangerous cities in the country are run by Democrats, and have been for decades. Thousands more African-Americans are victims of violent crime in these communities Joe Biden and the left ignore these American Victims. I NEVER WILL.

If the Radical Left takes power, they will apply their disastrous policies to every city, town, and suburb in America.

Just imagine if the so-called peaceful demonstrators in the streets were in charge of every lever of power in the U.S. Government.

Liberal politicians claim to be concerned about the strength of American institutions. But who, exactly, is attacking them? Who is hiring the radical professors, judges, and prosecutors? Who is trying to abolish immigration enforcement, and establish speech codes designed to muzzle dissent? In every case, the attacks on American institutions are being waged by the radical left.

Always Remember: they are coming after ME, because I am fighting for YOU.

We must reclaim our independence from the left's repressive mandates. Americans are exhausted trying to keep up with the latest list of approved words and phrases, and the ever-more restrictive political decrees. Many things have a different name now, and the rules are constantly changing. The goal of cancel culture is to make decent Americans live in fear of being fired, expelled, shamed, humiliated, and driven from society as we know it. The far-left wants to coerce you into saying what you know to be FALSE, and scare you out of saying what you know to be TRUE.

But on November 3rd, you can send them a thundering message they will never forget!

Joe Biden is weak. He takes his marching orders from liberal hypocrites who drive their cities into the ground while fleeing far from the scene of the wreckage. These same liberals want to eliminate school choice, while they enroll their children in the finest private schools in the land. They want to open our borders while living in walled-off compounds and communities. They want to defund the police, while they have armed guards for themselves.

This November, we must turn the page FOREVER on this failed political class. The fact is, I'm here, and they're not—and that's because of YOU. Together, we will write the next chapter of the Great American Story.

Over the next four years, we will make America into the Manufacturing Superpower of the World. We will expand Opportunity Zones, bring home our medical supply chains, and we will end our reliance on China once and for all.

We will continue to reduce taxes and regulations at levels not seen before.

We will create 10 million jobs in the next 10 months.

We will hire MORE police, increase penalties for assaults on law enforcement, and surge federal prosecutors into high-crime communities.

We will BAN deadly Sanctuary Cities, and ensure that federal healthcare is protected for American Citizens—not illegal aliens.

We will have strong borders, strike down terrorists who threaten our people, and keep America OUT of endless and costly foreign wars.

We will appoint prosecutors, judges, and justices who believe in enforcing the LAW—not their own political agenda.

We will ensure equal justice for citizens of every race, religion, color and creed.

We will uphold your religious liberty, and defend your Second Amendment right to keep and bear arms.

We will protect Medicare and Social Security.

We will always, and very strongly, protect patients with pre-existing conditions, and that is a pledge from the entire Republican Party.

We will END surprise medical billing, require price transparency, and further reduce the cost of prescription drugs and health insurance premiums.

We will greatly expand energy development, continuing to remain number one in the world, and keep America Energy Independent.

We will win the race to 5G, and build the world's best cyber and missile defense.

We will fully restore patriotic education to our schools, and always protect free speech on college campuses.

We will launch a new age of American Ambition in Space. America will land the first WOMAN on the moon—and the United States will be the first nation to plant its flag on Mars.

This is the unifying national agenda that will bring our country TOGETHER.

So tonight, I say again to all Americans: This is the most important election in the history of our country. There has never been such a difference between two parties, or two individuals, in ideology, philosophy, or vision than there is right now.

Our opponents believe that America is a depraved nation.

We want our sons and daughters to know the truth: America is the greatest and most exceptional nation in the history of the world!

Our country wasn't built by cancel culture, speech codes, and soul-crushing conformity. We are NOT a nation of timid spirits. We are a nation of fierce, proud, and independent American Patriots.

We are a nation of pilgrims, pioneers, adventurers, explorers and trailblazers who refused to be tied down, held back, or reined in. Americans have steel in their spines, grit in their souls, and fire in their hearts. There is no one like us on earth.

I want every child in America to know that you are part of the most exciting and incredible adventure in human history. No matter where your family comes from, no matter your background, in America, ANYONE CAN RISE. With hard work, devotion, and drive, you can reach any goal and achieve every ambition.

Our American Ancestors sailed across the perilous ocean to build a new life on a new continent. They braved the freezing winters, crossed the raging rivers, scaled the rocky peaks, trekked the dangerous forests, and worked from dawn till dusk. These pioneers didn't have money, they didn't have fame—but they had each other. They loved their families, they loved their country, and they loved their God!

When opportunity beckoned, they picked up their Bibles, packed up their belongings, climbed into covered wagons, and set out West for the next adventure. Ranchers and miners, cowboys and sheriffs, farmers and settlers—they pressed on past the Mississippi to stake a claim in the Wild Frontier.

Legends were born—Wyatt Earp, Annie Oakley, Davy Crockett, and Buffalo Bill.

Americans built their beautiful homesteads on the Open Range. Soon they had churches and communities, then towns, and with time, great centers of industry and commerce. That is who they were. Americans build the future, we don't tear down the past!

We are the nation that won a revolution, toppled tyranny and fascism, and delivered millions into freedom. We laid down the railroads, built the great ships, raised up the skyscrapers, revolutionized industry, and sparked a new age of scientific discovery. We set the trends in art and music, radio and film, sport and literature—and we did it all with style, confidence and flair. Because THAT is who we are.

Whenever our way of life was threatened, our heroes answered the call.

From Yorktown to Gettysburg, from Normandy to Iwo Jima, American Patriots raced into cannon blasts, bullets and bayonets to rescue American Liberty.

But America didn't stop there. We looked into the sky and kept pressing onward. We built a 6 million pound rocket, and launched it thousands of miles into space. We did it so that two brave patriots could stand tall and salute our wondrous American flag planted on the face of the Moon.

For America, nothing is impossible.

Over the next four years, we will prove worthy of this magnificent legacy. We will reach stunning new heights. And we will show the world that, for America, no dream is beyond our reach.

Together, we are unstoppable. Together, we are unbeatable. Because together, we are the proud CITIZENS of the UNITED STATES OF AMERICA. And on November 3rd, we will make America safer, we will make America stronger, we will make America prouder, and we will make America GREATER than ever before! Thank you, God Bless You. God Bless America—GOODNIGHT!

Activities

1. What were the differences in storytelling that you observe in the two speeches? What differences did you see in identifying elements of history? In assessing current problems? In offering visions of the future?

2. How did the two speakers differ in terms of how they understood their audiences? To whom did the speeches seem to be primarily addressed?

3. What differences did you discern in the use of evidence or analysis in the two speeches?

4. Summarize the most important issues and policy priorities identified in the two speeches. How did these differences align or differ from your understanding of the ideological priorities for each of the two political parties?
5. Which candidate did you think offered the more compelling case for his election? Why did you feel this way? How difficult was it for you to separate your own political beliefs from your objective assessment of each speech as a rhetorical argument?
6. What metaphors or linguistic devices did you observe in these speeches? How meaningful or effective were those devices?

Appendix B

Eulogy Speech

Former President Barack Obama's funeral tribute to Representative John Lewis, an icon of the civil rights movement[3]

James wrote to the believers, "Consider it pure joy, my brothers and sisters, whenever you face trials of many kinds, because you know that the testing of your faith produces perseverance. Let perseverance finish its work so that you may be mature and complete, lacking nothing."

It is a great honor to be back in Ebenezer Baptist Church, in the pulpit of its greatest pastor, Dr. Martin Luther King, Jr., to pay my respects to perhaps his finest disciple—an American whose faith was tested again and again to produce a man of pure joy and unbreakable perseverance—John Robert Lewis.

To those who have spoken to Presidents Bush and Clinton, Madam Speaker, Reverend Warnock, Reverend King, John's family, friends, his beloved staff, Mayor Bottoms—I've come here today because I, like so many Americans, owe a great debt to John Lewis and his forceful vision of freedom.

Now, this country is a constant work in progress. We were born with instructions: to form a more perfect union. Explicit in those words is the idea that we are imperfect; that what gives each new generation purpose is to take up the unfinished work of the last and carry it further than anyone might have thought possible.

John Lewis—the first of the Freedom Riders, head of the Student Nonviolent Coordinating Committee, youngest speaker at the March on Washington, leader of the march from Selma to Montgomery, Member of Congress representing the people of this state and this district for 33 years, mentor to young people, including me at the time, until his final day on this Earth—he not only embraced that responsibility, but he made it his life's work.

Which isn't bad for a boy from Troy. John was born into modest means—that means he was poor—in the heart of the Jim Crow South to parents who picked somebody else's cotton. Apparently, he didn't take to farm work—on days when he was supposed to help his brothers and sisters with their labor, he'd hide under the porch and make a break for the school bus when it showed up. His mother, Willie Mae Lewis, nurtured that curiosity in this shy, serious child. "Once you learn something," she told her son, "once you get something inside your head, no one can take it away from you."

As a boy, John listened through the door after bedtime as his father's friends complained about the Klan. One Sunday as a teenager, he heard Dr. King preach on the radio. As a college student in Tennessee, he signed up for Jim Lawson's workshops on the tactic of nonviolent civil disobedience. John Lewis was getting something inside his head, an idea he couldn't shake that took hold of him—that nonviolent resistance and civil disobedience were the means to change laws, but also change hearts, and change minds, and change nations, and change the world.

So he helped organize the Nashville campaign in 1960. He and other young men and women sat at a segregated lunch counter, well-dressed, straight-backed, refusing to let a milkshake poured on their heads, or a cigarette extinguished on their backs, or a foot aimed at their ribs, refused to let that dent their dignity and their sense of purpose. And after a few months, the Nashville campaign achieved the first successful desegregation of public facilities in any major city in the South.

John got a taste of jail for the first, second, third ... well, several times. But he also got a taste of victory. And it consumed him with righteous purpose. And he took the battle deeper into the South.

That same year, just weeks after the Supreme Court ruled that segregation of interstate bus facilities was unconstitutional, John and Bernard Lafayette bought two tickets, climbed aboard a Greyhound, sat up front, and refused to move. This was months before the first official Freedom Rides. He was doing a test. The trip was unsanctioned. Few knew what they were up to. And at every stop, through the night, apparently the angry driver stormed out of the bus and into the bus station. And John and Bernard had no idea what he might come back with or who he might come back with. Nobody was there to protect them. There were no camera crews to record events. You know, sometimes, we read about this and kind of take it for granted. Or at least we act as if it was inevitable. Imagine the courage of two people Malia's age, younger than my oldest daughter, on their own, to challenge an entire infrastructure of oppression.

John was only twenty years old. But he pushed all twenty of those years to the center of the table, betting everything, all of it, that his example could challenge centuries of convention, and generations of brutal violence, and countless daily indignities suffered by African Americans.

Like John the Baptist preparing the way, like those Old Testament prophets speaking truth to kings, John Lewis did not hesitate—he kept on getting on board buses and sitting at lunch counters, got his mug shot taken again and again, marched again and again on a mission to change America.

Spoke to a quarter million people at the March on Washington when he was just 23.

Helped organize the Freedom Summer in Mississippi when he was just 24.

At the ripe old age of 25, John was asked to lead the march from Selma to Montgomery. He was warned that Governor Wallace had ordered troopers to use violence. But he and Hosea Williams and others led them across that bridge anyway. And we've all seen the film and the footage and the photographs, and President Clinton mentioned the trench coat, the knapsack, the book to read, the apple to eat, the toothbrush—apparently jails weren't big on such creature comforts. And you look at those pictures and John looks so young and he's small in stature. Looking every bit that shy, serious child that his mother had raised and yet, he is full of purpose. God's put perseverance in him.

And we know what happened to the marchers that day. Their bones were cracked by billy clubs, their eyes and lungs choked with tear gas. As they knelt to pray, which made their heads even easier targets, and John was struck in the skull. And he thought he was going to die, surrounded by the sight of young Americans gagging, and bleeding, and trampled, victims in their own country of state-sponsored violence.

And the thing is, I imagine initially that day, the troopers thought that they had won the battle. You can imagine the conversations they had afterwards. You can imagine them saying, "Yeah, we showed them." They figured they'd turned the protesters back over the bridge; that they'd kept, that they'd preserved a system that denied the basic humanity of their fellow citizens. Except this time, there were some cameras there. This time, the world saw what happened, bore witness to Black Americans who were asking for nothing more than to be treated like other Americans. Who were not asking for special treatment, just the equal treatment promised to them a century before, and almost another century before that.

When John woke up, and checked himself out of the hospital, he would make sure the world saw a movement that was, in the words of Scripture, "hard pressed on every side, but not crushed; perplexed but not in despair; persecuted, but not abandoned; struck down, but not destroyed." They returned to Brown Chapel, a battered prophet, bandages around his head, and he said more marchers will come now. And the people came. And the troopers parted. And the marchers reached Montgomery. And their words reached the White House—and Lyndon Johnson, son of the South, said "We shall overcome," and the Voting Rights Act was signed into law.

The life of John Lewis was, in so many ways, exceptional. It vindicated the faith in our founding, redeemed that faith; that most American of ideas; that idea that any of us ordinary people without rank or wealth or title or fame can somehow point out the imperfections of this nation, and come together, and challenge the status quo, and decide that it is in our power to remake this country that we love until it more closely aligns with our highest ideals. What a radical ideal. What a revolutionary notion. This idea that any of us, ordinary people, a young kid from Troy can stand up to the powers and principalities and say no this isn't right, this isn't true, this isn't just. We can do better. On the battlefield of justice, Americans like John, Americans like the Reverends Lowery and C.T. Vivian, two other patriots that we lost this year, liberated all of us that many Americans came to take for granted.

America was built by people like them. America was built by John Lewises. He as much as anyone in our history brought this country a little bit closer to our highest ideals. And someday, when we do finish that long journey toward freedom; when we do form a more perfect union—whether it's years from now, or decades, or even if it takes another two centuries—John Lewis will be a founding father of that fuller, fairer, better America.

And yet, as exceptional as John was, here's the thing: John never believed that what he did was more than any citizen of this country can do. I mentioned in the statement the day John passed, the thing about John was just how gentle and humble he was. And despite this storied, remarkable career, he treated everyone with kindness and respect because it was innate to him—this idea that any of us can do what he did if we are willing to persevere.

He believed that in all of us, there exists the capacity for great courage, that in all of us there is a longing to do what's right, that in all of us there is a willingness to love all people, and to extend to them their God-given rights to dignity and respect. So many of us lose that sense. It's taught out of us. We start feeling as if, in fact, that we can't afford to extend kindness or decency to other people. That we're better off if we are above other people and looking down on them, and so often that's encouraged in our culture. But John always saw the best in us. And he never gave up, and never stopped speaking out because he saw the best in us. He believed in us even when we didn't believe in ourselves. As a Congressman, he didn't rest; he kept getting himself arrested. As an old man, he didn't sit out any fight; he sat in, all night long, on the floor of the United States Capitol. I know his staff was stressed.

But the testing of his faith produced perseverance. He knew that the march is not yet over, that the race is not yet won, that we have not yet reached that blessed destination where we are judged by the content of our character. He knew from his own life that progress is fragile; that we have to be vigilant against the darker currents of this country's history, of our own history, with their whirlpools of violence and hatred and despair that can always rise again.

Bull Connor may be gone. But today we witness with our own eyes police officers kneeling on the necks of Black Americans. George Wallace may be gone. But we can witness our federal government sending agents to use tear gas and batons against peaceful demonstrators. We may no longer have to guess the number of jelly beans in a jar in order to cast a ballot. But even as we sit here, there are those in power are doing their darnedest to discourage people from voting—by closing polling locations, and targeting minorities and students with restrictive ID laws, and attacking our voting rights with surgical precision, even undermining the Postal Service in the run-up to an election that is going to be dependent on mailed-in ballots so people don't get sick.

Now, I know this is a celebration of John's life. There are some who might say we shouldn't dwell on such things. But that's why I'm talking about it. John Lewis devoted his time on this Earth fighting the very attacks on democracy and what's best in America that we are seeing circulate right now.

He knew that every single one of us has a God-given power. And that the fate of this democracy depends on how we use it; that democracy isn't automatic, it has to be nurtured, it has to be tended to, we have to work at it, it's hard. And so he knew it depends on whether we summon a measure, just a measure, of John's moral courage to question what's right and what's wrong and call things as they are. He said that as long as he had breath in his body, he would do everything he could to preserve this democracy. That as long as we have breath in our bodies, we have to continue his cause. If we want our children to grow up in a democracy—not just with elections, but a true democracy, a representative democracy, a big-hearted, tolerant, vibrant, inclusive America of perpetual self-creation—then we are going to have to be more like John. We don't have to do all the things he had to do because he did them for us. But we have got to do something. As the Lord instructed Paul, "Do not be afraid, go on speaking; do not be silent, for I am with you, and no one will attack you to harm you, for I have many in this city who are my people." Just everybody's just got to come out and vote. We've got all those people in the city but we can't do nothing.

Like John, we have got to keep getting into that good trouble. He knew that nonviolent protest is patriotic; a way to raise public awareness, put a spotlight on injustice, and make the powers that be uncomfortable.

Like John, we don't have to choose between protest and politics, it is not an either-or situation, it is a both-and situation. We have to engage in protests where that is effective but we also have to translate our passion and our causes into laws and institutional practices. That's why John ran for Congress thirty-four years ago.

Like John, we have got to fight even harder for the most powerful tool we have, which is the right to vote. The Voting Rights Act is one of the crowning achievements of our democracy. It's why John crossed that bridge. It's why he spilled his blood. And by the way, it was the result of Democratic and Republican efforts. President Bush, who spoke here earlier, and his father, both signed its renewal when they were in office. President Clinton didn't have to because it was the law when he arrived so instead he made a law that made it easier for people to register to vote.

But once the Supreme Court weakened the Voting Rights Act, some state legislatures unleashed a flood of laws designed specifically to make voting harder, especially, by the way, state legislatures where there is a lot of minority turnout and population growth. That's not necessarily a mystery or an accident. It was an attack on what John fought for. It was an attack on our democratic freedoms. And we should treat it as such.

If politicians want to honor John, and I'm so grateful for the legacy of work of all the Congressional leaders who are here, but there's a better way than a statement calling him a hero. You want to honor John? Let's honor him by revitalizing the law that he was willing to die for. And by the way, naming it the John Lewis Voting Rights Act, that is a fine tribute. But John wouldn't want us to stop there, trying to get back to where we already were. Once we pass the John Lewis Voting Rights Act, we should keep marching to make it even better.

By making sure every American is automatically registered to vote, including former inmates who've earned their second chance.

By adding polling places, and expanding early voting, and making Election Day a national holiday, so if you are someone who is working in a factory, or you are a single mom who has got to go to her job and doesn't get time off, you can still cast your ballot.

By guaranteeing that every American citizen has equal representation in our government, including the American citizens who live in Washington, D.C. and in Puerto Rico. They are Americans.

By ending some of the partisan gerrymandering—so that all voters have the power to choose their politicians, not the other way around.

And if all this takes eliminating the filibuster—another Jim Crow relic—in order to secure the God-given rights of every American, then that's what we should do.

And yet, even if we do all this—even if every bogus voter suppression law was struck off the books today—we have got to be honest with ourselves that too many of us choose not to exercise the franchise; that too many of our citizens believe their vote won't make a difference, or they buy into the cynicism that, by the way, is the central strategy of voter suppression, to make you discouraged, to stop believing in your own power.

So we are also going to have to remember what John said: "If you don't do everything you can to change things, then they will remain the same. You only pass this way once. You have to give it all you have." As long as young people are protesting in the streets, hoping real change takes hold, I'm hopeful but we cannot casually abandon them at the ballot box. Not when few elections have been as urgent, on so many levels, as this one. We cannot treat voting as an errand to run if we have some time. We have to treat it as the most important action we can take on behalf of democracy.

Like John, we have to give it all we have.

I was proud that John Lewis was a friend of mine. I met him when I was in law school. He came to speak and I went up and I said, "Mr. Lewis, you are one of my heroes. What inspired me more than anything as a young man was to see what you and Reverend Lawson and Bob Moses and Diane Nash and others did." And he got that kind of—aw shucks, thank you very much.

The next time I saw him, I had been elected to the United States Senate. And I told him, "John, I am here because of you." On Inauguration Day in 2008, 2009, he was one of the first people that I greeted and hugged on that stand. I told him, "This is your day too."

He was a good and kind and gentle man. And he believed in us—even when we don't believe in ourselves. It's fitting that the last time John and I shared a public forum was on Zoom. I am pretty sure that neither he nor I set up the Zoom call because we didn't know how to work it. It was a virtual town hall with a gathering of young activists who had been helping to lead this summer's demonstrations in the wake of George Floyd's death. And afterwards, I spoke to John privately, and he could not have been prouder to see this new generation of activists standing up for freedom and equality; a new generation that was intent on voting and protecting the right to vote; in some cases, a new generation running for political office.

I told him, all those young people, John—of every race and every religion, from every background and gender and sexual orientation—John, those are your children. They learned from your example, even if they didn't always know it. They had understood, through him, what American citizenship requires, even if they had only heard about his courage through the history books.

"By the thousands, faceless, anonymous, relentless young people, Black and white . . . have taken our whole nation back to those great wells of democracy which were dug deep by the founding fathers in the formulation of the Constitution and the Declaration of Independence."

Dr. King said that in the 1960s. And it came true again this summer.

We see it outside our windows, in big cities and rural towns, in men and women, young and old, straight Americans and LGBTQ Americans, Blacks who long for equal treatment and whites who can no longer accept freedom for themselves while witnessing the subjugation of their fellow Americans. We see it in everybody doing the hard work of overcoming complacency, of overcoming our own fears and our own prejudices, our own hatreds. You see it in people trying to be better, truer versions of ourselves.

And that's what John Lewis teaches us. That's where real courage comes from. Not from turning on each other, but by turning towards one another. Not by sowing hatred and division, but by spreading love and truth. Not by avoiding our responsibilities to create a better America and a better world, but by embracing those responsibilities with joy and perseverance and discovering that in our beloved community, we do not walk alone.

What a gift John Lewis was. We are all so lucky to have had him walk with us for a while, and show us the way.

God bless you all. God bless America. God bless this gentle soul who pulled it closer to its promise.

ACTIVITIES

1. What aspects of Representative Lewis's character and/or life experiences are cited as arguments in this eulogy?
2. How did former President Obama argue that we should emulate those aspects of character?
3. What constitutes the evidence or proof offered in support of Obama's arguments?
4. What rhetorical and argumentative techniques does Obama use not only in an effort to secure Representative Lewis's memory as a consummate politician but also as a figure that transcends partisan politics?
5. What metaphors, literary devices, and other figures of speech are used to support arguments in this speech?

Appendix C

Case Study for Analysis

Kevin Cooper escaped from the California Institute for Men, a state prison in Chino, California, on June 2, 1983. He admitted that he hid for two days and two nights in a vacant house (the Lease house) near the prison. On Saturday night three members of the Ryen family (Doug and Peggy Ryen and their 10-year-old daughter Jessica) who lived next door to the Lease house were hacked to death, as was Chris Hughes, an 11-year-old neighbor child spending the night at the Ryen's house. A fifth victim, 8-year-old Josh Ryen, was left with serious injuries. Cooper was ultimately arrested and charged with four counts of first-degree murder and one count of attempted murder in the first degree, as well as with escape from a state prison. On February 19, 1985, he was convicted of the crimes; following a separate penalty hearing he was sentenced to death. On May 6, 1991, the California Supreme Court affirmed the convictions and the death sentence, and the United States Supreme Court declined to hear the case. Cooper's attorneys continued to pursue additional appeals, alleging that there were serious errors made in the investigation of the case and the presentation of evidence to the jury. We have included an order filed by the United States Court of Appeals for the Ninth Circuit on February 8, 2004. This order provides a fascinating illustration of the intricacies and complexities of arguments in a legal forum. Cooper was offered a last meal and was in a holding area outside the execution chamber when the Ninth Circuit granted a stay of execution on February 9, 2004.

The *New York Times* writer Nicholas Kristoff first wrote about the case in 2017 and published an investigative essay in May 2018.[4] In 2021, he summarized his findings: "It was an unimaginable tragedy, and it has been followed by another unimaginable tragedy, one that has lasted almost 38 years: A man who is very likely innocent appears to have been framed for that crime and remains on death row today."[5] Kristoff wrote that he hoped the governor of California would create a panel to review Cooper's case but cautioned that the criminal justice system emphasizes closure and finality, placing significant impediments to freeing a convicted person even when new information comes to light. On May 28, 2021, Governor Gavin Newsom signed an executive order for an independent law firm to examine Cooper's claims of innocence and appeal for clemency by reviewing his trial, his appeals and the facts underlying the conviction.[6]

After reading the arguments in the 2004 decision, answer the following questions.

1. From the Ninth Circuit Court's summary of the case, can you identify the primary elements of the prosecution's narrative? What was the motive attributed to the defendant? How did the prosecutor establish issues related to the defendant's means and opportunity to commit these crimes? What were the most compelling forms of evidence found to support a claim of guilt? How do you believe such evidence would likely influence jurors' perceptions of guilt or innocence? What elements of this evidence did you find less than fully convincing? Why?

2. Reading the Ninth Circuit's presentation, can you Identify the primary elements of Kevin Cooper's narrative of the case. In what ways was the defendant's narrative

incompatible with that offered by the prosecution? What evidence did the defendant offer to support his narrative? How effectively did the defendant's attorneys refute key elements of the prosecution's evidence? Why do you believe the jury failed to accept the defendant's position in the initial court proceedings? Why do these same claims find some support among the appellate justices?

3. What were the substantive questions of law and/or procedure advanced in the appeal? How did the different justices evaluate these arguments? What was the final court ruling? Do you agree or disagree with this ruling?

4. What arguments did you find to be missing from these transcripts? What additional arguments might you offer to support either the approval or denial of a stay of execution?

5. Why do you think Nicholas Kristoff has become convinced that Cooper was wrongfully convicted? What evidence did you not find in this court brief that might explain his position?

6. How might your personal political beliefs, ideology, experiences, or values influence your reading and evaluation of these arguments? To what extent might recent events regarding policing and race influence your understanding and analysis of this case?

KEVIN COOPER, Petitioner, v. JEANNE WOODFORD, Warden, San Quentin State Prison, San Quentin, California, Respondent.*

Judges: Before: James R. Browning, Pamela Ann Rymer, and Ronald M. Gould, Circuit Judges. Order; Dissent by Judge Browning.

Order

Kevin Cooper, a California death row inmate whose execution is scheduled for Tuesday, February 10, 2004 at 12:01 a.m., has filed an application to file a successor petition for writ of habeas corpus under 28 U.S.C. § 2244(b)(3), and a request for stay of execution. His request for an order authorizing the district court to consider this petition—his third application [*2][†] in the federal system following denial of his original habeas petition—is premised on the existence of evidence with respect to a blood spot, cigarette butts, and shoe print impressions that he asserts was manufactured by the state and which, if known to the jury, would have weakened the links in the state's chain of circumstantial evidence. He asks for another chance affirmatively to demonstrate his innocence through available mitochondrial DNA testing of hairs found in one of the victim's hands, and testing for the presence of a preservative agent EDTA on a T-shirt. However, with immaterial exceptions, this application turns on facts that have long since been known and that have already been presented and resolved adversely to Cooper in state court evidentiary hearings, proceedings before the California Supreme Court on direct and collateral review, in his original habeas petition in federal court, and in connection with his applications in this court to file second or successive petitions. To the extent that the claims are formulated differently in the petition he now asks to file, they are nevertheless based on facts that were available and could previously have been discovered [*3] with the exercise of due diligence. For this reason, Cooper fails to make the showing that the Anti-Terrorism and Effective Death Penalty Act of 1996 (AEDPA) requires for approval of his application. 28 U.S.C. § 2244(b)(3)(C).

In addition, Cooper's petition does not set forth facts that are sufficient to show by clear and convincing evidence that, in light of the evidence as a whole, no reasonable factfinder would have found him guilty of the offenses charged. The few items of evidence upon which

---

* 357 F.3d 1019 (9th Cir. 2004) No. 04-70578; (February 8, 2004, Filed). Retrieved online 8/31/04 from LexisNexis.

† The starred numbers that appear in brackets represent itemized pieces of evidence introduced in the trial.

Cooper now relies that were not before the jury have little or no probative value and fall short of showing that it is more likely than not that no reasonable juror would have convicted him.

Cooper has made no showing of actual innocence, nor has he shown that it would be manifestly unjust for the courts to decline to revisit the same issues again. Accordingly, we deny the application to file this successive petition. Given this decision, there is no basis for granting a stay.

I.

On June 2, 1983, Cooper escaped from the California Institute for Men (CIM), a state prison.[1] He admitted that he stayed in a vacant house (the Lease house) next door to the Ryens' residence [*4] on Thursday night, all day Friday, and Friday night; he hid in the bathroom when one of the owners of the Lease house stopped by on Saturday morning. The murders happened Saturday night. Using a hatchet or axe and a knife, he hacked to death Douglas and Peggy Ryen (37 separate wounds for Douglas, 32 for Peggy), their ten-year-old-daughter Jessica (46 wounds), and eleven-year-old Christopher Hughes (26 wounds), who was spending the night at the Ryens' home. Cooper also inflicted chopping wounds to the head, and stabbing wounds to the throat, of eight-year-old Joshua Ryen, who survived.

At the Lease house, a blood-stained khaki green button identical to the buttons on field jackets issued at the state prison from which Cooper escaped was found on the rug. Tests revealed the presence of blood in the shower and bathroom sink of the Lease home, and hair found in the bathroom sink was consistent with that of Jessica and [*5] Doug Ryen. A bloodstained rope in the Lease house bedroom was similar to a bloodstained rope found on the Ryens' driveway. A hatchet covered with dried blood and human hair that was found near the Ryens' home was missing from the Lease house, and the sheath for the hatchet was found in the bedroom where Cooper stayed. Buck knives and at least one ice pick were also missing from the Lease home, though a strap from one buck knife was found on the floor.

Blood found in the Ryens' home was the victims', except for one drop on a wall near where the murders occurred. It belonged to an African-American male, which Cooper is. Two partial shoe prints and one nearly complete shoe print found in the Ryens' house were consistent both with Cooper's size and the Pro Keds shoes issued at CIM.

The Ryens' vehicle, which had been parked outside their house, was missing when the bodies were discovered but was later found in Long Beach. A hand-rolled cigarette butt and "Role-Rite" tobacco that is provided to inmates at CIM (but not sold at retail) was in the car. Similar loose leaf tobacco was found in the bedroom of the Lease house where Cooper had stayed. A witness testified that Cooper smoked hand-rolled [*6] cigarettes using Role-Rite tobacco. A hair fragment discovered in the car was consistent with Cooper's pubic hair and a spot of blood found in the car could have come from one of the victims but not from Cooper.

Cooper was charged with four counts of first degree murder and one count of attempted murder in the first degree, and with escape from state prison. He pled guilty to escaping from state prison. On February 19, 1985, a jury convicted Cooper of the first degree murders of Franklyn Douglas Ryen, Jessica Ryen, Peggy Ann Ryen and Christopher Hughes, and of attempted murder in the first degree of Joshua Ryen. The jury found true the special circumstance of multiple murders, which made Cooper death-eligible under California's sentencing scheme. The jury also found true the special circumstance that Cooper intentionally inflicted great bodily injury on Joshua Ryen. The jury then determined the penalty as death on the four murder counts. On May 6, 1991, the California Supreme Court affirmed the convictions and sentence. *See People v. Cooper,* 53 Cal. 3d 771, 281 Cal. Rptr. 90, 809 P.2d 865 (1991). The United States Supreme Court denied a petition for writ of certiorari on December 16, 1991. [*7] *Cooper v. California,* 502 U.S. 1016, 116 L. Ed. 2d 755, 112 S. Ct. 664 (1991).

On March 24, 1992 Cooper requested appointment of counsel and a stay of execution from the United States District Court for the Southern District of California. He then filed a petition for writ of habeas corpus in the district court on August 11, 1994, and an amended petition on April 12, 1996. Meanwhile, he returned to state court to exhaust a number of claims. On February 19,

1996, the California Supreme Court denied Cooper's state habeas petition. Cooper then filed a supplemental petition in district court on June 20, 1997. Following an evidentiary hearing, the petition was denied on August 25, 1997. We affirmed in *Cooper v. Calderon*, 255 F.3d 1104 (9th Cir. 2001), and Cooper's petition for a writ of certiorari was denied by the United States Supreme Court. 537 U.S. 861, 154 L. Ed. 2d 100, 123 S. Ct. 238 (2002). Cooper filed numerous additional papers in state court, and another federal petition for writ of habeas corpus on April 20, 1998. We treated his appeal from the district court's denial of that petition as an application for authorization to file a second or successive petition for writ of habeas [*8] corpus based on trial counsel's ineffective assistance with respect to the Koon confession, which we denied. *Cooper v. Calderon*, 274 F.3d 1270 (9th Cir. 2001). Cooper then filed a request to file another successor petition that involved DNA testing and tampering, which we also denied; *Cooper v. Calderon*, 2003 U.S. App. LEXIS 27035, No. 99-71430 (9th Cir. Feb. 14, 2003), 2003 U.S. App. LEXIS 27036 (Apr. 7, 2003) (orders).

Cooper has filed six writs of habeas corpus in the California Supreme Court, the most recent of which was filed on February 2, 2004 and denied February 5, 2004. The petition before the California Supreme Court raised similar claims to those asserted in this application (actual innocence, tampering with evidence, failure to disclose exculpatory evidence, offering unreliable eye witness testimony of Joshua Ryen, denying Cooper the effective assistance of counsel during post-conviction DNA proceedings, and refusal of the state superior court to accept his petition for filing). The supreme court denied all claims on the merits and also denied those having to do with evidence tampering, failure to disclose exculpatory evidence/submission of false testimony to the jury, and offering Ryen's unreliable testimony [*9] as untimely, *In re Robbins*, 18 Cal. 4th 770, 780, 77 Cal. Rptr. 2d 153, 959 P.2d 311 (1998).

II.

Cooper's application is governed by AEDPA. Under AEDPA, in order for us to grant Cooper's application to file a successive petition, he must present a claim that was not previously presented in a federal habeas petition, and that relies on either a new rule of constitutional law made retroactive to cases on collateral review by the Supreme Court, or a factual predicate which could not have been discovered through due diligence and that would be sufficient to establish by clear and convincing evidence that, but for constitutional error, no reasonable factfinder would have found him guilty of the offense. 28 U.S.C. §§ 2244(b)(1), 2244(b)(2). We must decide whether his application makes a prima facie showing that satisfies these requirements. 28 U.S.C. § 2244(b)(3)(C).

Cooper argues that he has satisfied these prerequisites because evidence that he says is newly discovered through DNA proceedings, including evidence of false statements by the criminalist and continuing attempts to prevent Cooper from proving his innocence, provide factual predicates for compelling [*10] constitutional claims. As we will explain, findings by the state trial court after an evidentiary hearing are directly to the contrary. Cooper further contends that the evidence as a whole, including a confession by Kevin Koon, establishes by clear and convincing evidence that, but for the state's treachery, no reasonable factfinder would have been led to find Cooper guilty. As we will also explain, the district court found that the Koon confession would have had no effect on the outcome of the trial, and this court denied Cooper's request to file a second or successive petition on the same issue.

Further, Cooper submits that a claim is not subject to the requirements of § 2244(b) when the events that give rise to the claim occurred after resolution of the prior habeas petition. For this he relies on *Stewart v. Martinez-Villareal*, 523 U.S. 637, 644-45, 140 L. Ed. 2d 849, 118 S. Ct. 1618 (1998), and *Hill v. State of Alaska*, 297 F.3d 895, 898-99 (9th Cir. 2002). These cases are not helpful, however, because both involved issues such as competence to be executed that could not have been included in an earlier petition.

Finally, Cooper maintains that the requirements [*11] of § 2244(b)(2) need not be satisfied for a second or successive habeas corpus application to be considered by the district court because actual innocence is a constitutional safety valve. *See Schlup v. Delo*, 513 U.S. 298, 130 L. Ed. 2d 808, 115 S.

Ct. 851 (1995); *Herrera v. Collins,* 506 U.S. 390, 122 L. Ed. 2d 203, 113 S. Ct. 853 (1993); *McCleskey v. Zant,* 499 U.S. 467, 113 L. Ed. 2d 517, 111 S. Ct. 1454 (1991). We do not decide in this case whether or not this is so, because as we shall explain, Cooper has neither affirmatively proven actual innocence nor shown that it is more likely than not that, in light of all the evidence, including reliable new evidence of actual innocence, no reasonable juror would have found him guilty beyond a reasonable doubt. *See Carriger v. Stewart,* 132 F.3d 463, 478 (9th Cir. 1997) (adopting this standard).

III.

The petition that Cooper asks for leave to file asserts nine claims. We consider them in turn.

Actual innocence (claim one). Cooper's application repeats his theory of defense—that he did not commit the murders and the prosecution provided no motive. He relies on evidence, or the lack of it, that he also relied [*12] upon at trial or presented in his first federal habeas petition and applications for second or successive petitions: that Joshua Ryen referred to several assailants and said he had never seen Cooper before; that three suspicious men were observed in the vicinity of the murders on the night they occurred; that the number of weapons used indicates multiple assailants were involved; that law enforcement ignored information about other possible suspects, in particular Diana Roper's that Lee Furrow (her boyfriend) may have participated in the murders and left "bloody" coveralls in her closet; that the police destroyed the coveralls; that the state ignored a purported confession by Kevin Koon; and that cigarette butts were tampered with. All of this, except perhaps for the cigarette butts (which we consider in connection with the second claim), has been known since the time of trial, but regardless, does not show that Cooper is probably innocent.

Evidence that Joshua Ryen said that three strangers had been at the house earlier looking for work and at one point said that he believed they may have been involved was before the jury. It lacks probative force given that he also testified that [*13] he only saw one person in the house when the murders occurred. Other people could have been at the house, too, yet Cooper's innocence would not be shown because his blood was on the wall and strong circumstantial evidence connected him with the house and the Ryens' car. Cooper's reliance on the Roper evidence is misplaced, because that evidence would show that Roper had a "vision" that the coveralls might have some importance to the Ryen murders, and that the law enforcement official to whom the coveralls were given believed they looked stained but not *blood*-stained. That officer testified at an evidentiary hearing in state court that the coveralls had hair, sweat, dirt, and manure on them. He testified similarly at trial. Thus, the evidence *was* considered by the jury. In addition, both the state trial court after an evidentiary hearing, and the district court on Cooper's first habeas petition, determined that the coveralls had no exculpatory value at the time they were destroyed and that there was no factual basis for finding any bad faith on the part of the prosecutor or sheriff. The first federal petition likewise resolved that the Koon "confession" was not material. Another [*14] inmate (Anthony Wisely) told officers that Koon confessed, but Koon himself said that he had not. It is not more likely than not that no reasonable juror would have found Cooper guilty based on this.

Cooper points to one piece of evidence that is newly discovered, that an inmate at the Chino Institute for Men where Cooper was incarcerated before his escape recanted (on January 8, 2004) his trial testimony that he gave Cooper a pair of Pro Keds tennis shoes shortly before Cooper escaped. Even if the inmate's recantation could not have been discovered previously through the exercise of due diligence, this evidence alone lacks clear and convincing force and is not sufficient to show that no reasonable factfinder would have found Cooper guilty if this fact had been known. The same applies to Cooper's claim that evidence exists that Pro Keds shoes were also available to the military and were not special-issue to CIM. The reason is that no matter what the source of the shoes, the same print impression was found outside the Ryen master bedroom, on a sheet on the Ryen bedroom waterbed, and in the game room of the Lease house. This connected Cooper, who stayed in the Lease house, to the scene [*15] of the crime. Considered in light of all the evidence, the newly discovered recantation would not be sufficient to establish that no reasonable juror would have found Cooper guilty.

Cooper's successive petition also alleges that his innocence would be manifest by mitochondrial DNA testing on blond hair clutched by one of the victims and EDTA testing on a bloody T-shirt, and would have been manifest but for mishandling of Exhibit A-41 (the blood spot found in the hallway of the Ryens' home), cigarette butts from the Ryen car and the Lease house, and a shoe impression. Information about how the exhibits were treated and tested is not newly discovered. Dr. Gregonis, the criminalist who analyzed the blood spot (Exhibit A-41), was extensively cross-examined at trial about his analysis and about the fact that he had changed his original analysis. The trial court found after an evidentiary hearing that all tests had been conducted in good faith. The post-conviction DNA testing claims were also before us, and resolved, in connection with Cooper's application for a second and successive petition. That application (in Case No. 99-71430) and Cooper's request for us to reconsider our denial of [*16] it, which we treated as if it were a new application, were based on DNA testing, asserted deficiencies in the testing process, and tampering. We concluded that there was no basis for a petition based on any of these claims. *Cooper v. Calderon,* 2003 U.S. App. LEXIS 27035, Case No. 99-71430 (9th Cir. Feb. 14, 2003) (noting that DNA tests to which the state and Cooper agreed are not exculpatory and denying motion to file a second habeas corpus petition as Cooper failed to present newly discovered facts establishing his innocence); *Cooper v. Calderon,* 2003 U.S. App. LEXIS 27036, Case No. 99-71430 (9th Cir. Apr. 7, 2003) (order denying Cooper's petition for rehearing that was based on asserted deficiencies in the testing and tampering). These issues may not be revisited. 28 U.S.C. § 2244(b)(1).

In addition, there was a three-day evidentiary hearing in June 2003 with respect to whether further mitochondrial testing was warranted on the hairs in the victims' hands, and whether law enforcement personnel tampered with or contaminated the evidence that was analyzed using nuclear DNA testing. The trial court found that Cooper had not shown that mtDNA testing of the hairs recovered from the victims' hands was material [*17] to the identity of the perpetrator, and that even if the results were favorable to him, it would not create a reasonable probability that a different verdict would have been returned by the jury. The trial court also found that Gregonis (and other San Bernardino officials) credibly testified as to the chain of custody of the evidence in question, that Gregonis did not contaminate or tamper with any piece of evidence, and that Cooper made no showing that law enforcement personnel tampered with or contaminated any evidence in his case. *Order Denying Motion For Mitochondrial DNA Testing, Claim of Evidence Tampering, and Request for Post-Conviction Discovery,* Case No. CR 72787 (Superior Court of the State of California in and for the County of San Diego, July 2, 2003). These findings are presumptively correct, 28 U.S.C. § 2254(e)(1), and no clear and convincing evidence alleged by Cooper rebuts them.[2]

[*18]

Evidence tampering, destruction, and withholding (claim two). Cooper argues that the heart of his claim is that the state at trial, and through today, continues a pattern of deception and manipulation of evidence, inept and corrupt practices, and concealing official misconduct. In particular, he faults the work of criminalist Daniel Gregonis about most of which, as his application notes, the courts are well aware. The application points to newer evidence that Gregonis and Department of Justice criminalist Myers mishandled and contaminated evidence in 1999 and thereafter in connection with DNA testing, that Gregonis tampered with Exhibit A-41, that the state failed to deal with other blood samples in the vicinity of Exhibit A-41, that cigarette butts were mishandled, that evidence (such as the footprint, and sheath) were planted, and that leads were not pursued. The application also asserts that some of the officials involved in the investigation of the Cooper case were themselves at some time the subject of criminal investigations, the most significant of which in his view was San Bernardino Sheriff's Department Crime Lab manager William Baird. The district court already considered [*19] Cooper's allegation that the prosecution should have informed him about Baird's termination from the Sheriff's Department in 1988 (three years after the trial and five years after the investigation occurred), and determined that there was no *Brady* or *Agurs* violation[3] and no reasonable probability that, had the evidence been disclosed, the result of the proceeding would have been different. That other officials have been investigated for matters unrelated to the Cooper case is largely irrelevant. Cooper suggests that the *Brady* duty extends through post-conviction proceedings, but even if so the duty would be to disclose information that was material to trial. Finally, so far as tampering with the DNA testing (which occurred during post-conviction proceedings) is concerned, the state trial court determined in its evidentiary hearing that Cooper's claims lacked merit, and we resolved in connection with Cooper's motion for a second habeas corpus petition that nothing claimed about the DNA testing satisfies the requirements for a second or successive application.

[*20]

Failure to disclose exculpatory evidence (claim three). Cooper's application asserts that the prosecution knew about, and suppressed, Baird's alleged heroin use, failed to disclose information that three Hispanic males who were in jail on other charges in the summer of 1984 discussed their participation in the Ryen murders, and that the warden did not think that the tennis shoes that left the prints were particularly unique. However, none of this information is newly discovered.

Unreliable or altered testimony of Joshua Ryen (claim four). Cooper claims that Joshua Ryen's perceptions and recollections changed and were unduly influenced by law enforcement. Cooper also claims that the state's interference deprived him of relevant testimony. However, this is not newly discovered.

Denial of access to the courts (claim five). Cooper claims that he was denied access to the courts because the state trial court refused on January 23, 2004 to accept his most recent petition for writ of habeas corpus and two discovery motions, and the California Supreme Court denied his petition without requesting informal briefing. We discern no constitutional violation cognizable on federal habeas [*21] review. There is nothing untoward about the superior court deferring to the supreme court, particularly given the time exigencies involved, and Cooper's claims were adjudicated by the supreme court on the merits. The superior court had already denied Cooper's request for additional, mitochondrial DNA testing and found that it would shed no light on the outcome of the trial.

Evidence about bloody coveralls (claim six). As Cooper acknowledges, the claim regarding the destruction of the bloody coveralls has been raised in every available forum, and has been denied in every forum.

Ineffective assistance of counsel (claims seven, eight and nine). Cooper raises three claims that he was denied effective assistance of counsel with respect to the Koon confession, the bloody coveralls together with Lee Furrow's possible participation in the murders, and evidence of brown and blond hairs in the victims' hands that could not have come from Cooper. Nothing averred about the Koon confession is newly discovered. We previously determined that an ineffective assistance claim based on it would be a second or successive petition and denied leave to proceed with respect to it. *Cooper v. Calderon*, 274 F.3d at 1275. [*22] In any event, as the district court determined, the Koon confession was not material so even if counsel were deficient, there would be no prejudice. Nor is there anything new about connecting the coveralls to Lee Furrow or the fact that the victims were clutching hairs or fibers differently colored from Cooper's.

Either because the claims were previously raised and are now barred, 28 U.S.C. § 2244(b)(1), or were previously known or discoverable, 28 U.S.C. § 2244(b)(2)(B)(i), and because the facts underlying the claims in light of the evidence as a whole do not show clearly and convincingly that no reasonable factfinder would have found Cooper guilty, 28 U.S.C. § 2244(b)(2)(B)(ii), Cooper's application fails to satisfy the requirements of AEDPA and must be dismissed.

IV.

Cooper argues that apart from AEDPA, he has shown actual innocence sufficient to preclude imposition of the death penalty, *Herrera*, 506 U.S. 390, 122 L. Ed. 2d 203, 113 S. Ct. 853, or that he has at least made a strong enough showing of innocence to permit consideration of procedurally barred claims under *Schlup*, 513 U.S. 298, 130 L. Ed. 2d 808, 115 S. Ct. 851. [*23] *Carriger*, 132 F.3d 463. We do not believe that the standard for either is met.

There are two types of actual innocence claims. A free-standing claim of actual innocence does not require due diligence, and protects the entirely innocent. The threshold for establishing actual innocence regardless of constitutional error at trial is "extraordinarily high." *Carriger,* 132 F.3d at 476 (quoting *Herrera,* 506 U.S. at 417 (O'Connor, J., concurring)). We have held that it is higher than the standard to invalidate a conviction because of insufficient evidence, which is that no rational finder of fact could convict beyond a reasonable doubt in light of all the presently available evidence. *Id.* Rather, a freestanding claim of innocence requires affirmative proof of innocence. *Id.* Put differently, a petitioner making a freestanding claim of actual innocence "'must present evidence of innocence so strong that his execution would be 'constitutionally intolerable even if his conviction was the product of a fair trial.'" *Id.* at 478 (quoting *Schlup,* 513 U.S. at 316).

Cooper has not affirmatively proved his actual [*24] innocence by "'reliable evidence not presented at trial.'" *Calderon v. Thompson,* 523 U.S. 538, 559, 140 L. Ed. 2d 728, 118 S. Ct. 1489 (1998) (quoting *Schlup,* 513 U.S. at 324). At most he alleges the stuff of which cross-examination is made, not evidence that he did not do it. *See Carriger,* 132 F.3d at 477 ("Although the postconviction evidence he presents casts a vast shadow of doubt over the reliability of his conviction, nearly all of it serves only to undercut the evidence presented at trial, not affirmatively to prove Carriger's innocence.").

However, "while a petitioner making a *Herrera* claim must present evidence of innocence so strong that his execution would be 'constitutionally intolerable *even if* his conviction was the product of a fair trial,' a petitioner making a miscarriage of justice claim need only present evidence of innocence strong enough 'that a court cannot have confidence in the outcome of the trial *unless* the court is also satisfied that the trial was free of nonharmless constitutional error.'" *Carriger,* 132 F.3d at 478 (quoting *Herrera,* 506 U.S. at 442-44 (Blackmun, J., dissenting)) [*25] (italics in original) (internal quotation marks omitted). To permit consideration of a procedurally barred claim, a petitioner must show that "in light of all the evidence, including new evidence, 'it is more likely than not that no reasonable juror would have found petitioner guilty beyond a reasonable doubt.'" *Id.* (quoting *Schlup,* 513 U.S. at 327).

Other circuits have stated that the *Schlup* "gateway" has been codified in AEDPA and requires a petitioner to show a factual predicate which could not have been discovered through due diligence, and that would be sufficient to establish by clear and convincing evidence that, but for constitutional error, no reasonable factfinder would have found him guilty of the offense. *See, e.g., David v. Hall,* 318 F.3d 343, 347 n.5 (1st Cir. 2003) ("In AEDPA Congress adopted a form of actual innocence test as one component of its threshold requirements for allowing a second or successive habeas petition; but it also provided that this second petition is allowed only where the factual predicate for the claim of constitutional error could not have been discovered previously through the exercise of due diligence. [*26] ") (citing 28 U.S.C. § 2244(b)(2)(B)); *Flanders v. Graves,* 299 F.3d 974, 977 (8th Cir. 2002) (stating that the *Schlup* "gateway" to consider otherwise procedurally barred claims is "partially codified" in AEDPA at § 2244(b)(2)(B)(ii)); *see also In re Minarik,* 166 F.3d 591, 600 (3rd Cir. 1999) (stating that AEDPA "significantly altered" the showing a petitioner is "required to make in order to proceed on new claims in a second petition," by requiring a petitioner to show actual innocence and that the factual predicate for the claim could not have been previously discovered through due diligence); *cf. United States v. Barrett,* 178 F.3d 34, 48 (1st Cir. 1999) (referring to the "actual innocence" exception to the bar on second or successive petitions as part of the pre-AEDPA test).

Were we to adopt this reasoning of other circuits, Cooper's lack of due diligence would foreclose his actual-innocence-as-a-gateway argument. But we do not need to resolve this question because Cooper cannot show actual innocence under either the "clear and convincing" AEDPA § 2244(b)(2)(B)(ii) requirement, or the "more likely than [*27] not" *Schlup* requirement. To the extent that AEDPA does not codify *Schlup,* we believe for the same reasons that no sufficient showing for a second or successive application is made, that none is made for purposes of *Schlup.*

In addition to what we have already explained, even if Cooper were entirely correct that the post-conviction DNA testing to which he agreed was deficient, and even if Dan Gregonis, the San Bernardino County criminalist who Cooper claims contaminated evidence to incriminate him did contaminate evidence to which he had access, the *other* items of evidence to which the criminalist did *not* have access also inculpate Cooper. That would include a hand-rolled cigarette butt recovered from the Ryen station wagon, a hatchet (one of the murder weapons) with blood and hair evidence, that part of the blood-stained T-shirt which matched Cooper's DNA, and a blood-stained button found in the Lease house. Of course, the jury convicted Cooper without the benefit of DNA evidence, and a reasonable jury could find him guilty even without the incriminating results and even if cross-examination of the criminalist would show that he was negligent or corrupt or both [*28] in connection with it. In any event, the state trial court explicitly found that no such conduct occurred. Finally, there is no reasonable likelihood that mitochondrial DNA testing would be probative of innocence, for any number of people could have come and gone through the Ryen house leaving hairs.

In sum, neither singly nor in combination do these items establish Cooper's innocence, or show that it is more likely than not that no reasonable juror would have convicted him in light of the new evidence. To the contrary, there was clear and compelling evidence that linked Cooper to the crime. After escaping from prison, he stayed at the Lease house that was next door to the Ryens' home; his blood was found on the hallway wall opposite the master bedroom door of the Ryen house; shoe print impressions in the Lease house matched the pattern of prison-issued shoes and one of them was bloody; cigarette butts and tobacco in the Lease house and Ryens' station wagon were prison-issued; a blood-stained khaki green button identical to buttons on field jackets worn by inmates at Chino Institute for Men was found on the rug in the bedroom that Cooper used in the Lease house after the murders; [*29] a hatchet was missing from the Lease house and its sheath was found in the bedroom that Cooper used; and that bedroom and its bathroom, which had been cleaned earlier that day, showed signs of blood after the murders. *See People v. Cooper,* 53 Cal.3d at 795-800 (detailing the evidence of guilt).

As we deny Cooper's application for authorization to file this successor petition, and no other ground appears for issuing a stay, we also deny his request for a stay of execution.

APPLICATION DENIED.

DISSENT: James R. Browning, Senior Circuit Judge

Kevin Cooper is scheduled to be executed at one minute after midnight on Tuesday, February 10, 2004. He seeks two things.

First, Cooper wants to test two pieces of blood evidence for the presence of a preservative. Recent DNA tests of a blood spot and a bloody t-shirt have produced a positive DNA match for Cooper. Cooper contends there has been tampering and that his blood was placed on the evidence after it was collected. A simple and inexpensive test for a preservative in the blood will determine whether he is correct. The test would show whether the blood on the spot and on the t-shirt had [*30] a chemical used by crime laboratories to preserve blood samples in their possession.

Second, Cooper wants to test strands of long blond or light brown hair found clutched in the hand of Jessica Ryen, one of the murder victims. We already know the hair did not come from Cooper, an African-American. Cooper contends Jessica pulled the hair from one of her killers. Photographs in the record clearly show that the amount of hair is substantial, and it is clutched in Jessica's hand. The test could rule out the hair having come from one of the victims. There is evidence in the record to indicate that the crime was committed by three Caucasian men. Thus the test could also corroborate that evidence.

The State has been asked to permit these two tests, but refuses. As justification for its refusal, it states that Cooper had a fair trial, that the evidence of Cooper's guilt is overwhelming, and that it needs to proceed with Cooper's execution.

Contrary to the State's assurances, Cooper did not have a fair trial. Cooper has presented a sworn declaration of a state prison warden that, if believed, suggests that the State fabricated crucial evidence linking Cooper to the murders for which he has [*31] been convicted. Nor is the evidence of Cooper's guilt overwhelming. Indeed, as the evidence mounts that the State used unreliable and fabricated evidence to convict Cooper, the evidence of his guilt correspondingly diminishes.

There should be no hurry to execute Cooper. If he is truly guilty, these simple tests will resolve the matter. If he is truly innocent, those same tests will tell us that. When the stakes are so high, when the evidence against Cooper is so weak, and when the newly discovered evidence of the State's malfeasance and misfeasance is so compelling, there is no reason to hurry and every reason to find out the truth.

I. Nature of the Current Proceedings

Cooper has applied for authorization to file a second or successive petition for habeas corpus under 28 U.S.C. § 2244(b)(3)(A). We must grant authorization if we find that Cooper has made a *prima facie* case for relief under a second or successive petition. "By '*prima facie* showing' we understand simply a sufficient showing of *possible* merit to warrant a fuller exploration by the district court." *Woratzeck v. Stewart*, 118 F.3d 648, 650 (9th Cir. 1997) (quoting *Bennett v. United States*, 119 F.3d 468, 469 (7th Cir. 1997)) [*32] (emphasis added).

There are two possible standards that Cooper must satisfy.

First, if Cooper's claims are entirely governed by 28 U.S.C. § 2244 because he is seeking to file a second or successive petition, he must show that

> (B)(i) the factual predicate for the claim could not have been discovered previously through the exercise of due diligence; and

> (ii) the facts underlying the claim, if proven and viewed in light of the evidence as a whole, would be sufficient to establish by clear and convincing evidence that, but for constitutional error, no reasonable factfinder would have found the applicant guilty of the underlying offense.

28 U.S.C. §§ 2244(b)(2)(B)(i) and (ii).

Cooper has presented newly discovered evidence, including evidence of a constitutional violation in the form of a significant violation of *Brady v. Maryland*, 373 U.S. 83, 10 L. Ed. 2d 215, 83 S. Ct. 1194 (1963). Based on the record before us, there is a *prima facie* case that Cooper could not previously have discovered this evidence through the exercise of due diligence. In addition, Cooper has presented previously known evidence that is newly relevant [*33] because of intervening events since he last sought authorization to file a second or successive petition. Cooper's new evidence constitutes a "factual predicate" for the claims he seeks to present in his petition for habeas corpus. If Cooper's new evidence is believed and "viewed in light of the evidence as a whole," he has made out a *prima facie* case that such evidence would be "sufficient to establish by clear and convincing evidence that, but for constitutional error, no reasonable factfinder would have found him guilty of the underlying offense." 28 U.S.C. § 2244(b)(2)(B)(ii).

Second, if Cooper's claims are governed by the more lenient standard of *Schlup v. Delo*, 513 U.S. 298, 130 L. Ed. 2d 808, 115 S. Ct. 851 (1995), he need not satisfy the "clear and convincing evidence" requirement of § 2244(b)(2)(B)(ii). As long as he has satisfied the requirement of § 2244(b)(2)(B)(i) that the factual predicate of his claim "could not have been discovered previously through the exercise of due diligence," *Schlup* would require only that he "show that it is more likely than not that no reasonable juror would have convicted him in the light of the new evidence." [*34] 513 U.S. at 327. If Cooper's new evidence is believed, and considered in light of the record as a whole, Cooper has made out a *prima facie* case that would entitle him to relief under the "more likely than not" standard of *Schlup*.

We do not need to decide whether the "clear and convincing evidence" standard of § 2244(b)(2)(B)(ii) or the "more likely than not standard" of *Schlup* applies. Cooper has made out a *prima facie* case under either standard.

II. Background

On June 2, 1983, Cooper escaped from the minimum security area of the California Institute for Men ("CIM") where he was incarcerated. He broke into and hid in an empty house in

Chino Hills, about two miles away, in San Bernardino County, southeast of Los Angeles. The house was owned by a man named "Lease." Cooper made telephone calls from the Lease house to his girlfriend asking for money, but she refused to help him. Cooper's last call from the house was at about 8:00 pm on June 4.

The Ryens lived next door, about 125 yards away from the Lease house. During the night of June 4, 1983, the members of the Ryen household were viciously attacked. Doug and Peggy Ryen, the father and mother, were [*35] killed, as were their ten-year-old daughter, Jessica, and an eleven-year-old house-guest, Chris Hughes. Doug and Peggy's eight-year-old son, Josh, was left for dead but survived. The bodies of Doug, Peggy, Jessica, and Chris, as well as the still-living Josh, were discovered the next day by Chris's father. All of the murder victims were killed by multiple chopping, cutting, and puncture wounds. Josh suffered the same type of wounds. Jessica was found clutching a substantial amount of long blond or light brown hair in her hand, some of which had roots attached.

Cooper was apprehended at the end of July 1983, and he was tried for capital murder in late 1984 and early 1985. Cooper took the stand and testified that he was innocent. He has consistently maintained his innocence. Cooper testified at trial that he never went to the Ryen house. He testified that he left the Lease house after that last phone call at 8:00 pm on June 4 and hitchhiked to Mexico. Uncontradicted evidence at trial indicated that Cooper checked into a hotel in Tijuana at about 4:30 pm the next day, June 5. After seven days of deliberation, the jury found Cooper guilty of death-eligible first degree murder. After four [*36] additional days of deliberation, the jury sentenced Cooper to death.

III. Newly Discovered Evidence

Cooper seeks authorization to file a second or successive habeas application based on newly discovered evidence. Cooper attaches two new sworn declarations, both signed in January 2004, which, if believed, would indicate that crucial evidence may have been fabricated. Evidence presented at trial showed that Cooper left a bloody shoe print on a sheet in the Ryens' bedroom. A newly presented declaration by the then-Warden of CIM at Chino, if believed, demonstrates both that the State committed a clear violation of *Brady v. Maryland*, and that the State likely fabricated the evidence of the shoe print.

Cooper also presents new evidence, as well as pre-existing but newly relevant evidence, pertaining to recent DNA testing by the State. In 2001, the State tested three items of evidence for the presence of Cooper's DNA: a blood spot in the hallway of the Ryen house; blood on a t-shirt found beside the road three days after the murders; and saliva on two hand-rolled cigarettes the State claims to have found in the Ryens' abandoned station wagon. Cooper seeks additional testing of the [*37] blood to determine if a preservative is present. The presence of a preservative would show that Cooper's blood was planted. If believed, Cooper's evidence—both new and newly relevant—would suggest evidence tampering.

Finally, Cooper presents a declaration of Christine Slonaker, who states that she was in a Chino Hills bar on the night of the murders. She says she encountered two blond Caucasian men—one in a light colored t-shirt and jeans, the other in overalls, and both wearing tennis shoes—who were inebriated and spotted with blood. The declaration is new evidence, dated February 7, 2004, and if believed, would further corroborate pre-existing but newly relevant evidence that Cooper was not the man who committed the Ryen/Hughes murders.

A. The Bloody Shoe Print

Only two pieces of evidence at trial directly connected Cooper to the Ryen house. One was a bloody tennis shoe print found on a sheet in Doug and Peggy's bedroom. The other was a single spot of blood found on a wall in the hallway.

Several people testified at trial about the shoe print found on the Ryens' bedsheet. Several testified that Cooper had a new or close-to-new pair of "Pro-Ked Dude" tennis shoes. One [*38] key witness testified that prints from a "Pro-Ked Dude" shoe were found on the sheet in the Ryen house, on the shower sill in the Lease house, and in the game room in the Lease house.

"Pro-Ked Dude" tennis shoes are manufactured by Stride Rite solely for distribution in prisons and other institutions. They are not distributed to the general public.

The testimony of two witnesses, William Baird and James Taylor, was particularly important on this point. The California Supreme Court specifically discussed and relied on their testimony in sustaining Cooper's conviction on direct appeal. *People v. Cooper,* 53 Cal. 3d. 771, 797-98, 281 Cal. Rptr. 90, 809 P.2d 865 (1991).

William Baird was the Crime Laboratory Manager, in charge of collecting and analyzing evidence connected to the Ryen/Hughes murders. The sheet from the Ryens' bedroom was not initially thought to have any footprints. A bloody footprint was discovered on the sheet after it was taken to the lab. Baird's assistant, David Stockwell, testified that the foot-print could be seen when the sheet was folded the same way it had been folded when in the Ryens' bedroom (thereby bringing together two parts of the footprint that [*39] were separated when the sheet was flat). (Exhibit 191.)[4] Baird testified that the shoe print on the sheet matched two prints found in the Lease house, and that the prints had been made by a close-to-new "Pro-Ked Dude" shoe, made for and distributed only to prisons. (Exhs. 99, 210). Baird further testified that he had a close-to-new "Pro Ked Dude" shoe of approximately the same size in his lab, previously obtained from another prison. He testified that this shoe allowed him to analyze the print on the sheet and determine that it came from a prison-issued "Pro-Ked Dude" shoe. (Exh. 210.)

James Taylor was an inmate at the CIM during the time Cooper was incarcerated there. Taylor was a recreation attendant at the prison. As part of that job, he issued tennis shoes to inmates. Taylor testified at trial that he initially gave Cooper a pair of "P.F. Flyer" tennis shoes. He testified that Cooper, then imprisoned [*40] under the false name of David Trautman, exchanged his "P.F. Flyers" for a pair of black "Pro-Ked Dudes" a few days before he was transferred to the minimum security area. (Exh. 103.) Cooper escaped from the prison soon after he was transferred to the minimum security area.

Cooper attaches two recent declarations as exhibits to the habeas petition he seeks to file. The first is a handwritten sworn declaration of James Taylor, dated January 8, 2004, which states:

> 1. I was an inmate at the Reception Center West (RC-W) at the California Institute for Men in Chino California in May and June of 1983.
>
> 2. During that period of time, I met David Trautman, whose real name I understand to be Kevin Cooper. I met Kevin when he tried out for the basketball team. My job at the prison was recreation attendant. I was responsible for issuing basketball shoes to men in our unit who played on the team.
>
> 3. I issued only one pair of shoes to Kevin Cooper. I issued him a pair of P.F. Flyers. This brand was the best brand of shoe for basketball that the prison stocked. Kevin did not trade these shoes in to me for a pair of Keds, nor did he trade these shoes in to me for any other pair. (Exh. [*41] 100.)

Second, and more important, Cooper attaches a sworn declaration of Midge Carroll, who was Warden of CIM at Chino while Cooper was incarcerated there. Warden Carroll's declaration, dated January 30, 2004, states:

> 1. I was the Superintendent, or Warden, of the California Institution for Men at Chino, California, from 1982 through 1985. As Warden of this state penal facility, I had extensive contact with members of the San Bernardino Sheriff's Department who were responsible for the investigation of Kevin Cooper as a suspect in what became known as the Chino Hills Murders.
>
> 2. I was employed by the California Department of Corrections from 1966 until I permanently retired in 1999. . . .
>
> 3. As the Warden of the California Institute for Men at Chino, my contact with San Bernardino County deputy sheriffs about aspects of the investigation in the

Kevin Cooper case included conversations with one of the lead detectives about shoeprint evidence found at the crime scene. I communicated to one of the lead investigators that the notion that the shoeprints in question likely came only from a prison-issue tennis shoe was inaccurate. I came to this conclusion after conducting a personal [*42] inquiry of the appropriate staff, including the deputy warden, the business manager responsible for procurement, and the personnel responsible for warehousing. I learned that the shoes we carried were not prison-manufactured or specially designed prison-issue shoes. I learned that the shoes were common tennis shoes available to the general public through Sears and Roebuck and other such retail stores. I passed this information along to the detective. Had I been contacted, I would have testified to this on behalf of either the prosecution or defense, and I would have provided supporting documentation.

(Exh. 101.)

Both the Taylor and the Carroll declarations are newly discovered evidence. The Taylor declaration, by itself, is not particularly helpful to Cooper. It is, of course, a recantation of extremely important evidence introduced at trial, but a mere recantation by a non-governmental agent, absent an accompanying constitutional violation, is not a sufficient ground for habeas relief.

The Carroll declaration, on the other hand, discloses a clear *Brady* violation. Under *Brady v. Maryland,* 373 U.S. 83, 10 L. Ed. 2d 215, 83 S. Ct. 1194 (1963), the prosecution has a constitutional [*43] obligation to turn material exculpatory evidence over to the defendant. This obligation is independent of any specific request by the defendant for such information. *United States v. Agurs,* 427 U.S. 97, 107, 49 L. Ed. 2d 342, 96 S. Ct. 2392 (1976). The duty extends to impeachment as well as exculpatory evidence. Evidence is material "if there is a reasonable probability that, had the evidence been disclosed to the defense, the result of the proceeding would have been different." *United States v. Bagley,* 473 U.S. 667, 676, 87 L. Ed. 2d 481, 105 S. Ct. 3375 (1985); *see also Strickler v. Greene,* 527 U.S. 263, 280, 144 L. Ed. 2d 286, 119 S. Ct. 1936 (1999); *Kyles v. Whitley,* 514 U.S. 419, 433-34, 131 L. Ed. 2d 490, 115 S. Ct. 1555 (1995).

The significance of Warden Carroll's communication must have been clear to the San Bernardino Sheriff's Department investigators. They knew they had little or no direct evidence connecting Cooper to the Ryen house. The "Pro-Ked Dude" tennis shoe print provided that evidence. Because of the testimony of Baird and Taylor, the State was able to tell a damaging story about the presence of a bloody "Pro-Ked Dude" footprint in the bedroom of the murder victims, [*44] a footprint only Cooper, an escaped prisoner, could have left. But if Warden Carroll had been put on the stand and had been believed by the jury, the State's story would have been shown to be untrue.

The failure of the State to provide Cooper with the information that Warden Carroll gave to the San Bernardino Sheriff's Department, and that she now provides in her declaration, was unquestionably a *Brady* violation. Such a *Brady* violation meets the threshold requirement in 28 U.S.C. § 2244(b)(2)(B)(i) that "the factual predicate for the claim could not have been discovered previously through the exercise of due diligence."

It is the State's withholding of the Warden's evidence, rather than any lack of diligence, that explains why Cooper's attorneys have not presented this evidence before. *See Jaramillo v. Stewart,* 340 F.3d 877, 882 (9th Cir. 2003) (explaining in the context of cause for procedural default that failure to discovery a *Brady* claim lies with the state if the petitioner had no reason to know of state's withholding); *cf. Strickler,* 527 U.S. at 287-88 ("[A] defendant cannot conduct the 'reasonable and [*45] diligent investigation' . . . to preclude a finding of procedural default when the evidence is in the hands of the state."); *Julius v. Jones,* 875 F.2d 1520, 1525 (11th Cir.), *cert. denied,* 493 U.S. 900, 107 L. Ed. 2d 207, 110 S. Ct. 258 (1989) (*Brady* claim not procedurally barred because defendant may "rely on a belief that prosecutors will comply with the Constitution and will produce *Brady* material on request"). If the Warden's declaration is believed, the State misled Cooper's attorneys by asserting that the prison issued "Pro-Ked Dude" shoes. We should not penalize Cooper by transforming the State's constitutional violation into Cooper's lack of diligence.

B. DNA Testing

As soon as DNA testing became technologically possible, Cooper asked that it be done on the evidence in his case. The State finally consented to DNA testing on three items: a spot of blood found in the hall of the Ryen house; a t-shirt found beside the road three days after the murders; and two hand-rolled cigarette butts the State purportedly found in the Ryens' abandoned station wagon in Long Beach, California.

The DNA testing was performed by a laboratory of the California Department [*46] of Justice in Berkeley, California in 2001. The result was a positive match for Cooper for all three items. Cooper seeks to present newly discovered evidence surrounding the DNA testing. Cooper also seeks to present previously known but newly relevant evidence—evidence that takes on a new meaning in light of the DNA testing.

1. The Blood Spot from the Hall

A blood spot, marked in evidence as A-41, was taken from the hall in the Ryen house. Daniel Gregonis, the criminologist for the San Bernardino Sheriff's Department, testified at trial that this blood was consistent with Cooper's. Gregonis was impeached at trial based on deficiencies in his testing of the physical evidence, particularly including the A-41 spot.

Cooper presents newly discovered evidence of tampering with A-41 prior to DNA testing. When it came time for the DNA testing, Cooper's defense team noticed that Gregonis had simultaneously checked out A-41, as well as samples of Cooper's blood and saliva, for a 24-hour period on August 13 and 14, 1999. (Exh. 146.) According to Gregonis, this was done at the direction of the District Attorney in order to determine whether A-41 still existed. (Exh. 105.) Although [*47] Gregonis claims that he did not open the glass bindle that contained the pillbox that contained the A-41 sample when it arrived for testing at the DNA lab in 2001, Gregonis's initials were present on the tape that seals the package. (Exhs. 36, 38, 94.) In common laboratory practice, a seal with an individual's initials on it indicates that the individual opened a bag, and constitutes the only record of the evidence bag being opened. (Exh. 106.) The presence of Gregonis's initials suggests that, contrary to his sworn testimony, Gregonis opened the bag containing A-41. Further, the seal protecting A-41 from contamination was different when counsel viewed it in 2001, compared to when it was viewed in 1998. (Exhs. 36, 38.)

Cooper also presents evidence, not available at trial, that the sample has changed physical form since the trial. In 1995, A-41 consisted of plaster chips in a metal pillbox. In 1998, however, it consisted of a capped vial that contained white chips and the metal pillbox, inside of which was a smaller vial containing more white chips. In 2001, A-41 consisted of a vial with white chips and a metal pillbox with an empty vial inside.

The evidence of tampering with A-41 was [*48] not available to the defense at the time of trial. Moreover, Cooper presented this evidence to the California courts as soon as they learned of it, when DNA testing occurred in 2001. Cooper's counsel could not have reasonably been expected spontaneously and repeatedly to check all of the evidence logs when there was no reason for the State to have checked out the evidence. Rather, they discovered that Gregonis had accessed the evidence when the sample was taken to be tested in 2001. They raised the issue before the state courts soon thereafter.

This newly discovered evidence suggests the possibility that A-41 was contaminated with Cooper's blood or saliva, both of which he had also checked out at the same time. Such contamination would, of course, invalidate the results of the DNA testing. The newly discovered evidence of tampering is particularly important when considered in light of other mishandling of evidence adduced at trial. Gregonis testified that he had conducted a blind study of A-41, in which he tested the sample without knowing that Cooper was a suspect. (Ex. 147.) However, his own notes belie that fact. He knew Cooper was a suspect and had a sample of his semen by which [*49] he would have known which enzymes in the blood in A-41 would tie Cooper to the sample.

This was not the only time Gregonis may have used an improper scientific technique or contradicted himself at trial. When Gregonis conducted further testing, he did so by placing A-41 and Cooper's blood side-by-side for comparison. Although he initially denied doing so, he changed testimony when given his own laboratory notes that indicated otherwise. (Exh. 151.) Reflecting the problems of not having performed a blind study, Gregonis apparently changed his initial results of tests on A-41 so that Mr. Cooper's enzyme profile would match that of the donor of the A-41 sample, admitting that he had changed his notes after the fact only when confronted by counsel at trial. (Exhs. 152, 12.)

2. The Bloody T-Shirt

Cooper presents no newly discovered evidence directly relevant to the bloody t-shirt. As already recounted, however, Cooper has presented newly discovered evidence suggesting that the "Pro-Ked Dude" shoe print on the sheet from the Ryens' bedroom may have been fabricated. Cooper has also presented evidence from which one may draw a conclusion of possible tampering with the A-41 sample. The inference [*50] of tampering with that sample is, of course, made stronger if it is shown that the same was done with other evidence.

As detailed below, there is also already-known evidence linking the t-shirt to a potential suspect, Eugene Leland ("Lee") Furrow. Furrow's girlfriend, Diana Roper, and Roper's sister, Karee Kellison, have provided declarations stating that Furrow came home early in the morning on the night of the murders, driven in a brown station wagon containing several people. Previously that evening, Furrow had been wearing a Fruit-of-the-Loom t-shirt that Roper described as identical to the bloody t-shirt found beside the road and introduced into evidence. Furrow was no longer wearing the t-shirt. Instead, he was wearing coveralls that were spattered with blood. Furrow took off the coveralls, put them in the closet, and departed quickly. Roper strongly suspected that Furrow was involved in the Ryen/Hughes murders and turned the coveralls in to the police. As will be recounted below, these coveralls were never turned over to the defense, but were, instead, thrown away by the police into a dumpster.

Cooper has not been able to determine the precise mechanism by which his blood [*51] might have been placed after the fact on the t-shirt. However, he has provided enough evidence, both newly discovered and already known, to raise a reasonable suspicion that there has been tampering with the t-shirt.

3. The Hand-Rolled Cigarettes

Cooper presents newly discovered evidence that the hand-rolled cigarette butts tested for the presence of his DNA were not those introduced as evidence at trial in 1984. One of the butts, designated V-12, had measured 4 mm long when it was introduced at trial. (Exh. 95.) However, when it was tested in 2001 for the presence of Cooper's DNA, that same butt measured 7 mm in length. (Exh. 98.) This suggests either mishandling or tampering, and calls into question the DNA test linking Cooper to the Ryens' station wagon in which the butts were supposedly found. As with the A-41 sample, Cooper had no reason to check the length of the cigarette butt until the DNA testing occurred.

The import of this new evidence becomes clear in light of evidence available at trial that the origin of the cigarette butts was questionable, and that the butts, like other evidence, changed in form between trial and DNA testing. The circumstances of how the cigarette [*52] butts were found is somewhat suspicious. Although police found in the Lease house several cigarette butts of the type ultimately found in the Ryen car in Long Beach, only one of those cigarette butts was logged into evidence. (Exhs. 33, 18.) During an initial investigation of the station wagon, Detective Hall made no mention of any hand-rolled cigarette butts of the type smoked by Cooper. He did, however, find and inventory other small pieces of evidence in the area in which the cigarette butts were ultimately found. (Exh. 17.) Further, Detective Hall found other cigarettes in the car, although these cigarettes were subsequently lost. Only during a second search of the car, conducted by other criminologists, was one cigarette butt of a type issued in prisons found. (Exh. 22.) This is the butt (V-12) on which the DNA testing was done.

V-12 appears to have been mishandled before and during trial. During a pre-trial hearing on July 12, 1984, Gregonis testified that V-12 appeared to have been Cooper's. However, he said that independent verification of this fact would be impossible due to the fact that he "exhausted the sample." (Exh. 169.) However, V-12 appeared at trial, albeit not in [*53] cigarette form but rather in a metal container containing tobacco and the tobacco paper. (Exh. 97.) This disappearance and reappearance of V-12 is similar to the disappearance and reappearance of A-41, the blood spot which was also supposedly exhausted, only to reappear when further testing was needed. (Exhs. 12, 153.)

Given this evidence of mishandling, it is a permissible inference that the cigarette butt tested for DNA was not actually the butt introduced at trial; that the tested butt had not been found in the Ryens' car in Long Beach; or that, in any event, the cigarette butt evidence had been so mishandled as to render any DNA test, at the very least, unreliable.

C. Slonaker Declaration

In a declaration dated February 7, 2004, Christine Slonaker provides new information about the night of the Ryen/Hughes murders. (Exh. 212.) Slonaker recounts that on that night, she was with two friends at the Canyon Corral Bar in Chino Hills, and two men came into the bar. "Both men were Caucasian and had blond hair. One of them was wearing a light colored t-shirt and jeans. The other man was wearing overalls. Both men were wearing tennis shoes . . . they appeared to be under the influence of [*54] drugs." From afar, she thought that they were covered in mud, but they approached her and her friends, and while they were engaged in conversation, Slonaker realized that it was not mud. "The spots on them were blood. Most of the blood was on their shoes and the front portion of their clothes. They also had blood splatters on their face and arms." Slonaker recalls asking them: "Do you realized you are covered in blood?" One of Slonaker's friends also told one of the men: "Get off of me. You're covered in blood."

Slonaker recounts that the men were refused service, and escorted out of the bar. Shortly thereafter, a police officer arrived at the bar. The following morning, Slonaker heard about the Ryen/Hughes murders, but did not report what she had seen because she assumed that the police had been aware of the two strange men after seeing an officer that night at the bar.

The Slonaker declaration is a new piece of evidence suggesting that someone other than Cooper committed the Ryen/Hughes murders. It corroborates and reinforces evidence discussed below.

IV. Other Evidence

The newly discovered evidence, particularly the *Brady* evidence introduced by the Carroll declaration, substantially [*55] changes the State's case against Cooper. Under either 28 U.S.C. § 2244(b)(2)(B)(ii) or *Schlup*, our task is to evaluate the newly discovered evidence in light of all the other evidence in the record. In the material that follows, I summarize both evidence that was presented at trial and evidence that has been unearthed since then. Viewing the totality of this evidence in light of the Carroll declaration, I conclude that Cooper has made out a *prima facie* case that entitles him to file his second or successive petition for habeas corpus.

Warden Carroll's declaration casts doubt on the authenticity of the shoe print on the sheet taken from the Ryens' bedroom. The State knew from Warden Carroll that the prison did not have special prison-issue shoes. Nevertheless, the State put on witnesses testifying to precisely the contrary. William Baird, the Crime Laboratory Manager, testified that he had a "Pro-Ked Dude" shoe in his lab, to which he matched the "Pro-Ked Dude" print on the Ryens' sheet. But we now know from Warden Carroll that it was highly unlikely for there to have been a "Pro-Ked Dude" print on the sheet, because "Pro-Ked Shoes" are special-issue [*56] prison shoes. We also know from Warden Carroll that Cooper could not have had such shoes, and we know that there is no reasonable possibility that anyone else would have had such shoes. Failing to turn over this information was a clear *Brady* violation, and the reliability of the "Pro-Ked Dude" evidence was undermined.

The following is the evidentiary picture into which we must fit this new knowledge. We know that during the night of June 4, 1983, the members of the Ryen household were viciously attacked, and that four out of the five members of the household were killed. Josh, the Ryens' eight-year-old son, survived. Josh had been cut in the throat and was unable to speak when he was first taken to the hospital. But he was able to communicate by pointing to letters and numbers. He told his interviewers that three or four men had done the killings. (Exhs. 53, 54, and 55.) He was separately asked if any of the men were black or had dark skin. He said no. (Exh.

53.) While still in the hospital, he saw a picture of Cooper on television. He said that Cooper had not done it. (Exh. 60.) Detective Hector O'Campo took notes of the interviews. He left out of his notes Josh's statements about [*57] multiple killers. (Exh. 68.) Several other people in the hospital (including a nurse, a doctor, and his grandmother) heard Josh say that there were multiple killers, and that he had never seen Cooper before. (Exhs. 57, 59, 61.)

A year and a half later, Josh testified by videotape that Cooper had done the killing. At trial, he recounted seeing a man with a "puff of hair." At the time of his arrest, a month and a half after the murders, Cooper wore his hair in an Afro; Cooper was seen on television at the time of his arrest in his Afro. However, at the time he escaped from prison, Cooper wore his hair in braids. (Exh. 73.) There were no recovered hairs from a black person in the Lease house, indicating that Cooper had not combed out his braids in the house. (Exh. 167.)

The pathologist who performed autopsies on the victims initially believed that multiple people had done the killings, given the number and varied nature of the wounds. (Exh. 63.) He later testified that the killings could have been done by a single person, and testified that he only considered this after it was suggested to him by investigating officers. (Exh. 63.)

A blood-stained hatchet was found beside the road some [*58] distance from the house. A beige Fruit-of-the-Loom t-shirt was also found beside the road (at a different location) about 3 days after the killings. Cooper did not have such a t-shirt when he left prison, and the owner/occupants of the Lease house had no such t-shirt. (Exh. 29.) There was also no evidence that the t-shirt came from the Ryen house.

The Ryens kept a truck and a brown station wagon in their driveway. They left their keys in the ignitions of both vehicles. (Exh. 78.) After the murders, the brown station wagon was missing. It was found several days later (different witnesses testify to different dates) in a church parking lot in Long Beach. (Exh. 17.) Long Beach is on the coast, just south of Los Angeles. It is almost 50 miles due west of Chino Hills. Tijuana, where Cooper checked into a hotel at 4:30 pm on June 5, is just across the border into Mexico, slightly over 100 miles south of Chino Hills.

Nothing appears to have been taken from the Ryen house. Money left exposed on the counter remained. (Exh. 79.) Peggy Ryen's purse, containing money and numerous credit cards, was left undisturbed. (Exh. 78.)

The police testified that the following things were found in the [*59] Lease house: hand-rolled cigarettes butts with a type of tobacco issued in California prisons; a blood-stained button consistent with those found on jackets issued by California prisons; a blood-stained hatchet sheath; and evidence that there might have been some washed-away blood (visible through the use of "Luminol") in the shower and sink, and in spots in the hall that could have been footprints.

Although Cooper smoked many hand-rolled cigarettes while he was in the Lease house, only one was logged into evidence. (Exhs. 33, 167.) As discussed above, the State's handling of the cigarette butt evidence was dubious. The hatchet sheath was found in plain sight on a bedroom floor during a second search of the Lease house, but that was after it had been searched previously and the sheath was not detected. The police officer who had previously searched the bedroom denied that he had been in it; however, his finger-prints were found on a closet in the bedroom.

The evidence presented by the State of washed-away blood is also weak. Luminol reacts to blood, but also to certain metals, vegetable matter, and cleaning agents. It is impossible to tell without follow-up testing which of the possible [*60] reactants is causing the reaction. Furthermore, Luminol is extremely sensitive, detecting at a sensitivity level of between 1 part per million and 1 part per ten million. It can detect reactants that have existed unnoticed for years and after many washings. The fact that Luminol reacted with the sink and shower does not even establish clearly that there was any blood in them, let alone when it had been deposited.

Cooper's blood was not found in the Ryen house, except (perhaps) on the disputed spot on the wall in the hallway, A-41. That spot was tested and mishandled by state criminalist, Daniel Gregonis, as described above.

Not only is the evidence that was presented by the State at trial weak, there is also considerable evidence that the Ryen/Hughes murders were committed by three other men. In a declaration dated November 21, 1998, Diana Roper told the following story which was never presented at trial: during the early morning hours on the night of the murders, her then-boyfriend, Lee Furrow, came home, in a car driven by others. "Lee and Debbie walked through the front door. They were in a hurry. I heard the car depart. Lee was wearing long sleeve coveralls with a zipper in the [*61] front. The coveralls were splattered with blood. . . . He did not have the beige T-shirt or Levis on that he was wearing earlier in the day." (Exh. 82.) Furrow left the coveralls and quickly departed with Debbie on a motorcycle. (*Id.*)

Roper recounted that the bloody t-shirt introduced into evidence was similar to the t-shirt Furrow had worn the day of the murders: "The T-shirt in this photograph looks exactly like the T-shirt Lee was wearing on June 4, 1983 including the manufacturer, the size, the color and the pocket. I am absolutely positive the photograph of this T-shirt matches the T-shirt that Lee was wearing at our house the afternoon of June 4, 1983." (*Id.*) According to Roper, this was the same t-shirt she had previously bought for Furrow.

It is unclear, by contrast, how Cooper would have obtained a t-shirt like the one later found bloodied. No Fruit-of-the-Loom t-shirts were distributed at the prison. The occupants of the Lease house have provided evidence that none of them had such a t-shirt. And there was no such t-shirt in the Ryen house.

Roper also thought that she recognized the hatchet: "[A] few days after the murders I heard on the news that a hatchet was [*62] found near the crime scene in Chino. I immediately walked to the washer area of our house. Lee's hatchet was missing. . . . The hatchet [introduced into evidence at the trial] looks like the hatchet . . . , which I found missing after the Ryen/Hughes murders. I cannot say for sure if it is the same hatchet that Lee owned but the curvature of the handle is the same. Even more striking in similarity than the curvature of the handle is the style of the handle, which has a sort of an American Indian pattern to it." (*Id.*)

In the same declaration, Roper recounted: "Prior to meeting me, Lee was convicted of the murder of Mary Sue Kitts. Lee confided in me that he not only killed Mary Sue Kitts, but he also dismembered her body and threw the body parts in the Kern River." (*Id.*) Furrow strangled Mary Sue Kitts at the direction of Clarence Ray Allen. *People v. Allen*, 42 Cal. 3d. 1222, 1237-38, 232 Cal. Rptr. 849, 729 P.2d 115 (1986). Allen is currently held under sentence of death in a California prison.

Roper's sister Karee Kellison was in the house with Roper that night. In a declaration dated November 15, 1998, Kellison recounted the same story about the arrival and departure of [*63] Lee and Debbie. "Lee was wearing long sleeve coveralls, which were spattered with blood." (Exh. 197.) She also recounted, "I saw Lee and Debbie get out of a car. There was not sufficient light to identify who the other occupants in the car were. However, there was enough light to see that it was a station wagon, kind of brown in color." (*Id.*)

Christine Slonaker's February 7, 2004 declaration, (Exh. 212.), corroborates Roper's and Kellison's accounts of the night of the Ryen/Hughes murders. Slonaker encountered two Caucasian men—one wearing a light-colored t-shirt—at the Canyon Corral Bar in Chino Hills on the night of the murders, both of whom were covered in blood. Slonaker's account is supported by pre-existing evidence from Canyon Corral Bar employees. The bartender and manager testified that Caucasian men, whom they described as being extremely inebriated, had been in the bar on the night of the murders, one wearing a light-colored or beige t-shirt. (Exhs. 30, 31.) The bartender testified that the men were refused service and asked to leave the bar, corroborating Slonaker's account.

After Roper heard about the murders, Roper called her father to ask him to come to her [*64] house to confirm her opinion that they were spattered with blood. He agreed with her that they were. Five days after the murders, Roper gave the coveralls to Detective Eckley and told him that she thought they were connected to the Ryen/Hughes murders. Eckley then contacted Detective Benge, who instructed him to write a report and forward it to Sergeant Arthur, the chief investigating officer in the homicide division. (Exh. 194.) On June 10, 1983, Sergeant Stodelle told Arthur about the contents of Eckley's report about the coveralls. (Exh. 200.) Eckley's report clearly recounts Roper's story that Furrow had come home with the bloody coveralls on the night of the murder; that he had left them in the closet at her house; that he had been paroled three years before from his sentence for killing Mary Sue Kitts; and that she believed that the coveralls were connected to the Ryen/Hughes murders. (Exh. 194.)

Arthur made no attempt to recover the coveralls from Eckley. (Exh. 83.) Eckley made several attempts to contact the homicide division in June and July 1983, but his telephone calls were not returned. (Exh. 185.) The preliminary hearing in Cooper's case began on November 9, 1983. On [*65] December 1, the day the defense began its presentation, Eckley threw away the coveralls in a dumpster. (Exh. 185.) In May 1984, the Kellison-Roper family contacted Cooper's trial counsel about the coveralls. This was the first information he had received about them. It was not until December 1998 that an investigator for Cooper discovered a disposition report for the coveralls. It contained the initials "K.S.," which suggests that Eckley did not act independently in disposing of the coveralls.

Independent information given investigators in 1984 by Anthony Wisely, then an inmate at Vacaville, develops more fully the account provided by Roper and Kellison. Wisely told Detective Woods on December 19, 1984, that he had smoked marijuana with a certain Kenneth Koon while in prison. (Exh. 85.) He recounted to Woods that Koon had told him that he had participated in the Ryen/Hughes murders. (*Id.*) Roper was romantically involved with both Koon and Furrow around the time of the murders.

In his report, Woods wrote that Wisely told him that Koon told him the following. Koon was with two other men that were in the BRAND or the Aryan Brotherhood, and they had driven to a residence in Chino [*66] on the night of the Ryen/Hughes murders. Two men got out of the car and were in the house for about ten or fifteen minutes. One of the men was carrying two axes or hatchets, and also was wearing gloves. When the men returned to the car, one of them stated that "the debt was officially collected." Wisely said that "Koon thinks they hit the wrong house[.]" Koon said that one of the men involved "was very upset because they apparently had left one kid alive." (Exh. 85.)

Roper stated in her declaration, "I heard Lee say many times there are three rules to follow anytime you do a crime. They are wear gloves, never wear your own shoes and never leave a witness alive." (Exh. 82.) Nikol Gilberson, in a declaration signed November 21, 1998, stated that she was Lee Furrow's girlfriend from late 1983 to late 1984. She recounted in her affidavit that Lee Furrow "on several occasions" told her these same three rules.

This evidence against Cooper, taken as a whole and viewed in the light of the State's *Brady* violation, is extremely weak. There is also a plausible story told by Roper, Kellison, Slonaker and Koon (told through Wisely) that the true murderers are Furrow, Koon and another person. [*67] Cooper has clearly made out a *prima facie* case that entitles him to file his second or successive petition for habeas corpus.

V. Conclusion

Based on the foregoing I would authorize Cooper to file his proposed petition for habeas corpus. I would also grant a stay of execution.

ENDNOTES

[1] Matt Stevens, "Joe Biden Accepts Presidential Nomination: Full Transcript," *The New York Times*, August 20, 2020. https://www.nytimes.com/2020/08/20/us/politics/biden-presidential-nomination-dnc.html?smid=fb-nytimes&smtyp=cur&fbclid=IwAR1UTCrtHY40J0QaLd3CQGwFcNm6S_CKndoTlfEylXOBuzSh4c9MJffrj40

[2] Transcript: Donald Trump's RNC Speech. CNN, August 28, 2020. https://www.cnn.com/2020/08/28/politics/donald-trump-speech-transcript/index.html

[3] Read the full transcript of Obama's eulogy for John Lewis. *The New York Times*, August 19, 2020. https://www.nytimes.com/2020/07/30/us/obama-eulogy-john-lewis-full-transcript.html

[4] Nicholas Kristoff, "Was Kevin Cooper Framed for Murder?" *The New York Times*, May 17, 2018. https://www.nytimes.com/interactive/2018/05/17/opinion/sunday/kevin-cooper-california-death-row.html

[5] Nicholas Kristoff, "Is This an Innocent Man on Death Row?" *The New York Times,* January 24, 2021, p. SR3.

[6] Timothy Bella, "A Black Death Row Inmate Claims Police Framed Him in Quadruple Murder," *The Washington Post*, May 29, 2021. https://www.washingtonpost.com/nation/2021/05/29/kevin-cooper-newsom-investigation-murder/

Index

Abortion, 12–14, 79, 90, 176, 178, 264, 329
Abstraction, principle of, 65–66
Abu Graib, 70–71
Academic debate
   controlling the ground, 251–252
   cross-examination, 228–229, 253–254
   fact debates, 225
   fiat in, 251
   flow sheeting, 237–241
   format, 227–229
   hasty generalizations in, 246–248
   parliamentary, 255–257
   permutation, 250–251
   plans and counterplans in, 248–251
   policy debates, 226, 229, 231–232, 236, 237, 246–252
   presumption in prima facie case, 225
   procedural arguments in, 229–230
   resolution of, 224–225
   specialized formats, 253–257
   strategic thinking in, 251–253
   substantive arguments in, 229, 230–237
   value debates, 225–226, 229–231
Adherence, securing, 165–168
Adjacency pairs, 325

Advocacy, organization of, 168–170
Affirmative action, 131, 235
Affordable Care Act (ACA), 44, 65, 98, 120, 275
Afghanistan, 26, 81, 119, 273
AIDS
   functional cure, 139
   quilt, 206–207
   time frame analysis, 112
al-Assad, Bashar, 24, 25
al Qaeda, 208
Ambiguity of language, 176
American Dream, 131, 264
American exceptionalism, 28–29
Analogy
   argumentative metaphors vs., 79, 81
   false reasoning by, 110
   Hussein as Hitler, 23–25, 33, 70, 274–275
   importance in gaining adherence, 7, 126, 165, 166
   inductive arguments by, 106–113
   literal vs. figurative, 109
   9/11–Pearl Harbor, 26
Anger, 286, 324, 327, 329–330
Argument culture, 8, 321, 328
Argument(s)/argumentation
   in academic debate, 37, 223–242
   argument1/argument2, 6, 7, 8, 303
   and audiences, 43–52

   building, 151–170
   in business and organizations, 303–318
   climate for, 17, 36
   constructive, 9, 322
   conversational theory of, 322, 325–328
   critical evaluation of, 190
   critical thinking and, 87–105
   and decision making, 6, 9–10
   deductive, 107, 113–115
   defining, 6
   disadvantage, 234–236
   ethics and, 15–17, 100, 144, 152, 155, 289
   evaluating, 52–53, 175–183
   fields of, 43–61
   foundations of, 21–41
   and golden rule, 17
   grounds for, 125
   as human symbolic activity, 3–20
   inductive, 107–113
   interpersonal, 184, 186, 324, 329, 330, 331
   language of, 63–86
   legal, 34, 94, 285, 287, 290, 292
   limits of, 35–36, 324, 329
   metaphorical vs. analogical, 81
   as narrative, 29, 33, 35
   non sequitur, 183
   political, 10, 221, 261, 263, 265, 275–276

refuting, 173–193
Toulmin model/diagram of, 55–58
types of, 107–124
and values, 12–15
visual, 195–220
Aristotle, 34, 46, 92, 126, 140, 144, 153
Arlington National Cemetery, 204
Artistic proofs
examples as, 133–134, 145
logos, pathos, and ethos, 126
personal knowledge as, 126–127
Attorneys
argumentative role of, 288
role during the trial, 293–299
role in pretrial phases, 288–293
Audience(s)
age influence, 46–48
assessing, 45–46
background and experience of, 51
culture of, 51–52
education/knowledge level of, 50–51
evaluation of credibility, 140
expectations of, 168
gender of, 48–50
identification of, 43–44
organizing advocacy around, 168–170
in parliamentary debating, 256
and shared premises, 128–130
social affiliations of, 48
universal, 53
Authority, 28, 64, 77, 121, 167, 308, 309, 310, 321

Backing (support of warrant), 119, 120–121
Ballot harvesting, 263
Barr, William, 131, 141
Barré-Sinoussi, Françoise, 139
Bearing Witness While Black, 209
Bennett, W. Lance, 34, 268, 290
Benoit, Pamela, 328

Benoit, William, 328
Biden, Joe, 26, 31, 45, 48, 49, 55, 65, 76, 98, 110, 162, 185, 261, 266, 267, 269, 270, 276, 337–341
bin Laden, Osama, 28
Birdsell, David S., 200
Bitzer, Lloyd, 168
Black Lives Matter, 4, 27, 76, 79, 180
Blair, Carole, 204, 205
Blair, Tony, 274
Blame, for inherent ills, 96, 97, 98
Body image, 200
Branch Davidians, 57
Briefs, 186
Brockriede, Wayne, 16, 323
Burden of proof
in academic debate, 224–225, 227
in the courtroom, 182, 291
Burden of rejoinder, 224
Burger, Warren, 283
Burke, Kenneth, 4, 12, 63, 67, 76, 168, 323
Bush, George H. W., 23–24, 26, 27, 30, 70
Bush, George W., 66, 70, 75, 133, 145, 176, 182, 265, 271, 274
Buskell, Andrew, 3

Capability, 141
Capitol insurrection (January 6, 2021), 160, 162, 180, 203, 234, 273
Case flow, 237
Causal correlation, 110–111, 112, 114, 121, 122, 179
Causal generalization, 110, 114–115, 179
Character(s)
characterological coherence, 272
depiction in stories, 67–71
importance in political campaigns, 270–272
importance in storytelling, 32
type, 67–68
Charlie Hebdo, 208
Chauvin, Derek, 209, 284, 286

Chiang Kai-shek, 24
Circumvention, 233–234
Civility, 9, 10–11, 15–16
Claims/claims-making
argument as a vehicle for making, 8
of fact, value, and policy, 119–120
four levels for considering, 94
inductive vs. deductive, 107–115
refutation of, 173–193
Climate change, 50–51, 125–126, 139, 185, 186, 187–188, 234
Clinton, Bill, 15, 73–75, 271–272,
Clinton, Hillary, 23, 32, 54, 177
Coalitions, 310
Collins, Susan, 44
Comparative advantage case, 169–170
Compromise/consensus, 316, 327, 329
Confederate symbols, 133, 203
Conflict resolution, 322–325
Connotative meaning, 64, 65
Conspiracy theories, 30–31, 72, 94, 141–142, 160, 201–202, 216
Conversational argument
strategic dimensions of, 328–330
theory of, 325–328
Cooper, Kevin, case study, 357–375
Cost, stock issue of, 98–99
Cost-benefit analysis, 99, 100
Counter-criteria, 230
COVID-19, 4, 12, 13, 30, 31, 35, 45, 50, 55, 69, 91, 97, 98, 99, 113, 114, 119, 120, 122, 127, 134, 135, 136, 142, 159, 161, 177, 178, 201, 225, 231, 232, 261, 262, 267, 270, 274, 283, 324
Credibility
competence as measure of, 140–145
importance in narrative, 32
Crimean Peninsula, 22–23

Criteria case, 170
Critical thinking
 critical evaluation of arguments, 175–183
 Dewey's reflective thinking model, 95
 evaluating argumentative propositions, 89
Cross-Examination Debate Association (CEDA), 243, 253–254
Culture(s)
 argument strategies/styles in, 51–52
 and knowledge, 127–128
 lack of shared premises, 130
 organizational, 303, 304
Cupach, William R., 330
Cure, proposing for inherent ills, 97–98

DACA, 265, 266
Decision calculus, 99–100
Decision making
 individual vs. democratic, 9–12
 as objective for arguments, 6–9
Deductive arguments
 from causal generalization, 114–115
 from sign, 113–114
 in syllogistic form, 115–118
Deductive vs. inductive reasoning, 107
Deepfakes, 160–161
Democracy, importance of argumentation in, 10–12
Deng Xiaoping, 80–81
Denotative meaning, 64, 65
Desert Storm, 23
Dewey, John, 95
Disadvantage arguments, 234–235
 brink of disadvantage, 235
 linear disadvantages, 235
 take out response in, 236
 time frame as critical in, 235–236
 turnaround responses in, 236
 uniqueness of disadvantage, 235

Doublespeak, 176
Douglas, Stephen A., 27
Dreamers, 265–266, 268

Empirical evidence
 resolving propositions of fact with, 89
 supporting arguments through, 126
Equivocation, 177–179
Ethics, 15–17, 100, 144, 152, 155, 289
Ethos, 126, 140, 152
Euphemism, 176
Evidence
 hearsay, 58, 144, 184, 296–297
 in Lincoln-Douglas Debate, 226, 254
Example(s)
 as grounds for argument, 133–134
 inductive arguments by, 107–109
 intersectionality with statistics, 145
Exclusionary rule, 291

Facebook, 141, 159, 262
Fallacy/false reasoning
 ad hominem, 179–180
 ad populum, 180
 begging the question, 182
 of composition, 181
 of division, 181
 of false dichotomy, 182
 false reasoning by analogy, 110
 false reasoning by causal generalization, 115
 false reasoning by sign, 114
 hasty generalization, 109, 167, 246–248
 irrelevant reasoning, 179–181
 miscasting the issue, 181–182
 misdirecting the issue, 182–183
 post hoc ergo propter hoc, 113
 red herring, 182–183
 shifting burden of proof, 182
 straw man, 182

Fallows, James, 25
Fear
 appeal to, 180
 consequences of waging a war on, 26
 provoking through visual images, 217
Feinstein, Diane, 49
Feldman, Martha S., 34, 290
Fiat, 251
Fisher, Walter R., 17, 31, 32, 33, 34, 131, 264, 265
Floyd, George, 27, 209, 210, 284
Flow sheeting as systematic note taking, 237–241
 case flow/off-case flow, 237
 truncated sample flow, 238–240
Ford, Christine Blasey, 49
Ford, Gerald R., 277
Forrest Gump, 68

Gaddafi, Muammar, 24, 25, 28
Garner, Eric, 209
Gates, Robert, 210
Gender, 48–50
Gen Z, 46, 47
Giuliani, Rudy, 141
Glasser, Susan, 141
Goals case, 170
Google, 8, 155, 159, 160, 161, 164
Gore, Al, 75, 271, 274
Groarke, Leo, 201
Green, Marjorie Taylor, 201
Grounds for argument
 analysis of, 183
 artistic vs. inartistic proof, 126
 claims as, 6
 defining, 126
 examples as, 133–134
 premises as, 126–133
 research as, 151
 statistics as, 134–140
 testimony as, 140–145

Hall, Stuart, 214
Hart, Roderick, 275
Hearing vs. listening, 174
Hermagoras, 94, 95

Index

Heroes, character types of, 67–71
Hersh, Seymour, 70
Hitler, Adolf, 23–25, 33
Homeland Security Act, 132
Hong Kong, 71–73
Hultzen, Lee, 95
Hussein, Saddam, 23–25, 33, 70, 274–275

Ill, stock issue of, 95–96
Image(s)
  physical, 199–212
  in political campaigns, 269–270
  power of, 212–214
Immigration, 177–178, 181, 265–266, 268
Impeachment, 74–75, 272, 273
Inartistic proofs, 126, 133, 134, 145, 256
Incivility, 11
Inductive arguments, 107–113
  by analogy, 109–110
  by causal correlation, 110–113
  by example, 107–109
Infante, Dominic, 328
Inherency (of ills), 96–98, 232
Internet, 138, 152, 154, 155, 158–162, 212, 216, 274
Interpersonal argumentation
  conflict avoidance in, 322–325
  conversational argument, 327–330
  conversational theory of argument, 325–328
  and empathic listening, 331
  incompatibility as cause of, 328
  mediation strategies in, 322–325
  and self-esteem, 330–331
  social dimensions of, 323–324
  verbal aggression in, 328
Iraq, 23, 24, 25, 28, 33, 70, 71, 134, 145, 181, 182, 200, 201, 274
ISIS, 211, 212
Israeli–Palestinian conflict, 15, 77–78

Jackson, Michael, 289, 290
Jackson, Sally, 325, 327
Jacobs, Scott, 325, 327
Janik, Alan, 55, 58
Jargon, 50, 153, 156, 157, 245, 255, 256, 312
Jeppeson, Marsha S., 205
Johnson, Dwayne, 68
Johnson, Mark, 81
Jones, Paula, 73, 74
Judges
  instructions to jurors, 297, 298
  voir dire process of, 292
Jury nullification, 286
Jury selection
  for cause challenge, 292
  challenge to the array, 292
  consultants specializing in, 293
  peremptory challenge, 293

Kavanaugh, Brett, 49, 50
Klapp, Orrin, 67, 68
Knightley, Keira, 215–216

Lakoff, George, 81
Language
  abstraction of, 65–66
  ambiguity in, 66, 176–177
  defining, 63–65
  doublespeak, 176
  epistemic function of, 63
  good stories and, 66–78
  importance in argumentation, 63–64
  jargon, 312
  power of metaphor in, 79
  power of naming in, 79–81
  precision in, 66
  system of (grammar), 64
  terministic screen, 76
Legal argumentation
  adversarial nature, 285
  attorney-client relationship and, 288
  citizen jurors, 285–286
  civil/criminal cases in, 283, 284, 288
  court system structure, 284
  dispute resolution, 286–288
  in jury selection, 292–293
  in pretrial phases, 288–293
  propositions of fact in, 287
  during the trial, 293–299
Legare, Christine, 3
Lewinsky, Monica, 74
Lewis, John, 351–355
LGBTQ, 49, 103, 234–235, 264, 268
Lincoln, Abraham, 27, 28, 30, 127, 273
Lincoln-Douglas (L-D) Debate, 226, 254–255
Listening
  empathic, 331
  factors affecting, 174–175
  hearing vs., 174
Lodge, Milton, 262
Logos, 126
Lott, Trent, 132, 133

Marcos, Ferdinand, 24
Marine Corps War Memorial, 202
Materialistic myth, 264
Matlon, Ronald, 296
McCain, John, 44, 178, 271
McConnell, Mitch, 261
McLuhan, Marshall, 212
Meaning, denotative vs. connotative, 64
Media
  bias chart, 156
  political role of, 275
  spin on contemporary political debates, 277
  toxic culture of, 322
Meme, 162, 208
Metaphor(s)
  American Dream, 131, 264
  argumentative, 79–80
  in Chinese politics, 80–81
  generative capability of, 81
  ornamental, 79
  war, 81, 321
#MeToo, 75, 272, 310
Mill, John Stuart, 111
Millennials, 46, 47
Milley, Mark, 210
Misinformation, 80, 142, 159, 161–162
Mitchell, W. T., 199
Mr. Smith Goes to Washington, 68

Muhammad, 208
Munayyer, Yousef, 78
Murkowski, Lisa, 44

Naming, 75–78
Narrative
   analysis of, 183
   character of key actors in, 32
   creating our world to fit our stories, 27
   critiquing/evaluating, 29
   effects of cultural worldviews on, 28–29, 213
   fidelity, 31, 33, 127, 224, 289
   historical, 23, 26, 273
   paradigm, 29–35
   probability, 32, 272, 289
   of Putin's Crimean takeover, 22–23
   of Saddam Hussein as villain, 23–25, 33, 70, 274–275
   and values, 21–22
   of war on terror, 26–29
   of World War II, 25
   See also Stories/storytelling
National Debate Tournament (NDT), 243, 253–254
National Parliamentary Debate Association, 243, 255–256
Needs case, 169
Netanyahu, Benjamin, 78
Nicaragua, 69
Nimmo, Dan, 67
Non sequitur, 183
Note taking, 237–241

Obama, Barack, 14, 15, 24, 30, 44, 49, 65, 177, 178, 185, 216, 265, 266, 270, 271, 273, 275
Obfuscation, 65, 176, 274
Ocasio-Cortez, Alexandria, 10–11, 125
Off-case flow, 237, 252
Olbrechts-Tyteca, L., 52–54
Oral presentations, 54, 313, 314–315
Organizational argumentation
   assessing power, 310
   assessing the audience, 310, 312
   clarifying objectives, 309
   competing interests in organizations, 303–308
   determining communication style, 308–309
   formats for, 312–313
   forming coalitions, 310–311
   in oral presentation, 314–315
   resistance, 315–317
O'Rourke, Sean Patrick, 10
Otero, Vanessa, 156

Pathos, 126
Patriot Act, 132
Peele, Jordan, 216
Peltzman, Sam, 130
Pence, Mike, 65, 201
Perelman, Chaim, 52, 53, 54
Permutations, 250–251
Perry, Rick, 277
Photo manipulation, 215–216
Pinochet, August, 24
Pity, appeal to, 180
Point of Information (POI), 256
Point of Order (POO), 256, 257
Point of Personal Privilege (PPP), 256–257
Police violence, 4, 76, 136, 209–210, 284
Political argumentation, 273
   ambiguity of language in, 176–177, 265
   attitudes reinforced in echo chamber, 262
   and cynicism, 267
   debates, 275–278
   equivocation, 177–179
   importance of character in, 270–272
   importance of image in, 269–270
   materialistic and moralistic myths, 264–265
   and media influence, 262, 263, 269–270, 272, 274, 275, 276
   and partisanship, 268
   and polarization, 261–263, 266–268
   as stories, 268–274
   structure and form of campaign arguments, 274–275
   voter interests, 263–266
Polls, 44, 55, 74, 75, 134, 137–138, 142, 261, 263, 266, 272
Postman, Neil, 154, 212
Power
   in interpersonal relationships, 323
   significance in effective organizational advocacy, 310
Precedent, 287, 292
Premises
   contradictory, 130–132
   and cultural knowledge, 127–128
   definition of, 126
   and examples, 133–134
   and personal knowledge, 126–127
   rituals as shared knowledge, 127–128
   shared, 128–130
   and statistics, 134–140
   symbols as reflection of values, 128
   and testimony, 140–145
   testing, 129–133
Preponderance of evidence, 58, 287, 298
Presence, principle of, 53–55
Pretrial
   developing the theory of the case, 289–291
   discovery phase of, 288
   jury selection, 292–293
   motions, 291–292
Prima facie case, 225, 297
Procedural arguments
   criteria arguments, 230
   topicality arguments, 229–230
Proof, artistic vs. inartistic, 126
Proposition(s)
   analyzing, 92–99
   decision calculus, 99–100
   definition of, 87–88
   evaluation of, 87–89
   of fact, 89

key terms, 92–93
point of clash, 93–95
of policy, 90–92
stock issues, 95–99
systems analysis, 100–104
of value, 89–90
Pucci, Enrico, Jr., 205
Putin, Vladimir, 23, 32, 79, 80

QAnon, 30, 160, 202, 328
Questions/questioning
  cross-examination, 189, 228
  direct examination/cross-examination, in legal trials, 294–297
  follow-up, 190
  of precedent, 287
  for testing visual arguments, 214–217

Racism, 132–133, 161, 310, 325
Reagan, Ronald, 69, 70, 178, 270, 273
Reasonable doubt, 287, 297
Reasoning
  evaluating the process of, 179–183
  inductive vs. deductive, 107–108
  through narrative structures 26, 32
Recency, 144, 164
Redundancy/repetition, 66
Refugees, 195–198, 232–233
Refutation
  briefs, 186–188
  critically evaluating arguments, 175–179
  declarative, 188–189
  defined, 173–174
  by denial, 184–185
  evaluating grounds, 183
  finding fallacies in reasoning, 179–183
  focused listening, 174–175
  formulating a response, 183–186
  by mitigation, 185
  preparing for, 186–188
  presenting the response, 188–190
  by questioning, 189–190

by reducing to absurdity, 185–186
strategy, 184
tactics, 184–186
by turning the tables, 186
Rejoinder, burden of, 224
Research
  definition of, 151
  evaluating the relevance of the evidence, 165–168
  for grounds supporting a claim, 151
  how to record the evidence, 163–165
  planning process for, 152–153
Research sources
  books, 162–163
  government, 158
  internet, 155–156, 158–162
  interviewing, 153–155
  journals, 157, 159, 160
  magazines, 155, 156
  newspapers, 155, 156
  specialized, 156–158
Resolution
  affirmative burdens, 224
  constructing topicality arguments, 244–246
  in cross-examination debate, 254
  in Lincoln-Douglas debate, 255
  negative burdens, 224
  negative burdens/burden of rejoinder, 224
  operational definitions in, 243
  in parliamentary debate, 256–257
  presumption and burden of proof, 224–225, 226
Richards, I. A., 64, 245
Richardson, Alyssa, 209
Rieke, Richard, 55, 58
Rituals, 127, 128
Rokeach, Milton, 13
Rosenthal, Joe, 202
Rosling, Hans, 202

Sampling
  inferential statistics, 134
  interval, 137

random, 136–137
stratified, 137
Samsara, 199
Sanders, Bernie, 45, 48, 98
Sapir Whorf hypothesis, 76
Scene, depicted in stories, 71–73
Scheckels, Theodore, 257
Self-esteem, 330–331
Sexual harassment, 49, 73, 75–76, 138, 139, 272, 306
Shared premises, 128–130
Simpson, O. J., 215
Smith, Larry K., 269
Snowden, Edward, 132
Social media, 79, 159, 162, 167, 197, 201, 216, 262, 277
Specialized debate formats
  Cross-Examination Debate Association (CEDA), 243, 253
  National Debate Tournament (NDT), 253
  National Forensic Association's Lincoln-Douglas (L-D) debate, 226, 254, 255
  National Parliamentary Debate Association, 255–256
Speeches
  campaign, 276–277
  constructive, 227, 252, 254, 256
  oral presentations, 313
  rebuttal, 227–228
Spitzberg, Brian H., 330
Starr, Kenneth, 74, 75
Stasis, 93–95, 126, 184
Statistics, 167
  abusing percentages, 139–140
  category definition as a test of, 138–139
  defined, 134
  descriptive, 134
  gathering methods as a test of, 135–138
  as grounds for argument, 134–140
  inferential, 134
  intersectionality with examples, 145

time frame as a test of, 139
underreporting vs. overreporting, 135
Status quo, 165–166, 169, 170
Sterling, Donald, 209
Stewart, Jimmy, 68
Stock issues
　blame, 96–97
　cost, 98–99
　cure, 97–98
　decision calculus applied to, 99–100
　ill, 95–96
　systems analysis applied to, 100–104
Stories/storytelling
　arguments as, 34
　connection to life experiences, 34
　courtroom arguments as, 289–290
　cultural knowledge transmitted through, 127
　depicting characters in, 67–71
　depicting events in, 73–75
　depicting scene in, 71–73
　integrity in, 32–33
　in interpersonal relationships, 322
　as a means of legal reasoning, 290–291
　organizational culture as source for, 303–304
　origin, 28–29
　political campaigns as, 268–274
　self-concept affirmation through, 34, 42
　See also Narrative(s)
Stowe, Harriet Beecher, 29, 30
Stuckey, Mary E., 10
Syllogism
　categorical, 115
　conditional, 117
　deductive, 115–118
　disjunctive, 118
　structural validity vs. material truth in, 118
　validity of, 115, 116
Symbols
　as expression of identities, 4
　and ideology, 13, 202

naming/shaping experience, 12
　as reflection/deflection of reality, 63
　and values, 14, 63, 128
Syria, 24, 78, 194, 197, 198, 211, 232, 233
Systems analysis, 100–104
　benefits of applying systems theory, 104
　comparative advantage case, 169–170
　of a policy proposition, 101–104
　systems theory model for, 101

Tabor, Charles, 262
Take outs, 236
Taliban, 26
Tannen, Deborah, 8, 320, 322, 328
Temper, controlling, 46, 257, 315, 325, 329–330
Terrorism
　Afghanistan, 26
　conflicting narratives about, 27, 73, 76–77
　conspiracy narratives, 30
　ISIS, 211–212
　9/11, 26–27, 214–215
　Osama bin Laden, 28
　provocation of fear, 26
Testimony
　competence as test of, 141–143
　delivery of, 145
　descriptive, 140
　as grounds for argument, 140–145
　historical, 144
　interpretive, 140
　reluctant, 143
　trustworthiness of, 143–145
Thompson, Derek, 50
Thurmond, Strom, 132–133
The Three Servicemen Statue, 205
Topicality arguments
　better definition, 229–230
　breadth, 245
　context, 245
　field definitions, 245

impact, 246
limiting, 244–245
precision, 244
reverse voting issue standard in, 246
standards, 244
unique meaning, 244
violation, 245–246
Toulmin, Stephen, 55, 57, 58, 119–122
Toulmin model
　claim component of, 119–120
　grounds component of, 120
　modality element of, 121
　rebuttal component of, 121–122
　six components of, 118–119
　warrant and backing elements of, 120–121
Transgender Law Center, 49
Trapp, Robert, 256, 328, 330
Trial
　closing arguments, 297–298
　direct examination/cross-examination, 294–297
　opening statement, 293–294
　summary judgment, 297
Trump, Donald, 14, 30, 31, 32, 44, 49, 54–55, 65–66, 76, 133, 141, 142, 159, 160, 161, 162, 185, 209–210, 263, 265–266, 267, 270, 274, 275, 276, 341–349
Trustworthiness
　consistency in testimony, 143
　lack of, in politicians, 275
　recency in testimony, 144
　and reluctant testimony, 143
　and verifiability of testimony, 143–144
Turnaround/turning the tables, 186
Twinkie defense, 112
Twitter, 76, 159, 197, 262

Ukraine, 22–23, 32
Uncle Tom's Cabin (Stowe), 29

Value(s)
    competing, 13–14, 130–131, 263
    and ethical reasoning, 15–17
    and narrative/storytelling, 21–23, 26–29, 43, 75, 224, 269, 273, 298, 329
    organizing advocacy around, 169
    propositions, 89–90
Vietnam Veterans Memorial, 204–205
Vietnam Women's Memorial, 205
Villains, character type of, 67, 68
Visual aids in oral presentations, 313, 314
Visual argument
    importance of in communication, 195–199
    physical images used in, 199–212
    power of images in, 212–214
    tests of, 214–217
Visual images
    determining accuracy of, 214–217
    emotional reactions provoked by, 217
    relevance of, 216
Visualization(s)
    dominant reading of, 214
    negotiated reading of, 214
    oppositional reading of, 214
    power of, 212–214
Voir dire, 292
Voters
    attitudes of, 266–268
    candidate appeals to interests of, 12, 43–45, 263
    issues and, 263–266
    political alienation of, 266–268
Voting rights, 142, 234–235, 263, 267–268

War crimes, 78, 211–212
Warfield, Annette, 257
Warrants, 120–121
Warren, Elizabeth, 45
Watkins, Michael, 303
Weiner, Anthony, 32
Willard, Charles Arthur, 56, 57
Williams, Brian, 32–33
Williams, Rick, 212
Wingard, Jason, 79–80
Woods, Tiger, 142

Xiaoping, Deng, 80

Yoho, Ted, 10, 11
YouTube, 66, 159, 202, 279